Mastering JavaScript

Mastering™ JavaScript

James Jaworski

SYBEX®

San Francisco • Paris • Düsseldorf • Soest

Associate Publisher: Gary Masters
Acquisitions Manager: Kristine Plachy
Acquisitions & Developmental Editor: Dan Brodnitz
Editor: Doug Robert
Book Designer: Catalin Dulfu
Graphic Illustrator: Inbar Berman
Desktop Publisher: Maureen Forys
Production Coordinator: Anton Reut
Proofreader: Theresa Gonzalez
Indexer: Ted Laux
Cover Designer: Design Site
Cover Illustrator: Design Site

Library of Congress Card Number: 96-71650
ISBN: 0-7821-2014-8

Manufactured in the United States of America

10 9 8 7 6 5 4 3 2 1

To Lucyle Pawloski

ACKNOWLEDGEMENTS

I'd like to thank everyone who helped to see this book to completion. In particular, I'd like to thank Margot Maley of Waterside Productions for making it possible and all the great folks at Sybex for their terrific support—especially Doug Robert and Dan Brodnitz. I'd also like to thank my wife Lisa, for her patience, love, and understanding, my son Jason, for making great coffee, and my daughter Emily, for her endless entertainment.

Special thanks go out to Keith MacDonald of Helios Software Solutions for contributing the shareware version of the extraordinary TextPad program to this book's CD. I used TextPad for creating almost all of the HTML, JavaScript, and Java programming examples. I'd also like to thank Sun Microsystems for permission to include the JDK 1.1.1 on the CD, and the World Wide Web Consortium (W3C) for their HTML 3.2 and Cascading Style Sheets documents.

CONTENTS AT A GLANCE

TABLE OF CONTENTS

18 Communicating with Applets   567

INTRODUCTION

With all of the available Web development technologies, such as HTML, Java, and ActiveX, you are probably wondering why you should invest the time to learn JavaScript. The answer to this question is apparent when you compare the capabilities provided by the current set of Web programming languages:

- HTML is great for creating static Web pages. However, it provides no capabilities to design pages that dynamically respond to user inputs. *JavaScript provides these capabilities.*

- Java and ActiveX are excellent languages for creating components that can be embedded in a Web page. However, their output display is confined, for security reasons, to a limited area of the browser window. In addition, if you want to develop Java and ActiveX components, you'll be undertaking a significant programming investment. *JavaScript provides the capability to develop scripts that can access all aspects of the browser display, and in a secure and easy-to-develop manner.*

JavaScript enables you to integrate HTML documents, Web components (which may have been written in Java and ActiveX), and multimedia plug-ins so that you can develop Web applications that are dynamic, respond to a variety of user inputs, and access advanced browser capabilities such as multimedia, VRML, layers, and style sheets. Further, the LiveConnect feature of Netscape browsers allows JavaScript to directly access the variables and methods of Java applets and to exercise a fine level of control over the operation of plug-ins. If these are not compelling enough reasons to learn JavaScript, read on.

JavaScript can also be used to develop server-side Web applications. Both Netscape and Microsoft Web servers support server-side JavaScript. You can use JavaScript to replace all of your CGI scripts that are written in Perl, C, and shell programming languages. Also, Netscape's LiveWire add-on lets you develop integrated client- and server-side applications using JavaScript, greatly simplifying browser-server communication and automatically making the output of server-side scripts available as HTML to browser clients.

Finally, JavaScript is the language used by Netscape's LiveWire Pro to provide connectivity between Web servers and server-external databases. You can use this capability to integrate your Web applications with full-scale databases containing information about your products, customer orders, shipping, or whatever you want.

In this book you'll cover all aspects of JavaScript programming. You'll learn to program Web browsers using client-side JavaScript and LiveConnect. You'll learn how to program Web servers using server-side JavaScript and LiveWire. You'll also learn how to program database-enabled applications using server-side JavaScript, LiveWire Pro, and Structured Query Language (SQL). More important, you'll learn how to combine all of these facets of JavaScript programming to develop integrated Web applications that are attractive, informative, and easy to use.

Conventions Used in This Book

Certain conventions are used in this book to make it easier for you to work with:

- **Upper or Lower Case?** Even though the case does not matter for HTML and JavaScript elements, to help keep them distinct I use all uppercase letters for HTML elements and all lowercase letters for JavaScript elements. (Case *does* matter for Java elements; in my discussions of Java items I use whatever case is commonly required.)

- **Fonts:** I use a `monospaced font` to display JavaScript objects, methods, functions, and variables. (The names of files and directories are also displayed in that font.) Words identifying program parameters or arguments within a syntax explanation (some books refer to these words as "descriptive place-holders") are displayed in *italic*.

- **➥:** Within a script or code listing, you'll see this continuation arrow to indicate a line that is a continuation of the line above it, and which has been broken only to fit it into the book's margins. If you need to type that line of code into a text editor, you should neither break the line nor type a special arrow character. Simply enter both lines of code on a single long line.

- **URLs:** Web addresses are given in *italics*.

Some Experience Required: HTML

This book is aimed at those who want to learn and master JavaScript. You do not require any previous programming experience or knowledge of JavaScript. However, you should have a basic familiarity with HTML, the Hypertext Markup Language. Appendix A of this book provides an HTML reference manual. If you are new to HTML, I recommend that you use one of the many online tutorials that are available on the Web to get up to speed. To find one of these tutorials, use your browser's search capabilities to search for the text "HTML tutorial."

Hardware and Software Requirements

This book is oriented toward Windows 95 users. However, the JavaScript that you will learn will run on any platform that supports Netscape Communicator. These include Windows NT, Macintosh, Linux, and Unix variations. To use this book with Windows 95 and Netscape Communicator, I recommend that you have a 486 or better processor with at least 16 megabytes of RAM. You can get away with a 386 processor and 8 megabytes of RAM, but your browser will start and run very slowly.

You can develop LiveWire applications using Windows 95, but to run those applications you will need a Netscape Web server that supports LiveWire. These servers only run on Windows NT (Workstation or Server) and Unix—there is no Mac version available. I recommend getting Windows NT Workstation—it is far less expensive than either NT Server or Unix, and as far as LiveWire and LiveWire Pro are concerned it works just as well. To run LiveWire and LiveWire Pro, you will need to boost your RAM to a minimum of 32 megabytes.

What Browser Should I Use?

To make the best use of this book, I recommend that you use Netscape Communicator. This book covers JavaScript 1.2, which is fully supported only by the Navigator 4.0 browser provided with Communicator. However, many of the book's examples also work with Navigator 3.0; as proof, those examples that work with Navigator 3.0 are shown with Navigator 3.0 screen shots.

Version 3.0 of Microsoft Internet Explorer only supports JavaScript 1.0. Thus, it is not capable of displaying many of this book's examples.

Using the Companion CD

In addition to containing all the *listings* (scripts, code, and supporting files and graphics) presented and discussed in this book, the CD accompanying this book contains Sun's *Java Developers Kit* (complete, version 1.1.1); *TextPad* (shareware version), an extraordinarily good editor for editing HTML and JavaScript files; and HTML reference files detailing the latest developments in JavaScript and related standards.

NOTE
Note to Windows NT 3.51 users: If you are using Windows NT 3.51 (or earlier), you will not be able to read the CD format successfully. However, you can use the CD's contents if you obtain them via the Web instead of from the CD—just use your browser to access the Sybex home page (at http://*www.sybex.com*), then click on Downloads and follow the links to Mastering JavaScript. The files available for downloading include the complete and unmodified listings (i.e., all the book's scripts, code, and supporting files and graphics). Links to the other contents of the CD are also displayed.

How This Book Is Organized

The chapters in this book have three basic elements: background information on a particular aspect of JavaScript, a discussion of how to apply that aspect of JavaScript to the development of Web applications, and programming examples that show JavaScript in action.

This is a large book because there is a lot that you can do with JavaScript, and plenty to learn if you want to master all aspects of JavaScript programming. The book is organized into 7 parts, consisting of 32 chapters and 4 appendixes, as described here:

Part I: Getting Started with JavaScript

In Part I, you'll cover the elements of the JavaScript language and learn how to write simple scripts. Part I introduces you to JavaScript's syntax, and gives you a feel for its use in browser programming. You learn about JavaScript's support of object-based programming and are introduced to JavaScript's predefined objects.

These predefined objects enable your scripts to control the way information is displayed by your browser and also how your browser responds to user events. Mastery of these objects is critical to becoming a proficient JavaScript programmer.

Part II: Using Predefined Objects and Methods

In Part II, you'll learn the details of JavaScript's predefined objects, and learn how to use the properties and methods of these objects in sample scripts. When you finish Part II, you will have been thoroughly introduced to JavaScript browser programming and you'll be prepared to go on in Part III to learning how to use JavaScript to create a number of very useful and entertaining scripts.

Part III: Sample JavaScript Applications

In this part, you'll learn how to use JavaScript to create some useful enhancements to your Web pages.

- In Chapter 12, you'll learn how to use JavaScript to implement attractive Web page widgets—small, eye-catching components that will help to make your pages more attractive and memorable.

- In Chapter 13, you'll learn how to implement common desktop accessories in JavaScript and how to integrate them with your Web pages.

- In Chapter 14, you'll learn how to develop Web-based catalogs, using JavaScript instead of CGI programs.

- In Chapter 15, you'll learn how to use JavaScript to interface with existing search engines and to implement browser-side search capabilities.

- In Chapter 16, you'll learn how to program card and board games using JavaScript.

Part IV: Integrating Java and JavaScript

In Part IV, you'll be introduced to the Java language and learn how to combine it with JavaScript. Chapter 17 introduces the Java language and describes how Java and JavaScript complement each other. Chapter 18 explains how to use JavaScript to load, control, and communicate with Java applets. It also explains how a Java applet can invoke JavaScript functions. Chapter 19 shows how JavaScript and Java can be integrated to produce combined Web applications.

Part V: Working with Plug-Ins

Part V describes how browser plug-ins work, and shows how to use JavaScript to load and communicate with plug-ins. Chapter 20 provides an overview of plug-ins, discussing how they work and describing some of the most popular ones. Chapter 21 shows how to access plug-ins from JavaScript. Chapter 22 covers advanced LiveConnect applications.

Part VI: Advanced Applications

In this part we cover the development of advanced Web applications using new features of JavaScript 1.2. Chapter 23 provides an overview of style sheets and shows how JavaScript style sheets can be used to easily control the ways in which Web documents are presented. Chapter 24 explains how layers can be used to develop advanced multimedia applications. Chapter 25 introduces the Virtual Reality Modeling Language (VRML) and discusses how JavaScript can be used with Navigator's Live3D plug-in to include virtual-reality effects in your Web presentations.

Part VII: Server Programming

In Part VII, you'll learn how to use JavaScript to develop server-side applications. Part VII is fairly long—seven chapters. However, when you finish these chapters you'll know how to use JavaScript for both client- and server-side Web programming. Chapter 26 covers the Common Gateway Interface (CGI) and shows how server-side CGI scripts interact with client-side JavaScript scripts. Chapter 27 introduces LiveWire, and shows how to use JavaScript to create server-side JavaScript applications. Chapter 28 introduces LiveWire Pro and shows how to use JavaScript to link your Web server to database applications. Chapter 29 demonstrates the use of JavaScript to implement the three-tier architecture of distributed systems. Chapter 30 discusses the components that are available for developing Web applications, and how JavaScript is used to integrate these components. Chapter 31 discusses the differences between Internet and intranet applications, and identifies how JavaScript's capabilities can be maximized in building a company's intranet. Chapter 32 identifies security issues you must consider when developing JavaScript-based Web applications.

The Appendixes

Four appendixes are included that provide reference manuals for the HTML, JavaScript, and Java languages, as well as the most current information on the ECMA standards. So that readers may continue to have access to the latest ECMA developments, the ECMA appendix will be kept up to date via this book's Web page, which is accessible via the Sybex home page at *http://www.sybex.com*.

Updates to This Book Online

The publisher will be posting updates to this book with the latest news about ECMA standardization of JavaScript and information concerning future releases of Netscape Communicator and Microsoft Internet Explorer. Use your Web browser to access the Sybex home page at *http://www.sybex.com*, then follow the links to this book's own Web page for the most current information.

PART I

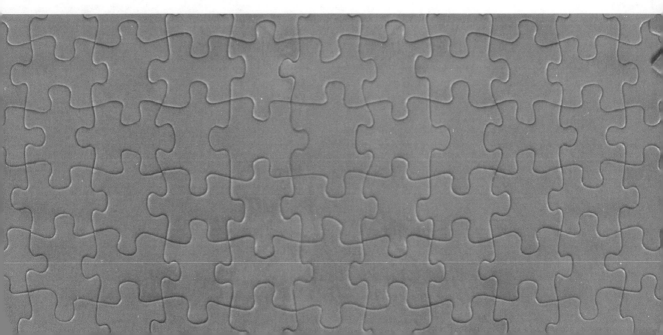

Getting Started with JavaScript

CHAPTER
ONE

1

Fundamentals

- The Web

- The Hypertext Markup Language

- Helper Applications, External Viewers, and Plug-Ins

- Universal Resource Locators

- The Hypertext Transfer Protocol

- Common Gateway Interface Programs

- LiveWire and LiveWire Pro Development Toolkits

- Intranets, Extranets, and Distributed Applications

■magine being able to create interactive multimedia adventure games that anyone can play over the World Wide Web. Imagine being able to create animated product catalogs that not only help your customers find the products they want but enable them to purchase them using secure online payment systems. Imagine being able to create database applications solely for use by your company's sales force and accessible to them from anywhere in the country. With JavaScript, you can do it all.

JavaScript is a new and powerful programming language for the World Wide Web. It not only enables the development of truly interactive Web pages, it is the glue that integrates *Java applets*, *browser plug-ins*, *server scripts*, and other Web *objects*, permitting developers to create *distributed applications* for use over the Internet and over corporate *intranets* as well.

If all the terms in the preceding paragraphs are a bit confusing to you, you've come to the right place to begin your involvement with JavaScript and the world of interactive Web page development. In this chapter, I will provide all the background information you need to begin mastering the JavaScript language. We'll start with the concepts that are essential to understanding the operation of the World Wide Web.

NOTE JavaScript is supported by both Netscape and Microsoft browsers and is an essential tool for advanced Web development. Throughout this book I will be emphasizing Netscape's Navigator implementation of the language, because it provides more powerful and interesting capabilities than those provided by Microsoft's Internet Explorer.

Although I've written this book to show you how to use JavaScript 1.2 for Navigator 4.0 (the browser component of Netscape's *Communicator* package), many of the examples I'll be presenting will also work fine with JavaScript 1.1 browsers, like Navigator 3.0. This is an important consideration, because you'll probably want your Web pages to be useful to the greatest number of Web users, and many of them may not have upgraded by the time you make your Web pages and applications available.

NOTE   In this book I will be using Navigator 3 screen shots to illustrate the examples that can be used both by Nav 4 and Nav 3 levels of browsers, sort of as proof that Nav 3-level browsers *can* run these scripts. In other words, just because they're in a Nav 4 book doesn't mean you can't use a lot of them for the previous version. Relatedly, I'll show Nav 4 screen shots only for the examples that are in any way limited to Nav 4-level browser capabilities. For instance, only Nav 4-level browsers will be able to take full advantage of many of the features we discuss in the second half of the book, such as JavaScript style sheets and layer objects.

The Web

The World Wide Web, or simply *the Web* for short, is one of the most popular services provided via the Internet. At its best, it combines the appeal of exploring exotic destinations with the excitement of playing a video game, listening to a music CD, or even directing a movie, and you can do it all by means of an intuitive, easy to use, graphical user interface. Probably the most appealing aspect of the Web, however, is the fact that it isn't just for spectators. Once you have some experience with Web *authoring tools*, you can publish yourself—and offer over the Web anything you want to make available, from your company's latest research results to your own documentary on the lives of the rich and famous.

A little history: What exactly *is* the Web? The Web is the collection of all browsers, servers, files, and browser-accessible services available through the Internet. It was created in 1989 by a computer scientist named Tim Berners-Lee; its original purpose was to facilitate communication between research scientists. Berners-Lee, working at the *Conseil Européen pour la Recherche Nucléaire* (CERN), the European Laboratory for Particle Physics, located in Geneva, Switzerland, designed the Web in such a way that documents located on one computer on the Internet could provide links to documents located on other computers on the Internet.

To many, the most familiar element of the Web is the *browser*. A browser is the user's window to the Web, providing the capability to view Web documents and access Web-based services and applications. The most popular browsers are Netscape's Navigator and Microsoft's Internet Explorer, both of which support JavaScript. Both browsers are descendants of the *Mosaic* browser, which was developed by Marc Andreessen at the National Center for Supercomputing Applications (NCSA), located at the University of Illinois, Urbana-Champaign.

Mosaic's slick graphical user interface (GUI, pronounced "gooey") transformed the Web from a research tool to the global publishing medium that it has become today.

Today's Web browsers extend Mosaic's GUI features with multimedia capabilities and with *browser programming languages* such as Java and JavaScript. These programming languages make it possible to develop Web documents that are highly interactive, meaning they do more than simply connect you to another Web page elsewhere on the Internet. *Web documents created with JavaScript can actually contain programs*—which you, as the user of a browser, can run entirely within the context of the Web page that is currently displayed. This is a major advance in Web publishing technology. It means, for one thing, that you can now use your computer to run your company's intranet programs or play games without having to install any additional software on your machine—because now the Web page can deliver the software to your machine (albeit only for the duration of the time you are accessing the page that contains that software).

In order to publish a document on the Web, it must be made available to a Web *server*. Web servers retrieve Web documents in response to browser requests and forward the documents to the requesting browsers via the Internet. Web servers also provide gateways that enable browsers to access Web-related applications, such as database searches and electronic payment systems, as well as other Internet services, such as Gopher and Wide Area Information Search (WAIS).

The earliest Web servers were developed by CERN and NCSA. These servers were the mainstay of the Web throughout its early years. Since then, commercial Web servers, developed by Netscape, Microsoft, and other companies, have become increasingly popular on the Web. These servers are designed for higher performance and to facilitate the development of complex Web applications. In particular, Netscape and Microsoft now offer servers that support the development of server-based applications using JavaScript and Java. Code written in these languages can be integrated very tightly with the server, with the result that server-side programs are executed very efficiently. The capability to support server-side JavaScript and Java programs has enabled Netscape and Microsoft to capture a major part of the Web server market.

Because the Web uses the Internet as its communication medium, it must follow Internet communication *protocols*. A protocol is a set of rules governing the procedures for exchanging information. The Internet's Transmission Control Protocol (TCP) and Internet Protocol (IP) enable worldwide connectivity between browsers and servers. In addition to using the TCP/IP protocols for communication across the Internet, the Web also uses its own protocol, called the Hypertext Transfer Protocol (HTTP), for exchanges between browsers and servers. HTTP is used by browsers to request documents from servers and by servers to return requested documents to browsers. Figure 1.1 shows an analogy between, on the one hand, HTTP and TCP/IP over the Internet, and on the other hand, the English language and telephony protocols over the phone system. Browsers and servers communicate via HTTP over the Internet in the same way that an American writer and a British editor would communicate via English over a phone system.

FIGURE 1.1

An analogy. Browsers and servers communicate via HTTP over the Internet in the same way that an American writer and a British editor would communicate via English over a phone system.

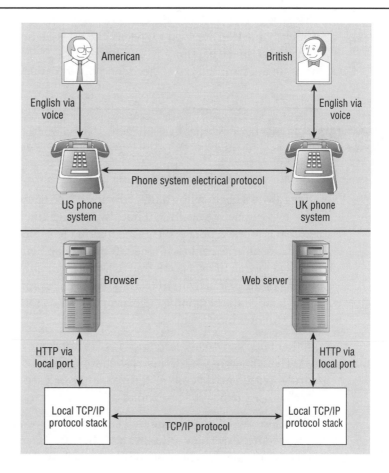

The Hypertext Markup Language

The Hypertext Markup Language, or HTML, is the *lingua franca* of the Web. It is used to create Web pages and is similar to the codes used by some word processing programs, notably WordPerfect.

HTML uses ordinary ASCII text files to represent Web pages. The files consist of the text to be displayed and the *tags* that specify *how* the text is to be displayed. For example, the following line from an HTML file shows the text of a title between the appropriate title tags.

```
<TITLE>Mastering JavaScript</TITLE>
```

The use of tags to define the elements of a Web document is referred to as *markup*. Some tags are used to specify the title of a document, others are used to identify headings, paragraphs, and hyperlinks. Still others are used to insert forms, images, multimedia objects, and other features in Web documents.

NOTE This book assumes that you already have a working knowledge of HTML. This section briefly reviews the important aspects of the language.

Tags always begin with < and end with >. The name of the tag is placed between these two symbols. Usually, but not always, tags come in pairs, to surround the text that is marked up. Such tags are referred to as *surrounding* tags. For example, HTML documents begin with the <HTML> tag and end with the </HTML> tag. The first tag of a pair of tags is referred to as the *beginning* or *opening* tag and the second tag of the pair is referred to as the *ending* or *closing* tag. The ending tag has the same name as the beginning tag except that a / (a forward slash character) immediately follows the <.

Other tags, known as *separating* tags, do not come in pairs, and have no closing tags. These tags are used to insert such things as line breaks, images, and horizontal rules within marked up text. An example of a separating tag is the <HR> tag, which is used to insert a horizontal rule (a line) across a Web page.

Both surrounding and separating tags make use of *attributes* to specify properties of marked up text. These attributes and their *attribute values*, if any, are included in the tag. For example, a horizontal rule 10 pixels wide may be specified using the following tag:

```
<HR SIZE="10">
```

The above HR tag contains a SIZE attribute that is assigned an attribute value of 10.

Attributes and attribute values are placed in the opening tag of a pair of surrounding tags.

Listing 1.1 contains a sample HTML document that illustrates the use of tags in marking up a Web page. Figure 1.2 shows how this HTML document is displayed by Netscape Navigator. The <HTML> and </HTML> tags are used to identify the beginning and end of the HTML document. The document contains a head, identified by the <HEAD> and </HEAD> tags, and a body, identified by the <BODY> and </BODY> tags. The document's head contains a title which is marked by the <TITLE> and </TITLE> tags. (The title appears at the top of the Navigator window.)

FIGURE 1.2

A browser display of the HTML document shown in Listing 1.1.

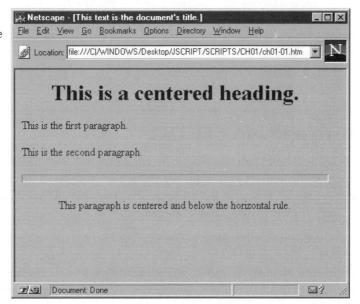

Listing 1.1. Example HTML Document (ch01-01.htm)

```
<HTML>
<HEAD>
<TITLE>This text is the document's title.</TITLE>
</HEAD>
<BODY>
<H1 ALIGN="CENTER">This is a centered heading.</H1>
```

```
<P>This is the first paragraph.</P>
<P>This is the second paragraph.</P>
<HR SIZE="10">
<P ALIGN="CENTER">This paragraph is centered and below the
➥ horizontal rule.</P>
</BODY>
</HTML>
```

Here are a few items to notice within this listing:

- The document's body contains a level-one heading that is marked by the `<H1>` and `</H1>` tags. The opening `<H1>` tag uses the `ALIGN` attribute to center the heading.

- Two paragraphs immediately follow the heading. These paragraphs are marked by the paragraph tags `<P>` and `</P>`.

- Following these two paragraphs is a horizontal rule with its `SIZE` attribute set to 10.

- The last element of the document's body is a paragraph that uses the `ALIGN` attribute to center the paragraph.

The Development of HTML

HTML was originally developed by Tim Berners-Lee at CERN. Since then, it has evolved through several major revisions. Each revision adds new tags that increase the expressive power of the language. For example, HTML 2.0 added the capability to include forms within Web documents.

As of this writing (spring 1997) HTML 3.2 is the latest official version of the HTML language. An HTML version 3.0 was initiated, but attempted to add so many new elements to the language that it failed to be adopted by browser developers. HTML 3.2 formalizes new elements that were already supported by many popular browsers. HTML 3.2 thus includes tags for tables, and also defines document style sheets and tags that support the use of JavaScript and Java.

Although HTML is periodically standardized, the language continues to grow as the result of new tags, attributes, and attribute values that are introduced by browser developers. Since Netscape and Microsoft hold the largest share of the browser market, they have taken the lead in defining new additions to HTML. Since these additions are not part of the official HTML language, they are referred to as *extensions*. Most of these extensions will eventually be integrated into the next official version of HTML. Among the latest extensions to HTML is the layer tag, which allows multiple overlapping document layers to be included in Web pages.

> **NOTE**   Appendix A describes new HTML extensions introduced by Netscape Navigator 4.0.

Helper Applications

Most graphical Web browsers provide support for viewing images in common graphics formats, such as GIF and JPEG. Some can even play audio files. However, most browsers do not provide much more than that in terms of multimedia features. Instead of building ever larger, ever more complicated browsers that are capable of handling the ever growing list of file formats, browser developers have opted to design their browsers to rely on other programs, referred to as *helper applications*, to support the broad range of multimedia and other file formats. When a browser encounters a file type that it does not know how to handle, it searches its list of helper applications (some come with the browser, but users may have downloaded and configured others since the time they installed the browser) to see if it has one that is capable of dealing with the file. If a suitable helper is found, then the browser executes the helper and passes it the name of the file to be run. If an appropriate helper cannot be found, then the browser prompts the user to identify which helper to use or to save the file for later display.

External Viewers and Plug-Ins

Early helper programs operated independently of the Web browser. These programs, referred to as *external viewers*, were executed separate from the browser and created their own windows to display various types of files. Netscape and Microsoft developed the capability for their second-generation browsers to use *plug-in* or *add-in modules*, which not only execute automatically when needed, but display their output in the browser window. Since then, numerous companies have developed plug-in modules to support everything from the three-dimensional worlds created by the Virtual Reality Modeling Language (VRML) to CD-quality audio.

Plug-in modules are generally quicker to load and more efficient than external viewers. Since they execute with the browser, they can be accessed from within the browser environment. Netscape recently added the capability to control plug-in modules from Java and JavaScript code via its LiveConnect toolkit. You'll learn how to work with plug-ins and LiveConnect in Part 5 of this book.

Using MIME Types to Identify Helpers for File Formats

So far, we've described how browsers use helper applications to display different types of files, but how does a browser know which helpers to use for a given file? The answer lies in MIME types.

MIME stands for Multipurpose Internet Mail Extensions. MIME was originally developed as a standard for including different types of files in electronic mail. It was subsequently adopted by Web servers and browsers to identify the types of files referenced in a Web page.

MIME identifies file types using a *type/subtype* naming scheme. Examples of common MIME types are text/plain, text/html, image/gif, and video/quicktime. The first component of a MIME type identifies the general type of a file, while the second part identifies the specific type within the general category. For example, the text/plain and text/html types both belong to the text category, but they differ in their subtypes. Table 1.1 lists some common MIME types.

Web servers contain configuration files that match file extensions with their MIME types. For example, files that end with the extensions .htm or .html are associated with the text/html MIME type and files that end with .jpg, .jpe, or .jpeg are associated with the image/jpeg MIME type.

Browsers also contain configuration information about MIME types. This information is used to map MIME types to the helper application that displays files of that type.

When a browser requests a file from a Web server, the server uses the file's extension to look up the file's MIME type. The server then identifies the file's MIME type to the browser. The browser uses the file's MIME type to determine which helper application, if any, is to be used to display the file. If the file is to be displayed by an external viewer, the browser waits until the file has been completely received before launching the viewer. If the file is to be displayed by a plug-in, the browser launches the plug-in and passes the file to the plug-in as the file is received. This enables the plug-in to begin displaying the file before it is fully loaded, an important capability of audio and video streaming applications.

TABLE 1.1   Example MIME Types

MIME Type	Description
text/plain	Generic ASCII text file.
text/html	Text file containing HTML.
image/gif	Image in Graphics Interchange Format.
image/jpeg	Image in Joint Photographic Experts Group format.
audio/x-wav	File containing sounds stored in the Windows audio file format.
video/mpeg	Video in the Moving Pictures Experts Group format.
video/quicktime	Video in the Apple QuickTime format.
application/octet-stream	Raw (unformatted) stream of bytes.
application/x-javascript	File containing JavaScript source code.

Universal Resource Locators

A *universal resource locator*, or URL, is the notation used to specify the addresses of an Internet file or service. You have probably seen numerous examples of URLs. They are included in TV commercials, they're shown on billboards, and they appear in magazine ads. I've even heard people announce them, slash by slash and dot by dot, on the radio. Examples of URLs include *http://home.netscape.com*, *http://www.microsoft.com*, and *ftp://ftp.cdrom.com*.

A URL always contains a protocol identifier, like http or ftp, and a host name, as in the examples above. Commonly used protocol identifiers are http, ftp, and file. The protocol identifier is also referred to as a *scheme*. When writing a URL, the protocol identifier is followed by :// and then the host name of the computer to which the protocol applies. (In URLs, path names are written using / forward slash characters rather than \ back slash characters.) For example, to access the main home page of Microsoft on the host named www.microsoft.com, you would use the URL *http://www.microsoft.com*. To access the root directory of the File Transfer Protocol (FTP) server hosted at ftp.cdrom.com, you would use the URL *ftp://ftp.cdrom.com.*

In addition to the host name, the URL can specify the path and file name of a file to be accessed by adding a single / character followed by the name. For example, the home page for this book is located in the `javascript` subdirectory of my Web server's root directory, in the file `index.htm`. The URL for this file is therefore:

http://www.jaworski.com/javascript/index.htm

(Actually, since my Web server is set up to use the file name `index.htm` by default, it can be omitted from the URL. The URL *http://www.jaworski.com/javascript* would be sufficient to locate the file.)

NOTE URLs may also contain additional addressing components, such as a port name before the path and file name, and a file offset after the file name.

The "File" Protocol in URLs

The `file` protocol can be used by your browser to access files located on your local machine. Suppose the file `test.htm` was located on your Windows 95 desktop. The path to this file would be `c:\windows\desktop\test.htm`. To open the file with your browser, you would use the following URL:

file://localhost/C|/WINDOWS/Desktop/test.htm

The host name `localhost` in the URL above is used to refer to the local file system and may be omitted safely. The slash following `localhost`, however, should be retained. The above URL could thus be written as follows:

file:///C|/WINDOWS/Desktop/test.htm

Note that in both examples above the `c:` drive designation that you are probably most familiar with from DOS conventions is written as `c|` instead.

The Hypertext Transfer Protocol

As mentioned earlier in this chapter, HTTP is the protocol used for communication between browsers and Web servers. HTTP uses a request/response model of communication. A browser establishes a connection with a server and sends URL requests to the server. The server processes the browser's request and sends a response back to the browser.

A browser connects with a Web server by establishing a TCP connection at port 80 of the server. This port is the address at which Web servers "listen" for browser requests. Once a connection has been established, a browser sends a request to the server. This request specifies a request method, the URL of the document, program, or other resource being requested, the HTTP version being used by the browser, and other information related to the request.

Several request methods are available. GET, HEAD, and POST are the most commonly used ones.

- The GET method is used to retrieve the information contained at the specified URL. This method may also be used to *submit* data collected in an HTML *form* (the topic of Chapter 7) or to invoke a Common Gateway Interface program (a topic I discuss in the next section, below). When the server processes a GET request, it delivers the requested information (if it can find it), but appends at the front of the information an HTTP header that provides data about the server, identifies any errors that occurred in processing the request, and describes the type of information being returned as a result.

- The HEAD method is similar to the GET method except that when a Web server processes a HEAD request it only returns the HTTP header data and not the information that was the object of the request. The HEAD method is used to retrieve information about a URL without actually obtaining the information addressed by the URL.

- The POST method is used to inform the server that the information appended to the request is to be sent to the specified URL. The POST method is typically used to send form data and other information to Common Gateway Interface programs. The Web server responds to a POST request by sending back header data followed by any information generated by the CGI program as the result of processing the request.

Common Gateway Interface Programs

The *Common Gateway Interface* is a standard that specifies how external programs may be used by Web servers. Programs that adhere to the Common Gateway Interface standard are referred to as CGI programs. CGI programs may be used to process data submitted with forms, to perform database searches, and to support other types of Web applications such as clickable image maps.

A browser request for a CGI program takes the form of the CGI program's URL. The request comes about as the result of a user clicking a link or submitting a form. The browser makes the request using HTTP. When a Web server receives the request, the Web server executes the CGI program and also passes it any data that was submitted by the browser. When the CGI program performs its processing it usually generates data in the form of a Web page, which it returns via the Web server to the requesting browser.

The CGI standard specifies how data may be passed from Web servers to CGI programs and how data should be returned from CGI programs to the Web server. Table 1.2 summarizes these interfaces. In Chapters 7 and 26, you'll study the CGI and learn how to create CGI programs.

TABLE 1.2 CGI Summary

Method of Communicating	Interface	Description
Command-line arguments	Web server to CGI program	Data is passed to the CGI program via the command line used to execute the program. Command-line arguments are passed to CGI programs as the result of ISINDEX queries.
Environment variables	Web server to CGI program	A Web server passes data to the CGI program by setting special variables, referred to as environment variables, that are available to the CGI program via its environment.
Standard input stream	Web server to CGI program	A Web server passes data to a CGI program by sending the data to the standard character input stream associated with the CGI program. The CGI program reads the data as if it were manually entered by a user at a character terminal.
Standard output stream	CGI program to Web server	The CGI program passes data back to the Web server by writing it to its standard output stream (e.g., to a terminal). The Web server intercepts this data and sends it back to the browser that made the CGI request.

Java Applets

The Java language, developed by Sun Microsystems, Inc., has realized tremendous popularity in the last two years. Although it was originally developed as a language for programming consumer electronic devices, Java has increasingly been adopted as a hardware and software-independent platform for developing advanced Web applications. Java may be used to write stand-alone applications, but the primary impetus for its popularity is its ability to develop programs that can be executed by a Web browser.

The Java programs that can be executed by the Web browser are called *applets* rather than applications, because they cannot be run outside of the browser's own window. ("Application" usually implies a complete, stand-alone program.) Programmers create Java applets using built-in programming features of the Java Developer's Kit (JDK). Web pages, written in HTML, reference Java applets using the <APPLET> tag, in much the same way that images are referenced using the <IMAGE> tag. When a Web page that references a Java applet is loaded by a browser, the browser requests the applet code from the Web server. When the browser receives the applet code, it executes the code and allocates a fixed area of the browser window. This area is identified by attributes specified with the applet tag. The applet is not allowed to update the browser display or handle events outside of its allocated window area.

By way of comparison, JavaScript provides access to the entire Web page, but does not support many of the more advanced object-oriented programming features of Java.

Netscape Navigator 4.0 provides the capability for Java applets to invoke JavaScript functions. It also provides the capability for JavaScript scripts to load Java applets and invoke Java methods. Part 4 of this book shows how JavaScript and Java can be combined to produce advanced Web applications.

A Brief History of JavaScript

Often, one programming language will evolve from another. For example, Java evolved from C++, which evolved from C, which evolved from other languages. This is also the case for JavaScript. Netscape originally developed a language called *LiveScript* to add a basic scripting capability to both Navigator and its

Web-server line of products; when it added support for Java applets in its release of Navigator 2.0, Netscape replaced LiveScript with JavaScript. Although the initial version of JavaScript was little more than LiveScript renamed, JavaScript has been subsequently updated with each new beta release of Navigator.

This book's description is based on the final release of Netscape Navigator 4.0. Microsoft has also implemented JavaScript in its Internet Explorer 3.0. However, while Netscape has concentrated on introducing new features to JavaScript, Microsoft has focused on its ActiveX technology, in direct competition to both JavaScript and Java.

JavaScript supports both Web browser and server scripting. Browser scripts are used to create dynamic Web pages that are more interactive, more responsive, and more tightly integrated with plug-ins and Java applets. JavaScript supports these features by providing special programming capabilities, such as the ability to dynamically generate HTML and to define custom event-handling functions.

JavaScript scripts are included in HTML documents via the HTML <SCRIPT> tag. When a JavaScript-capable browser loads an HTML document containing scripts, it evaluates the scripts as they are encountered. The scripts may be used to create HTML elements that are added to the displayed document or to define functions, called event handlers, that respond to user actions, such as mouse clicks and keyboard entries. Scripts may also be used to control plug-ins and Java applets.

On the server side, JavaScript is used to more easily develop scripts that process form data, perform database searches, and implement custom Web applications. Server-side scripts are more tightly integrated with the Web server than CGI programs. Developers must use Netscape's LiveWire toolkit to develop server-side scripts.

LiveWire

LiveWire is a graphical environment for developing and managing Web sites. It was created by Netscape for use with Netscape servers. One of LiveWire's features is that it supports the development of server-based programs using the JavaScript language. These programs are used in the same way as CGI programs, but they are more closely integrated with Web servers and the HTML pages that reference them. An advanced version of LiveWire, referred to as LiveWire Pro, also provides a Structured Query Language (SQL) type of database and a report generator.

Server-based JavaScript programs are compiled with HTML documents into a platform-independent bytecode format. When a compiled document is requested by a Web browser, it is translated back into HTML format and sent out to the browser. The server-based scripts remain with the server and are loaded to perform any server-side processing. The HTML document loaded by the browser communicates with the server-side scripts to implement advanced Web applications that are distributed between the browser, server, and other server-side programs, such as database and electronic commerce applications.

LiveWire provides a number of programming objects which can be used by JavaScript scripts to implement CGI-style programs. These objects simplify the communication between browsers, Web servers, and server-side scripts. Chapter 27 introduces LiveWire and shows how it is used to develop server-side scripts.

Intranets, Extranets, and Distributed Applications

In the last couple of years, corporations have begun to look at ways of deploying TCP/IP networks inside of their companies to take advantage of the full range of standards-based services provided by the Internet. These "company-internal internets" have become known as *intranets*. Intranets may be private networks that are physically separate from the Internet, internal networks that are separated from the Internet by a firewall, or simply a company's internal extension of the Internet.

Companies deploy intranets so that they can make Internet services available to their workers. E-mail,Web browsing, and Web publishing are the most popular of these services. Many companies make Web servers available for their employees' intranet publishing needs. These intranet Web servers allow departments, groups, and individuals within a company to conveniently share information while usually limiting access to the information to company employees.

The popularity of intranets as a way of communicating and of sharing information within a company has brought about a demand for more powerful and sophisticated intranet applications. The eventual goal is for the intranet to provide a common application framework from which a company's core information processing functions can be implemented and accessed. Netscape, Sun, Microsoft, and other Web software providers are focusing on the intranet as the primary application framework for the development of business software. Netscape's

Open Network Environment, known as *Netscape ONE*, documents Netscape's approach to building network-centric applications for a company's intranet and for the "extranet" as well—*extranet* being the term that refers to that portion of a company's network that is accessible outside of the company. The extranet links a company to its customers, vendors, and suppliers.

Because of its client/server architecture and user-friendly browser software, the Web is the perfect candidate for implementing this common intranet application framework. The approach taken by Netscape and other Web software developers is to use the Web browser as the primary interface by which users connect to the intranet and run intranet and extranet applications. These applications are referred to as *distributed applications* since their execution is distributed in part on the browser (via JavaScript, Java, ActiveX, VBScript, and other languages), in part on the server (via CGI programs and JavaScript and Java server-side programs), and in part on database and other enterprise servers.

Distributed intranet and extranet applications use HTML, JavaScript, Java, and other languages for programming the browser-based user interface portion of the distributed application. They also use JavaScript and Java to perform server-side programming. In Netscape ONE and other distributed application development approaches, Java is seen as a key technology for developing the components of distributed applications and JavaScript is seen as the essential glue which combines these components into fully distributed Web-based intranet and extranet applications.

Summary

This chapter covered the concepts that are essential to understanding the operation of the Web. You learned about HTML, HTTP, CGI, MIME-types, plug-ins, Java applets, JavaScript, and LiveWire. You should have a basic understanding of how these elements work together to develop Web applications. In the next chapter, you'll begin the exciting process of learning to use JavaScript to write some sample scripts.

CHAPTER
TWO

2

Introduction to JavaScript

- JavaScript and Browsers, JavaScript and Servers

- Embedding JavaScript in HTML

- Telling Non-JavaScript Browsers to Ignore Your Code

- JavaScript Comments

- Generating HTML

- Types and Variables

This chapter introduces you to the JavaScript language. I'll show you how JavaScript works with both browsers and Web servers, and how to embed JavaScript statements in HTML documents. I'll then cover JavaScript's use of *types* and *variables*, and show you how to use *arrays*. By the time you have finished this chapter, you'll be able to write simple scripts and include them in your Web pages.

JavaScript and Browsers, JavaScript and Servers

JavaScript is a script-based programming language that supports the development of both client and server components of Web-based applications. On the client side, it can be used to write programs that are executed by a Web browser within the context of a Web page. On the server side, it can be used to write Web server programs that can process information submitted by a Web browser and then update the browser's display accordingly. Figure 2.1 provides an overview of how JavaScript supports both client and server Web programming.

FIGURE 2.1

JavaScript supports both client and server Web applications.

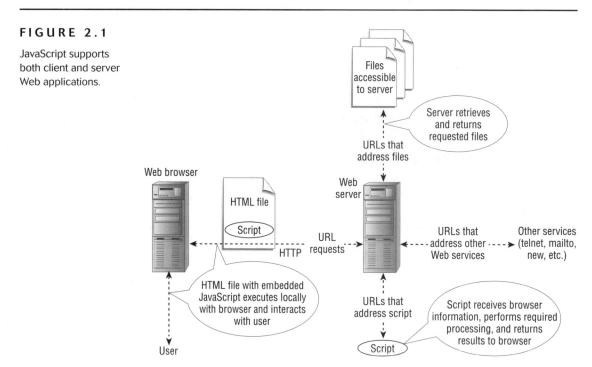

On the left side of the figure, a Web browser displays a Web page, which, as I mentioned in Chapter 1, is a result of the browser acting on the instructions contained in an HTML file. The browser reads the HTML file and displays elements of the file as they are encountered. In this case, the HTML file (which the browser has retrieved from a Web server, seen on the right) contains embedded JavaScript code. The process of reading the HTML file and identifying the elements contained in the file is referred to as *parsing*. When a script is encountered during parsing, the browser executes the script before continuing with further parsing.

The script can perform actions, such as generating HTML code that affects the display of the browser window. The script can also define JavaScript language elements that are used by other scripts or by the browser itself. Figure 2.2 summarizes the parsing of HTML files that contain JavaScript scripts.

Some scripts may define functions for handling *events* that are generated by user actions. For example, you might write a script to define a function for handling the event "filling in a form" or "clicking a link." The event handlers can

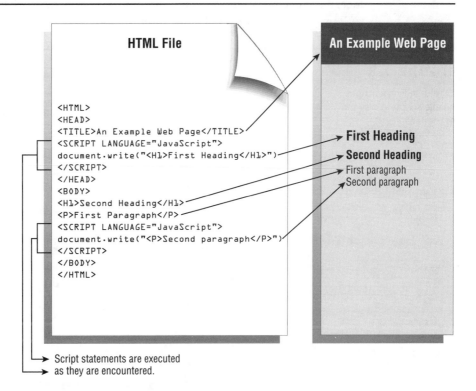

FIGURE 2.2

HTML files are parsed and displayed one element at a time.

```
<HTML>
<HEAD>
<TITLE>An Example Web Page</TITLE>
<SCRIPT LANGUAGE="JavaScript">
document.write("<H1>First Heading</H1>")
</SCRIPT>
</HEAD>
<BODY>
<H1>Second Heading</H1>
<P>First Paragraph</P>
<SCRIPT LANGUAGE="JavaScript">
document.write("<P>Second paragraph</P>")
</SCRIPT>
</BODY>
</HTML>
```

HTML File

An Example Web Page

First Heading

Second Heading

First paragraph
Second paragraph

Script statements are executed
as they are encountered.

then perform actions such as validating the form's data, generating a custom URL for the link, or loading a new Web page.

JavaScript's event-handling capabilities provide greater control over the user interface than HTML alone. For example, when a user submits an HTML form, a browser that isn't implementing JavaScript handles the "submit form" event by sending the form data to a CGI program for further processing. The CGI program processes the form data and returns the results to the Web browser, which displays the results to the user. By comparison, when a user submits an HTML form using a browser that *is* implementing JavaScript, a JavaScript event-handling function is called to process the form data. This processing may vary from validating the data (that is, checking to see that the data entered by the user is appropriate for the fields contained in the form) to performing all of the required form processing, eliminating the need for a CGI program. In other words, JavaScript's event-handling capabilities allow the *browser* to perform some, if not all, of the form processing. Figure 2.3 compares JavaScript's event-handling capabilities to those provided by HTML. Besides providing greater control over the user interface, these event-handling capabilities help to reduce network traffic, the need for CGI programs, and the load on the Web server.

FIGURE 2.3

Event-handling functions enable scripts to respond to user actions.

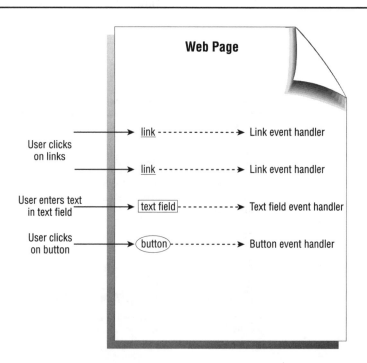

TIP I'll cover JavaScript's event-handling capabilities more fully in Chapter 4, "Event Handling."

While JavaScript's browser programming capabilities can eliminate the need for *some* server-side programs, others are still required to support more advanced Web applications, such as those that access database information, support electronic commerce, or perform specialized processing. To help developers create these server-side programs, Netscape Corporation offers its LiveWire and LiveWire Pro toolkits, which provide an integrated environment for developing JavaScript server-side programs.

- **LiveWire toolkit.** The LiveWire toolkit comes with a copy of Netscape Navigator Gold, the LiveWire Site Manager, the LiveWire JavaScript Compiler, and the LiveWire Database Connectivity Library, which are described below.

    - Netscape Navigator Gold is the same as the regular Navigator browser but with additional capabilities for creating, editing, and publishing Web documents.

    - The Site Manager is for building Web applications that are integrated into a Netscape Web server. These applications are written in JavaScript.

    - The JavaScript Compiler is for compiling server-side JavaScript scripts into a form that can be integrated with the Web server via the Site Manager.

    - The Database Connectivity Library is for providing an interface between Web applications controlled by Site Manager and external database programs.

- **LiveWire Pro toolkit.** The LiveWire Pro toolkit contains all of the elements of the LiveWire toolkit plus the Informix Online-Workgroup SQL database and the Crystal Reports Professional software. These programs provide the capability to integrate database applications with server-side JavaScript and Java programs.

Server-side JavaScript scripts are used to replace traditional CGI programs. Instead of a Web server calling a CGI program to process form data, perform searches, or implement customized Web applications, a JavaScript-enabled Web server can invoke a precompiled JavaScript script to perform this processing. The

Web server automatically creates JavaScript objects that tell the script how it was invoked and the type of browser requesting its services; it also automatically communicates any data supplied by the browser. The script processes the data provided by the browser and returns information to the browser, via the server. The browser then uses this information to update the user's display. Figure 2.4 illustrates how server-side scripts are used.

FIGURE 2.4

Server-side scripts are used to replace CGI programs.

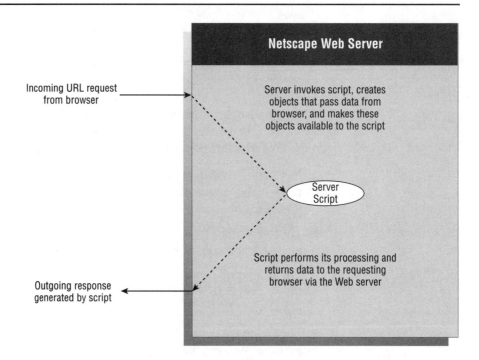

There are several advantages to using server-side JavaScript scripts on a Netscape Web server:

- Since the Netscape Web server's interface has been specially designed for executing the scripts, it is able to minimize the processing overhead that is usually associated with invoking the script, passing data, and returning the results of the script's processing.

- You can use the LiveWire Site Manager to manage all of the scripts that are used by the server. This eliminates the problems that are usually associated with multiple CGI programs, which may have been written in OS Shell, Perl, tcl, C and other languages. It also provides tighter control over the security of these server-side applications.

- You can use the JavaScript and Java languages to write server-side programs. These modern object-based and object-oriented languages provide a powerful, easy-to-use interface with the Web server.

- The database extensions integrated within LiveWire Pro provide a powerful capability for accessing information contained in compatible external databases.

The database connectivity supported by LiveWire Pro is a major accomplishment in Web programming. With these features, Netscape has enabled even beginning programmers to create server-side JavaScript programs to update databases with information provided by browsers (usually through forms) and to provide Web users with Web pages that are dynamically generated from database queries. You can imagine how exciting this is for researchers gathering and reporting information over the Web and for entrepreneurs who have catalogs full of products and services to sell over the Web. Figure 2.5 illustrates the use of JavaScript and LiveWire Pro to provide database connectivity to Web applications.

FIGURE 2.5

LiveWire provides database connectivity to server-side scripts.

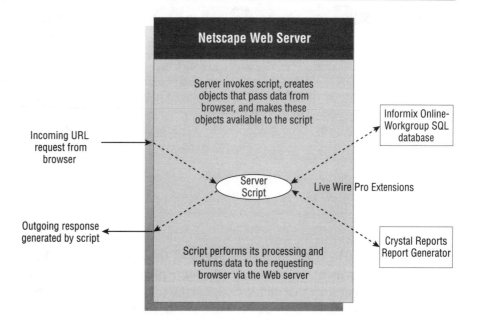

NOTE

In this section, I've provided an overview of the different ways in which JavaScript can be used for browser and server-side Web applications. JavaScript's syntax is the same for both browser *and* server programming; however, the examples I will be using in this chapter mainly reflect how JavaScript relates to browser programming. For examples of JavaScript *server* programming, see the seven chapters that make up Part 7 of this book.

Embedding JavaScript in HTML

JavaScript statements can be included in HTML documents by enclosing the statements between an opening `<script>` tag and a closing `</script>` tag. Within the opening tag, the LANGUAGE attribute is set to `"JavaScript"` to identify the script as being JavaScript as opposed to some other scripting language, such as Visual Basic Script.

NOTE

The LANGUAGE attribute can be set to JavaScript, JavaScript 1.1, or JavaScript 1.2. Use the JavaScript tag without a number only if you know your script will be usable by all earlier levels of JavaScript-enabled Web browser. If you are including elements that are of use only to later versions of Web browsers, include the appropriate JavaScript version number in your LANGUAGE attribute to prevent misleading or frustrating users of earlier browsers, which might not alert the user that the full content of the script is not being utilized.

The script tag is typically used as follows:

```
<script language="JavaScript">
  JavaScript statements
</script>
```

The script tag may be placed in either the *head* or the *body* of an HTML document. In many cases, it is better to place the script tag in the head of a document to ensure that all JavaScript definitions have been made before the body of the document is displayed. You'll learn more about this in the subsection "Use of the Document Head," later in this section.

The traditional first exercise with any programming language is to write a program to display the text *Hello World!* This teaches the programmer to display output, a necessary feature of most programs. A JavaScript script that displays this text is shown in Listing 2.1.

The body of our example document (the lines between the `<body>` and the `</body>` tags) contains a single element: a script, identified by the `<script>` and `</script>` tags. The opening script tag has the attribute `language="JavaScript"` to identify the script as JavaScript. The script has a single statement, `document.write("Hello World!")`, that writes the text *Hello World!* to the body of the current `document` object. Figure 2.6 shows how the HTML document is displayed by a JavaScript-enabled browser. The text written by the script becomes part of the HTML document displayed by the browser.

FIGURE 2.6

The very simple result of Listing 2.1, Hello World!, displayed by Netscape Navigator 3.0

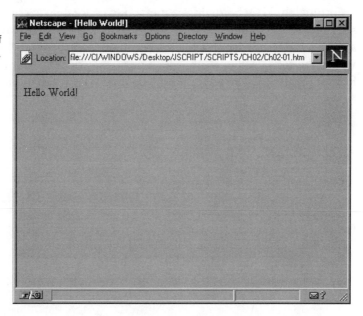

Listing 2.1. Hello World! (ch02-01.htm)

```
<html>
<head>
<title>Hello World!</title>
</head>
<body>
```

```
<script language="JavaScript">
document.write("Hello World!")
</script>
</body>
</html>
```

Telling Non-JavaScript Browsers to Ignore Your Code

Not all browsers support JavaScript. Older browsers, such as the Internet Explorer 2.0 and the character-based Lynx browser, do not recognize the script tag and, as a consequence, display as text all the JavaScript statements that are enclosed between <script> and </script>. Figures 2.7 and 2.8 show how the preceding JavaScript script is displayed by Internet Explorer 2.0 and by DosLynx.

Fortunately, HTML provides a method to conceal JavaScript statements from such JavaScript-challenged browsers. The trick is to use HTML *comment* tags to *surround* the JavaScript statements. Because HTML comments are displayed only within the code used to create a Web page, they do not show up as part of the browser's display. The use of HTML comment tags is as follows:

```
<!-- Begin hiding JavaScript
JavaScript statements
// End hiding JavaScript -->
```

FIGURE 2.7

Internet Explorer 2.0 displays the Hello World! script of Listing 2.1 instead of executing it.

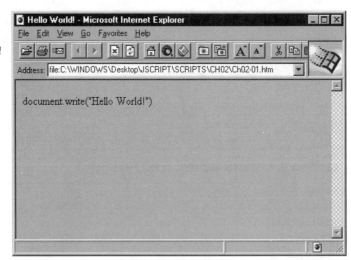

FIGURE 2.8

DosLynx displays the Hello World! script of Listing 2.1 instead of executing it.

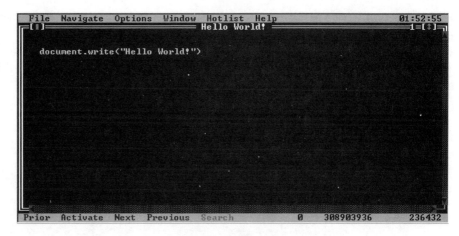

The < ! - - tag begins the HTML comment and the - - > tag ends the comment. The / / string identifies a JavaScript comment, as you'll learn later in this chapter in the section "JavaScript Comments."

The comment tags cause the JavaScript statements to be treated as comments by JavaScript-challenged browsers. JavaScript-enabled browsers, on the other hand, know to ignore the comment tags and process the enclosed statements as JavaScript. Listing 2.2 shows how HTML comments are used to hide JavaScript statements. Figure 2.9 shows how Internet Explorer 2.0 displays the HTML document shown in Listing 2.2.

Listing 2.2. Using HTML comments to hide JavaScript code (ch02-02.htm)

```
<html>
<head>
<title>Using HTML comments to hide JavaScript code</title>
</head>
<body>
<script language="JavaScript">
<!-- Begin hiding JavaScript
document.write("Hello World!")
// End hiding Javascript -->
</script>
</body>
</html>
```

FIGURE 2.9

Result of using HTML comments (Listing 2.2) with Internet Explorer 2.0. Compare to Figures 2.7 and 2.8.

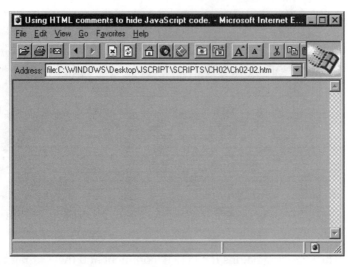

The *Noscript* Tag

Versions 2.0 and later of Netscape Navigator and versions 3.0 and later of Microsoft Internet Explorer support JavaScript. These browsers account for nearly 90% of browser use on the Web and their percentage of use is increasing. This means that most browser requests come from JavaScript-capable browsers. However, there are still popular browsers, such as Lynx, that do not support JavaScript. In addition, both Navigator and Internet Explorer provide users with the option of *disabling* JavaScript. The `<noscript>` tag was created for those browsers that can't or won't process JavaScript. It is used to display markup that is an alternative to executing a script. The HTML instructions contained inside the tag are displayed by JavaScript-challenged browsers (as well as by JavaScript-capable browsers that have JavaScript disabled). The script shown in Listing 2.3 illustrates the use of the noscript tag. Figure 2.10 shows the Web page of Listing 2.3 as displayed by a JavaScript-capable browser. Compare that display to Figure 2.11, which shows how it is displayed by Internet Explorer 2.0, a non-JavaScript browser.

FIGURE 2.10

Using the Noscript tag with Navigator, a JavaScript-capable browser (Listing 2.3)

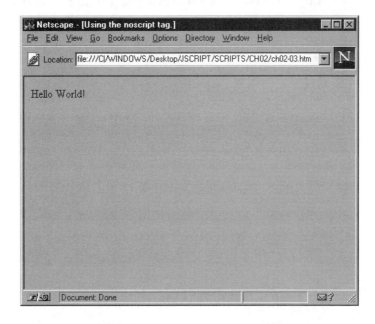

FIGURE 2.11

Using the Noscript tag with Internet Explorer 2.0, a non-JavaScript browser (Listing 2.3)

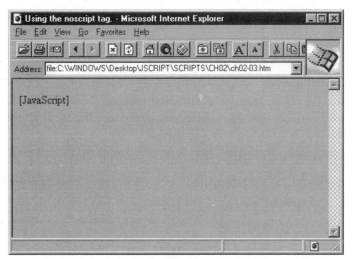

Listing 2.3. Using the Noscript Tag (ch02-03.htm)

```
<html>
<head>
<title>Using the noscript tag.</title>
</head>
<body>
<script language="JavaScript">
<!-- Begin hiding JavaScript
document.write("Hello World!")
// End hiding Javascript -->
</script>
<NOSCRIPT>
[JavaScript]
</NOSCRIPT>
</body>
</html>
```

The Script Tag's SRC Attribute

The script tag itself provides an alternative way to include JavaScript code in an HTML document, via the tag's SRC attribute, which may be used to specify a *file* containing JavaScript statements. Here's an example of the use of the SRC attribute:

```
<script language="JavaScript" SRC="src.js">
</script>
```

In the above example, the file src.js is a file containing JavaScript statements. (The file could have been named anything, but it should end with the .js extension; I just chose src.js to help you remember the src attribute.) Note that the closing </script> tag is still required.

If the file src.js contains the following code, then the HTML document shown in Listing 2.4 would produce the browser display shown in Figure 2.12.

```
<!-- Begin hiding JavaScript
document.write("This text was generated by code in the
➥ src.js file.")
// End hiding JavaScript -->
```

NOTE

The SRC attribute may have a URL as its attribute value. Web servers that provide the source file, however, *must* report the file's MIME type as `application/x-javascript`; otherwise, browsers will not load the source file.

Listing 2.4. Inserting Source JavaScript Files (ch02-04.htm)

```
<html>
<head>
<title>Using the SRC attribute of the script tag.</title>
</head>
<body>
<script language="JavaScript" SRC="src.js">
</script>
</body>
</html>
```

FIGURE 2.12

Using the SRC attribute of the script tag to include JavaScript code (Listing 2.4)

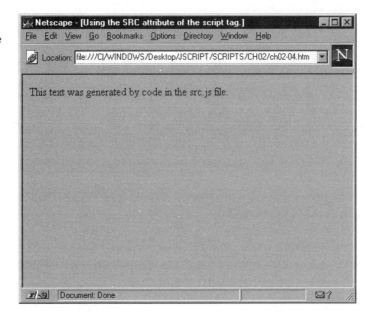

JavaScript Entities

JavaScript entities allow the value of an HTML attribute to be provided by a JavaScript *expression*. This allows attribute values to be dynamically calculated during the loading of a Web page.

A JavaScript entity begins with &{ and ends with };. The following example shows how the HREF attribute of a link may be specified by the JavaScript linkTo variable:

```
<A HREF="&{linkTo};">Click here.</A>
```

The value of linkTo, which must be calculated earlier in the script, must be a valid URL.

Listing 2.5 shows how the linkTo variable can be used to create a link to this book's Web page.

Listing 2.5. Using JavaScript Entities (ch02-05.htm)

```
<html>
<head>
<title>Using the JavaScript entities.</title>
<script language="JavaScript"><!--
linkTo="http://www.jaworski.com/javascript"
// -->
</script>
</head>
<body>
<A HREF="&{linkTo};">Click here.</A>
</body>
</html>
```

JavaScript Comments

The JavaScript language provides comments of its own. These comments are used to insert notes and processing descriptions into scripts. The comments are ignored (as intended) when the statements of a script are parsed by JavaScript-enabled browsers.

JavaScript comments use the syntax of C++ and Java. The // string identifies a comment that continues to the end of a line. An example of a single line comment follows.

```
// This JavaScript comment continues to the end of the line.
```

The /* and */ strings are used to identify comments that may span multiple lines. The comment begins with /* and continues up to */. An example of a multiple line comment follows.

```
/* This is
an example
of a multiple
line comment */
```

The script shown in Listing 2.6 illustrates the use of JavaScript comments. The script contains four statements that, if they weren't ignored, would write various capitalizations of the text *Hello World!* to the current document. However, since the first three of these statements are contained in comments, and since comments are ignored by browsers, these statements have no effect on the Web page generated by the script. Figure 2.13 shows how the JavaScript comments in Listing 2.6 are handled by a JavaScript-capable browser.

Listing 2.6. Using JavaScript comments (ch02-06.htm)

```
<html>
<head>
<title>Using JavaScript comments</title>
</head>
<body>
<script language="JavaScript">
<!-- Begin hiding JavaScript
// document.write("hello world!")
/* document.write("Hello world!")
document.write("Hello World!") */
document.write("HELLO WORLD!")
// End hiding Javascript -->
</script>
</body>
</html>
```

FIGURE 2.13

How JavaScript comments are handled by a JavaScript-capable browser (Listing 2.6)

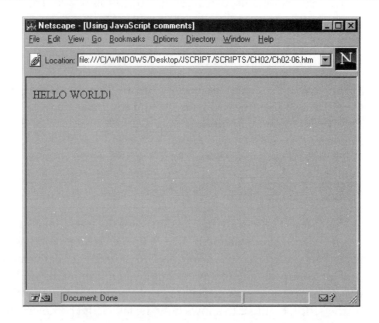

NOTE   Throughout the rest of the book, all browser references will be to JavaScript-capable browsers, unless otherwise specified.

Use of the Document Head

The head of an HTML document provides a great place to include JavaScript definitions. Since the head of a document is processed before its body, placing definitions in the head will cause them to be defined before they are used. This is important because any attempt to use a variable before it is defined results in an error. Listing 2.7 shows how JavaScript definitions can be placed in the head of an HTML document. The script contained in the document head defines a variable named *greeting* and sets its value to the string *Hi Web surfers!* (You'll learn all about variables in the "Variables" section later in this chapter.) The scriptcontained in the document's body then writes the value of the `greeting` variable to the current document. Figure 2.14 shows how this document is displayed.

Listing 2.7. Using the head for definitions (ch02-07.htm)

```
<HTML>
<HEAD>
<TITLE>Using the HEAD for definitions</TITLE>
<SCRIPT language="JavaScript">
<!--
greeting = "Hi Web surfers!"
// -->
</SCRIPT>
</HEAD>
<BODY>
<SCRIPT language="JavaScript">
<!--
document.write(greeting)
// -->
</SCRIPT>
</BODY>
</HTML>
```

FIGURE 2.14

How the greeting variable is displayed (Listing 2.7)

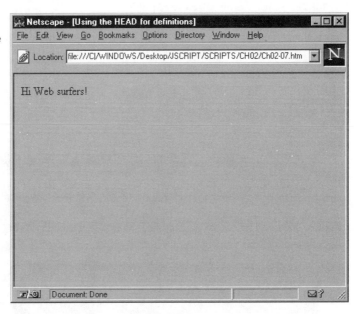

It is important to make sure that all definitions occur before they are used; otherwise an error will be displayed when your HTML document is loaded by a browser. Listing 2.8 contains an HTML document that will generate a "use before definition" error. In this listing, the head contains a JavaScript statement that writes the value of the `greeting` variable to the current document; however, the `greeting` variable is not defined until the body of the document. Figure 2.15 shows how this error is displayed by a browser.

Listing 2.8. Example of use before definition (ch02-08.htm)

```
<HTML>
<HEAD>
<TITLE>Use before definition</TITLE>
<SCRIPT language="JavaScript">
<!--
document.write(greeting)
// -->
</SCRIPT>
</HEAD>
<BODY>
<SCRIPT language="JavaScript">
<!--
greeting = "Hi Web surfers!"
// -->
</SCRIPT>
</BODY>
</HTML>
```

FIGURE 2.15

JavaScript generates an error when a variable is used before it is defined. (Listing 2.8)

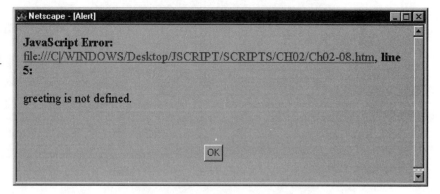

Netscape - [Alert]

JavaScript Error:
file:///C|/WINDOWS/Desktop/JSCRIPT/SCRIPTS/CH02/Ch02-08.htm, **line 5:**

greeting is not defined.

OK

Generating HTML

The examples presented so far have shown how you can use JavaScript to write simple text to the `document` object. By including HTML tags in your JavaScript script, you can also use JavaScript to generate HTML elements that will be displayed in the current document. The example shown in Listing 2.9 illustrates this concept. Figure 2.16 shows how the Web page generated by this script is displayed.

Listing 2.9. Using JavaScript to create HTML tags (ch02-09.htm)

```
<HTML>
<HEAD>
<TITLE>Using JavaScript to create HTML tags</TITLE>
<SCRIPT LANGUAGE="JavaScript">
<!--
greeting = "<H1>Hi Web surfers!</H1>"
welcome = "<P>Welcome to <CITE>Mastering JavaScript</CITE>.</P>"
// -->
</SCRIPT>
</HEAD>
<BODY>
<SCRIPT LANGUAGE="JavaScript">
<!--
document.write(greeting)
document.write(welcome)
// -->
</SCRIPT>
</BODY>
</HTML>
```

In the script contained in the head of the HTML document, the variables `greeting` and `welcome` are assigned text strings containing embedded HTML tags. These text strings are displayed by the script contained in the body of the HTML document:

- The `greeting` variable contains the heading *Hi Web surfers!*, which is surrounded by the HTML heading tags `<H1>` and `</H1>`.

- The `welcome` variable is assigned the string *Welcome to Mastering JavaScript*.

- The citation tags , `<CITE>` and `</CITE>`, cause the `welcome` variable's string to be cited as a literary reference (which means it shows up in italic).

- The paragraph tags, `<P>` and `</P>`, that surround the `welcome` text are used to mark it as a separate paragraph.

The resulting HTML document generated by the script is equivalent to the following:

```
<HTML>
<HEAD>
<TITLE>Using JavaScript to create HTML tags</TITLE>
</HEAD>
<BODY>
<H1>Hi Web surfers!</H1>
<P>Welcome to <CITE>Mastering JavaScript</CITE>.</P>
</BODY>
</HTML>
```

So far, I've been making use of variables, such as `greeting` and `welcome`, without having explicitly defined what they are. In the next section, I formally introduce variables.

FIGURE 2.16

Generating HTML from
JavaScript (Listing 2.9)

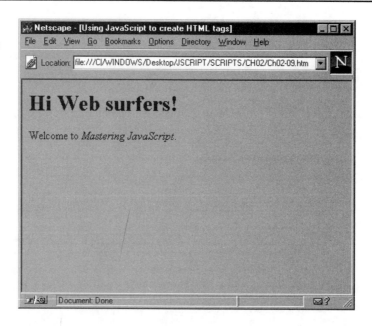

Variables

JavaScript, like other programming languages, uses variables to store values so they can be used in other parts of a program. Variables are names that are associated with these stored values. For example, the variable `imageName` may be used to refer to the name of an image file to be displayed and the variable `totalAmount` may be used to display the total amount of a user's purchase.

Variable names can begin with an uppercase letter (A through Z), lowercase letter (a through z), or an underscore character (_). The remaining characters can consist of letters, the underscore character, or digits (0 through 9). Examples of variable names are as follows:

```
orderNumber2
_123
SUM
Image7
Previous_Document
```

Variable names are case sensitive. This means that a variable named `sum` refers to a different value than one named `Sum`, `sUm`, or `SUM`.

WARNING Since variable names are case sensitive, it is important to make sure that you use the same capitalization each time you use a variable.

Types and Variables

Unlike Java and some other programming languages, JavaScript does not require you to specify the *type* of data contained in a variable. (It doesn't even allow it.) In fact, the same variable may be used to contain a variety of different values, such as the text string *Hello World!*, the integer *13*, the floating-point value *3.14*, or the logical value *true*. The JavaScript interpreter keeps track of and converts the type of data contained in a variable.

JavaScript's automatic handling of different types of values is a double-edged sword. On one side, it frees you from having to explicitly specify the type of data contained in a variable and from having to convert from one data type to another. On the other side, since JavaScript automatically converts values of one type to another, it is important to keep track of what types of values should be contained in a variable and how they are converted in expressions involving variables of other types. The next section, "Types and Literal Values," identifies the types of values supported by JavaScript. The section following it, "Conversion between Types," discusses important issues related to type conversion.

Types and Literal Values

JavaScript supports four primitive types of values, and supports complex types, such as arrays and objects. *Primitive types* are types that can be assigned a single literal value, such as a number, string, or boolean value. Here are the primitive types supported by JavaScript:

- Integers

- Floating-point numbers

- Logical or boolean values

- Strings

In addition, JavaScript has the *null* value, which is a value common to all four of these types. The null value is used to represent a default or unspecified value.

> **NOTE** You'll learn about the complex types, such as arrays and objects, later in this chapter, in the section "Complex Types."

In JavaScript, you do not declare the type of a variable, as you do in other languages, such as Java and C++. Instead, the type of a variable is implicitly defined based on the literal values that you assign to it. For example, if you assign the integer *123* to the variable `total`, then `total` will support integer operations. If you assign the string value *The sum of all accounts* to total, then `total` will support string operations. Similarly, if you assign the logical value *true* to `total`, then it will support logical operations.

It is also possible for a variable to be assigned a value of one type and then later in the script's execution be assigned a value of another type. For example, the variable `total` could be assigned *123*, then *The sum of all accounts*, and then *true*.

The type of the variable would change with the type of value assigned to it. The different types of literal values that can be assigned to a variable are covered in the following subsections.

Number Types: Integers and Floating-Point Numbers

When working with numbers, JavaScript supports both integer and floating-point values. It transparently converts from one type to another as values of one type are combined with values of other types in numerical expressions. For example, integer values are converted to floating-point values when they are used in floating point expressions.

Integer Literals   Integers can be represented in JavaScript in decimal, hexadecimal, or octal form.

- *A decimal (base ten) integer* is what nonprogrammers are used to seeing: the digits 0 through 9, with each new column representing a higher power of ten.

- *A hexadecimal (base sixteen) integer* in JavaScript must always begin with the characters 0x or 0X in the two leftmost columns. Hexadecimal uses the letters 0 through 9 to represent the values zero through nine and the letters A through F to represent the values normal people know as ten through fifteen.

- *An octal (base eight) integer* in JavaScript must always begin with the character 0 in the leftmost column. Octal uses only the digits 0 through 7.

Examples of decimal, hexadecimal, and octal integers are provided in Table 2.1.

TABLE 2.1   Examples of decimal, hexadecimal, and octal integers for the same values

Decimal Number	Hexadecimal Equivalent	Octal Equivalent
19	0x13	023
255	0xff	0377
513	0x201	01001
1024	0x400	02000
12345	0x3039	030071

The program shown in Listing 2.10 illustrates the use of JavaScript hexadecimal and octal integers. Figure 2.17 shows how the Web page generated by this program is displayed. Note that the hexadecimal and octal integers are converted to decimal before they are displayed.

FIGURE 2.17

Using hexadecimal
and octal integers
(Listing 2.10)

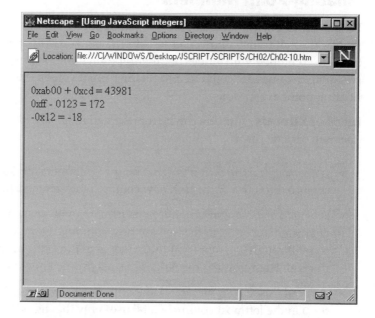

Listing 2.10. Using JavaScript integers (ch02-10.htm)

```
<HTML>
<HEAD>
<TITLE>Using JavaScript integers</TITLE>
</HEAD>
<BODY>
<SCRIPT LANGUAGE="JavaScript">
<!--
document.write("0xab00 + 0xcd = ")
document.write(0xab00 + 0xcd)
document.write("<BR>")
document.write("0xff - 0123 = ")
document.write(0xff - 0123)
document.write("<BR>")
document.write("-0x12 = ")
```

```
document.write(-0x12)
// -->
</SCRIPT>
</BODY>
</HTML>
```

Floating-Point Literals Floating-point literals are used to represent numbers that require the use of a decimal point, or very large or small numbers that must be written using exponential notation.

A floating-point number must consist of either a number containing a decimal point or an integer followed by an exponent. The following are valid floating-point numbers:

```
-4.321
55.
12e2
1e-2
7e1
-4e-4
.5
```

As you can see in the examples above, floating-point literals may contain an initial integer, followed by an optional decimal point and fraction, followed by an optional exponent ("e" or "E") and its integer exponent value. Also, the initial integer and integer exponent value may be signed as positive or negative (+ or −).

The script shown in Listing 2.11 and Figure 2.18 shows how these values are displayed by JavaScript. Notice that JavaScript simplifies the display of these numbers whenever possible.

Listing 2.11. Using floating-point numbers (ch02-11.htm)

```
<HTML>
<HEAD>
<TITLE>Using floating-point numbers</TITLE>
</HEAD>
<BODY>
<SCRIPT LANGUAGE="JavaScript">
<!--
document.write(-4.321)
document.write("<BR>")
document.write(55.)
```

```
document.write("<BR>")
document.write(12e2)
document.write("<BR>")
document.write(1e-2)
document.write("<BR>")
document.write(7e1)
document.write("<BR>")
document.write(-4e-4)
document.write("<BR>")
document.write(.5)
// -->
</SCRIPT>
</BODY>
</HTML>
```

FIGURE 2.18

How floating-point num-
bers are displayed by
JavaScript (Listing 2.11)

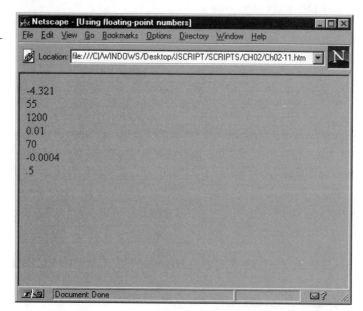

Logical Values

JavaScript, like Java and unlike C, supports a pure boolean type that consists of
the two values *true* and *false*. Several logical operators may be used in boolean
expressions, as you'll learn in Chapter 3 (in the section "Logical Operators").
JavaScript automatically converts the boolean values *true* and *false* into *1* and *0*

when they are used in numerical expressions. The script shown in Listing 2.12 illustrates this automatic conversion. Figure 2.19 shows the results of this conversion as displayed by Navigator.

A *boolean value* is a value that is either true or false. The word *boolean* is taken from the name of the mathematician George Boole, who developed much of the fundamental theory of mathematical logic.

FIGURE 2.19

How logical values are converted to other types (Listing 2.12)

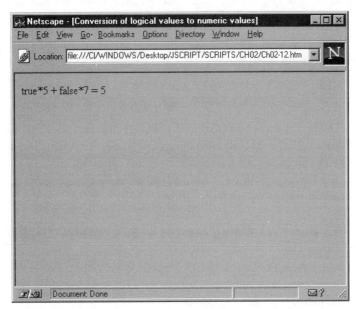

Listing 2.12. Conversion of logical values to numeric values (ch02-12.htm)

```
<HTML>
<HEAD>
<TITLE>Conversion of logical values to numeric values</TITLE>
</HEAD>
<BODY>
<SCRIPT LANGUAGE="JavaScript">
<!--
```

```
document.write("true*5 + false*7 = ")
document.write(true*5 +false*7)
// -->
</SCRIPT>
</BODY>
</HTML>
```

String Values

JavaScript provides built-in support for strings of characters. A string is a sequence of zero or more characters that are enclosed by double (") or single quotes ('). If a string begins with a double quote then it must end with a double quote. Likewise, if a string begins with a single quote then it must end in a single quote.

To insert a quote character in a string, you must precede it by the backslash (\) escape character. The following are examples of the use of the escape character to insert quotes into strings:

```
"He asked, \"Who owns this book?\""
'It\'s Bill\'s book.'
```

The script shown in Listing 2.13 illustrates the use of quotes within strings. Figure 2.20 shows how the strings are displayed. Note that single quotes do not need to be coded with escape characters when they are used within double-quoted strings. Similarly, double quotes do not need to be coded when they are used within single-quoted strings.

Listing 2.13. Using quotes within strings (ch02-13.htm)

```
<HTML>
<HEAD>
<TITLE>Using quotes within strings</TITLE>
</HEAD>
<BODY>
<SCRIPT LANGUAGE="JavaScript">
<!--
document.write("He said, \"That's mine!\"<BR>")
document.write('She said, "No it\'s not."<BR>')
document.write('That\'s all folks!')
// -->
</SCRIPT>
</BODY>
</HTML>
```

FIGURE 2.20

How quotes are inserted
into strings (Listing 2.13)

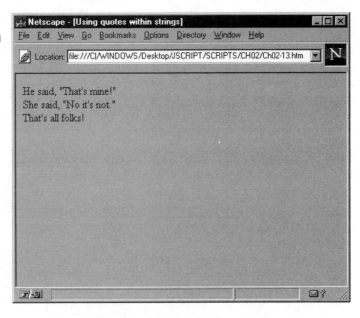

He said, "That's mine!"
She said, "No it's not."
That's all folks!

JavaScript defines five special formatting characters for use in strings. These characters are identified in Table 2.2.

TABLE 2.2   Special formatting characters

Character	Meaning
\n	new line
\r	carriage return
\f	form feed
\t	horizontal tab
\b	backspace

The script shown in Listing 2.14 shows how these formatting characters are used. Figure 2.21 displays the Web page generated by this script. The Web page uses the HTML *preformatted text* tags to prevent the formatting characters from being treated as HTML whitespace characters. (If you are unfamiliar with the preformatted text tag consult Appendix A, "HTML Reference.") Notice that the backspace character is incorrectly displayed, the form feed character is ignored, and that the carriage return character is displayed in the same manner as the new line character. Even though these characters are not fully supported in the display of Web pages they may still be used to insert formatting codes within data and files that are produced by JavaScript.

FIGURE 2.21

How formatting characters are handled (Listing 2.14). Note that not all characters are processed by your Web browser.

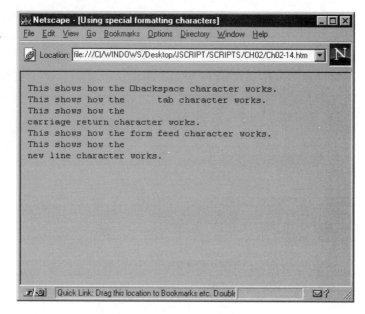

Listing 2.14. Using special formatting characters (ch02-14.htm)

```
<HTML>
<HEAD>
<TITLE>Using special formatting characters</TITLE>
</HEAD>
<BODY>
<PRE>
<SCRIPT LANGUAGE="JavaScript">
<!--
document.write("This shows how the \bbackspace character
➡ works.\n")
```

```
document.write("This shows how the \ttab character works.\n")
document.write("This shows how the \rcarriage return character
➡ works.\n")
document.write("This shows how the \fform feed character
➡ works.\n")
document.write("This shows how the \nnew line character
➡ works.\n")
// -->
</SCRIPT>
</PRE>
</BODY>
</HTML>
```

The null Value

The *null* value is a value that is common to all JavaScript types. It is used to set a variable to an initial value that is different from other valid values. Use of the *null* value prevents the sort of errors that result from using uninitialized variables. The *null* value is automatically converted to default values of other types when used in an expression, as you'll see in the following section, "Conversion between Types."

Conversion between Types

JavaScript automatically converts values from one type to another when they are used in an expression. This means that you can combine different types in an expression and JavaScript will try to perform the type conversions that are necessary for the expression to make sense. For example, the expression, `"test"` + 5 will convert the numeric 5 to a string *"5"* and append it to the string *"test"*, producing *"test5"*. JavaScript's automatic type conversion also allows you to assign a value of one type to a variable and then later assign a value of a different type to the same variable.

How does JavaScript convert from one type to another? The process of determining when a conversion should occur and what type of conversion should be made is fairly complex. JavaScript converts values when it evaluates an expression or assigns a value to a variable. When JavaScript assigns a value to a variable it changes the type associated with the variable to the type of the value that is assigns.

When JavaScript evaluates an expression, it parses the expression into its component unary and binary expressions based upon the order of precedence of the operators it contains. It then evaluates the component unary and binary expressions of the parse tree. Figure 2.22 illustrates this process. Each expression is evaluated according to the operators involved. If an operator takes a value of a type that is different than the type of an operand, then the operand is converted to a type that is valid for the operator.

Some operators, such as the + operator, may be used for more than one type. For example, "a"+"b" results in the string *"ab"* when the + operator is used with string values, but it assumes its typical arithmetic meaning when used with numeric operands. What happens when JavaScript attempts to evaluate "a"+3? JavaScript converts the integer 3 into the string *"3"* and yields *"a3"* for the expression. In general, JavaScript will favor string operators over all others, followed by floating-point, integer, and logical operators.

NOTE Expressions are covered in the section "Operators and Expressions," in Chapter 3.

FIGURE 2.22

Expressions are evaluated based on the types of operators involved.

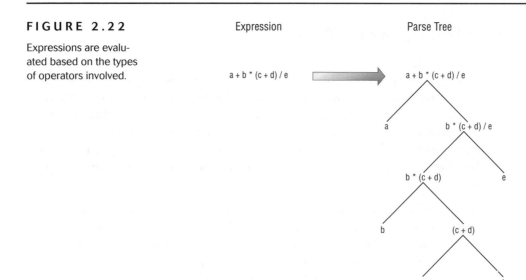

Expression

Parse Tree

The script shown in Listing 2.15 illustrates JavaScript conversion between types when the + operator is used. Figure 2.23 shows how the Web page resulting from this script is displayed. Note that in all cases where string operands are used with a non-string operator, JavaScript converts the other operator into a string:

- Numeric values are converted to their appropriate string value.

- Boolean values are converted to *1* and *0* to support numerical operations.

- The *null* value is converted to *"null"* for string operations, *false* for logical operations, and *0* for numerical operations.

Listing 2.15. Automatic conversion between types (ch02-15.htm)

```
<HTML>
<HEAD>
<TITLE>Implicit conversion between types</TITLE>
<SCRIPT LANGUAGE="JavaScript">
<!--
s1="test"
s2="12.34"
i=123
r=.123
lt=true
lf=false
n=null
// -->
</SCRIPT>
</HEAD>
<BODY>
<H1>Implicit conversion between types</H1>
<TABLE BORDER=2>
<SCRIPT LANGUAGE="JavaScript">
<!--
// Column headings for table
document.write("<TR>")
document.write("<TH>row + column</TH>")
document.write("<TH>string \"12.34\"</TH>")
document.write("<TH>integer 123</TH>")
document.write("<TH>float .123</TH>")
document.write("<TH>logical true</TH>")
document.write("<TH>logical false</TH>")
document.write("<TH>null</TH>")
document.write("</TR>")
```

```
// First operand is a string
document.write("<TR>")
document.write("<TH>string \"test\"</TH>")
document.write("<TD>")
document.write(s1+s2)
document.write("</TD><TD>")
document.write(s1+i)
document.write("</TD><TD>")
document.write(s1+r)
document.write("</TD><TD>")
document.write(s1+lt)
document.write("</TD><TD>")
document.write(s1+lf)
document.write("</TD><TD>")
document.write(s1+n)
document.write("</TD>")
document.write("</TR>")
// First operand is an integer
document.write("<TR>")
document.write("<TH>integer 123</TH>")
document.write("<TD>")
document.write(i+s2)
document.write("</TD><TD>")
document.write(i+i)
document.write("</TD><TD>")
document.write(i+r)
document.write("</TD><TD>")
document.write(i+lt)
document.write("</TD><TD>")
document.write(i+lf)
document.write("</TD><TD>")
document.write(i+n)
document.write("</TD>")
document.write("</TR>")
// First operand is a float
document.write("<TR>")
document.write("<TH>float .123</TH>")
document.write("<TD>")
document.write(r+s2)
document.write("</TD><TD>")
document.write(r+i)
document.write("</TD><TD>")
document.write(r+r)
```

```
document.write("</TD><TD>")
document.write(r+1t)
document.write("</TD><TD>")
document.write(r+1f)
document.write("</TD><TD>")
document.write(r+n)
document.write("</TD>")
document.write("</TR>")
// First operand is a logical true
document.write("<TR>")
document.write("<TH>logical true</TH>")
document.write("<TD>")
document.write(1t+s2)
document.write("</TD><TD>")
document.write(1t+i)
document.write("</TD><TD>")
document.write(1t+r)
document.write("</TD><TD>")
document.write(1t+1t)
document.write("</TD><TD>")
document.write(1t+1f)
document.write("</TD><TD>")
document.write(1t+n)
document.write("</TD>")
document.write("</TR>")
// First operand is a logical false
document.write("<TR>")
document.write("<TH>logical false</TH>")
document.write("<TD>")
document.write(1f+s2)
document.write("</TD><TD>")
document.write(1f+i)
document.write("</TD><TD>")
document.write(1f+r)
document.write("</TD><TD>")
document.write(1f+1t)
document.write("</TD><TD>")
document.write(1f+1f)
document.write("</TD><TD>")
document.write(1f+n)
document.write("</TD>")
document.write("</TR>")
// First operand is null
```

```
document.write("<TR>")
document.write("<TH>null</TH>")
document.write("<TD>")
document.write(n+s2)
document.write("</TD><TD>")
document.write(n+i)
document.write("</TD><TD>")
document.write(n+r)
document.write("</TD><TD>")
document.write(n+lt)
document.write("</TD><TD>")
document.write(n+lf)
document.write("</TD><TD>")
document.write(n+n)
document.write("</TD>")
document.write("</TR>")
// -->
</SCRIPT>
</TABLE>
</BODY>
</HTML>
```

FIGURE 2.23

Conversion table for the + operator (Listing 2.15)

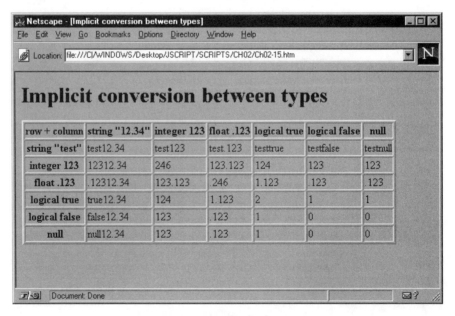

Netscape - [Implicit conversion between types]

File Edit View Go Bookmarks Options Directory Window Help

Location: file:///C|/WINDOWS/Desktop/JSCRIPT/SCRIPTS/CH02/Ch02-15.htm

Implicit conversion between types

row + column	string "12.34"	integer 123	float .123	logical true	logical false	null
string "test"	test12.34	test123	test.123	testtrue	testfalse	testnull
integer 123	12312.34	246	123.123	124	123	123
float .123	.12312.34	123.123	.246	1.123	.123	.123
logical true	true12.34	124	1.123	2	1	1
logical false	false12.34	123	.123	1	0	0
null	null12.34	123	.123	1	0	0

Document: Done

Let's take a look at Listing 2.15. The script in the document head defines the variables to be used in the table's operations. The s1 and s2 variables are assigned string values. The i and r variables are assigned integer and floating-point values. The lt and lf variables are assigned logical values. The n variable is assigned the *null* value.

The script in the document body is fairly long. However, most of the script is used to generate the HTML tags for the cells of the conversion table. The script is surrounded by the tags <TABLE BORDER=2> and </TABLE>. The script then generates the cells of the table one row at a time. The <TR> and </TR> tags mark a row of the table. The <TH> and </TH> tags mark header cells. The <TD> and </TD> tags identify normal non-header table cells.

First, the column header row is displayed. Then each row of the table shown in Figure 2.23 is generated by combining the operand at the row heading with the operand at the table heading using the + operator.

Conversion Errors

If JavaScript cannot convert a value to a type that is valid for an operation it will generate a *runtime error*. An error will typically occur if a conversion from a string value to a numerical or logical value is required and the string value does not represent a value of the target type. The script shown in Listing 2.16 provides an example of a string conversion that results in a runtime error. The integer *123* is multiplied by the string *"test"*. Since the * operator is a numeric operator and not a string operator, JavaScript attempts to convert *"test"* into a number. Because the *"test"* value does not represent a valid number, a conversion error is generated. Figure 2.24 shows the error message that results from the script in Listing 2.16.

FIGURE 2.24

Example of a conversion error (Listing 2.16)

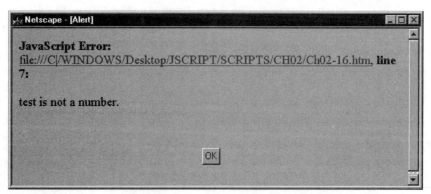

Listing 2.16. String conversion error (ch02-16.htm)

```
<HTML>
<HEAD>
<TITLE>String conversion error</TITLE>
</HEAD>
<BODY>
<SCRIPT language="JavaScript">
<!--
document.write(123*"test")
// -->
</SCRIPT>
</BODY>
</HTML>
```

Conversion errors do not normally occur for numeric or logical values or the *null* value. A numeric value can always be converted to its string equivalent. Most logical operators also support numeric operations.

> **NOTE**
>
> JavaScript 1.2 has made significant changes to the equality and inequality operators (== and !=). These operators, discussed in Chapter 3, are used to compare expressions. If a script has its LANGUAGE attribute set to Java-Script1.2 then the equality and inequality operators will no longer convert values from one type to another before testing for equality or inequality.

Conversion Functions

Functions are collections of JavaScript code that perform a particular task, and often return a value. A function may take zero or more parameters. These parameters are used to specify the data to be processed by the function. You'll learn more about functions in the section of Chapter 3 named "Function Calls."

JavaScript provides three functions which are used to perform explicit type conversion. These are eval(), parseInt(), and parseFloat().

> **NOTE**
>
> Functions are referenced by their name with the empty parameter list "()" appended. This makes it easier to differentiate between functions and variables in the discussion of scripts.

The eval() function is used to convert a string expression to a numeric value. For example, the statement total = eval("432.1*10"), results in the value *4321* being assigned to the total variable. The eval() function takes the string value *"432.1*10"* as a parameter and returns the numeric value *4321* as the result of the function call. If the string value passed as a parameter to the eval() function does not represent a numeric value, then use of eval() results in an error being generated.

The parseInt() function is used to convert a string value into an integer. Unlike eval(), parseInt() returns the first integer contained in the string or *0* if the string does not begin with an integer. For example, parseInt("123xyz") returns *123* and parseInt("xyz") returns *0*. The parseInt() function also parses hexadecimal and decimal integers.

The parseFloat() function is similar to the parseInt() function. It returns the first floating-point number contained in a string or *0* if the string does not begin with a valid floating-point number. For example, parseFloat("2.1e4xyz") returns *21000* and parseFloat("xyz") returns *0*.

The script shown in Listing 2.17 illustrates the use of JavaScript's explicit conversion functions. Figure 2.25 shows how the Web page generated by this script is displayed.

Listing 2.17. Explicit conversion functions (ch02-17.htm)

```
<HTML>
<HEAD>
<TITLE>Using Explicit Conversion Functions</TITLE>
</HEAD>
<BODY>
<H1 ALIGN="CENTER">Using Explicit Conversion Functions</H1>
<SCRIPT LANGUAGE="JavaScript"><!--
document.write('eval("12.34*10") = ')
document.write(eval("12.34*10"))
document.write("<BR>")
document.write('parseInt("0x10") = ')
document.write(parseInt("0x10"))
document.write("<BR>")
document.write('parseFloat("5.4321e6") = ')
document.write(parseFloat("5.4321e6"))
// --></SCRIPT>
</BODY>
</HTML>
```

FIGURE 2.25

Using the JavaScript conversion functions (Listing 2.17)

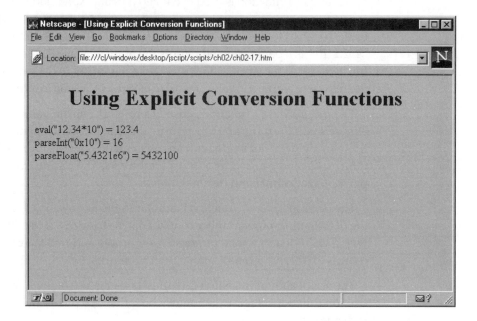

Complex Types

In addition to the primitive types discussed in the previous sections, JavaScript supports two other variable types—arrays and objects. These types are referred to as complex data types because they are built from the primitive string, numeric, and logical types.

NOTE   Arrays are a special type of JavaScript object.

Arrays

Arrays are objects which are capable of storing a sequence of values. These values are stored in indexed locations within the array. For example, suppose you have a company with five employees and you want to display the names of your employees on a Web page. You could keep track of their names in an array variable named `employee`. You would declare the array using the statement

```
employee = new Array(5)
```

and store the names of your employees in the array using the following statements.

```
employee[0] = "Bill"
employee[1] = "Bob"
employee[2] = "Ted"
employee[3] = "Alice"
employee[4] = "Sue"
```

You could then access the names of the individual employees by referring to the individual elements of the array. For example, you could display the names of your employees using statements such as the following.

```
document.write(employee[0])
document.write(employee[1])
document.write(employee[2])
document.write(employee[3])
document.write(employee[4])
```

The script shown in Listing 2.18 illustrates the use of arrays. Figure 2.26 shows how the Web page generated by this script is displayed.

Listing 2.18. Using JavaScript arrays (ch02-18.htm)

```
<HTML>
<HEAD>
<TITLE>Using Arrays</TITLE>
</HEAD>
<BODY>
<H1 ALIGN="CENTER">Using Arrays</H1>
<SCRIPT LANGUAGE="JavaScript"><!--
employee = new Array(5)
employee[0] = "Bill"
employee[1] = "Bob"
employee[2] = "Ted"
employee[3] = "Alice"
employee[4] = "Sue"
document.write(employee[0]+"<BR>")
document.write(employee[1]+"<BR>")
document.write(employee[2]+"<BR>")
document.write(employee[3]+"<BR>")
document.write(employee[4])
// --></SCRIPT>
</BODY>
</HTML>
```

FIGURE 2.26

Arrays allow multiple values to be stored with a single variable. (Listing 2.18)

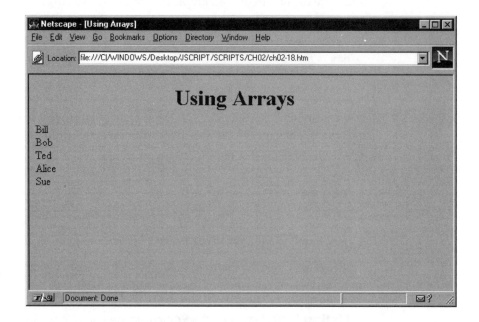

The *length* of an array is the number of elements that it contains. In the example script of Listing 2.18, the length of the employee array is 5. The individual elements of an array are referenced using the name of the array followed by the index of the array element enclosed in brackets. Because the first index is 0, the last index is one less than the length of the array. For example, suppose that you have an array named `day` of length 7 that contains the names of the days of the week. The individual elements of this array would be accessed as `day[0]`, `day[1]`, ..., `day[6]`.

Declaring Arrays An array must be declared before it is used. An array may be declared using either of the following two statement forms:

- `arrayName = new Array(arrayLength)`
- `arrayName = new Array()`

> **NOTE** A third form of array declaration is discussed in the section "Constructing Dense Arrays," which follows later in this chapter.

In the first form, the length of the array is explicitly specified. An example of this form is:

```
days = new Array(7)
```

In the above example, `days` corresponds to the array name and 7 corresponds to the array length.

When an array is declared of a specified length, JavaScript initializes the values of the elements of the array to *null*.

In the second array declaration form, the length of the array is not specified and results in the declaration of an array of length 0. An example of using this type of array declaration follows:

```
order = new Array()
```

This declares an array of length 0 that is used to keep track of customer orders. JavaScript automatically extends the length of an array when new array elements are initialized. For example, the following statements create an order array of length 0 and then subsequently extend the length of the array to 100 and then 1000.

```
order = new Array()
order[99] = "Widget #457"
order[999] = "Delux Widget Set #10"
```

When JavaScript encounters the reference to `order[99]`, in the above example, it extends the length of the array to 100, initializes `order[0]` through `order[98]` to *null*, and initializes `order[99]` to *"Widget #457"*. When JavaScript encounters the reference to `order[999]` in the third statement, it extends the length of order to 1000, initializes `order[100]` through `order[998]` to *null*, and initializes `order[999]` to *"Delux Widget Set #10"*.

Even if an array is initially declared to be of fixed initial length, it still may be extended by referencing elements that are outside the current size of the array. This is accomplished in the same manner as with zero-length arrays. Listing 2.19 shows how fixed-length arrays are expanded as new array elements are referenced. Figure 2.27 shows the how the Web page generated by this script is displayed.

Listing 2.19. Extending the length of an array (ch02-19.htm)

```
<HTML>
<HEAD>
<TITLE>Extending Arrays</TITLE>
</HEAD>
<BODY>
<H1 ALIGN="CENTER">Extending Arrays</H1>
<SCRIPT LANGUAGE="JavaScript"><!--
order = new Array()
document.write("order.length = "+order.length+"<BR>")
order[99] = "Widget #457"
document.write("order.length = "+order.length+"<BR>")
order[999] = "Delux Widget Set #10"
document.write("order.length = "+order.length+"<BR>")
// --></SCRIPT>
</BODY>
</HTML>
```

FIGURE 2.27

An array's length dynamically expands as new elements are referenced. (Listing 2.19)

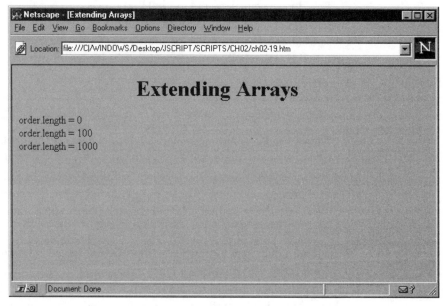

Constructing Dense Arrays A *dense array* is an array that is initially declared with each element being assigned a specified value. Dense arrays are used in the same manner as other arrays. They are just declared and initialized in a more efficient manner. Dense arrays are declared by *listing* the values of the array elements in the array declaration, in place of the array length. Dense array declarations take the following form:

```
arrayName = new Array(value_0, value_1, ... , value_n)
```

In the above declaration, because we start counting at zero, the length of the array is n+1.

When creating short length arrays, the dense array declaration is very efficient. For example, an array containing the three-letter abbreviations for the days of the week may be declared using the following statement:

```
day = new Array('Sun','Mon','Tue','Wed','Thu','Fri','Sat')
```

The Elements of an Array JavaScript does not place any restrictions on the values of the elements of an array. These values could be of different types, or could refer to other arrays or objects. For example, you could declare an array as follows:

```
junk = new Array("s1",'s2',4,3.5,true,false,null,new
Array(5,6,7))
```

The junk array has length 8 and its elements are as follows:

```
junk[0]="s1"
junk[1]='s2'
junk[2]=4
junk[3]=3.5
junk[4]=true
junk[5]=false
junk[6]=null
junk[7]=a new dense array consisting of the values 5, 6, & 7
```

The last element of the array, junk[7], contains an array as its value. The three elements of junk[7] can be accessed using *a second set of subscripts*, as follows:

```
junk[7][0]=5
junk[7][1]=6
junk[7][2]=7
```

The script shown in Listing 2.20 illustrates the use of arrays within arrays. Figure 2.28 shows the Web page that results from execution of this script.

FIGURE 2.28

An array may contain another array as the value of one of its elements. (Listing 2.20)

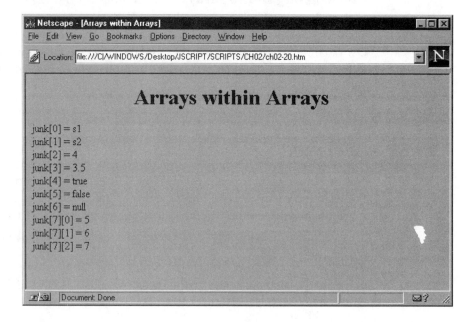

Listing 2.20. An array within an array (ch02-20.htm)

```
<HTML>
<HEAD>
<TITLE>Arrays within Arrays</TITLE>
</HEAD>
<BODY>
<H1 ALIGN="CENTER">Arrays within Arrays</H1>
<SCRIPT LANGUAGE="JavaScript"><!--
junk = new Array("s1",'s2',4,3.5,true,false,null,
➥ new Array(5,6,7))
document.write("junk[0] = "+junk[0]+"<BR>")
document.write("junk[1] = "+junk[1]+"<BR>")
document.write("junk[2] = "+junk[2]+"<BR>")
document.write("junk[3] = "+junk[3]+"<BR>")
document.write("junk[4] = "+junk[4]+"<BR>")
document.write("junk[5] = "+junk[5]+"<BR>")
document.write("junk[6] = "+junk[6]+"<BR>")
document.write("junk[7][0] = "+junk[7][0]+"<BR>")
document.write("junk[7][1] = "+junk[7][1]+"<BR>")
```

```
document.write("junk[7][2] = "+junk[7][2])
// --></SCRIPT>
</BODY>
</HTML>
```

Objects and the *length* Property

JavaScript arrays are implemented as *objects*. Objects are named collections of data that have *properties* and may be accessed via *methods*.

- A *property* returns a value that identifies some aspect of the state of an object.

- *Methods* are used to read or modify the data contained in an object.

The length of an array is a property of an array. You can access the property of any object in JavaScript by appending a period plus the name of the property to the name of the object, as shown here:

```
objectName.propertyName
```

For example, the length of an array is determined as follows:

```
arrayName.length
```

For example, consider the following array.

```
a = new Array(2,4,6,8,10)
```

The value returned by a.length is 5.

The process of declaring and using JavaScript objects is covered in Chapter 5, "Objects in JavaScript."

Summary

This chapter introduced you to the JavaScript language. You learned how JavaScript works and how JavaScript statements are embedded in HTML documents. You learned about JavaScript's use of types and variables, and how JavaScript automatically converts values of one type to another. In the next chapter, you'll be introduced to JavaScript's operators and programming statements, and learn how functions are created and invoked.

CHAPTER

THREE

3

Operators, Statements, and Functions

- Operators and Expressions

- Operator Precedence

- Statements and Declarations

- Functions and Function Calls

- Local and Global Variables

- Accessing Objects in Statements

This chapter continues your introduction to the JavaScript language. You'll cover all of the operators provided by JavaScript and learn how expressions are evaluated. You'll learn to use JavaScript's programming statements and develop sample scripts that demonstrate the use of each statement. You'll also learn how to create and invoke *functions*. When you have finished this chapter, you'll be able to write JavaScript scripts that use JavaScript's operators and statements to perform a variety of computations.

Operators and Expressions

In the previous chapter, you have used some of the basic operators provided by JavaScript. These include the + operators used with string and numeric types and the = assignment operator. In this section, you'll be introduced to all of the operators provided by JavaScript. These operators are organized into the following categories:

- Arithmetic
- Logical
- Comparison
- String
- Bit manipulation
- Assignment
- Conditional

Let's start with a little terminology. An *operator* is used to transform one or more values into a single resultant value. The values to which the operator applies are referred to as *operands*. The combination of an operator and its operands is referred to as an *expression*.

Expressions are *evaluated* in order to determine the value of the expression. This value is the value that results when the operator is applied to the operands. Some operators, like the = (assignment) operator, result in a value being assigned to a *variable*. Others produce a value that may be used in other expressions.

NOTE

For some operators, such as the * multiplication operator, the *order* of the operands does not matter—for example, x * y = y * x is true for all integers and floating-point numbers. Other operators, such as the + (string concatenation) operator, yield different results for different orderings of their operands. For example, "ab" + "cd" does not equal "cd" + "ab".

Unary operators are operators that are used with only one operand. For example, the unary operator ! is applied to a logical value and returns the *logical not* of that value. Most JavaScript operators are *binary* operators, operators that have two operands. An example of a binary operator is the * (multiplication) operator, which is used to calculate the product of two numbers. For example, the expression 7 * 6 is evaluated as 42 by applying the * operator to the operands 7 and 6.

So far we've only been dealing with simple expressions. More complex expressions can be constructed by combining simple unary and binary expressions. In order to evaluate complex expressions we must *parse* them into their component unary and binary expressions, applying the rules of order or *precedence* (for example, evaluating groups before adding or multiplying them). You'll learn more about parsing expressions later in the chapter, under "Operator Precedence."

Arithmetic Operators

Arithmetic operators are the most familiar operators because we use them every day to perform common mathematical calculations. The mathematical operators supported by JavaScript are listed in Table 3.1.

Logical Operators

Logical operators are used to perform boolean operations on boolean operands, such as *logical and*, *logical or*, and *logical not*. The logical operators supported by JavaScript are listed in Table 3.2.

Comparison Operators

Comparison operators are used to determine whether two values are equal or to compare numerical values to determine which value is greater than the other. The comparison operators supported by JavaScript are listed in Table 3.3.

TABLE 3.1   Arithmetic Operators

Operator	Description
+	addition
-	subtraction or unary negation
*	multiplication
/	division
%	modulus
++	increment and then return value (or return value and then increment)
--	decrement and then return value (or return value and then decrement)

NOTE   The % (modulus) operator calculates the *remainder* of dividing two integers. For example, 17 % 3 = 2, since 17/3 = 5 with a remainder of 2.

TABLE 3.2   Logical Operators

Operator	Description
&&	logical and
||	logical or
!	logical not

TABLE 3.3   Comparison Operators

Operator	Description
==	equal
!=	not equal
<	less than

TABLE 3.3   Comparison Operators (continued)

Operator	Description
<=	less than or equal
>	greater than
>=	greater than or equal

NOTE   If the LANGUAGE attribute of the <SCRIPT> tag is set to JavaScript1.2, the == and != operators do not attempt to convert operands to a common type before comparison takes place. In this case, 5=="5" evaluates to false and 5!="5" evaluates to true.

String Operators

String operators are used to perform operations on strings. JavaScript currently supports only the + *string concatenation* operator.

Bit Manipulation Operators

Bit manipulation operators perform operations on the bit representation of a value, such as shifting the bits to the right or the left. The bit manipulation operators supported by JavaScript are listed in Table 3.4.

TABLE 3.4   Bit Manipulation Operators

Operator	Description
&	and
|	or
^	exclusive or
<<	left shift
>>	sign-propagating right shift
>>>	zero-fill right shift

Assignment Operators

Assignment operators are used to update the value of a variable. Some assignment operators are combined with other operators to perform a computation on the value contained in a variable and then update the variable with the new value. The assignment operators supported by JavaScript are listed in Table 3.5.

TABLE 3.5   Assignment Operators

Operator	Description
=	Set the variable on the left of the = operator to the value of the expression on its right.
+=	Increment the variable on the left of the += operator by the value of the expression on its right.
-=	Decrement the variable on the left of the -= operator by the value of the expression on its right.
*=	Multiply the variable on the left of the *= operator by the value of the expression on its right.
/=	Divide the variable on the left of the /= operator by the value of the expression on its right.
%=	Take the modulus of the variable on the left of the %= operator using the value of the expression on its right.
<<=	Left shift the variable on the left of the <<= operator using the value of the expression on its right.
>>=	Take the sign-propagating right shift of the variable on the left of the >>= operator using the value of the expression on its right.
>>>=	Take the zero-filled right shift of the variable on the left of the >>>= operator using the value of the expression on its right.
&=	Take the bitwise *and* of the variable on the left of the &= operator using the value of the expression on its right.
|=	Take the bitwise *or* of the variable on the left of the |= operator using the value of the expression on its right.
^=	Take the bitwise exclusive *or* of the variable on the left of the ^= operator using the value of the expression on its right.

Conditional Expressions

JavaScript supports the conditional expression operator ? : found in Java, C, and C++. This operator is a *ternary* operator since it takes three operands—a condition to be evaluated and two alternative values to be returned based on the truth or falsity of the condition. The format for a conditional expression is as follows:

```
condition ? value1 : value2
```

A condition is an expression that results in a logical value—i.e., true or false.

If the condition is true, *value1* is the result of the expression. Otherwise, *value2* is the result. An example of using this expression follows:

```
(x > y) ? 5 : 7
```

If the value stored in variable x is greater than the value contained in variable y then 5 is the result of the expression. If the value stored in x is less than or equal to the value of y then 7 is the result of the expression.

Operator Summary Table

The script shown in Listing 3.1 illustrates the use of the JavaScript operators introduced in the preceding subsections. It generates the HTML table shown in Figure 3.1.

Listing 3.1. JavaScript Operators

```
<html>
<head>
<title>JavaScript Operators</title>
</head>
<body>
<h1>JavaScript Operators</h1>
<table BORDER="2" CELLPADDING="4" ALIGN="CENTER">
<tr><td>Category</td>
<td>Operator</td>
<td>Description</td>
<td>Usage Example</td>
<td>Value/Result</td></tr>
<tr><td>String</td>
```

```
<td>+</td>
<td>concatenation</td>
<td>&quot;Java&quot; + &quot;Script&quot;</td>
<td><script><!--
document.write("Java"+"Script")
// --></script>
</td></tr>
<tr><td ROWSPAN="10">Arithmetic</td>
<td>+</td>
<td>addition</td>
<td>2 + 3</td>
<td><script><!--
document.write(2+3)
// --></script>
</td></tr>
<tr><td ROWSPAN="2">-</td>
<td>subtraction</td>
<td>6 - 4</td>
<td><script><!--
document.write(6-4)
// --></script>
</td></tr>
<tr><td>unary negation</td>
<td>-9</td>
<td><script><!--
document.write(-9)
// --></script>
</td></tr>
<tr><td>*</td>
<td>multiplication</td>
<td>3 * 4</td>
<td><script><!--
document.write(3*4)
// --></script>
</td></tr>
<tr><td>/</td>
<td>division</td>
<td>15/3</td>
<td><script><!--
document.write(15/3)
// --></script>
</td></tr>
<tr><td>%</td>
<td>modulus</td>
<td>15%7</td>
```

```
<td><script><!--
document.write(15%7)
// --></script>
</td></tr>
<tr><td ROWSPAN="2">++</td>
<td>increment and then return value</td>
<td>x=3; ++x</td>
<td><script><!--
x=3
document.write(++x)
// --></script>
</td></tr>
<tr><td>return value and then increment</td>
<td>x=3; x++</td>
<td><script><!--
x=3
document.write(x++)
// --></script>
</td></tr>
<tr><td ROWSPAN="2">--</td>
<td>decrement and then return value</td>
<td>x=3; --x</td>
<td><script><!--
x=3
document.write(--x)
// --></script>
</td></tr>
<tr><td>return value and then decrement</td>
<td>x=3; x--</td>
<td><script><!--
x=3
document.write(x--)
// --></script>
</td></tr>
<tr><td ROWSPAN="6">Bit Manipulation</td>
<td>&amp;</td>
<td>and</td>
<td>10 &amp; 7</td>
<td><script><!--
document.write(10&7)
// --></script>
</td></tr>
<tr><td>|</td>
<td>or</td>
```

```
<td>10 | 7</td>
<td><script><!--
document.write(10|7)
// --></script>
</td></tr>
<tr><td>^</td>
<td>exclusive or</td>
<td>10 ^ 7</td>
<td><script><!--
document.write(10^7)
// --></script>
</td></tr>
<tr><td>&lt;&lt;</td>
<td>left shift</td>
<td>7 &lt;&lt; 3</td>
<td><script><!--
document.write(7<<3)
// --></script>
</td></tr>
<tr><td>&gt;&gt;</td>
<td>sign-propagating right shift</td>
<td>-7 &gt;&gt; 2</td>
<td><script><!--
document.write(-7>>2)
// --></script>
</td></tr>
<tr><td>&gt;&gt;&gt;</td>
<td>zero-fill right shift</td>
<td>-7 &gt;&gt;&gt; 2</td>
<td><script><!--
document.write(-7>>>2)
// --></script>
</td></tr>
<tr><td ROWSPAN="3">Logical</td>
<td>&amp;&amp;</td>
<td>logical and</td>
<td>true &amp;&amp; false</td>
<td><script><!--
document.write(true&&false)
// --></script>
</td></tr>
<tr><td>||</td>
<td>logical or</td>
<td>true || false</td>
<td><script><!--
```

```
document.write(true||false)
// --></script>
</td></tr>
<tr><td>!</td>
<td>not</td>
<td>!true</td>
<td><script><!--
document.write(!true)
// --></script>
</td></tr>
<tr><td ROWSPAN="6">Comparison</td>
<td>==</td>
<td>equal</td>
<td>3 == 7</td>
<td><script><!--
document.write(3==7)
// --></script>
</td></tr>
<tr><td>!=</td>
<td>not equal</td>
<td>3 != 7</td>
<td><script><!--
document.write(3!=7)
// --></script>
</td></tr>
<tr><td>&lt;</td>
<td>less than</td>
<td>3 &lt; 7</td>
<td><script><!--
document.write(3<7)
// --></script>
</td></tr>
<tr><td>&lt;=</td>
<td>less than or equal</td>
<td>3 &lt;= 7</td>
<td><script><!--
document.write(3<=7)
// --></script>
</td></tr>
<tr><td>&gt;</td>
<td>greater than</td>
<td>3 &gt; 7</td>
<td><script><!--
document.write(3>7)
// --></script>
```

```
</td></tr>
<tr><td>&gt;=</td>
<td>greater than or equal</td>
<td>3 &gt;= 7</td>
<td><script><!--
document.write(3>7)
// --></script>
</td></tr>
<tr><td>Conditional Expression</td>
<td>(condition) ? value1 : value2</td>
<td>if condition is true then value1 else value2</td>
<td>true ? 3 : 7</td>
<td><script><!--
document.write(true?3:7)
// --></script>
</td></tr>
</table>
</body>
</html>
```

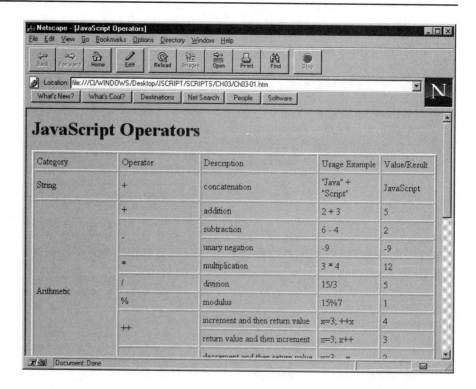

Operator Precedence

The *precedence* of the operator determines which operations are evaluated before others during the parsing and execution of complex expressions. For example, when you evaluate the expression 3 + 4 * 5, you should come up with 23 as your answer and not 35. This is because the multiplication operator * has a higher precedence than the addition operator +. JavaScript defines the precedence and therefore the order of evaluation of all it operators. Table 3.6 summarizes the precedence of the JavaScript operators.

TABLE 3.6   Operator Precedence

Precedence	Operator
1	parentheses, function call, or array subscript
2	!, ~, -, ++, -- (see note)
3	*, /, % (see note)
4	+, - (see note)
5	<<, >>, >>> (see note)
6	<, <=, >, >= (see note)
7	==, != (see note)
8	&
9	^
10	|
11	&&
12	||
13	?:
14	=, +=, -=, *=, /=, %=, <<=, >>=, >>>=, &=, ^=, |= (see note)

NOTE: Where more than one operator is listed at a given level, those operators are all of equal priority—I don't mean to imply that =, for example, has a slightly higher priority than += or -= in level 14 above. Rather, it means that as JavaScript reads an expression from left to right at that level of precedence, it will evaluate any of those operators as it comes across them.

To see how you would use Table 3.6 to determine the order of evaluation, consider the following complex expression:

```
a = 3 * (9 % 2) - !true >>> 2 - 1
```

Since parentheses surround 9 % 2 ("nine modulo two"), we evaluate that term first, resulting in the following:

```
a = 3 * 1 - !true >>> 2 - 1
```

NOTE As mentioned previously, the % (modulus) operator calculates the remainder of dividing two integers. For example, 9 % 2 = 1, since 9/2 = 4 with a remainder of 1.

The highest precedence operator is now the ! negation operator. After evaluation of !true we get:

```
a = 3 * 1 - false >>> 2 - 1
```

The * operator is the next to be evaluated, resulting in:

```
a = 3 - false >>> 2 - 1
```

The two - operators now have the highest precedence. The logical value *false* is converted to *0* and the simple expression 2 - 1 is evaluated to *1*, yielding the following:

```
a = 3 >>> 1
```

Then, since >>> has a higher precedence than =, the expression is evaluated to:

```
a = 3
```

Finally, the = assignment operator assigns the integer value *3* to variable a.

Statements

The statements of any programming language are the instructions from which programs are written. Most programming languages support a common core set of statements, such as assignment statements, if statements, loop statements, and others. These languages differ only in the syntax used for their statements and the degree to which the languages support software development paradigms and programming features such as object-oriented programming, abstract data definition, inference rules, and list processing.

JavaScript provides a complete range of basic programming statements. While it is not an object-oriented programming language, it *is* an object-*based* language, and supports objects, object properties, and methods. You'll learn more about these object-based programming features in Chapter 5.

The statements provided by JavaScript are summarized in Table 3.7 and covered in the following subsections.

TABLE 3.7 JavaScript Statement Summary

Statement	Purpose	Example
assignment	Assign the value of an expression to a variable.	`x = y + z`
data declaration	Declare a variable (and optionally assign a value to it).	`card = new Array(52)`

if	Alter program execution based on the value of a condition.	`if (x>y) {`
		`  z = x`
		`}`

switch	Alter program execution based on the value of a condition.	`switch(i) {case 0:`
		`  x=true`
		`  break`
		`case 1:`
		`  x=!x`
		`  break`
		`default:`
		`  x=true`
		`}`

while	Repeatedly execute a set of statements until a condition becomes false.	`while (x!=7) {`
		`  x %= n`
		`  --n`
		`}`

for	Repeatedly execute a set of statements until a condition becomes false.	`for(i=0;i<7;++i){`
		`  document.write(x[i])`
		`}`

TABLE 3.7   JavaScript Statement Summary (continued)

Statement	Purpose	Example
do while	Repeatedly execute a set of statements until a condition becomes false.	```do { i*=I ++j } while (i<100) ;```
break	Immediately terminate a *while* or *for* statement.	`if(x>y) break`
continue	Immediately terminate the current iteration of a *while* or *for* statement.	`if(x>y) continue`
function call	Invoke a function.	`x=abs(y)`
return	Return a value from a function call.	`return x*y`
method invocation	Invoke a method of an object.	`document.write("Hello!")`

Here are a few things to keep in mind when writing a series of statements:

- More than one statement may occur on a single line of text, provided that each statement is separated by a semicolon (;). The semicolon is the JavaScript "line separator" indicator.

- No semicolon is needed between statements that occur on separate lines.

- A long JavaScript statement may be written using multiple lines of text. No line-continuation identifier is required for such multi-line statements.

As of JavaScript 1.2, statements may be preceded by an optional label, which is used by the `break` and `continue` statements to determine where program execution should resume. The format of the label is as follows:

```
label: statement
```

Assignment Statements

The most basic statement found in almost any programming language is the *assignment* statement. The assignment statement updates the value of a variable based upon an assignment operator and an expression (and, optionally, the current value of the variable being updated). You have seen numerous examples of assignment statements in the earlier sections of this chapter and in Chapter 2.

Data Declarations

Data declarations identify a variable to the JavaScript interpreter. So far you have been declaring simple variables through assignment statements. For example, the statement

```
a = 25
```

causes a to be implicitly declared as an integer variable and initialized to 25. The variable a is referred to as a *global* variable. This means that it can be accessed by all scripts defined in an HTML document. Later in this chapter, in the section titled "Local Variable Declarations," you'll learn how to declare variables that are *local* to a function definition.

Array declarations are another example of data declaration statements. For example, the following array declarations declare array variables:

```
// Declares an array of zero elements
customerNum = new Array()

// Declares an array of 100 null valued elements
productCode = new Array(100)
```

Dense array declarations provide the capability to declare an array and assign initial values to all of the elements of the array. Here are two examples of these declaration statements:

```
// Declares and initializes a seven-element array
day = new Array("Sun","Mon","Tue","Wed","Thu","Fri","Sat")

// Declares and initializes a four-element array
name = new Array("Bob","Sybil","Ricky","Mad Dog")
```

Another type of variable declaration involves the creation of an instance of an object. You'll learn about objects and their creation in Chapter 5. For now, instances of objects are created using statements of the following form:

```
variableName = new objectConstructor(p1,p2,....,pn)
```

where *variableName* is the name of a variable that is assigned the newly created object, new is the new object creator, *objectConstructor()* is a function that is used to create the object, and *p1* through *pn* are an optional list of parameters that are used in the object's creation.

The If Statement

The if statement provides the capability to alter the course of a program's execution based on an expression that yields a logical value. If the logical value is *true*, a specified set of statements is executed. If the logical value is *false*, the set of statements is skipped (and, optionally, a second set of statements is executed). The if statement comes in two forms. The syntax of the first form is as follows:

```
if ( condition ) {
 statements
 }
```

If the specified condition is true, then the statements identified within the braces { and } are executed. Execution then continues with the statement following the if statement. If the specified condition is false, then the statements enclosed by braces are skipped and execution continues with the statement following the if statement. For example, the following statement writes the text *Good morning* to the current Web document when the value of the hour variable is less than 12.

```
if(hour<12){
  document.write("Good morning")
 }
```

The syntax of the second form of the if statement is similar to the first form except that an else clause is added. The syntax of the second form is as follows:

```
if ( condition ) {
 first set of statements
 } else {
 second set of statements
 }
```

If the specified condition is true, then the first set of statements is executed. If the specified condition is false, then the second set of statements is executed. In both cases, execution continues with the statement following the if statement.

An example of the second form of the if statement follows:

```
if(hour<12){
  document.write("Good morning")
 }else{
  document.write("Hello")
 }
```

The if statement results in the current document being updated with the text *Good morning* if the value of the hour variable is less than 12 or with the text *Hello* if hour is greater than or equal to 12.

> **NOTE**
> The braces enclosing the statements in the if and else clauses can be omitted if only one statement is enclosed.

Loop Statements

Loop statements are used to repeat the execution of a set of statements while a particular condition is *true*. JavaScript supports two types of loop statements: the while statement and the for statement. It also provides the break and continue statements. The break statement is used to terminate all loop iteration. The continue statement is used to cause a single loop iteration to end immediately and proceed to the next loop iteration.

While Statement

The while statement is a basic loop statement, used to repeat the execution of a set of statements while a specified condition is true. The syntax of the while statement is as follows:

```
while ( condition ) {
  statements
 }
```

The while statement evaluates the condition, and if the condition evaluates to *true*, executes the statements enclosed within braces. When the condition evaluates to *false*, it transfers control to the statement following the while statement.

Listing 3.2 provides an example of how the while statement can be used to generate the content of an HTML document. Figure 3.2 shows how the document generated by this script is displayed by a Web browser. The script iterates from 1 to 6, generating six levels of HTML headings. The index variable is incremented each time it passes through the loop.

Listing 3.2. The While statement

```
<HTML>
<HEAD>
```

```
<TITLE>Using the While Statement</TITLE>
</HEAD>
<BODY>
<SCRIPT><!--
i=1
while(i<7){
 document.write("<H"+i+">This is a level "+i+" heading."
 ➥ +"</H"+i+">")
 ++i
}
// --></SCRIPT>
</BODY>
</HTML>
```

FIGURE 3.2

Using the While state-
ment to generate
an HTML document
(Listing 3.2)

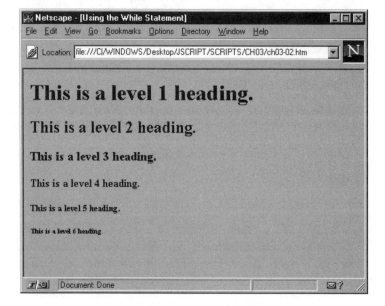

The Do While Statement

The do while statement, introduced in JavaScript 1.2, is similar to the while
statement. The only difference is that the looping condition is checked at the
end of the loop, instead of at the beginning. This ensures that the enclosed

statements are executed at least once. The syntax of the do while statement is as follows:

```
do {
  statements
} while (condition);
```

For example, the following statements display the integers 1 through 10:

```
i=0
do {
  ++i
  document.writeln(i+"<BR>")
} while (i<10);
```

For Statement

The for statement is similar to the while statement in that it repeatedly executes a set of statements while a condition is true. It is different from the while statement in that it is designed to update a variable after each loop iteration. The syntax of the for statement is:

```
for ( initializationStatement; condition; updateStatement ) {
  statements
}
```

The initialization statement is executed only at the beginning of the for statement's execution. The condition is then tested, and if it is true, the statements enclosed within braces are executed. If the condition is false, the loop is terminated and the statement following the for statement is executed.

If the statements enclosed within the braces of the for statement are executed, the update statement is executed, and then the condition is retested. The enclosed statements and update statement are repeatedly executed until the condition becomes false.

NOTE The initialization statement, condition, and update statement are optional and may be omitted.

An example `for` statement follows:

```
a = new Array(2,4,6,8,10)
sum = 0
for (i = 0;i < a.length;++i) {
  sum += a[i]
}
```

The first statement of the above example creates a five-element array with the values 2, 4, 6, 8, and 10. The second statement initializes the variable `sum` to 0. The `for` statement begins by initializing the variable `i` to 0 and tests the length of a to see if it is greater than `i`. Since `i` is 0 and `a.length` is 5, the statement enclosed within the braces is executed and the value of `sum` is incremented by `a[i]`, which is 2.

The update statement, `++i`, is then executed. This causes `i` to be incremented to 1. The condition is retested and since `i` is less than 5 the statement enclosed within braces is then reexecuted. This time `sum` is incremented by 4 and its value becomes 6.

The update statement, `++i`, is executed a second time and the condition is retested. From here, you should be able to follow the remainder of the `for` statement's execution. The `for` loop continues to iterate until `i < a.length` is no longer true. This happens when `i` becomes 5. At this point, `sum` has become the sum of all the elements of a and its value is 30.

Listing 3.3 shows how the script shown in Listing 3.2 can be updated to use a `for` statement instead of a `while` statement. The Web page resulting from the execution of this script is the same as that displayed in Figure 3.2.

Listing 3.3. Use of the For statement

```
<HTML>
<HEAD>
<TITLE>Using the For Statement</TITLE>
</HEAD>
<BODY>
<SCRIPT><!--
for(i=1;i<7;++i)
  document.write("<H"+i+">This is a level "+i+" heading."
  +"</H"+i+">")
// --></SCRIPT>
</BODY>
</HTML>
```

The braces enclosing the statements in the `for`, `while`, **and** `do while` statements can be omitted if only one statement is enclosed.

The Break Statement

The `break` statement is used to terminate execution of a loop and transfer control to the statement following the loop. The `break` statement consists of the single word `break`. When the `break` statement is encountered, the loop is immediately terminated. An example of its use follows:

```
a = new Array(5,4,3,2,1)
sum = 0
for (i = 0;i < a.length;++i) {
 if (i == 3) break;
 sum += a[i]
}
```

The above `for` statement executes for i equal to 0, 1, 2, and 3. When i equals 3 the condition of the `if` statement is true and the `break` statement is executed. This causes the `for` statement to immediately terminate. The value of `sum` is 12 upon termination of the `for` statement.

As of JavaScript 1.2, the `break` statement may take a label as an argument:

```
break label
```

If a label is specified, then the `break` statement breaks out of the enclosing statement identified by the label. The enclosing statement may be an `if` or `switch` statement, or a loop statement.

Listing 3.4 provides a script that illustrates the use of the `break` statement. Figure 3.3 shows the Web page generated by this script. The script loops to test the integers from 100 to 1 until it finds one which is evenly divisible by 17. When it finds such a number, it terminates the loop.

Listing 3.4. The Break statement

```
<HTML>
<HEAD>
<TITLE>Using the Break Statement</TITLE>
</HEAD>
<BODY>
```

```
<SCRIPT><!--
for(i=100;i>0;--i){
 document.write(i+"<BR>")
 if(i%17==0) break
}
// --></SCRIPT>
</BODY>
</HTML>
```

FIGURE 3.3

Using the Break statement (Listing 3.4)

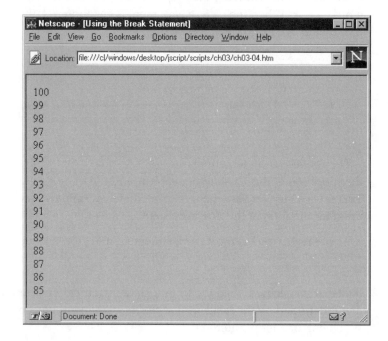

The Continue Statement

The continue statement is similar to the break statement in that it affects the execution of the for or while statement in which it is contained. It differs from the break statement in that it does not completely terminate the loop's execution but only terminates the execution of the statements in the loop's current iteration.

When a continue statement is encountered in a while or for loop, the rest of the statements being iterated are skipped and control of execution returns to the condition of the loop.

Consider the following `while` loop as an example:

```
i = 1
sum = 0
while(i<10) {
  i *= 2;
  if (i == 4) continue
  sum += i + 1
}
```

The `while` loop iterates for `i` equal to 1, 2, 4, and 8 at the beginning of each loop. However, `sum` is only updated when `i` equals 1, 4, and 8. When `i` equals 2 at the beginning of the loop, it is doubled to 4 as the result of the first statement of the loop's execution. This causes the condition of the `if` statement to be true and the `continue` statement to be executed. Execution of the `continue` statement causes the last statement in the loop to be skipped and control to return to the evaluation of the condition of the `while` statement. The final value of `sum` is 29.

As of JavaScript 1.2, the `continue` statement may take a label as an argument:

```
continue label
```

The label is used to specify which loop statement is to be continued. This is used in nested loops to continue outer loops from within inner loops.

Listing 3.5 provides a script that illustrates the use of the `continue` statement. Figure 3.4 shows the Web page generated by this script. The script prints out the integers between 1 and 10, but uses the `continue` statement to skip all odd integers.

Listing 3.5. The Continue statement

```
<HTML>
<HEAD>
<TITLE>Using the Continue Statement</TITLE>
</HEAD>
<BODY>
<SCRIPT><!--
for(i=1;i<10;++i){
  if(i%2!=0) continue
  document.write(i+"<BR>")
}
// --></SCRIPT>
</BODY>
</HTML>
```

FIGURE 3.4

Using the Continue
statement (Listing 3.5)

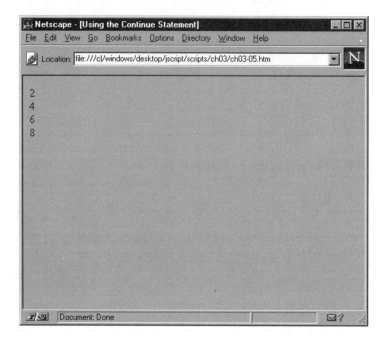

FIGURE 3.4

Using the Continue
statement (Listing 3.5)

Function Calls

Most programming languages support function calls. *Functions* are named blocks
of statements that are referenced and executed as a unit. Data that is required for
the execution of a function may be passed as *parameters* to the function. Functions
may return a value, but are not required to do so. When a function returns a
value, the invocation of the function is usually part of an expression. For example, the following statement invokes the `factorial()` function, passing it the
integer value 5 as a parameter:

```
n = factorial(5)
```

In the above example, the function call, `factorial(5)`, returns a value which
is assigned to the variable n. The `factorial()` function is a hypothetical function and is not defined by JavaScript.

When a function does not return a value, it is usually used to perform an operation that updates a variable or an object that is external to JavaScript. The invocation
of a non-value returning function is a complete statement, not merely part of a

larger expression. For example, consider the function invocation in the following statement.

```
notifyUser("Product code is invalid")
```

In the above statement, the function `notifyUser()` takes the string *"Product code is invalid"* as a parameter. It then displays this string to the user. The function does not return a value, and therefore, is not on the right side of an assignment statement.

Defining Functions

A function must be defined before it can be used. Function definitions are usually placed in the head of an HTML document, although it is not mandatory to do so. Placing function definitions in the head, however, ensures that the definition occurs before the function is used. The syntax of a function definition is as follows:

```
function functionName(p1, p2, ..., pn) {
 statements
 }
```

The function name is the name used to refer to the function in function calls. The parameters are the names of variables that receive the values passed to the function when the function is invoked. The statements enclosed in braces are executed as the result of a function call.

For example, consider the following function definition:

```
function display(text) {
 document.write(text)
 }
```

If the above function is invoked with the statement `display("xyz")`, the text *xyz* is written to the current Web document. The `display("xyz")` function call is thus equivalent to the statement `document.write("xyz")`.

Listing 3.6 provides an example of a function definition. Figure 3.5 shows the Web page generated by this script.

Listing 3.6. A function definition

```
<HTML>
<HEAD>
<TITLE>A function definition</TITLE>
<SCRIPT LANGUAGE="JavaScript"><!--
```

```
function displayTaggedText(tag, text) {
 document.write("<"+tag+">")
 document.write(text)
 document.write("</"+tag+">")
}
// -->
</SCRIPT>
</HEAD>
<BODY>
<SCRIPT LANGUAGE="JavaScript"><!--
displayTaggedText("H1","This is a level 1 heading")
displayTaggedText("P","This text is the first paragraph of the
➥ document.")
// -->
</SCRIPT>
</BODY>
</HTML>
```

The script in the document head defines the function, `displayTaggedText()`, that takes two parameters, `tag` and `text`. Actual values for `tag` and `text` are passed to the function via these parameters when the function is invoked. The

FIGURE 3.5

Defining and using a function (Listing 3.6)

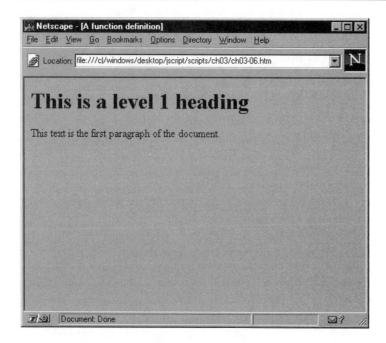

function consists of three statements. The first statement writes the left angle bracket, followed by the value of the `tag` parameter plus a right angle bracket to the current document. The second `write()` statement writes the value of the `text` variable to the current document. The third statement writes the string `</`, followed by the value of the `tag` variable followed by the right angle bracket, to the current document. The `displayTaggedText()` function does not return a value.

The script in the body of the document executes two function call statements that invoke the `displayTaggedText()` function to write a level-1 HTML heading and a paragraph of text to the current document. The parameters passed in the first invocation are `"H1"` and `"This is a level 1 heading"`. The `"H1"` string is passed to the `displayTaggedText()` function via the `tag` variable. The `"This is a level 1 heading"` string is passed via the `text` variable. The second invocation of `displayTaggedText()` is handled in the same manner. The string `"P"` is passed via `tag` and `"This is a level 1 heading"` is passed via `text`.

Defining Functions with a Variable Number of Parameters

JavaScript provides the capability to define functions that take a variable number of parameters, using the `arguments` array. The `arguments` array is automatically created by JavaScript for each function invocation. Suppose function `f` is invoked with the parameters `"test"`, `true`, and `77` as in the following statement:

```
f("test",true,77)
```

The array `f.arguments` contains the values of these parameters. In this case, the variables are as follows:

```
f.arguments.length = 3
f.arguments[0] = "test"
f.arguments[1] = true
f.arguments[2] = 77
```

The following function definition illustrates the use of the `arguments` array.

```
function sum() {
 n = sum.arguments.length
 total = 0
 for(i=0;i<n;++i) {
  total += sum.arguments[i]
```

```
  }
  return total
}
```

The sum() function is designed to add an arbitrary list of parameters. The variable n is assigned the length of the sum.arguments array. The total variable is used to add the elements of sum.arguments.

Local Variable Declarations

When defining a function, it is often necessary to define variables that will be used to store values calculated by the function. You could declare variables using the declaration statements that you studied in the section "Data Declarations" earlier in the chapter. However, this causes the function definition to be dependent on these global variables and, as a result, less modular and more difficult to debug. Instead, it is better to declare variables that are used only within the function. These variables, referred to as *local variables*, are accessible only within the function that they are declared. Figure 3.6. illustrates the difficulties inherent with using global variables within functions.

FIGURE 3.6

Using global variables within functions

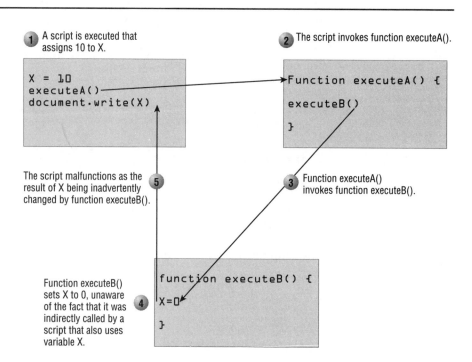

1. A script is executed that assigns 10 to X.

2. The script invokes function executeA().

```
X = 10
executeA()
document.write(X)
```

```
Function executeA() {

  executeB()

}
```

5. The script malfunctions as the result of X being inadvertently changed by function executeB().

3. Function executeA() invokes function executeB().

4. Function executeB() sets X to 0, unaware of the fact that it was indirectly called by a script that also uses variable X.

```
function executeB() {

  X=0

}
```

Local variables are declared in the same manner as global variables, except that local variable declarations are preceded by the keyword var. The following are examples of local variable declarations.

```
// Declares temp as a local variable
var temp

// Declares index as a local variable and initializes it to 1
var index = 1

/* Declares the product array with an initial
   capacity of 100 elements */
var product = new Array(100)
```

Local variables may have the same name as global variables. In the case that a local variable and global variable have the same name, all references to the variable name within the function that the local variable is defined refer to the local variable of that function and not to the global variable. All references to the variable name outside of the function which defines the local variable are to the global variable. Listing 3.7 provides a script that illustrates the use of global and local variables with the same names. Figure 3.7 displays the Web page that is generated by this script. The variable x is a local variable in the displaySquared() function and a global variable in the script contained in the document body. Note that the local and global x variables may be updated independently.

Listing 3.7. Use of global and local variables

```
<HTML>
<HEAD>
<TITLE>Global and Local Variables</TITLE>
<SCRIPT LANGUAGE="JavaScript"><!--
function displaySquared(y) {
var x = y * y
document.write(x+"<BR>")
}
// -->
</SCRIPT>
</HEAD>
<BODY>
<SCRIPT LANGUAGE="JavaScript"><!--
for(x=0;x<10;++x)
 displaySquared(x)
// -->
```

```
</SCRIPT>
</BODY>
</HTML>
```

FIGURE 3.7

Use of global and local variables (Listing 3.7)

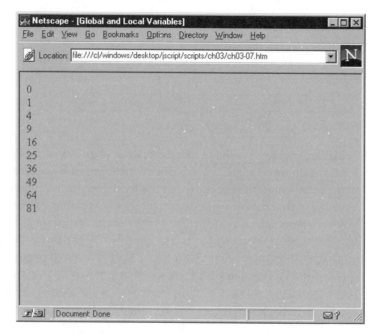

The Return Statement

The `return` statement is used to return a value as the result of the processing performed by a function. This value is returned to the statement which invokes the function. The syntax of the `return` statement is:

```
return expression
```

The expression evaluates to the value to be returned by the function. When the `return` statement is encountered, the expression is evaluated and the value to which the expression evaluates is immediately returned by the function. No subsequent statements of the function are processed.

An example of the use of the `return` statement is shown in the following function definition:

```
function factorial(n) {
  var sum = 1
```

```
for(i=1;i<=n;++i)
  sum *= i
return sum
}
```

In the above example, `sum` is calculated as the product of all integers from `1` through n. This value is then returned via the `return` statement.

Object-Access Statements

Objects are complex JavaScript data structures that both contain data and provide functions, referred to as *methods*, that are used to perform operations on this data. The individual variables comprising an object are referred to as *properties*. Properties provide access to the data contained in an object.

NOTE JavaScript objects are covered in Chapter 5. This section focuses on programming statements that use object properties and methods.

Since properties provide access to the values contained in the variables comprising an object, they are usually used in expressions that appear in the right or left side of an assignment statement. For example, suppose the `employee` variable refers to an object of type `employeeRecord` that has the `employeeID` property. The following assignment statement retrieves the value of the `employeeID` property and assigns it to the `id` variable.

```
id = employee.employeeID
```

The general syntax used to access the property of an object is

```
variableName.propertyName
```

where the variable name is the name of a variable that refers to an object and the property name is the name of the property to be retrieved.

When a property reference appears in the left side of an assignment statement, the property of the referenced object is updated. In the following example, the `employeeID` property of the object referred to by the `employee` variable is updated with the value stored in the `id` variable.

```
employee.employeeID = id
```

The methods of an object are functions that are used to perform operations on the object. These methods are invoked in a similar manner as properties. However, since methods are functions, they must include the method's parameter list. An empty parameter list is specified in the same manner as for function calls. The general syntax of a method invocation is shown here:

```
variableName.methodName(p1,p2,...,pn)
```

where the variable name is the name of a variable that refers to an object and the method name is the name of the method to be invoked. The parameters *p1* through *pn* are an optional list of method parameters.

Some methods do not return a value. Their invocation is a complete statement in itself. A common example that you've been using so far is the `write()` method of the `document` object:

```
document.write("text to be displayed")
```

Some methods return a value. In this case, the method invocation may appear as part of a larger expression, as in the following example:

```
payroll=0
for(i=0;i<employee.length;++i)
  payroll += employee[i].netPay()
```

In the above example, `employee` is an array of `employeeRecord` objects. The `netPay()` method calculates the net pay of each employee based on data contained in the properties of the `employeeRecord` objects.

The With Statement

The `with` statement is provided as a convenience to eliminate retyping the name of an object that is to be referenced in a series of property references and method invocations. The syntax of the `with` statement is as follows:

```
with(variableName){
  statements
}
```

The variable name identifies the default object to be used with the statements enclosed in braces. An example of the `with` statement follows:

```
with(document) {
  write("<H1>With It</H1>")
```

```
write("<P>")
write("Eliminate object name references with with")
write("</P>")
}
```

In the above example, the need to prefix each `write()` method invocation with the `document` object is eliminated because `document` is identified in the `with` statement.

The For In Statement

You learned how the `for` statement is used to iterate a set of statements based on a loop condition and an update statement. The `for in` statement is similar to a `for` statement in that it repeatedly executes a set of statements. However, instead of iterating the statements based on the loop condition, it executes the statements for all properties that are defined for an object.

The syntax of the `for in` statement is as follows:

```
for (variableName in objectName) {
  statements
}
```

The `for in` loop executes the statements enclosed in braces one time for each property defined for `objectName`. Each time the statements are executed, the variable specified by `variableName` is assigned a string identifying the current property name. For example, consider the execution of the following `for in` statement in the case of the `employee` object having the properties `employeeID`, `employeeName`, and `employeeLocation`.

```
for(prop in employee)
    document.write(prop+"<BR>")
```

The above `for in` statement would cause the following text to be written to the current document:

employeeID

employeeName

employeeLocation

The Switch Statement

JavaScript 1.2 has added the `switch` statement to the list of statements that it supports. Its syntax is the same as in Java and C++:

```
switch (expression) {
  case value1:
    statements
    break
          .
          .
          .
  case valuen2:
    statements
    break
  default:
    statements
}
```

The `switch` statement evaluates the expression and determines if any of the values (*value1* through *valuen*) match the expression's value. If one of them matches, then the statements for that particular case are executed, and statement execution then continues after the `switch` statement. If there is no matching value, then the statements for the `default` case are executed.

The `break` statements may be omitted. If they are omitted, however, execution continues with the next case (if any).

The following `switch` statement prints the string value of the number corresponding to 1, 2, or 3, or prints *I don't know* otherwise.

```
switch (i) {
case 1:
  document.writeln("one")
  break
case 2:
  document.writeln("two")
  break
case 3:
  document.writeln("three")
  break
default:
  document.writeln("I don't know")
  break
}
```

Summary

This chapter introduced you to more elements of the JavaScript language. You covered all of the operators provide by JavaScript and learned how expressions are evaluated using operator precedence. You learned to use JavaScript's programming statements and developed sample scripts that demonstrated the use of these statements. You also learned how to create and invoke functions. In the next chapter, you'll extend your JavaScript programming expertise by learning how JavaScript supports the handling of user-generated events.

CHAPTER
FOUR

4

Event Handling

- How JavaScript Handles Events

- Link Events

- Window Events

- Image Events

- Form Events

- Setting Event Handlers from within JavaScript

- Event Emulation Methods

Events are the mechanism by which browsers respond to user actions. JavaScript's event-handling features give you the ability to alter the standard way in which a browser reacts to these actions. This enables you to develop Web pages that are more interactive, more responsive, and easier to use.

This chapter illustrates the use of JavaScript's event-handling features. It describes JavaScript's approach to event handling and identifies the event handlers that are predefined by JavaScript. It shows you how to write your own event-handling functions and how to associate them with user interface actions. By the time you finish this chapter, you'll be able to use event-handling functions to develop highly interactive Web pages.

What Are Events?

Events describe actions that occur as the result of user interaction with a Web page. For example, when a user clicks on a hyperlink or a button, or enters data in a form, an event is generated informing the browser that an action has occurred and that further processing is required. The browser waits for events to occur, and when they do, it performs whatever processing is assigned to those events. The processing that is performed in response to the occurrence of an event is known as *event handling*. The code that performs this processing is called an *event handler*. Figure 4.1 illustrates the notion of an event and the process of event handling.

For a simple example of event processing, consider what normally happens when a user clicks on a URL that is displayed on a Web page. The default HTML action arising from such an event is that the browser loads and displays the page

FIGURE 4.1

Events and event handling

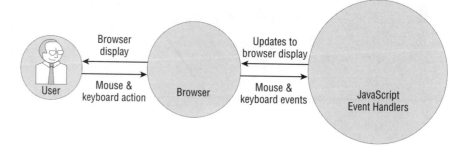

associated with that URL. With JavaScript, however, you can change that default action by writing a different event handler. Here are just a few things you can do with events using JavaScript event handlers:

- You can define an event handler that displays a dialog box when a user moves the mouse over a link.
- You can define an event handler that validates the data a user has just entered into a form.
- You can define an event handler that loads and displays an animation sequence when a user clicks on a button.
- You can even define event handlers that interact with Java applets and browser plug-ins.

JavaScript's event-handling features are what enables JavaScript to create Web pages that come alive and interact with Web users.

How JavaScript Handles Events

JavaScript's approach to event handling is a two-step process:

1. Defining the events that can be handled by scripts
2. Providing a standard method of connecting these events to user-supplied JavaScript code

JavaScript defines events for links, images, image maps, form elements, and windows. It also defines special attributes for the tags corresponding to these HTML elements. The values of these attributes are text strings that identify the event-handling code.

As previously mentioned, JavaScript defines events for links, images, image maps, form elements, and windows. (The windows I'm referring to include both the body of a document containing HTML content and the frame set of a frame layout document. Refer to Appendix A, "HTML Reference," and Chapter 6, "Windows and Frames," for more information on these objects.) Table 4.1 summarizes the events defined by JavaScript. The first two columns identify the name and tags of the HTML element. The third and fourth columns identify and describe the events that JavaScript defines for the HTML element. We'll provide examples of these events in later sections of this chapter. For now, just try to get a feel for the kinds of events that can be handled through JavaScript.

TABLE 4.1   Events defined by JavaScript

HTML Element	HTML Tags	JavaScript Event	Description
link	`<A> ... </A>`	click	The mouse is clicked on a link.
		mouseOver	The mouse is moved over a link.
		mouseOut	The mouse is moved from within a link to outside of that link.
image	`<IMG>`	abort	The loading of an image is aborted as the result of a user action.
		error	An error occurs during the loading of an image.
		load	An image is loaded and displayed.
area	`<AREA>`	mouseOver	The mouse is moved over an area of a client-side image map.
		mouseOut	The mouse is moved from within an image map area to outside of that area.
document body	`<BODY> ... </BODY>`	blur	A document loses the current input focus.
		error	An error occurs when a document is loaded.
		focus	A document receives the current input focus.
		load	The loading of a document is completed.
		unload	The user exits a document.

TABLE 4.1   Events defined by JavaScript (continued)

HTML Element	HTML Tags	JavaScript Event	Description
frame set	`<FRAMESET> ... </FRAMESET>`	blur	A frame set loses the current input focus.
		error	An error occurs when a frame set is loaded.
		focus	A frame set receives the current input focus.
		load	The loading of a frame set is completed.
		unload	The user exits a frame set.
frame	`<FRAME> ... </FRAME>`	blur	A frame loses the current input focus.
		focus	A frame receives the current input focus.
form	`<FORM> ... </FORM>`	submit	A form is submitted by the user.
		reset	A form is reset by the user.
text field	`<INPUT TYPE = "text">`	blur	A text field loses the current input focus.
		focus	A text field receives the current input focus.
		change	A text field is modified and loses the current input focus.
		select	Text is selected within a text field.
text area	`<TEXTAREA> ... </TEXTAREA>`	blur	A text area loses the current input focus.
		focus	A text area receives the current input focus.
		change	A text area is modified and loses the current input focus.
		select	Text is selected within a text area.
button	`<INPUT TYPE = "button">`	click	A button is clicked.

TABLE 4.1   Events defined by JavaScript (continued)

HTML Element	HTML Tags	JavaScript Event	Description
submit	`<INPUT TYPE = "submit">`	click	A submit button is clicked.
reset	`<INPUT TYPE = "reset">`	click	A reset button is clicked.
radio button	`<INPUT TYPE = "radio">`	click	A radio button is clicked.
checkbox	`<INPUT TYPE = "checkbox">`	click	A checkbox is clicked.
selection	`<SELECT> ... </SELECT>`	blur	A selection element loses the current input focus.
		focus	A selection element receives the current input focus.
		change	A selection element is modified and loses the current input focus.

JavaScript recognizes special event-handling attributes for each of the HTML elements identified in Table 4.1. These attributes are used to specify the JavaScript code to be executed in response to a particular event. For example, suppose we wanted to handle the event associated with a user moving the mouse over a particular link. We would connect the link to the event-handling code as follows:

```
<A HREF="http://www.jaworski.com" onMouseOver=
➡ "event-handling code">
text associated with link</A>
```

The `onMouseOver` attribute identifies the event handler to be associated with the `mouseOver` event. The actual code is placed between the quotes. Listing 4.1 provides an example of using the `onMouseOver` attribute.

Listing 4.1. Example event handler (ch04-01.htm)

```
<HTML>
<HEAD>
<TITLE>Example Event Handler</TITLE>
```

```
</HEAD>
<BODY>
<H1>Example Event Handler</H1>
<P><A HREF="http://www.jaworski.com/javascript"
onMouseOver="alert('Link to the Mastering JavaScript Home
➥ Page.')">Move your mouse over this link and a popup window
➥ is displayed.</A></P>
</BODY>
</HTML>
```

In Listing 4.1, the JavaScript event-handling code is the following:

```
alert('Link to the Mastering JavaScript Home Page.')
```

This code consists of a call to the `alert()` method of the window object with the string `'Link to the Mastering JavaScript Home Page.'` passed as a parameter. The `alert()` method displays a popup window with the specified text. Figure 4.2 shows the Web page that is displayed before the mouse is moved over the link. Figure 4.3 shows the popup window that is displayed as the result of handling the `mouseOver` event. Note that if you click on the link, the popup window is not displayed. The `click` event is handled by a different event handler. This event handler is specified by the `onClick` attribute.

FIGURE 4.2

Initial display of the event-handling example from Listing 4.1

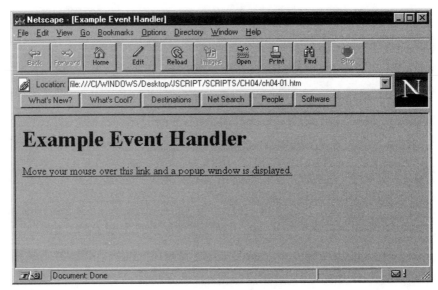

FIGURE 4.3

Popup window resulting from mouseOver event of Listing 4.1

The attribute for the `mouseOver` event is `onMouseOver`. The JavaScript code that is executed as the result of the event is provided as the attribute value of the `onMouseOver` attribute. In general, the name of the event-handling attribute is the name of the event prefixed by "on". The attributes are case insensitive—which means that you can use `onMouseOver`, `onmouseover`, `ONMOUSEOVER`, or any other upper and lower case character combinations.

Table 4.2 lists and describes the event-handling attributes of the HTML elements that were presented in Table 4.1. In the following section, you'll learn how to write event handlers for each of these attributes.

TABLE 4.2   Event-handling attributes

Event-handling Attribute	Identifies Code to Execute When...
onAbort	when the loading of an image is aborted as the result of a user action.
onBlur	when a document, frame set, text field, text area, or selection loses the current input focus.
onChange	when a text field, text area, or selection is modified and loses the current input focus.
onClick	when a link, client-side image map area, button, submit button, reset button, radio button, or checkbox is clicked.
onError	when an error occurs during the loading of an image.
onFocus	when a document, frame set, text field, text area, or selection receives the current input focus.
onLoad	when an image, document, or frame set is loaded.
onMouseOut	when the mouse is moved out of a link or an area of a client-side image map.

TABLE 4.2	Event-handling attributes (continued)
Event-handling Attribute	**Identifies Code to Execute When...**
onMouseOver	when the mouse is moved over a link or an area of a client-side image map.
onReset	when a user resets a form by clicking on the form's reset button.
onSelect	when text is selected in a text field or text area.
onSubmit	when a form is submitted.
onUnload	when the user exits a document or frame set.

NOTE From now on, we'll follow Netscape's approach and refer to events by the names of their event-handling attributes.

Handling JavaScript Events

To handle any of the JavaScript events identified in Table 4.1, all you have to do is include the event-handling attribute for that event in an appropriate HTML tag and then specify the event-handling JavaScript code as the attribute's value. You've seen an example of this in Listing 4.1. In the following subsections, you'll encounter many more examples of JavaScript event-handling. Before we go off to develop these examples, I'll spend a short time discussing the best way to insert code for the value of an event-handling attribute.

In general, you can insert any JavaScript code for the value of an event-handling attribute. However, if you surround the attribute value with double quotes, you must use single quotes within your event-handling code. Likewise, if you use single quotes to surround the attribute value, you must use double quotes within your event-handling code. Multiple JavaScript statements must be separated by semicolons. Listing 4.2 provides an example of an event handler that inserts multiple statements within the event-handling attribute.

Listing 4.2. Event handler with multiple statements in attribute value (ch04-02.htm)

```
<HTML>
<HEAD>
<TITLE>Event Handler With Multiple Statements</TITLE>
<SCRIPT LANGUAGE="JavaScript">
<!--
count=0
//-->
</SCRIPT>
</HEAD>
<BODY>
<H1>Event Handler With Multiple Statements</H1>
<P><A HREF="http://www.jaworski.com" ONMOUSEOVER='++count;
alert("You moved your mouse here "+count+" times!")'>Displays
the number of times you move your mouse over this link.</A></P>
</BODY>
</HTML>
```

In the above example, the variable count is initialized to 0 in the document's head. The onMouseOver event handler consists of the following statements:

```
++count; alert("You moved your mouse here "+count+" times!")
```

The semicolon is needed to separate the two statements. The first statement, ++count, increments count each time the mouse passes over the link. The second statement creates a popup window that displays this information to the user. Figure 4.4 shows how this information is displayed.

FIGURE 4.4

Popup window that displays the number of times a link was passed over (Listing 4.2)

As a matter of good style, it is best to have a single function call as the value of an event-handling attribute. This makes the event-handling code easier to debug, more modular, and more capable of being reused in other Web pages. Listing 4.3 shows a more complex event handler that is accessed via a single function call.

Listing 4.3. Using functions as event handlers (ch04-03.htm)

```
<HTML>
<HEAD>
<TITLE>Using functions as event handlers</TITLE>
<SCRIPT LANGUAGE="JavaScript">
<!--
function confirmLink() {
 alert("The contents of this link may be objectionable to anyone
➥ over the age of ten.")
 if(confirm("Are you ten years old or younger?")) {
  window.location="http://www.jaworski.com"
 }
}
//-->
</SCRIPT>
</HEAD>
<BODY>
<H1>Using functions as event handlers</H1>
<P><A HREF="somewhere" onClick="return false" onMouseOver="
➥ confirmLink()">Confirms
whether you want to connect via this link.</A></P>
</BODY>
</HTML>
```

The `confirmLink()` function is defined in the head of the document. This
function is the event handler for the `onMouseOver` event of the link defined in
the body of the document. The `confirmLink()` function invokes the `alert()`
method of the current window to display a warning to the user. This message is
shown in Figure 4.5. It then uses the current window's `confirm()` method to
determine the user's age (see Figure 4.6). If the user presses Cancel in the confirm
dialog box then the `confirm()` method returns `false` and no further action is
performed. If the user presses OK in the confirm dialog box then the `confirm()`
method returns `true` and the `location` property of the current window is set to
a new URL. This causes the new document to be loaded without the user ever
clicking on a link to that document. In fact, the destination of the link in the body
of the Web document is just the dummy URL `"somewhere"`. However, the clicking of this link is disabled by setting the `onClick` event handler to return *false*.
Whenever a *false* value is returned, the action associated with a click event is canceled. You'll learn more about this feature in later examples.

The important point about Listing 4.3 is that the onMouseOver event handling is performed via a single function call to confirmLink(). This allows confirmLink() to be developed without having to worry about quoting or trying to fit all of its statements in a single attribute value. The result is a much cleaner implementation of the event handler.

FIGURE 4.5

Age warning popup window (Listing 4.3)

FIGURE 4.6

Confirming the user's age (Listing 4.3)

NOTE The event handling examples I present in this chapter are geared to providing a simple explanation of the mechanics of event handling. I'll develop more sophisticated examples throughout the course of the book after I've covered JavaScript *objects* beginning in the next chapter.

Handling Link Events

So far you've seen several examples of handling events associated with links. Let's complete the discussion of link event handling before moving on to handling events associated with other HTML elements.

There are only three events that are associated with a link. These are shown in Table 4.3. In Listings 4.1 through 4.3 I already covered the handling of the first one—onMouseOver. The onMouseOver event is for providing the user with warnings or other information about a link before the user clicks on it.

TABLE 4.3. Link Events

Event	Event-handling Attribute
The mouse is moved over a link.	onMouseOver
The mouse is moved away from a link.	onMouseOut
The user clicks on the link.	onClick

The second link event, onMouseOut, is similar to the onMouseOver event, except that it is triggered when the user *leaves* a link, not when they approach it. As such, onMouseOut event handlers generally try to provide information to a user after they have left a link. Listing 4.4 provides an example of an onMouseOut event handler.

Listing 4.4. Handling onMouseOut for links (ch04-04.htm)

```
<HTML>
<HEAD>
<TITLE>Handling onMouseOut for links</TITLE>
<SCRIPT LANGUAGE="JavaScript">
<!--
function advertiseLink() {
 alert("The ACME Widget Company is having a 50% off sale on their
 ➡ best widgets.")
 if(confirm("Would you like to visit them and save 50% on an ACME
 ➡ widget?")) {
  window.location="http://www.jaworski.com/javascript/acme.htm"
 }
}
//-->
</SCRIPT>
</HEAD>
<BODY>
<H1>Handling onMouseOut for links</H1>
<P><A HREF="somewhere" ONMOUSEOUT="advertiseLink()">Tells you
➡ why you should connect to this link.</A></P>
</BODY>
</HTML>
```

In the above listing, an advertiseLink() function is defined in the document head. This function is set up to be the event handler for onMouseOut events and is set in the link defined in the body of the HTML document. When a user moves the mouse away from the link, the advertiseLink() function is invoked. The advertiseLink() function first notifies the user via the alert() method that the ACME Widget Company is having a fifty-percent-off sale (Figure 4.7). It then uses a confirm() method to ask the user if they want to visit the ACME Widget Company (Figure 4.8). If the user responds by clicking OK, then advertiseLink() sets the location property of the window to cause the ACME Web page to be loaded (Figure 4.9). If the user clicks Cancel, then the event handling is terminated.

FIGURE 4.7

Alerting the user to ACME Widget Company (Listing 4.4)

FIGURE 4.8

Asking the user to link to ACME Widget Company (Listing 4.4)

FIGURE 4.9

The ACME Widget Company Home Page is loaded (Listing 4.4)

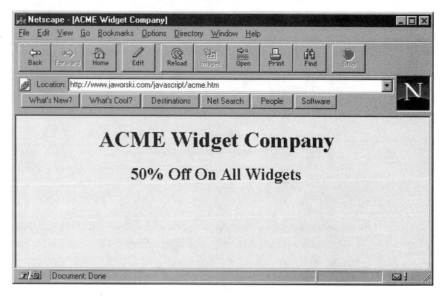

The advertiseLink() function presented above is just one example of how the onMouseOut event can be handled. Of course, it may be an annoying nuisance to your Web users if you badger them with an advertisement every time they refrain from following a link, so exercise a little creativity when you use anything similar to this example.

The last link event handling attribute, onClick, allows the clicking of a hyperlink to be handled in a custom manner. If the onClick event handler returns the value *false*, then the action associated with the click—in this case, the linking to a new document—is canceled. This capability lets the onClick event handler query the user to confirm or deny whether they want to proceed with a link. Listing 4.5 provides an example of this type of onClick event handling. The confirmLink() function is defined in the document head. It alerts the user to the fact that they have selected the Mastering JavaScript home page and then asks the user to confirm whether they want to link to this page (Figure 4.10). The results of the confirm() method are then returned. Notice that in the onClick event handler, the confirmLink() method is not invoked directly, but rather is invoked as part of a return statement:

```
return confirmLink()
```

This is because the value returned by confirm() and confirmLink() must be propagated to the point where the event handler was invoked in order for a false value to cancel the action associated with the clicking of the link. Try removing the return statement and calling confirmLink() directly. You will find that canceling the link is no longer an option.

Listing 4.5. Handling onClick for links (ch04-05.htm)

```
<HTML>
<HEAD>
<TITLE>Handling onClick for links</TITLE>
<SCRIPT LANGUAGE="JavaScript">
<!--
function confirmLink() {
  alert("This is the Mastering JavaScript Home Page.")
  return confirm("Are you sure you want to load this document?")
}
//-->
</SCRIPT>
</HEAD>
<BODY>
<H1>Handling onClick for links</H1>
```

```
<P><A HREF="http://www.jaworski.com/javascript"
ONCLICK="return confirmLink()">Asks you to confirm
your selection of this link.</A></P>
</BODY>
</HTML>
```

FIGURE 4.10

Confirming a user selection (Listing 4.5)

Handling Window Events

Window events apply to normal HTML documents that contain a body and produce a display; they also apply to layout documents that replace the document body with a frame set. (Layout documents are used to organize the display of other documents via frames—if you're unfamiliar with these objects, turn to Appendix A, "HTML Reference," and Chapter 6, "Windows and Frames," for more information.) In this section, we'll look at the event handling associated with both types of documents. Table 4.4 summarizes the events that are associated with these window objects.

TABLE 4.4 Window Events

Event	Event-handling Attribute
A window is loaded.	onLoad
A window is exited.	onUnload
An error occurs when a window is loaded.	onError
A window receives the input focus.	onFocus
A window loses the input focus.	onBlur

Listing 4.6 illustrates the handling of the onLoad and onUnload events for a normal displayable HTML document. When the document is first loaded, the

alert message shown in Figure 4.11 is displayed. As you exit the document (but not the browser), the alert message shown in Figure 4.12 is displayed.

Listing 4.6. Handling load events in a content document (ch04-06.htm)

```
<HTML>
<HEAD>
<TITLE>Handling load events in a content document</TITLE>
</HEAD>
<BODY onLoad="alert('Hello!')" onUnload="alert('Bye Bye!')">
<H1>Handling load events in a content document</H1>
<P>This document has a body and is displayed in typical
fashion.</P>
</BODY>
</HTML>
```

FIGURE 4.11

The onLoad message
(Listing 4.6)

FIGURE 4.12

The onUnload message
(Listing 4.6)

The onLoad event handler is typically used to perform any necessary initialization for Web pages that use Java or plug-ins, or to make a grand entrance by playing an audio file or an animation sequence. The onUnload event handler performs a similar function—terminating Java applets and plug-ins or enabling a dramatic exit. You'll see examples of using onLoad and onUnload for these uses in later chapters. The following example shows how onLoad and onUnload can be used with layout documents.

Listing 4.7. Handling load events in a layout document (ch04-07.htm)

```
<HTML>
<HEAD>
<TITLE>Handling load events in a layout document</TITLE>
<SCRIPT LANGUAGE="JavaScript"><!--
function selectFrames(){
 base="frames/"
 newFrames=new
Array("red.htm","yellow.htm","blue.htm","green.htm","white.htm")
 window.firstFrame.location=base+newFrames[Math.round
 ➥ (5*Math.random())%5]
 window.secondFrame.location=base+newFrames[Math.round
 ➥ (5*Math.random())%5]
}
//-->
</SCRIPT>
</HEAD>
<FRAMESET
COLS="*,*" ONLOAD="selectFrames()" ONUNLOAD="alert('Thanks for
stopping by!')">
<FRAME SRC="frames/grey.htm" NAME="firstFrame">
<FRAME SRC="frames/grey.htm" NAME="secondFrame">
</FRAMESET>
</HTML>
```

NOTE If you are not familiar with Netscape frames, refer to Appendix A, "HTML Reference," and Chapter 6, "Windows and Frames".

The HTML document shown in Listing 4.7 defines the `selectFrames()` function to handle the `onLoad` event. Before we describe the processing performed by the `setFrames()` function, let's discuss what's going on in the frame set part of the document. The frame set tags specify that two frames are to be contained in the document. The frames are to be organized into columns with the first frame named *firstName* and the second named *secondFrame*. Initially, both frames display the document at the relative URL *frames/grey.htm*. The `onLoad` attribute of the frame set tag specifies that the `selectFrames()` function should handle the event associated with the frame's loading. The `onUnload` event just displays the popup window with the text *Thanks for stopping by!* when the frame set is exited.

The `selectFrames()` function randomly loads two new documents into `firstFrame` and `secondFrame`. The `newFrames` array contains the names of five documents. A document is randomly selected from the list using the `random()` and `round()` methods of the `Math` object to calculate an index into the `newFrames` array. The `location` property of `firstFrame` and `secondFrame` are set to the randomly selected documents. (You'll learn all about the `Math` and `window` objects in the next chapter.)

When you load Listing 4.7 it opens a two-frame document with both the left and right frames initially set to gray. As soon as the document is loaded, the `onLoad` event is generated and `selectFrames()` is invoked to load new frame documents as shown in Figure 4.13. When you exit the document, the message shown in Figure 4.14 is displayed.

FIGURE 4.13

The onLoad event causes new frames to be loaded (Listing 4.7).

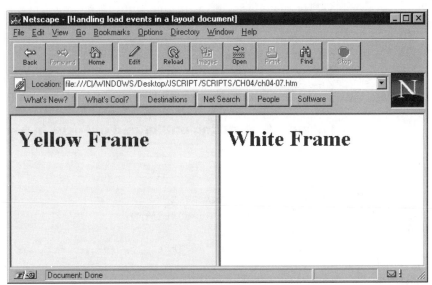

FIGURE 4.14

The onUnload message displayed when the frame set is exited (Listing 4.7)

While the onLoad and onUnload events are generated at the beginning and end of a document's existence, the onFocus and onBlur events can be triggered several times while a document is loaded. The onFocus event is generally used to restore a document to a default starting state or to continue previously interrupted processing. The onBlur event is used to interrupt the processing being performed on a page, such as the playing of an audio file or an animation, before a new page or area within the current page is activated. Listing 4.8 presents an example of the use of onLoad and onUnload event handlers. The frames are organized in column order.

Listing 4.8. Defining the frame set (ch04-08.htm)

```
<!-- ch04-08.htm -->
<HTML>
<HEAD>
<TITLE>Handling onFocus and onBlur events in a frame</TITLE>
</HEAD>
<FRAMESET COLS="*,*">
<FRAME SRC="frames/doc1.htm">
<FRAME SRC="frames/doc2.htm">
</FRAMESET>
</HTML>
```

Listing 4.9. Handling onBlur and onFocus in frames (doc1.htm)

```
<!-- doc1.htm -->
<HTML>
<HEAD>
<TITLE>Document 1</TITLE>
<SCRIPT LANGUAGE="JavaScript">
function gotFocus() {
 document.bgColor="#FFFFFF"
}
function lostFocus() {
 document.bgColor="#FF0000";
}
</SCRIPT>
</HEAD>
<BODY onFocus="gotFocus()" onBlur="lostFocus()"
BGCOLOR="#FF0000">
<H1>Document 1</H1>
</BODY>
</HTML>
```

Listing 4.10. Displaying an alternative background color (doc2.htm)

```
<!-- doc2.htm -->
<HTML>
<HEAD>
<TITLE>Document 2</TITLE>
</HEAD>
<BODY BGCOLOR="#FF0080">
<H1>Document 2</H1>
</BODY>
</HTML>
```

The file `doc1.htm` is the heart of this example. When it is loaded, it displays a reddish-orange color and lists a simple heading. The body tag specifies that the event handlers, `gotFocus()` and `lostFocus()`, are used for the `onFocus` and `onBlur` events. The document head defines these functions. The `gotFocus()` function sets the background color of the frame occupied by the document to white. The `lostFocus()` function resets the color of the frame back to its original color.

Figure 4.15 shows the original state of the frame set. Figure 4.16 shows how the background of the first frame changes to white when it receives the input focus.

The file `doc2.htm` is a simple document that merely displays a heading and dark pink background color. It is used to provide contrast for `doc1.htm`.

FIGURE 4.15

The frame set in its initial state (Listings 4.8 through 4.10)

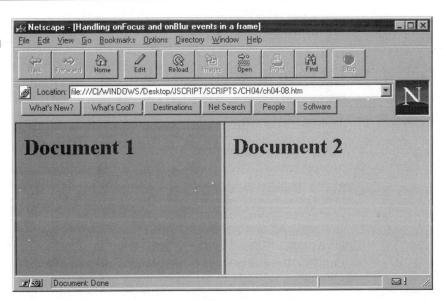

FIGURE 4.16

The frame set after the
first frame receives
the input focus (List-
ings 4.8 through 4.10)

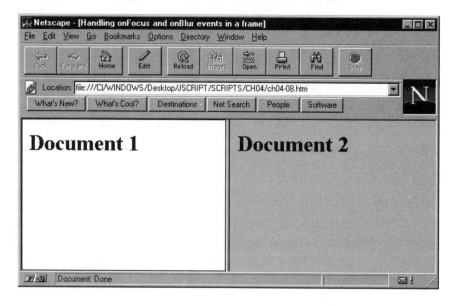

Handling Image Events

Image events are used to monitor the progress of image loading. Usually, images
are the longest loading element of a Web document. In many applications, it is
important to know whether they have been loaded, are in the process of loading,
or have had their loading interrupted. The image events provide this capability.
They are summarized in Table 4.5.

TABLE 4.5   Image Events

Event	Event-handling Attribute
An image has been loaded and displayed.	onLoad
The loading of an image has been aborted by the user.	onAbort
An error has occurred during the loading of an image.	onError

The onLoad event occurs when an image's loading and display has been completed. In many cases, such as in an image map application, it may be important
to wait for the onLoad event to occur before further processing is allowed. The

onAbort and onError events are used to respond to any exceptions that may occur in the loading process. Listing 4.11 illustrates the use of these event-handling capabilities.

Listing 4.11. Image event handling (ch04-11.htm)

```
<HTML>
<HEAD>
<TITLE>Image Event Handling</TITLE>
<SCRIPT LANGUAGE="JavaScript"><!--
function imageLoaded() {
 document.bgColor="#FFFFFF"
 window.defaultStatus=document.images[0].src+" has been loaded."
}
function imageAborted() {
 alert("Hey! You just aborted the loading of the last image!")
}
function imageError() {
 alert("Error loading image!")
}
//-->
</SCRIPT>
</HEAD>
<BODY>
<H1>Image Event Handling</H1>
<P>An image is loaded after this paragraph.</P>
<IMG SRC="image1.gif"
 onLoad="imageLoaded()"
 onAbort="imageAborted()"
 onError="imageError()">
</BODY>
</HTML>
```

The document shown in Listing 4.11 displays a heading, a one-line paragraph, and an image. The image has event handlers that respond to the onLoad, onAbort, and onError events. The onLoad event is handled by the image-Loaded() function. When an image has been loaded, the imageLoaded() function changes the document background color to white and displays a status message at the bottom of the browser window to identify the name of the image and the fact that it has been loaded. Figure 4.17 shows the document window after the onLoad event has been handled.

FIGURE 4.17

Handling the onLoad
event for images
(Listing 4.11)

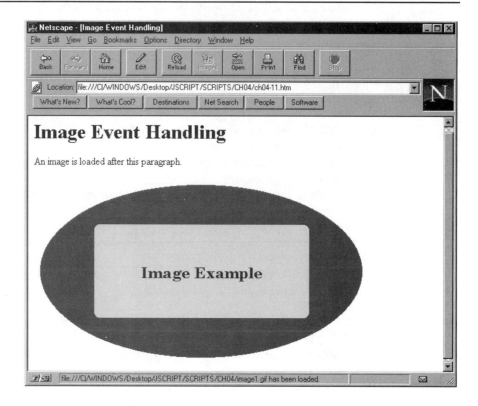

The onAbort event occurs as the result of a user action that causes image loading to be aborted, such as clicking the Stop button or changing to a new document. It is handled by the imageAborted() function, which simply notifies the
user that they have caused the image's loading to be aborted. Figure 4.18 shows
the result of processing the onAbort event.

FIGURE 4.18

Handling the onAbort
event for images
(Listing 4.11)

The `onError` event occurs as the result of an error which prevents an image from loading. A common example of this type of an error is the failure of a Web browser to locate the image. The `imageError()` function handles the `onError` event by displaying a notification to the user. Figure 4.19 shows how the `onError` event is handled as the result of the image file being moved from its specified location.

FIGURE 4.19

Handling the onError
event for images
(Listing 4.11)

Handling Image Map Events

Image maps are a popular feature found on many Web pages. An image map consists of an image that is divided into different areas or regions. When the user clicks on a particular location within the image, a connection is made to the URL associated with that location. This allows the image map to exhibit different responses based on the area clicked by the user. Figure 4.20 summarizes the basic mechanics of image maps.

FIGURE 4.20

How image maps work

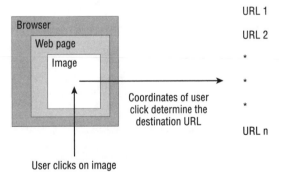

Two types of image maps are supported by JavaScript: server-side image maps and client-side image maps. Server-side image maps were developed first. As their name implies, most of the processing is performed on the server. The server contains a map file that defines the various regions of the image and associates these regions with specific URLs. When a user clicks on a location in the image, the coordinates of the location are passed to the Web server. The server determines which region was selected and returns the URL associated with that region. The user's browser then connects to this URL. Figure 4.21 summarizes server-side image map processing.

FIGURE 4.21

How server-side image maps work

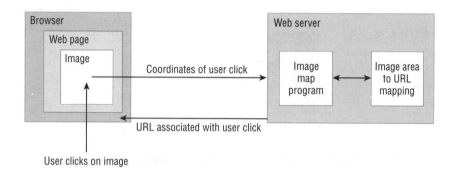

Client-side image maps are a very efficient improvement over server-side image maps. Instead of the map file being maintained on the server, it is embedded in the map element of the HTML file being browsed. This allows the browser to perform all of the processing required to determine which map area was selected by the user and to select the destination URL. Figure 4.22 summarizes client-side image map processing.

FIGURE 4.22

How client-side image maps work

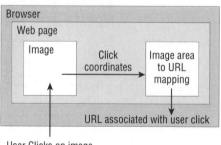

NOTE Appendix A, "HTML Reference," discusses the HTML tags used to implement client-side image maps.

JavaScript provides event-handling capabilities that support the processing of client-side image maps. The events supported for image maps are the same as those supported for links, and are summarized in Table 4.6. These events enable custom handling of user image-map clicks and mouse movements around a particular map area.

TABLE 4.6   Image Map Events

Event	Event-handling Attribute
The mouse is moved over an area.	`onMouseOver`
The mouse is moved away from an area.	`onMouseOut`

TIP

In order to use the `onMouseOver` and `onMouseOut` events with the `AREA` tag, you may have to set the `HREF` attribute. If the `NOHREF` attribute is present, these events may not function properly.

Listing 4.12 presents an example of the handling of `onMouseOver` and `onMouseOut` events. The document displays a heading and an image that is used as a client-side image map. Note that the image sets the `USEMAP` attribute to *#blockman*, which is the name of the image map described by the map tags. The image used in the image map is `blockman.gif`. It is shown in Figure 4.23 along with the coordinates of various points within the image. These coordinates are used to create the parameters for the area tags that are enclosed by the map tags.

Listing 4.12. Image map event handling (ch04-12.htm)

```
<HTML>
<HEAD>
<TITLE>Image Map Event Handling</TITLE>
<SCRIPT LANGUAGE="JavaScript"><!--
firstTimeOnHead=true
function onHead() {
 if(firstTimeOnHead) {
  alert("You're on my head!")
  firstTimeOnHead=false
 }
}
```

```
function myEye() {
 alert("Be careful or you'll poke out my eye!")
}
function myNose() {
 alert("Aaacchhooo!")
}
function myMouth() {
 alert("Get out of my mouth!")
}
//-->
</SCRIPT>
</HEAD>
<BODY>
<H1>Image Map Event Handling</H1>
<IMG SRC="blockman.gif" USEMAP="#blockman">
<MAP NAME="blockman">
<AREA COORDS="80,88,120,125" HREF="ch04-10.htm"
onMouseOver="myEye()">
<AREA COORDS="169,88,208,125" HREF="ch04-10.htm"
onMouseOver="myEye()">
<AREA COORDS="124,147,165,181" HREF="ch04-10.htm"
onMouseOut="myNose()">
<AREA COORDS="92,210,192,228" HREF="ch04-10.htm"
onMouseOut="myMouth()">
<AREA COORDS="6,4,292,266" HREF="ch04-10.htm"
onMouseOver="onHead()">
</MAP>
</BODY>
</HTML>
```

The first and second area tags describe rectangles which enclose block man's eyes. Both tags specify that the myEye() function should be called to handle the onMouseOver event. The third area tag describes the rectangle formed by block man's nose. It specifies that the myNose() function should handle the onMouse-Out event. The fourth area tag describes the rectangle formed by block man's mouth. It specifies that the onMouseOut event should be handled by the myMouth() function. Finally, the fifth area tag describes the larger rectangle that handles block man's head. This tag handles the onMouseOver event via the onHead() function.

FIGURE 4.23

Coordinates within
blockman.gif
(Listing 4.12)

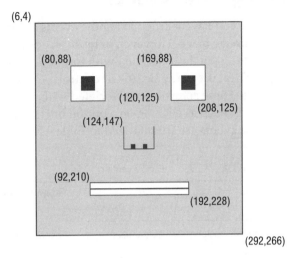

The `area` tags are processed in a first-come, first-handled order. The browser checks the location of a mouse action with each `area` tag in the order that the tags appear in the `map` tag. If the browser gets to the last tag, it is processing a mouse action that occurred outside the other `area` tags but within the outline of block man's head.

The event-handling functions in this listing are quite simple. The `myEye()`, `myNose()`, and `myMouth()` functions display cute messages using the `alert()` method. The `onHead()` function is just a tad more sophisticated. The `first-TimeOnHead` variable is initialized to *true* when the HTML document is first loaded. The `onHead()` function displays a message when `firstTimeOnHead` is *true* and then sets `firstTimeOnHead` to *false*. This causes the alert message to be displayed only once. Figure 4.24 shows the Web page displayed by a browser as the result of handling the initial `onMouseOver` event for block man's head.

FIGURE 4.24

Handling `onMouseOver`
for AREA tags (Listing 4.12)

Handling Form Events

So far you have learned to handle events associated with links, windows, images and image maps. However, in most practical JavaScript applications the event handling will be associated with forms. Forms provide a number of sophisticated graphical user interface (GUI) controls such as buttons, check boxes, and text fields. These controls are associated with a number of events that reflect user actions, such as clicking on a button or checkbox or selecting text in a text field. These events are summarized in Table 4.7.

TABLE 4.7   Form Events

Event	Form Element	Event-Handling Attribute
The form is submitted by the user.	overall form	onSubmit
The form is reset by the user.	overall form	onReset
The text field or text area loses the input focus.	text field or text area	onBlur
The text field or text area receives the input focus.	text field or text area	onFocus
The text field or text area is modified and loses the current input focus.	text field or text area	onChange
Text is selected within the text field or text area.	text field or text area	onSelect
The button or check box is clicked.	button, submit button, reset button, radio button, or check box	onClick
The selection element loses the input focus.	selection	onBlur
The selection element receives the input focus.	selection	onFocus
The selection element is modified and loses the current input focus.	selection	onChange

We'll present three examples that cover most of the events in Table 4.7. The first example, shown in Listing 4.13, illustrates events associated with text field and text area buttons and the onSubmit form event. The second example is presented in Listing 4.14. It illustrates the onClick event used with different types of buttons and check boxes. The third example is shown in Listing 4.15 and shows how the onChange selection element event is handled.

Listing 4.13. Text field and text area event handling (ch04-13.htm)

```
<HTML>
<HEAD>
<TITLE>Text Field and Text Area Events</TITLE>
<SCRIPT LANGUAGE="JavaScript"><!--
function nameSelect() {
 if(isBlank(""+document.contest.last.value)) {
  document.contest.last.value="Surname"
  document.contest.last.focus()
  document.contest.last.select()
 }
}
function isBlank(s) {
 var len=s.length
 var i
 for(i=0;i<len;++i) {
  if(s.charAt(i)!=" ") return false
 }
 return true
}
function validate(fieldName,fieldValue) {
 if(isBlank(fieldValue)) {
  alert(fieldName+" cannot be left blank.")
  return false
 }
 return true
}
function validateEmail() {
 validate("The e-mail field",document.contest.email.value)
}
function validateEssay() {
 validate("The essay field",document.contest.essay.value)
}
```

```
function validateForm() {
 if(!validate("The last name field",document.contest.last.value))
  return false
 if(!validate("The e-mail field",document.contest.email.value))
  return false
 if(!validate("The essay field",document.contest.essay.value))
  return false
}
//--></SCRIPT>
</HEAD>
<BODY>
<FORM NAME="contest" ONSUBMIT="return validateForm()">
<H2 ALIGN="CENTER">Contest Application</H2>
<P>Last name:
<INPUT TYPE="TEXT" NAME="last" SIZE="16"
 ONCHANGE="nameSelect()">
First name:
<INPUT TYPE="TEXT" NAME="first" SIZE="12">
Middle Initial:
<INPUT TYPE="TEXT" NAME="initial" SIZE="2"></P>
<P>E-mail address:
<INPUT TYPE="TEXT" NAME="email" SIZE="32"
 ONCHANGE="validateEmail()"></P>
<P>In 50 words or less, state why you should win the contest:</P>
<TEXTAREA NAME="essay" ROWS="5" COLS="40"
 ONCHANGE="validateEssay()"></TEXTAREA>
<P>Submit your winning entry:
<INPUT TYPE="SUBMIT" NAME="go" VALUE="Make me a winner!"></P>
</FORM>
</BODY>
</HTML>
```

The previous listing presents the contest application form shown in Figure 4.25. Event handlers are associated with the last, email, and essay fields of the form as well as with the form as a whole. The last and email fields are text fields and the essay field is a text area field. The onChange event of the last field uses the nameSelect() function to handle the event associated with the changes to the field's contents. The nameSelect() function uses the isBlank() function to determine if the user made changes to the field that resulted in it becoming blank. If the field is left blank, then the field's value is set to *Surname*, the current focus is set to the field, and the text is selected. Figure 4.26 shows the result of the nameS-elect() processing.

FIGURE 4.25

Contest application form
(Listing 4.13)

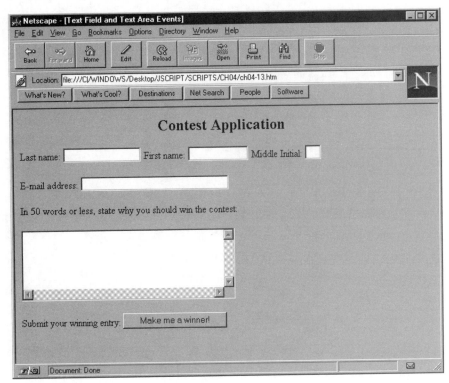

The email field uses the `validateEmail()` function to handle the `onChange` event. This function invokes the `validate()` function to check whether the field had been left blank and uses the `alert()` function to send a notification to the user that the field cannot be blank. The `validateEssay()` function is used in the same manner by the `essay` field. The form tag specifies that the `onSubmit` event should be handled by the statement `return validateForm()`. When the user clicks on the button labeled *Make me a winner!*, the `validateForm()` function is invoked to check whether the `last`, `email`, or `essay` fields are blank and to notify the user if any field is blank. It returns *false* to prevent the form from being submitted with these fields being blank.

The script shown in Listing 4.14 presents the survey form shown in Figure 4.27. This form illustrates the handling of the `onClick` event for buttons and check boxes. When any of the radio buttons or check boxes are checked, the `results` text field displays the checked fields. When the button labeled *To Upper Case* is

FIGURE 4.26

Result of `nameSelect()`
processing (Listing 4.13)

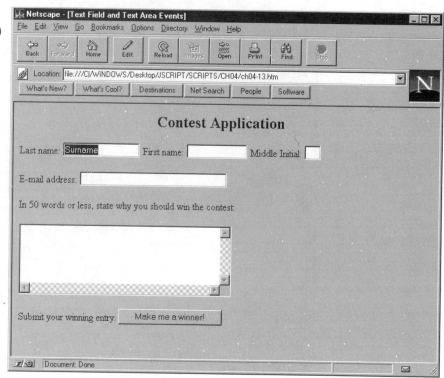

clicked, the `results` field is converted to upper case. When the Submit or Reset
button is clicked, a confirmation window is displayed. Note that the effect of the
Submit button may be canceled—with the result that the form is not submitted.

Listing 4.14. Button and check box event handling (ch04-14.htm)

```
<HTML>
<HEAD>
<TITLE>Button and Check Box Events</TITLE>
<SCRIPT LANGUAGE="JavaScript"><!--
function showResults() {
 var resultMsg=""
 if(document.survey.age[0].checked) resultMsg+="under 30, "
 if(document.survey.age[1].checked) resultMsg+="between 30
➥ and 60, "
 if(document.survey.age[2].checked) resultMsg+="over 60, "
```

```
 if(document.survey.sex[0].checked) resultMsg+="male, "
 if(document.survey.sex[1].checked) resultMsg+="female, "
 if(document.survey.reading.checked) resultMsg+="reading, "
 if(document.survey.eating.checked) resultMsg+="eating, "
 if(document.survey.sleeping.checked) resultMsg+="sleeping, "
 document.survey.results.value=resultMsg
}
function upperCaseResults() {
 var newResults=document.survey.results.value
 document.survey.results.value=newResults.toUpperCase()
}
//--></SCRIPT>
</HEAD>
<BODY>
<FORM NAME="survey">
<H2 ALIGN="CENTER">Survey Form</H2>
<P><B>Age:</B>
<INPUT TYPE="RADIO" NAME="age" VALUE="under30"
 ONCLICK="showResults()">Under 30
<INPUT TYPE="RADIO" NAME="age" VALUE="30to60"
 ONCLICK="showResults()">30 - 60
<INPUT TYPE="RADIO" NAME="age" VALUE="over60"
 ONCLICK="showResults()">Over 60</P>
<P><B>Sex: </B>
<INPUT TYPE="RADIO" NAME="sex" VALUE="male"
 ONCLICK="showResults()">Male
<INPUT TYPE="RADIO" NAME="sex" VALUE="female"
 ONCLICK="showResults()">Female</P>
<P><B>Interests: </B>
<INPUT TYPE="CHECKBOX" NAME="reading"
 ONCLICK="showResults()"> Reading
<INPUT TYPE="CHECKBOX" NAME="eating"
 ONCLICK="showResults()"> Eating
<INPUT TYPE="CHECKBOX" NAME="sleeping"
 ONCLICK="showResults()"> Sleeping</P>
<P>
<INPUT TYPE="BUTTON" NAME="makeUpper"
 VALUE="To Upper Case" ONCLICK="upperCaseResults()"></P>
<P><B>Results: </B><INPUT TYPE="TEXT" NAME="results"
➥ SIZE="50"></P>
<INPUT TYPE="SUBMIT" NAME="submit" VALUE="Submit"
 ONCLICK='return confirm("Sure?")'>
```

```
<INPUT TYPE="RESET" NAME="reset"
 ONCLICK='return confirm("Sure?")'>
</FORM>
</BODY>
</HTML>
```

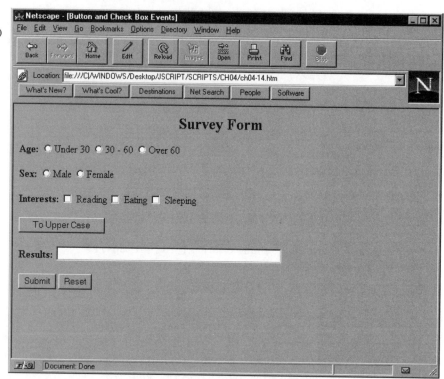

FIGURE 4.27

Survey Form (Listing 4.14)

The radio and check boxes in Listing 4.14 use a single event-handling function—`showResults()`. This function checks the status of these fields and creates a text message, which it displays in the `results` field. The `upperCaseResults()` function handles the `onClick` event of the `makeUpper` button by converting the contents of the `results` field to upper case. You'll learn more about the mechanics of how this happens in the next chapter on JavaScript objects.

The script in Listing 4.15 presents a menu for the Web Diner page, as shown in Figure 4.28. This form consists of a multiple selection list, from which fast food items are selected, and a text area field, which displays the results of the user's selection. The `updateOrder()` function handles the `onChange` event associated with the selection list. It checks through all of the options in the selection list to see which have been selected and displays a formatted text string in the text area field which summarizes the user's selection.

Listing 4.15. Selection list event handling (ch04-15.htm)

```
<HTML>
<HEAD>
<TITLE>Handling Selection List Events</TITLE>
<SCRIPT LANGUAGE="JavaScript"><!--
function updateOrder() {
 var orderString=""
 var n=document.diner.entries.length
 for(i=0;i<n;++i) {
  if(document.diner.entries.options[i].selected) {
   orderString+=document.diner.entries.options[i].value+"\n"
  }
 }
 document.diner.summary.value=orderString
}
//--></SCRIPT>
</HEAD>
<BODY>
<FORM NAME="diner">
<H2 ALIGN="CENTER">The Web Diner</H2>
<P><B>Place your order:</B></P>
<SELECT NAME="entries" SIZE="4" MULTIPLE="MULTIPLE"
 ONCHANGE="updateOrder()">
<OPTION VALUE="Hamburger">Hamburger</OPTION>
<OPTION VALUE="Hot Dog">Hot Dog</OPTION>
<OPTION VALUE="Chicken Sandwich">Chicken Sandwich</OPTION>
<OPTION VALUE="French Fries">French Fries</OPTION>
<OPTION VALUE="Onion Rings">Onion Rings</OPTION>
<OPTION VALUE="Soda">Soda</OPTION>
<OPTION VALUE="Milk Shake">Milk Shake</OPTION>
<OPTION VALUE="Coffee">Coffee</OPTION></SELECT>
<P><B>You ordered: </B></P>
<P>
<TEXTAREA NAME="summary" ROWS="4" COLS="20"></TEXTAREA></P>
```

```
<P><INPUT TYPE="SUBMIT" NAME="order" VALUE="Let me have it!"></P>
</FORM>
</BODY>
</HTML>
```

FIGURE 4.28

Web Diner Menu
(Listing 4.15)

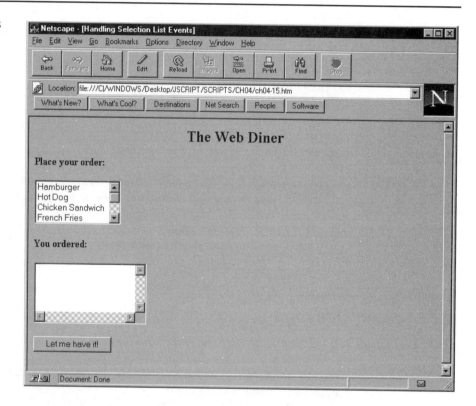

Setting Event Handlers from within JavaScript

Until now, we have been explicitly identifying event handlers using the event attribute of the tag to which the event handlers apply. This is the traditional, preferred way of identifying event handlers. With Netscape, you also have the capability to specify event handlers from within JavaScript. While this capability adds greater flexibility in specifying event handlers, you should use it with care—the flexibility that you gain from this approach can also lead to code that is less structured and more difficult to debug. I'll discuss the pros and cons of this approach after I have introduced it and illustrated it with an example.

As you'll learn in Chapter 5, "Objects in JavaScript," most of the individual elements of an HTML document can be accessed as objects that are automatically created by JavaScript. These objects have *properties* that specify the values of data items associated with the object. For example, in Listing 4.15, the entries selection list is identified by the following object:

```
document.diner.entries
```

The number of options in the selection list is a property of the list and is identified by the following:

```
document.diner.entries.length
```

Objects that are associated with events, such as links and form elements, have properties that identify the functions used to handle these events. For example, in Listing 4.15, the onChange event handler associated with the entries selection list is identified by the following property:

```
document.diner.entries.onchange
```

Instead of specifying updateOrder() as the event handler for entries in its input tag definition, we could have used the following JavaScript statement:

```
document.diner.entries.onchange=updateOrder
```

If we used this approach, the above statement would need to be placed in a script that is executed *after* the entries input tag definition, or else a JavaScript error would result.

When an event-handling function is explicitly assigned to the event property of an object, the trailing parentheses () are omitted. It is important that both the object and the function be defined prior to the assignment statement.

Listing 4.16 illustrates the process of setting event handlers from within JavaScript, and Figure 4.29 shows the Web page that is generated. It consists of a single clickMe button that, when clicked, causes the text *Set by handler1* or *Set by handler2* to be alternately displayed in a text field. The input tag of the Click Me! button does not identify a event handler via the onClick attribute. Instead, a script follows the form definition which assigns handler1 to document.test.clickMe.onclick. This script causes the initial event handler for the onClick event of the Click Me! button to be handler1().

Listing 4.16. Setting event handlers from within JavaScript (ch04-16.htm)

```
<HTML>
<HEAD>
<TITLE>Setting event handlers from within JavaScript</TITLE>
<SCRIPT LANGUAGE="JavaScript"><!--
function handler1() {
 document.test.result.value="Set by handler1"
 document.test.clickMe.onclick=handler2
}
function handler2() {
 document.test.result.value="Set by handler2"
 document.test.clickMe.onclick=handler1
}
//--></SCRIPT>
</HEAD>
<BODY>
<FORM NAME="test">
<INPUT TYPE="BUTTON" NAME="clickMe" VALUE="Click Me!">
<P><INPUT TYPE="TEXT" NAME="result" SIZE="20"></P>
</FORM>
<SCRIPT LANGUAGE="JavaScript"><!--
 document.test.clickMe.onclick=handler1
//--></SCRIPT>
</BODY>
</HTML>
```

When handler1() is invoked to handle the onClick event, it sets the result text field to *Set by handler1* and then changes the onClick event handler to handler2(). The next time the Click Me! button is clicked, handler2() handles the onClick event. The handler2() function sets the result field to *Set by handler2* and changes the onClick event handler back to handler1().

This simple example illustrates the flexibility and power of explicitly assigning event handlers from within JavaScript. However, when you use this approach, it is much more difficult to determine which events are handled by which functions.

This makes your code more difficult to debug. As a general practice, if the event handler associated with an event will be the same throughout a script's execution, then you should assign it using the event attribute of the HTML element to which it applies. If an event requires multiple event handlers, then change event handlers using JavaScript.

FIGURE 4.29

Setting event handlers from within JavaScript (Listing 4.16)

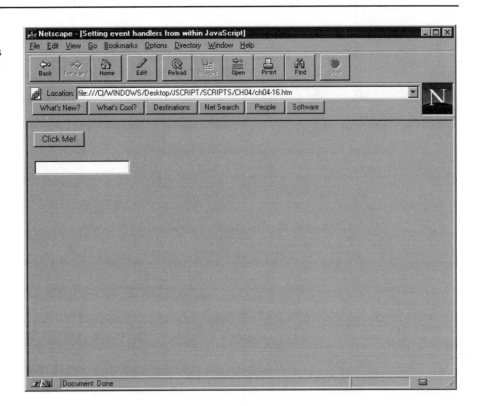

Event Emulation Methods

In the previous section, you learned how HTML elements are represented by JavaScript objects, and how certain properties of these objects can be used to assign event handlers. In addition to these properties, some objects have methods which can be used to *emulate* the occurrence of events. When an event emulation method is invoked, the object to which it refers acts as if the event is taking place. However, no event is actually generated. For example, button objects have the `click()` method that, when invoked, causes a button to *appear* as if it is being clicked. However, the button's event handler is not invoked.

Listing 4.17 provides an example of event emulation. Figure 4.30 shows the Web page displayed by this document. It consists of two buttons—button1, labeled *Click Me*, and button2, labeled *Watch Me*. When you click on button1, the function `clickButton2()` is invoked; it executes the following statement:

```
document.test.button2.click()
```

which causes button2 to appear as if it is being clicked.

You are probably wondering why you would ever want the capability to emulate events. Consider a script that instructs a user how to use a Web page. The script could inform the user to click certain buttons to obtain different types of results. Rather than just telling the user what buttons to click, you can use event emulation to actually *show* the user what buttons to click.

You'll learn the details of which objects and methods support event emulation in the next chapter, "Objects in JavaScript."

Listing 4.17. Emulating events (ch04-17.htm)

```
<HTML>
<HEAD>
<TITLE>Emulating Events</TITLE>
<SCRIPT LANGUAGE="JavaScript"><!--
function clickButton2() {
 document.test.button2.click()
}
//--></SCRIPT>
</HEAD>
<BODY>
<FORM NAME="test">
<INPUT TYPE="BUTTON" NAME="button1" VALUE="Click Me"
 ONCLICK="clickButton2()">
<INPUT TYPE="BUTTON" NAME="button2" VALUE="Watch Me">
</FORM>
</BODY>
</HTML>
```

FIGURE 4.30

An event emulation
example (Listing 4.17)

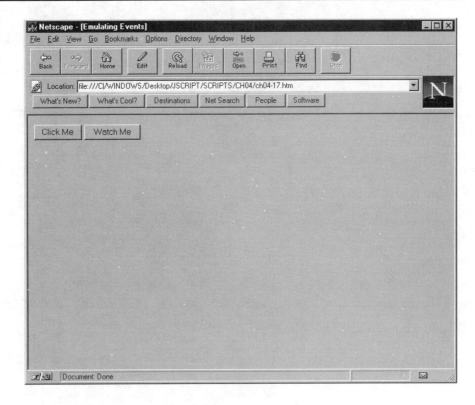

Summary

This chapter illustrated the use of JavaScript's event-handling capabilities. It
described JavaScript's approach to event handling and identified the event handlers that are predefined by JavaScript. You learned how to write your own
event-handling functions and how to associate them with user interface actions.
In the next chapter, you'll learn about JavaScript's support of objects and how to
create your own objects and methods in JavaScript.

Objects in JavaScript

- Object-Oriented Programming

- JavaScript Object-Based Programming Features

- Navigator Objects

- Other Predefined Object Types

- Color Constants

- Arrays Are Objects

- Using Functions as Objects

One of the most important features of JavaScript is that it is an object-based language. This simplifies the design of JavaScript programs and enables them to be developed in a more intuitive, modular, and reusable manner.

This chapter describes JavaScript's support of objects and object-based programming. It introduces the JavaScript Object Model and summarizes the predefined JavaScript objects. It also shows how to create your own object types. When you finish this chapter, you'll be able to define and use objects in your Web pages.

TIP	The chapters in Part 2 of this book, "Using Predefined Objects and Methods," provide detailed descriptions and examples of JavaScript's predefined objects.

What Are Objects?

Most people know that objects are entities that exist in the real world of people, places, and things. But they also exist in the cyber world of computers and networking. Examples of real-world objects include you, the book you are reading, and the lamp that you use to provide you with light. Examples of cyber-world objects are the Web pages that you create and the individual HTML elements they contain. It is these types objects that I will be discussing in relation to JavaScript.

An object consists of two things:

- A collection of *properties* that contain data
- *Methods* that enable operations on the data contained in those properties

When you view something as an object, then you look at it in terms of its properties and methods. Table 5.1 identifies some of the properties and methods that could apply to common objects.

You've already seen several examples of JavaScript objects. You've used the document object and its write() method in many of the scripts in previous chapters. You've also used the alert() method of the window object to display messages to the user. The fields of a form are also objects. You've seen how the value property of a field can be used to test and set the field's value. By the time you finish this chapter, you will have encountered all of the predefined JavaScript objects and learned how to create objects of your own.

TABLE 5.1   Examples of objects, properties, and methods

Object	Properties	Methods

You
(real-world object)
	`height`
	`weight`
	`hairColor`
		`eat()`
		`exercise()`
		`grow()`

This book
(real-world object)
	`pages`
	`currentPage`
		`turnPageForward()`
		`turnPageBackward()`
		`goToPage()`

A lamp (real-world object)	`onOffState` `turnOff()`	`turnOn()`

A Web page
(cyber-world object)
	`title`
	`bgColor`
	`links`
		`open()`
		`close()`
		`write()`

An HTML button (cyber-world object)	`name` `value`	`click()`

NOTE   JavaScript is not a full object-oriented language—there are a few object-oriented programming features that it lacks. However, JavaScript *is* an object-*based* language, and provides several important object-oriented programming features. In order to learn why these features are important and how to use these features correctly, we'll begin by reviewing object-oriented programming in general, and then identify which object-oriented programming features are supported by JavaScript.

What Is Object-Oriented Programming?

The field of software engineering has evolved over the fifty or so years of the computer's popular existence. This evolution has brought about different approaches and strategies to the task of creating high-quality software while minimizing development time and costs. The most successful development approach currently in use is the object-oriented approach. This approach *models* the elements of a software application as objects—by modeling I mean object types are named, their properties are identified, and their methods are described. Once an object type is defined, it can then be used to create specific instances of other objects of that type and to construct other, more complex object types.

NOTE   An object type is referred to as a *class* in object-oriented languages such as Java and C++.

Object Types and Instances

An object type is a template from which specific objects of that type are created. It defines the properties and methods that are common to all objects of that type. For example, let's consider a person's mailing address as an object type. I'll name it `mailAddress` and give it the properties of `streetAddress`, `city`, `state`, and `postalCode`. In addition to these properties, I'll define `changeAddress()` as a method for changing one person's address and `findAddress()` as a method for finding out another person's address. Don't worry about how I'm doing this— you'll learn that later—for this explanation just focus on what's being done.

When I define the `mailAddress` object type, I haven't specified anyone's address. I've only developed a template for the creation of an address—kind of like a blank Rolodex card. The address type can be *instantiated*, which is the programming term for creating a specific *instance* of that type of object; in this case it would mean creating a specific person's address record. This is similar to producing a Rolodex card, filling it in, and sticking it in the Rolodex.

The capability to define an object type from which specific object instances can then be created is a very basic but important feature of object-oriented software development.

Creating Object Types

While the definition and instantiation of object types is a basic feature of object-oriented languages, it is not the only feature these languages provide. The ability to use object types to define *other* object types is what really gives object-oriented programming its power. There are two major ways in which this is accomplished: *object composition* and *inheritance*.

Object Composition

One approach to developing object types is to define primitive object types which serve as simple building blocks from which more complex types may be composed. This approach is referred to as *object composition*. Consider the process of building a house. At some point, somebody must construct the boards, nails, and glass panes that are used as the basic building blocks for constructing most homes. These building objects are assembled into more complex objects such as doors, windows, and prefabricated walls. These more complex objects are then, in turn, assembled into larger objects which eventually are integrated into a finished home. In the same way that boards, nails, glass panes, and other simple objects are used to construct a wide variety of different homes, simple object types are used in programming to create more complex object types which are eventually integrated into a final software application. For example, the `mailAddress` object may be used to create an employment application form, which is itself used to create a personnel database system.

Object composition is closely related to and depends on the capability to support *object re-use*. When an object type is defined, it is often very desirable that it be defined in such a way that it can be re-used in other software applications. This simplifies the development of other applications, and naturally leads to cost and schedule savings. The re-use of software objects is just as important as the re-use of technology in other engineering disciplines. Imagine the state of the automotive industry if the wheel had to be reinvented for every new type of car that's been developed.

Encapsulation Software objects are re-useable when they follow certain design principles. One of the most important of these principles is *encapsulation*. Encapsulation is the packaging of the properties and methods of an object into a container with an appropriately defined interface. The object's interface must provide the methods and properties that enable the object to be used in the manner that is intended, and must do it without providing methods or properties that would allow the object to be misused. If this abstract description is difficult to fathom, consider the interface of an automobile. Auto designers provide steering, braking, and throttling capabilities in all cars, since these capabilities are basic to driving. However, no automobile manufacturer provides drivers with the capability to manually control the firing of spark plugs from the dashboard. Even if drivers were interested in this capability, they more than likely could not use it to any advantage.

Modularity and Information Hiding Encapsulation depends upon two important concepts for its success. The first concept, *modularity*, refers to an object's being complete in and of itself and not accessing other objects outside their defined interfaces. Modular objects are said to be "loosely coupled," which means that dependencies between objects are minimized, and internal changes to an object do not require changes in other objects that make use of the object. The second concept, *information hiding*, refers to the practice of limiting information about an object to that which is required to use the object's interface. It is accomplished by removing information about the internal operation of an object from the object's interface.

Inheritance

The second major way of constructing object types from other object types is through *inheritance*. In this approach, higher level, more abstract object types are defined from which lower level, more concrete object types are derived. When a lower level object type is created, it identifies one or more higher level object types as its *parent* types. The *child* type inherits all of the properties and methods of its parents. This eliminates the need to redefine these properties and methods. The child type is free to redefine any of the methods that it inherits or to add new properties and methods. This enables the child type to tailor its inherited characteristics to new situations.

As an example, consider the various types of objects that may be constructed to implement a scrolling marquee. At the highest level, a `genericMarquee` may be constructed that has the basic properties `scrolledText` and `scrollRate`. It may provide basic methods, such as `startScrolling()` and `stopScrolling()`. From this generic marquee, more complex marquees may be created. For example, `horizontalMarquee` and `verticalMarquee` object types may be constructed that add the property `scrollDirection` to those inherited from `generic-Marquee`. These, in turn, may be further refined into marquees which use colored text and backgrounds. The properties `textColor` and `backgroundColor` and the methods `randomTextColor()` and `randomBackgroundColor()` could be added.

Using inheritance, more sophisticated, custom-tailored object types can be created from those that are already defined, by just adding the properties and methods needed to differentiate the new objects from their parents. Once a useful object type is created, it can then be re-used many times to create several child objects and numerous generations of offspring.

Classification and Inheritance Object-oriented programming languages, such as Java and C++ (but not JavaScript), refer to an object's type as its "class," and provide the capability to develop child classes from parent classes using inheritance. The resulting class structure is referred to as a *classification scheme*. The classification schemes that result from object-oriented development mimic those that are fundamental to the way we as human beings acquire and organize knowledge. For example, we develop general class names, such as "animal," that we use to refer to large groups of real-world objects. We then develop names of subclasses, such as "mammal," "bird," and "insect," which we use to refine our concept of animal. We continue to develop more detailed classes that differentiate between objects of the same class. The same sort of classification process is carried out by developers of object-oriented programs.

Single and Multiple Inheritance Part of the reason that inheritance is a successful approach to object development is that it mimics the way we acquire and organize knowledge—it is therefore *intuitive* to us. In addition to this, inheritance is *efficient*, because it only requires you to define the properties and methods that are unique for an object's type.

Some languages, notably Java, enforce a more restricted form of inheritance, known as *single inheritance*. Single inheritance requires that a child class have only one parent. However, a parent may have multiple children. Since a child class inherits its properties and methods from a single parent, it is an exact duplicate of its parent before it adds its own unique properties and methods.

Other languages, notably C++, support *multiple inheritance*. As you might expect, multiple inheritance allows child classes to inherit their properties and methods from more than one parent class. Multiple inheritance is much more powerful than single inheritance, because it allows independent, but complementary, branches of the class structure to be fused together into a single branch.

Multiple inheritance does, however, introduce some difficulties with respect to name resolution. Suppose that class C is the child of both class A and class B. Suppose also that both class A and B define different `save()` methods. Which of these two methods is inherited by class C? How does the compiler determine which method to use for objects of class C? Although it is certainly possible to develop naming schemes and compilers that resolve naming difficulties resulting from multiple inheritance, these solutions often require a significant amount of additional compilation and runtime processing.

Polymorphism While at first it may appear to be undesirable to have many methods of the same name, the capability to do so is actually a feature of object-oriented programming. *Polymorphism* is the capability to take on different forms. It allows an object type to define several different implementations of a method. These methods are differentiated by the types and number of parameters they accept. For example, several different `print()` methods may be defined, each of which is used to print objects of different object types. Other `print()` methods may be defined which take a different number of parameters. The interpreter, compiler, or runtime system selects the particular `print()` method that is most appropriate for the object being printed. Polymorphism allows the programmer to use a standard method, e.g., `print()`, to perform a particular operation and to define different forms of the method to be used with different parameters. This promotes standardization and reusable software and eliminates the need to come up with many slightly different names to distinguish the same operation being performed with different parameters.

JavaScript Object-Based Programming Features

In the previous section, you learned about the capabilities that are common to object-oriented programming languages. Several of the capabilities described are not supported by JavaScript, but are supported by Java. You won't be studying Java until Part 4 of this book, but it is worth your while to become familiar with the object-oriented programming capabilities described in the previous section so that when you do get to Part 4, you'll be ready to start learning how Java applets can be integrated with JavaScript scripts.

In this section, you'll learn which object-oriented programming capabilities are supported by JavaScript and how they are used to develop object-based JavaScript programs.

JavaScript is not a full object-oriented programming language. It does not support the basic object-oriented programming capabilities of classification, inheritance, encapsulation, and information hiding. However, this is not as bad as it first appears. JavaScript is a scripting language, not a full programming language. The features that it does provide are geared toward providing a capability to quickly and easily generate scripts which execute in the context of a Web page or a server-side application.

JavaScript is referred to as an *object-based* language. It supports the development of object types and the instantiation of these types to create object instances. It provides great support for object composition, but only fair support for modularity and object re-use. Table 5.2 summarizes JavaScript's object-based programming capabilities.

TABLE 5.2   JavaScript's object-based programming capabilities

Capability	Description
Object types	JavaScript supports both predefined and user-defined object types. However, JavaScript does not provide capabilities for type enforcement. An object of any type may be assigned to any variable.
Object instantiation	Object types are instantiated using the `new` operator to create specific object instances.
Object composition	Object types may be defined in terms of other predefined or user-defined object types.
Modularity	JavaScript code may be defined in a modular fashion, but JavaScript does not provide any features that enforce modular software development.
Object re-use	JavaScript software may be re-used via the `SRC` attribute of the `SCRIPT` tag. Software may be made available for re-use via the Internet.
Information hiding	JavaScript does not provide any capabilities to support information hiding.
Encapsulation	Since JavaScript lacks information hiding capabilities, it cannot be used to develop encapsulated object types. Any method or property that is defined for a type is always directly accessible.
Inheritance	JavaScript does not provide any language features that support inheritance between object types.
Classification	Since JavaScript does not support inheritance, it cannot be used to develop a hierarchy of object types.
Polymorphism	JavaScript supports polymorphism using the arguments array for function definitions.

Although JavaScript does not provide all of the features of full object-oriented programming languages, such as Java, it does provide a suite of object-based features that are specially tailored to browser and server scripting. These features include a number of predefined browser and server objects and the capability to access related objects through the properties and methods of other objects. If this seems very abstract at this point, don't worry—you'll see several concrete examples of these features throughout this chapter as well as in the chapters of Part 2.

The JavaScript Object Model

JavaScript supports a simple object model which is supported by a number of predefined objects. The *JavaScript Object Model* centers around the specification of object types that are used to create specific object instances. Object types under this model are defined in terms of properties and methods:

- Properties are used to access the data values contained in an object. Properties, by default, can be updated as well as read, although some properties of the predefined JavaScript objects are read-only.

- Methods are functions which are used to perform operations on an object. Methods use the object's properties to perform these operations.

Using Properties

An object's properties are accessed by combining the object's name and its property name as follows:

```
objectName.propertyName
```

For example, the background color of the current Web document is identified by the `bgColor` property of the predefined `document` object. If you wanted to change the background color to white, you could use the following JavaScript statement:

```
document.bgColor="white"
```

The above statement assigns the string `"white"` to the `bgColor` property of the predefined `document` object. Listing 5.1 shows how this statement can be used in an example script. Figure 5.1 shows the Web page that it produces. Several buttons are displayed with the names of different colors. When a button is clicked, the button's `onClick` event handler changes the background of the document by setting the `document.bgColor` property.

Listing 5.1. Using JavaScript properties (ch05-01.htm)

```
<HTML>
<HEAD>
<TITLE>Using Properties</TITLE></HEAD>
<BODY>
<H1>Using Properties</H1>
<FORM>
<P><INPUT TYPE="BUTTON" NAME="red" VALUE="Red"
 ONCLICK='document.bgColor="red"'></P>
<P><INPUT TYPE="BUTTON" NAME="white" VALUE="White"
 ONCLICK='document.bgColor="white"'></P>
<P><INPUT TYPE="BUTTON" NAME="blue" VALUE="Blue"
 ONCLICK='document.bgColor="blue"'></P>
</FORM>
</BODY>
</HTML>
```

FIGURE 5.1

Using properties to change background colors (Listing 5.1)

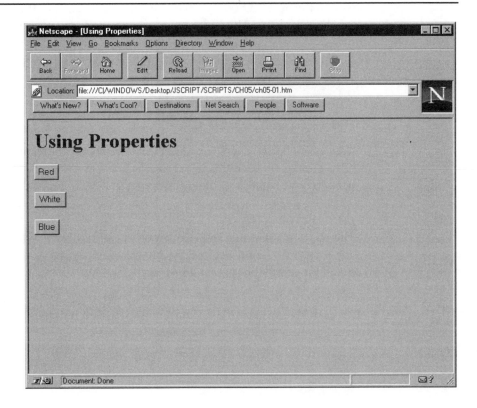

Using Methods

An object's methods are accessed in the same manner as its properties:

```
objectName.methodName(parameterList)
```

The parameters, if any, are separated by commas. The parentheses must be used even if no parameters are specified. An example of a method invocation is:

```
r=Math.random()
```

The `random()` method of the predefined `Math` object is invoked. This method returns a random floating-point number between 0 and 1. The number is then assigned to the r variable.

You have been using the methods of predefined JavaScript objects since your first script in Chapter 2. You've used the `write()` method of the `document` object to generate HTML entities that are written to the current document. You've also used the `alert()` method of the `window` object to display popup dialog boxes. In the next section, you'll be introduced to some of the objects that are automatically created by Netscape Navigator and other JavaScript-capable browsers. Later in this chapter, all of the predefined JavaScript objects will be introduced in summary form. Part 2 of this book will show you how to use each of these predefined objects in your Web pages.

Creating Instances of Objects

Instances of objects of a particular object type are created using the `new` operator. You've previously used the `new` operator to create array objects. The same syntax is used to create objects of other types:

```
variable = new objectType(parameters)
```

The `objectType(parameters)` portion of the above statement is referred to as the *constructor*. Some object types have more than one constructor. Constructors differ in the number of parameters that they allow.

For example, `Date` is a predefined JavaScript object type. To create an instance of `Date` with the current date and time and assign it to the `currentDate` variable, you would use the following statement:

```
currentDate = new Date()
```

In the above statement, the `Date()` constructor does not take any parameters. The `Date` object type also allows object instances to be created for a specified date. For example, the following statement creates an instance of `Date` for January 1, 1999:

```
currentDate = new Date(99,1,1)
```

The constructor used in the above statement, `Date(99,1,1)`, takes three parameters. The `Date` object type provides other constructors in addition to the ones described in this section. (The `Date` object type is formally introduced later in this chapter in the section "The `Date` Object.")

Navigator Objects

When a Web page is loaded by Navigator or another JavaScript-capable browser, the browser creates a number of JavaScript objects that provide access to the Web page and the HTML elements it contains. These objects are used to update and interact with the loaded Web page. Table 5.3 identifies these objects and summarizes their use.

TABLE 5.3   Navigator objects

Object	Use
window	To access a browser window or a frame within a window. The `window` object is assumed to exist and does not require the `window.` prefix when referring to its properties and methods.
document	To access the document that is currently loaded into a window. A document refers to an HTML document that provides content—i.e., that has HEAD and BODY tags.
location	To represent a URL. It can be used to create a URL object, access parts of a URL, or modify an existing URL.
history	To maintain a history of the URLs accessed within a window.
frame object frames array	To access an HTML frame. The `frames` array is used to access all frames within a window.
link object links array	To access a text- or image-based source anchor of a hypertext link. The `links` array is used to access all link objects within a document.

TABLE 5.3   Navigator objects (continued)

Object	Use
`anchor` object `anchors` array	To access the target of a hypertext link. The `anchors` array is used to access all anchor objects within a document.
`image` object `images` array	To access an image that is embedded in an HTML document. The `images` array is used to access all `image` objects within a document.
`area`	To access an area within a client-side image map.
`applet` object `applets` array	To access a Java applet. The `applets` array is used to access all applets in a document.
`form` object `forms`	To access an HTML form. The `forms` array is used to access all forms within a document.
`elements`	To access all form elements (fields or buttons) contained within a form.
`embeds`	To access embedded plug-ins.
`layer` object `layers` array	To access HTML layers.
`text`	To access a text field of a form.
`textarea`	To access a text area field of a form.
`radio`	To access a set of radio buttons of a form.
`checkbox`	To access a checkbox of a form.
`button`	To access a form button that is not a submit or reset button.
`submit`	To access a submit button of a form.
`reset`	To access a reset button of a form.
`select option`	To access a select list of a form. The `option` object is used to access the elements of a select list.
`password`	To access a password field of a form.
`hidden`	To access a hidden field of a form.
`FileUpload`	To access a file upload element of a form.

TABLE 5.3 Navigator objects (continued)

Object	Use
navigator	To access information about the browser that is executing a script.
mimeType object mimeTypes array	To access information about a particular MIME type supported by a browser. The mimeTypes array is an array of all mimeType objects supported by a browser.
plugin object plugins array	To access information about a particular browser plug-in. The plugins array isan array of all plug-ins supported by a browser.

Table 5.3 summarizes the predefined objects that are created by Netscape Navigator when a Web page is loaded. JavaScript also supports object types that are independent of the Web page that is loaded. These objects are described in the section "Other Predefined Object Types," later in this chapter.

The Navigator Object Hierarchy

The objects presented in Table 5.3 are created by Navigator as the results of Web pages that you design. For example, if you create a Web page with three forms, then the forms array will contain three form objects corresponding to the forms that you have defined. Similarly, if you define a document with seven links, then the links array will contain seven link objects that correspond to your links.

The Navigator objects are organized into a hierarchy that corresponds to the structure of loaded Web documents and the current state of the browser. This hierarchy is referred to as an *instance hierarchy*. The window and navigator objects are the highest-level objects in this hierarchy.

The Window Object The window object represents a Navigator window, and it has properties that are used to identify the objects of the HTML elements that comprise that window. For example, the frames array is a property of a window object. If the window uses the frame set tag to define multiple frames, then the frames array contains the frame object associated with each frame. The window's location property refers to the location object that contains the URL associated with the window.

If a window contains displayable content, as opposed to a frame set tag, then the window object's document property refers to the document object associated with the window. The document object contains properties that reference objects that are displayed in the window. These properties include the links, anchors, images, and forms arrays. The links array identifies all link objects contained in a document. The anchors array identifies all named anchors. Link objects refer to the source of a hyperlink, while anchor objects refer to the named destinations of a link. The images, applets, and forms arrays identify all image, applet, and form objects contained in a document. A document's area property refers to an area within a client-side image map that is defined in the document. A document's history property refers to a history object that contains a list of URLs that the user has visited within a particular window.

A document object's forms array identifies all form objects that are defined in the document. Although a document may define any number of forms, usually only one form is defined. The form object provides access to the individual elements defined for a particular form via the elements array. The elements array refers to text, textarea, radio, checkbox, button, submit, reset, select, password, hidden, and FileUpload form fields. These fields may also be individually accessed by their names. You'll learn how to use form-related objects in Chapter 7.

The Navigator Object The navigator object, like the window object, is a top-level object in the Navigator hierarchy. The navigator object is used to describe the configuration of the browser being used to display a window. Two of its properties, mimeTypes and plugins, contain the list of all MIME types and plug-ins supported by the browser.

Hierarchical Object Identifiers

Since Navigator organizes the various objects of a Web page according to the instance hierarchy described in the previous section, a hierarchical naming scheme is used to identify these objects. For example, suppose an HTML document defines three forms, and the second form has seven elements. Also suppose the fifth element of the second form is a radio button. You can access the name of this radio button using the following identifier:

```
document.forms[1].element[4].name
```

The above identifier refers to the name of the fifth element of the second form of the current document. (Remember that array indices begin at 0.) You could display this name using the following statement:

```
document.write(document.forms[1].element[4].name)
```

> **NOTE** You do not have to identify the `window` object when you refer to the current window's properties and methods—your browser will assume the current `window` object by default. There is one exception, however: in event handling code, it is the current `document` object that is assumed by default.

In most cases, you can refer to a property or method of a Navigator-created object by starting with `document` and using the property names of the objects that contain the object (such as `links`, `anchors`, `images`, and `forms`) to identify the object within the instance hierarchy. When you have named the object in this fashion, you can then use the object's property or method name to access the data and functions defined for that object.

Listing 5.2 provides an example of using hierarchical names to access the elements defined within a Web document. The document defines a number of functions in the document head. It begins by invoking the `open()` method of the `window` object to open a second browser window. This second window is assigned to the `outputWindow` variable and is used to write the description of the objects defined for the HTML document shown in Listing 5.2. The `open()` method takes two parameters—the URL of the document to be loaded in the window and a window name. Since we don't want to load a document at another URL, we set the URL parameter to a blank string.

Listing 5.2. Using hierarchical object identifiers (ch05-02.htm)

```
<HTML>
<HEAD>
<TITLE>Using Hierarchical Object Identifiers</TITLE>
<SCRIPT LANGUAGE="JavaScript"><!--
outputWindow = open("","output")
function setupWindow() {
 outputWindow.document.write("<HTML><HEAD><TITLE>Output
 Window</TITLE></HEAD><BODY>")
}
function describeNavigator() {
 outputWindow.document.write("<H2>Navigator Properties</H2>")
 outputWindow.document.write(navigator.appCodeName+" ")
 outputWindow.document.write(navigator.appName+" ")
 outputWindow.document.write(navigator.appVersion+"<BR>")
```

```
   outputWindow.document.write(navigator.mimeTypes.length+" MIME
    types are defined. ")
   outputWindow.document.write(navigator.plugins.length+"
    plug-ins are installed.")
  }
function describeWindow() {
  outputWindow.document.write("<H2>Window Properties</H2>")
  outputWindow.document.write("Frames: "+frames.length+"<BR>")
  outputWindow.document.write("URL: "+location.href+"<BR>")
  }
function describeDocument() {
  outputWindow.document.write("<H2>Document Properties</H2>")
  describeLinks()
  describeForms()
  }
function describeLinks(){
  outputWindow.document.write("<H3>Links</H3>")
  outputWindow.document.write("This document contains "
   +document.links.length+" links:<BR>")
  for(i=0;i<document.links.length;++i)
   outputWindow.document.write(document.links[i].href+"<BR>")
  }
function describeForms() {
  outputWindow.document.write("<H3>Forms</H3>")
  for(i=0;i<document.forms.length;++i) describeForm(i)
  }
function describeForm(n) {
  outputWindow.document.write("Form "+n+" has "
   +document.forms[n].elements.length+" elements:")
  for(j=0;j<document.forms[n].elements.length;++j)
   outputWindow.document.write(" "
    + document.forms[n].elements[j].name)
  outputWindow.document.write("<BR>")
  }
function finishWindow() {
  outputWindow.document.write("<FORM><INPUT Type='button'
   Value='Close Window' onClick='window.close()'></FORM>")
  outputWindow.document.write("</BODY></HTML>")
  }
// --></SCRIPT></HEAD>
<BODY>
<H1>Using Hierarchical Object Identifiers</H1>
```

```
<P><A HREF="http://www.jaworski.com/javascript">Link to
  Mastering JavaScript home page.</A></P>
<P><A HREF="http://home.netscape.com/">Link to Netscape's home
 page.</A></P>
<FORM>
<P><INPUT TYPE="TEXT" NAME="textField1"
 VALUE="Enter text here!"></P>
<P><INPUT TYPE="CHECKBOX" NAME="checkbox1"
 CHECKED="CHECKED">I'm checkbox1.</P>
<P><INPUT TYPE="CHECKBOX" NAME="checkbox2"> I'm checkbox2.</P>
<INPUT TYPE="SUBMIT" NAME="submitButton" VALUE="Click here!">
</FORM>
<SCRIPT LANGUAGE="JavaScript"><!--
setupWindow()
describeNavigator()
describeWindow()
describeDocument()
finishWindow()
// --></SCRIPT>
</BODY>
</HTML>
```

The `setupWindow()` function is used to generate the head of the second document and its opening body tag. It uses the `outputWindow` variable to select the second window as the target for writing. This function and other functions in the script write their output using statements of the form:

```
outputWindow.document.write()
```

These statements tell JavaScript to write to the `document` object of the `window` object identified by the `outputWindow` variable.

The `describeNavigator()` function displays some of the `navigator` object's properties to the second window. It also uses the `outputWindow` variable to select this window. It displays the `appCodeName`, `appName`, `appVersion`, and uses the `length` property of the `mimeTypes` and `plugins` arrays to determine the number of MIME types and plug-ins supported by the browser.

The `describeWindow()` function displays some properties of the original (first) window. It displays the number of frames defined by the window and the URL of the document loaded into the window. Since the window does not define any frames, the length of the `frames` array is 0. The `href` property of the window's `location` object is used to get the text string corresponding to the

URL. The URL displayed when you execute the script will be different depending on the directory from which you run the files of this chapter.

The `describeDocument()` function displays some of the properties associated with the current document in the second window. It invokes the `describe-Links()` and `describeForms()` functions to perform this processing.

The `describeLinks()` function uses the `length` property of the `links` array to identify the number of links contained in the document. It then executes a `for` loop to display the URL associated with each of these links. The `href` attribute of the `link` object is used to get the text string corresponding to the URL.

The `describeForms()` function uses the `length` property of the `forms` array to iterate through the document's links and display each one. The `displayForm()` function is used to display each form.

The `displayForm()` function uses the `length` property of the `elements` array of each `form` object to identify the number of elements contained in a form. It takes a single parameter, identified by the n variable. This parameter identifies the index into the forms array of the `form` object being displayed. The name of each field element is displayed by referencing the `name` property of each object contained in the `elements` array of each `form` object identified in the `forms` array. This is a good example of using hierarchical object naming to access the low-level elements of an HTML document.

The `finishWindow()` function appends the following HTML to the body of the document displayed in the second window:

```
<FORM>
<INPUT Type='button' Value='Close Window'
 onClick='window.close()'>
</FORM>
</BODY>
</HTML>
```

The form is used to create a button, labeled *Close Window*, that is used to close the second window. The `onClick` attribute is assigned the event handling code, `window.close()`, which is used to close the window upon clicking of the button. The `window` object should be explicitly referenced in event handlers to ensure that the current window is closed and not the current document. The `</BODY>` and `</HTML>` tags are used to end the displayed document.

The main body of the HTML document defines two links—one to the *Mastering JavaScript* home page and one to Netscape's home page. The document then defines a form with four elements—a text field, two check boxes, and a submit button.

The script contained in the main body of the document invokes the `setup-Window()`, `describeNavigator()`, `describeWindow()`, `describe-Document()`, and `finishWindow()` functions to display the contents of the first window in the second window referenced by the `outputWindow` object. This script is placed at the end of the document so that the various HTML elements of the document are defined when the script is invoked.

A second window is created to display the various properties of the document. This second window is displayed by the Web browser as shown in Figure 5.2. When the Close Window button is clicked by the user, the original document, shown in Figure 5.3, is displayed. You can also use your browser's Window pull-down menu to switch between the two windows.

FIGURE 5.2

The Output window
(Listing 5.2)

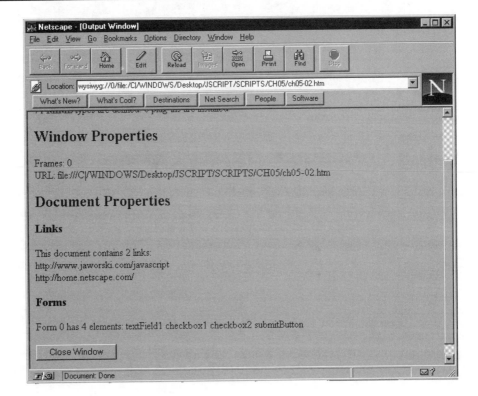

FIGURE 5.3

The Original Document window (Listing 5.2)

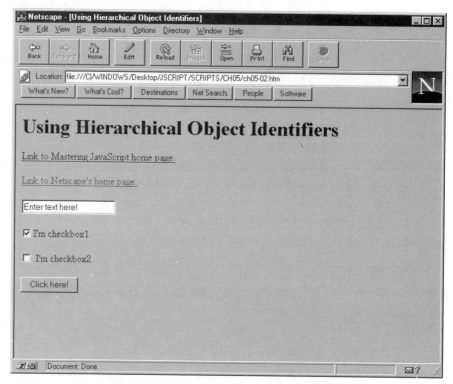

Other Predefined Object Types

In addition to the predefined Navigator objects discussed in earlier sections, Java-Script also provides two general-purpose object types that support common operations. These object types are `Date` and `string`. In addition, the predefined `Math` object may be used to access standard mathematical functions and constants. The `Date` and `string` object types and the `Math` object are described in the following sections.

The *Date* Object Type

The `Date` object type provides a common set of methods for working with dates and times. These methods are summarized in Table 5.4. The `Date` object type does not define any properties. Instances of the `Date` object type may be created with any of the four constructors shown in Table 5.5. Listing 5.3 illustrates the use of the `Date` object type.

TABLE 5.4   Methods of the Date object

Method	Description
`getDate()`	Returns the day of the month of the `Date` object.
`getDay()`	Returns the day of the week of the `Date` object.
`getHours()`	Returns the hour of the `Date` object.
`getMinutes()`	Returns the minutes of the `Date` object.
`getMonth()`	Returns the month of the `Date` object.
`getSeconds()`	Returns the seconds of the `Date` object.
`getTime()`	Returns the time of the `Date` object.
`getTimeZoneOffset()`	Returns the time zone offset (in minutes) of the `Date` object.
`getYear()`	Returns the year of the `Date` object.
`parse()`	Returns the number of milliseconds since midnight January 1, 1970 local time.
`setDate(integer)`	Sets the day of the month of the `Date` object.
`setHours(integer)`	Sets the hours of the `Date` object.
`setMinutes(integer)`	Sets the minutes of the `Date` object.
`setMonth(integer)`	Sets the month of the `Date` object.
`setSeconds(integer)`	Sets the seconds of the `Date` object.
`setTime(integer)`	Sets the time of the `Date` object.
`setYear(integer)`	Sets the year of the `Date` object.
`toGMTString()`	Converts a date to a string in Internet GMT (Greenwich Mean Time) format.

TABLE 5.4   Methods of the Date object (continued)

Method	Description
`toLocaleString()`	Converts a date to a string in *locale* format, which means the format commonly used in the geographical region in which the user is located.
`UTC()`	(Universal Coordinated Time) Returns the number of milliseconds since midnight January 1, 1970 GMT.

TABLE 5.5   Date constructors

Constructor	Description
`Date()`	Creates a `Date` instance with the current date and time.
`Date(dateString)`	Creates a `Date` instance with the date specified in the `dateString` parameter. The format of the `dateString` is *"month day, year hours:minutes:seconds"*.
`Date(year, month, day)`	Creates a `Date` instance with the date specified by the year, month, and day integers. The year parameter is between 0 and 99.
`Date(year, month, day, hours, minutes, seconds)`	Creates a `Date` instance with the date specified by the year, month, day, hours, minutes and seconds integers. The year parameter is between 0 and 99.

Listing 5.3. Using the Date object (ch05-03.htm)

```
<HTML>
<HEAD>
<TITLE>Using the Date Object Type</TITLE>
</HEAD>
<BODY>
<H1>Using the Date Object Type</H1>
<SCRIPT LANGUAGE="JavaScript"><!--
currentDate = new Date()
with (currentDate) {
  document.write("Date: "+getMonth()+"/ "+getDate()+"/ "+getYear()
   +"<BR>")
```

```
document.write("Time: "+getHours()+": "+getMinutes()+": "
    +getSeconds())
}
// --></SCRIPT>
</BODY>
</HTML>
```

The above document uses the methods of the `Date` object type to write the current date and time to the current `document` object. The `currentDate` variable is assigned a new `Date` object that is created using the `new` operator and the `Date()` constructor. A `with` statement is used to make the object stored with `currentDate` the default object for object references. The two `write()` method invocations use the `getMonth()`, `getDate()`, `getYear()`, `getHours()`, `getMinutes()`, and `getSeconds()` methods to access the various components of a `Date` object. Figure 5.4 shows the Web page generated by Listing 5.3.

FIGURE 5.4

Using the `Date` object type (Listing 5.3)

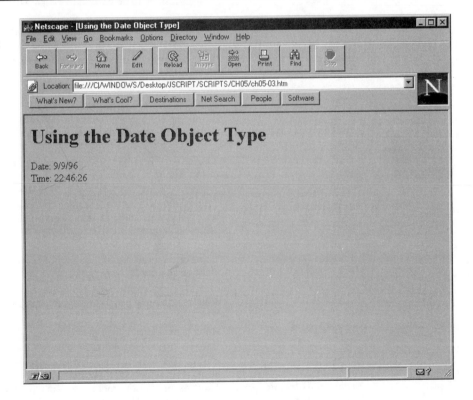

The *string* Object Type

The `string` object type provides a set of methods for manipulating strings. These methods are summarized in Table 5.6. Any JavaScript string value or variable containing a string value is able to use these methods. The `string` object also defines the `length` property which returns the length of a string in characters.

TABLE 5.6   `String` methods

Method	Description
`anchor(anchorName)`	Causes a string to be displayed as a hypertext anchor with the specified anchor name. The string may be written to a document using the `document.write()` or `document.writeln()` methods.
`big()`	Causes a string to be displayed using the *big* HTML tags.
`blink()`	Causes a string to be displayed using the *blink* HTML tags.
`bold()`	Causes a string to be displayed using the *bold* HTML tags.
`charAt(index)`	Returns a string that consists of the character at the specified index of the string to which the method is applied.
`fixed()`	Causes a string to be displayed using the *teletype* HTML tags.
`fontcolor(color)`	Causes a string to be displayed in the specified color.
`fontsize(size)`	Causes a string to be displayed at the specified font size. The `size` parameter must be between 1 and 7.
`indexOf(pattern)`	Returns the index of the first string specified by the `pattern` parameter that is contained in a string. Returns *-1* if the pattern is not contained in the string.
`indexOf(pattern, startIndex)`	Same as the previous method except that searching starts at the position specified by `startIndex`.
`italics()`	Causes a string to be displayed using the *italics* HTML tags.
`lastIndexOf(pattern)`	Returns the index of the last string specified by the *pattern* parameter that is contained in a string. Returns *-1* if the pattern is not contained in the string.
`lastIndexOf(pattern, startIndex)`	Same as the previous method except that searching starts at the position specified by `startIndex`.

TABLE 5.6   `String` methods (continued)

Method	Description
`link(href)`	Causes a string to be displayed as a hypertext link to the URL specified by the `href` parameter.
`small()`	Causes a string to be displayed using the *small* HTML tags.
`split(separator)`	Separates a string into an array of substrings based upon the `separator`.
`strike()`	Causes a string to be displayed using the *strikeout* HTML tags.
`sub()`	Causes a string to be displayed using the *subscript* HTML tags.
`substring(startIndex, endIndex)`	Returns the substring of a string beginning at `startIndex` and ending at `endIndex`.
`sup()`	Causes a string to be displayed using the *superscript* HTML tags.
`toLowerCase()`	Returns a copy of the string converted to lower case.
`toUpperCase()`	Returns a copy of the string converted to upper case.

Listing 5.4 illustrates the use of the `string` object type. The script in the document body begins by defining the function `displayParagraph()`, which displays text surrounded by the `<P>` and `</P>` paragraph tags. The `displayParagraph()` function is used to display several text strings which are modified using sample string methods. The text "`This is big.`" is modified using the `big()` method, causing it to be displayed in a larger font. The text "`This is small.`" and "`This is blinking text.`" are similarly modified using the `small()` and `blink()` methods. The `sup()` method is then used to create exponents for x and y. The `link()` method is used to create a link from the text "`Mastering JavaScript`" to the URL *http://www.jaworski.com/javascript*. Figure 5.5 shows the Web page generated by Listing 5.4.

Listing 5.4. Using the string object type (ch05-04.htm)

```
<HTML>
<HEAD>
<TITLE>Using the String Object Type</TITLE>
</HEAD>
```

```
<BODY>
<H1>Using the String Object Type</H1>
<SCRIPT LANGUAGE="JavaScript"><!--
function displayParagraph(text) {
 document.write("<P>"+text+"</P>")
}
displayParagraph("This is big.".big())
displayParagraph("This is small.".small())
displayParagraph("This is blinking text.".blink())
displayParagraph("x"+"2".sup()+"+y"+"2".sup())
displayParagraph("Mastering JavaScript".link
 ('http://www.jaworski.com/javascript'))
// --></SCRIPT>
</BODY>
</HTML>
```

FIGURE 5.5

Using the `string` object (Listing 5.4)

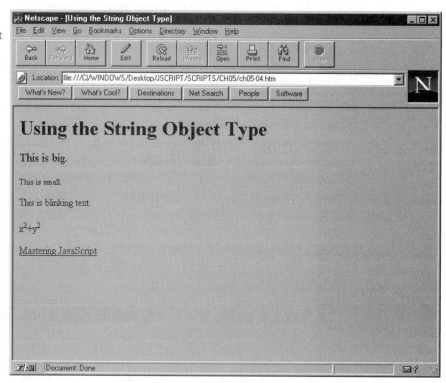

184

Creating *string* Objects

`String` objects may be created in the same manner as other JavaScript objects using the `new` operator. For example, the variable `text` may be assigned the string `"I am a string"` using the statement:

```
text = new String("I am a string")
```

The above statement is equivalent to:

```
text = "I am a string"
```

The *Math* Object

The `Math` object provides a standard library of mathematical constants and functions. The constants are defined as properties of `Math`, and are listed in Table 5.7. The functions are defined as methods of `Math`, and are summarized in Table 5.8. Specific instances of `Math` are not created, because `Math` is a built-in object and not an object type. Listing 5.5 illustrates the use of the `Math` object; Figure 5.6 shows the Web page it generates.

TABLE 5.7 Math properties

Property	Description
E	Euler's constant.
LN2	The natural logarithm of 2.
LN10	The natural logarithm of 10.
LOG2E	The base 2 logarithm of e.
LOG10E	The base 10 logarithm of e.
PI	The constant π.
SQRT1_2	The square root of ½.
SQRT2	The square root of 2.

TABLE 5.8   Math methods

Method	Description
abs(x)	Returns the absolute value of x.
acos(x)	Returns the arc cosine of x in radians.
asin(x)	Returns the arc sine of x in radians.
atan(x)	Returns the arc tangent of x in radians.
atan2(x,y)	Returns the angle of the polar coordinate corresponding to (x,y).
ceil(x)	Returns the least integer that is greater than or equal to x.
cos(x)	Returns the cosine of x.
exp(x)	Returns e^x.
floor(x)	Returns the greatest integer that is less than or equal to x.
log(x)	Returns the natural logarithm of x.
max(x,y)	Returns the greater of x and y.
min(x,y)	Returns the lesser of x and y.
pow(x,y)	Returns x^y.
random()	Returns a random number between 0 and 1.
round(x)	Returns x rounded to the closest integer.
sin(x)	Returns the sine of x.
sqrt(x)	Returns the square root of x.
tan(x)	Returns the tangent of x.

Listing 5.5. Using the Math object (ch05-05.htm)

```
<HTML>
<HEAD>
<TITLE>Using the Math Object</TITLE>
</HEAD>
<BODY>
<H1>Using the Math Object</H1>
<SCRIPT LANGUAGE="JavaScript"><!--
document.write(Math.PI+"<BR>")
document.write(Math.E+"<BR>")
document.write(Math.ceil(1.234)+"<BR>")
document.write(Math.random()+"<BR>")
document.write(Math.sin(Math.PI/2)+"<BR>")
document.write(Math.min(100,1000)+"<BR>")
// --></SCRIPT>
</BODY>
</HTML>
```

FIGURE 5.6

Example of using the Math object (Listing 5.5)

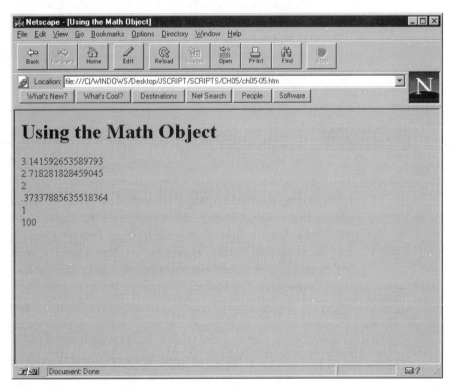

187

Color Constants

JavaScript defines a number of color constants that can be used with methods and functions that take color parameters. Some of these color constants are `"red"`, `"orange"`, `"yellow"`, `"green"`, `"blue"`, `"white"`, `"black"`, and `"brown"`. A complete list of the color constants can be found in Appendix B, "JavaScript Reference."

Defining Object Types

JavaScript provides the capability for you to define your own object types and create specific object instances. To create a new object type, you simply define a function that is used to construct specific instances of the object type. Essentially, this constructor function does two things:

- It assigns values to the object type's properties.
- It identifies other functions to be used as the object type's methods.

As an example of defining a new object type, we'll create the `table` object type. This object type will be used to create simple tables using JavaScript, and write them to the current document.

> **NOTE** The function used as a constructor of an object type must have the same name as the object type.

Identifying and Assigning Properties The first thing that we'll do is identify the properties of the `table` object type. The number of rows and columns of the table are obvious properties with which to start. Let's name these properties `table.rows` and `table.columns`. We'll also need to define a property to store the elements of the table. Let's call this property `table.data` and let it be an array of the following length:

```
table.rows * table.columns
```

Since HTML allows some table cells to be designated as header cells, let's also define the property `table.header` as an array of the same length as above, `table.rows * table.columns`, where each element is a boolean value indicating whether a table cell is a header cell. Finally, let's define a property, `table.border`, that identifies the border width of the table. The following code shows how the table constructor would be defined using the items items we just identified.

```
function table(rows,columns) {
  this.rows = rows
  this.columns = columns
  this.border = 0
  this.data = new Array(rows*columns)
  this.header = new Array(rows*columns)
}
```

- As you can see, the `table()` constructor takes the parameters `rows` and `columns`, and assigns them to `this.rows` and `this.columns`. The `this` prefix is a special keyword that is used to refer to the current object. For example, the statement `this.rows = rows` assigns the value stored in the `rows` parameter to the `rows` property of the current object. Similarly, `this.columns = columns` assigns the `columns` parameter to the `columns` property of the current object. The parameters to the `table()` constructor do not have to be named rows and columns—they could have been named x and y. However, it is common to see parameters named after the object type properties to which they are assigned.

- The `border` property of the current object is set to the default value of 0. This results in the creation of a borderless table. As mentioned earlier, the `data` and `header` properties are each assigned an array of size `rows * columns`.

In order to create an object that is an instance of the `table` object type, you use the `new` operator in conjunction with the `table` constructor. For example, the following statement creates a table of three rows by four columns and assigns it to the t variable:

```
t = new table(3,4)
```

Defining Methods So far, we've defined the properties of the `table` object type. However, we'll need to define some methods to update the values of the `data`, `header`, and `border` properties and to write the `table` object to a `document` object.

Methods are defined by assigning the name of an already defined function to a method name in an object type constructor. For example, suppose the `table_setValue()` function is defined as follows. This function sets the value of the table cell at the specified `row` and `column` parameters to the `value` parameter.

```
function table_setValue(row,col,value) {
  this.data[row*this.columns+col]=value
}
```

We can use the above-defined `table_setValue()` function as the `setValue()` method of the `table` object type by including the following statement in the `table` constructor:

```
this.setValue = table_setValue
```

Note that trailing parentheses are not used in the above statement. The new table constructor is as follows:

```
function table(rows,columns) {
  this.rows = rows
  this.columns = columns
  this.border = 0
  this.data = new Array(rows*columns)
  this.header = new Array(rows*columns)
  this.setValue = table_setValue
}
```

An example of invoking the `setValue()` method for the table object stored in the `t` variable follows:

```
t.setValue(2,3,"Hello")
```

The above statement sets the table `data` value at row 2 and column 3 to `"Hello"`.

Definition of *table.js*

Listing 5.6 provides a complete definition of the `table` object. Note that functions must be defined before they can be assigned to a method name.

Listing 5.6. Definition of the table object (ch05-06.htm)

```
function table_getValue(row,col) {
  return this.data[row*this.columns+col]
}
function table_setValue(row,col,value) {
  this.data[row*this.columns+col]=value
}
```

```
function table_set(contents) {
 var n = contents.length
 for(var j=0;j<n;++j) this.data[j]=contents[j]
}
function table_isHeader(row,col) {
 return this.header[row*this.columns+col]
}
function table_makeHeader(row,col) {
 this.header[row*this.columns+col]=true
}
function table_makeNormal(row,col) {
 this.header[row*this.columns+col]=false
}
function table_makeHeaderRow(row) {
 for(var j=0;j<this.columns;++j)
  this.header[row*this.columns+j]=true
}
function table_makeHeaderColumn(col) {
 for(var i=0;i<this.rows;++i)
  this.header[i*this.columns+col]=true
}
function table_write(doc) {
 doc.write("<TABLE BORDER="+this.border+">")
 for(var i=0;i<this.rows;++i) {
  doc.write("<TR>")
  for(var j=0;j<this.columns;++j) {
   if(this.header[i*this.columns+j]) {
    doc.write("<TH>")
    doc.write(this.data[i*this.columns+j])
    doc.write("</TH>")
   }else{
    doc.write("<TD>")
    doc.write(this.data[i*this.columns+j])
    doc.write("</TD>")
   }
  }
  doc.writeln("</TR>")
 }
 doc.writeln("</TABLE>")
}
function table(rows,columns) {
 this.rows = rows
 this.columns = columns
```

```
this.border = 0
this.data = new Array(rows*columns)
this.header = new Array(rows*columns)
this.getValue = table_getValue
this.setValue = table_setValue
this.set = table_set
this.isHeader = table_isHeader
this.makeHeader = table_makeHeader
this.makeNormal = table_makeNormal
this.makeHeaderRow = table_makeHeaderRow
this.makeHeaderColumn = table_makeHeaderColumn
this.write = table_write
}
```

Listing 5.6 adds the getValue(), set(), isHeader(), makeHeader(),
makeNormal(), makeHeaderRow(), makeHeaderColumn(), and write()
methods to the table definition introduced in the previous section.

The getValue() method returns the data value stored at a specified row and
column. The set() method stores an array of values as the contents of a table. The
makeHeader() and makeNormal() methods are used to identify whether a cell
should or should not be a header cell. The makeHeaderRow() and makeHeader-
Column() methods are used to designate an entire row or column as consisting of
header cells. The write() method is used to write a table to a document object.

Using the *table* Object

Listing 5.7 provides an example of the use of the table object. The document's
body contains a script that creates, initializes, and displays a three-row by four-
column table object. Using the SRC attribute of the script tag, it includes the
table.js file presented in the previous section. It begins by creating a table
object and assigning it to the t variable. It then creates an array, named contents,
that contains a list of values. The set() method is invoked to assign the contents
array to the cells of the table stored at t. The table's border property is set to 4
pixels, and the cells of column 0 are designated as header cells. Finally, the write()
method is used to write the table to the current document object. Figure 5.7 shows
the Web page resulting from the script of Listing 5.7.

Listing 5.7. Using the table object (ch05-07.htm)

```
<HTML>
<HEAD>
```

```
<TITLE>Defining Object Types</TITLE>
<SCRIPT LANGUAGE="JavaScript" SRC="table.js"><!--
// --></SCRIPT>
</HEAD>
<BODY>
<H1>Defining Object Types</H1>
<SCRIPT LANGUAGE="JavaScript"><!--
t = new table(3,4)
contents = new Array("This","is","a","test","of","the","table",
 "object.","Let's","see","it","work.")
t.set(contents)
t.border=4
t.makeHeaderColumn(0)
t.write(document)
// --></SCRIPT>
</BODY>
</HTML>
```

FIGURE 5.7

An example table
(Listing 5.7)

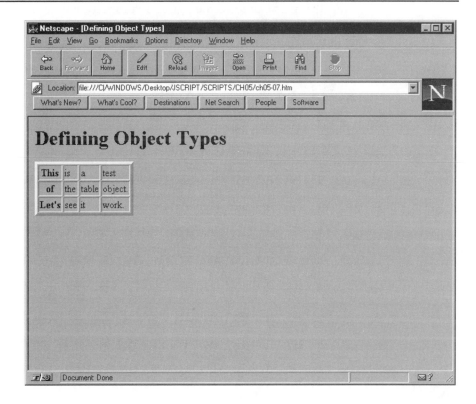

193

Adding Properties and Methods to an Object Type

Object types that can be instantiated with the new operator are referred to as *instantiable* object types. They include all user-defined object types and the pre-defined Date and string object types. JavaScript provides the capability to add properties and methods to already defined instantiable object types via the prototype property.

For example, suppose we wanted to add a background color attribute to the table object type defined in previous section. We could add the new attribute with the following statement:

```
table.prototype.bgColor = "white"
```

The above statement uses the prototype property of the table object type to create a new property called bgColor to represent the background color of the table.

Now that we've defined the bgColor property, we should create an additional method called colorWrite() that writes a table using the bgColor property. The following function performs this processing:

```
function table_colorWrite(doc) {
 doc.write("<TABLE BORDER="+this.border+"BGCOLOR="
 +this.bgColor+">")
 for(var i=0;i<this.rows;++i) {
  doc.write("<TR>")
  for(var j=0;j<this.columns;++j) {
   if(this.header[i*this.columns+j]) {
    doc.write("<TH>")
    doc.write(this.data[i*this.columns+j])
    doc.write("</TH>")
   }else{
    doc.write("<TD>")
    doc.write(this.data[i*this.columns+j])
    doc.write("</TD>")
   }
  }
  doc.writeln("</TR>")
 }
 doc.writeln("</TABLE>")
}
```

We can use the `table_colorWrite()` function in the listing above as the `colorWrite()` method by including the following statement in our script:

```
table.prototype.colorWrite=table_colorWrite
```

Listing 5.8 updates the script shown in Listing 5.7 to make use of the new `bgColor` property and the `colorWrite()` method. Figure 5.8 shows the Web page that results from Listing 5.8. Note that we did not have to modify the original `table.js` file that is included via the `SRC` attribute.

TIP

Always *create* an object of the object type being modified before using the object type's `prototype` property. This will ensure that any new properties and methods are correctly added.

Listing 5.8. Updating an object type definition (ch05-08.htm)

```
<HTML>
<HEAD>
<TITLE>Updating Object Types</TITLE>
<SCRIPT LANGUAGE="JavaScript" SRC="table.js"><!--
// --></SCRIPT>
</HEAD>
<BODY>
<H1>Updating Object Types</H1>
<SCRIPT LANGUAGE="JavaScript"><!--
function table_colorWrite(doc) {
 doc.write("<TABLE BORDER="+this.border+" BGCOLOR=
 ➥"+this.bgColor+">")
 for(var i=0;i<this.rows;++i) {
  doc.write("<TR>")
  for(var j=0;j<this.columns;++j) {
   if(this.header[i*this.columns+j]) {
    doc.write("<TH>")
    doc.write(this.data[i*this.columns+j])
    doc.write("</TH>")
   }else{
    doc.write("<TD>")
    doc.write(this.data[i*this.columns+j])
    doc.write("</TD>")
   }
  }
```

```
  doc.writeln("</TR>")
 }
 doc.writeln("</TABLE>")
}

t = new table(3,4)
table.prototype.bgColor="white"
table.prototype.colorWrite=table_colorWrite
contents = new Array("This","is","a","test","of","the",
➥"table","object.",
 "Let's","see","it","work.")
t.set(contents)
t.border=4
t.makeHeaderColumn(0)
t.colorWrite(document)
// --></SCRIPT>
</BODY>
</HTML>
```

FIGURE 5.8

Color tables (Listing 5.8)

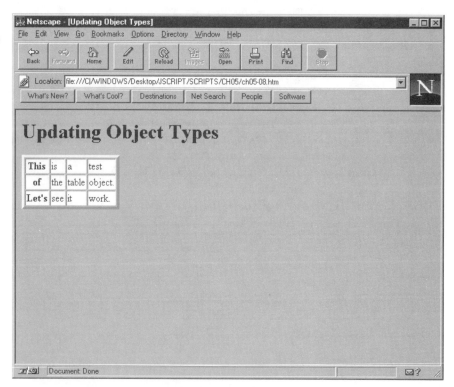

Arrays Are Objects

Arrays are implemented as objects in JavaScript. You have probably already noticed the similarity between the ways arrays and objects are constructed. The statement

```
a = new Array(25)
```

invokes the `Array` constructor with the parameter 25 and assigns the constructed array to the a variable. Array objects have the `length` and `prototype` properties. The `length` property identifies the length of an array. The `prototype` property is used as discussed in the previous section. Arrays also have three methods, as summarized in Table 5.9.

TABLE 5.9   Array methods

Method	Description
join(*separator*)	Joins all elements of an array into a string where each element is separated by *separator*.
reverse()	Reverses the elements of an array.
sort([*compare*])	Sorts the elements of an array according to the specified *compare* function. The *compare* function is an optional parameter. If it is omitted then the array is sorted in dictionary order.

The `sort()` method provides a powerful capability to sort arrays. When used with the *compare* parameter it allows an array to be sorted by the specified compare function. The compare function should take two parameters and return *-1* if the first parameter is less than the second, *0* if the parameters are equal, and *1* if the first parameter is greater than the second. Listing 5.9 presents an example of the use of the sort() method.

Listing 5.9. The sort() method

```
<HTML>
<HEAD>
<TITLE>Sorting Arrays</TITLE>
<SCRIPT LANGUAGE="JavaScript"><!--
function isGreater(a,b) {
 if(Math.abs(a) < Math.abs(b)) return -1
 else if(Math.abs(b) == Math.abs(a)) return 0
 return 1
}
```

```
// -->></SCRIPT>
</HEAD>
<BODY>
<H1>Sorting Arrays</H1>
<SCRIPT LANGUAGE="JavaScript"><!--
 numericalOrder = new Array(-3,-2,-1,0,1,2,3)
 document.write("<PRE>Numerical order: "+numericalOrder.join
  (" ")+"<BR>")
 absoluteOrder = numericalOrder.sort(isGreater)
 document.write("Absolute order:   "+absoluteOrder.join(" ")
  +"</PRE>")
// -->></SCRIPT>
</BODY>
</HTML>
```

The isGreater() function is defined in the document head. This function is used to compare two numbers based on their absolute value, and is used as a compare function in the second script contained in the document body. The second script defines the numericalOrder array and initializes it to the integers from –3 to 3 arranged in numerical order. This array is displayed using the join() method to convert the array to a string. The absoluteOrder array is created by applying the sort() method with the isGreater() function passed as a parameter. Note that the parentheses () are stripped from the function name. The sorted array is then displayed to the document window. Figure 5.9 shows the output displayed by the Web page.

Using Functions as Objects

A function may be created as an object and assigned to a variable using the Function() constructor. The syntax of the function constructor is as follows:

```
variable = new Function([arg1,…,argn],functionBody)
```

The parameters *arg1, …, argn* are arguments to the function being created. The *functionBody* parameter is string containing the code of the function body. The function is accessed using the name of the variable to which it is assigned. For example, the following JavaScript code can be used to create a function that triples the value of a number:

```
triple = new Function("n","return 3*n")
```

FIGURE 5.9

Using the `sort()`
method (Listing 5.9)

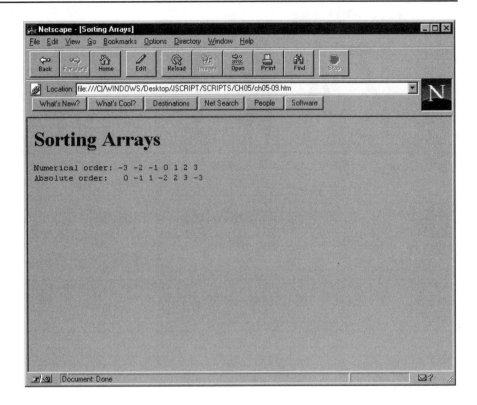

The above function may be invoked using a statement such as the following:

```
x = triple(100)
```

which sets the value of **x** to 300.

Summary

This chapter described JavaScript's support of objects and object-based programming. It introduced the JavaScript Object Model and summarized the predefined JavaScript objects. It also showed you how to create your own objects and methods. In the next chapter, you'll learn how to use predefined JavaScript objects that allow you to create and manage multiple frames and windows.

PART II

Using Predefined Objects and Methods

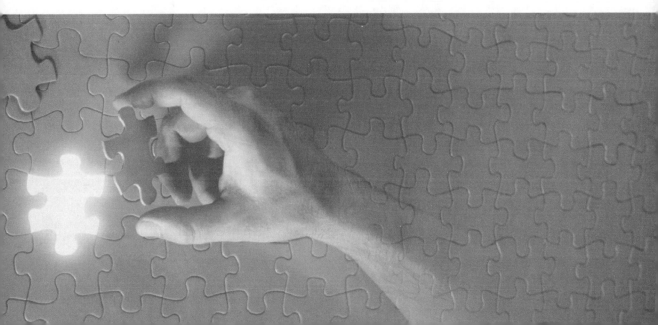

CHAPTER

SIX

6

Windows and Frames

- Opening and Closing Windows

- Simple Communication Windows: Messages, Prompts, and Status Bars

- Using the Window "Synonyms"

- Frames and Frame Sets

- Generating Document Contents

- Working with Colors

This chapter shows you how to use three important JavaScript objects: the `window`, `frame`, and `document` objects. It describes how to use these objects to create and manage multiple frames and windows in your Web pages. When you have finished this chapter, you'll be able to use frames and windows to effectively organize your Web pages.

The *Window* Object

The `window` object is fundamental to all browser scripts. Like the `navigator` object, the `window` object is a top-level object that is automatically defined by your browser. A separate `window` object is defined for each window that is opened. These windows are listed on your browser's Window pull-down menu as shown in Figure 6.1.

FIGURE 6.1

Your browser's Window pull-down menu lists all of the windows that are currently opened.

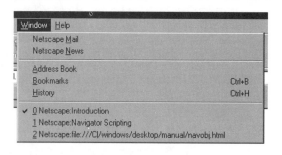

The `window` object is so important to writing browser scripts that the current `window` object is assumed by default in many cases and may be omitted. For example, when you use the statement:

```
document.write("Write this text to the current window.")
```

in a script, JavaScript assumes that you are referring to the current window object and executes the following statement:

```
window.document.write("Write this text to the current window.")
```

In addition, the `window` object has several *synonyms* that let you refer to the current `window` object being displayed by your browser, as well as to other related window objects. These synonyms are implemented as properties of the window object. You'll learn about these synonyms in the section "Using the Window Synonyms" later in this chapter.

Tables 6.1 and 6.2 summarize the properties and methods of the window object. These properties and methods are described in the following sections.

TABLE 6.1   Properties of the window object

Property	Description
closed	Identifies whether a window has been closed.
defaultStatus	Specifies the default status message that appears on the status bar on the bottom of the browser window.
document	An object that refers to the current document being displayed in a window.
frame	An object that refers to a single frame. The frames array provides access to all the frame objects contained within a window.
frames	An array that consists of all frame objects contained in a window object.
length	Identifies the number of frames contained in a window.
location	An object that identifies the URL associated with a window object.
name	Identifies the name of the window.
opener	Identifies the window object that caused a window to be opened.
parent	A synonym that identifies the window containing a particular window.
self	A synonym that identifies the current window being referenced.
status	Specifies a temporary message that appears on the status bar on the bottom of the browser window.
top	A synonym that refers to the topmost browser window in a series of nested windows.
window	A synonym that identifies the .current window being referenced.

TABLE 6.2   Methods of the `window` object

Method	Description
`alert(text)`	Displays an alert dialog box.
`blur()`	Removes focus from a window.
`clearTimeout(timer)`	Clears a previously set timeout.
`close()`	Closes the specified window.
`confirm(text)`	Displays a confirm dialog box.
`focus()`	Gives focus to a window.
`open(url,name,[options])`	Opens a new window and creates a new window object.
`prompt(text,defaultInput)`	Displays a prompt dialog box.
`scroll(x,y)`	Scrolls a window to the specific location.
`setTimeout(expression,milliseconds)`	Evaluates an expression after a timeout period has elapsed.
`clearInterval(ID)`	Clears a timeout created by `setInterval()`.
`moveBy(horiz,vert)`	Move the window by the specified amount.
`moveTo(x,y)`	Move to the specified location.
`resizeBy(horiz,vert)`	Resize the window by moving the bottom right corner.
`resizeTo(width,height)`	Resize the window to the specified dimensions.
`scrollBy(horiz,vert)`	Scroll the window.
`scrollTo(x,y)`	Scroll to the specified position.
`setInterval(function,time,[args])`	Repeatedly invoke a function or evaluate an expression after a timeout (in milliseconds) has expired.
`setTimeout(function,time,[args])`	Invoke a function after a timeout (in milliseconds) has expired.

Opening and Closing Windows

When you launch your browser it creates and opens a window to display your startup page. This is the most common way that a `window` object is created. In most cases, the window that you open during browser startup stays open until you exit your browser. When you open a new Web document or a local file with your browser, you usually *replace* the document contained in the opened window and do not create or open a new window. In Netscape Navigator, new windows are created and opened when you select the New Web Browser menu item from the File menu. In Microsoft Internet Explorer, you use the New Window menu item to create a new window. When a new window is created, it can be accessed from the browser's Window pull-down menu as shown in Figure 6.1.

The `open()` and `close()` methods may be used from within JavaScript to open and close browser windows. The `open()` method opens a new Web browser window at a specified URL with a given set of options. A newly created object is returned as the result of invoking `open()`. This object is usually assigned to a variable which is used to keep track of the window. The syntax of the `open()` method is as follows:

```
variable = open(url, name, [options])
```

where *variable* is the name of the variable to which the `window` object is assigned, *url* is the URL of the document to open in the window, *name* is the name to be associated with the window, and *options* can be used to specify different characteristics of the window. The name may be used in the target attribute of a `<form>` tag or an `<a>` tag.

The options, if supplied, consist of a set of comma-separated *option=value* pairs. The options and their values are shown in Table 6.3.

TABLE 6.3   Options of the `open()` method

Option	Values	Description
toolbar	yes no	Does the window have a tool bar?
location	yes no	Does the window display its location?
directories	yes no	Does the window provide directory buttons?
status	yes no	Does the window have a status bar?

TABLE 6.3   Options of the `open()` method (continued)

Option	Values	Description
menubar	yes no	Does the window have a menu bar?
scrollbars	yes no	Does the window provide scroll bars?
resizable	yes no	Is the window resizable?
width	*integer*	The width of the window in pixels.
height	*integer*	The height of the window in pixels.
outerWidth	*integer*	The outer width of the window.
outerHeight	*integer*	The outer height of the window.
left	*integer*	Distance from the left of the screen.
top	*integer*	Distance from the top of the screen.
alwaysRaised	yes no	Create a raised, floating window.
z-lock	yes no	Create a window which stays in the background.

NOTE: The values 1 and 0 may be used instead of yes and no.

An example of the use of the `open()` method follows:

```
win = open("http://www.sybex.com","sybex")
```

The above statement opens a new window and loads the Sybex home page located at *http://www.sybex.com* into the window. The window is given the name *sybex* and is assigned to the `win` variable.

The `close()` method is used to close a window that has been opened. For example, `win.close()` can be used to close the window opened above.

Listings 6.1 and 6.2 provide a colorful example of how the `open()` and `close()` methods are used in an example Web page. Listing 6.1 creates a Web page that announces a New Year's Eve party. Figure 6.2 shows the party invitation that is generated by Listing 6.1.

FIGURE 6.2

A party invitation
(Listing 6.1)

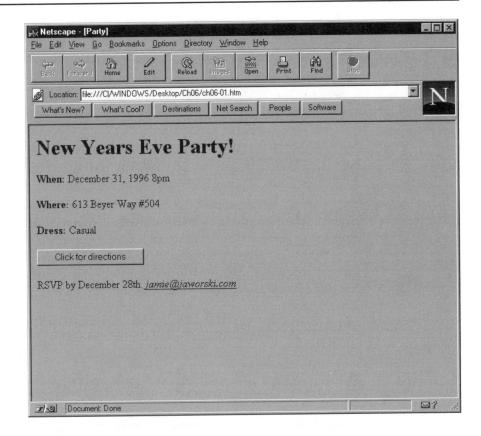

Listing 6.1. Opening a new window (ch06-01.htm)

```
<HTML>
<HEAD>
<TITLE>Party</TITLE>
<SCRIPT LANGUAGE="JavaScript"><!--
function directions() {
 open("ch06-02.htm","map")
}

// --></SCRIPT>
</HEAD>
<BODY>
```

```
<H1>New Years Eve Party!</H1>
<P><B>When:</B> December 31, 1996 8pm</P>
<P><B>Where:</B> 613 Beyer Way #504</P>
<P><B>Dress:</B> Casual </P>
<FORM>
<INPUT TYPE="BUTTON" VALUE="Click for directions"
 ONCLICK="directions()">
</FORM>
<P>RSVP by December 28th.
<A HREF="mailto:jamie@jaworski.com">
 <I>jamie@jaworski.com</I></A></P>
</BODY>
</HTML>
```

When a user clicks on the "Click for directions" button shown in Figure 6.2, a new window is created and opened using the document of Listing 6.2. This window is shown in Figure 6.3. (If you click on the Window pull-down menu, you can verify that a new window has been created—see Figure 6.4.) Clicking on the Close window button closes the second window.

The `directions()` function of Listing 6.1 uses the `open()` method to open the file ch06-02.htm (see Listing 6.2). It assigns the name `"map"` to the newly created window.

As shown in Listing 6.2, the `onClick` event handler of the Close window button invokes the `close()` method to close and dispose of the second window.

Listing 6.2. Closing a window (ch06-02.htm)

```
<HTML>
<HEAD>
<TITLE>Directions</TITLE>
</HEAD>
<BODY ONLOAD="defaultStatus='It\'s at the big star!'">
<FORM>
<INPUT TYPE="BUTTON" VALUE="Close window"
 ONCLICK="window.close()">
</FORM>
<IMG SRC="map.gif">
</BODY>
</HTML>
```

FIGURE 6.3

Directions to the party
(Listing 6.2)

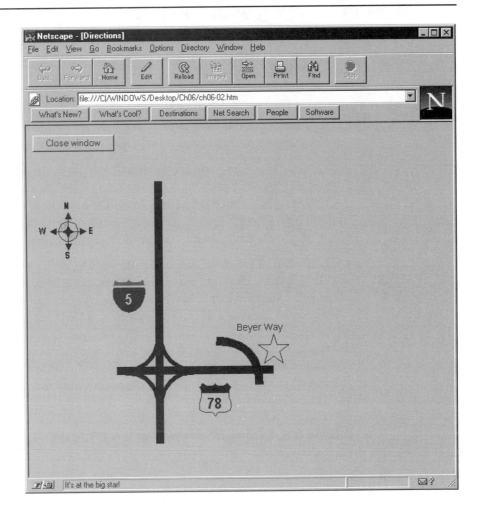

FIGURE 6.3

Directions to the party
(Listing 6.2)

FIGURE 6.4

A new window is
created. (Listings 6.1
and 6.2)

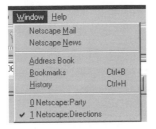

Communicating with the User

Some of the most useful methods provided by the `window` object are those that support dialog with the user. These methods are `alert()`, `confirm()`, and `prompt()`. You've used these methods in Chapters 4 and 5.

- The `alert()` method displays a dialog box containing a message and an OK button. You use the `alert()` method to provide the user with critical information that must be acknowledged, usually by means of an OK button.

- The `confirm()` method is similar to the `alert()` method except that it produces a dialog box with a message, an OK button, and a Cancel button. The `confirm()` method returns *true* if the user clicks OK and *false* if the user clicks Cancel. You use the `confirm()` method to inform the user and ask him to confirm whether he wants to perform a particular action.

- The `prompt()` method displays a message to the user and prompts the user to type information into a text field. It provides the capability to display default text in the text field. You use the `prompt()` method to obtain text input from the user such as a password or a URL.

Listing 6.3 provides an example of the use of each of these three methods. Figure 6.5 shows the initial page displayed by this script. When you open this script in your browser, you can click on the buttons provided to see an example of each type of dialog box.

Listing 6.3. Dialog box demo (ch06-03.htm)

```
<HTML>
<HEAD>
<TITLE>Dialog box demo</TITLE>
</HEAD>
<BODY>
<FORM>
<INPUT TYPE="BUTTON" VALUE="Alert"
 ONCLICK="alert('An alert dialog box.')">
<INPUT TYPE="BUTTON" VALUE="Confirm"
 ONCLICK="confirm('A confirm dialog box.')">
<INPUT TYPE="BUTTON" VALUE="Prompt"
 ONCLICK="prompt('A prompt dialog box.','Type something!')">
</FORM>
</BODY>
</HTML>
```

FIGURE 6.5

Dialog box demo opening display (Listing 6.3)

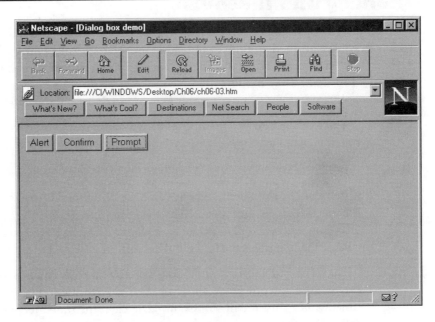

Displaying Status Information

The window object provides two properties that can be used to display status information in the browser's status bar:

- The defaultStatus property specifies a permanent default status message.

- The status property specifies a transient status message that appears as the result of a user action such as moving a mouse to a particular window location.

Using the Window Synonyms

As mentioned earlier, the window object provides several properties which are used as synonyms to identify the current window object as well as related objects. The window and self properties both refer to the current window being referenced. The parent property is used in multiframe windows and refers to the window that contains a particular window. The opener property refers to the window from which a particular window was opened. The top property is used with framed windows. It refers to the topmost window containing a particular window.

Working with Timeouts

The setTimeout() and clearTimeout() methods provide a clever way to wait a specified amount of time for a user to perform a particular action and, if the action does not occur within the specified time, perform timeout processing. The setTimeout() method identifies an expression to be evaluated after a specified number of milliseconds; it is this expression that performs the timeout processing.

The setTimeout() method returns a value that is used to identify the timeout. It is usually assigned to a variable as shown in the following example:

```
timVar = setTimeout("timeoutProcessing()",10000)
```

In the above statement, the setTimeout() method is invoked to perform the timeout processing specified by the timeoutProcessing() function after 10,000 milliseconds (10 seconds) have elapsed. The setTimeout() method returns a value that identifies the timeout. This value is assigned to the timVar variable.

The clearTimeout() method is used to cancel a timeout before it occurs and prevent the timeout processing from being performed. It takes the value of the timeout as an argument. For example, to clear the timeout created above, use the following statement:

```
clearTimeout(timVar)
```

The above statement clears the timeout identified by timVar. This prevents the timeoutProcessing() from being invoked after the timeout period has occurred.

The setInterval() and clearInterval() methods are similar to setTimeout() and clearTimeout(). The setInterval() method differs from setTimeout() in that it repeatedly executes a function or evaluates an expression after the timeout is expired.

Listing 6.4 provides a more concrete example of performing timeout processing. It generates the Web page shown in Figure 6.6 and sets a ten-second timeout for the user to click on the provided button. If the user does not click on the button within ten seconds the alert dialog box shown in Figure 6.7 is displayed. If the user does click on the button within ten seconds the button's onClick event handler clears the timeout and congratulates the user.

Listing 6.4. A timeout processing example (ch06-04.htm)

```
<HTML>
<HEAD>
```

```
<TITLE>Timeout Program</TITLE>
<SCRIPT LANGUAGE="JavaScript"><!--
function setTimer() {
 timer=setTimeout("alert('Too slow!')",10000)
}
function clearTimer() {
 clearTimeout(timer)
 alert("Congratulations!")
}
// --></SCRIPT>
</HEAD>
<BODY>
<SCRIPT LANGUAGE="JavaScript"><!--
setTimer()
// --></SCRIPT>
<FORM>
<INPUT TYPE="BUTTON" VALUE="Click here within ten seconds."
 ONCLICK="clearTimer()">
</FORM>
</BODY>
</HTML>
```

FIGURE 6.6

Opening window for timeout processing example (Listing 6.4)

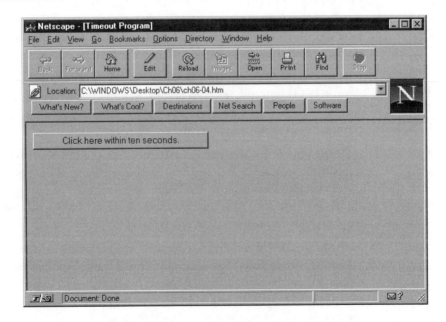

FIGURE 6.7

What happens when
a timeout occurs
(Listing 6.4)

The *Frame* Object

Frames are an HTML innovation developed by Netscape. They enable you to partition a window into independent display areas and organize and control the information displayed in these areas in powerful ways. You've already been exposed to frames in Chapter 4, "Event Handling." Frames are covered in detail in Appendix A, "HTML Reference," but are also summarized in this section in preparation for introducing the `frame` object.

An HTML file can contain either a document body or a *frame set*. You already know what a document body is, but what is a frame set? Frame sets are used to organize frames. If a file contains a document body, it uses the `<body>` tags to specify the document's contents. If a file contains a frame set, it uses the `<frameset>` tags instead of the `<body>` tags, to enclose one or more <frame> tags which are used to identify the individual frames contained in the frame set. The `<frame>` tags identify other HTML files to be loaded in the frame. These files can contain a document body or another (nested) frame set.

The `<frameset>` tag supports the ROWS and COLS attributes. These attributes are used to lay out the frames contained in the frame set. By default, they specify the dimensions of the frame set, in pixels. Refer to Appendix A for details on other ways in which these attributes are used.

`Frame` objects are automatically created by your browser and enable your scripts to control how frames are used. These `frame` objects allow you to load, based on user-generated events, new documents into frames. For example, a common use of frames is to use one frame as a clickable table of contents and use another frame to display the sections the user has selected.

The properties of the `frame` object are similar to the `window` object. That's because `frame` objects are also windows in the sense that a frame can also contain a document body or a frame set. This important characteristic of frames allows multiple nested frame sets to be displayed in a single browser window. The properties of the `frame` object are summarized in Table 6.4.

TABLE 6.4   Properties of the frame object

Property	Description
frames	An array which identifies all the frames contained within a window or frame set.
name	Identifies the name of the frame as specified in the name attribute of the <frame> tag.
length	Identifies the length of the frames array.
parent	A synonym that refers to the frame containing the current frame.
self	A synonym that refers to the current frame.
window	A synonym that refers to the current frame.

The frame object has six methods: blur(), focus(), setInterval(), clearInterval(), setTimeout(), and clearTimeout().

Tic Tac Toe

In order to learn how to use frames and have some fun at the same time, in this section you're going to use frames to create a Tic Tac Toe game. Several HTML and JavaScript files work together to implement this game.

Listing 6.5 shows the contents of the ttt.htm file, which provides the main entry point into the game. When you open the ttt.htm file with your browser it displays the window shown in Figure 6.8. It displays a 3-by-3 Tic Tac Toe grid in the upper left corner and a Restart button in the lower right corner.

Listing 6.5. The main Tic Tac Toe file (ttt.htm)

```
<HTML>
<HEAD>
<TITLE>Tic Tac Toe</TITLE></HEAD>
<FRAMESET ROWS="300,*" COLS="300,*" BORDER=0>
<FRAME SRC="board.htm">
<FRAME SRC="values.htm">
<FRAME SRC="blank.htm">
<FRAME SRC="control.htm">
</FRAMESET>
</HTML>
```

FIGURE 6.8

The initial Tic Tac Toe
display (Listing 6.5)

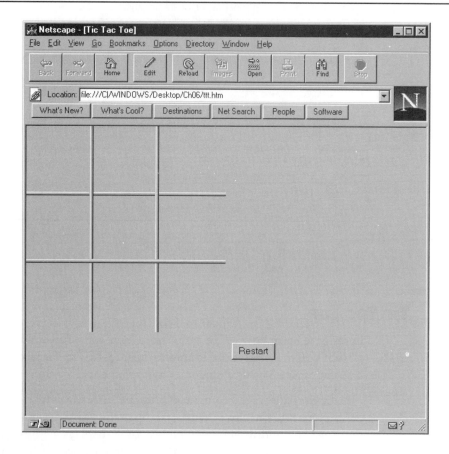

The Top-Level Frame Set

The ttt.htm file is the top-level frame set. This file creates a frame set that has
two rows and two colums. The first row and first column are 300 pixels wide and
the second row and column use the rest of the window. The frame set does not
have a border.

The four frames comprising the frame set load the HTML files board.htm,
values.htm, blank.htm, and control.htm. The Tic Tac Toe grid is created by
the board.htm file that is loaded into the first frame. The Restart button is created
by the control.htm file that is loaded in the fourth frame. The files values.htm
and blank.htm do not display information in their respective frames.

board.htm Listing 6.6 shows the contents of board.htm. This file creates a second-level nested frame set, which is displayed in the first frame of the top-level frame set (which is itself defined in ttt.htm). The frame set defined by board.htm is organized into a 3-by-3 grid of 100-pixel-by-100-pixel squares. The documents loaded into these squares are contained in the files square0.htm through square8.htm.

Listing 6.6. The frames of the Tic Tac Toe board (board.htm)

```
<HTML>
<HEAD>
<TITLE>Tic Tac Toe</TITLE></HEAD>
<FRAMESET ROWS="100,100,100" COLS="100,100,100">
<FRAME SRC="square0.htm">
<FRAME SRC="square1.htm">
<FRAME SRC="square2.htm">
<FRAME SRC="square3.htm">
<FRAME SRC="square4.htm">
<FRAME SRC="square5.htm">
<FRAME SRC="square6.htm">
<FRAME SRC="square7.htm">
<FRAME SRC="square8.htm">
</FRAMESET>
</HTML>
```

Before going on to see what's in the square files, let's look at the remaining three frames defined in ttt.htm.

values.htm The values.htm file is shown in Listing 6.7. It contains a single form with nine hidden fields, each assigned the value of *no one*. Later on in the discussion I'll show how this hidden form is used.

Listing 6.7. A hidden form (values.htm)

```
<HTML>
<HEAD>
<TITLE>Values</TITLE>
</HEAD>
<BODY>
<FORM>
<INPUT TYPE="HIDDEN" VALUE="no one" NAME="sq0">
<INPUT TYPE="HIDDEN" VALUE="no one" NAME="sq1">
```

```
<INPUT TYPE="HIDDEN" VALUE="no one" NAME="sq2">
<INPUT TYPE="HIDDEN" VALUE="no one" NAME="sq3">
<INPUT TYPE="HIDDEN" VALUE="no one" NAME="sq4">
<INPUT TYPE="HIDDEN" VALUE="no one" NAME="sq5">
<INPUT TYPE="HIDDEN" VALUE="no one" NAME="sq6">
<INPUT TYPE="HIDDEN" VALUE="no one" NAME="sq7">
<INPUT TYPE="HIDDEN" VALUE="no one" NAME="sq8">
</FORM>
</BODY>
</HTML>
```

blank.htm   The file `blank.htm`, shown in Listing 6.8, contains a blank HTML file that is used as a dummy placeholder to fill up the third frame defined in `ttt.htm`. It does not display any information in the browser window.

Listing 6.8. A blank document (blank.htm)

```
<HTML>
<HEAD>
<TITLE>Blank</TITLE>
</HEAD>
<BODY>
</BODY>
</HTML>
```

control.htm   Listing 6.9 shows the contents of the `control.htm` file. It implements the restart button by invoking the `restart()` function. This function restarts the Tic Tac Toe game to its original state using the following statement:

```
parent.location.href="ttt.htm"
```

This statement uses the `parent` property of the current window to access the window containing the frame set defined by `ttt.htm`. It then sets the `href` property of the window's location, causing the `ttt.htm` file to be reloaded.

Listing 6.9. Implementing the Restart button (control.htm)

```
<HTML>
<HEAD>
<TITLE>Blank</TITLE>
<SCRIPT LANGUAGE="JavaScript"><!--
```

```
function restart() {
 parent.location.href="ttt.htm"
}
// --></SCRIPT>
</HEAD>
<BODY>
<FORM>
<P ALIGN="CENTER">
<INPUT TYPE="Button" VALUE="Restart" onClick="restart()">
</P>
</FORM>
</BODY>
</HTML>
```

The Second-Level Frame Set

Now that we've covered the top-level frame set defined by ttt.htm, let's look
into the second-level frame set defined by board.htm. As shown in Listing 6.6,
this frame set defines nine frames containing the files square0.htm through
square8.htm. Listing 6.10 shows as an example the contents of the square4.htm
file. All nine files are identical except that the fourth line of each file sets the cell
variable to a value that indicates which grid cell is occupied by a square. For
instance, square0.htm sets cell to 0, square1.htm sets cell to 1, and
square8.htm sets cell to 8.

Listing 6.10. A sample square (square4.htm)

```
<HTML>
<HEAD>
<TITLE>Blank</TITLE>
<SCRIPT LANGUAGE="JavaScript"><!--
cell=4
// --></SCRIPT>
</HEAD>
<SCRIPT LANGUAGE="JavaScript" SRC="ttt.js"><!--
// --></SCRIPT>
</HEAD>
<BODY onFocus="playerMoves()">
</BODY>
</HTML>
```

The important point to notice about the square files is that the onFocus event of each file invokes the playerMoves() function. You may wonder where this function is defined. It's defined in the ttt.js file, which is included in each square file via the SRC attribute of the <script> tag included in each file's head. The ttt.js file provides the JavaScript code that is at the heart of the Tic Tac Toe game's operation. This file is shown in Listing 6.11.

Listing 6.11. The JavaScript code that implements the Tic Tac Toe game (ttt.js)

```
function isBlank(n) {
 if(owns("player",n) || owns("computer",n)) return false
 return true
}
function owns(who,i) {
 var fr = parent.parent.frames[1]
 var doc = fr.document
 var field = doc.forms[0].elements[i]
 if(field==null || field.value==who) return true
 else return false
}
function setOwner(who,n) {
 var fr = parent.parent.frames[1]
 var doc = fr.document
 var field = doc.forms[0].elements[n]
 field.value=who
}
function ticTacToe(who,n1,n2,n3) {
 if(owns(who,n1) && owns(who,n2) && owns(who,n3)) {
  var color=parent.frames[0].document.bgColor
  for(var i=0;i<9;++i)
   parent.frames[i].document.bgColor="black"
  parent.frames[n1].document.bgColor=color
  parent.frames[n2].document.bgColor=color
  parent.frames[n3].document.bgColor=color
  return true
 }
 return false
}
function isTicTacToe(who) {
```

```
    if(ticTacToe(who,0,1,2)) return true
    if(ticTacToe(who,3,4,5)) return true
    if(ticTacToe(who,6,7,8)) return true
    if(ticTacToe(who,0,3,6)) return true
    if(ticTacToe(who,1,4,7)) return true
    if(ticTacToe(who,2,5,8)) return true
    if(ticTacToe(who,0,4,8)) return true
    if(ticTacToe(who,2,4,6)) return true
    return false
}
function computerMoves() {
  var moved=false
  while(!moved){
    var newMove = Math.round(9*Math.random())
    if(isBlank(newMove)){
      setOwner("computer",newMove)
      var fr=parent.frames[newMove]
      fr.location.href="x.htm"
      moved=true
    }
  }
}
function playerMoves() {
  if(isBlank(cell)){
    setOwner("player",cell)
    location.href="o.htm"
    if(!isTicTacToe("player")) computerMoves()
    isTicTacToe("computer")
  }
}
```

In order to understand just what `ttt.js` does, open `ttt.htm` with your browser, and after the document has been loaded, click on one of the Tic Tac Toe squares, as shown in Figure 6.9. An **O** appears in the square that you click; the computer responds by marking an **X** in another square.

Click again and the computer responds again; continue clicking on blank squares until the game is over. The computer plays randomly, so you *should* win at least once in a while. If you or the computer wins, then the Tic Tac Toe squares are identified by blacking out the other squares, as shown in Figure 6.10. If neither of you wins, all of the squares are filled in, as in the paper version of the game.

FIGURE 6.9

Playing Tic Tac Toe

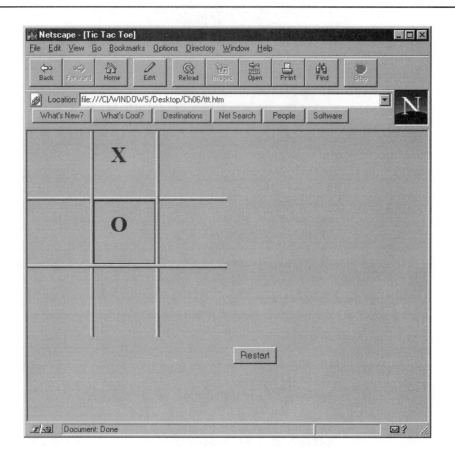

Investigating *ttt.js*

Now that you know how the game works, let's analyze `ttt.js`. It defines seven functions: `isBlank()`, `owns()`, `setOwner()`, `ticTacToe()`, `isTicTacToe()`, `computerMoves()`, and `playerMoves()`.

The `playerMoves()` function is invoked when you click on a square in the Tic Tac Toe grid. It uses the `isBlank()` function to determine whether the square is empty. The `cell` variable identifies which square has been clicked on. If the cell is blank, the `setOwner()` function is invoked to set the owner of the cell as the player. It then loads the `o.htm` file into the cell by setting the `href` property of the document's location. This marks the cell with an **O** to indicate that it belongs to the player. The `isTicTacToe()` function is invoked to determine whether

FIGURE 6.10

A winning combination

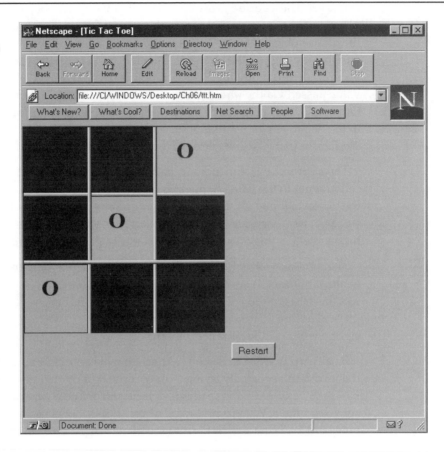

the player has made a straight line of three **O**s: Tic Tac Toe. If the player has not made Tic Tac Toe, then the `computerMoves()` method is invoked to select a cell for the computer. The `isTicTacToe()` function is then invoked again to see if the computer has made Tic Tac Toe with three **X**s.

The `isBlank()` function uses the `owns()` function to determine whether the player or the computer currently owns a cell. If either owns a cell then it returns *false*. Otherwise, it returns *true*.

The `owns()` function performs some fairly intricate processing. It sets the `doc` variable to the document loaded in the second frame of the top-level frame set. This is the document created when the `values.htm` file is loaded. We could have used the `top` property instead of `parent.parent` to access the top-level frame set. The `frames` array contains all of the `frame` objects in the frame set. The element `frames[1]` refers to the second frame. The `document` property of the `frame` object refers to the document that is loaded in the frame. The `field` variable is assigned the element of the index (`i`) of the first form contained in the `values.htm` document. The value of this field is checked to see if it equals the value passed via the `who` argument. If the values match, then *true* is returned. Otherwise *false* is returned. The values of the hidden fields of the form contained in the document generated by `values.htm` are used to maintain the state of the Tic Tac Toe game. You'll learn more about using hidden fields in Chapter 8.

The `setOwner()` function updates the ownership of a cell by setting the *n*th cell's owner to the value of the `who` parameter. It uses `parent.parent` to access the top-level frame set, `frames[1].document` to access the frame containing the `values.htm` document, and `elements[n].value` to access the value of the *n*th hidden field in this document. It then assigns the value of `who` to this field.

The `ticTacToe()` function checks to see if the player identified by `who` owns all three of the cells specified by `n1`, `n2`, and `n3`. If Tic Tac Toe has occurred, it sets the background color of all cells except the Tic Tac Toe cells to black. The `isTicTacToe()` function uses the `ticTacToe()` function to check each of the eight possible Tic Tac Toe combinations.

Finally, the `computerMoves()` function makes a random move for the computer. It does this by repeatedly trying to move until it finds an unused cell. It uses the `random()` and `round()` methods of the `Math` object to generate random integers between 0 and 8. When it finds a blank cell, it sets the owner of the cell to the computer and loads the `x.htm` file into the frame associated with the cell.

Listing 6.12. Displaying an O (o.htm)

```
<HTML>
<HEAD>
<TITLE>O</TITLE>
</HEAD>
<BODY>
<H1 ALIGN="CENTER">O</H1>
</BODY>
</HTML>
```

Listing 6.13. Displaying an X (x.htm)

```
<HTML>
<HEAD>
```

```
<TITLE>X</TITLE>
</HEAD>
<BODY>
<H1 ALIGN="CENTER">X</H1>
</BODY>
</HTML>
```

The *Document* Object

The document object is a very important JavaScript object. It allows you to update a document that has been or is being loaded and to access the HTML elements contained in a loaded document. It provides many properties that help you to access these elements, as shown earlier in Table 6.5. Many of these properties are objects that we'll be studying in subsequent chapters. Table 6.6 identifies the methods of the document object. The document object does not have any event handlers.

TABLE 6.5   Properties of the document object

Property	Description
alinkColor	Identifies the value of the alink attribute of the <body> tag.
anchor	An object that refers to an array contained in a document. See Chapter 9.
anchors	An array of all the anchors contained in a document. See Chapter 9.
applet	An object which refers to an applet that is contained in a document. See Chapter 18.
applets	An array of all the applets contained in a document. See Chapter 18.
area	An object that refers to an image map area contained in a document. See Chapter 10.
bgColor	Identifies the value of the bgcolor attribute of the <body> tag.
cookie	Identifies the value of a cookie. See Chapter 8.
domain	Identifies the domain name of the server from which the document is served.
embeds	An array of all the plugins contained in a document. See Chapter 20.

TABLE 6.5   Properties of the `document` object (continued)

Property	Description
fgColor	Identifies the value of the `text` attribute of the `<body>` tag.
form	An object that refers to a form contained in a document. See Chapter 7.
forms	An array of all the forms contained in a document. See Chapter 7.
history	A list of URLs that have been visited in a window. See Chapter 9.
image	An object that refers to an image contained in a document. See Chapter 10.
images	An array of all the images contained in a document. See Chapter 10.
lastModified	The date that a document was last modified.
link	An object that refers to a link contained in a document. See Chapter 9.
links	An array of all the links contained in a document. See Chapter 9.
linkColor	Identifies the value of the `link` attribute of the `<body>` tag.
plugin	An object that refers to a plugin contained in a document. See Chapter 20.
referrer	The URL of the document that provided the link to a document. See Chapter 9.
title	The document's title.
URL	The URL of a document. See Chapter 9.
vlinkColor	Identifies the value of the `vlink` attribute of the `<body>` tag.

TABLE 6.6.   Methods of the `document` object

Method	Description
close()	Closes a stream (see note nearby) used to create a document object.
open(*[mimeType]*)	Opens a stream used to create a document object with the optional MIME type.
write(*expr1[,expr2,...,exprN]*)	Writes the values of the expressions to a document.
writeln(*expr1[,expr2,...,exprN]*)	Writes the values of the expressions to a document followed by a new line character.

The term *stream* in Table 6.6 refers to a sequence of input or output characters. In the case of the `open()` and `close()` methods, it refers to the sequence of characters that constitute the document being created.

Generating Document Contents

You already know how to use the methods of the `document` object to generate HTML. For instance, you've used `write()` and `writeln()` extensively to write HTML code to a document as it is loaded in a window. The `document` object also provides two additional methods—`open()` and `close()`—that can help you to generate the contents of a document. Both of these additional methods work with the `write()` and `writeln()` methods.

The `open()` method allows you to update a document that is in a window other than the current window. For example, suppose the variable `win2` refers to a window that you have created. You can use `open()` to generate the document loaded into `win2` as follows:

```
win2.document.open()
  .
  .
  .
win2.document.write()
win2.document.writeln()
  .
  .
  .
win2.document.close()
```

In the above example, the `open()` method opens the document for writing, the `write()` and `writeln()` methods are used to write to the document, and the `close()` method is used to close the document after writing has been completed.

The `open()` method takes an optional string parameter that specifies the MIME type of the document being generated. If this parameter is omitted, the *text/html* MIME type is assumed.

Your browser will display the document according to its MIME type. For example, if you open a document with the *image/gif* MIME type, then it will display the document as a GIF image. However, in order to create the GIF image you must write the GIF header and pixel data to the document.

If you use open() with a MIME type that is not supported directly by your browser it will look to see if it has a plugin that supports the MIME type. If a suitable plugin exists, your browser will load the plugin and pass the contents of the document to the plugin as the document is written. You'll learn more about using open() and close() with plugins in Chapter 20.

> **NOTE** If open() is unable to open a document for any reason, then it returns the value null. If open() is able to open a document it will return a value other than null.

Accessing Document Contents

The document object provides several properties which can be used to access the contents of an HTML document. These properties were listed in Table 6.5 earlier in the chapter. In many cases the document properties refer to objects that are contained within the displayed document. You'll learn how to use these objects in subsequent chapters.

Listing 6.14 provides an example of using the properties of the document object to summarize the objects that are contained in a document. (That is, it lists the objects that are contained in the document and displays a count of how many of each type are contained.) This example also shows how to use the open() method to generate the contents of a document that is contained in another window.

Listing 6.14. Accessing document contents (ch06-14.htm)

```
<HTML>
<HEAD>
<TITLE>Accessing Document Contents</TITLE>
<SCRIPT LANGUAGE="JavaScript"><!--
function createSummary() {
 win2 = open("","window2")
 win2.document.open("text/plain")
 win2.document.writeln("Title: "+document.title)
 win2.document.writeln("Links: "+document.links.length)
 win2.document.writeln("Anchors: "+document.anchors.length)
```

```
win2.document.writeln("Forms:  "+document.forms.length)
win2.document.writeln("Images: "+document.images.length)
win2.document.writeln("Applets: "+document.applets.length)
win2.document.writeln("Embeds: "+document.embeds.length)
win2.document.close()
}
// --></SCRIPT>
</HEAD>
<BODY>
<A NAME="#top"></A>
<P><A HREF="http://www.jaworski.com/javascript">
 <IMG SRC="master.gif"></A>
<A HREF="http://www.sybex.com/"><IMG SRC="sybex.gif"></A></P>
<FORM>
<INPUT TYPE="BUTTON" NAME="Help" VALUE="Help"
    ONCLICK="alert('Click one of the above images.')">
</FORM>
<SCRIPT LANGUAGE="JavaScript"><!--
setTimeout("createSummary()",5000)
// --></SCRIPT>
</BODY>
</HTML>
```

When you open the file shown in Listing 6.14, it generates the Web page shown in Figure 6.11. This Web page has two images that are used as the source of links. It also contains a form with one button and an internal anchor (not visible) that names the top of the document. After five seconds, your browser creates a new window and displays the document shown in Figure 6.12. This action is caused by the script contained in the body of Listing 6.14. It contains a single statement that sets a five-second timeout before invoking the createSummary() function.

The createSummary() function is defined in the document's head. It creates a new window using the open() method of the window object. This new window is blank; it is assigned to the win2 variable. The document contained in the new window is opened using the text/plain MIME type. A series of writes to the document are performed and then the document is closed. The write statements access the properties of the document that is displayed in the first window, and summarize these properties in the second window. These properties describe the document title and identify the number of links, anchors, forms, images, applets, and plugins contained in the document.

FIGURE 6.11

The opening window
(Listing 6.14)

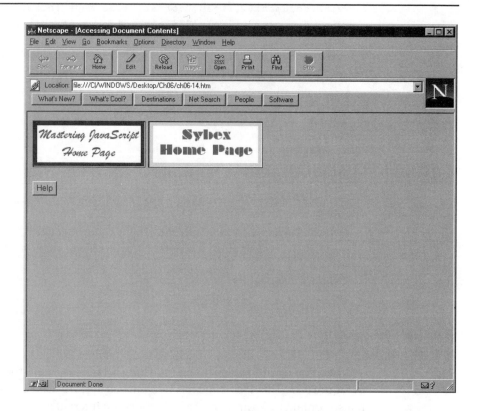

Working with Colors

The document object provides several properties that allow you to change the colors used to display Web pages. Unfortunately, most of these properties must be specified before the body of a document has been laid out. This means that the properties must be set by scripts that execute when the document's header is processed. An exception to this is the bgColor property. It can be used to change a document's background color at any time.

The fgColor property allows you to change the color of text that is displayed in a document. It applies to all text that is not part of a link. The linkColor property specifies the color for links that have not been visited (i.e., that have not been clicked on), and the vlinkColor property specifies the color of visited links. Finally, the alinkColor property specifies the color of a link as it is to appear while it is being clicked.

FIGURE 6.12

The document summary
window (Listing 6.14)

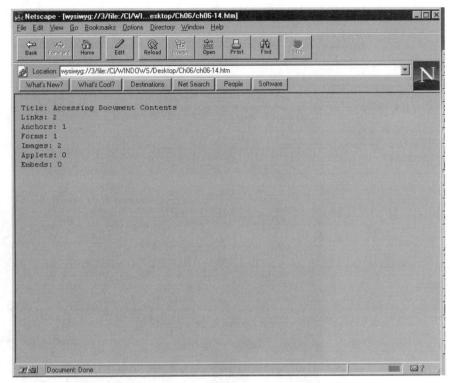

Listing 6.15 provides an example of using the bgColor, fgColor, and link-
Color attributes. It generates the document display shown in Figure 6.13. Note
that these attributes are set in the document header so that they can go into effect
when the document body is laid out.

Listing 6.15. Using color attributes (ch06-15.htm).

```
<HTML>
<HEAD>
<TITLE>Changing Colors</TITLE>
<SCRIPT LANGUAGE="JavaScript"><!--
document.bgColor="black"
document.fgColor="white"
document.linkColor="yellow"
// --></SCRIPT>
</HEAD>
<BODY>
```

```
<H1>Changing Colors</H1>
<P>This Web page shows how document colors can be changed.</P>
<P>Here is a <A HREF="nowhere">sample link</A>.</P>
</BODY>
</HTML>
```

FIGURE 6.13

A grayscale version of the document generated by Listing 6.15.

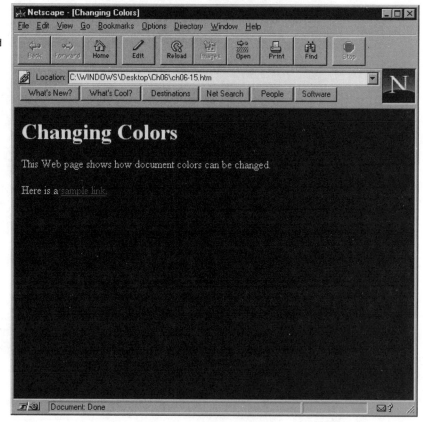

Summary

This chapter showed you how to use the predefined window, frame, and document objects to create and manage Web pages with multiple windows and frames. It also provided several examples of using windows and frames to organize your Web pages. In the next chapter, you'll learn how to use predefined JavaScript objects to implement local form-processing functions.

CHAPTER
SEVEN

7

Forms Processing

- ■ The `Form` Object

- ■ Accessing Forms within JavaScript

- ■ Accessing Form Elements

- ■ Using Form Event Handlers

- ■ Performing Local Form Processing

- ■ Working with CGI Scripts

Forms provide you with an important capability for Web page development—they allow you to gather information from individuals who browse your Web pages. This is especially important if you use your Web site to advertise or sell your products. Forms make it easy to collect information from your Web page users. They provide a full range of Graphical User Interface (GUI) controls and they automatically submit the data they collect to your Web server. This data can then be processed by CGI programs or server-side JavaScript scripts built upon Netscape's LiveWire.

JavaScript provides a number of features that can be used to enhance the forms that you develop for your particular Web applications. These features allow you to validate form data before it is submitted to your server and to exercise greater control of the interaction between your forms and Web users.

This chapter introduces the form object and discusses the JavaScript objects that are associated with form fields and GUI controls. It shows how to use the properties and methods of these objects, and how to handle form-related events. When you finish this chapter you will know how to use JavaScript to create forms that perform local processing and will be able to use these forms to communicate with CGI programs.

NOTE	If you are unfamiliar with the HTML tags used to create forms, consult Appendix A, "HTML Reference."

The *Form* Object

JavaScript provides the form object to enable your scripts to interact with and exercise control over HTML forms. The form object is a property of the document object. Your browser creates a unique form object for every form that is contained in a document.

The form object is important because it provides you with access to the forms contained in your documents and allows you to respond to form-related events. Table 7.1 lists the properties of the form object. These properties provide access to a form's attributes and allow you to work with a form's fields and GUI controls.

The `form` object provides two methods, `submit()` and `reset()`, which are used to submit a form or reset a form's entries to their default values. (The events that are handled by forms are covered in Chapter 4 and in the section "Using Form Event Handlers" of this chapter.)

TABLE 7.1   Properties of the `form` object

Property	Description
`action`	Provides access to the `action` attribute of the `<form>` tag.
`button`	An object representing a button GUI control.
`checkbox`	An object representing a check box field.
`elements`	An array containing all the fields and GUI controls contained in a form.
`encoding`	Provides access to the `enctype` attribute of the `<form>` tag.
`FileUpload`	An object representing a file-upload form field.
`hidden`	An object representing a hidden form field.
`length`	Provides access to the length of the elements array.
`method`	Provides access to the `method` attribute of the `<form>` tag.
`name`	Identifies the name of the form.
`password`	An object representing a password field.
`radio`	An object representing a radio button field.
`reset`	An object representing a reset button.
`select`	An object representing a selection list.
`submit`	An object representing a submit button.
`target`	Provides access to the `target` attribute of the `<form>` tag.
`text`	An object representing a text field.
`textarea`	An object representing a text area field.

Accessing Forms within JavaScript

Since `form` objects are properties of documents, they are accessed by referencing the documents in which they are contained. If you name a form when you create it, then you can access the form by its name. Forms are named using the form's name attribute. For example, if you create a form named `employeeData` you can access the form's `method` property using `employeeData.method`.

You can also use the `forms` property of the `document` object to access the forms contained in a particular document. The `forms` property is an array that contains an entry for each form contained in a document. Suppose that the `employeeData` form is the third form contained in the document loaded into the current window. You can access the form's method property using `document.forms[2].method`.

Accessing Form Elements

A form may contain a wide variety of fields and GUI controls. These form components are referred to as *elements* of the form and are objects in their own right. Table 7.2 lists and summarizes the objects that may be contained in a form.

TABLE 7.2   The objects that may be contained in a form

Object	Description
button	A general-purpose button for implementing GUI controls.
checkbox	A clickable field which allows multiple selections from within a group.
FileUpload	A field which allows a user to specify a file to be submitted as part of the form.
hidden	A field which may contain a value but is not displayed within a form.
password	A text field in which the values entered by a user are hidden via mask characters.
radio	A clickable field which allows only a single selection from within a group.
reset	A button which is used to reset the contents of a form to its default state.
select	A list from which individual list items may be selected.

TABLE 7.2   The objects that may be contained in a form (continued)

Object	Description
submit	A button which is used to submit the data entered into a field.
text	A single-line field for entering text.
textarea	A multi-line field for entering text.

If the elements of a form are named using an HTML name attribute, then the element can be accessed using this name. For example, suppose that you have a form named form1 that contains a text field named ssn. You can access the value of this field using form1.ssn.value.

In most cases, you will access the elements of a form using the elements array property of the form object. This array contains an object for each element of a form. Suppose that the ssn field of the form1 form is the seventh element defined in the form. You can access the value of the ssn field using form1.elements[6].value.

The objects described in Table 7.2 reference the elements of a form and have properties and methods of their own as summarized in Tables 7.3 and 7.4.

TABLE 7.3   Properties of form elements

Object	Property	Description
button	name	Provides access to the button's name attribute.
	type	Identifies the object's type.
	value	Identifies the object's value.
checkbox	checked	Identifies whether the checkbox is currently checked.
	defaultChecked	Identifies whether the checkbox is checked by default.
	name	Provides access to the object's name attribute.
	type	Identifies the object's type.
	value	Identifies the object's value.
FileUpload	name	Provides access to the object's name attribute.
	type	Identifies the object's type attribute.

TABLE 7.3   Properties of form elements (continued)

Object	Property	Description
	value	Identifies the object's value.
hidden	name	Provides access to the object's name attribute.
	type	Identifies the object's type.
	value	Identifies the object's value.
password	defaultValue	Identifies the object's default value.
	name	Provides access to the object's name attribute.
	type	Identifies the object's type.
	value	Identifies the object's value.
radio	checked	Identifies whether the radio button is currently checked.
	defaultChecked	Identifies whether the radio button is checked by default.
	length	Identifies the number of radio buttons in a group.
	name	Provides access to the object's name attribute.
	type	Identifies the object's type.
	value	Identifies the object's value.
reset	name	Provides access to the object's name attribute.
	type	Identifies the object's type.
	value	Identifies the object's value.
select	length	Identifies the length of the select list.
	name	Provides access to the object's name attribute.
	options	An array which identifies the options supported by the select list.
	selectedIndex	Identifies the first selected option within the select list.
	type	Identifies the object's type.
submit	name	Provides access to the object's name attribute.

TABLE 7.3   Properties of form elements (continued)

Object	Property	Description
	type	Identifies the object's type.
	value	Identifies the object's value.
text	defaultValue	Identifies the default text to be displayed in the text field.
	name	Provides access to the object's name attribute.
	type	Identifies the object's type.
	value	Identifies the object's value.
textarea	defaultValue	Identifies the default text to be displayed in the text area field.
	name	Provides access to the object's name attribute.
	type	Identifies the object's type.
	value	Identifies the object's value.

NOTE All form elements have the form property. This property references the form in which the element is contained.

TABLE 7.4   Methods of form elements

Object	Method	Description
button	click()	Simulates the button being clicked.
	blur()	Removes focus from the button.
	focus()	Gives focus to the button.
checkbox	click()	Simulates the checkbox being clicked.
	blur()	Removes focus from the button.
	focus()	Gives focus to the button.

TABLE 7.4   Methods of form elements (continued)

Object	Method	Description
FileUpload	blur()	Removes focus from the FileUpload field.
	focus()	Gives focus to the FileUpload field.
hidden	none	
password	blur()	Removes input focus from the password field.
	focus()	Gives input focus to the password field.
	select()	Highlights the text displayed in the password field.
radio	click()	Simulates the clicking of the radio button.
	blur()	Removes focus from the radio button.
	focus()	Gives focus to the radio button.
reset	click()	Simulates the clicking of the reset button.
	blur()	Removes focus from the reset button.
	focus()	Gives focus to the reset button.
select	blur()	Removes focus from the selection list.
	focus()	Gives focus to the selection list.
submit	click()	Simulates the clicking of the submit button.
	blur()	Removes focus from the submit button.
	focus()	Gives focus to the submit button.
text	blur()	Removes focus from the text field.
	focus()	Gives focus to the text field.
	select()	Highlights the text in the text field.
textarea	blur()	Removes focus from the text area.
	focus()	Gives focus to the text area.
	select()	Highlights the text in the text area.

Listing 7.1 shows how the individual forms and form elements can be accessed in multiform documents. It creates the three form document shown in Figure 7.1. When you click on the Submit button of the first form, the `onSubmit()` handler invokes the `displayFormData()` function. Note that it does this in the context of a `return` statement. This causes the form submission to be aborted when `displayFormData()` returns a *false* value. This is always the case because `displayFormData()` always returns *false*.

The `displayFormData()` function creates and opens a separate window and assigns the `window` object to the `win2` variable. It then opens the window's document with a text/plain MIME type. It uses the `forms` array of the `document` object of the first window to determine how many forms are contained in the document. It then writes this information to the document contained in `win2`. Next, it identifies the number of elements in each form using the `length` property of the form's `elements` array. Finally, it displays the `type` property of each form element via `win2`, as shown in Figure 7.2.

Listing 7.1. Accessing the elements of a form (form-acc.htm)

```
<HTML>
<HEAD>
<TITLE>Multiform Document Example</TITLE>
<SCRIPT LANGUAGE="JavaScript"><!--
function displayFormData() {
 win2=open("","window2")
 win2.epsument.open("text/plain")
 win2.epsument.writeln("This document has "+
  document.forms.length+" forms.")
 for(i=0;i<document.forms.length;++i) {
  win2.epsument.writeln("Form "+i+" has "+
   document.forms[i].elements.length+" elements.")
  for(j=0;j<document.forms[i].elements.length;++j) {
   win2.epsument.writeln((j+1)+" A "+
    document.forms[i].elements[j].type+" element.")
  }
 }
 win2.epsument.close()
 return false
}
// --></SCRIPT>
</HEAD>
```

```
<BODY>
<H1>Multiform Document Example</H1>
<FORM ACTION="nothing" onSubmit="return displayFormData()">
<H2>Form 1</H2>
<P>Text field: <INPUT TYPE="TEXT" NAME="f1-1"
 VALUE="Sample text"></P>
<P>Password field: <INPUT TYPE="PASSWORD" NAME="f1-2"></P>
<P>Text area field:
<TEXTAREA ROWS="4" COLS="30"
  NAME="f1-3">Write your novel here.</TEXTAREA></P>
<P><INPUT TYPE="SUBMIT" NAME="f1-4" VALUE="Submit">
<INPUT TYPE="RESET" NAME="f1-5"></P>
</FORM>
<HR>
<FORM>
<H2>Form 2</H2>
```

FIGURE 7.1

A multiform document
(Listing 7.1)

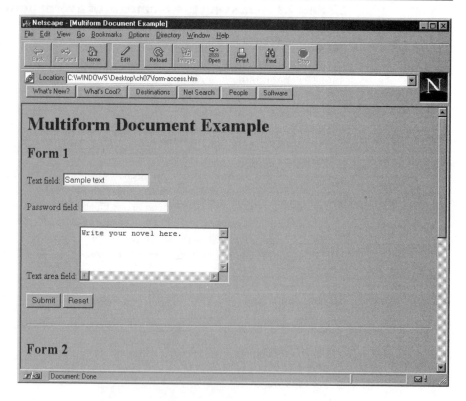

```
<P><INPUT TYPE="CHECKBOX" NAME="f2-1" VALUE="1"
  CHECKED> Check me!</P>
<P><INPUT TYPE="CHECKBOX" NAME="f2-1" VALUE="2"> No.
  Check me!</P>
  <P><INPUT TYPE="CHECKBOX" NAME="f2-1" VALUE="3"> Check all of
  us!</P>
  <P><INPUT TYPE="RADIO" NAME="f2-2" VALUE="1"> AM</P>
  <P><INPUT TYPE="RADIO" NAME="f2-2" VALUE="2" CHECKED> PM</P>
  <P><INPUT TYPE="RADIO" NAME="f2-2" VALUE="3"> FM</P>
  <INPUT TYPE="FILE" NAME="f2-3">
  </FORM>
  <HR>
  <FORM>
  <H2>Form 3</H2>
  <INPUT TYPE="HIDDEN" NAME="f3-1">
  <SELECT NAME="f3-2" SIZE="4">
  <OPTION VALUE="">Item 1</OPTION>
```

FIGURE 7.2

A summary of the contents of the multiform document (Listing 7.1)

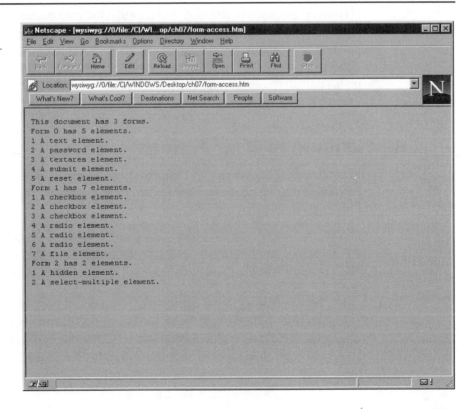

```
<OPTION VALUE="">Item 2</OPTION>
<OPTION VALUE="" SELECTED>Item 3</OPTION>
<OPTION VALUE="">Item 4</OPTION>
<OPTION VALUE="">Item 5</OPTION>
</SELECT>
</FORM>
</BODY>
</HTML>
```

Using Form Event Handlers

JavaScript's ability to handle form-related events is a very powerful tool for customizing form behavior. It allows you to control the user's interaction with your forms and to process form data as it is entered by the user. It also allows you to process form data locally at the user's browser, reducing the load on your communication bandwidth and on your Web server.

Form event handlers respond to events that indicate the user has performed an input action, such as filling in a text field, clicking on a button, or submitting an entire form. These event handlers check the data entered by the user and then either prompt the user to correct any errors or provide the user with other feedback on the data that was entered. Form event handlers may also be used to adaptively present new forms to a user based upon the user's response to prior forms.

Responding to User Actions

Event handling in general, and form event handling in particular, are introduced in Chapter 4. If you have not already read Chapter 4 you should do so before continuing on in this chapter.

Within Chapter 4, Table 4.2 identifies all of the JavaScript event-handling attributes and Table 4.7 identifies which event-handling attributes apply to forms and form elements. From Table 4.7 you can see that form events fall into the following categories:

- *Clicks and checks.* These are the most common types of form events. A user clicks on a button or checks a checkbox to provide information or to perform an action. These events are handled by providing feedback on the results of the click or updating the browser window as the result of performing an action.

- *Text changes.* Text changes are another common type of form event. The user enters data into a text field or text area, an event is generated, and the event handler validates the user's entry and performs further processing based on the user's input.

- *List selection.* When a user selects an item from a selection list, event-handling code is used to verify that the selection is consistent with other inputs and to perform any processing indicated by the selection.

- *Change of focus.* Change-of-focus events occur when a form element, such as a text field or selection list, receives or loses the current input focus. These events usually do not require special event handing. However, JavaScript provides the capability to do so, when required.

- *Form submission and reset.* These events are generated when a user clicks on a submit or reset button. Form submission events are typically handled by validating all of the data entered by the user, performing any local processing on that data, and then forwarding the data to a CGI program or other server-side script.

Since you have already covered form event handling in Chapter 4, I'm not going to bore you with any more trivial examples. Instead we'll use JavaScript's event-handling capabilities to create a form-based Hangman game—something which is impossible to do in HTML alone.

Hangman is a game where you try to guess a word, one letter at a time. You are initially presented with a word pattern where each letter of the word to be guessed is represented by an underscore (_) character. This tells you how many letters are in the word, but nothing more. When you guess a letter that is in the word, the underscore representing that letter is replaced by the letter you guessed correctly. This tells you that you've guessed the correct letter and shows you where the letter appears in the word. You continue to guess until you run out of guesses or you guess all of the letters of the word.

Your status in terms of guesses is depicted in a gallows—that's why its called Hangman. Each time you guess incorrectly, a "body part" is added to the victim being hanged. You are only allowed seven incorrect guesses (head, upper and lower torso, two arms, two legs) before the game is over. The purpose of the game is not to be morbid, but to improve your word recognition skills.

Before going on to learn how the game is implemented using form event handling, you should play a few games. Start the game by opening `hangman.htm` in your browser. At startup, it presents the display shown in Figure 7.3. Play the game by clicking on any of the buttons labeled A through Z. If you guess correctly, the game will display the position of the letter in the *Word to guess* text field as shown in Figure 7.4. If you guess incorrectly, a part of your body will be hung in the gallows as shown in Figure 7.5. If you continue to guess incorrectly, your complete effigy will be hung (see Figure 7.6), an alert dialog box will tell you that you lost, and the game will start again. If you are clever enough to guess the word before you are hung, an alert dialog box will tell you that you won and the game will start over. Clicking on the Start Again button will immediately restart the game with a new word to guess.

NOTE   If you try to modify any of the form's text fields an alert message will be displayed that tells you not to mess with that field.

FIGURE 7.3

The Hangman opening display (Listing 7.2)

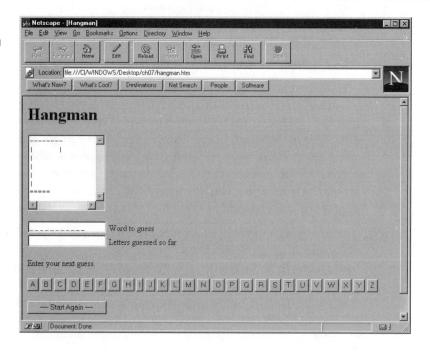

FIGURE 7.4

You guessed correctly.
(Listing 7.2)

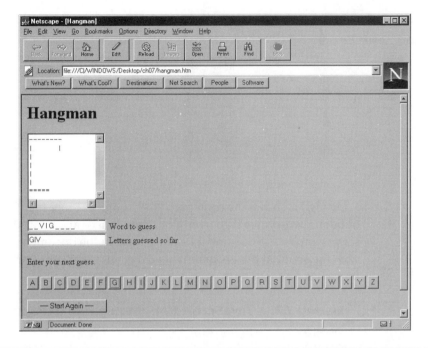

FIGURE 7.5

You guessed incorrectly.
(Listing 7.2)

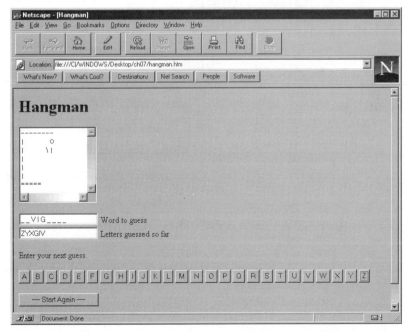

FIGURE 7.6

You're hung. (Listing 7.2)

Listing 7.2 shows the contents of the hangman.htm file. This file is fairly long, but don't worry; we'll go over it one small piece at a time. The file contains two scripts: one in the document head and one in the document body. We'll start with the script in the document head, because that's the part your browser processes first.

Listing 7.2. A JavaScript Hangman game (hangman.htm)

```
<HTML>
<HEAD>
<TITLE>Hangman</TITLE>
<SCRIPT LANGUAGE="JavaScript"><!--
gallows = new Array("--------\n|        |\n|\n|\n|\n|\n=====",
"--------\n|        O\n|\n|\n|\n|\n=====",
"--------\n|        O\n|        |\n|\n|\n|\n=====",
"--------\n|        O\n|       \\ |\n|\n|\n|\n=====",
"--------\n|        O\n|       \\ |/\n|\n|\n|\n=====",
"--------\n|        O\n|       \\ |/\n|        |\n|\n|\n=====",
"--------\n|        O\n|       \\ |/\n|        |        /\n|\n=====",
"--------\n|        O\n|       \\ |/\n|        |       / \\\n|\n=====")
guessChoices = new
Array("JavaScript","Navigator","LiveConnect","LiveWire")
function startAgain() {
 guesses = 0
 max = gallows.length-1
 guessed = " "
 len = guessChoices.length - 1
 toGuess = guessChoices[Math.round(len*Math.random())]
 .toUpperCase()
 displayHangman()
```

```
 displayToGuess()
 displayGuessed()
}
function stayAway() {
 alert("Don't mess with this form element!")
}
function displayHangman() {
 document.game.status.value=gallows[guesses]
}
function displayToGuess() {
 pattern=""
 for(i=0;i<toGuess.length;++i) {
  if(guessed.indexOf(toGuess.charAt(i)) != -1)
   pattern += (toGuess.charAt(i)+" ")
  else pattern += "_ "
 }
 document.game.toGuess.value=pattern
}
function displayGuessed() {
 document.game.guessed.value=guessed
}
function badGuess(s) {
 if(toGuess.indexOf(s) == -1) return true
 return false
}
function winner() {
 for(i=0;i<toGuess.length;++i) {
  if(guessed.indexOf(toGuess.charAt(i)) == -1) return false
 }
 return true
}
function guess(s){
 if(guessed.indexOf(s) == -1) guessed = s + guessed
 if(badGuess(s)) ++guesses
 displayHangman()
 displayToGuess()
 displayGuessed()
 if(guesses >= max){
 alert("You're dead. The word you missed was "+toGuess+".")
  startAgain()
 }
 if(winner()) {
  alert("You won!")
  startAgain()
```

```
          }
        }
        // --></SCRIPT>
        </HEAD>
        <BODY>
        <H1>Hangman</H1>
        <FORM NAME="game">
        <PRE>
        <TEXTAREA NAME="status" ROWS="7" COLS="16"
         ONFOCUS="stayAway()"></TEXTAREA>
        </PRE><P>
        <INPUT TYPE="TEXT" NAME="toGuess"
         ONFOCUS="stayAway()"> Word to guess<BR>
        <INPUT TYPE="TEXT" NAME="guessed"
         ONFOCUS="stayAway()"> Letters guessed so far<BR>
        <P>Enter your next guess.</P>
        <INPUT TYPE="BUTTON" VALUE=" A " ONCLICK="guess('A')">
        <INPUT TYPE="BUTTON" VALUE=" B " ONCLICK="guess('B')">
        <INPUT TYPE="BUTTON" VALUE=" C " ONCLICK="guess('C')">
        <INPUT TYPE="BUTTON" VALUE=" D " ONCLICK="guess('D')">
        <INPUT TYPE="BUTTON" VALUE=" E " ONCLICK="guess('E')">
        <INPUT TYPE="BUTTON" VALUE=" F " ONCLICK="guess('F')">
        <INPUT TYPE="BUTTON" VALUE=" G " ONCLICK="guess('G')">
        <INPUT TYPE="BUTTON" VALUE=" H " ONCLICK="guess('H')">
        <INPUT TYPE="BUTTON" VALUE=" I " ONCLICK="guess('I')">
        <INPUT TYPE="BUTTON" VALUE=" J " ONCLICK="guess('J')">
        <INPUT TYPE="BUTTON" VALUE=" K " ONCLICK="guess('K')">
        <INPUT TYPE="BUTTON" VALUE=" L " ONCLICK="guess('L')">
        <INPUT TYPE="BUTTON" VALUE=" M " ONCLICK="guess('M')">
        <INPUT TYPE="BUTTON" VALUE=" N " ONCLICK="guess('N')">
        <INPUT TYPE="BUTTON" VALUE=" O " ONCLICK="guess('O')">
        <INPUT TYPE="BUTTON" VALUE=" P " ONCLICK="guess('P')">
        <INPUT TYPE="BUTTON" VALUE=" Q " ONCLICK="guess('Q')">
        <INPUT TYPE="BUTTON" VALUE=" R " ONCLICK="guess('R')">
        <INPUT TYPE="BUTTON" VALUE=" S " ONCLICK="guess('S')">
        <INPUT TYPE="BUTTON" VALUE=" T " ONCLICK="guess('T')">
        <INPUT TYPE="BUTTON" VALUE=" U " ONCLICK="guess('U')">
        <INPUT TYPE="BUTTON" VALUE=" V " ONCLICK="guess('V')">
        <INPUT TYPE="BUTTON" VALUE=" W " ONCLICK="guess('W')">
        <INPUT TYPE="BUTTON" VALUE="7 X " ONCLICK="guess('X')">
        <INPUT TYPE="BUTTON" VALUE=" Y " ONCLICK="guess('Y')">
        <INPUT TYPE="BUTTON" VALUE=" Z " ONCLICK="guess('Z')"><P>
        <INPUT TYPE="BUTTON" NAME="restart" VALUE="----
           Start Again ----"
```

```
    ONCLICK="startAgain()">
    <SCRIPT LANGUAGE="JavaScript"><!--
    startAgain()
    // --></SCRIPT>
    </FORM>
    </BODY>
    </HTML>
```

The script defines two arrays, `gallows` and `guessChoices`, and eight functions—`startAgain()`, `stayAway()`, `displayHangman()`, `displayToGuess()`, `displayGuessed()`, `badGuess()`, `winner()`, and `guess()`. Each of these is discussed in the following paragraphs.

gallows: This array contains eight string entries that correspond to the eight states that the gallows pole may be in: empty, head hanging, head and upper torso hanging, and so on. The strings may look very cryptic. That's because new lines are represented by the new line character (`\n`) and back slashes are represented by a pair of back slashes (`\\`). These are the standard escape characters used by JavaScript, Java, C, and C++. Try decoding and drawing each of the strings in the gallows array to get a better feel for how these escape characters are used.

guessChoices: This array contains four words. These are the words that the user is required to guess. One word from this array is randomly selected for each play of the game. You can add or replace the words contained in this array to tailor Hangman with your own word list.

startAgain0: This function starts and restarts the Hangman game. It initializes variables used by the program and then invokes the functions required to display the hangman, show the word to be guessed, and display the letters that the user has already guessed. The `guesses` variable keeps track of how many incorrect guesses the user has made. It is used to select which element of the `gallows` array is to be displayed. The `max` variable determines how many guesses the user can make before he or she is hung. The `guessed` variable is initialized to `" "` (one space) to indicate that the user has not yet guessed any letters.

> **NOTE** The value " " is used instead of "" (no space) because the `indexOf()` method of the `string` object does not work correctly for the value "".

The `len` variable is used to calculate the maximum array subscript of the `guessChoices` array. The `toGuess` variable is set to a randomly selected word in the guessChoices array. This word is then converted to upper case. The displayHangman() function displays the hangman figure in the status text area. The displayToGuess() function displays the word being guessed in the toGuess text field. The displayGuessed() function displays the letters guessed by the user in the guessed text field. When the game is first started or restarted, the displayGuessed() function is used to blank out the guessed text field.

stayAway(): This function is called by the onFocus event handlers of the form's text fields to warn the user not to mess around with these fields. This is to discourage the user from trying to change the content of these fields.

displayHangman(): This function displays the hangman character figure in the status text area. It does this by setting the value property of the status field of the game form of the current document to the gallows array entry corresponding to the number of incorrect guesses.

displayToGuess(): This function displays a word pattern based on the word to be guessed and the letters the user has currently guessed. If a user has guessed a letter of the word then that letter is displayed. Otherwise an underscore character is displayed in place of the letter. It loops through each letter of the word contained in toGuess and uses the indexOf() method of the string object to determine whether that letter is contained in the guessed string. The word pattern is then written to the toGuessed text field.

displayGuessed(): This function writes the value of the guessed variable to the guessed text field to inform the user of the letters that he or she has already tried. The guessed variable is updated each time a user makes a new letter guess.

badGuess(): This function returns *true* if the letter represented by the s parameter is not in the word contained in the toGuess variable. It returns *false* otherwise. It is used to determine whether the user has guessed incorrectly.

winner(): This function checks each letter in the word contained in the toGuess variable and returns *false* if any letter is not in the string contained in the guessed variable. It returns *true* otherwise. It is used to determine whether the user has correctly guessed all letters of the toGuess word.

guess(): This function is invoked whenever the user clicks on a button with the letters A through Z. It is invoked by the button's onClick event handler and passes the letter associated with the button via the s parameter. Here's how it works:

- The guess() function first checks to see if the letter is currently in the list of letters the user has already guessed, and adds the letter to the list if it is not.

- It then checks to see if the letter is an incorrect guess, and increments the `guesses` variable accordingly.

- Next, it invokes the appropriate functions to redisplay the form's text fields.

- It then checks to see if the user has run out of guesses, and if so, alerts the user that he has been hung.

- Finally, it invokes the `winner()` function to determine if the user has correctly guessed all letters of the `toGuess` word, and, if so, tells the user that they have won.

The form displayed by the browser is named `game`. It contains the text area named `status`, the text fields named `toGuess` and `guessed`, the buttons labeled A through Z, and the Start Again button. Each of these form elements performs event handling which supports the processing of the Hangman game. This event handling is as follows:

status, toGuess, and guessed: These fields handle the `onFocus` event by invoking the `stayAway()` function to tell the user to not mess with the field's contents.

A through Z: These buttons handle the `onClick` event by invoking the `guess()` function and passing as a parameter the letter associated with the button.

Start Again: This button invokes the `startAgain()` function to reinitialize the game's variables and restart the game.

The script contained in the document body contains the single statement, `startAgain()`, which initializes the variables used in the game and displays the contents of the form's text fields.

Performing Local Form Processing

The Hangman game of the previous section is a great example of the power of local form processing. However, unless your sole purpose in Web programming is to entertain those who browse your Web page, you'll probably want to use forms to return some data to your Web server. This brings up the very important question of which processing should be performed locally via browser-side scripts and which should be performed on the server? For the most part this question is easy to answer: "If it can be performed on the browser then do it." It's a pretty good rule of thumb. However, as with most rules of thumb, there are cases which create exceptions to the rule. For example, if you don't want anyone to know how you process the form data, then don't do it locally on the browser. Anyone can figure out your processing approach by examining your JavaScript code. Another consideration is performance. If your Web application requires a time- or resource-intensive computation, you can avoid upsetting your user by having the data sent back to your high-performance server for processing. However, in most cases forms processing is short and quick and no noticeable impact is made on browser performance.

Working with CGI Scripts

Before the advent of JavaScript, the data the forms collected from users was submitted to CGI programs. The CGI programs performed all processing on the form data and sent the results of that processing back to the browser so that it could be displayed to users. The sections "The Hypertext Transfer Protocol" and "Common Gateway Interface Programs" of Chapter 1 provide a summary of the methods by which browsers communicate with CGI programs. In this section, we'll show how to use JavaScript scripts to communicate with CGI programs. More importantly, we'll show how to use JavaScript to perform local processing of form data before sending the data to CGI programs.

Sending Form Data to a CGI Program

When a form sends data to a CGI program it uses either the GET or POST method. This method is specified by setting the `method` attribute of the form to either `"get"` or `"post"`. If the GET method is used, the form encodes and appends its data to the URL of the CGI program. When a Web server receives the encoded URL, it passes the form data to the CGI program via a program variable known as an *environment* variable. If the POST method is used, the Web server passes the form's data to the CGI program via the program's standard input. The POST method is preferred over the GET method because of data size limitations associated with environment variables. The `method` property of the `form` object allows a form's method to be set within JavaScript.

A form's `ACTION` attribute specifies the URL of the CGI program to which a form's data is to be sent. The `action` property of the `form` object allows this URL to be set or changed within JavaScript. This allows a script to send a form's data to one of several CGI programs, depending upon the form's contents as entered by a user. For example, you can have a general-purpose form that collects information on users interested in your product line and then process that data in different ways depending upon the demographic data supplied by the user.

In most cases, form data is encoded using the URL encoding scheme identified by the following MIME type:

application/x-www-form-urlencoded

However, it is likely that another scheme:

multipart/form-data encoding

will become popular because of its support for file uploads. This encoding scheme is discussed in RFC 1867, which can be found at the URL *http://www.jaworski.com/ javascript/rfc1867.txt*. The `encoding` property of the `form` object identifies what encoding scheme was specified by the form's `ENCTYPE` attribute. The `encoding` property may also be used to change this attribute.

NOTE   An RFC (literally a *Request For Comments*) is a document that is used to describe a particular aspect of the Internet, such as a protocol standard or a coding scheme.

Performing Local Form Processing

Having covered the basic form properties that control a form's interaction with a CGI program, let's investigate how JavaScript can be used to locally process a form's data and then send the processed data to the Web server.

When a form is submitted, either as the result of a user clicking on a submit button or the invocation of a form's `submit()` method, all of the data contained in the form's fields are sent to the Web server. This is both inefficient and undesirable since we can use JavaScript to preprocess a form's data.

The secret to using JavaScript to send processed form data to CGI programs is to use a *summary form* to hold the data that is the result of any local form processing. Once a form's data has been initially processed, it is put into a summary form, and then the summary form is sent to the CGI program for any additional processing that is required. Listing 7.3 illustrates this concept. A Web page is designed with two forms. The first form is visible to the user and is the form used to collect raw input data. This form is shown in Figure 7.7. It provides the user with four selection lists with which the user can select a particular type of automobile.

Listing 7.3. Using a summary form to support local processing (orderfrm.htm)

```
<HTML>
<HEAD>
<TITLE>Submitting the results of local form processing</TITLE>
<SCRIPT LANGUAGE="JavaScript"><!--
function processOrder() {
 order = ""
 order += document.orderForm.model.selectedIndex
 order += document.orderForm.doors.selectedIndex
 order += document.orderForm.color.selectedIndex
 sel = document.orderForm.accessories
 for(i=0;i<sel.length;++i)
  if(sel.options[i].selected) order += i
 document.submitForm.result.value = order
 document.submitForm.submit()
 return false
}
// --></SCRIPT>
</HEAD>
<BODY>
<H1>Select your next car:</H1>
<PRE>Model          Doors     Color    Accessories</PRE>
<FORM ACTION="" NAME="orderForm"
 ONSUBMIT="return processOrder()">
<SELECT NAME="model" SIZE="3">
<OPTION>Big Blob</OPTION>
<OPTION>Wild Thing</OPTION>
<OPTION>Penny Pincher</OPTION>
<OPTION>Class Act</OPTION>
</SELECT>
<SELECT NAME="doors" SIZE="3">
<OPTION>2 doors</OPTION>
<OPTION>4 doors</OPTION>
</SELECT>
<SELECT NAME="color" SIZE="3">
<OPTION>red</OPTION>
<OPTION>white</OPTION>
<OPTION>blue</OPTION>
<OPTION>black</OPTION>
```

```
<OPTION>brown</OPTION>
<OPTION>silver</OPTION>
<OPTION>pink</OPTION>
</SELECT>
<SELECT NAME="accessories" SIZE="3" MULTIPLE="MULTIPLE">
<OPTION>air conditioning</OPTION>
<OPTION>CD player</OPTION>
<OPTION>bigger engine</OPTION>
<OPTION>fancy dashboard</OPTION>
<OPTION>leather seats</OPTION>
</SELECT>
<P><INPUT TYPE="SUBMIT" NAME="order" VALUE="I'll take it!"></P>
</FORM>
<FORM ACTION="http://www.jaworski.com/cgi-bin/echo"
      METHOD="POST" NAME="submitForm">
<INPUT TYPE="HIDDEN" NAME="result">
</FORM>
</BODY>
</HTML>
```

FIGURE 7.7

The form that is presented to the user (Listing 7.3)

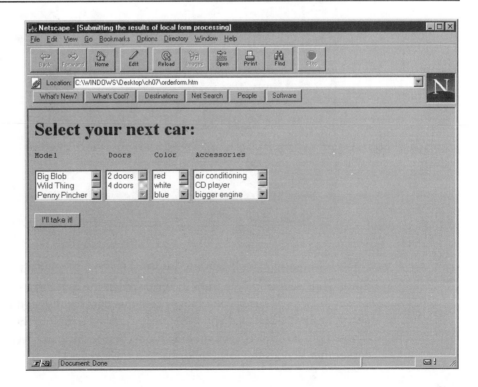

When the first form is submitted, the `onSubmit` event handler invokes the `processOrder()` function as the argument of a `return` statement. If the `return` statement returns *false* then the form is not submitted. If the `return` statement returns *true* then the form *is* submitted. Since `processOrder()` *always* returns *false*, the form will never be submitted. Instead, `processOrder()` fills in the invisible field in the second form and submits the second form to a CGI program located on my Web server. This CGI program is located at the URL *http://www.jaworski.com/ cgi-bin/echo*. It merely echoes back any form fields that it has received from the browser. Figure 7.8 provides an example of the CGI program's output.

FIGURE 7.8

The form data that is echoed by the Web server (Listing 7.3)

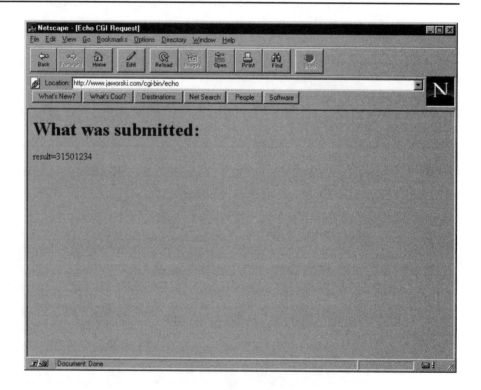

Let's summarize what we've covered so far. The first form is used to gather automobile selection data from the user. When the first form is submitted, `processOrder()` is invoked to process this data locally on the user's browser. `processOrder()` then inserts the processed data into the second form (named `submitForm`) and submits the second form to my Web server. The Web server then echoes the form fields back to the browser.

The processing performed by processOrder() is quite simple, but it illustrates how locally processed form data can be sent to a Web server. Here are the steps:

1. processOrder() begins by setting the order variable to a string that contains the indices of the list items selected in the model, doors, and colors selection lists. Each of these three lists is a single-selection list.

2. For each item in the multiple-selection accessories list, processOrder() checks to see if the item has been selected, and appends the index of each selected accessories item to the string stored in the order variable.

3. It then sets the invisible results field of submitForm to the value stored in order. By doing so, it has placed all of the first form's results into a single field in submitForm.

4. It then invokes the submit() method of submitForm to send the result field to my Web server.

While you may not be impressed by the complexity of the processing performed by processOrder(), you should realize the value of the approach that it takes. This approach allows you to design your forms so that they are most appealing to your end users. When the user submits a filled-out form, you can process the form's results and send the results to your Web server in whatever format is most efficient for your CGI or other server-side programs.

Summary

This chapter introduced the form object and discussed the JavaScript objects that are associated with form fields and GUI controls. It showed you how to use the properties and methods of these objects and how to handle form-related events. In the next chapter, you will learn how to enhance your forms by using hidden form fields and "cookies."

CHAPTER
EIGHT

8

Hidden Fields and Cookies

The Web was originally designed to be *stateless*, in the sense that all Web servers would process URL requests in the same manner, independent of any previous requests. This enabled the first Web servers to be fast and efficient by not requiring them to maintain information about the browsers requesting URLs. Browsers also operated in a stateless fashion, processing new URL requests independent of previous requests.

The stateless design of the Web works well in most cases. When a browser requests a particular Web page, the Web server that provides that page will serve it up to the browser in the same way every time. Similarly, all Web browsers requesting a particular Web page always request that page in the same way. However, there are situations in which you *want* the processing of one Web page to be dependent on the processing of previous pages. For example, you may want to enable a user to complete a series of forms where the user's responses to the first form determine which forms are provided next. For example, you may want to create a form that collects general information about the user, such as name and address, and link it to subsequent forms to collect more information, but those forms will vary depending on what country the user has entered in the first form.

A number of capabilities have been successively introduced to enable Web applications to be built upon the stateless design of the Web. *Hidden form fields* were introduced first, followed by HTTP "*cookies.*" These capabilities were introduced to allow CGI programs to maintain information about individual Web browsers. With JavaScript's support of browser-side scripting, the use of hidden fields and cookies can be taken to new levels.

In this chapter you'll learn how to use hidden fields and cookies to maintain browser state information and how you can use this information in your scripts to develop more capable and powerful Web applications. When you've finished this chapter you'll be able to read and update hidden fields and cookies using JavaScript, and locally implement on the browser side much of the complex state-related processing that would otherwise be performed by server-side CGI programs.

Maintaining State Information

To gain a greater understanding of the problem of maintaining state information, let's explore the example discussed in this chapter's introduction. Suppose that you want to develop a Web page that presents a related series of forms to a user as follows:

- Form 1. Collects the user's name, address, phone number, and e-mail address.

- Form 2. Asks the user which of your products he or she currently uses.

- Form 3. Asks the user to evaluate the products that he or she uses.

Say the user receives the first form, fills it out and submits it. It goes to a CGI program located on your Web server. This CGI program processes the form's data and sends the second form to the user. The user fills out the second form and submits it. It goes to the same or perhaps a different CGI program on your server. When this CGI program receives the second form's data it has no way of knowing that the second form's data is related to the data of the first form, and so it cannot combine the results of the two forms in its database. The same problem occurs with the CGI program that receives the third form's data.

There is a work-around to this problem. You can have the user enter some small piece of common information, like his e-mail address, in all three forms. When the second and third forms are submitted to your Web server, then a CGI program can combine their data based upon the common e-mail address. This work-around allows your CGI programs to continue to operate in a stateless manner. However, your users suffer by having to reenter their e-mail address in all three forms. While this may not seem to be much of an inconvenience, it is noticeable, and it detracts from the appeal of your forms.

What would be even better is if somehow your CGI program could remember the e-mail address that was entered into the first form and attach it to the second and third forms that it sends to your browser. *Hidden form fields* were invented to provide CGI programs with this specific capability.

Using Hidden Form Fields

Hidden form fields are text fields that are not displayed and cannot be modified by a user. Forms with hidden fields are dynamically generated by CGI programs as the result of processing data submitted by other forms.

A CGI program sets a hidden field to a particular value when the server sends a form to a browser. When a user fills out and submits a form containing a hidden field, the value originally stored in the field is returned to the server. The server uses the information stored in the hidden field to maintain state information about the user's browser. To see how this works, let's examine how hidden fields can be used in the three-form example discussed in the previous section.

When a user fills out the name and address information and submits form 1, the CGI program on your server processes the form data by creating a record in a database and sending form 2 back to the user. However, instead of sending a static form 2, it dynamically *generates* a form 2 that contains a hidden field, with the field's value set to the e-mail address that was submitted in the first form.

When the user fills out and submits form 2, the hidden field (still with the user's e-mail address) is sent to your CGI program. Your CGI program can now relate the data of the second form with that of the first, because they both have the same value in the e-mail address field (even though the user did not have to retype their e-mail address in the second form). The same process is carried out for the third form, after which the CGI program sends back a Web page to the user, thanking him or her for filling out the forms.

JavaScript and Hidden Form Fields

At this point, you are probably wondering what any of this has to do with JavaScript. JavaScript's browser-side programming features take full advantage of and enhance the capabilities provided by hidden fields. With JavaScript, you can eliminate the need to send three forms back and forth between the user's browser and your CGI programs. A JavaScript script can perform the processing of all three forms locally on the user's browser and then consolidate the forms' results before sending them to a CGI program.

To see how JavaScript can use hidden fields to implement our three-form customer survey, open the `survey.htm` file with your browser. Your browser will display the first form of a three-form series, as shown in Figure 8.1. Fill out this form and click the Next button. Make sure you that you fill in the *E-mail address* field; otherwise you will receive the alert message shown in Figure 8.2.

FIGURE 8.1

The first form of the customer survey asks the user to enter general name and address information. (Listing 8.3)

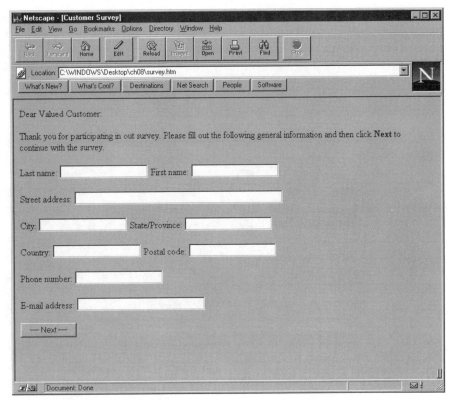

FIGURE 8.2

If the user skips the *E-mail address* field, the form validation alert notifies the user that this information is necessary. (Listing 8.3)

After you click the Next button, the form shown in Figure 8.3 is displayed. This form asks you to identify which products you use. Click on the check box of at least one of these fictitious products.

FIGURE 8.3

The second form of the customer survey asks users what products they use. (Listing 8.4)

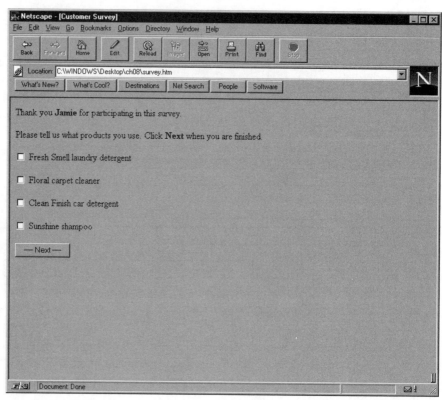

> **NOTE** If you do not select at least one of the four products, the third part of the form will be skipped.

After you click the Next button of the second form, the third form is displayed, as shown in Figure 8.4. The third form asks you to evaluate the products that you selected in the second form. Use the radio buttons to perform your product evaluation.

When you click the Next button on the third form, all of the values of the three forms are collectively sent to the CGI program located at *http://www.jaworski.com/cgi-bin/thanks*. This CGI program reads these values and then sends back the thank-you message shown in Figure 8.5.

FIGURE 8.4

The third form of the customer survey asks customers how they like the products. (Listing 8.5)

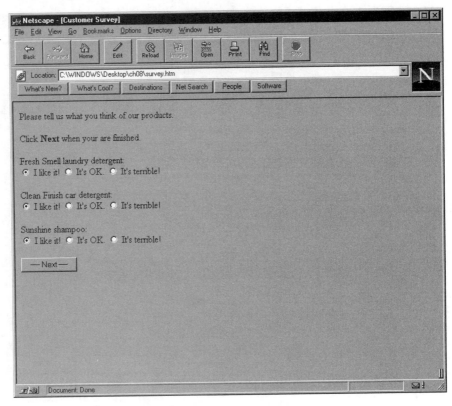

The processing performed in the example all takes place on the user's browser. A CGI program is not required until after all three forms have been filled out. The values of these forms are stored in a separate invisible form that consists entirely of hidden fields. As the user completes each form, the values of the current form are stored in the hidden fields of the invisible form. When the user has completed the third form (or completed the second form without checking any products) the invisible form is submitted to the CGI program. This is much more efficient than having a CGI program process the results of each form separately.

TIP   If you were creating a real survey, you would dress up the form with graphics and a catchier layout.

FIGURE 8.5

The thank-you message is displayed after the user completes the survey.

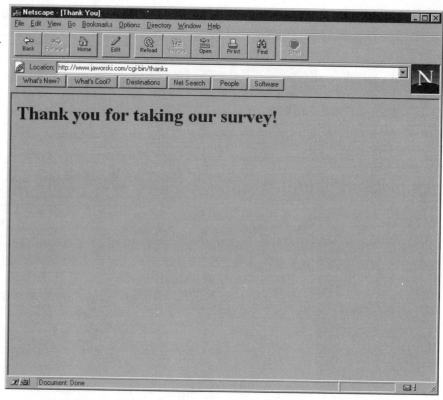

The survey.htm file shown in Listing 8.1 defines a two-frame set. The first frame loads the file form1.htm (Listing 8.3) and the second frame loads control.htm (Listing 8.2). The border attribute of the frame set is set to 0 to avoid displaying a distracting border between frames.

Listing 8.1. Defining the survey's frame set (survey.htm)

```
<HTML>
<HEAD>
<TITLE>Customer Survey</TITLE>
</HEAD>
<FRAMESET COLS="*,10" BORDER=0>
<FRAME SRC="form1.htm">
<FRAME SRC="control.htm">
</FRAMESET>
</HTML>
```

Listing 8.2. The survey's hidden form (control.htm)

```
<HTML>
<HEAD>
<SCRIPT LANGUAGE="JavaScript"><!--
// --></SCRIPT>
</HEAD>
<BODY>
<FORM ACTION="http://www.jaworski.com/cgi-bin/thanks"
 NAME="controlForm"
 METHOD="post" TARGET="_top">
<INPUT TYPE="HIDDEN" NAME="lastName" VALUE="">
<INPUT TYPE="HIDDEN" NAME="firstName" VALUE="">
<INPUT TYPE="HIDDEN" NAME="street" VALUE="">
<INPUT TYPE="HIDDEN" NAME="city" VALUE="">
<INPUT TYPE="HIDDEN" NAME="state" VALUE="">
<INPUT TYPE="HIDDEN" NAME="country" VALUE="">
<INPUT TYPE="HIDDEN" NAME="zip" VALUE="">
<INPUT TYPE="HIDDEN" NAME="phone" VALUE="">
<INPUT TYPE="HIDDEN" NAME="email" VALUE="">
<INPUT TYPE="HIDDEN" NAME="products" VALUE="">
<INPUT TYPE="HIDDEN" NAME="evaluation" VALUE="">
</FORM>
</BODY>
</HTML>
```

The control.htm file defines a form with 11 hidden fields. Since all of the form's fields are hidden, the form is not displayed. These fields are filled in with the data collected by the three visible forms that are displayed to the user.

The form's NAME attribute is set to "controlForm". This allows the form to be referenced by name by the JavaScript code that executes with the forms contained in the first frame.

The form's ACTION attribute is set to the URL of my CGI program and its METHOD attribute is set to "post". When the form is submitted, this CGI program receives the data that has been stored in the hidden fields and returns a thank-you message to the user. The form's TARGET attribute is "_top". This causes the thank-you message to be displayed in the full window occupied by survey.htm rather than in the frame occupied by control.htm.

The form1.htm file displays the form shown in Figure 8.1 in the first frame of the frame set. It contains a single script that defines the processForm1() function. This function handles the onClick event that is generated when the user clicks on the Next button. It sets the form1 variable to document.form1 so that it can be used as a shortcut (to avoid having to retype the `document` prefix). It then checks to see if the `email` field is blank. If it is blank then it displays an alert dialog box to the user, otherwise it continues on with its processing. The `controlForm` variable is used as a shortcut to the hidden form stored in the second frame. All of the fields from `form1` are then copied into the hidden fields of `controlForm`. Finally, the `form2.htm` (Listing 8.4) file is loaded into the first frame and `form2` replaces `form1`.

Listing 8.3. The first form of the survey (form1.htm)

```
<HTML>
<HEAD>
<TITLE>Customer Survey: General Information</TITLE>
<SCRIPT LANGUAGE="JavaScript"><!--
function processForm1() {
 form1 = document.form1
 if(form1.email.value=="")
  alert("You must fill in your e-mail address!")
 else {
  controlForm = parent.frames[1].document.controlForm
  controlForm.lastName.value=form1.lastName.value
  controlForm.firstName.value=form1.firstName.value
  controlForm.street.value=form1.street.value
  controlForm.city.value=form1.city.value
  controlForm.state.value=form1.state.value
  controlForm.country.value=form1.country.value
  controlForm.zip.value=form1.zip.value
  controlForm.phone.value=form1.phone.value
  controlForm.email.value=form1.email.value
  location.href="form2.htm"
 }
}
// --></SCRIPT>
</HEAD>
<BODY>
<P>Dear Valued Customer:</P>
<P>Thank you for participating in our survey. Please fill out
 the following general information and then click <B>Next</B> to
 continue with the survey.</P>
<FORM ACTION="" NAME="form1">
<P>Last name: <INPUT TYPE="TEXT" NAME="lastName">
 First name: <INPUT TYPE="TEXT" NAME="firstName"></P>
<P>Street address: <INPUT TYPE="TEXT" SIZE="50" NAME="street">
 </P>
```

```
<P>City: <INPUT TYPE="TEXT" NAME="city">
 State/Province: <INPUT TYPE="TEXT" NAME="state"></P>
<P>Country: <INPUT TYPE="TEXT" NAME="country">
 Postal code: <INPUT TYPE="TEXT" NAME="zip"></P>
<P>Phone number: <INPUT TYPE="TEXT" NAME="phone"></P>
<P>E-mail address: <INPUT TYPE="TEXT" SIZE="30" NAME="email">
 </P>
<P></P>
<INPUT TYPE="BUTTON" NAME="next" VALUE="---- Next ----"
 onClick="processForm1()">
</FORM>
</BODY>
</HTML>
```

The `form2.htm` file displays the form shown in Figure 8.3. It contains two scripts—one in the document head and the other in the document body. The script in the document body is executed when the Web page is generated. This script is used to insert the first name of the user into the text that is displayed above the form.

Listing 8.4. The second form of the survey (form2.htm)

```
<HTML>
<HEAD>
<TITLE>Customer Survey: Product Usage</TITLE>
<SCRIPT LANGUAGE="JavaScript"><!--
function processForm2() {
 controlForm = parent.frames[1].document.controlForm
 form2 = document.form2
 products = ""
 if(form2.laundry.checked) products += "1"
 else products += "0"
 if(form2.carpet.checked) products += "1"
 else products += "0"
 if(form2.car.checked) products += "1"
 else products += "0"
 if(form2.shampoo.checked) products += "1"
 else products += "0"
 controlForm.products.value=products
 location.href="form3.htm"
}
// --></SCRIPT>
</HEAD>
<BODY>
<SCRIPT LANGUAGE="JavaScript"><!--
```

```
document.write("<P>Thank you <B>"+parent.frames[1].document
  .controlForm.firstName.value+"</B> ")
document.writeln("for participating in this survey.</P>")
// --></SCRIPT>
<P>Please tell us what products you use. Click <B>Next</B> when you are
finished.</P>
<FORM NAME="form2">
<P><INPUT TYPE="CHECKBOX" NAME="laundry"> Fresh Smell laundry
  detergent</P>
<P><INPUT TYPE="CHECKBOX" NAME="carpet"> Floral carpet cleaner</P>
<P><INPUT TYPE="CHECKBOX" NAME="car"> Clean Finish car detergent</P>
<P><INPUT TYPE="CHECKBOX" NAME="shampoo"> Sunshine shampoo</P>
<P></P>
<P><INPUT TYPE="BUTTON" NAME="next" VALUE="---- Next ----"
onClick="processForm2()"></P>
</FORM>
</BODY>
</HTML>
```

The script in the document head defines the processForm2() function. This function handles the onClick event that is generated when the user clicks on the Next button. It sets the hidden products field of controlForm based upon the products the user has checked off. It then loads form3.htm (Listing 8.5) as the replacement for form2.htm in the first frame.

Listing 8.5. The third form of the survey (form3.htm)

```
<HTML>
<HEAD>
<TITLE>Customer Survey: Product Evaluation</TITLE>
<SCRIPT LANGUAGE="JavaScript"><!--
function usesProducts() {
 productsUsed = parent.frames[1].document.controlForm.products.value
 usage = new Array(productsUsed.length)
 productsInUse=false
 for(i=0;i<usage.length;++i) {
  if(productsUsed.charAt(i)=="0") usage[i]=false
  else{
   usage[i]=true
   productsInUse=true
  }
 }
 return productsInUse
}
```

```
function askAboutProducts() {
 document.writeln('<P>Please tell us what you think of our
  products.</P>')
 document.writeln('<P>Click <B>Next</B> when your are
  finished.</P>')
 document.writeln('<FORM NAME="form3">')
 if(usage[0]){
  document.writeln('<P>Fresh Smell laundry detergent:<BR>')
  document.writeln('<INPUT TYPE="RADIO" NAME="laundry"')
  document.writeln('VALUE="like" CHECKED> I like it!')
  document.writeln('<INPUT TYPE="RADIO" NAME="laundry"')
  document.writeln('VALUE="ok"> It\'s OK.')
  document.writeln('<INPUT TYPE="RADIO" NAME="laundry"')
  document.writeln('VALUE="dislike"> It\'s terrible!')
  document.writeln('</P>')
 }
 if(usage[1]){
  document.writeln('<P>Floral carpet cleaner:<BR>')
  document.writeln('<INPUT TYPE="RADIO" NAME="carpet"')
  document.writeln('VALUE="like" CHECKED> I like it!')
  document.writeln('<INPUT TYPE="RADIO" NAME="carpet"')
  document.writeln('VALUE="ok"> It\'s OK.')
  document.writeln('<INPUT TYPE="RADIO" NAME="carpet"')
  document.writeln('VALUE="dislike"> It\'s terrible!')
  document.writeln('</P>')
 }
 if(usage[2]){
  document.writeln('<P>Clean Finish car detergent:<BR>')
  document.writeln('<INPUT TYPE="RADIO" NAME="car"')
  document.writeln('VALUE="like" CHECKED> I like it!')
  document.writeln('<INPUT TYPE="RADIO" NAME="car"')
  document.writeln('VALUE="ok"> It\'s OK.')
  document.writeln('<INPUT TYPE="RADIO" NAME="car"')
  document.writeln('VALUE="dislike"> It\'s terrible!')
  document.writeln('</P>')
 }
 if(usage[3]){
  document.writeln('<P>Sunshine shampoo:<BR>')
  document.writeln('<INPUT TYPE="RADIO" NAME="shampoo"')
  document.writeln('VALUE="like" CHECKED> I like it!')
  document.writeln('<INPUT TYPE="RADIO" NAME="shampoo"')
  document.writeln('VALUE="ok"> It\'s OK.')
  document.writeln('<INPUT TYPE="RADIO" NAME="shampoo"')
  document.writeln('VALUE="dislike"> It\'s terrible!')
  document.writeln('</P>')
```

```
          }
          document.writeln('<P></P><P>')
          document.writeln('<INPUT TYPE="BUTTON" NAME="next"')
          document.writeln('VALUE="---- Next ----" ')
          document.writeln(' onClick="processForm3()"></P>')
          document.writeln('</FORM>')
         }
         function processForm3() {
          controlForm = parent.frames[1].document.controlForm
          form3 = document.form3
          evaluation = ""
          for(i=0;i<form3.elements.length-1;++i)
           if(form3.elements[i].checked)
            evaluation += form3.elements[i].value + " "
          controlForm.evaluation.value=evaluation
          controlForm.submit()
         }
         // --></SCRIPT>
         </HEAD>
         <BODY>
         <SCRIPT LANGUAGE="JavaScript"><!--
         if(usesProducts()) askAboutProducts()
         else parent.frames[1].document.controlForm.submit()
         // --></SCRIPT>
         </BODY>
         </HTML>
```

The form3.htm file, unlike form1.htm and form2.htm, consists almost entirely of JavaScript code. Most of the code is contained in the script located in the document's head. A small script is contained in the document's body. This script invokes the usesProducts() function to determine whether the user had checked any products when he filled out form2. If the user had checked at least one product then the askAboutProducts() function is invoked to generate form3. Otherwise, the controlForm is submitted as is, without the user having to fill in form3.

The script in the document head defines three functions: usesProducts(), askAboutProducts(), and processForm3(). These functions perform the following processing.

usesProducts() This function checks the hidden products field of control-Form to determine what products the user checked off when filling in form2. It initializes the usage array based upon this information. It sets productsInUse to *true* if the user has checked off any products in form2 and to *false* otherwise. It then returns this value as a result.

askAboutProducts()   This function generates the HTML content of `form3`. It creates a short text introduction to the form, generates the `<form>` tag, and then generates a set of three radio buttons for each product the user selected in `form2`. It then generates a Next button for the form, setting the form's `onClick` event handler to `processForm3()`. Finally, it generates the closing `</form>` tag.

processForm3()   This function handles the `onClick` event generated when the user clicks on the Next button after filling out form3. It summarizes the radio buttons checked by the user and stores this summary in the hidden `evaluation` field of `controlForm`. It then submits the data contained in `controlForm`.

Cookies

Hidden form fields were introduced to enable CGI programs to maintain state information about Web browsers. They work well in situations where the state information is to be maintained for a short period of time, as is the case when a user fills out a series of forms. However, hidden fields do not allow state information to be maintained in a *persistent* manner. That is, hidden fields can only be used within a single browser session. When a user exits the browser, the information contained in a hidden form field is lost forever.

Netscape developed the *cookie* as a means to store state-related and other information in a persistent manner. The information stored in a cookie is maintained between browser sessions; it survives when the user turns off their machine. Cookies allow CGI programs to store information on Web browsers for significantly longer time periods.

A cookie consists of information sent by a server-side program in response to a URL request by the browser. The browser stores the information in the `cookies.txt` file ("the cookie jar") according to the URL of the CGI program sending the cookie. This URL may be generalized, based upon additional information contained in the cookie.

When a browser requests a URL from a Web server, the browser first searches `cookies.txt` to see if the URL of any of its cookies matches the URL that it is requesting. The browser then sends, as part of the URL request, the Web server the information contained in the matching cookie or cookies.

Cookies provide CGI programs with the capability to store information on browsers. Browsers return this information to CGI programs when they request the URL of the CGI program. CGI programs update cookies when they respond to browser URL requests. In this manner, a CGI program can use browsers to maintain state information and have the browsers return this information whenever they invoke the CGI program.

To get a better feel for how cookies work, let's revisit the three-form example introduced in the beginning of this chapter. The goal is to implement a sequence of forms where each form expands upon the information gathered in previous forms. In order to do this, a CGI program must be able to relate the data received in later forms with that received in earlier forms. The solution is for the CGI program to identify related forms using data that is common to these forms. A person's e-mail address is a common example of this identifying data.

Cookies provide a persistent mechanism for storing identifying data. When a browser submits form 1 to a CGI program, the CGI program responds by sending form 2 to the browser. A cookie containing the user's e-mail address accompanies this second form. When the browser submits form 2, it returns any cookies that match the CGI program to which the form is submitted. This causes the user's e-mail address to be returned with the submitted form 2 data. The CGI program then sends form 3 to the browser. When the user submits form 3, the browser again checks `cookies.txt` and sends any related cookies.

Cookies are obviously more powerful than hidden form fields. Since cookies persist between browser sessions, they may be used to store permanent user data, such as identification information (e-mail address) and preferences (frames, background colors, etc.), as well as state information (the current page in an online book).

How Is Information Stored in a Cookie?

A cookie is created when a CGI program includes a Set-Cookie header as part of an HTTP response. This response is generated when a browser requests the URL of the CGI program. The syntax of the Set-Cookie header is:

```
Set-Cookie: NAME=VALUE
[; expires=DATE] [; path=PATH] [; domain=DOMAIN_NAME] [; secure]
```

The *NAME=VALUE* field is required. The other fields are optional; however, they should all appear on the same line as the Set-Cookie header.

NOTE More than one Set-Cookie header may be sent in a single HTTP response.

NAME=VALUE This field contains the essential data being stored in a cookie. For example, when used to store my e-mail address it could appear as `email=jamie@jaworski.com`. A semicolon, comma, or white-space character is not allowed in the *NAME=VALUE* string. Applications are free to develop their own encoding scheme for these strings.

expires=DATE This field specifies the expiration date of a cookie. If it is omitted then the cookie expires at the end of the current browser session. The date is specified in the following format:

```
Weekday, DD-Mon-YY HH:MM:SS GMT
```

Weekday is the day of the week. *DD* is the day of the month. *Mon* is the first three letters of the month. *YY* is the year (e.g., 97). *HH* is hours. *MM* is minutes. *SS* is seconds. The GMT time zone is always used. An example date is:

```
Friday, 20-Sep-96 12:00:00 GMT
```

The above date is noon GMT on September 20th, 1996.

TIP Cookies that specify long-term user preferences should specify an expiration date of several years to help ensure that the cookies will be available as needed in the future. Cookies that specify short-term state information should expire in days, at which point the expired (stale) cookies are automatically destroyed.

domain=DOMAIN_NAME When a cookie is stored in the `cookies.txt` file, it is organized by the URL of the CGI program that sent the cookie. The `domain` field is used to specify a more general domain name to which the cookie should apply. For example, suppose the URL of the CGI program that sends a cookie has the domain *athome.jaworski.com*. A `domain=jaworski.com` field in a cookie would associate that cookie with all hosts in the *jaworski.com* domain, not just the single host *athome.jaworski.com*. The domain field cannot be used to associate cookies with top-level domains *.com*, *.mil*, *.edu*, *.net*, *.org*, *.gov*, and *.int*. Any domain name that is not part of the top-level domains (for example, *ca.us*) must include an extra subdomain. For example, *sd.ca.us* is allowed, but *ca.us* is not.

path=PATH This field is used to specify a more general path for the URL associated with a cookie. For example, suppose the URL of a CGI program is *http://www.jaworski.com/cgi-bin/js-examples/ch08/test*. The *path* of that CGI program is /cgi-bin/js-examples/ch08/. In order to associate a cookie with all of my CGI programs in this example, I could set `path=/cgi-bin`.

secure If the `secure` field is specified, then a cookie is only sent over a secure communication channel (HTTPS servers).

When a browser sends matching cookies back to a Web server, it sends an HTTP request header in the following format:

```
Cookie: NAME1=VALUE1; NAME2=VALUE2; ... NAMEN=VALUEN
```

NAME1 through *NAMEN* identify the cookie names and *VALUE1* through *VALUEN* identify their values.

Using JavaScript with Cookies

Cookies provide a powerful feature for Web application development, but using them with CGI programs can be somewhat messy. You have to design your programs to send cookies via the HTTP response header and to receive cookies via the HTTP request header. While this is not difficult to implement, it means that more processing is performed on the server and not on the browser.

JavaScript, on the other hand, can take full advantage of cookies by reading and setting them locally on the browser, eliminating the need for the cookies to be processed by CGI programs. A JavaScript script can then forward any information the CGI program requires to perform its processing. By using JavaScript to maintain cookies and perform as much processing as possible on the browser, CGI programs can be greatly simplified, and in most cases, eliminated.

The cookie associated with a document is set using the document's `cookie` property. When you set a cookie you must provide the same cookie fields that would be provide by a CGI program. For example, consider the following statements:

```
email="jamie@jaworski.com"
expirationDate="Thursday, 01-Dec-99 12:00:00 GMT"
document.cookie="email="+email+";expires="+expirationDate
```

These statements set the value of the `cookie` property of the current document to the string `"email=jamie@jaworski.com; expires=Thursday,`

01-Dec-99 12:00:00 GMT". Note that the `expires` field is required to keep the cookie from expiring after the current browser session. `Domain`, `path` and `secure` fields can also be used when a `cookie` property is set.

When the value of the cookie is retrieved using the following statement

```
cookieString=document.cookie
```

the `cookieString` variable will be assigned the value "`email=jamie @jaworski.com`". If multiple cookies had been set for the current document then `cookieString` would contain a list of semicolon-separated *name*=*value* pairs. For example, consider the following statements:

```
email="jamie@jaworski.com"
firstName="Jamie"
lastName="Jaworski"
expirationDate="Thursday, 01-Dec-99 12:00:00 GMT"
document.cookie="email="+email+";expires="+expirationDate
document.cookie="firstName="+firstName
 +";expires="+expirationDate
document.cookie="lastName="+lastName+";expires="+expirationDate
cookieString=document.cookie
```

The value of `cookieString` includes the *name*=*value* pairs of the `email`, `firstName`, and `lastName` cookies. This value is "`email=jamie@jaworski .com; firstName=Jamie; lastName=Jaworski`".

In order to get a feel for how cookies are accessed via JavaScript, run the file `cooktest.htm` shown in Listing 8.6. It will display the form shown in Figure 8.6. This form allows you to enter the text of a cookie and then set the cookie by clicking the Set Cookie button. The new value of the cookie is displayed at the top of the Web page.

Listing 8.6. A cookie test program (cooktest.htm)

```
<HTML>
<HEAD>
<TITLE>Cookie Test</TITLE>
<SCRIPT LANGUAGE="JavaScript"><!--
function updateCookie() {
 document.cookie=document.form1.cookie.value
 location.reload(true)
}
// --></SCRIPT>
```

```
</HEAD>
<BODY>
<SCRIPT LANGUAGE="JavaScript">
 <!--document.write("Your current cookie value is: '"+
   document.cookie+"'")// -->
</SCRIPT>
<FORM ACTION="" NAME="form1">
<P>Enter new cookie: <INPUT TYPE="TEXT" SIZE="60"
 NAME="cookie"></P>
<INPUT TYPE="BUTTON" NAME="setCookie" VALUE="Set Cookie"
 onClick="updateCookie()">
</FORM>
</BODY>
</HTML>
```

FIGURE 8.6

The cookie test program's opening screen tells the user what the current cookie value is and prompts them to enter a new cookie. (Listing 8.6)

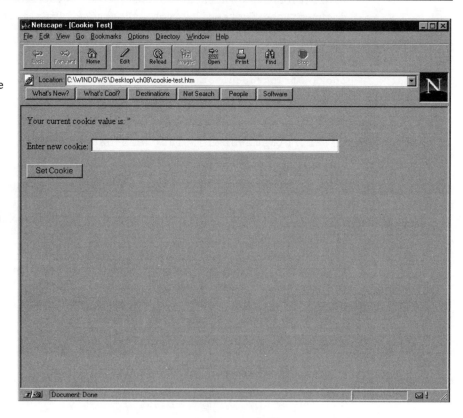

To see how this script works, enter the cookie shown in Figure 8.7 and click on the Set Cookie button. The new cookie is displayed as shown in Figure 8.8. Experiment with this program by entering cookies with different or no expiration dates, terminating your browser, and restarting it to see what cookies have persisted between browser sessions.

FIGURE 8.7

An example of how to enter the text of a cookie (Listing 8.6)

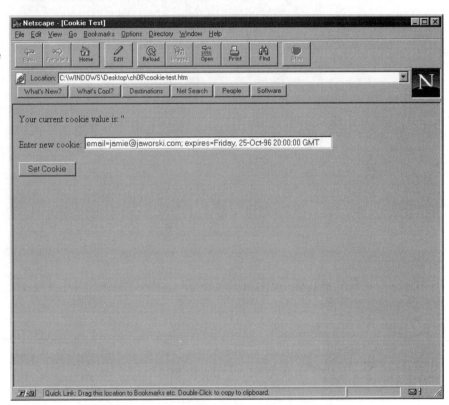

The cookie test program is very simple. This attests to the power and flexibility with which JavaScript supports cookies. The program consists of two scripts—one in the document head and one in the document body. The script in the document body displays the current cookie values that are available to the document. The script in the document head handles the onClick event associated with the Next Cookie button by setting a cookie with the value entered by the user. It then reloads the current cooktest.htm document so that the updated cookie value is displayed. Note that the cookie test program runs locally without the need for a

FIGURE 8.8

When the page reloads, the new cookie is displayed. (Listing 8.6)

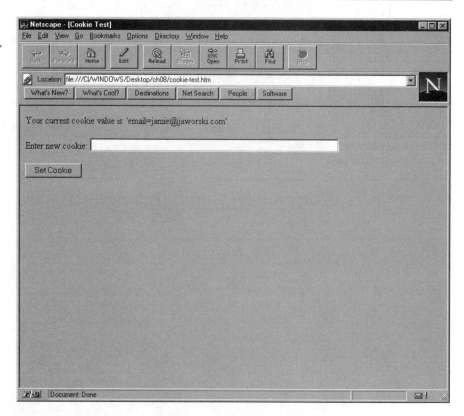

CGI program. For Web applications that do not require you to collect information from users, the combination of JavaScript and cookies can, in many cases, eliminate the need to develop CGI programs.

Example: A History Quiz

As another example of how JavaScript and cookies can be combined to build Web applications that execute entirely on the browser, we'll develop a JavaScript application that quizzes users about their understanding of historical facts.

Open `quiz.htm` with your browser, and it displays the Web page shown in Figure 8.9. Click on the radio button corresponding to the correct answer and then click on the Continue button. The Web page is redisplayed with a new question and an updated score. If you select the wrong answer, you are notified with an alert message and the question is redisplayed. When you have successfully answered all of the questions in the quiz you will be congratulated with the Web page shown in Figure 8.10.

The `quiz.htm` file is shown in Listing 8.7. It consists almost entirely of JavaScript code. This code is organized into three scripts. Two of the scripts are in the document's head and the other, a short script, is located in the document's body. The second script of the document's head loads the JavaScript code contained in the `history.js` file (Listing 8.8), which contains the questions that are used in the quiz. The quiz questions are contained in a separate file so that the quiz can be easily tailored to different sets of questions.

TIP	You can improve the quiz by adding graphics and links to related topics.

FIGURE 8.9

The Quiz Program opening display lists a quiz question and a group of possible answers. (Listing 8.7)

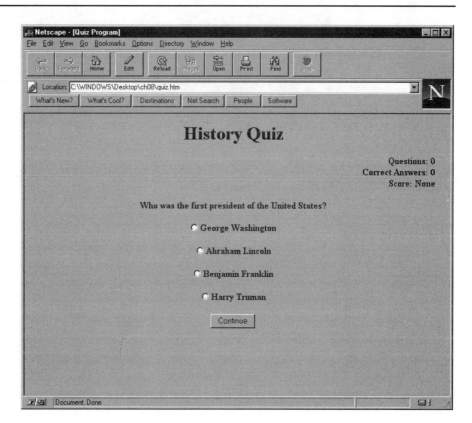

FIGURE 8.10

The Quiz Program final display tells users how well they scored. (Listing 8.7)

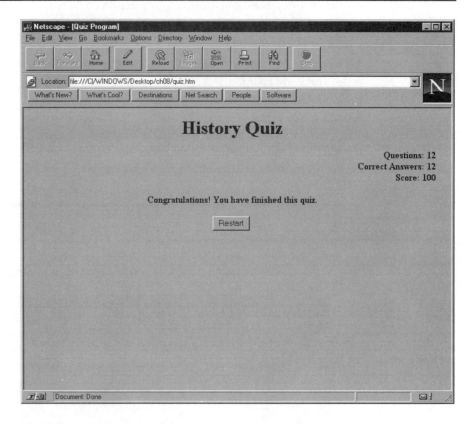

Listing 8.7. Quiz program (quiz.htm)

```
<HTML>
<HEAD>
<TITLE>Quiz Program</TITLE>
<SCRIPT LANGUAGE="JavaScript"><!--
//Question object
function Question() {
 this.question=Question.arguments[0]
 var n=Question.arguments.length
 this.answers = new Array(n-2)
 for(var i=1; i<n-1; ++i) this.answers[i-1]=Question.arguments[i]
 this.correctAnswer=Question.arguments[n-1]
}
```

```
function readCookie() {
 currentQuestion=0
 numberOfQuestions=0
 correctAnswers=0
 score="None"
 cookie=document.cookie
 currentQuestion=getNumberValue(cookie,"currentQuestion")
 numberOfQuestions=getNumberValue(cookie,"numberOfQuestions")
 correctAnswers=getNumberValue(cookie,"correctAnswers")
 if(numberOfQuestions>0) score=Math.round(correctAnswers*100/ numberOfQuestions)
}
function getNumberValue(s,n) {
 s=removeBlanks(s)
 var pairs=s.split(";")
 for(var i=0;i<pairs.length;++i) {
  var pairSplit=pairs[i].split("=")
  if(pairSplit[0]==n) {
   if(pairSplit.length>1) return parseInt(pairSplit[1])
   else return 0
  }
 }
 return 0
}
function removeBlanks(s) {
 var temp=""
 for(var i=0;i<s.length;++i) {
  var c=s.charAt(i)
  if(c!=" ") temp += c
 }
 return temp
}
function askNextQuestion() {
 document.writeln("<H4 ALIGN='CENTER'>"+qa[currentQuestion].question+"</H4>")
 displayAnswers()
}
function displayAnswers() {
 document.writeln('<FORM NAME="answerForm">')
 for(var ii=0;ii<qa[currentQuestion].answers.length;++ii) {
  document.writeln('<H4 ALIGN="CENTER">')
  document.writeln('<INPUT TYPE="RADIO" NAME="answer">'
   +qa[currentQuestion].answers[ii])
```

```
  if(ii+1==qa[currentQuestion].answers.length) {
   document.writeln('<BR><BR><INPUT TYPE="BUTTON" NAME="continue"
    VALUE="Continue" ')
   document.writeln(' onClick="checkAnswers()">')
  }
  document.writeln('</H4>')
 }
 document.writeln('</FORM>')
}
function checkAnswers() {
 var numAnswers=qa[currentQuestion].answers.length
 var correctAnswer=qa[currentQuestion].correctAnswer
 for(var jj=0;jj<numAnswers;++jj) {
  if(document.answerForm.elements[jj].checked) {
   if(jj==correctAnswer){
    correct()
     break
   }else{
     incorrect()
     break
   }
  }
  if(jj==numAnswers){
   incorrect()
   break
  }
 }
}
function correct() {
 ++currentQuestion
 ++numberOfQuestions
 ++correctAnswers
 updateCookie()
 location="quiz.htm"
}
function incorrect() {
 ++numberOfQuestions
 updateCookie()
 alert("Incorrect!")
 location="quiz.htm"
}
```

```
function updateCookie() {
 document.cookie="currentQuestion="+currentQuestion
 document.cookie="numberOfQuestions="+numberOfQuestions
 document.cookie="correctAnswers="+correctAnswers
}
function endQuiz() {
 document.cookie="currentQuestion=0"
 document.cookie="numberOfQuestions=0"
 document.cookie="correctAnswers=0"
 document.writeln('<FORM NAME="finishedForm">')
 document.write("<H4 ALIGN='CENTER'>")
 document.write("Congratulations! You have finished this quiz.")
 document.writeln('<BR><BR><INPUT TYPE="BUTTON" NAME="restart"
 VALUE="Restart" ')
 document.writeln(' onClick="restartQuiz()">')
 document.writeln("</H4>")
 document.writeln('</FORM>')
}
function restartQuiz() {
 location="quiz.htm"
}
// --></SCRIPT>
<SCRIPT LANGUAGE="JavaScript" SRC="history.js"><!--
// --></SCRIPT>
</HEAD>
<BODY>
<SCRIPT LANGUAGE="JavaScript"><!--
readCookie()
document.writeln("<H1 ALIGN='CENTER'>"+pageHeading+"</H1>")
document.writeln("<P ALIGN='RIGHT'><B>Questions:
 "+numberOfQuestions+"<BR>")
document.writeln("Correct Answers: "+correctAnswers+"<BR>")
document.writeln("Score: "+score+"</B></P>")
if(currentQuestion >= qa.length) endQuiz()
else askNextQuestion()
// --></SCRIPT>
</BODY>
</HTML>
```

We'll examine the code contained in the body of quiz.htm and then study the code in the document's head. After that we'll cover history.js.

Body Code

The code in the body of `quiz.htm` is very short. The `readCookie()` function is invoked to read the cookies associated with the document and use the cookie's *name=value* pairs to initialize the script's variables to the current state of the quiz. The cookies contain the number of the current question, the number of questions asked so far, and the number of correct answers. Next, the script creates a document heading based on the value of the `pageHeading` variable. (The `pageHeading` variable is initialized in `history.js`.)

The number of questions asked, number of correct answers, and quiz score are then displayed. The script checks to see if the value of `currentQuestion` is equal to or greater than the length of the `qa` array. (The `qa` array is also defined in `history.js`.) It is used to store all of the quiz's questions and answers. If the `currentQuestion` variable is greater than or equal to the length of the `qa` array, then all questions have been asked and the `endQuiz()` function is invoked to end the quiz. Otherwise, the `askNextQuestion()` function is invoked to present the user with another question.

Head Code

The first script in the head of `quiz.htm` defines twelve functions. These functions are used as follows:

Question() This function is used in `history.js` to create `Question` objects. It uses the `arguments` property of the `function` object to determine how many arguments were passed in the `Question()` invocation. The first argument is the text of the question. The last argument is an integer that identifies the correct answer. All arguments between the first and the last are used to define the answers to a question.

readCookie() This function reads the cookies of the current document and sets the `currentQuestion`, `numberOfQuestions`, and `correctAnswers` variables. It then uses these values to calculate the value of the `score` variable.

getNumberValue() This function is used by `readCookie()` to parse the cookie string `s` and return the value associated with a particular name `n`. It does this by removing all blanks from `s` and then splitting `s` by means of the field separator "`;`". Having separated the string into *name=value* fields, it then separates these fields by "`=`". It checks to see if the name component of the split field matches `n`, and returns the value associated with the name as an integer. If the name does not have a value it returns 0.

removeBlanks() This function removes all blanks contained in a string and returns this value as a result.

askNextQuestion() This function displays the current question in a centered level-4 heading. It then invokes `displayAnswers()` to display the possible answers associated with this question.

displayAnswers() This function displays the possible answers of the current question as a form. A radio button is displayed with each answer. A Continue button follows the answers. The Continue button's `onClick` event handler is set to the `checkAnswers()` function.

checkAnswers() This function is invoked when a user answers a question and clicks on the Continue button. It determines how many answers are associated with a question and then checks the radio button of each answer to see if it is checked. When it finds a checked button it determines whether the checked button is the correct answer. If the answer is correct it invokes the `correct()` function; otherwise it invokes the `incorrect()` function. If no radio buttons have been clicked the `incorrect()` function is invoked.

correct() This function increments the `currentQuestion, numberOf-Questions`, and `correctAnswers` variables and invokes `updateCookie()` to write the values of these variables to the document's cookie jar. It then reloads the `quiz.htm` file to process the next question.

incorrect() This function increments the `numberOfQuestions` variable and invokes `updateCookie()` to write the value of this variable to the document's cookie jar. It then reloads the `quiz.htm` file to reprocess the same question.

updateCookie() This function uses the document's cookie jar to temporarily store the program's state while the `quiz.htm` file is reloaded. It stores the values of the `currentQuestion, numberOfQuestions`, and `correctAnswers` variables.

endQuiz() This function ends the quiz by setting the document's cookies back to their initial state. It then displays a form that congratulates the user for finishing the quiz, and displays a Restart button so that the user can restart the quiz if they wish. The `onClick` event handler for the Restart button is `restartQuiz()`.

restartQuiz() This function handles the clicking of the Restart button by reloading the `quiz.htm` file so that the quiz may be restarted.

The Source File

Having gone through the description of `quiz.htm`, the `history.js` file is easy to understand. It defines the `pageHeading` variable that is used to display the heading on each quiz page. It then creates the `qa` array. Each element of `qa` is a `Question` object. Twelve questions are defined. Feel free to add your own questions or delete the ones that I've created—you can change the entire content of the quiz by modifying `history.js`. You can also substitute your own question file for `history.js` by modifying the `SRC` attribute value of the second script of `quiz.htm`.

This example showed how JavaScript can use cookies to create a complex Web application without the use of a CGI program. All of the cookie processing was performed locally on the browser.

Listing 8.8. Quiz questions (history.js)

```
//Heading displayed on the quiz page
pageHeading="History Quiz"

//Questions
qa = new Array()
qa[0] = new Question("Who was the first president
  of the United States?",
 "George Washington",
 "Abraham Lincoln",
 "Benjamin Franklin",
 "Harry Truman",
 0)
qa[1] = new Question("When did Columbus discover America?",
 "1249",
 "1942",
 "1492",
 "1294",
 2)
qa[2] = new Question("Who commanded the Macedonian army?",
 "Napoleon",
 "Alexander the Great",
 "Cleopatra",
 "George Patton",
 1)
qa[3] = new Question("Where did Davy Crockett lose his life?",
 "The Spanish Inquisition",
```

```
        "The Alamo",
        "Miami, Florida",
        "On the Oregon Trail",
        1)
    qa[4] = new Question("Who was the first man to
        walk on the moon?",
        "Louis Armstrong",
        "Buzz Armstrong",
        "Jack Armstrong",
        "Neil Armstrong",
        3)
    qa[5] = new Question("Who wrote the <I>Scarlet Letter</I>?",
        "Michael Crichton",
        "Ernest Hemingway",
        "Nathaniel Hawthorne",
        "Charles Dickens",
        2)
    qa[6] = new Question("Eli Whitney invented:",
        "Mad Cow's Disease",
        "the Cotton Gin",
        "whisky",
        "the automobile",
        1)
    qa[7] = new Question("Who was known as the King of the Fauves?",
        "Salvatore Dali",
        "Henri Matisse",
        "Pablo Picasso",
        "Vincent Van Gogh",
        1)
    qa[8] = new Question("Who discovered the force of gravity?",
        "Isaac Newton",
        "Galileo",
        "Copernicus",
        "Albert Einstein"
        ,0)
    qa[9] = new Question("Who created HTML?",
        "Tim Berners-Lee",
        "Marc Andreessen",
        "Bill Gates",
        "Jim Barksdale",
        0)
    qa[10] = new Question("Leonardo da Vinci was born in Greece.",
```

```
"True",
"False",
1)
qa[11] = new Question("Louisiana was purchased from France.",
"True",
"False",
0)
```

Comparison: Cookies vs. Hidden Form Fields

Now that you've learned how both hidden fields and cookies can be used to maintain state information, you might be wondering which one you should use and when. In general, cookies are the preferred option because they allow persistent storage of state information and hidden fields do not. However, cookies may not be the right choice for all applications. Table 8.1 summarizes the tradeoffs between cookies and hidden fields.

Both cookies and hidden fields are easy to use; however, both also have some coding overhead associated with them. Cookie strings need to be parsed when they are read. Hidden fields require invisible forms to be set up. As far as ease of use is concerned, I prefer cookies because all of the setup processing is performed in JavaScript.

Even though cookies are supported by Navigator, Internet Explorer, and other browsers, they are not supported by all browsers. On the other hand, hidden fields are supported by all HTML 2.0-compatible browsers.

Cookies are not supported by all Web servers; hidden fields are. Cookies are not as performance-efficient as hidden fields, because cookie operations require disk I/O to the `cookies.txt` file. However, in most applications this performance difference is not noticeable.

Cookies provide persistent storage. That is their biggest advantage and why they were developed in the first place. If you require persistent storage then you have to use cookies.

Cookies may not always be available to your scripts. Although the cookie specification states that a browser cannot claim that it is cookie-capable unless it provides a minimum cookie storage capacity of 300 (currently, this limit is not a problem for most browsers), with the increase in cookie popularity, it could be an issue in the future. Hidden fields do not have any practical limits.

TABLE 8.1   Cookies vs. hidden fields

Trade Off	Cookies	Hidden Fields
Ease of use	Requires cookie string parsing	Requires form setup and access
Browser support	Navigator, Internet Explorer, other browsers	Almost all browsers
Server support	May not be supported by some servers	Supported by all servers
Performance	Slower—requires disk I/O	Faster—implemented in RAM
Persistent storage	Supported	Not Supported
Availability	Maximum cookie storage may be reached	No practical storage limitation

Summary

In this chapter you learned how to use hidden fields and cookies to maintain browser state information. You learned how JavaScript enhances the capabilities provided by both hidden fields and cookies by maximizing local processing and reducing the need for CGI programming. In the next chapter, you'll learn how to work with the *link-related objects* provided by JavaScript. You'll learn how to attach scripts to link events and how to work with the document history maintained by your browser.

CHAPTER
NINE

9

Working with Links

The ability to quickly move from one Web page to another in search of information (and entertainment) is at the heart of the Web's popularity. With a click of the mouse, we can travel from a Web page about native cultures to recipes of exotic foods. The single-click simplicity with which we traverse the Web is provided by *links*.

Most links are *static*. Static links always take you to the same destination. This type of link can be written entirely in HTML. Other links are *dynamic*, such as those used to link forms to CGI programs. When you submit a form, especially a search form, the Web page to which you link is often a page that is generated according to data submitted with the form. Until JavaScript, most dynamic links were created using CGI programs. Now, with JavaScript, you can develop browser-side dynamic links, which can eliminate the need for CGI programming and reduce the load on your Web server.

In this chapter you'll learn how to use JavaScript objects that provide control over the way that links are implemented. You'll learn how to use the `location` object to load documents at various URLs, how to attach JavaScript code to a document's links, and how to use the `history` object to keep track of the URLs that have been visited within a window. When you finish this chapter you'll be able to use link-related objects to implement dynamically programmable links within your own Web pages.

URLs

A universal resource locator, or URL, is the standard type of Internet address used on the Web. It is used to locate resources and services associated with a variety of protocols. These include (but are not limited to) Web pages, files on FTP servers, and e-mail and newsgroup addresses. Examples of URLs are provided in Table 9.1.

TABLE 9.1   Examples of URLs

URL	Description
http://www.jaworski.com/javascript	This book's home page
ftp://ftp.cdrom.com	The Walnut Creek FTP server
mailto:jamie@jaworski.com	The author's e-mail address
news://news.scruznet.com/comp.language.javascript	The JavaScript newsgroup

The syntax of a URL varies with the particular protocol used to access a resource or service. For example, most URLs do not contain spaces, but URLs that use the *javascript:* protocol may include spaces, as you'll learn later in this section.

The most common format of a URL is as follows:

```
protocol//hostname[:port] path search hash
```

- The `protocol` element of the URL syntax above identifies the protocol to be used to access a resource or service. Examples of protocols include *http:*, *ftp:*, *mailto:*, and *file:*. More-specialized JavaScript protocols are presented later in this section.

- The `hostname` element of the URL identifies the fully qualified domain name of the host where the resource is located. Examples are *home.netscape.com*, *www.microsoft.com* and *java.sun.com*.

- The `port` element of the URL identifies the TCP port number to use with the protocol. The port is optional. If it is omitted, the colon preceding the port is also omitted, and the protocol's "well-known" port is assumed. *Well-known ports* are the ports that servers "listen to" when implementing a protocol. For example, the well-known port of HTTP is 80.

- The `path` element of the URL is the directory/file path to the resource. It is written in the Unix forward-slash format. An example path is `/javascript/index.htm`. The path is usually relative to a directory used by the server. For example, my Web server uses the following directory,

  ```
  /usr/local/etc/httpd/htdocs
  ```

  as the base directory from which it services HTTP requests. Thus, the URL

  http://www.jaworski.com/javascript/index.htm

  addresses the following file:

  ```
  /usr/local/etc/httpd/htdocs/javascript/index.htm.
  ```

- The `search` element of the URL identifies a query string passed in a URL. Query strings are data that is passed to CGI programs via the QUERY_STRING environment variable. The query string begins with a question mark (?) followed by the query data. Spaces are encoded using plus (+) signs. Other codings used for special characters and binary data are discussed in Appendix A. For example, the query string *?tall+dark+handsome* passes the words *tall*, *dark*, and *handsome* to a CGI program.

- The *hash* element of the URL identifies a named file offset. It consists of a hash character (#) (some of you may know this as a pound sign) followed by the name of the anchor associated with the file offset. For example, if you want to create a link to the part of the file associated with the anchor section3, you would append the hash #section3 to the link's URL.

The *javascript:* and *about:* Protocols

In addition to the standard protocols used with URLs, Netscape Navigator supports the *javascript:* and *about:* protocols.

The *javascript:* Protocol   This protocol is used to evaluate a JavaScript expression and load a Web page that contains the value of the expression. If the expression does not evaluate to a defined value, then no Web page is loaded.

> **NOTE**   Spaces may be included in URLs that use the *javascript:* protocol.

In order to see how the *javascript:* protocol works, open your browser and load the following URL:

javascript:Date()

As shown in Figure 9.1, this URL (which, incidentally, contains a space) opens a document that displays the value of the current date.

Try opening the following URL:

javascript:"<H1>"+"What's up?"+"</H1>"

This one results in the document shown in Figure 9.2 being displayed. Note that the H1 tags were used to display *What's up?* as a level 1 heading.

> **NOTE**   The URL *javascript:void(0)* can be used to create a link that does nothing when the user clicks on it. The void() operator is used to evaluate an expression without returning a value.

FIGURE 9.1

Using the *javascript:* protocol to display the current date

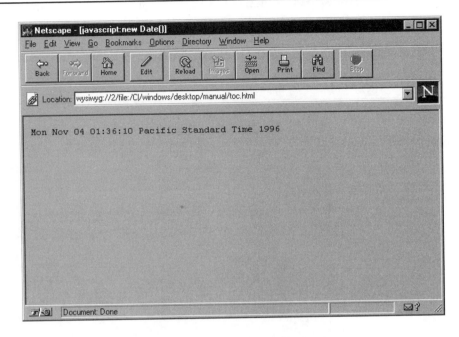

FIGURE 9.2

Using the *javascript:* protocol to display HTML tags

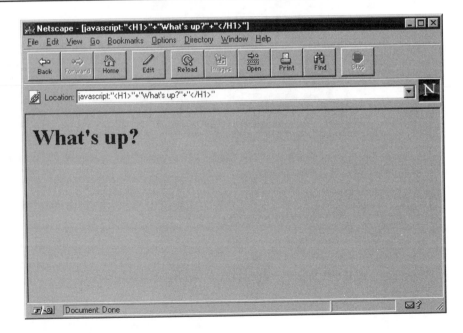

The *about:* Protocol This protocol provides access to built-in Navigator information. The URL *about:* loads a Web page that identifies the current Navigator version and other related information as shown in Figure 9.3. Loading *about:* has the same result as selecting About Netscape from the Navigator Help pull-down menu.

FIGURE 9.3

Loading *about:* displays
the same information
as selecting About
Netscape from Naviga-
tor's Help menu.

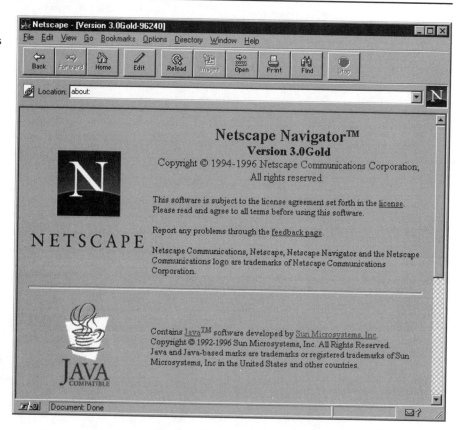

If the *about:cache* URL is loaded, then Navigator displays statistics on the current state of its cache, as shown in Figure 9.4.

If the *about:plugins* URL is loaded, then Navigator displays information about the plugins that are currently configured, as shown in Figure 9.5. The resulting display is the same as that obtained by selecting About Plugins from the Help menu.

FIGURE 9.4

Loading *about:cache* displays information about the current state of the disk cache.

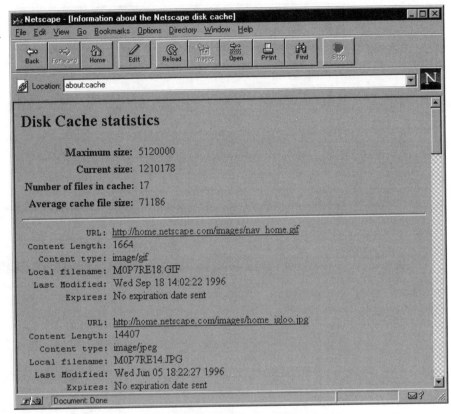

The *location* Object

JavaScript uses the `location` object to access the URL of the current document that is loaded in a window. The `location` object contains properties that describe the various parts of the URL. These properties are summarized in Table 9.2.

TABLE 9.2   Properties of the `location` object

Property	Description
hash	The anchor part of the URL (if any).
host	The hostname:port part of the URL.

TABLE 9.2   Properties of the `location` object (continued)

Property	Description
hostname	The hostname part of the URL.
href	The entire URL.
pathname	The pathname part of the URL.
port	The port part of the URL.
protocol	The protocol part of the URL. It includes the colon following the protocol name.
search	The query string part of the URL.

FIGURE 9.5

Loading *about:plugins* displays information about the plug-ins your browser has installed.

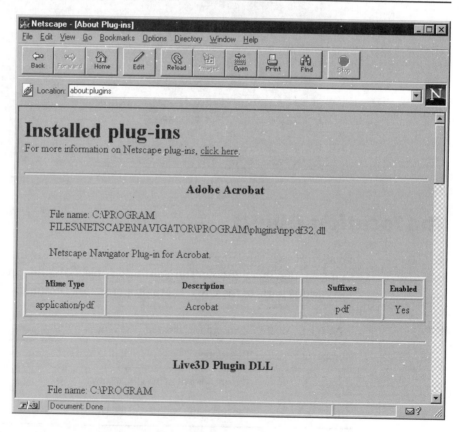

The location object is a property of the window object. If the location object of a window is modified, then the browser attempts to load the document specified by the modified URL into the window. For this reason, you should use the href property to modify the entire URL at a single time, rather than sequentially modifying each of the parts of the URL.

NOTE The document object also contains a location property. This property is read-only and cannot be modified to load a new document. You should not plan on using this property, because it will be deleted in future versions of JavaScript. Instead, use the href property of the location property of the window object.

The location object has two methods—reload() and replace(). The reload() method causes the current document of a window to be reloaded according to the policy used by the browser's Reload button. This policy allows a document to be reloaded from the server in one of the following three ways:

- *Every time.* The document is reloaded from the server every time.

- *Once per session.* The document is reloaded from the server once per session if the document's date on the server indicates that it is newer than the document stored in cache. If the document is not in the cache, it is loaded from the server.

- *Never.* The document is reloaded from cache, if possible. Otherwise, it is loaded from the server.

If true is passed as an argument to the reload() method, then the document is unconditionally loaded from the server.

The replace() method takes a URL as a parameter, and loads the document at the specified URL over the current document in the current document history list. This prevents the user from returning to the previous document by clicking the browser's Back button.

The location object does not have any events.

Example Application Using *location*

The location object is a simple object with which to work. It is usually used to load a new document or to access individual parts of a document's URL. Listing 9.1 provides an example of the location object's use.

Open the file load-url.htm with your browser and it will display the form shown in Figure 9.6. This form lets you enter simple URLs that use the file:, http:, and ftp: protocols. You can enter a host name and path to further specify the URLs. When you click on the Load URL button, the document at the specified URL is displayed in the bottom frame of the window, as shown in Figure 9.7.

The load-url.htm file is shown in Listing 9.1. It sets up a two-row frame set. The file url-form.htm is loaded in the top row and blank.htm is loaded in the bottom row. The url-form.htm file is shown in Listing 9.2 and the blank.htm file is shown in Listing 6.8 of Chapter 6.

FIGURE 9.6

The Load URL form lets you enter a URL part by part. (Listing 9.1)

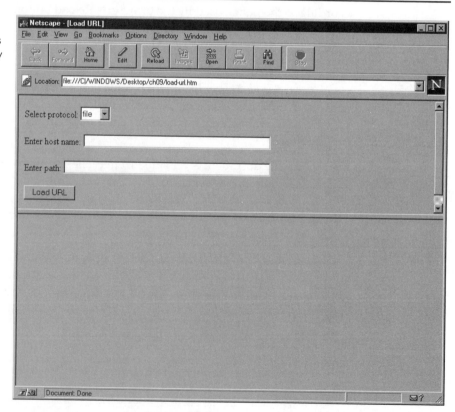

FIGURE 9.7

The Load URL form lets you load Netscape's home page. (Listing 9.1)

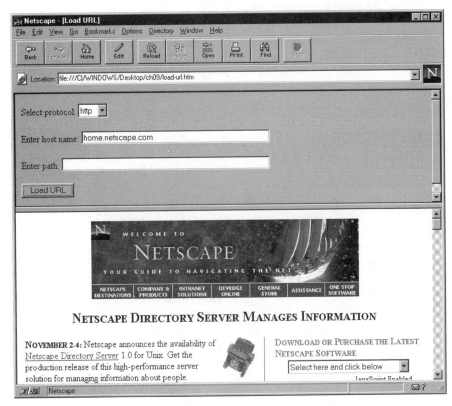

Listing 9.1. Using the location object (load-url.htm)

```
<HTML>
<HEAD>
<TITLE>Load URL</TITLE>
</HEAD>
<FRAMESET ROWS="200,*" BORDER=10>
<FRAME SRC="url-form.htm">
<FRAME SRC="blank.htm">
</FRAMESET>
</HTML>
```

Listing 9.2. A form for entering a URL (url-form.htm)

```
<HTML>
<HEAD>
```

```
<TITLE>Load URL</TITLE>
<SCRIPT LANGUAGE="JavaScript"><!--
function loadFrames() {
 ix = document.URLform.protocol.options.selectedIndex
 urlString = document.URLform.protocol.options[ix].value+"//"
 urlString += document.URLform.hostname.value
 path =      document.URLform.path.value
 if(path.length > 0) {
  if(path.charAt(0)!="/") path = "/"+path
 }
 urlString += path
 parent.frames[1].location.href=urlString
}
// --></SCRIPT>
</HEAD>
<BODY>
<FORM ACTION="" NAME="URLform">
<P>Select protocol:
<SELECT NAME="protocol" SIZE="1">
<OPTION VALUE="file:" SELECTED="SELECTED">file</OPTION>
<OPTION VALUE="http:">http</OPTION>
<OPTION VALUE="ftp:">ftp</OPTION></SELECT></P>
<P>Enter host name:
<INPUT TYPE="TEXT" NAME="hostname" SIZE="45"></P>
<P>Enter path:
<INPUT TYPE="TEXT" NAME="path" SIZE="50"></P>
<P></P>
<INPUT TYPE="BUTTON" NAME="load" VALUE="Load URL"
 ONCLICK="loadFrames()">
</FORM>
</BODY>
</HTML>
```

There is a single script in the head of url-form.htm. This script defines the
loadFrames() function, which is invoked to handle the onClick event of the
Load URL button. It determines which of the protocol options were selected and
uses that option to build urlString. It appends the string "//" and the value of
the hostname field to urlString followed by the value of the path variable. The
path variable is set based on the value of the path field. If the first character of
the path field is not "/" then it prepends a slash to the path variable before appending
its value to urlString. Finally, it loads the document specified by urlString in
the second frame by setting the frame's location.href property to urlString.

The *link* Object

The link object encapsulates a text or image link contained in a document. It is a property of the document object. The links array is an array of all links contained in a document and is also a property of the document object. A link object is similar to a location object in that it contains a URL. Because of this, link objects have many of the same properties as location objects; these properties are shown in Table 9.3. The only additional property that the link object has in comparison with the location object is the target property. This property is the target attribute of the link, and identifies the window where the document referenced by the link's URL is to be loaded.

TABLE 9.3   Properties of the link object

Property	Description
hash	The anchor part of the URL (if any).
host	The hostname:port part of the URL.
hostname	The hostname part of the URL.
href	The entire URL.
pathname	The pathname part of the URL.
port	The port part of the URL.
protocol	The protocol part of the URL. It includes the colon following the protocol name.
search	The query string part of the URL.
target	The link's target attribute.

The link object does not have any methods. It has three events—onClick, onMouseOver, and onMouseOut as described in Chapter 4.

NOTE   The following section presents an example of using the link object. After this example, the JavaScript link() method is introduced.

Example Application Using *link*: A Pair-Matching Game

To see how the `link` object may be used in a Web application, we'll develop a JavaScript version of a familiar pattern-matching game. In this game, you are faced with an array of 16 cards. These 16 cards represent eight pairs of matching images, randomly arranged. Initially, you see only the backs of the cards; the images are hidden face-down. Your goal is to turn over one card and then another to see if the images on the cards match. If they do, the pair remains face-up, and you take another turn; that is, you try to find another pair by choosing two of the remaining cards. Whenever the second card of one of your attempts doesn't match the first card, both of those two cards flip over again, and you must take another turn. You continue taking turns until you have uncovered all the matching pairs.

To get a better feel for how the game is played, open the file `click1.htm` with your browser. You will see a display similar to the one shown in Figure 9.8. In order to play the game, click on any one of the cards, as shown in Figure 9.9. Now click on any other card, as shown in Figure 9.10. Your objective is to click on a card whose image matches the first. Your odds at getting it right are 1 out of 15. However, with repeated tries you will be able to improve those odds. If the card you clicked on is a match, the matching images will remain face-up until the end of the game. If you missed, click on the Continue button to try again. The mismatched pair you clicked are then hidden (i.e., turned face-down) again. Continue taking turns until you have finally turned over all of the pairs, two cards at a time. By the time you have won a game you will be ready to go on to see how the game is implemented.

> **NOTE**
> In Chapter 10 you will learn how to enhance the pair match program with JavaScript's dynamic image display capabilities.

Listing 9.3 contains the code of the `click1.htm` file. This file is rather short, considering the complexity of the pair-matching application, and consists mostly of JavaScript code. The code is organized into three scripts—two in the header and one in the body.

FIGURE 9.8

The pair match opening
screen shows all cards
turned over. (Listing 9.3)

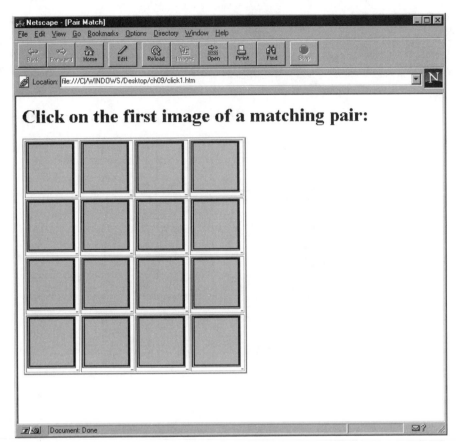

FIGURE 9.8

The pair match opening
screen shows all cards
turned over. (Listing 9.3)

The script in the document's body invokes the `readCookie()` function to
read the cookies used by `click1.htm`. (Cookies were covered in Chapter 8. If
you skipped Chapter 8, you should go back and read it before going on.) The
`displayTable()` function is used to display the table of images shown in
Figure 9.8.

The first header script imports JavaScript code from the `pairs.js` file (Listing 9.4). The code in `pairs.js` is common to `click2.htm` (Listing 9.5) and
`match.htm` (Listing 9.6) which are also used in the pair-matching program.

A single image has been clicked—try to find a match! (Listing 9.3)

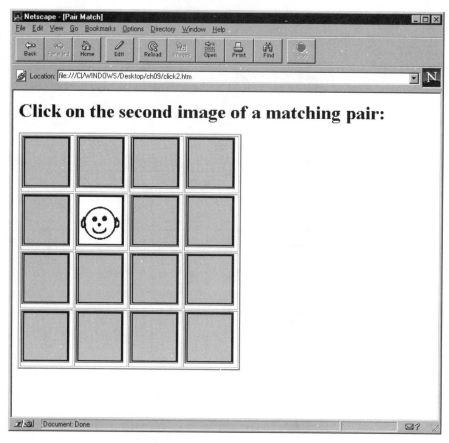

The second header script contains the functions `readCookie()`, `displayCell()` and `useClick()`. These functions are unique to `click1.htm`. However, modified versions of these functions are used in `click2.htm` and `match.htm`. Their use in `click1.htm` is described in the following paragraphs:

NOTE

To fully understand `readCookie()`, `displayCell()` and `userClick()` you'll need to read the description of `pairs.js` (Listing 9.4 later in this section).

FIGURE 9.10

Two images have been clicked. They don't match, so you must click the Continue button to take your next turn. (The images will automatically flip face-down again.) (Listing 9.5)

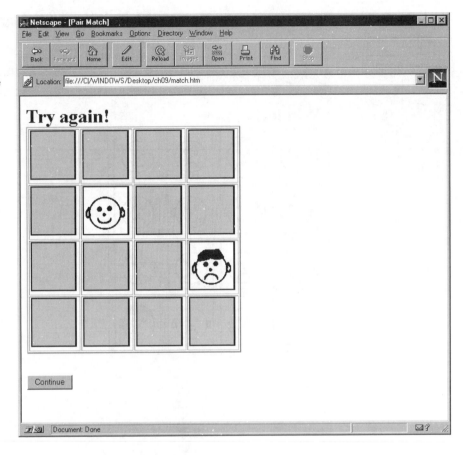

readCookie() This function reads the cookies that are available to click1.htm and looks for cookies that have the names displayedImages and imageSequence. The displayedImages cookie contains 16 characters which are either 0 or 1. The value 1 at position n indicates that the user has successfully matched the nth image. The value 0 indicates that they have not. The imageSequence is a permuted string that identifies which of the 16 image positions are occupied by image pairs 0 through 7. The initializeImageArray() function is invoked to initialize the images array with the file names of the images that are at each image position. The initializeDisplayedArray() is invoked to initialize the displayed array with boolean values based upon the displayedImages cookie.

FIGURE 9.11

The game has been won—all images have been matched. (Listing 9.6)

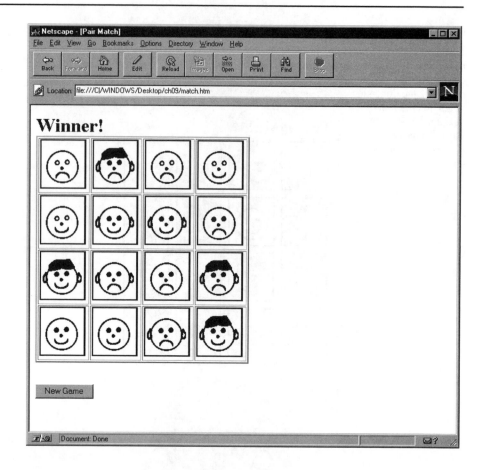

displayCell() This function creates the image link of each cell of the 4-row-by-4-column image table shown in Figure 9.8. Each cell links to the click2.htm file. The image associated with the link is either none.gif (corresponding to a hidden image) or one of the images contained in the images array. The onClick event of the link is handled by the userClick() function, which is passed the index (n) of the table cell being displayed. When userClick() returns, the click2.htm file is loaded, since it is the HREF attribute of the image link.

userClick() This function handles the onClick event associated with each of the table's image link cells. It updates the document's displayedImages and imageSequence cookies, and creates a third cookie, click1, which stores the index of the cell that was clicked.

Listing 9.3. The startup file for the pair matching game (click1.htm)

```
images = new Array(16)
displayed = new Array(16)

function nameDefined(c,n) {
 var s=removeBlanks(c)
 var pairs=s.split(";")
 for(var i=0;i<pairs.length;++i) {
  var pairSplit=pairs[i].split("=")
  if(pairSplit[0]==n) return true
 }
 return false
}
function removeBlanks(s) {
 var temp=""
 for(var i=0;i<s.length;++i) {
  var c=s.charAt(i)
  if(c!=" ") temp += c
 }
 return temp
}
function getCookieValue(c,n) {
 var s=removeBlanks(c)
 var pairs=s.split(";")
 for(var i=0;i<pairs.length;++i) {
  var pairSplit=pairs[i].split("=")
  if(pairSplit[0]==n) return pairSplit[1]
 }
 return ""
}
function permuteString(s) {
 var len=s.length
 var sArray = new Array(len)
 for(var i=0;i<len;++i) sArray[i]=s.charAt(i)
 for(var i=0;i<len;++i) {
  var currentValue=sArray[i]
  ix=Math.round(Math.random()*(len-1))
  sArray[i]=sArray[ix]
  sArray[ix]=currentValue
 }
 t=""
 for(var i=0;i<len;++i) t+=sArray[i]
```

```
   return t
  }
function initializeImageArray() {
 for(var i=0;i<16;++i) {
  var ch=imageSequence.charAt(i)
  var n=parseInt(ch)
  if(n>3) images[i]="frown"+(n-3)+".gif"
  else images[i]="smile"+(n+1)+".gif"
  }
 }
function initializeDisplayedArray() {
 for(var i=0;i<16;++i) {
  var ch=displayedImages.charAt(i)
  if(ch=="1") displayed[i]=true
  else displayed[i]=false
  }
 }
function displayTable(){
 document.writeln('<TABLE BORDER="2">')
 for(var i=0;i<4;++i) {
  document.writeln('<TR>')
  for(var j=0;j<4;++j) {
   document.writeln('<TD>')
   displayCell(i*4+j)
   document.writeln('</TD>')
   }
  document.writeln('</TR>')
  }
 document.writeln('</TABLE>')
 }
```

The pairs.js file shown in Listing 9.4 contains the common code used by
click1.htm, click2.htm, and match.htm. It defines the images and
displayed arrays, and seven functions: nameDefined(), removeBlanks(),
getCookieValue(), permuteString(), initializeImageArray(), ini-
tializeDisplayedArray(), and displayTable(). These arrays and functions are used as follows:

images This array contains the names of the image files that are displayed in
each cell of the table.

displayed This array consists of 16 boolean values, indicating which images
have been matched by the user.

nameDefined() This function checks the cookie passed via the c argument to see if it contains a *name=value* pair with the name passed by the n argument. It returns true if a matching name is found and false otherwise.

removeBlanks() This function returns a string that has all blank spaces removed.

getCookieValue() This function returns the value of the *name=value* pair of the cookie passed via the c argument and the name passed via the n argument.

permuteString() This function is passed a string s and returns a string t where t is a random permutation of s. It is used to randomly distribute the images contained in the image table.

initializeImageArray() This function is invoked by readCookie() to initialize the images array based upon the imageSequence cookie value. The files smile1.gif through smile4.gif correspond to imageSequence values 0 through 3. The files frown1.gif through frown4.gif correspond to image-Sequence values 4 through 7.

initializeDisplayedArray() This function initializes the boolean displayed array based on the displayedImages cookie.

displayTable() This function displays the image link table. It generates the HTML code for the table as a whole, as well as for each of its rows and for all of its cells. It invokes the displayCell() function to generate the contents of each table cell. The displayCell() function is invoked when the table is being formatted.

Listing 9.4. Common code for the pair-matching game (pairs.js)

```
images = new Array(16)
displayed = new Array(16)

function nameDefined(c,n) {
 var s=removeBlanks(c)
 var pairs=s.split(";")
 for(var i=0;i<pairs.length;++i) {
  var pairSplit=pairs[i].split("=")
  if(pairSplit[0]==n) return true
 }
 return false
}
function removeBlanks(s) {
 var temp=""
 for(var i=0;i<s.length;++i) {
  var c=s.charAt(i)
```

```
   if(c!=" ") temp += c
  }
  return temp
}
function getCookieValue(c,n) {
 var s=removeBlanks(c)
 var pairs=s.split(";")
 for(var i=0;i<pairs.length;++i) {
  var pairSplit=pairs[i].split("=")
  if(pairSplit[0]==n) return pairSplit[1]
 }
 return ""
}
function permuteString(s) {
 var len=s.length
 var sArray = new Array(len)
 for(var i=0;i<len;++i) sArray[i]=s.charAt(i)
 for(var i=0;i<len;++i) {
  var currentValue=sArray[i]
  ix=Math.round(Math.random()*(len-1))
  sArray[i]=sArray[ix]
  sArray[ix]=currentValue
 }
 t=""
 for(var i=0;i<len;++i) t+=sArray[i]
 return t
}
function initializeImageArray() {
 for(var i=0;i<16;++i) {
  var ch=imageSequence.charAt(i)
  var n=parseInt(ch)
  if(n>3) images[i]="frown"+(n-3)+".gif"
  else images[i]="smile"+(n+1)+".gif"
 }
}
function initializeDisplayedArray() {
 for(var i=0;i<16;++i) {
  var ch=displayedImages.charAt(i)
  if(ch=="1") displayed[i]=true
  else displayed[i]=false
 }
}
function displayTable(){
 document.writeln('<TABLE BORDER="2">')
```

```
for(var i=0;i<4;++i) {
 document.writeln('<TR>')
 for(var j=0;j<4;++j) {
  document.writeln('<TD>')
  document.writeln('<SCRIPT LANGUAGE="JavaScript">')
  document.writeln('displayCell('+(i*4+j)+')')
  document.writeln('</SCRIPT>')
  document.writeln('</TD>')
 }
 document.writeln('</TR>')
 }
 document.writeln('</TABLE>')
 }
```

When a user clicks on any image link displayed by click1.htm, the
userClick() function is invoked to handle the event. Each image displayed
by click1.htm is used as the anchor of a link. The destination of this link is
click2.htm; this file processes the second click of a pair of clicks. Its code
is shown in Listing 9.5.

The only differences between click2.htm and click1.htm are in click2's
implementation of the readCookie(), displayCell(), and userClick()
functions. These differences are as follows:

readCookie() In click2.htm, readCookie() reads three cookies:
displayedImages, imageSequence, and click1. The additional click1 cookie
contains the index of the image that the user selected with his or her first click.

displayCell() In click2.htm, the displayCell() function displays an image
face-up if it has already been matched by the user (i.e., if displayed[n] is true)
or if it was selected on the user's first click. Also, all links created by click2.htm
now point to match.htm. When a user clicks on a link, userClick() is invoked
to handle the onClick event, then match.htm is loaded.

userClick() In click2.htm, the userClick() function creates an additional
cookie, click2, that records the user's second image selection.

Listing 9.5. The document used to process the second click (click2.htm)

```
<HTML>
<HEAD>
<TITLE>Pair Match</TITLE>
<SCRIPT LANGUAGE="JavaScript" SRC="pairs.js"><!--
```

```
// --></SCRIPT>
<SCRIPT LANGUAGE="JavaScript"><!--
function readCookie() {
 var cookie=document.cookie
 displayedImages=getCookieValue(cookie,"displayedImages")
 imageSequence=getCookieValue(cookie,"imageSequence")
 click1=parseInt(getCookieValue(cookie,"click1"))
 initializeImageArray()
 initializeDisplayedArray()
}
function displayCell(n) {
 var f="none.gif"
 if(displayed[n] || click1==n) f=images[n]
 document.write('<A HREF="match.htm" ')
 document.write('onClick="userClick('+n+')">')
 document.write('<IMG SRC="'+f+'" WIDTH="80" HEIGHT="83">')
 document.write('</A>')
}
function userClick(n) {
 document.cookie="displayedImages="+displayedImages
 document.cookie="imageSequence="+imageSequence
 document.cookie="click1="+click1
 document.cookie="click2="+n
}
// --></SCRIPT>
</HEAD>
<BODY BGCOLOR="#FFFFFF">
<H1>Try to find a match!</H1>
<SCRIPT LANGUAGE="JavaScript"><!--
readCookie()
displayTable()
// --></SCRIPT>
</BODY>
</HTML>
```

The match.htm file is loaded each time the user has clicked on two cards. It checks to see if the images match and whether the game has been won. It is similar to click1.htm and click2.htm but has some changes and additional functions, as follows:

Script in Document Body The script in the document's body invokes the displayMatchStatus() function before going on to display the image table. The `displayMatchStatus()` determines whether the user has matched a pair of images, and it displays an appropriate heading. After the image table is displayed, a form with a single button is generated. The button's label is *New Game* if the user has just matched all image pairs and *Continue* otherwise. Clicking on the button results in `click1.htm` being reloaded.

readCookie() The `readCookie()` function reads four cookies: `displayed-Images`, `imageSequence`, `click1`, and `click2`.

displayCell() The `displayCell()` function displays an image if its index is `click1` or `click2` or if that image has already been matched. It does not generate image links for the table's cells. Simple images are used instead. By the time a user gets to `match.htm` they will not be clicking on an image. Instead, they'll click on the New Game or Continue button.

displayMatchStatus() This function checks to see if a user has matched two images. In this case, `click1` must be different from `click2` (the user can't click on the same image twice) and the value of the `images` array for both clicks must be the same (the image files match). If the user has successfully matched two images then the value of the `displayed` array is updated to reflect the fact that the images match. The `displayedImages` cookie value is then updated, based upon the revised `displayed` array. The `winner()` function is invoked to determine whether all images have been matched, and an appropriate heading is displayed.

winner() This function checks to see if all images have been matched. If they have, then it returns `true`. Otherwise, it returns `false`.

Listing 9.6. The document used to check for matching clicks (match.htm)

```
<HTML>
<HEAD>
<TITLE>Pair Match</TITLE>
<SCRIPT LANGUAGE="JavaScript" SRC="pairs.js"><!--
// --></SCRIPT>
<SCRIPT LANGUAGE="JavaScript"><!--
function readCookie() {
 var cookie=document.cookie
 displayedImages=getCookieValue(cookie,"displayedImages")
 imageSequence=getCookieValue(cookie,"imageSequence")
 click1=parseInt(getCookieValue(cookie,"click1"))
 click2=parseInt(getCookieValue(cookie,"click2"))
```

```
 initializeImageArray()
 initializeDisplayedArray()
}
function displayCell(n) {
 var f="none.gif"
 if(displayed[n] || click1==n || click2==n) f=images[n]
 document.write('<IMG SRC="'+f+'" WIDTH="80" HEIGHT="83">')
}
function displayMatchStatus() {
 if(click1!=click2 && images[click1]==images[click2]){
  displayed[click1]=true
  displayed[click2]=true
  displayedImages=""
  for(var i=0;i<16;++i) {
   if(displayed[i]) displayedImages+="1"
   else displayedImages+="0"
  }
  if(winner()){
   document.writeln("<H1>Winner!")
   displayedImages="0000000000000000"
   imageSequence=permuteString("0123456701234567")
   state="winner"
  }else{
   document.writeln("<H1>They matched!")
   state="matched"
  }
 }else{
  document.writeln("<H1>Try again!")
  state="notMatched"
 }
 document.cookie="displayedImages="+displayedImages
 document.cookie="imageSequence="+imageSequence
}
function winner() {
 for(var i=0;i<16;++i)
  if(displayed[i]!=true) return false
 return true
}
// --></SCRIPT>
</HEAD>
<BODY BGCOLOR="#FFFFFF">
<SCRIPT LANGUAGE="JavaScript"><!--
```

```
readCookie()
displayMatchStatus()
displayTable()
document.write('<FORM><INPUT TYPE="BUTTON" NAME="goToClick1"')
if(state=="winner") document.writeln(' VALUE="New Game" ')
else document.writeln(' VALUE="Continue" ')
document.write('onClick="window.location.href=')
document.write("'click1.htm'")
document.writeln('"></FORM>')
// --></SCRIPT>
</BODY>
</HTML>
```

The *link()* Method

The link object is not the only way of creating a link. A link may be created using the link() method of the String object. This method takes the hypertext reference (HREF) attribute of the link as a parameter and creates a link to the specified HREF. For example, the following statements create a link to the *Mastering JavaScript* home page.

```
mjLink="Mastering
JavaScript".link("http://www.jaworski.com/javascript/")

document.writeln(mjLink)
```

The above statements result in the following HTML being generated for the current document:

```
<A HREF="http://www.jaworski.com/javascript/">Mastering
➥ JavaScript</A>
```

As another example, consider Listing 9.7. It contains the code of the linkx.htm file and generates the Web page shown in Figure 9.12. It creates an array of strings, called text, with the following anchor text:

> Mastering JavaScript Home Page
> Sybex Home Page
> Netscape Home Page
> Microsoft Home Page
> JavaSoft Home Page

It then creates an array of links, called `linkx`, using the `link()` method of the `String` object. These links are to the following URLs:

- *http://www.jaworski.com/javascript/*
- *http://www.sybex.com*
- *http://home.netscape.com*
- *http://www.microsoft.com*
- *http://www.javasoft.com*

Finally, it writes these links to the current document using the `writeln()` method of the `document` object.

Listing 9.7. Using the link() method (linkx.htm)

```
<HTML>
<HEAD>
<TITLE>Using the link() Method</TITLE>
</HEAD>
<BODY>
<H1>Using the link() Method</H1>
<SCRIPT LANGUAGE="JavaScript"><!--
text=new Array(5)
text[0]="Mastering JavaScript Home Page"
text[1]="Sybex Home Page"
text[2]="Netscape Home Page"
text[3]="Microsoft Home Page"
text[4]="JavaSoft Home Page"
linkx=new Array(5)
linkx[0]=text[0].link("http://www.jaworski.com/javascript/")
linkx[1]=text[1].link("http://www.sybex.com")
linkx[2]=text[2].link("http://home.netscape.com")
linkx[3]=text[3].link("http://www.microsoft.com")
linkx[4]=text[4].link("http://www.javasoft.com")
for(var i=0;i<linkx.length;++i)
  document.writeln("<P>"+linkx[i]+"</P>")
// --></SCRIPT>
</BODY>
</HTML>
```

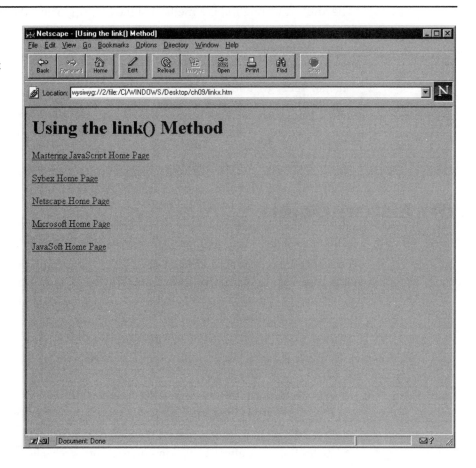

The *anchor* Object

The anchor object represents an anchor that is used as a named offset within an HTML document. It is a property of the document object. The anchors array contains all of the anchors of a document. The anchor object has no properties, methods, or events. It is used to keep track of the named offsets that are defined relative to an HTML document. For example, anchors.length can be used to step through all of a document's anchors.

An anchor object is also a link object if it contains an HREF attribute. In this case, it will have an entry in both the anchors and links arrays.

The `anchor()` method is a method of the `String` object that can be used to generate the hypertext used to create an `anchor` object. It is similar to the `link()` method. For example, the following code can be used to create an anchor in the current document:

```
anchorString="Section 5".anchor("sect5")
document.write(anchorString)
```

The anchor created by the above code is equivalent to the following HTML:

```
<A NAME="sect5">Section 5</A>
```

The *history* Object

The `history` object is used by Navigator to keep track of the URLs that have been displayed within a window. It displays this information in the history list that is accessed via Navigator's Go menu. The `history` object is a property of the `document` object. The `history` object has no events, but it has one property, `length`, that identifies the length of the history list.

The `history` object has three methods—`back()`, `forward()`, and `go()`— which can be used to travel to documents contained in the history list.

- The `back()` method loads the previous document in the history list. It produces the same effect as clicking on your browser's Back button.

- The `forward()` method loads the next document in the history list. It produces the same effect as clicking on your browser's Forward button.

- The `go()` method goes to a specific document in the history list. It can take either an integer parameter or a string parameter.

  - `go(n)` —When $n>0$, this method loads the document that is n entries ahead (forward) in the history list. When $n=0$, it reloads the current document. When $n<0$, go loads the document that is n entries behind (back) in the history list.

  - `go(string)` —When used in this manner, `go()` loads the closest document in the history list whose URL contains this string as a substring. For example, `history.go("chargers")` loads the closest history entry that contains the string `"chargers"` in its URL.

Standardized Navigation Scripts

The JavaScript `history` object may be used to help your users navigate your site. For example, it can be used to create simple direction buttons that allow users to revisit previously traversed Web pages. More elaborate navigation aids may be developed using a standard site navigation form.

Make sure that you are connected to the Internet, and then open `navigate.htm` with your browser. The Web page shown in Figure 9.13 is displayed. It contains navigation image links in the left frame and the *Mastering JavaScript* home page in the right frame. Click on the W3C HTML Page link. It causes the Web page shown in Figure 9.14 to be displayed in the right frame. Click on the link to HTML 3.2 and the Web page shown in Figure 9.15 is loaded into the right frame. Now click on the navigation image links to move backward and forward one or two documents at a time in the history list. These navigation aids provide a handy way for users to move through a long list of Web pages that they have visited. If your Web site contains documents that are distributed over a large number of Web pages, then these type of navigation aids may make navigating your site easier for your users.

> **NOTE**
>
> The navigation controls in this example work by accessing the history list; therefore the user cannot use these controls to go "forward" any further than they have already gone previously. In other words, in a ten page site, if a user has read only up to page four, they can only forward as far as page four.

The `navigate.htm` file sets up a two-column frame set, with the `nav.htm` file (the navigation aids) loaded into the left column and the *Mastering JavaScript* home page loaded in the right column.

Listing 9.8. The navigation frame set (navigate.htm)

```
<HTML>
<HEAD>
<TITLE>Navigation Aids</TITLE>
</HEAD>
<FRAMESET Cols="225,*" BORDER="0">
<FRAME SRC="nav.htm">
<FRAME SRC="http://www.jaworski.com/javascript">
</FRAMESET>
</HTML>
```

The nav.htm file creates a table of image links that implement the navigation buttons. The goBack2(), goForward2(), goBack(), goForward(), and goHome() functions use the history and location objects to cause the appropriate Web pages to be loaded.

Listing 9.9. Implementing the navigation aids (nav.htm)

```
<HTML>
<HEAD>
<TITLE>Navigation Aids</TITLE>
<SCRIPT LANGUAGE="JavaScript"><!--
home="http://www.jaworski.com/javascript"
function goBack2() {
 parent.frames[1].history.go(-2)
}
```

FIGURE 9.13

The navigation aids (Listing 9.8)

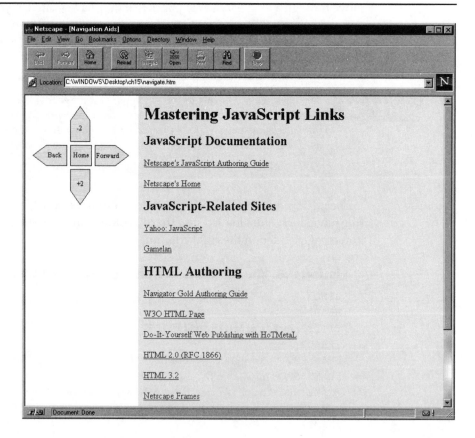

```
function goForward2() {
 var len=parent.frames[1].history.length
 parent.frames[1].history.go(2)
}
function goBack() {
 parent.frames[1].history.back()
}
function goForward() {
 parent.frames[1].history.forward()
}
function goHome() {
 parent.frames[1].location.href=home
}
// --></SCRIPT>
</HEAD>
```

FIGURE 9.14

A W3C page that covers HTML (Listing 9.8)

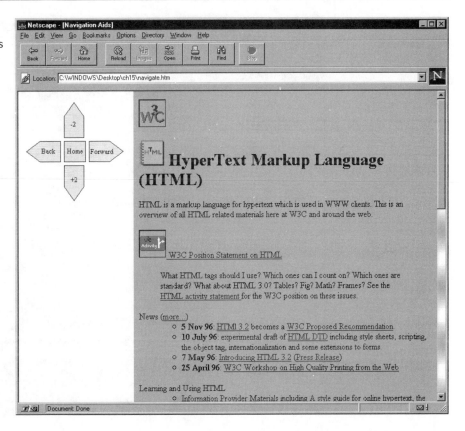

```
<BODY BGCOLOR="white">
<TABLE>
<TR><TD></TD>
<TD><A HREF="javascript:void(0)" onClick="goBack2()">
<IMG SRC="back2.gif" border="0"></A></TD>
<TD></TD></TR>
<TR><TD><A HREF="javascript:void(0)" onClick="goBack()">
<IMG SRC="back.gif" border="0"></A></TD>
<TD><A HREF="javascript:void(0)" onClick="goHome()">
<IMG SRC="home.gif" border="0"></A></TD>
<TD><A HREF="javascript:void(0)" onClick="goForward()">
<IMG SRC="forward.gif" border="0"></A></TD></TR>
<TR><TD></TD>
<TD><A HREF="javascript:void(0)" onClick="goForward2()">
<IMG SRC="forward2.gif" border="0"></A></TD>
```

FIGURE 9.15

A W3C page on
HTML 3.2 (Listing 9.8)

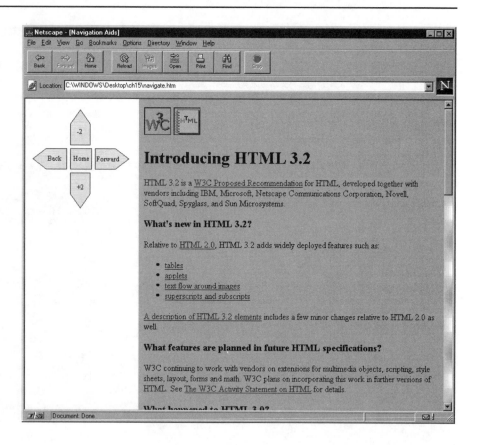

```
<TD></TD></TR>
</TABLE>
</BODY>
</HTML>
```

Summary

In this chapter you learned how to use link-related objects to exercise greater control over your document's links. You learned how to load documents via the `location` object, how to attach JavaScript code to a document's links, and how to use the `history` object to keep track of the URLs that have been visited within a window. In the next chapter you'll learn how to use JavaScript's `image` and `area` objects to perform animation and to implement advanced client-side image map programs.

CHAPTER

TEN

10

Using Images

- The `image` Object and Its Properties

- Dynamic Image Display

- Images and Animation

- Image Maps and the `area` Object

- Working with Image Maps

The old adage that a picture is worth a thousand words has never been more appropriate than it is to the Web. Images transform Web pages from fancy formatted text to professional graphical presentations. They allow drawings, photographs, and other graphics to be used to present the information that words alone cannot describe. Images can also be used as the source anchor for links or as clickable image maps. When images are used with links, they provide a highly intuitive approach to navigating the Web.

Until JavaScript, however, images could not be displayed dynamically, because HTML's image-display capabilities have one significant limitation—once you've displayed an image, you cannot change it without loading a new Web page. JavaScript overcomes the static image-display limitations of HTML by allowing you to dynamically update images without having to load a new Web page. This single JavaScript feature can greatly enhance the attractiveness of your Web pages. It allows you to provide timely graphical feedback in response to user actions and can be used to include sophisticated animation sequences in your Web pages.

In this chapter you'll learn how to use the excellent image-handling features provided by JavaScript. You'll cover the image object and learn how to control the way images are displayed with respect to surrounding text. You'll learn how to dynamically display images in your Web pages and how to use dynamic images to create animation effects. You'll also learn how to develop sophisticated client-side image maps using the area object. When you've finished this chapter, you'll be able to use images to create Web applications that are highly informative, user-friendly, and entertaining.

The *image* Object

The image object provides access to the images that are loaded with a document. It is a property of the document object. The images array contains an entry for each <img> tag that is specified within a document. The images array is also a property of the document object.

The properties of the image object are shown in Table 10.1. These properties reflect the attributes of the <img> tag. The image object has no methods, but has three events—onAbort, onError, and onLoad, as described in Chapter 4.

TABLE 10.1   Image object properties

Property	Description
border	The value of the `<img>` tag's BORDER attribute
complete	Identifies whether an image has been completely loaded
height	The value of the `<img>` tag's HEIGHT attribute
hspace	The value of the `<img>` tag's HSPACE attribute
lowsrc	The value of the `<img>` tag's LOWSRC attribute
name	The value of the `<img>` tag's NAME attribute
prototype	Used to add user-specified properties to an `image` object
src	The value of the `<img>` tag's SRC attribute
vspace	The value of the `<img>` tag's VSPACE attribute
width	The value of the `<img>` tag's WIDTH attribute

The `image` object type differs from other Navigator object types in that it allows new `image` objects to be explicitly created via a *constructor* (which were introduced in Chapter 5). The `Image()` constructor is used to create and preload images that aren't initially displayed as part of a Web page. These `image` objects are stored in the browser's cache and are used to replace images that have already been displayed.

An example of creating a cached image via the `Image()` constructor follows:

```
cachedImage = new Image()
cachedImage.src = "myImage.gif"
```

The first statement creates a new `image` object and assigns it to the `cachedImage` variable. The second statement sets the `image` object's `src` property to the image file `myImage.gif`. This causes `myImage.gif` to be loaded into the browser cache. The loaded image can then be referenced using the `cachedImage` variable.

NOTE   Images that are created using the `Image()` constructor are not accessible via the `images` array.

Image Display Properties

Before we get into dynamic image display we'll cover the image properties that affect the way an image is displayed with respect to surrounding text. These properties reflect the attributes of the `<img>` tag used to place an image in a document.

The `border` property identifies the thickness of an image's border in pixels. Images that are created using the `Image()` constructor have their border set to 0. The `border` property is read-only.

The `height` and `width` properties of an image specify the height and width of the window area in which the image is to be displayed. If the image is larger than the specified area the browser will scale the image to fit in the allocated space. The `height` and `width` properties can be specified in pixels or as a percentage of the window's dimensions; a percent sign is used to specify a percentage value. Images that are created using the `Image()` constructor have their `height` and `width` properties set to their actual dimensions. The `height` and `width` properties are read-only.

The `hspace` and `vspace` properties are used to specify a margin between an image and surrounding text. The `hspace` attribute specifies the size of an image's left and right margins in pixels. The `vspace` attribute specifies an image's top and bottom margins in pixels. Images that are created using the `Image()` constructor have their `hspace` and `vspace` properties set to 0. These properties are read-only.

Other Image Properties

The `image` object has other properties which can be used to monitor and control image loading and display:

- The `name` property is a read-only property that specifies the image's `name` attribute.

- The `lowsrc` property can be modified to quickly load and display a low-resolution image while a slower loading high-resolution image is being loaded.

- The `src` property is used to load a new image in the place of a currently displayed image. You'll learn more about this property in the next section on dynamic image display.

- The `complete` property is a read-only property that indicates whether an image has been completely loaded.

- The `prototype` property allows other user-defined properties to be created for all objects of the `image` object type. This property is covered in Chapter 5.

Dynamic Image Display

JavaScript's dynamic image display capabilities are easy to use. Just follow these three steps:

1. Use the `Image()` constructor to create `image` objects for storing the images that you'll display dynamically.

2. Load the image files associated with the newly created images by setting the image's `src` attribute to the image file's name.

3. Display the images by setting the `src` attribute of an image in the document's `images` array to the `src` attribute of a cached image.

For example, suppose you have a document that contains two `<img>` tags. When the document is loaded by your browser, the image files that are specified in the `<img>` tags' `src` attributes are displayed. You can load and display two new images using the following JavaScript code:

```
//Step 1: Create image objects
newImage1 = new Image()
newImage2 = new Image()

//Step 2: Load the image files
newImage1.src = "new1.gif"
newImage2.src = "new2.gif"

//Step 3: Display the images
document.images[0].src = newImage1.src
document.images[1].src = newImage2.src
```

In Chapter 9, you developed an image pair-matching program. This program was designed to illustrate link event handling and to develop your skills in using cookies. The program did not take advantage of JavaScript's dynamic image display capabilities, and as a result required a new Web page to be loaded whenever a new image was displayed. Now that you know how to display images dynamically, let's revise the pair-matching program to take advantage of these capabilities.

A revised pair-matching program is contained in Listing 10.1. This single file (pairs.htm) takes the place of the click1.htm, click2.htm, match.htm, and pairs.js files used in Chapter 9. It also implements the image map program in a much smoother fashion, because it does not load an entire Web page to display a single image. Figure 10.1 shows the program's opening display. Figure 10.2 provides a sample snapshot of a game in mid-progress. You can play the new game by opening the pairs.htm file with your browser. You should immediately notice the improvement in the way the program displays images.

FIGURE 10.1

The revised pair-matching program takes advantage of dynamic image display. (pairs.htm)

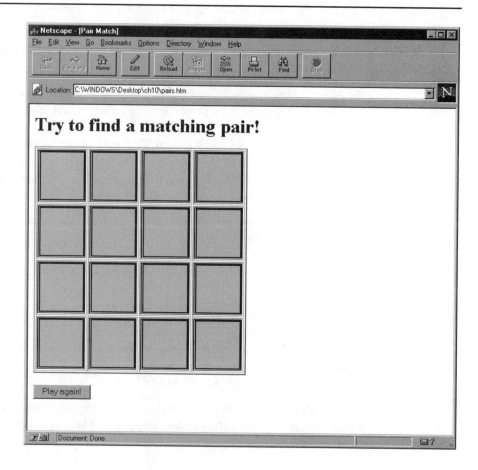

FIGURE 10.2

A snapshot of the pair matching program's display—recognize anyone? (pairs.htm)

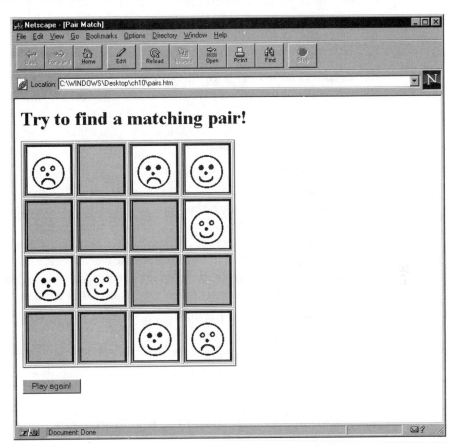

The pairs.htm file contains a large script in the document's head and a small script in the document's body. The script in the document's body invokes the initialize() function to initialize the arrays and variables used in the program. It invokes the displayTable() function to display the table of image links.

The script in the document's head defines four functions: initialize(), displayTable(), userClick(), and resetImages(). The use of these functions is described in the following paragraphs.

initialize() This function initializes the arrays and variables used throughout the script. The imageSource array is used to load and cache the images to be displayed throughout the script's execution. The imageSequence array is used to identify in which table cells the images are to be stored. It randomizes the location of pairs of the digits 0 through 7. These digits correspond to the first eight images stored in `imageSource`. The `click` variable is used to keep track of whether the user has clicked on the first or second image of the two-image sequence. The `click1` and `click2` variables identify the index of the image that the user clicked.

displayTable() This function displays the initial image link table. It is similar to the `displayTable()` function used in Chapter 9. However, it displays the table only once—when the document is loaded. Thus, it displays the `none.gif` image in each table cell. The table images are updated dynamically by the `userClick()` function.

userClick() This function handles the `onClick` event that is generated when a user clicks on an image link. If the user has clicked on the first image of the two-click sequence, then the `click` variable is set to 1, `click1` is set to the index of the clicked cell, and the image associated with the cell is displayed. If the user has clicked on the second image of the two-click sequence, then the `click` variable is reset to 0, `click2` is set to the index of the clicked cell, and the image associated with the cell is displayed. If the images do not match, then the `resetImages()` function is invoked to reset the image display after a timeout period.

resetImages() This function waits between one and two seconds and then resets the table cells pointed to by the `click1` and `click2` variables; it resets them to the `none.gif` image. The timing delay is implemented by checking the `getSeconds()` method of the `Date` object to determine when at least one second has expired.

Listing 10.1. Pair matching revisited (pairs.htm)

```
<HTML>
<HEAD>
<TITLE>Pair Match</TITLE>
<SCRIPT LANGUAGE="JavaScript"><!--
function initialize() {
 imageSource=new Array(9)
 for(var i=0;i<9;++i) imageSource[i]=new Image()
 imageSource[0].src="smile1.gif"
 imageSource[1].src="smile2.gif"
 imageSource[2].src="smile3.gif"
 imageSource[3].src="smile4.gif"
 imageSource[4].src="frown1.gif"
 imageSource[5].src="frown2.gif"
 imageSource[6].src="frown3.gif"
 imageSource[7].src="frown4.gif"
```

```
    imageSource[8].src="none.gif"
    imageSequence=new Array(16)
    for(var i=0;i<16;++i) imageSequence[i]=i%8
    for(var i=0;i<16;++i) {
     var currentValue=imageSequence[i]
     var ix=Math.round(Math.random()*(15))
     imageSequence[i]=imageSequence[ix]
     imageSequence[ix]=currentValue
    }
    click=0
    click1=0
    click2=0
 }
 function displayTable(){
  document.writeln('<TABLE BORDER="2">')
  for(var i=0;i<4;++i) {
   document.writeln('<TR>')
   for(var j=0;j<4;++j) {
    document.writeln('<TD>')
    document.write('<A HREF="javascript:void(0)" ')
    document.write('onClick="userClick('+(i*4+j)+')">')
    document.write('<IMG SRC="none.gif" WIDTH="80" HEIGHT="83">')
    document.write('</A>')
    document.writeln('</TD>')
   }
   document.writeln('</TR>')
  }
  document.writeln('</TABLE>')
 }
 function userClick(n) {
  if(click==0){
   click=1
   click1=n
   document.images[n].src=imageSource[imageSequence[n]].src
  }else if(click==1){
   click=0
   click2=n
   document.images[n].src=imageSource[imageSequence[n]].src
   if(click1==click2 ||
     imageSequence[click1]!=imageSequence[click2]) resetImages()
  }
 }
 function resetImages() {
```

```
var d1=new Date()
var t1=d1.getSeconds()
for(;;){
 var d2=new Date()
 var t2=d2.getSeconds()
 if(Math.abs(t1-t2)>1) break;
 }
document.images[click1].src=imageSource[8].src
document.images[click2].src=imageSource[8].src
}
// --></SCRIPT>
</HEAD>
<BODY BGCOLOR="#FFFFFF">
<H1>Try to find a matching pair!</H1>
<SCRIPT LANGUAGE="JavaScript"><!--
initialize()
displayTable()
// --></SCRIPT>
<FORM>
<P ALIGN="CENTER">
<INPUT TYPE="BUTTON" NAME="replay" VALUE="Play again!"
 ONCLICK="window.location='pairs.htm'">
</P>
</FORM>
</BODY>
</HTML>
```

Images and Animation

JavaScript's dynamic image display capabilities can be used to create animation effects. Animation basically involves displaying one image after another in sequence. The quality of the animation depends on the quality of the images displayed, the delay between successive image displays, and the ability of your browser to reduce any deviations in this delay.

The quality of the images displayed depends on your taste in choosing images or your artistic skills in creating them; we can't provide you with much help in those areas. The delay between images is usually a fraction of a second. Higher-performance computers may be able to minimize this delay and reduce deviations in the average delay. These deviations are caused by the performance load on your system that results from other concurrently executing tasks.

Even if you already know the basics of how to perform animation, there are a few tips that will improve your results. These are as follows:

1. Make sure that all images are loaded before you start your animation sequence. This will eliminate any additional delays associated with image loading.

2. Use the `setInterval()` method of the `window` object to implement delays between images. This method will help to reduce any deviations in your average delay.

3. Experiment with the delay value to see what delay is best for your animation. Although a lower delay value provides a smoother animation, a delay that is too small can result in images being displayed at a comically quick pace.

The file `animate.htm` provides a simple example of JavaScript animation. It displays a rectangle with five rows of colors: blue, green, red, purple, and cyan. It displays successive images that cycle the colors, giving the appearance that the colors are moving downward across the rectangle. Refer to Figure 10.3. Admittedly this is not a very exciting animation, but it illustrates the principles of animation without getting wrapped up in the images being displayed. You can apply these principles to your own animation needs. If you haven't already done so, open `animate.htm` with your browser. Experiment with the faster and slower buttons to change the delay between successive images. Notice how this delay affects the quality of the animation.

The `animate.htm` file is rather short compared to other scripts. The script in the document's body simply invokes the `initialize()` function to create and load the animation images, set the value of the `delay` variable, and initialize other variables. Note that the `onLoad` event of the `<img>` tag sets the `start` variable to `true` in order to start the animation.

The script in the document's head defines four functions: `initialize()`, `startAnimation()`, `animate()`, `goFaster()`, and `goSlower()`. The use of these functions is described in the following paragraphs.

initialize() This function creates and loads the images used in the animation and sets the `delay` variable to 500. Since the delay is specified in milliseconds, this initial delay is a half second. The `delta` variable is set to 100. This variably is used to increment or decrement the delay when the user clicks on the Slower or Faster buttons. The `nextImage` variable identifies the next image to be displayed.

FIGURE 10.3

A snapshot of the animation sequence shows one of the images displayed. (animate.htm)

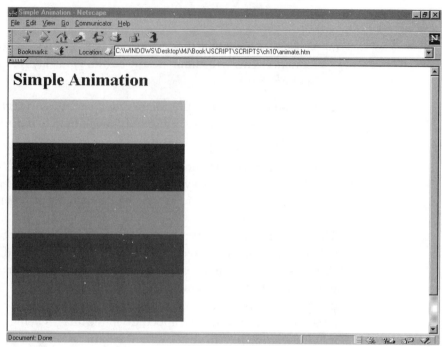

startAnimation() This function invokes the `setInterval()` method of the `window` object to start the animation with the specified `delay`.

animate() This function performs the actual animation. It displays the next image, and updates `nextImage` to point to a new image.

goFaster() This function handles the `onClick` event associated with the Faster button by decreasing the `delay` value by the amount indicated by the `delta` variable.

goSlower() This function handles the `onClick` event associated with the Slower button by increasing the `delay` value by the amount indicated by the `delta` variable.

> **NOTE**
>
> Note that the `goFaster()` and `goSlower()` functions invoke `clearInterval()` to clear the animation timer before changing the `delay` variable.

Listing 10.2. JavaScript animation (animate.htm)

```
<HTML>
<HEAD>
<TITLE>Simple Animation</TITLE>
<SCRIPT LANGUAGE="JavaScript"><!--
function initialize() {
 start=false
 imageSource=new Array(5)
 for(var i=0;i<5;++i){
  imageSource[i]=new Image()
  imageSource[i].src="image"+i+".gif"
 }
 delay=500
 delta=100
 nextImage=1
 startAnimation()
}
function startAnimation() {
 interval=setInterval('animate()',delay)
}
function animate() {
 if(start==true){
  i=nextImage
  ++nextImage
  nextImage%=5
  document.display.src=imageSource[i].src
 }
}
function goFaster() {
 clearInterval(interval)
 delay-=delta
 if(delay<100) delay=100
 startAnimation()
}
function goSlower() {
 clearInterval(interval)
 delay+=delta
 startAnimation()
}
// --></SCRIPT>
```

```
</HEAD>
<BODY BGCOLOR="#FFFFFF">
<SCRIPT LANGUAGE="JavaScript"><!--
initialize()
// --></SCRIPT>
<H1>Simple Animation</H1>
<IMG NAME="display" SRC="image0.gif" onLoad="start=true">
<BR>
<FORM>
<INPUT TYPE="BUTTON" NAME="faster" VALUE="Faster"
ONCLICK="goFaster()">
<INPUT TYPE="BUTTON" NAME="slower" VALUE="Slower"
ONCLICK="goSlower()">
</FORM>
</BODY>
</HTML>
```

Image Maps and the
area Object

Clickable image maps provide a graphical, intuitive, and easy-to-use way to navigate the Web. An image map is an image that is divided into different areas, each of which is associated with its own URL. When a user clicks on a particular area of the image map, the document at the URL associated with the area is loaded. Chapter 4 introduces image maps and shows how to handle image map events.

JavaScript supports client-side image maps and provides the area object as a way of handling user actions related to specific image areas. These areas are defined by the <area> tag. For more information on how to use these tags, consult Appendix A, "HTML Reference."

The properties of the area object are shown in Table 10.2. These properties reflect the HREF and TARGET attributes of the <area> tag and are equivalent to those of the location and link objects that you studied in Chapter 9. The area object does not have any methods. It has two events, onMouseOut and onMouseOver, as described in Chapter 4.

TABLE 10.2   Area object properties

Property	Description
hash	The file offset part of an `area` object's HREF attribute
host	The host name part of an `area` object's HREF attribute
hostname	The host:port part of an `area` object's HREF attribute
href	An `area` object's complete HREF attribute
pathname	The path name part of an `area` object's HREF attribute
port	The port part of an `area` object's HREF attribute
protocol	The protocol part of an `area` object's HREF attribute
search	The query string part of an `area` object's HREF attribute
target	An `area` object's TARGET attribute

Working with Image Maps

The HTML `<map>` and `<area>` tags can be used to implement effective client-side image maps. However, as is usually the case, JavaScript provides some additional features that further enhance the capabilities of HTML. With respect to image maps, these features are the `onMouseOver` and `onMouseOut` events associated with the `area` object. The `onMouseOver` event is generated when a user moves the mouse pointer over an image area. The `onMouseOut` event is generated when a user moves the mouse pointer away from an image area. Of the two events, the `onMouseOver` event is generally more useful. To illustrate its use, we'll create an image map for lazy people. With this image map, users will not have to *click* on the image for an action to be performed—they only have to move the mouse over an image area.

Open `imap.htm` with your Web browser; the two-frame document shown in Figure 10.4 is displayed. When you move your mouse over the What's New? circle, the second frame displays the relevant page, as shown in Figure 10.5. When you move your mouse over the Our Products circle, the second frame shows the document shown in Figure 10.6. Move your mouse over the Our Company and Our Field circles and the frame shows the documents shown in Figures 10.7 and 10.8. Isn't this much more efficient than having to move *and* click on individual image areas?

FIGURE 10.4

The image map opening display provides an interesting company home page. (Listing 10.3)

FIGURE 10.5

The What's New? document display provides up-to-date news about a company. (Listing 10.5)

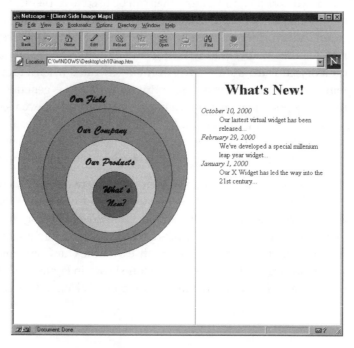

FIGURE 10.6

The Our Products document display provides access to information about a company's products. (Listing 10.6)

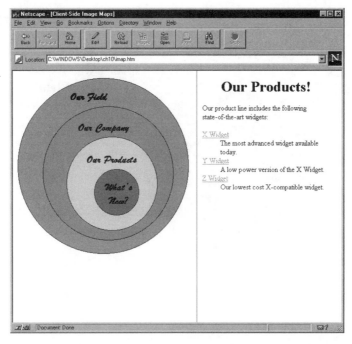

FIGURE 10.7

The Our Company document display provides high-level information about a company. (Listing 10.7)

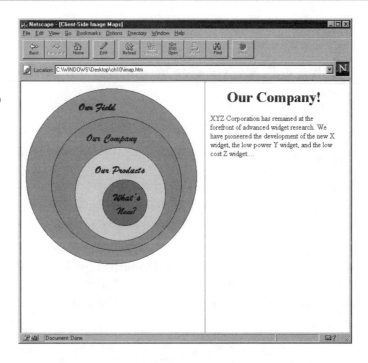

FIGURE 10.8

The Our Field document display provides new information about the technical fields in which the company is engaged. (Listing 10.8)

The `imap.htm` file is shown in Listing 10.3. It creates a simple two-frame document with `map.htm` (Listing 10.4) loaded in the first frame.

Listing 10.3. A client-side image map (imap.htm)

```
<HTML>
<HEAD>
<TITLE>Client-Side Image Maps</TITLE>
</HEAD>
<FRAMESET COLS="415,*" BORDER="1">
<FRAME SRC="map.htm">
<FRAME SRC="blank.htm">
</FRAMESET>
</HTML>
```

The `map.htm` file creates a client-side image map and defines four `<area>` tags. These `<area>` tags correspond to each of the four circles of the `map.gif` file. The HREF attribute of each `<area>` tag is set to the URL *javascript:void(0)*. This URL causes user clicks to be ignored. The `onMouseOver` events of the four

`<area>` tags are handled by invoking the `goWhatsNew()`, `goProducts()`, `goCompany()`, and `goField()` functions, as appropriate. These functions display the files shown in Listings 10.5 through 10.8. (In a real company home page, the files shown in Listings 10.5 through 10.8 would contain real links, as opposed to the fake ones shown in the example.)

Listing 10.4. Creating the image map (map.htm)

```
<HTML>
<HEAD>
<TITLE>Client-Side Image Maps</TITLE>
<SCRIPT LANGUAGE="JavaScript"><!--
function goWhatsNew() {
 parent.frames[1].location.href="whatsnew.htm"
}
function goProducts() {
 parent.frames[1].location.href="products.htm"
}
function goCompany() {
 parent.frames[1].location.href="company.htm"
}
function goField() {
 parent.frames[1].location.href="field.htm"
}
// --></SCRIPT>
</HEAD>
<BODY BGCOLOR="#FFFFFF">
<MAP NAME="bizmap">
  <AREA NAME="whatsNew" COORDS="219,250,50" shape="circle"
   HREF="javascript:void(0)" onMouseOver="goWhatsNew();
     return true">
  <AREA NAME="products" COORDS="205,226,100" shape="circle"
   HREF="javascript:void(0)" onMouseOver="goProducts();
     return true">
  <AREA NAME="company" COORDS="192,202,155" shape="circle"
   HREF="javascript:void(0)" onMouseOver="goCompany()">
  <AREA NAME="field" COORDS="183,189,188" shape="circle"
   HREF="javascript:void(0)" onMouseOver="goField()">
</MAP>
<IMG SRC="map.gif" BORDER="0" USEMAP="#bizmap">
</HTML>
```

Listing 10.5. What's New! (whatsnew.htm)

```
<HTML>
<HEAD>
<TITLE>What's New!</TITLE>
</HEAD>
<BODY BGCOLOR="#FFFFFF">
<H1 ALIGN="CENTER">What's New!</H1>
<DL>
<DT><I>October 10, 2000</I></DT>
<DD>Our lastest virtual widget has been released...</DD>
<DT><I>February 29, 2000</I></DT>
<DD>We've developed a special millenium leap year widget...</DD>
<DT><I>January 1, 2000</I></DT>
<DD>Our X Widget has led the way into the 21st century...</DD>
</DL>
</BODY>
</HTML>
```

Listing 10.6. Our Products! (products.htm)

```
<HTML>
<HEAD>
<TITLE>Our Products!</TITLE>
</HEAD>
<BODY BGCOLOR="#FFFFFF">
<H1 ALIGN="CENTER">Our Products!</H1>
<P>Our product line includes the following
 state-of-the-art widgets:</P>
<DL>
<DT><A HREF="javascript:void(0)">X Widget</A></DT>
<DD>The most advanced widget available today.</DD>
<DT><A HREF="javascript:void(0)">Y Widget</A></DT>
<DD>A low power version of the X Widget.</DD>
<DT><A HREF="javascript:void(0)">Z Widget</A></DT>
<DD>Our lowest cost X-compatible widget. </DD>
</DL>
</BODY>
</HTML>
```

Listing 10.7. Our Company! (company.htm)

```
<HTML>
<HEAD>
```

```
<TITLE>Our Company!</TITLE>
</HEAD>
<BODY BGCOLOR="#FFFFFF">
<H1 ALIGN="CENTER">Our Company!</H1>
<P>XYZ Corporation has remained at the forefront of advanced
 widget research. We have pioneered the development of the
 new X widget, the low power Y widget, and the low cost Z
 widget....</P>
</BODY>
</HTML>
```

Listing 10.8. Our Field! (field.htm)

```
<HTML>
<HEAD>
<TITLE>Our Field!</TITLE>
</HEAD>
<BODY BGCOLOR="#FFFFFF">
<H1 ALIGN="CENTER">Our Field!</H1>
<P>Our field has witnessed a number of breakthroughs in the
 last year. Advanced widget research at the university level
 has led to whole new ways of designing widgets. New widget
 designs have revolutionized the end products built from these
 widgets....</P>
</BODY>
</HTML>
```

Summary

In this chapter you learned how to use the image-handling features provided by JavaScript. You were introduced to the image object and learned how to control the way images are formatted with respect to surrounding text. You also learned how to dynamically display images in your Web pages. You covered the basics of animation and learned how to use dynamic images to create animation effects. You also learned how to use the area object to enhance the attractiveness of client-side image maps. You've covered quite a bit of material in this chapter. The following chapter will be much lighter. You'll learn how to use the mathematical constants and functions provided by JavaScript's Math object.

CHAPTER
ELEVEN

11

Doing Math

- The `Math` Object

- Mathematical Constants

- Mathematical Functions

- Using Math Functions in Scripts

Almost every useful or entertaining program performs some sort of mathematical computation. Game programs use random number generators to shuffle cards, roll dice, or add variety to computer actions. Word processing programs use plenty of tedious arithmetic to determine how pages should be displayed or laid out in hardcopy form. Graphics programs use trigonometric functions to display different geometrical shapes. And so on.

Web programs have an equal affinity for math. Most of the game programs that you've developed so far have used a random number generator. Web sales forms calculate sales totals based on the prices of the products that a user selects. Search engines rank the search value of Web pages based on a variety of formulae ranging from simple to complex.

In this chapter you'll learn about the extensive library of mathematical functions and constants that are provided by JavaScript's Math object. You'll learn how to use the Math object to perform simple computations, and you'll create a JavaScript calculator that illustrates the use of the constants and functions provided by Math. When you finish this chapter you'll have a thorough understanding of JavaScript's math capabilities.

The *Math* Object

The Math object is a predefined JavaScript object. However, it is not part of the Navigator object hierarchy and cannot be instantiated like Date and String to create specific object instances. Think of Math as a library of mathematical constants and functions. The constants are properties of Math and the functions are its methods. Learning to use the Math object involves familiarizing yourself with these properties and methods.

Mathematical Constants

For a scripting language, JavaScript provides a rich collection of mathematical constants—more than you'll need unless you are a mathematician, engineer, or scientist. These constants are described in Table 11.1.

TABLE 11.1 Math constants used in JavaScript

Constant	Description
E	Euler's constant. It is found everywhere in computational math and is the base for natural logarithms.
LN2	The natural logarithm of 2. This is a handy constant for converting between natural logarithms and base 2 logarithms.
LN10	The natural logarithm of 10. Like LN2, it is used in logarithm conversions.
LOG2E	The base 2 logarithm of E. It is used in base 2 to base E logarithm conversions.
LOG10E	The base 10 logarithm of E. It is used in base 10 to base E logarithm conversions.
PI	Another famous mathematical constant, PI is the ratio of the circumference of a circle to its diameter.
SQRT1_2	The square root of ½ is used in many trigonometric calculations.
SQRT2	The square root of 2 is commonly used in algebraic formulas.

The mathematical constants are accessed as Math.*constant* where *constant* is one of the constants listed above. For example, pi times Euler's constant divided by the square root of two is written as follows:

```
Math.PI*Math.E/Math.SQRT2
```

Mathematical Functions

The Math object provides 18 mathematical functions which cover the gamut from rounding to random number generation. These functions have been organized into the following categories:

- Rounding
- Comparison
- Algebraic
- Logarithmic and exponential

- Trigonometric

- Random number generation

To use any of the mathematical functions, invoke them as methods of the `Math` object. For example, the cosine of pi divided by 2 is written as

```
Math.cos(Math.PI/2))
```

The categories of Math functions are described in the following paragraphs.

Rounding Functions

The `round()`, `floor()`, and `ceiling()` functions are used to approximate floating-point numbers with integers. The `round()` function returns the closest integer to a floating-point number. The `floor()` function returns the greatest integer that is less than or equal to a floating-point number. Similarly, the `ceiling()` function returns the least integer that is greater than or equal to a floating-point number.

Comparison Functions

The `min()` and `max()` functions are used to compare two numbers. The `min()` function returns the lesser of the two numbers, and the `max()` function returns the greater. These functions are often used in operations that rely on sorting.

Algebraic Functions

The `abs()` function calculates the absolute value of a number. It is very useful in calculating the distance between two numbers. It is also commonly found in solutions to algebraic problems.

Logarithmic and Exponential Functions

JavaScript provides the natural logarithm function, `log()`. Base 2 or 10 logarithms can be calculated using the logarithm constants (LN2, LN10, LOG2E, LOG10E) to convert between different bases.

The power function, `pow()`, calculates a number raised to a power.

The exponential function, `exp()`, calculates Euler's constant raised to a power. The function `exp(x)` is the same as `pow(Math.E,x)`.

Trigonometric Functions

JavaScript provides seven trigonometric function: `cos()`, `sin()`, `tan()`, `acos()`, `asin()`, `atan()`, and `atan2()`. Trig functions are used to calculate the position and relationship of points on circles, ellipses, waves, and other curved objects with respect to Cartesian coordinates. You probably won't use these functions unless you are involved in science or engineering.

Random Number Generation

The `random()` function generates a pseudo-random number between 0 and 1. You'll continue to use `random()` with many of the examples of this book—especially with games.

Using Math Functions in Scripts

When you use `Math` constants or functions in a script you must precede the constant or function reference with the keyword `Math`. However, this often brings clutter to your scripts. You can use the `with` statement to help eliminate this clutter in math-intensive scripts. For example, the following two statements are equivalent:

Statement 1

```
with (Math) {
  y=sqrt(pow(cos(x),2)+pow(sin(x),2))
}
```

Statement 2

```
y=Math.sqrt(Math.pow(Math.cos(x),2)+ Math.pow(Math.sin(x),2))
```

Example Project: A JavaScript Calculator

Math can be a somewhat passionless subject. The same is true for the Math object. We've already covered all of JavaScript's mathematical constants and functions. To liven things up a bit, let's use these constants and functions to build an advanced scientific calculator.

Open math.htm with your browser. It displays the calculator shown in Figure 11.1. This calculator is the same as most calculators that you've used before except that it has some of JavaScript's mathematical constants and functions attached to it. The purpose of the calculator is not to come up with a new calculator design but to illustrate the use of the JavaScript Math object. For example, click on the e button. Your browser display should look like Figure 11.2. Select log(x) from the Functions selection list, as shown in Figure 11.3. Now click on the Apply button to calculate the natural log of e. The answer is 1—just as you'd expect. Figure 11.4 shows the result of this calculation. Play with the calculator to get a good feel for how it operates.

FIGURE 11.1

This calculator's keys are attached to JavaScript Math methods. (Listing 11.1)

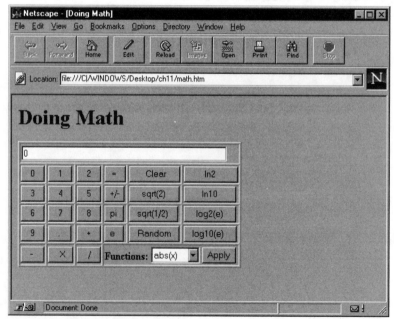

FIGURE 11.2

Clicking the e button causes Euler's constant to be displayed. (Listing 11.1)

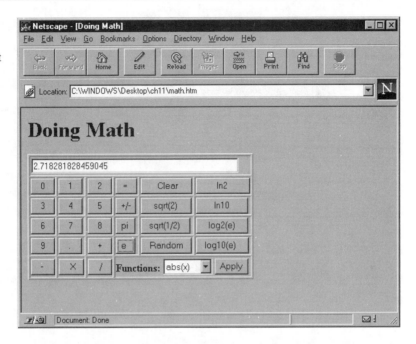

FIGURE 11.3

Selecting log(x) allows you to apply log(x) to e. (Listing 11.1)

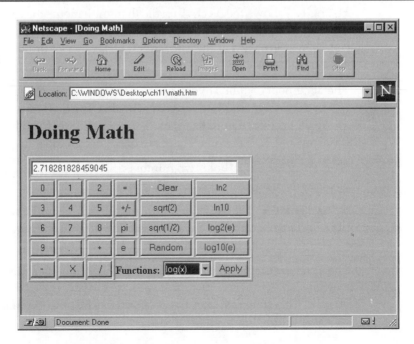

FIGURE 11.4

Applying log(x) to e
results in an answer of 1.
(Listing 11.1)

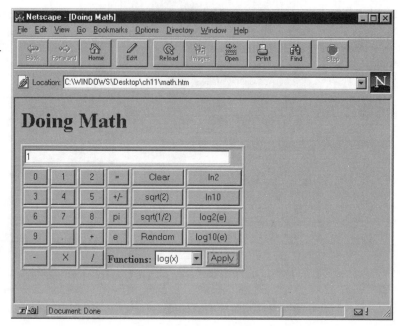

Listing 11.1 shows the `math.htm` file that implements the calculator. This is a fairly long file and is about half HTML and half JavaScript. The HTML creates the nice-looking form used as the calculator. The JavaScript provides the computations behind the buttons.

The document contains two scripts: one in the head and one in the body. The script in the document's body invokes the `setStartState()` function to perform all necessary initializations. The script in the document's head defines the r array and 12 functions. These are described in the following paragraphs.

r This array is used to hold two numbers, entered by the user, that are used as the operands of an arithmetic calculation.

setStartState() This function performs all variable initialization. It sets the `state` variable to *start*, the current operands to *0*, the current `operator` to *""* (null string), and the index of the current operand (`ix`) to *0*.

The `state` variable may be set to any of the following states:

* *start*. This state indicates the program has just loaded/reloaded or that the Clear button has been pressed.

- *gettingInteger*. This state is entered when the user tries to enter an integer via the calculator's keypad.

- *gettingFloat*. This state is entered when the user tries to enter a floating-point number. It is entered when the user clicks the decimal point button.

- *haveOperand*. This state is entered when the user completes the entry of an integer or floating-point number by pressing = or a JavaScript constant, or selecting/applying a JavaScript function.

- *getOperand2*. This state is entered when the user clicks an arithmetic operator (+, -, X, or /).

addDigit()   This function handles the clicking of a digit (0 through 9). If the current `state` is *gettingInteger* or *gettingFloat*, then the digit is appended to the current operand. Otherwise, the current operand is initialized to the digit and the `state` is set to *gettingInteger*. The calculator's `total` field is then updated.

appendDigit()   This function is invoked by `addDigit()` to append a digit to the current operand. If the value of the current operand is *0*, then the digit becomes the value of the current operand. Otherwise, it is appended to the current operand. Note that operands are maintained as string values.

display()   This function displays a string (usually the current operand) in the `total` field of the calculator form.

addDecimalPoint()   This function handles the clicking of the decimal point button. If the current state is *gettingFloat*, then the decimal point is ignored. Otherwise, it appends a decimal point to the current operand or creates a new operand equal to *0.* (zero followed by a decimal point). It then sets the current `state` to *gettingFloat* and updates the value of the `total` field.

clearDisplay()   This function invokes the `setStartState()` function to reinitialize the calculator, and invokes `display()` to update the `total` field.

changeSign()   This function handles the clicking of the change sign (+/-) button. It converts the current operand from negative to positive or vice versa. It then updates the calculator's `total` field.

setTo()   This function handles the clicking of any of the JavaScript constants. It sets the value of the current operand to the constant and the current `state` to *haveOperand*. The `decimal` flag is set to `false` to indicate that a decimal point is not longer in effect. The calculator's `total` field is then updated with the value of the new operand.

calc() This function handles the clicking of the calculate (=) key. If the current `state` is *gettingInteger*, *gettingFloat*, or *haveOperand*, it checks `ix` to determine if the current operand is *1* or *0*. If `ix` is *1* then the user has entered two operands and an operator. The `calculateOperation()` function is invoked to calculate the result of applying the operator to the two operands. The resultant value is stored in the first operand and the number of operands (`ix`) is set to *0*.

If the current `state` is *getOperand2*, then `calculateOperation()` is invoked to calculate the result of applying the current `operator` to the first operand and itself. The resultant value is stored in the first operand and the number of operands (`ix`) is set to *0*.

After performing `state`-specific processing, the current `state` is set to *haveOperand*, the `decimal` flag is set to *false*, and the calculator's `total` field is updated.

calculateOperation() This function is invoked by the `calc()` and `performOp()` functions to calculate the value of applying a binary operator to two operands. It handles addition, subtraction, multiplication, and division operations. It also checks for division by 0.

performOp() This function handles the clicking of a binary (two-value) operator, such as +, -, X, or /. If the current `state` is *start*, it increments the number of operands and sets the `operator` variable to the operator selected by the user.

If the current `state` is *gettingInteger*, *gettingFloat*, or *haveOperand*, then this function checks the number of operands in use (`ix`). If `ix` is *0*, indicating that the current operand is the first operand, then it increments the number of operands and sets the `operator` variable to the operator selected by the user. If `ix` is *1*, the `calculateOperation()` method is invoked to calculate the current operation entered by the user. The result is assigned to the first operand, and this operand is displayed in the calculator's `total` field. The `operator` variable is assigned the new operator.

applyFunction() This function responds to the clicking of the Apply button by applying the currently selected JavaScript function to the current operand. It then displays the new operand value in the calculator's `total` field.

Listing 11.1. A JavaScript Calculator (math.htm)

```
<HTML>
<HEAD>
<TITLE>Doing Math</TITLE>
```

```
<SCRIPT LANGUAGE="JavaScript"><!--
r = new Array(2)
function setStartState(){
 state="start"
 r[0] = "0"
 r[1] = "0"
 operator=""
 ix=0
}
function addDigit(n){
 if(state=="gettingInteger" || state=="gettingFloat")
  r[ix]=appendDigit(r[ix],n)
 else{
  r[ix]=""+n
  state="gettingInteger"
 }
 display(r[ix])
}
function appendDigit(n1,n2){
 if(n1=="0") return ""+n2
 var s=""
 s+=n1
 s+=n2
 return s
}
function display(s){
 document.calculator.total.value=s
}
function addDecimalPoint(){
 if(state!="gettingFloat"){
  decimal=true
  r[ix]+="."
  if(state=="haveOperand" || state=="getOperand2") r[ix]="0."
  state="gettingFloat"
  display(r[ix])
 }
}
function clearDisplay(){
 setStartState()
 display(r[0])
}
```

```
function changeSign(){
 if(r[ix].charAt(0)=="-") r[ix]=r[ix].substring(1,r[ix].length)
 else if(parseFloat(r[ix])!=0) r[ix]="-"+r[ix]
 display(r[ix])
}
function setTo(n){
 r[ix]=""+n
 state="haveOperand"
 decimal=false
 display(r[ix])
}
function calc(){
 if(state=="gettingInteger" || state=="gettingFloat" ||
  state=="haveOperand"){
  if(ix==1){
   r[0]=calculateOperation(operator,r[0],r[1])
   ix=0
  }
 }else if(state=="getOperand2"){
  r[0]=calculateOperation(operator,r[0],r[0])
  ix=0
 }
 state="haveOperand"
 decimal=false
 display(r[ix])
}
function calculateOperation(op,x,y){
 var result=""
 if(op=="+"){
  result=""+(parseFloat(x)+parseFloat(y))
 }else if(op=="-"){
  result=""+(parseFloat(x)-parseFloat(y))
 }else if(op=="*"){
  result=""+(parseFloat(x)*parseFloat(y))
 }else if(op=="/"){
  if(parseFloat(y)==0){
   alert("Division by 0 not allowed.")
   result=0
  }else result=""+(parseFloat(x)/parseFloat(y))
 }
 return result
}
```

```
function performOp(op){
 if(state=="start"){
  ++ix
  operator=op
 }else if(state=="gettingInteger" || state=="gettingFloat" ||
  state=="haveOperand"){
  if(ix==0){
   ++ix
   operator=op
  }else{
   r[0]=calculateOperation(operator,r[0],r[1])
   display(r[0])
   operator=op
  }
 }
 state="getOperand2"
 decimal=false
}
function applyFunction(){
 var selectionList=document.calculator.functions
 var selIX=selectionList.selectedIndex
 var sel=selectionList.options[selIX].value
 if(sel=="abs") r[ix]=Math.abs(r[ix])
 else if(sel=="acos") r[ix]=Math.acos(r[ix])
 else if(sel=="asin") r[ix]=Math.asin(r[ix])
 else if(sel=="atan") r[ix]=Math.atan(r[ix])
 else if(sel=="ceil") r[ix]=Math.ceil(r[ix])
 else if(sel=="cos") r[ix]=Math.cos(r[ix])
 else if(sel=="exp") r[ix]=Math.exp(r[ix])
 else if(sel=="floor") r[ix]=Math.floor(r[ix])
 else if(sel=="log") r[ix]=Math.log(r[ix])
 else if(sel=="sin") r[ix]=Math.sin(r[ix])
 else if(sel=="sqrt") r[ix]=Math.sqrt(r[ix])
 else r[ix]=Math.tan(r[ix])
 decimal=false
 display(r[ix])
}
// --></SCRIPT>
</HEAD>
<BODY>
<SCRIPT LANGUAGE="JavaScript"><!--
setStartState()
// --></SCRIPT>
```

```
<H1>Doing Math</H1>
<FORM NAME="calculator">
<TABLE BORDER="BORDER" ALIGN="CENTER">
<TR>
<TD COLSPAN="6"><INPUT TYPE="TEXT" NAME="total" VALUE="0"
 SIZE="44"></TD></TR>
<TR>
<TD><INPUT TYPE="BUTTON" NAME="n0" VALUE="   0   "
 ONCLICK="addDigit(0)"></TD>
<TD><INPUT TYPE="BUTTON" NAME="n1" VALUE="   1   "
 ONCLICK="addDigit(1)"></TD>
<TD><INPUT TYPE="BUTTON" NAME="n2" VALUE="   2   "
 ONCLICK="addDigit(2)"></TD>
<TD><INPUT TYPE="BUTTON" NAME="equals" VALUE="   =   "
 ONCLICK="calc()"></TD>
<TD ROWSPAN="1"><INPUT
TYPE="BUTTON" NAME="clearField" VALUE="   Clear   "
 ONCLICK="clearDisplay()"></TD>
<TD COLSPAN="1"><INPUT
TYPE="BUTTON" NAME="1n2" VALUE="      ln2      "
 ONCLICK="setTo(Math.LN2)"></TD></TR>
<TR>
<TD><INPUT TYPE="BUTTON" NAME="n3" VALUE="   3   "
 ONCLICK="addDigit(3)"></TD>
<TD><INPUT TYPE="BUTTON" NAME="n4" VALUE="   4   "
 ONCLICK="addDigit(4)"></TD>
<TD><INPUT TYPE="BUTTON" NAME="n5" VALUE="   5   "
 ONCLICK="addDigit(5)"></TD>
<TD COLSPAN="1" ROWSPAN="1"><INPUT TYPE="BUTTON"
 NAME="sign" VALUE=" +/- " ONCLICK="changeSign()"></TD>
<TD ROWSPAN="1"><INPUT TYPE="BUTTON" NAME="sqrt2"
 VALUE="  sqrt(2)   " ONCLICK="setTo(Math.SQRT2)"></TD>
<TD COLSPAN="1" ROWSPAN="1"><INPUT TYPE="BUTTON" NAME="1n10"
 VALUE="      ln10      " ONCLICK="setTo(Math.LN10)"></TD></TR>
<TR>
<TD><INPUT TYPE="BUTTON" NAME="n6" VALUE="   6   "
 ONCLICK="addDigit(6)"></TD>
<TD><INPUT TYPE="BUTTON" NAME="n7" VALUE="   7   "
 ONCLICK="addDigit(7)"></TD>
<TD><INPUT TYPE="BUTTON" NAME="n8" VALUE="   8   "
 ONCLICK="addDigit(8)"></TD>
<TD COLSPAN="1" ROWSPAN="1"><INPUT
```

```
TYPE="BUTTON" NAME="pi" VALUE=" pi   "
 ONCLICK="setTo(Math.PI)"></TD>
<TD COLSPAN="1" ROWSPAN="1"><INPUT
TYPE="BUTTON" NAME="sqrt12" VALUE="sqrt(1/2) "
 ONCLICK="setTo(Math.SQRT1_2)"></TD>
<TD COLSPAN="1" ROWSPAN="1"><INPUT
TYPE="BUTTON" NAME="log2e" VALUE="  log2(e)   "
 ONCLICK="setTo(Math.LOG2E)"></TD></TR>
<TR>
<TD><INPUT TYPE="BUTTON" NAME="n9" VALUE="   9    "
 ONCLICK="addDigit(9)"></TD>
<TD><INPUT TYPE="BUTTON" NAME="decimal" VALUE="   .    "
 ONCLICK="addDecimalPoint()"></TD>
<TD><INPUT TYPE="BUTTON" NAME="plus" VALUE="   +    "
 ONCLICK="performOp('+')"></TD>
<TD COLSPAN="1" ROWSPAN="1"><INPUT TYPE="BUTTON" NAME="e"
 VALUE=" e    " ONCLICK="setTo(Math.E)"></TD>
<TD COLSPAN="1" ROWSPAN="1"><INPUT TYPE="BUTTON"
 NAME="random" VALUE="Random"
 ONCLICK="setTo(Math.random())"></TD>
<TD COLSPAN="1" ROWSPAN="1"><INPUT TYPE="BUTTON" NAME="log10e"
 VALUE="log10(e)  " ONCLICK="setTo(Math.LOG10E)"></TD></TR>
<TR>
<TD><INPUT TYPE="BUTTON" NAME="minus" VALUE="   -    "
 ONCLICK="performOp('-')"></TD>
<TD><INPUT TYPE="BUTTON" NAME="multiply" VALUE="   X  "
 ONCLICK="performOp('*')"></TD>
<TD><INPUT TYPE="BUTTON" NAME="divide" VALUE="   /    "
 ONCLICK="performOp('/')"></TD>
<TD COLSPAN="3" ROWSPAN="1"><B>Functions: </B>
<SELECT NAME="functions" SIZE="1">
<OPTION VALUE="abs" SELECTED="SELECTED">abs(x)</OPTION>
<OPTION VALUE="acos">acos(x)</OPTION>
<OPTION VALUE="asin">asin(x)</OPTION>
<OPTION VALUE="atan">atan(x)</OPTION>
<OPTION VALUE="ceil">ceil(x)</OPTION>
<OPTION VALUE="cos">cos(x)</OPTION>
<OPTION VALUE="exp">exp(x)</OPTION>
<OPTION VALUE="floor">floor(x)</OPTION>
<OPTION VALUE="log">log(x)</OPTION>
<OPTION VALUE="sin">sin(x)</OPTION>
<OPTION VALUE="sqrt">sqrt(x)</OPTION>
```

```
<OPTION VALUE="tan">tan(x)</OPTION>
</SELECT>
<INPUT TYPE="BUTTON" NAME="apply" VALUE="Apply"
 onClick="applyFunction()"></TD></TR>
</TABLE>
</FORM>
</BODY>
</HTML>
```

Summary

In this chapter you learned how to use the mathematical functions and constants provided by JavaScript's Math object. You used these functions and constants to create a JavaScript calculator. This chapter marks the end of Part 2. You have now covered the important objects, methods, and properties that are predefined by JavaScript. In Part 3 you'll learn to use them in some practical Web applications. Chapter 12 begins Part 3 by providing several examples of JavaScript Web page widgets that can enhance the appearance of your Web pages.

PART III

Sample JavaScript
Applications

Web Page Widgets

- What's a Widget?

- Including Advertisements in Your Web Pages

- Usage Counters for Tabulating "Hits"

- Scrolling Messages

- Page Format Preferences

It seems like the most popular Web pages always have the latest adornments—scrolling text, animated icons, or dynamically updated advertisements. To some extent, these novelties help to contribute to the popularity of these pages. The Web, after all, is the showcase for everything that is new and cool.

In this chapter, we'll cover using JavaScript to create a variety of interesting widgets for your Web pages. These widgets can be used to simplify the development of your pages and to add features that your users will find helpful and interesting. I'll present a variety of ways in which JavaScript can be used to facilitate the way you display advertisements, and I'll show you how to develop and display the number of "hits" your Web sites and Web pages are enjoying. You'll also learn how to create scrolling text and images and animated icons. Finally, I'll present examples of features that allow users to control how your Web pages are displayed. When you finish this chapter you'll be able to enhance your Web pages with all of these new features.

What's a Widget?

Widgets are common components that can be used over and over. They have been developed to fill a common need, and can be easily tailored for use in a variety of situations.

In this chapter, you'll learn how to develop and use a variety of widgets with your Web pages. Some of the widgets, such as animated icons and scrolling text marquees, will need to be tailored for a particular application. Others, such as usage counters for measuring hits, can be reused with little or no tailoring required.

Including Advertisements in Your Web Pages

The Web has become a mecca for advertisement. It is hard to find a popular Web page that does not have some sort of colorful ad strategically positioned across the top or along the side of the page. And why not? It's a great way to generate interest in your products or services, and thus possibly some extra income to pay for Internet access. I can think of harder ways to make money!

In this section, you'll learn how JavaScript can be used to simplify the placement and management of ads in your Web pages. You'll learn how to display fixed ads, for specific time intervals, and how to randomly sequence your ads in a continuous display. You'll also learn how to tailor your ad display based on user preferences.

Fixed Ads

Fixed ads are ads that stay in place for a given period of time—a day, a week, a month, etc. After the ad's time interval expires, a new ad is displayed. JavaScript can be used to simplify the management of fixed ads by automatically displaying the next ad at the proper time.

Listing 12.1 provides an example of a script that displays a different ad for each day of the week. To see how it works, open the file `fixedad.htm` with your browser. Your browser will display a Web page similar to the one shown in Figure 12.1 except that the ad displayed by your browser will vary according to which day of the week it is.

FIGURE 12.1

This widget displays the ad of the day. (Listing 12.1)

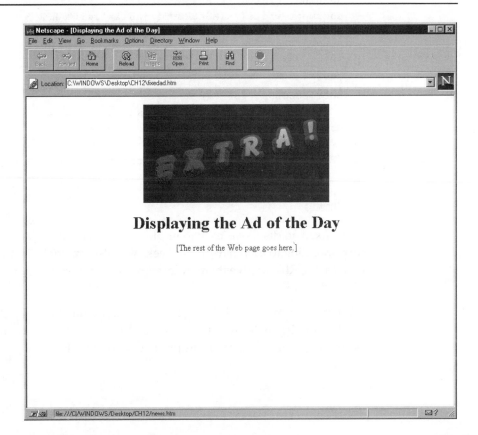

Listing 12.1. Displaying a new ad every day (fixedad.htm)

```
<HTML>
<HEAD>
<TITLE>Displaying the Ad of the Day</TITLE>
<SCRIPT LANGUAGE="JavaScript"><!--
urls = new Array("widgets.htm",
"webmstr.htm",
"coffee.htm",
"sports.htm",
"news.htm",
"stocks.htm",
"travel.htm")

function insertAd() {
 var today = new Date()
 adIX = today.getDay()
 document.write('<P ALIGN="CENTER"><A HREF="'+urls[adIX]+'">')
 document.write('<IMG SRC="i'+adIX+'.gif" BORDER="0">')
 document.writeln('</A></P>')
}
// --></SCRIPT>
</HEAD>
<BODY BGCOLOR="#FFFFFF">
<SCRIPT LANGUAGE="JavaScript"><!--
insertAd()
// --></SCRIPT>
</P><H1 ALIGN="CENTER">Displaying the Ad of the Day</H1>
<P ALIGN="CENTER">[The rest of the Web page goes here.]</P>
</BODY>
</HTML>
```

The fixed ad display is easy to implement. You create an array of URLs corresponding to each day of the week. You also create the ad images associated with each URL and give them indexed names—for example, i0.gif, i1.gif, i2.gif, etc.

When your Web page is being loaded, you use the Date object to determine what ad to display for the current month, date, day, hour, etc. The ad is displayed as an image link using the appropriate image and URL.

Random Ads

Random ads are ads that are randomly selected and displayed, usually each time a Web page is loaded. Random ads change often and are usually used by Web sites with lots of advertisers. JavaScript can be used to simplify the processing of these ads by randomly selecting and displaying a new ad each time a Web page is loaded.

Listing 12.2 shows how random ads can be implemented using JavaScript. Open `randad.htm` with your browser. It will display a Web page similar to the one shown in Figure 12.2 except that the ad displayed by your browser will probably differ, since the ad is randomly selected from a set of seven.

Click on your browser's Reload button and another randomly selected ad is displayed, as shown in Figure 12.3.

FIGURE 12.2

This widget displays a random ad. (Listing 12.2)

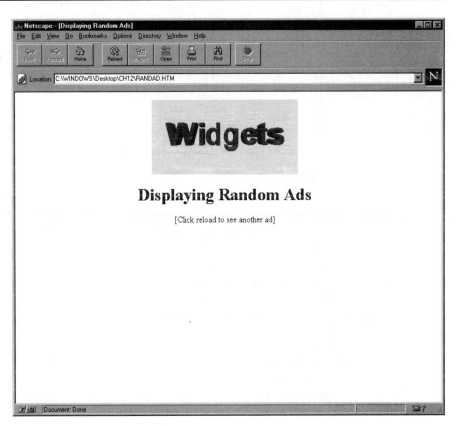

FIGURE 12.3

A different ad is
displayed with
each page reload.
(Listing 12.2)

Listing 12.2. A random ad display page (randad.htm)

```html
<HTML>
<HEAD>
<TITLE>Displaying Random Ads</TITLE>
<SCRIPT LANGUAGE="JavaScript"><!--
urls = new Array("widgets.htm",
"webmstr.htm",
"coffee.htm",
"sports.htm",
"news.htm",
"stocks.htm",
"travel.htm")
```

```
function insertAd() {
  adIX = Math.round(Math.random()*(urls.length-1))
  document.write('<P ALIGN="CENTER"><A HREF="'+urls[adIX]+'">')
  document.write('<IMG SRC="i'+adIX+'.gif" BORDER="0">')
  document.writeln('</A></P>')
}
// --></SCRIPT>
</HEAD>
<BODY BGCOLOR="#FFFFFF">
<SCRIPT LANGUAGE="JavaScript"><!--
insertAd()
// --></SCRIPT>
<H1 ALIGN="CENTER">Displaying Random Ads</H1>
<P ALIGN="CENTER">[Click reload to see another ad]</P>
</BODY>
</HTML>
```

The file `randad.htm` is very similar to `fixedad.htm`. It differs only in the way it selects the ad to be displayed. Instead of selecting an ad based on the `Date` object, it generates a random number which is used to select an ad.

User-Selected Ads

For an ad to be successful, a user must respond to it. Ideally, they will respond by buying the product or service you're advertising, but the first step to getting them to do that is usually getting them to click on the ad. There are a number of strategies that can be used to get users to click on an ad. For example, you can use off-beat messages, colorful image links, or animated icons in the hope of catching the user's attention. You can also display only ads that the user is likely to be interested in. For example, a Web page that is devoted to sports is a better place to advertise sports equipment than hand-made blankets.

In fact, it's a good idea to let the user decide what kind of ads he or she is interested in seeing. The Web page generated by Listing 12.3 does just that. It allows the user to set his or her ad preferences and it permanently stores the user's preference via a cookie.

To see how it works, open `prefad.htm` with your browser. It will display a Web page similar to that shown in Figure 12.4. Note that a small form is provided for you to select what type of ads you are interested in seeing. Select Travel from the selection list and click on the Update button. All the ads that you see in the future will now be travel-related ads, as shown in Figure 12.5.

FIGURE 12.4

Select ad preferences to determine what types of ads will be displayed. (Listing 12.3)

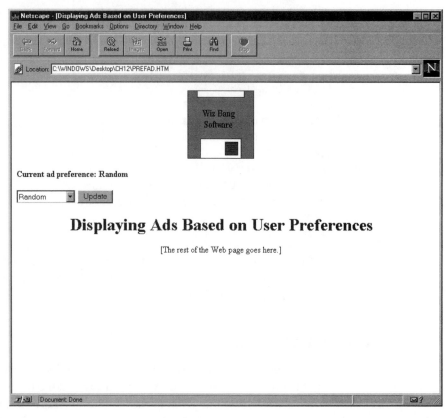

Listing 12.3. Code to display an ad based on user preferences (prefad.htm)

```
<HTML>
<HEAD>
<TITLE>Displaying Ads Based on User Preferences</TITLE>
<SCRIPT LANGUAGE="JavaScript"><!--
function nameDefined(c,n) {
 var s=removeBlanks(c)
 var pairs=s.split(";")
 for(var i=0;i<pairs.length;++i) {
  var pairSplit=pairs[i].split("=")
  if(pairSplit[0]==n) return true
 }
```

FIGURE 12.5

Now ads are
displayed based on
user preferences.
(Listing 12.3)

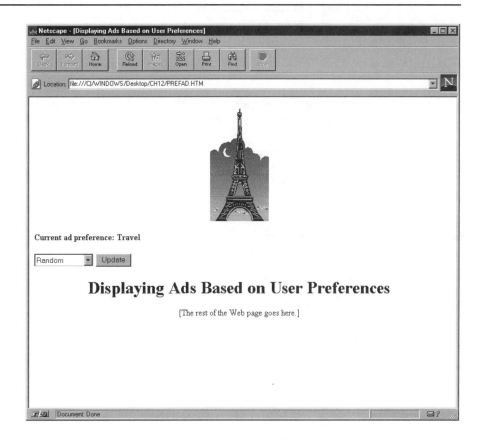

FIGURE 12.5

Now ads are
displayed based on
user preferences.
(Listing 12.3)

```
 return false
}
function removeBlanks(s) {
 var temp=""
 for(var i=0;i<s.length;++i) {
  var c=s.charAt(i)
  if(c!=" ") temp += c
 }
 return temp
}
function getCookieValue(c,n) {
 var s=removeBlanks(c)
 var pairs=s.split(";")
 for(var i=0;i<pairs.length;++i) {
```

```
  var pairSplit=pairs[i].split("=")
  if(pairSplit[0]==n) return pairSplit[1]
 }
 return ""
}

preferences = new Array("Random","Home","Business","Computers",
 "Travel","Entertainment")

urls = new Array("decorate.htm",
"coffee.htm",
"repair.htm",
"news.htm",
"stocks.htm",
"widgets.htm",
"software.htm",
"hardware.htm",
"webmstr.htm",
"travel.htm",
"travel2.htm",
"sports.htm",
"tv.htm")

prefIX=new Array(0,0,3,6,9,11)

function insertAd() {
 readCookie()
 setUserPreferences()
 displayAd()
}

function displayAd() {
 if(userPref==0){
   adIX = Math.round(Math.random()*(urls.length-1))
 }else{
  var startIX=prefIX[userPref]
  var numPrefs=urls.length-startIX
  if(userPref!=prefIX.length-1)
   numPrefs=prefIX[userPref+1] - startIX
  adIX = Math.round(Math.random()*(numPrefs-1))
  adIX += startIX
 }
```

```
    document.write('<P ALIGN="CENTER">')
    document.write('<A HREF="'+urls[adIX]+'">')
    document.write('<IMG SRC="ir'+adIX+'.gif" BORDER="0">')
    document.writeln('</A></P>')
    document.write('<FORM NAME="setPref">')
    document.write('<P><B> Current ad preference: ')
    document.write(preferences[userPref]+' ')
    document.write('</B></P>')
    displaySelectionList()
    document.write(' <INPUT TYPE="BUTTON" NAME="update"' )
    document.write('VALUE="Update" onClick="updatePrefs()">')
    document.writeln('</FORM>')
}

function displaySelectionList() {
 document.write('<SELECT NAME="prefsList">')
 for(var i=0;i<preferences.length;++i) {
  if(i==userPref)
    document.write('<OPTION DEFAULT>'+preferences[i])
  else document.write('<OPTION>'+preferences[i])
  }
 document.write('</SELECT>')
}

function updatePrefs() {
 var list = window.document.setPref.prefsList
 var selectedOption=list.options[list.selectedIndex].text
 var newCookie="adPref="+selectedOption
 newCookie += "; expires=Wednesday, 09-Nov-99 23:12:40 GMT"
 window.document.cookie=newCookie
 window.location="prefad.htm"
}

function setUserPreferences() {
 userPref=0
 for(var i=0;i<preferences.length;++i) {
  if(adPref==preferences[i]){
   userPref=i
   break
  }
 }
}
```

```
function readCookie() {
 var cookie=document.cookie
 adPref="random"
 if(nameDefined(cookie,"adPref"))
  adPref=getCookieValue(cookie,"adPref")
}
// --></SCRIPT>
</HEAD>
<BODY BGCOLOR="#FFFFFF">
<SCRIPT LANGUAGE="JavaScript"><!--
insertAd()
// --></SCRIPT>
<H1 ALIGN="CENTER">Displaying Ads Based on User Preferences</H1>
<P ALIGN="CENTER">[The rest of the Web page goes here.]</P>
</BODY>
</HTML>
```

Even though `prefad.htm` is noticeably longer than `fixedad.htm` and `randad.htm`, it is only slightly more complex. It consists of some familiar code. You're already familiar with `nameDefined()`, `removeBlanks()`, and `getCookieValue()`; these functions are used to parse cookies. The rest of the script's arrays and functions are as follows.

preferences This array identifies the ad categories that a user is allowed to select.

urls This array lists the URLs to be used in the ads.

prefIX This array identifies the index into the `urls` array of the first ad in each ad category specified by the `preferences` array.

insertAd0 This function is used to insert an ad and the preferences form into a document. It invokes `readCookie()` to load any preferences that were previously selected by the user, `setPreferences()` to set those preferences, and `displayAd()` to display the ad.

displayAd0 This function displays an ad based on user preferences. It sets `adIX` to the index of the ad (with respect to urls) to be displayed. It calculates this index (for non-random preferences) by selecting a random index within the portion of the `urls` array occupied by URLs of the user-preferred category.

After computing `adIX`, `displayAd()` displays the ad, followed by the preference selection form.

displaySelectionList() This function displays the selection list containing the ad categories identified in the `preferences` array.

updatePrefs() This function updates the `adPref` cookie with the value of the preference selected in the `prefsList` selection list. It then reloads the current document with the selected preference in effect.

setUserPreferences() This function sets the `userPref` variable to the index within the preferences array of the current user preferences, as identified by the `adPref` cookie.

readCookie() This function reads the `adPref` cookie value and stores it in the `adPref` variable.

> **NOTE**
>
> You may wonder why `displayAd()` generated the entire preferences selection form. Why not just put it in the HTML code? The reason for generating the HTML from JavaScript was to combine the ad and the preference selection form into a single widget, which could be inserted into a document using the simple `insertAd()` function invocation.

Usage Counters for Tabulating "Hits"

Many Web sites display usage counters of the form "This Web site has been visited 102,987 times." These counters help keep track of how many times a site has been visited (in Internet lingo, the visits are called *hits*) and display this number to users (and would-be advertisers).

In this section, we'll look at how you can use JavaScript to create usage counters that are tailored to the individual user rather than the mass of humanity that visits your Web site.

Web Page Access Counters

Most usage counters keep track of how many times any member of mankind, as a whole, has accessed a Web site. Wouldn't it be nice to have a counter that reported to each user how many times that individual user had accessed your site?

Let's start with tabulating individual user accesses to a Web page before we move on to tracking accesses to your Web site as a whole. The script shown in Listing 12.4 tallies Web page accesses. Run this script by opening `pagecnt.htm` with your browser. You will see the display shown in Figure 12.6. It tells you that you've loaded the Web page for the first time. Click your browser's Reload button and you will see the display shown in Figure 12.7. It tells you that you've accessed the Web page for the second time.

FIGURE 12.6

Opening a page for the first time results in this display being shown. (Listing 12.4)

FIGURE 12.7

Opening a page for the second time shows the counter in operation. (Listing 12.4)

Listing 12.4. A personal Web page access counter (pagecnt.htm)

```
<HTML>
<HEAD>
<TITLE>Keeping track of Web page access</TITLE>
<SCRIPT LANGUAGE="JavaScript"><!--
function nameDefined(c,n) {
 var s=removeBlanks(c)
 var pairs=s.split(";")
 for(var i=0;i<pairs.length;++i) {
  var pairSplit=pairs[i].split("=")
  if(pairSplit[0]==n) return true
 }
 return false
}
function removeBlanks(s) {
 var temp=""
 for(var i=0;i<s.length;++i) {
  var c=s.charAt(i)
  if(c!=" ") temp += c
 }
 return temp
}
function getCookieValue(c,n) {
 var s=removeBlanks(c)
 var pairs=s.split(";")
 for(var i=0;i<pairs.length;++i) {
  var pairSplit=pairs[i].split("=")
  if(pairSplit[0]==n) return pairSplit[1]
 }
 return ""
}

function insertCounter() {
 readCookie()
 displayCounter()
}

function displayCounter() {
 document.write('<H3 ALIGN="CENTER">')
 document.write("Welcome! You've accessed this page ")
 if(counter==1) document.write("for the first time.")
 else document.write(counter+" times!")
```

```
    document.writeln('</H3>')
  }

  function readCookie() {
   var cookie=document.cookie
   counter=0
   if(nameDefined(cookie,"pageCount"))
    counter=parseInt(getCookieValue(cookie,"pageCount"))
   ++counter
   var newCookie="pageCount="+counter
   newCookie += "; expires=Wednesday, 09-Nov-99 23:12:40 GMT"
   window.document.cookie=newCookie
  }
  // --></SCRIPT>
  </HEAD>
  <BODY BGCOLOR="#FFFFFF">
  <SCRIPT LANGUAGE="JavaScript"><!--
  insertCounter()
  // --></SCRIPT>
  <H1 ALIGN="CENTER">Keeping track of Web page access</H1>
  <P ALIGN="CENTER">[The rest of the Web page goes here.]</P>
  </BODY>
  </HTML>
```

The script in the document body invokes the insertCounter() function to generate and insert the counter in the Web page. The script in the document head defines three new functions—insertCounter(), readCookie(), and displayCounter(). These functions are used as follows.

insertCounter() This function invokes readCookie() to load the current access counter and displayCounter() to display the counter.

readCookie() This function reads the pageCount cookie, increments it by 1, and then stores it as an updated cookie.

displayCounter() This function displays the counter message.

Web Site Access Counters

The script shown in Listing 12.4 can be easily extended to report how many times a single user has accessed your Web site as a whole. This is accomplished by storing the usage counter in a cookie that has the path set to / (simply a forward slash). This causes the cookie to apply to all Web pages located on a particular host.

To see how the counter works, follow these steps:

1. Open `sitecnt.htm` (Listing 12.5) with your browser. It will display the Web page shown in Figure 12.8.

FIGURE 12.8

Opening `sitecnt.htm` (Listing 12.5) for the first time shows that you're visiting this site for the first time.

2. Close your browser and copy `sitecnt.htm` to another directory. This will demonstrate the effect of having two Web pages at your site.

3. Open the copied file. It will be displayed as shown in Figure 12.9. Note that the counter was updated even though the second file you opened was in another directory (representing a separate Web page at the same site).

FIGURE 12.9

The counter (Listing 12.5) tallies your additional accesses to the site, even though your accesses may be to different pages at the site.

In order for this counter to keep an accurate count of accesses to your Web site, you must copy the file `sitecnt.htm` to all the Web pages at your site.

Listing 12.5. Web site access counter (sitecnt.htm)

```
<HTML>
<HEAD>
<TITLE>Keeping track of Web site access</TITLE>
<SCRIPT LANGUAGE="JavaScript" SRC="counter.js"><!--
// --></SCRIPT>
</HEAD>
<BODY BGCOLOR="#FFFFFF">
<SCRIPT LANGUAGE="JavaScript"><!--
insertSiteCounter()
// --></SCRIPT>
<H1 ALIGN="CENTER">Keeping track of Web site access</H1>
<P ALIGN="CENTER">[The rest of the Web page goes here.]</P>
</BODY>
</HTML>
```

To show how easy it is to include a counter in your Web pages, I've separated the code that implements the counter from the code that displays it. The `sitecnt.htm` file shown in Listing 12.5 includes the `counter.js` file shown in Listing 12.6. In Listing 12.5, only a single JavaScript line is needed to insert the site counter into the Web page.

Listing 12.6. The code that implements the counter (counter.js)

```
function nameDefined(c,n) {
 var s=removeBlanks(c)
 var pairs=s.split(";")
 for(var i=0;i<pairs.length;++i) {
  var pairSplit=pairs[i].split("=")
  if(pairSplit[0]==n) return true
 }
 return false
}
function removeBlanks(s) {
 var temp=""
 for(var i=0;i<s.length;++i) {
```

```
  var c=s.charAt(i)
  if(c!=" ") temp += c
 }
 return temp
}
function getCookieValue(c,n) {
 var s=removeBlanks(c)
 var pairs=s.split(";")
 for(var i=0;i<pairs.length;++i) {
  var pairSplit=pairs[i].split("=")
  if(pairSplit[0]==n) return pairSplit[1]
 }
 return ""
}

function insertSiteCounter() {
 readCookie()
 displayCounter()
}

function displayCounter() {
 document.write('<H3 ALIGN="CENTER">')
 document.write("Welcome! You've accessed this site ")
 if(counter==1) document.write("for the first time.")
 else document.write(counter+" times!")
 document.writeln('</H3>')
}

function readCookie() {
 var cookie=document.cookie
 counter=0
 if(nameDefined(cookie,"siteCount"))
  counter=parseInt(getCookieValue(cookie,"siteCount"))
 ++counter
 var newCookie="siteCount="+counter
 newCookie += "; expires=Wednesday, 09-Nov-99 23:12:40 GMT"
 newCookie += "; path=/"
 window.document.cookie=newCookie
}
```

You probably noticed that counter.js is very similar to pagecnt.htm. The only significant difference between the two files is that counter.js stores the cookie with the path set to /. This enables the cookie to work with any file in any directory on your system.

Time Usage Counters

In some cases, you may be more interested in telling users how many hours or minutes they have spent at your Web site, rather than how many times they have accessed it. This is especially true if your Web site provides some sort of interactive content, like a game or tutorial. In this case, you may want to display a message of the form, "You've accessed this Web site for over 120 hours—Get a life!" This type of usage counter can be easily implemented with JavaScript, as shown in Listing 12.7. Note that this file uses `timecnt.js` (Listing 12.8).

NOTE	Don't rely on this technique being secure—mischievous users could manipulate their `cookies.txt` file to change the time value recorded.

Listing 12.7. Keeping track of user access time (timecnt.htm)

```
<HTML>
<HEAD>
<TITLE>Keeping track of Web site access time</TITLE>
<SCRIPT LANGUAGE="JavaScript" SRC="timecnt.js"><!--
// --></SCRIPT>
</HEAD>
<BODY BGCOLOR="#FFFFFF">
<SCRIPT LANGUAGE="JavaScript"><!--
insertTimeCounter()
// --></SCRIPT>
<H1 ALIGN="CENTER">Keeping track of Web site access time</H1>
<P ALIGN="CENTER">[The rest of the Web page goes here.]</P>
</BODY>
</HTML>
```

Open `timecnt.htm` with your browser. Your display should look like Figure 12.10. Wait a few seconds and then click your browser's Reload button. It should display the Web page shown in Figure 12.11. Notice how it tracked the time in which the page was loaded.

FIGURE 12.10

The time counter display shows that you're accessing this site for the first time. (Listing 12.7)

FIGURE 12.11

The time counter can also be used to track the amount of time the user has spent at your site. (Listing 12.7)

Listing 12.8. Implementing the time counter (timecnt.js)

```
function nameDefined(c,n) {
 var s=removeBlanks(c)
 var pairs=s.split(";")
 for(var i=0;i<pairs.length;++i) {
  var pairSplit=pairs[i].split("=")
  if(pairSplit[0]==n) return true
 }
 return false
}
```

```
function removeBlanks(s) {
 var temp=""
 for(var i=0;i<s.length;++i) {
  var c=s.charAt(i)
  if(c!=" ") temp += c
 }
 return temp
}
function getCookieValue(c,n) {
 var s=removeBlanks(c)
 var pairs=s.split(";")
 for(var i=0;i<pairs.length;++i) {
  var pairSplit=pairs[i].split("=")
  if(pairSplit[0]==n) return pairSplit[1]
 }
 return ""
}

function insertTimeCounter() {
 today = new Date()
 startTime = today.getTime()
 readCookie()
 displayCounter()
 setInterval("setCookie()",1000)
}

function displayCounter() {
 document.write('<H3 ALIGN="CENTER">')
 document.write("Welcome! You've accessed this site ")
 if(prevTime==0) document.write("for the first time.")
 else document.write("over "+displayTime())
 document.writeln('</H3>')
}

function displayTime() {
 var seconds=Math.round(prevTime/1000)
 var minutes=Math.round(seconds/60)
 var hours=Math.round(minutes/60)
 if(seconds<60) return ""+seconds+ " seconds."
 else if(minutes<60) return ""+minutes+ " minutes."
 else return ""+hours+" hours "
}
```

```
function readCookie() {
 var cookie=document.cookie
 prevTime=0
 if(nameDefined(cookie,"timeCount"))
   prevTime=parseInt(getCookieValue(cookie,"timeCount"))
}

function setCookie() {
 now = new Date()
 endTime = now.getTime()
 duration = endTime-startTime
 var newCookie="timeCount="+(prevTime+duration)
 newCookie += "; expires=Wednesday, 09-Nov-99 23:12:40 GMT"
 newCookie += "; path=/"
 window.document.cookie=newCookie
}
```

The `timecnt.js` file uses five new functions—`insertTimeCounter()`, `displayCounter()`, `displayTime()`, `readCookie()`, and `setCookie()`. These functions are used as follows.

insertTimeCounter() This function sets the starting time in which a page is loaded, invokes `readCookie()` to load the previous elapsed time, and then invokes `displayCounter()` to display the current elapsed time. The `setInterval()` method of the `window` object is used to invoke `setCookie()` at one second intervals.

displayCounter() This function displays the total time that a page was accessed up to the time that it was loaded.

displayTime() This function converts elapsed time from milliseconds to seconds, minutes, and hours.

readCookie() This function reads the `timeCount` cookie and stores its value in the `prevTime` variable.

setCookie() This function updates the `timeCount` cookie by adding the time in which a Web page is loaded to the previous value of the cookie.

Nag Counters

As a final example of usage counters, consider a situation in which you want to inform your users that they need to do something like registering or paying their usage bills. In this case, you may want to display a message along the lines of

"You've used this Web page 75 times and you still haven't registered!" These types of nag messages can be easily added to a usage counter. Listing 12.9 shows how. It uses the `counter.js` file that you studied in the "Web Site Access Counters" section earlier in this discussion, and displays an alert message after the user has accessed your Web site ten or more times. Figure 12.12 shows how this message is displayed. As a practical matter, you would also want to tie the alert message to the value of a cookie that tracked user registration.

Listing 12.9. Implementing a nag counter (nag.htm)

```
<HTML>
<HEAD>
<TITLE>Nagging the user to register</TITLE>
<SCRIPT LANGUAGE="JavaScript" SRC="counter.js"><!--
// --></SCRIPT>
</HEAD>
<BODY BGCOLOR="#FFFFFF">
<SCRIPT LANGUAGE="JavaScript"><!--
insertSiteCounter()
if(counter>=10) alert("Don't you think you its time you
registered?")
// --></SCRIPT>
<H1 ALIGN="CENTER">Nagging the user to register</H1>
<P ALIGN="CENTER">[The rest of the Web page goes here.]</P>
</BODY>
</HTML>
```

FIGURE 12.12

Nagging the user is easy using counters and alert dialog boxes. (Listing 12.9)

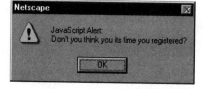

Scrolling Messages

Another popular way of attracting a user's attention is through the use of scrolling messages. These types of messages are very eye-catching and can be used to divert even the most focused Web surfer.

Scrolling Text

One of the easiest ways to implement scrolling messages is via scrolling text. There are a number of ways of accomplishing this. For example, you can scroll text in a form's text field, you can scroll it in the browser's status message area (the status bar), or you can get real fancy and scroll different images that contain separate parts (or even the separate characters) of your message. In this section we'll take a look at scrolling a single text message across the browser's status bar. We'll look at scrolling different messages or images in the section "Adding Simple Animation" later in this discussion.

NOTE   Use `setScrollText()` to tailor the scrolled message for your applications.

Listing 12.10 generates a catchy scrolling text message using the browser's status message area. Figure 12.13 shows the Web page that it displays. To run this script with your browser, open `textscrl.htm`.

Listing 12.10. Implementing a scrolling text message (textscrl.htm)

```
<HTML>
<HEAD>
<TITLE>Scrolling text in the status window</TITLE>
<SCRIPT LANGUAGE="JavaScript"><!--
function setScrollText(s) {
 scrollCount=0
 maxScroll=127
 scrolledText=s
}
function space(n) {
 result=""
 for(var i=0;i<n;++i) result+=" "
 return result
}
function scrollText() {
 var text=space(maxScroll-scrollCount)+scrolledText
 ++scrollCount
 scrollCount %= (maxScroll+1)
 window.defaultStatus=text
 window.setTimeout("scrollText()",500)
```

```
}
// --></SCRIPT>
</HEAD>
<BODY BGCOLOR="#FFFFFF">
<SCRIPT LANGUAGE="JavaScript"><!--
setScrollText("This is scrolling text!!!")
scrollText()
// --></SCRIPT>
<H1 ALIGN="CENTER">Scrolling text in the status window</H1>
<P ALIGN="CENTER">[The rest of the Web page goes here.]</P>
</BODY>
</HTML>
```

The script in the document's body sets the text to be scrolled using the setScrollText() function. It then invokes scrollText() to begin the

FIGURE 12.13

Scrolling text in the
status message area
is a good way to get
the user's attention.
(Listing 12.10)

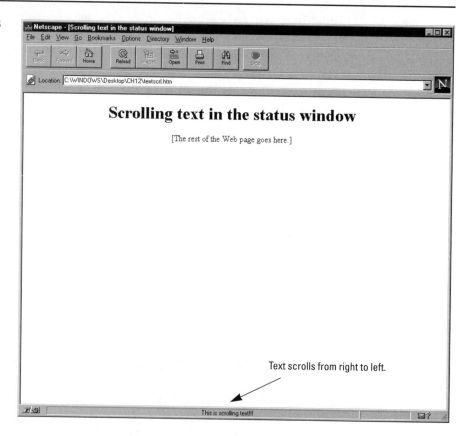

scrolling process. `scrollText()` prepends up to 127 spaces to the text to be scrolled, and gradually reduces the number of prepended spaces to create a right-to-left scrolling effect. A timeout is set to run `scrollText()` every half second.

Scrolling Images

Scrolling images are even more effective than scrolling text in getting a user's attention. Imagine a hand appearing on one side of a Web page and moving across the top of the Web page to point to a link. Wouldn't that get your attention? And wouldn't you be tempted to click on the link?

Open `imgscrl.htm` with your browser. Watch the hand scroll across the top of the browser screen as shown in Figure 12.14. Doesn't it catch your eye?

FIGURE 12.14

Scrolling a hand across the top of a Web page calls attention to an important part of your Web page. (Listing 12.11)

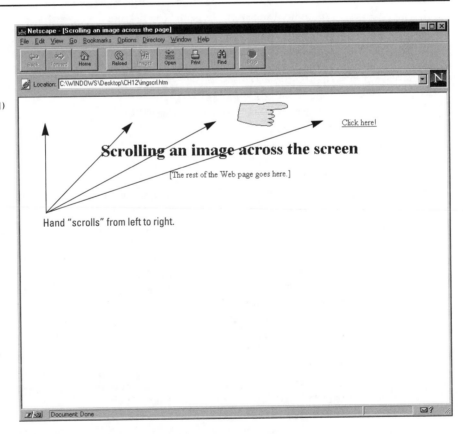

Listing 12.11. Implementing a scrolling image (imgscrl.htm)

```html
<HTML>
<HEAD>
<TITLE>Scrolling an image across the page</TITLE>
<SCRIPT LANGUAGE="JavaScript"><!--
function loadImages() {
 hand = new Image()
 blank = new Image()
 hand.src = "hand.gif"
 blank.src = "blnkhand.gif"
 max = 5
}
function scrollImage(force,n) {
 if(force || window.document.images[n].src==hand.src){
  window.document.images[n].src = blank.src
  window.document.images[(n+1)%max].src = hand.src
 }
}
// --></SCRIPT>
</HEAD>
<BODY BGCOLOR="#FFFFFF">
<SCRIPT LANGUAGE="JavaScript"><!--
loadImages()
// --></SCRIPT>
<P ALIGN="CENTER">
<IMG SRC="blnkhand.gif" BORDER="0"
 onLoad="setTimeout('scrollImage(false,0)',1000)">
<IMG SRC="blnkhand.gif" BORDER="0"
 onLoad="setTimeout('scrollImage(false,1)',1000)">
<IMG SRC="blnkhand.gif" BORDER="0"
 onLoad="setTimeout('scrollImage(false,2)',1000)">
<IMG SRC="blnkhand.gif" BORDER="0"
 onLoad="setTimeout('scrollImage(false,3)',1000)">
<IMG SRC="blnkhand.gif" BORDER="0"
 onLoad="setTimeout('scrollImage(false,4)',1000)">
<A HREF="javascript: void(0)">Click here!</A>
</P>
<H1 ALIGN="CENTER">Scrolling an image across the screen</H1>
<P ALIGN="CENTER">[The rest of the Web page goes here.]</P>
<SCRIPT LANGUAGE="JavaScript"><!--
scrollImage(true,4)
```

```
// --></SCRIPT>
</BODY>
</HTML>
```

The scrolling hand is very easy to implement. You create a GIF file with an image of the hand and a blank GIF file that is the same size as the hand. You then display five blank images in a row across the top of a page. These blank images are then successively replaced by the hand to create a scrolling effect.

The `loadImages()` function is used to load the two images into the `hand` and `blank` variables. The `scrollImage()` function performs the scrolling by changing the position where the hand is displayed. It uses the `force` parameter to unconditionally scroll the image. Otherwise, it only scrolls the image when it handles the `onLoad` event of an image where the hand is already loaded.

Adding Simple Animation

The example scrolling image that you created in the previous section is very catchy and is, in itself, an example of animation. However, the image remains fixed in shape while it travels across the Web page. To make it even more eye-catching, try using an animated image that travels across the page.

Listing 12.12 provides an example of this kind of animation. Open `aniscrl.htm` with your browser and watch the animated face move across the top of the page as shown in Figure 12.15.

Listing 12.12. Implementing an animated scrolling image (aniscrl.htm)

```
<HTML>
<HEAD>
<TITLE>Scroll and animate an image</TITLE>
<SCRIPT LANGUAGE="JavaScript"><!--
function loadImages() {
 hand = new Image()
 blank = new Image()
 faces = new Array(5)
 for(var i=0;i<faces.length;++i) {
  faces[i]=new Image()
  faces[i].src="face"+i+".gif"
 }
 blank.src = "blnkface.gif"
```

```
  max = faces.length
  timeout=500
}
function scrollImage(force,n) {
 if(force || window.document.images[n].src!=blank.src){
  window.document.images[n].src = blank.src
  window.document.images[(n+1)%max].src = faces[(n+1)%max].src
 }
}
// --></SCRIPT>
</HEAD>
<BODY BGCOLOR="#FFFFFF">
<SCRIPT LANGUAGE="JavaScript"><!--
loadImages()
// --></SCRIPT>
<P ALIGN="CENTER">
<IMG SRC="blnkface.gif" BORDER="0"
 onLoad="setTimeout('scrollImage(false,0)',timeout)">
<IMG SRC="blnkface.gif" BORDER="0"
 onLoad="setTimeout('scrollImage(false,1)',timeout)">
<IMG SRC="blnkface.gif" BORDER="0"
 onLoad="setTimeout('scrollImage(false,2)',timeout)">
<IMG SRC="blnkface.gif" BORDER="0"
 onLoad="setTimeout('scrollImage(false,3)',timeout)">
<IMG SRC="blnkface.gif" BORDER="0"
 onLoad="setTimeout('scrollImage(false,4)',timeout)">
<A HREF="javascript: void(0)">Click here!</A>
</P>
<H1 ALIGN="CENTER">Scroll and animate an image</H1>
<P ALIGN="CENTER">[The rest of the Web page goes here.]</P>
<SCRIPT LANGUAGE="JavaScript"><!--
scrollImage(true,max-1)
// --></SCRIPT>
</BODY>
</HTML>
```

Listing 12.12 is very similar to Listing 12.11. The major difference between the two is that Listing 12.12 displays a five-element array of faces rather than a single hand. This causes the simple animation effect of the changing face.

FIGURE 12.15

The scrolling face illustrates simultaneous animation and scrolling. (Listing 12.12)

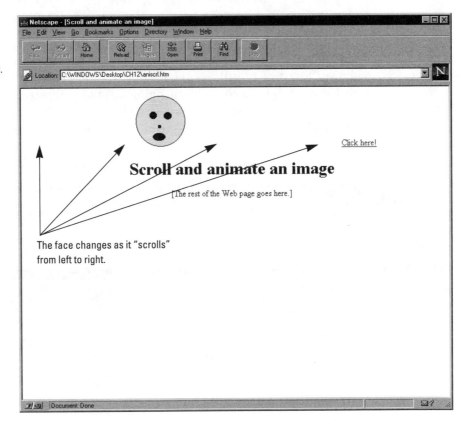

Page Format Preferences

As a final type of Web page widget you'll create a simple form that can be used to control the way that your Web pages are displayed. There are a number of page formatting and display options that you may wish to allow users to control:

- Whether to use frames.

- Whether to display images.

- What colors to use for the document background, text, and links.

- Whether to display navigation buttons, a usage clock, or other widgets.

By giving users control over these options you can get them more involved with your Web pages and heighten their awareness and interest in what you publish.

Listing 12.13 shows how simple page format controls can be added to a Web page to permit the user to change the text and background colors. Figure 12.16 shows the browser display that it produces. Experiment with the document's background and text colors by changing them to different color combinations. Doesn't this simple widget make you feel like you have greater control over what's displayed, and that you are interacting with and improving upon it?

NOTE In later chapters you'll see examples of implementing display navigation buttons, a usage clock, and other widgets.

FIGURE 12.16

With JavaScript, it's easy to change document colors. (Listing 12.13)

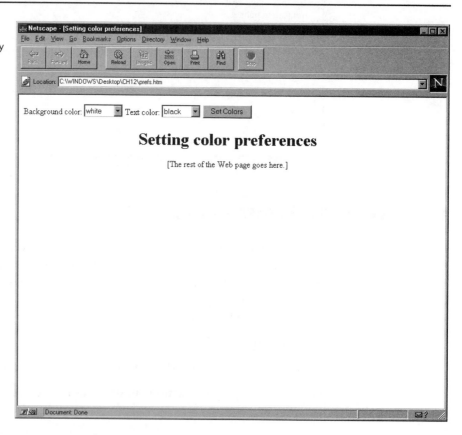

Listing 12.13. Implementing user preferences (prefs.htm)

```
<HTML>
<HEAD>
<TITLE>Setting color preferences</TITLE>
<SCRIPT LANGUAGE="JavaScript"><!--
function nameDefined(c,n) {
 var s=removeBlanks(c)
 var pairs=s.split(";")
 for(var i=0;i<pairs.length;++i) {
  var pairSplit=pairs[i].split("=")
  if(pairSplit[0]==n) return true
 }
 return false
}
function removeBlanks(s) {
 var temp=""
 for(var i=0;i<s.length;++i) {
  var c=s.charAt(i)
  if(c!=" ") temp += c
 }
 return temp
}
function getCookieValue(c,n) {
 var s=removeBlanks(c)
 var pairs=s.split(";")
 for(var i=0;i<pairs.length;++i) {
  var pairSplit=pairs[i].split("=")
  if(pairSplit[0]==n) return pairSplit[1]
 }
 return ""
}
function readCookie() {
 var cookie=document.cookie
 background="white"
 text="black"
 if(nameDefined(cookie,"background"))
  background=getCookieValue(cookie,"background")
 if(nameDefined(cookie,"text"))
  text=getCookieValue(cookie,"text")
}
function setCookie() {
```

```
    var newCookie="background="+background
    newCookie += "; expires=Wednesday, 09-Nov-99 23:12:40 GMT"
    window.document.cookie=newCookie
    var newCookie="text="+text
    newCookie += "; expires=Wednesday, 09-Nov-99 23:12:40 GMT"
    window.document.cookie=newCookie
    window.location="prefs.htm"
  }
  function prefsForm() {
   document.writeln('<FORM name="prefs">')
   document.writeln('Background color: ')
   document.writeln('<SELECT name="bg" size="1">')
   document.writeln('<OPTION>black')
   document.writeln('<OPTION SELECTED>white')
   document.writeln('<OPTION>red')
   document.writeln('<OPTION>orange')
   document.writeln('<OPTION>yellow')
   document.writeln('<OPTION>green')
   document.writeln('<OPTION>blue')
   document.writeln('<OPTION>brown')
   document.writeln('</SELECT>')
   document.writeln(' Text color: ')
   document.writeln('<SELECT name="fg" size="1">')
   document.writeln('<OPTION SELECTED>black')
   document.writeln('<OPTION>white')
   document.writeln('<OPTION>red')
   document.writeln('<OPTION>orange')
   document.writeln('<OPTION>yellow')
   document.writeln('<OPTION>green')
   document.writeln('<OPTION>blue')
   document.writeln('<OPTION>brown')
   document.writeln('</SELECT>')
   document.writeln('<INPUT type="button" value="Set Colors"
onClick="setPrefs()"')
   document.writeln('</FORM>')
  }
  function setPrefs() {
   bgField = window.document.prefs.bg
   bgIndex = bgField.selectedIndex
   background = bgField.options[bgIndex].text
   fgField = window.document.prefs.fg
```

```
fgIndex = fgField.selectedIndex
text = fgField.options[fgIndex].text
setCookie()
}
readCookie()
document.bgColor=background
document.fgColor=text
// --></SCRIPT>
</HEAD>
<BODY BGCOLOR="#FFFFFF">
<SCRIPT LANGUAGE="JavaScript"><!--
prefsForm()
// --></SCRIPT>
<H1 ALIGN="CENTER">Setting color preferences</H1>
<P ALIGN="CENTER">[The rest of the Web page goes here.]</P>
</BODY>
</HTML>
```

To insert the color preferences form into a Web page, you would invoke the prefsForm() function. Your document's head must include the seven functions shown in Listing 12.13 plus the following three lines of code:

```
readCookie()
document.bgColor=background
document.fgColor=text
```

The above statements are included in the head because the document's foreground (text) color must be set before the document's body is processed.

NOTE The SRC attribute of the script tag may be used to include the JavaScript code shown in the document head.

The new functions defined in the document's head are used as follows.

readCookie() This function reads the cookies containing the background and text colors.

setCookie() This function sets the background and text color cookies to the values selected by the user. It then reloads the Web page to bring the new values into effect.

prefsForm() This function displays the color preferences selection form.

setPrefs() This function handles the `onClick` event associated with the Set Colors button by reading the color values selected by the user and invoking `setCookie()` to store the cookie values.

Summary

In this chapter, you learned how to create a variety of interesting widgets for use in your Web pages. You learned how to develop and display ads and usage counters. You also learned how to create scrolling text and images and animated icons. Finally, you learned how to include format controls in your Web pages. In the next chapter you'll learn how to integrate common desktop accessories in your pages.

CHAPTER
THIRTEEN

13

Desktop Accessories

- Calendar

- Calculator

- To-Do List

- World Clock

- Assembling the Desktop

One of the reasons for the success of window-based operating systems is their ability to take the objects of your physical desktop—clock, calendar, notepad, calculator, files, etc.—and make them available in electronic form. Software like the MacOS and Microsoft Windows were developed around this desktop metaphor. The World Wide Web, on the other hand, was designed using the metaphor of a library—we access electronic documents and view electronic pages. Now the Web and the desktop are beginning to converge. The browser is being integrated into window-based operating systems, and desktop programs are being executed on the Web.

In the previous chapter you developed several widgets which enhance the effectiveness of your Web pages. These widgets are generic and can be tailored to a variety of needs. In this chapter, you'll learn how to develop JavaScript components that are not only eye-catching, but useful. As you have probably guessed by now, you'll be developing desktop accessories—a calendar, a calculator, a to-do list, and a clock—that you'll be able to use with your own Web pages and Web applications.

Calendar

The first accessory that you'll develop is a calendar. Calendars are required by anyone who works or lives by a schedule. I constantly consult a calendar to schedule meetings, conferences, travel, and parties. In most cases, a simple monthly view is all I need to make these scheduling decisions. Why would I want to put a calendar on a Web page? Well, if I were the leader of a rock band, I would like to tell my fans when and where to go for my next month's gigs. If I were an astronomer, I'd let people know when to look for interesting celestial events. If I were a soccer coach, I'd inform my players when practices and games would be held. Get the idea? In short, when there's a need to publicize a schedule, making it available electronically is a good way to do it.

The calendar that you'll develop in this section is only a calendar—it won't let you publish your schedule, it will just show you the days of the month. However, it can easily be added as an accessory to any schedule publishing application, as you'll see in Chapter 29.

When you run the calendar scripts of this chapter, they will display a calendar for the *current* month. The screen captures shown in this chapter were current for the month in which this chapter was written. Thus, your display and the chapter's screens will differ.

Listing 13.1 defines a `Calendar` object which displays the monthly calendar shown in Figure 13.1. The `calendar.js` file serves as a building block for a general calendar application. It defines six functions: the `Calendar()` constructor, `displayCalendar()`, `displayCalendarHeader()`, `displayDates()`, `numberOfDays()`, and `writeDate()`. These functions are used as follows:

Calendar() This is the constructor for the `Calendar` object. It checks the number of arguments passed to it and creates a calendar using the current date or a specified month and year. It also defines the `display()` method using the `displayCalendar()` function.

displayCalendar() This function displays a monthly calendar as an HTML table. It invokes `displayCalendarHeader()` to display the table header and `displayDates()` to display the actual calendar dates. If a day of the month is passed as an argument to this function then that day is highlighted in red when the calendar is displayed.

displayCalendarHeader() This function displays the calendar header—month, year, and days of the week.

displayDates() This function displays the days of the month. It figures out what day the month should begin on by creating a `Date` object for the first day of the month and by accessing its `getDay()` method. It invokes the `numberOfDays()` function to get the number of days in a particular month. It calculates the number of rows in the calendar table and then fills in those rows with the appropriate dates. If the `shade` argument is set to `true` then the specified day is highlighted in red. Calendar days outside of the current month are ignored (a non-breaking space, ` `, is used to fill the calendar entry of these days).

numberOfDays() This function calculates the number of days in a month. It takes leap years into account.

writeDate() This function writes the cells of the calendar table as centered level-3 headings.

FIGURE 13.1

Displaying the calendar
(Listing 13.2)

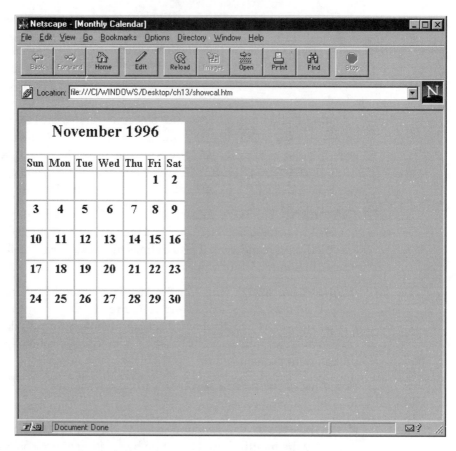

Listing 13.1. The Calendar object (calendar.js)

```
function Calendar() {
 var len = Calendar.arguments.length
 if(len == 2){
  this.month = Calendar.arguments[0]
  this.year = Calendar.arguments[1]
 }else{
  today = new Date()
  this.month = today.getMonth()
  this.year = today.getYear()
 }
 this.display = displayCalendar
```

```
}

function displayCalendar() {
 document.writeln("<TABLE BORDER='0' BGCOLOR='white'>")
 displayCalendarHeader(this.month,this.year)
 if(displayCalendar.arguments.length>0){
  var day = displayCalendar.arguments[0]-1
  displayDates(day,this.month,this.year,true)
 }else displayDates(0,this.month,this.year,false)
 document.writeln("</TABLE>")
}

function displayCalendarHeader(month,year) {
 var days = new Array("Sun","Mon","Tue","Wed","Thu",
  "Fri","Sat")
 var months = new Array("January","February","March","April",
  "May","June","July","August","September","October",
  "November","December")
 document.writeln("<TR><TH COLSPAN='7'><H2 ALIGN='CENTER'>")
 document.writeln(months[month])
 document.writeln(" 19"+year+"</H2></TH></TR>")
 document.writeln("<TR>")
 for(var i=0;i<days.length;++i)
  document.writeln("<TH> "+days[i]+" </TH>")
 document.writeln("</TR>")
}

function displayDates(day,month,year,shade) {
 d = new Date(year,month,1)
 var startDay = d.getDay()
 var numDays = numberOfDays(month,year)
 var numRows = Math.floor((numDays+startDay)/7)
 if((numDays+startDay)%7 > 1) ++numRows
 var currentDate=0
 for(var i=0;i<numRows;++i) {
  document.writeln("<TR>")
  for(var j=0;j<7;++j) {
   if(shade && day==currentDate)
    document.write("<TD BGCOLOR='red'>")
   else document.write("<TD>")
   if(currentDate>=numDays) document.write(" ")
   else if(currentDate>0){
    ++currentDate
```

```
    writeDate(currentDate)
   }else if(i*7+j>=startDay){
    ++currentDate
     writeDate(currentDate)
   }else document.write(" ")
   document.writeln("</TD>")
  }
  document.writeln("</TR>")
 }
}

function numberOfDays(month,year) {
 var numDays=new Array(31,28,31,30,31,30,31,31,30,31,30,31)
 n = numDays[month]
 if(month == 1 && year % 4 == 0) ++n
 return n
}

function writeDate(n) {
  document.write("<H3 ALIGN='CENTER'>"+n+"</H3>")
}
```

To see how the Calendar object and functions of the `calendar.js` file work, open `showcal.htm` (Listing 13.2) with your browser. It generates the display shown in Figure 13.1. The file `showcal.htm` is a simple HTML file with two scripts—one to read `calendar.js` and one to create and display a calendar. You can use `calendar.js` in your scripts in a similar fashion.

Listing 13.2. Displaying the calendar (showcal.htm)

```
<HTML>
<HEAD>
<TITLE>Monthly Calendar</TITLE>
<SCRIPT LANGUAGE="JavaScript" SRC="calendar.js"><!--
// --></SCRIPT>
</HEAD>
<BODY>
<SCRIPT LANGUAGE="JavaScript"><!--
cal=new Calendar()
cal.display()
// --></SCRIPT>
</BODY>
</HTML>
```

Since `calendar.js` is fairly modular, its functions can be used to build larger calendar applications. Let's do so now as a prelude to using `calendar.js` in your own Web applications.

Open `cal.htm` with your browser and it displays the Web page shown in Figure 13.2. At the top of your screen are three buttons for displaying different monthly views. If you click on the left arrow, the previous month is displayed, as shown in Figure 13.3. If you click on the right arrow, the next month is displayed. And of course, if you click on the Current Month button, the current month's calendar is displayed.

FIGURE 13.2

Calendar program opening display (Listing 13.3)

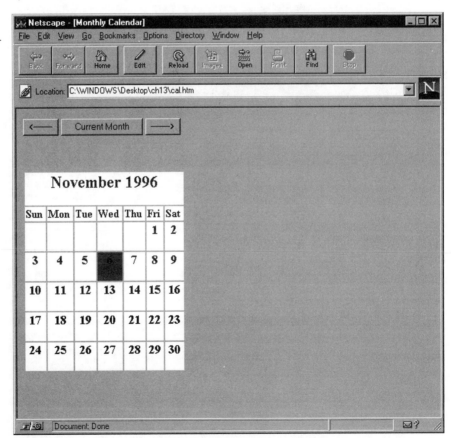

The button controls at the top of the calendar were added by creating a two-frame set. The buttons are placed in the top frame set and the calendar is displayed in the bottom frame set. Listing 13.3 shows how the frame sets were set up.

Listing 13.3. Setting up a two-frame calendar (cal.htm)

```
<HTML>
<HEAD>
<TITLE>Monthly Calendar</TITLE>
<FRAMESET ROWS="77,*" BORDER="0">
<FRAME SRC="control.htm">
<FRAME SRC="calendar.htm">
</FRAMESET>
</HTML>
```

FIGURE 13.3

Displaying the previous month (Listing 13.3)

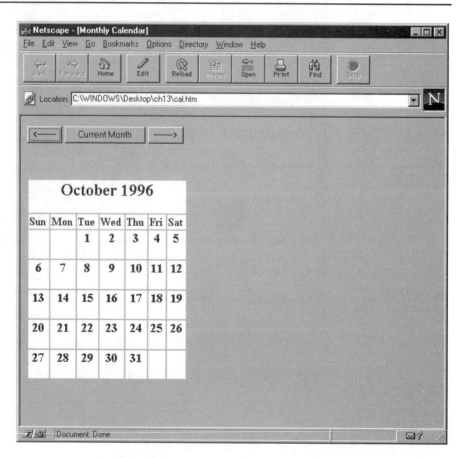

The `control.htm` file (Listing 13.4) is used to display the buttons in the top frame. Note that two hidden fields are used to hold the values of the current month and year of the calendar being displayed. These values are initially set to 99 and 0. The `calendar.htm` file recognizes these values as invalid and sets them to the values of the current month to mark them as invalid entries. (You can't have a month 99 and year 0 has long since passed.)

The `previousMonth()`, `currentMonth()`, and `nextMonth()` functions are used to handle the events associated with the clicking of the three buttons. They update the month and year as appropriate, and invoke `updateCalendar()` to store the new month and year values in the `monthValue` and `yearValue` hidden fields. The `updateCalendar()` function then reloads the bottom frame so that the calendar displayed reflects the new month and year values.

Listing 13.4. The calendar controls (control.htm)

```
<HTML>
<HEAD>
<TITLE>Monthly Calendar</TITLE>
<SCRIPT LANGUAGE="JavaScript"><!--
function updateCalendar(month,year) {
 document.forms[0].monthValue.value=month
 document.forms[0].yearValue.value=year
 parent.frames[1].location="calendar.htm"
}
function previousMonth() {
 month=document.forms[0].monthValue.value
 year=document.forms[0].yearValue.value
 --month
 if(month<0) {
  if(year==0) month=0
  else{
    --year
    month=11
  }
 }
 updateCalendar(month,year)
}
function currentMonth() {
 var today=new Date()
 updateCalendar(today.getMonth(),today.getYear())
}
```

```
function nextMonth() {
 month=document.forms[0].monthValue.value
 year=document.forms[0].yearValue.value
 ++month
 if(month>11) {
  if(year==99) month=11
  else{
   ++year
   month=0
  }
 }
 updateCalendar(month,year)
}
// --></SCRIPT>
</HEAD>
<BODY>
<FORM NAME="changeMonth">
<INPUT TYPE="HIDDEN" NAME="monthValue" VALUE="99">
<INPUT TYPE="HIDDEN" NAME="yearValue" VALUE="0">
<INPUT TYPE="BUTTON" NAME="previous" VALUE="<-------"
 onClick="previousMonth()">
<INPUT TYPE="BUTTON" NAME="current" VALUE="Current Month"
 onClick="currentMonth()">
<INPUT TYPE="BUTTON" NAME="next" VALUE="------->"
 onClick="nextMonth()">
</FORM>
</BODY>
</HTML>
```

The calendar.htm file (Listing 13.5) displays the calendar in the bottom frame. It uses the calendar.js file to accomplish this purpose. It contains a small script which reads the monthValue and yearValue fields of the control.htm file and creates a calendar for the specified month and year. If the month is 99 then the script sets the month and year to the current date and updates the monthValue and yearValue fields with these values. If the month and year are current, then the current date is highlighted in red on the calendar.

Listing 13.5. The calendar update frame (calendar.htm)

```
<HTML>
<HEAD>
<TITLE>Monthly Calendar</TITLE>
<SCRIPT LANGUAGE="JavaScript" SRC="calendar.js"><!--
```

```
// --></SCRIPT>
</HEAD>
<BODY>
<SCRIPT LANGUAGE="JavaScript"><!--
formRef = parent.frames[0].document.forms[0]
month = parseInt(formRef.monthValue.value)
year = parseInt(formRef.yearValue.value)
today = new Date()
if(month==99) {
 month = today.getMonth()
 year = today.getYear()
 formRef.monthValue.value=""+month
 formRef.yearValue.value=""+year
}
cal=new Calendar(month,year)
if(month==today.getMonth() && year==today.getYear())
 cal.display(today.getDate())
else cal.display()
// --></SCRIPT>
</BODY>
</HTML>
```

Calculator

You've already learned, in Chapter 11, how to develop the second desktop acces-sory—a calculator. However, the calculator that you developed in Chapter 11 was meant to help you learn how to use JavaScript's Math object and would be a little bit of an overkill for most users on a Web page. The calc.htm file shown in Figure 13.4 (Listing 13.6) removes all of the extra functions used to show off JavaScript's math library and won't scare off any of your Web users.

Why would you want to include a calculator on a Web page? A calculator is a nice feature if you are involved in any type of Web-based sales. When a customer selects a series of products and sees their total price automatically calculated, he or she often wants to double-check the calculations. Did they add the right sales tax? Did they charge the right shipping rate? Did they add the numbers correctly? Having a calculator available to your customers offers them a convenient way to perform these checks. They may even create a bookmark to your Web page just to have the calculator available from their browser!

FIGURE 13.4

The simplified calculator
(Listing 13.6)

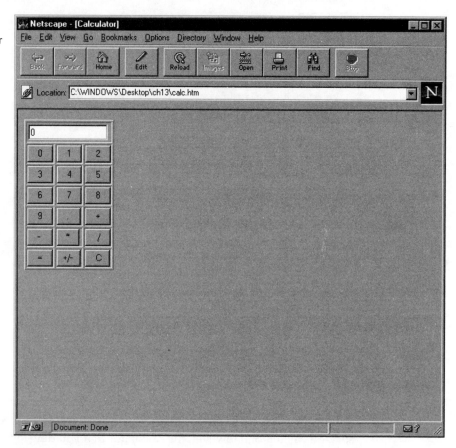

Listing 13.6. The revised calendar program (calc.htm)

```
<HTML>
<HEAD>
<TITLE>Calculator</TITLE>
<SCRIPT LANGUAGE="JavaScript"><!--
r = new Array(2)
function setStartState(){
 state="start"
 r[0] = "0"
 r[1] = "0"
 operand=""
 ix=0
}
```

```
function addDigit(n){
 if(state=="gettingInteger" || state=="gettingFloat")
  r[ix]=appendDigit(r[ix],n)
 else{
  r[ix]=""+n
  state="gettingInteger"
 }
 display(r[ix])
}
function appendDigit(n1,n2){
 if(n1=="0") return ""+n2
 var s=""
 s+=n1
 s+=n2
 return s
}
function display(s){
 document.calculator.total.value=s
}
function addDecimalPoint(){
 if(state!="gettingFloat"){
  decimal=true
  r[ix]+="."
  if(state=="haveOperand" || state=="getOperand2") r[ix]="0."
  state="gettingFloat"
  display(r[ix])
 }
}
function clearDisplay(){
 setStartState()
 display(r[0])
}
function changeSign(){
 if(r[ix].charAt(0)=="-") r[ix]=r[ix].substring(1,r[ix].length)
 else if(parseFloat(r[ix])!=0) r[ix]="-"+r[ix]
 display(r[ix])
}
function calc(){
 if(state=="gettingInteger" || state=="gettingFloat" ||
  state=="haveOperand"){
  if(ix==1){
   r[0]=calculateOperation(operand,r[0],r[1])
   ix=0
  }
```

```
 }else if(state=="getOperand2"){
  r[0]=calculateOperation(operand,r[0],r[0])
  ix=0
 }
 state="haveOperand"
 decimal=false
 display(r[ix])
}
function calculateOperation(op,x,y){
 var result=""
 if(op=="+"){
  result=""+(parseFloat(x)+parseFloat(y))
 }else if(op=="-"){
  result=""+(parseFloat(x)-parseFloat(y))
 }else if(op=="*"){
  result=""+(parseFloat(x)*parseFloat(y))
 }else if(op=="/"){
  if(parseFloat(y)==0){
   alert("Division by 0 not allowed.")
   result=0
  }else result=""+(parseFloat(x)/parseFloat(y))
 }
 return result
}
function performOp(op){
 if(state=="start"){
  ++ix
  operand=op
 }else if(state=="gettingInteger" || state=="gettingFloat" ||
  state=="haveOperand"){
  if(ix==0){
   ++ix
   operand=op
  }else{
   r[0]=calculateOperation(operand,r[0],r[1])
   display(r[0])
   operator=op
  }
 }
 state="getOperand2"
 decimal=false
}
```

```
// --></SCRIPT>
</HEAD>
<BODY>
<SCRIPT LANGUAGE="JavaScript"><!--
setStartState()
// --></SCRIPT>
<FORM NAME="calculator">
<TABLE BORDER="BORDER" ALIGN="CENTER">
<TR>
<TD COLSPAN="3"><INPUT TYPE="TEXT" NAME="total" VALUE="0"
 SIZE="15"></TD></TR>
<TR>
<TD><INPUT TYPE="BUTTON" NAME="n0" VALUE="   0   "
 ONCLICK="addDigit(0)"></TD>
<TD><INPUT TYPE="BUTTON" NAME="n1" VALUE="   1   "
 ONCLICK="addDigit(1)"></TD>
<TD><INPUT TYPE="BUTTON" NAME="n2" VALUE="   2   "
 ONCLICK="addDigit(2)"></TD>
</TR>
<TR>
<TD><INPUT TYPE="BUTTON" NAME="n3" VALUE="   3   "
 ONCLICK="addDigit(3)"></TD>
<TD><INPUT TYPE="BUTTON" NAME="n4" VALUE="   4   "
 ONCLICK="addDigit(4)"></TD>
<TD><INPUT TYPE="BUTTON" NAME="n5" VALUE="   5   "
 ONCLICK="addDigit(5)"></TD>
</TR>
<TR>
<TD><INPUT TYPE="BUTTON" NAME="n6" VALUE="   6   "
 ONCLICK="addDigit(6)"></TD>
<TD><INPUT TYPE="BUTTON" NAME="n7" VALUE="   7   "
 ONCLICK="addDigit(7)"></TD>
<TD><INPUT TYPE="BUTTON" NAME="n8" VALUE="   8   "
 ONCLICK="addDigit(8)"></TD>
</TR>
<TR>
<TD><INPUT TYPE="BUTTON" NAME="n9" VALUE="   9   "
 ONCLICK="addDigit(9)"></TD>
<TD><INPUT TYPE="BUTTON" NAME="decimal" VALUE="   .   "
 ONCLICK="addDecimalPoint()"></TD>
<TD><INPUT TYPE="BUTTON" NAME="plus" VALUE="   +   "
 ONCLICK="performOp('+')"></TD>
</TR>
```

```
<TR>
<TD><INPUT TYPE="BUTTON" NAME="minus" VALUE="   -    "
 ONCLICK="performOp('-')"></TD>
<TD><INPUT TYPE="BUTTON" NAME="multiply" VALUE="   *    "
 ONCLICK="performOp('*')"></TD>
<TD><INPUT TYPE="BUTTON" NAME="divide" VALUE="    /    "
 ONCLICK="performOp('/')"></TD>
</TR>
<TR>
<TD><INPUT TYPE="BUTTON" NAME="equals" VALUE="   =    "
 ONCLICK="calc()"></TD>
<TD COLSPAN="1" ROWSPAN="1"><INPUT TYPE="BUTTON"
 NAME="sign" VALUE="  +/-   " ONCLICK="changeSign()"></TD>
<TD><INPUT TYPE="BUTTON" NAME="clearField" VALUE="   C   "
 ONCLICK="clearDisplay()"></TD>
</TR>
</TABLE>
</FORM>
</BODY>
</HTML>
```

To-Do List

When you're browsing the Web, would you like to take notes on a particular Web page and have those notes available to you whenever you revisit the page? I know I would. You could take notes to summarize the important points of a Web-based document, to identify other relevant URLs, or to just keep track of when or why you last visited the page.

This section presents an approach to maintaining private notes on public Web sites. In keeping with the desktop metaphor, it implements this approach in terms of a to-do list—a very handy tool for people who have a lot to do! It can easily be tailored to a general-purpose notepad by just changing its heading.

Open notes.htm with your browser. It generates the display shown in Figure 13.5. Now type a list of things that you have to do—your to-do list—as shown in Figure 13.6. Exit your browser, wait a few seconds, and then reopen notes.htm. Your notes are still there, on that Web page! And the best thing about it is that nobody else can read them.

This may not seem to be all that exciting. But it is an important capability. You can add the same type of note area to your Web pages. People can jot down notes to themselves about your Web pages and when they return to your Web page, their notes will still be there—but only for their own use.

How does `notes.htm` (Listing 13.7) work? You probably guessed it—cookies. Cookies are used to store the notes entered by the user. These notes are stored on the user's system, so you don't have to worry about making disk space available for them. When the user revisits your Web page they are automatically reloaded by his or her browser.

FIGURE 13.5

The to-do list opening display (Listing 13.7)

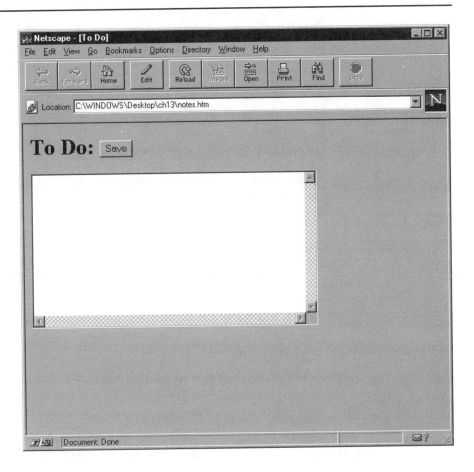

FIGURE 13.6

The to-do list reads the cookie next time it starts. (Listing 13.7)

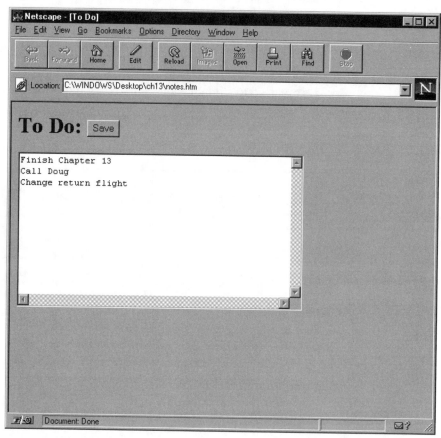

The notes.htm file uses the cookie-reading functions of cookie.js (Listing 13.8). You've already used these functions in Chapters 9 and 10. They are nameDefined(), removeBlanks(), and getCookieValue().

The file notes.htm defines four other functions—loadNotes(), saveNotes(), encode(), and decode()—to process the text that is entered into its text area field. These functions are used as follows:

loadNotes() This function uses nameDefined() and getCookieValue() to read the value of the toDo cookie. It invokes decode() to decode the cookie value.

saveNotes() This function reads the notes entered into the text area field and invokes encode() to encode them in a form that is suitable for storage in a cookie. It then creates a new `toDo` cookie with a 1999 expiration date. (I picked 1999 arbitrarily. There is no reason why you can't go beyond the year 2000.)

encode() White-space characters, semicolons, and commas cannot be stored as part of a cookie's *name=value* pair. This function encodes such strings into a form that is suitable for cookie storage. The conversions carried out by the `encode()` function are listed in Table 13.1.

decode() This function decodes a stored cookie string in accordance with Table 13.1.

TABLE 13.1 String-to-cookie encoding performed by `encode()` and `decode()`

String character	Cookie character
/	//
space	/b
,	/.
;	/:
\n	/n
\r	/r
\t	/t
\b	/b

Listing 13.7. The to-do list script (notes.htm)

```
<HTML>
<HEAD>
<TITLE>To Do</TITLE>
<SCRIPT LANGUAGE="JavaScript" SRC="cookie.js"><!--
// --></SCRIPT>
<SCRIPT LANGUAGE="JavaScript"><!--
function loadNotes() {
 var cookie=document.cookie
 if(nameDefined(cookie,"toDo")) {
  todo=getCookieValue(cookie,"toDo")
```

```
   todo=decode(todo)
  }else todo=""
  document.forms[0].notes.value=todo
}
function saveNotes() {
  todo=window.document.forms[0].notes.value
  todo=encode(todo)
  var newCookie = "toDo="+todo+"; expires="
  newCookie += "Wednesday, 09-Nov-99 23:12:40 GMT"
  document.cookie=newCookie
}
function encode(s) {
  t=""
  for(var i=0;i<s.length;++i) {
   ch=s.charAt(i)
   if(ch=="/") t += "//"
   else if(ch==" ") t += "/b"
   else if(ch==",") t += "/."
   else if(ch==";") t += "/:"
   else if(ch=="\n") t += "/n"
   else if(ch=="\r") t += "/r"
   else if(ch=="\t") t += "/t"
   else if(ch=="\b") t += "/b"
   else t += ch
  }
  return t
}
function decode(s) {
  // Decode the encoded cookie value
  t=""
  for(var i=0;i<s.length;++i) {
   var ch=s.charAt(i)
   if(ch=="/") {
    ++i
    if(i<s.length){
      ch=s.charAt(i)
      if(ch=="/") t += ch
      else if(ch==".") t += ","
      else if(ch==":") t += ";"
      else if(ch=="n") t += "\n"
      else if(ch=="r") t += "\r"
      else if(ch=="t") t += "\t"
```

```
      else if(ch=="b") t += "  "
    }
   }else t += ch
  }
 return t
}
// --></SCRIPT>
</HEAD>
<BODY>
<FORM>
<H3>To Do:
<INPUT NAME="save" TYPE="BUTTON" VALUE="Save"
 onClick="saveNotes()"></H3>
<TEXTAREA NAME="notes" ROWS="12" COLS="50"
 VALUE=""></TEXTAREA>
</FORM>
<SCRIPT LANGUAGE="JavaScript"><!--
 loadNotes()
// --></SCRIPT>
</BODY>
</HTML>
```

Listing 13.8. Common cookie functions (cookie.js)

```
function nameDefined(c,n) {
 var s=removeBlanks(c)
 var pairs=s.split(";")
 for(var i=0;i<pairs.length;++i) {
  var pairSplit=pairs[i].split("=")
  if(pairSplit[0]==n) return true
 }
 return false
}
function removeBlanks(s) {
 var temp=""
 for(var i=0;i<s.length;++i) {
  var c=s.charAt(i)
  if(c!=" ") temp += c
 }
 return temp
}
function getCookieValue(c,n) {
```

```
var s=removeBlanks(c)
var pairs=s.split(";")
for(var i=0;i<pairs.length;++i) {
 var pairSplit=pairs[i].split("=")
 if(pairSplit[0]==n) return pairSplit[1]
}
return ""
}
```

World Clock

The Web never sleeps. Someone could be browsing your Web page at any time of the day. They could be viewing it from Europe, Asia, Africa, Australia, or North or South America. In some cases, you may want to display the current date and time along with your Web page.

When people view your Web page, they are more concerned about the time of day where they are rather than the time of day where your Web page is located. If you add the time to your Web pages via a CGI program, you will have a hard time converting your time to the local time of your Web users. Fortunately, JavaScript can be easily used to display the user's local time and identify the user's time-zone offset from Greenwich Meridian Time (GMT).

Open clock.htm with your browser and your browser will display the day of the week, the date, your local time, and your time-zone offset from GMT, as shown in Figure 13.7. Take a closer look at your browser display. Notice the seconds tick by. Your browser updates the time on one-second intervals. This allows you to update the time as your Web page sits on your user's browser. You can even tell your user how long he or she has used your Web page—an important capability if you decide to charge someone based on access time.

The script used in clock.htm is fairly short, but it illustrates some important points. The clock text field takes its value directly from the dateTime() function. The tick() function is then invoked to start the clock running. This function updates the value of the clock field and then sets a one-second timeout so it can reinvoke itself. The dateTime() function returns a string containing the day, date, time, and time-zone offset.

FIGURE 13.7

The world clock display
(Listing 13.9)

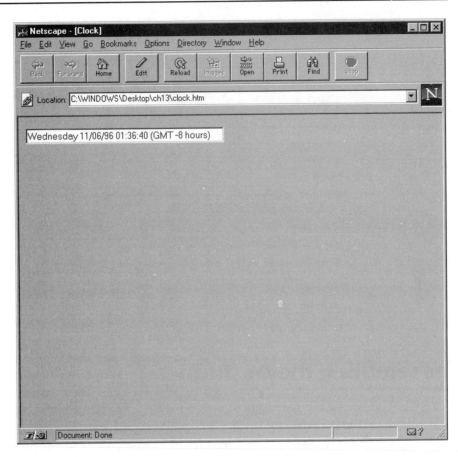

Listing 13.9. A clock script (clock.htm)

```
<HTML>
<HEAD>
<TITLE>Clock</TITLE>
<SCRIPT LANGUAGE="JavaScript"><!--
function dateTime() {
 var days = new Array("Sunday","Monday","Tuesday","Wednesday",
  "Thursday","Friday","Saturday")
 var now = new Date()
 var result = days[now.getDay()]+" "
 result += now.toLocaleString()
 var tzOffset=-now.getTimezoneOffset()/60
```

```
    if(tzOffset<0) result += " (GMT "+tzOffset+" hours)"
    else result += " (GMT +"+tzOffset+" hours)"
    return result
}
function tick() {
  document.forms[0].clock.value=dateTime()
  setTimeout("tick()",1000)
}
// --></SCRIPT>
</HEAD>
<BODY>
<FORM>
<INPUT NAME="clock" TYPE="TEXT" SIZE="40"
 VALUE="&{dateTime()};">
</FORM>
<SCRIPT LANGUAGE="JavaScript"><!--
tick()
// --></SCRIPT>
</BODY>
</HTML>
```

Assembling the Desktop

Now that you've developed the clock, calendar, calculator, and to-do list, wouldn't you like to put them all together in one Web page? You'll learn how to do that so you can see them working together and envision how to integrate them with your own Web pages. The hard part has been completed—the accessories have been developed. All you need to do now is to assemble them into a common desktop.

Open desktop.htm and you'll see the Web page shown in Figure 13.8. You can watch the clock tick, flip through the calendar, make some notes, or calculate how much your next raise should be.

The desktop.htm file (Listing 13.10) is the first of two levels of frame sets. It defines two colums which contain the files calclock.htm (Listing 13.11) and notescalc.htm (Listing 13.12). The calclock.htm file creates a frame set for displaying the clock and the calendar. The notescalc.htm file creates a frame set for displaying the to-do list and the calculator. Notice how simple it was to integrate all four accessories into a single Web application.

FIGURE 13.8

The desktop display integrates each of the desktop accessories. (Listing 13.10)

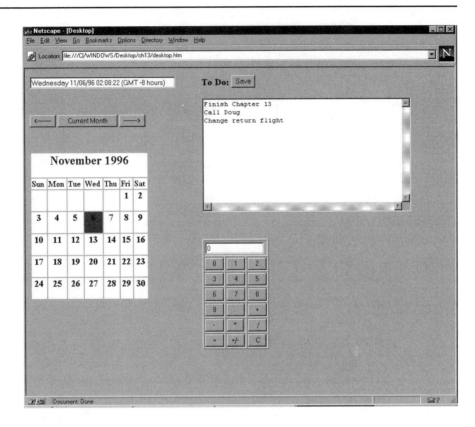

Listing 13.10. Defining the top level frame set (desktop.htm)

```
<HTML>
<HEAD>
<TITLE>Desktop</TITLE>
<FRAMESET COLS="350,*" BORDER="0">
<FRAME SRC="calclock.htm">
<FRAME SRC="notescalc.htm">
</FRAMESET>
</HTML>
```

Listing 13.11. Defining the left frame set (calclock.htm)

```
<HTML>
<HEAD>
<TITLE>Desktop</TITLE>
```

```
<FRAMESET ROWS="80,*" BORDER="0">
<FRAME SRC="clock.htm">
<FRAME SRC="cal.htm">
</FRAMESET>
</HTML>
```

Listing 13.12. Defining the right time set (notescalc.htm)

```
<HTML>
<HEAD>
<TITLE>Desktop</TITLE>
<FRAMESET ROWS="325,*" BORDER="0">
<FRAME SRC="notes.htm">
<FRAME SRC="calc.htm">
</FRAMESET>
</HTML>
```

Summary

In this chapter, you learned how to develop four common desktop accessories—a calendar, a calculator, a clock, and a to-do list—and integrate them into a Web page-based application: a Web desktop. You are finally learning how to develop scripts that are both useful and reusable. In the next chapter, you'll develop some examples of on-line catalogs and order forms that use JavaScript to simplify the customer ordering process.

CHAPTER

FOURTEEN

14

Online Catalogs

- Developing a Catalog without a CGI Program

- Tailoring a Catalog Based on User Preferences

- Adding Multimedia Features

The Web has become a showcase for almost everything that is new or innovative. New products, services, and technologies are frequently introduced to the world via corporate Web sites and through ads appearing on popular Web pages. Small companies with few products may be able to provide complete information on their products in a small number of Web pages. Large companies, like IBM, Microsoft, and Sun Microsystems, have so many products that they only describe their latest and greatest products on their top-level Web pages and provide access to everything else via online catalogs.

Catalogs are important to online merchants, both resellers and manufacturers. Sales catalogs must be highly attractive to stimulate interest in products and must be easy to use in order to help close the sale.

Online catalogs are used for reasons other than product information and sales. Web-based libraries use catalogs to provide information on book availability. Museums catalog their exhibits and collectors catalog their collections. Multimedia catalogs are especially impressive.

The primary purpose of a catalog is to facilitate access to information. HTML-based catalogs present static Web pages that use CGI programs to fetch product information. In these catalogs, a user fills out a catalog search form and submits it to a CGI program. The CGI program returns the Web page of the selected product. With JavaScript, much of the catalog processing can be performed on the browser. Catalogs can be dynamically tailored based on user preferences and can be implemented without the need for CGI programs. JavaScript catalogs can also make optimal use of multimedia features.

In this chapter, you'll learn to use JavaScript to create sophisticated catalogs. You'll learn how to develop catalogs that do not require CGI programs and that can be tailored to user preferences. When you finish this chapter you'll be able to develop catalogs that are attractive, informative, and easy to use.

Developing a Catalog without a CGI Program

Small catalogs are usually implemented entirely in HTML; ordinary links are used to guide users to the information they want. Large catalogs are typically implemented using a series of HTML forms that provide a front-end search interface for a CGI program; the user enters product search criteria into the HTML forms, submits them to the CGI program, and a Web page containing the requested product information is returned.

JavaScript can be used to implement small to medium catalogs without the need for CGI programs. Even if CGI programs are required, JavaScript can help to reduce their complexity.

When implementing a catalog in JavaScript, you should include as much catalog indexing information as possible within the script. This will allow your script to implement the catalog search functions locally without requiring CGI processing.

Figure 14.1 provides an example of a JavaScript-only product catalog. The catalog is organized according to the room of the house in which a product is used. Run this script by opening `catalog.htm` (Listing 14.1) with your browser. Select Bed Room from the *Room* selection list and click on the Select Room button. You'll see that the values of the *Types of products* selection list is updated based on the room that is selected. Select Electronics from this selection list and click on the Select Product Type button. The *Products* selection list is now updated with electronics products for the bedroom. Select Clock Radio from this list and click on the Select Product button. As you can see in Figure 14.2, the lower left frame identifies the product image file that would be displayed in that frame, and the lower right frame identifies the HTML file that would be loaded to describe the selected product. (I display the file's name here rather than the actual file only so that I wouldn't have to create 75 product images and 75 product descriptions for this example. For a real catalog, you would have to supply the images and descriptions appropriate to your products.)

Listing 14.1. The catalog's top-level frame set (catalog.htm)

```
<HTML>
<HEAD>
<TITLE>XYZ Company Catalog</TITLE>
</HEAD>
<FRAMESET ROWS="235,*" BORDER="10">
<FRAME SRC="catform.htm">
<FRAME SRC="products.htm">
</FRAMESET>
</HTML>
```

The `catalog.htm` file shown in Listing 14.1 sets up a top-level frame set that organizes the catalog into a two-row form. The `products.htm` file shown in Listing 14.2 sets up a two-column frame set for the bottom half of the window.

FIGURE 14.1

A JavaScript-only catalog
(Listing 14.1)

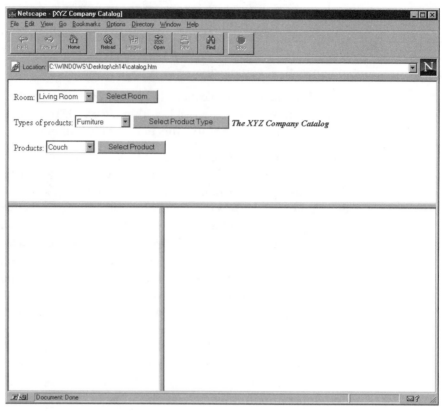

FIGURE 14.1

A JavaScript-only catalog
(Listing 14.1)

Listing 14.2. The frame set used to display the product image and description (products.htm)

```html
<HTML>
<HEAD>
<TITLE>XYZ Company Catalog</TITLE>
</HEAD>
<FRAMESET COLS="300,*" BORDER="10">
<FRAME SRC="blank.htm">
<FRAME SRC="blank.htm">
</FRAMESET>
</HTML>
```

FIGURE 14.2

Selecting a product from the catalog. To reduce the amount of file space and work involved in this example, we're displaying only the file names of the image files rather than the actual image. (Listing 14.1)

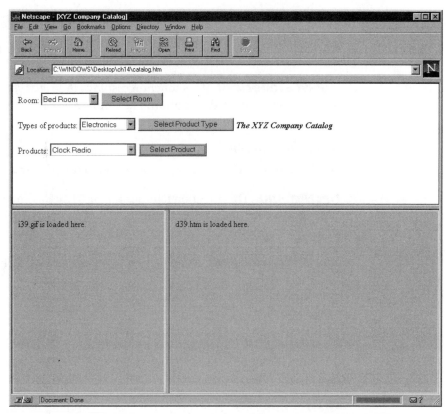

The `catform.htm` file implements the catalog form shown in the top half of the browser's display. It consists of four scripts—three in the document's head and one in the document's body. The script in the document's body invokes the `displayCatalogForm()` function to cause the catalog's form to be displayed. The first two scripts in the document's head insert code in the files `products.js` (Listing 14.5) and `cookie.js` (Listing 14.4). The third script in the document's head defines ten functions, which are used as follows.

displayCatalogForm()   This is the main function used to create the catalog form. It invokes the `readCookie()` function to read the user's current form selections. It then invokes the `displayRooms()`, `displayCategories()`, and `displayProducts()` functions to display the elements of the form.

readCookie() This function reads the `room` and `cat` cookie values to determine what form elements are currently selected by the user.

displayRooms() This function displays the *Room* selection list and the Select Room button. The `rooms` array is defined in the `products.js` file.

displayCategories() This function displays the *Types of products* selection list and the Select Product Type button. The `roomCategories` array is defined in the `products.js` file.

displayProducts() This function displays the *Products* selection list and the Select Product button. The `prod` array is defined in the `products.js` file.

selectRoom() This function handles the `onClick` event of the Select Room button. It sets `cat` to the first product category associated with the room and invokes `setCookie()` to store the `room` and `cat` variables as cookies.

selectProductType() This function handles the `onClick` event of the Select Product Type button. It updates the `cat` variable based on the user's selection and invokes `setCookie()` to store the updated `cat` variable as a cookie.

selectProduct() This function handles the `onClick` event of the Select Product button. It identifies the product image and description files that should be loaded in the lower frames of the window.

writeDocument() This function is used to update the lower window frames with the names of the files that should be displayed there. In a real catalog, you would display the file's contents, rather than just its name.

setCookie() This function updates the `room` and `cat` (product category) cookies and reloads the current document to update the catalog form's display.

Listing 14.3. The code that implements the catalog form (catform.htm)

```
<HTML>
<HEAD>
<TITLE>XYZ Company Catalog</TITLE>
<SCRIPT LANGUAGE="JavaScript" SRC="products.js"><!--
// --></SCRIPT>
```

```
<SCRIPT LANGUAGE="JavaScript" SRC="cookie.js"><!--
// --></SCRIPT>
<SCRIPT LANGUAGE="JavaScript"><!--
function displayCatalogForm() {
 readCookie()
 document.writeln('<FORM>')
 displayRooms()
 displayCategories()
 displayProducts()
 document.writeln('</FORM>')
}
function readCookie() {
 var cookie=document.cookie
 room="li"
 cat="fu"
 if(nameDefined(cookie,"room"))
  room=getCookieValue(cookie,"room")
 if(nameDefined(cookie,"cat"))
  cat=getCookieValue(cookie,"cat")
}
function displayRooms() {
 document.write('<P>')
 document.write('Room: ')
 document.writeln('<SELECT name="roomField">')
 for(var i=0;i<rooms.length;++i) {
  if(room==rooms[i]){
   document.write('<OPTION SELECTED')
  }else document.write('<OPTION')
  document.write(' VALUE="'+rooms[i]+'">')
  document.writeln(roomName(rooms[i]))
 }
 document.writeln('</SELECT>')
 document.write(' <INPUT type="BUTTON" value="Select Room" ')
 document.writeln('onClick="selectRoom()">')
 document.writeln('</P>')
}
function displayCategories() {
 document.write('<P>')
 document.write('Types of products: ')
 document.writeln('<SELECT name="catField">')
 for(var i=0;i<roomCategories.length;++i) {
```

```
  if(room==roomCategories[i].room) {
   if(cat==roomCategories[i].cat)
    document.write('<OPTION SELECTED')
   else document.write('<OPTION')
   document.write(' VALUE="'+roomCategories[i].cat+'">')
   document.writeln(categoryName(roomCategories[i].cat))
  }
 }
 document.writeln('</SELECT>')
 document.write(' <INPUT type="BUTTON" ')
 document.write('value="Select Product Type" ')
 document.writeln('onClick="selectProductType()">')
 document.writeln(' <B><I>The XYZ Company Catalog</B></I>')
 document.writeln('</P>')
}
function displayProducts() {
 document.write('<P>')
 document.write('Products: ')
 document.writeln('<SELECT name="productField">')
 for(var i=0;i<prod.length;++i) {
  if(room==prod[i].room) {
   if(cat==prod[i].category) {
    document.write('<OPTION VALUE="')
     document.write(i+'">')
    document.writeln(prod[i].name)
   }
  }
 }
 document.writeln('</SELECT>')
 document.write(' <INPUT type="BUTTON" ')
 document.write('value="Select Product" ')
 document.writeln('onClick="selectProduct()">')
 document.writeln('</P>')
}
function selectRoom() {
 var field=window.document.forms[0].roomField
 var ix=field.selectedIndex
 room=field.options[ix].value
 for(var i=0;i<roomCategories.length;++i) {
  if(room==roomCategories[i].room){
   cat=roomCategories[i].cat
```

```
  break
 }
 }
 setCookie()
}
function selectProductType() {
 var field=window.document.forms[0].catField
 var ix=field.selectedIndex
 cat=field.options[ix].value
 setCookie()
}
function selectProduct() {
 var field=window.document.forms[0].productField
 var ix=field.selectedIndex
 prodIX=field.options[ix].value
 writeDocument(0,prod[prodIX].image+" is loaded here.")
 writeDocument(1,prod[prodIX].desc+" is loaded here.")
}
function writeDocument(n,s) {
 var doc=parent.frames[1].frames[n].document
 doc.open()
 doc.writeln(s)
 doc.close()
}
function setCookie() {
 var newCookie = "room="+room
 window.document.cookie=newCookie
 newCookie = "cat="+cat
 window.document.cookie=newCookie
 window.location="catform.htm"
}
// --></SCRIPT>
</HEAD>
<BODY bgColor="white">
<SCRIPT LANGUAGE="JavaScript"><!--
displayCatalogForm()
// --></SCRIPT>
</BODY>
</HTML>
```

The `cookie.js` file includes the cookie-reading functions used in previous examples.

Listing 14.4. Functions for reading cookies (cookie.js)

```
function nameDefined(c,n) {
 var s=removeBlanks(c)
 var pairs=s.split(";")
 for(var i=0;i<pairs.length;++i) {
  var pairSplit=pairs[i].split("=")
  if(pairSplit[0]==n) return true
 }
 return false
}
function removeBlanks(s) {
 var temp=""
 for(var i=0;i<s.length;++i) {
  var c=s.charAt(i)
  if(c!=" ") temp += c
 }
 return temp
}
function getCookieValue(c,n) {
 var s=removeBlanks(c)
 var pairs=s.split(";")
 for(var i=0;i<pairs.length;++i) {
  var pairSplit=pairs[i].split("=")
  if(pairSplit[0]==n) return pairSplit[1]
 }
 return ""
}
```

The `products.js` file contains the product database used by the catalog. It consists of the following definitions.

rooms This array contains the two-letter room identifiers used as shortcuts to refer to rooms.

roomName() This function returns the full room name associated with a room identifier.

productCategories This array contains the two-letter product category identifiers used as shortcuts to refer to product categories.

categoryName() This function returns the full product category name associated with its two-character identifier.

Product() This function is the constructor for the `Product` object. It assigns the product's `id`, `name`, `cat`, and `room` properties. It also identifies the image and description files associated with the product.

roomProductCategory() This function is the constructor for the `roomProductCategory` object. It is used to map rooms to product categories.

roomCategories This array consists of `roomProductCategory` objects which are used to assign product categories to rooms.

prod This array identifies all of the products in the catalog.

Listing 14.5. The catalog's product database (products.js)

```
rooms = new Array("li","di","be","ki","ba")

function roomName(room) {
 if(room=="li") return "Living Room"
 if(room=="di") return "Dining Room"
 if(room=="be") return "Bed Room"
 if(room=="ki") return "Kitchen"
 if(room=="ba") return "Bath Room"
 return "Unknown"
}

productCategories = new Array("fu","ca","li","el","ac",
 "ap","cb","si","to","ba")

function categoryName(cat) {
 if(cat=="fu") return "Furniture"
 if(cat=="ca") return "Carpeting"
 if(cat=="li") return "Lighting"
 if(cat=="el") return "Electronics"
 if(cat=="ac") return "Accessories"
 if(cat=="ap") return "Appliances"
 if(cat=="cb") return "Cabinets"
 if(cat=="si") return "Sinks"
 if(cat=="to") return "Toilets"
 if(cat=="ba") return "Bath and Shower"
```

```
        return "Unknown"
    }

    function Product(id,name,category,room)        {
     this.id=id
     this.name=name
     this.category=category
     this.room=room
     this.image="i"+id+".gif"
     this.desc="d"+id+".htm"
    }


    function roomProductCategory(room,cat) {
     this.room=room
     this.cat=cat
    }


    var i=0
    roomCategories = new Array()
    roomCategories[i] = new roomProductCategory("li","fu"); ++i
    roomCategories[i] = new roomProductCategory("li","ca"); ++i
    roomCategories[i] = new roomProductCategory("li","li"); ++i
    roomCategories[i] = new roomProductCategory("li","el"); ++i
    roomCategories[i] = new roomProductCategory("li","ac"); ++i
    roomCategories[i] = new roomProductCategory("di","fu"); ++i
    roomCategories[i] = new roomProductCategory("di","ca"); ++i
    roomCategories[i] = new roomProductCategory("di","li"); ++i
    roomCategories[i] = new roomProductCategory("di","ac"); ++i
    roomCategories[i] = new roomProductCategory("be","fu"); ++i
    roomCategories[i] = new roomProductCategory("be","ca"); ++i
    roomCategories[i] = new roomProductCategory("be","li"); ++i
    roomCategories[i] = new roomProductCategory("be","el"); ++i
    roomCategories[i] = new roomProductCategory("be","ac"); ++i
    roomCategories[i] = new roomProductCategory("ki","ap"); ++i
    roomCategories[i] = new roomProductCategory("ki","cb"); ++i
    roomCategories[i] = new roomProductCategory("ki","li"); ++i
    roomCategories[i] = new roomProductCategory("ki","ac"); ++i
    roomCategories[i] = new roomProductCategory("ba","si"); ++i
    roomCategories[i] = new roomProductCategory("ba","to"); ++i
    roomCategories[i] = new roomProductCategory("ba","li"); ++i
    roomCategories[i] = new roomProductCategory("ba","ba"); ++i
    roomCategories[i] = new roomProductCategory("ba","ac"); ++i
```

```
var i=0
prod=new Array()

//Living room products
prod[i]=new Product(i,"Couch","fu","li"); ++i
prod[i]=new Product(i,"Sofa","fu","li"); ++i
prod[i]=new Product(i,"Arm chair","fu","li"); ++i
prod[i]=new Product(i,"Long table","fu","li"); ++i
prod[i]=new Product(i,"Side table","fu","li"); ++i
prod[i]=new Product(i,"Persian rug","ca","li"); ++i
prod[i]=new Product(i,"Cheap rug","ca","li"); ++i
prod[i]=new Product(i,"Ceiling light","li","li"); ++i
prod[i]=new Product(i,"Floor light","li","li"); ++i
prod[i]=new Product(i,"Table light","li","li"); ++i
prod[i]=new Product(i,"Big TV","el","li"); ++i
prod[i]=new Product(i,"Small TV","el","li"); ++i
prod[i]=new Product(i,"Entertainment Center","el","li"); ++i
prod[i]=new Product(i,"Stereo","el","li"); ++i
prod[i]=new Product(i,"Large painting","ac","li"); ++i
prod[i]=new Product(i,"Small painting","ac","li"); ++i
prod[i]=new Product(i,"Large fake plant","ac","li"); ++i
prod[i]=new Product(i,"Small fake plant","ac","li"); ++i
prod[i]=new Product(i,"Expensive knick knack","ac","li"); ++i
prod[i]=new Product(i,"Cheap knick knack","ac","li"); ++i

//Dining room products
prod[i]=new Product(i,"Expensive dining set","fu","di"); ++i
prod[i]=new Product(i,"Cheap dining set","fu","di"); ++i
prod[i]=new Product(i,"China cabinet","fu","di"); ++i
prod[i]=new Product(i,"Serving table","fu","di"); ++i
prod[i]=new Product(i,"Stain-proof rug","ca","di"); ++i
prod[i]=new Product(i,"Plastic floor covering","ca","di"); ++i
prod[i]=new Product(i,"Chandalier","li","di"); ++i
prod[i]=new Product(i,"Ceiling lamp","li","di"); ++i
prod[i]=new Product(i,"China set","ac","di"); ++i
prod[i]=new Product(i,"Silver set","ac","di"); ++i

//Bed room products
prod[i]=new Product(i,"King bed","fu","be"); ++i
prod[i]=new Product(i,"Queen bed","fu","be"); ++i
prod[i]=new Product(i,"Single bed","fu","be"); ++i
prod[i]=new Product(i,"In table","fu","be"); ++i
```

```
prod[i]=new Product(i,"Dresser","fu","be"); ++i
prod[i]=new Product(i,"Lamb skin carpet","ca","be"); ++i
prod[i]=new Product(i,"Bear skin carpet","ca","be"); ++i
prod[i]=new Product(i,"Ceiling lamp","li","be"); ++i
prod[i]=new Product(i,"Table lamp","li","be"); ++i
prod[i]=new Product(i,"Clock Radio","el","be"); ++i
prod[i]=new Product(i,"Electronic head board","el","be"); ++i
prod[i]=new Product(i,"Pillow set","ac","be"); ++i
prod[i]=new Product(i,"Linen set","ac","be"); ++i
prod[i]=new Product(i,"Bed spread","ac","be"); ++i

//Kitchen products
prod[i]=new Product(i,"Refrigerator","ap","ki"); ++i
prod[i]=new Product(i,"Stove - oven","ap","ki"); ++i
prod[i]=new Product(i,"Microwave oven","ap","ki"); ++i
prod[i]=new Product(i,"Toaster","ap","ki"); ++i
prod[i]=new Product(i,"Coffee maker","ap","ki"); ++i
prod[i]=new Product(i,"Dish washer","ap","ki"); ++i
prod[i]=new Product(i,"Deluxe cabinets","cb","ki"); ++i
prod[i]=new Product(i,"Standard cabinets","cb","ki"); ++i
prod[i]=new Product(i,"Deluxe counter","cb","ki"); ++i
prod[i]=new Product(i,"Standard counter","cb","ki"); ++i
prod[i]=new Product(i,"Ceiling light","li","ki"); ++i
prod[i]=new Product(i,"Counter light","li","ki"); ++i
prod[i]=new Product(i,"Cookware","ac","ki"); ++i
prod[i]=new Product(i,"Storage containers","ac","ki"); ++i
prod[i]=new Product(i,"Wall clock","ac","ki"); ++i

//Bath room products
prod[i]=new Product(i,"Deluxe sink","si","ba"); ++i
prod[i]=new Product(i,"Standard sink","si","ba"); ++i
prod[i]=new Product(i,"Deluxe toilet","to","ba"); ++i
prod[i]=new Product(i,"Standard toilet","to","ba"); ++i
prod[i]=new Product(i,"Ceiling light","li","ba"); ++i
prod[i]=new Product(i,"Wall light","li","ba"); ++i
prod[i]=new Product(i,"Deluxe bath tub","ba","ba"); ++i
prod[i]=new Product(i,"Standard bath tub","ba","ba"); ++i
prod[i]=new Product(i,"Shower stall","ba","ba"); ++i
prod[i]=new Product(i,"Wall cabinet","ac","ba"); ++i
prod[i]=new Product(i,"Towel rack","ac","ba"); ++i
prod[i]=new Product(i,"Towels","ac","ba"); ++i
```

Tailoring a Catalog Based on User Preferences

You now know how to implement catalogs using JavaScript, but JavaScript can do much more! HTML-only catalogs are not very user-friendly—it's pretty much take it or leave it when it comes to user preferences. That's because you have to program a CGI program to implement those preferences. With JavaScript, implementing preferences is a snap! For example, you can use cookies to store preferences between browser sessions. More importantly, you won't be wasting your server's CPU time running unneeded CGI programs.

Figure 14.3 shows how the catalog that was developed in the previous section can be enhanced to allow for user preference selection. Note the *Catalog view* selection list and the Select View Preference button which are used to select different views of the catalog. Start by selecting *By product category* from the selection list and then clicking on the Select View Preference button. The form is updated to allow selection by product category rather than by room. Now select *Electronics (Bed Room)* from the *Types of products* list and click on the Select Product Type button. The *Products* list is then updated with the bed room electronics products. Finally, select *Clock Radio* from the *Products* list and click on the Select Product button. The appropriate product image and description files would then be displayed in the lower frames of the window. (As in the previous section, for the purposes of this example you'll see only the *names* of the product image and description files, as in Figure 14.4.)

The `catalog2.htm` file updates the `catalog.htm` file to use the `catform2.htm` file instead of `catform.htm`.

Listing 14.6. The updated catalog's top-level frame set (catalog2.htm)

```
<HTML>
<HEAD>
<TITLE>XYZ Company Catalog</TITLE>
</HEAD>
<FRAMESET ROWS="235,*" BORDER="10">
<FRAME SRC="catform2.htm">
<FRAME SRC="products.htm">
</FRAMESET>
</HTML>
```

FIGURE 14.3

Adding catalog view
preferences (Listing 14.6)

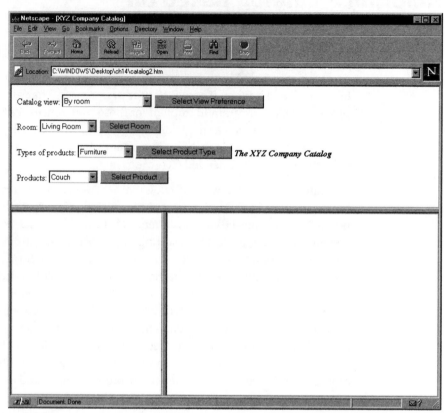

The catform2.htm file updates the catform.htm file from the previous discussion to provide alternative catalog views. The changes to catform.htm are as follows.

displayCategoryForm()   This function is updated to implement the room, product category, and product views.

readCookie()   This function reads an additional cookie—the view cookie—which is used to track the catalog view selected by the user.

displayByRoom()   This function displays the room-oriented catalog view.

displayByCat()   This function displays the product category-oriented catalog view.

FIGURE 14.4

Selecting a product via a
different view. Again, to
reduce the size of this
example, we're showing
only the file names of the
image files. (Listing 14.6)

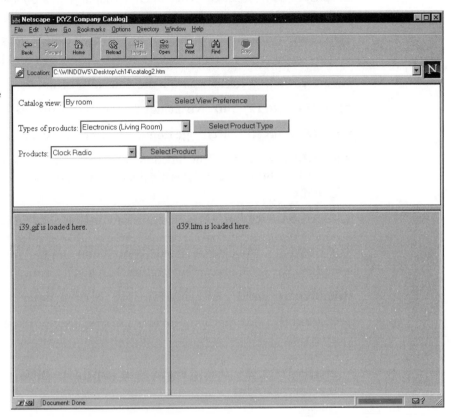

displayByProduct() This function displays the product-oriented
catalog view.

displayAltView() This function displays the *Catalog view* selection list and the
Select View Preference button.

displayRooms() No change from previous discussion.

displayCategories() No change from previous discussion.

displayProducts() No change from previous discussion.

displayCatList() This function displays the *Types of products* selection list and
Select Product Type button.

displayProductsList()   This function displays an alphabetical list of products. It identifies the room associated with each product.

altView()   This function handles the onClick event of the Select View Preference button by storing the user-selected view in a cookie.

selectRoom()   No change from previous discussion.

selectProductType()   No change from previous discussion.

selectProduct()   No change from previous discussion.

selectProductCat()   This function handles the onClick event of the Select Product Type button. It updates the document's cookies based on the user's selection.

selectFromBigList()   This function handles the onClick event of the Select Product button and invokes writeDocument() to display the product's image and description file names in the window's lower frames. In a real catalog, you would display the file's contents, rather than just its name.

writeDocument()   No change from previous discussion.

setCookie()   This function provides additional support to handle the view cookie.

Listing 14.7. A catalog form that supports different catalog views (catform2.htm)

```
<HTML>
<HEAD>
<TITLE>XYZ Company Catalog</TITLE>
<SCRIPT LANGUAGE="JavaScript" SRC="products.js"><!--
// --></SCRIPT>
<SCRIPT LANGUAGE="JavaScript" SRC="cookie.js"><!--
// --></SCRIPT>
<SCRIPT LANGUAGE="JavaScript"><!--
function displayCatalogForm() {
 readCookie()
 if(view=="byRoom") displayByRoom()
 else if(view=="byCat") displayByCat()
 else displayByProduct()
}
function readCookie() {
 var cookie=document.cookie
```

```
 room="li"
 cat="fu"
 view="byRoom"
 if(nameDefined(cookie,"room"))
  room=getCookieValue(cookie,"room")
 if(nameDefined(cookie,"cat"))
  cat=getCookieValue(cookie,"cat")
 if(nameDefined(cookie,"view"))
  view=getCookieValue(cookie,"view")
}
function displayByRoom() {
 document.writeln('<FORM>')
 displayAltView()
 displayRooms()
 displayCategories()
 displayProducts()
 document.writeln('</FORM>')
}
function displayByCat() {
 document.writeln('<FORM>')
 displayAltView()
 displayCatList()
 displayProducts()
 document.writeln('</FORM>')
}
function displayByProduct() {
 document.writeln('<FORM>')
 displayAltView()
 displayProductsList()
 document.writeln('</FORM>')
}
function displayAltView() {
 document.write('<P>')
 document.write('Catalog view: ')
 document.writeln('<SELECT name="viewField">')
 document.write('<OPTION VALUE="byRoom" SELECTED>By room')
 document.write('<OPTION VALUE="byCat">By product category')
 document.write('<OPTION VALUE="byProd">Alphabetical
  by product')
 document.writeln('</SELECT>')
 document.write(' <INPUT type="BUTTON" ')
 document.write('value="Select View Preference" ')
 document.writeln('onClick="altView()">')
```

```
   document.writeln('</P>')
}
function displayRooms() {
 document.write('<P>')
 document.write('Room: ')
 document.writeln('<SELECT name="roomField">')
 for(var i=0;i<rooms.length;++i) {
  if(room==rooms[i]){
   document.write('<OPTION SELECTED')
  }else document.write('<OPTION')
  document.write(' VALUE="'+rooms[i]+'">')
  document.writeln(roomName(rooms[i]))
 }
 document.writeln('</SELECT>')
 document.write(' <INPUT type="BUTTON" value="Select Room" ')
 document.writeln('onClick="selectRoom()">')
 document.writeln('</P>')
}
function displayCategories() {
 document.write('<P>')
 document.write('Types of products: ')
 document.writeln('<SELECT name="catField">')
 for(var i=0;i<roomCategories.length;++i) {
  if(room==roomCategories[i].room) {
   if(cat==roomCategories[i].cat)
    document.write('<OPTION SELECTED')
   else document.write('<OPTION')
   document.write(' VALUE="'+roomCategories[i].cat+'">')
   document.writeln(categoryName(roomCategories[i].cat))
  }
 }
 document.writeln('</SELECT>')
 document.write(' <INPUT type="BUTTON" ')
 document.write('value="Select Product Type" ')
 document.writeln('onClick="selectProductType()">')
 document.writeln(' <B><I>The XYZ Company Catalog</B></I>')
 document.writeln('</P>')
}
function displayProducts() {
 document.write('<P>')
 document.write('Products: ')
 document.writeln('<SELECT name="productField">')
 for(var i=0;i<prod.length;++i) {
```

```
 if(room==prod[i].room) {
  if(cat==prod[i].category) {
   document.write('<OPTION VALUE="')
    document.write(i+'">')
   document.writeln(prod[i].name)
  }
 }
}
document.writeln('</SELECT>')
document.write(' <INPUT type="BUTTON" ')
document.write('value="Select Product" ')
document.writeln('onClick="selectProduct()">')
document.writeln('</P>')
}
function displayCatList() {
 document.write('<P>')
 document.write('Types of products: ')
 document.writeln('<SELECT name="catListField">')
 for(var i=0;i<productCategories.length;++i) {
  for(var j=0;j<roomCategories.length;++j) {
   if(productCategories[i]==roomCategories[j].cat) {
    if(cat==productCategories[i])
     document.write('<OPTION SELECTED')
    else document.write('<OPTION')
     var optionValue=roomCategories[j].room
      +productCategories[i]
    document.write(' VALUE="'+optionValue+'">')
    document.write(categoryName(productCategories[i])+" ")
     document.writeln('('+roomName(roomCategories[j].room)+')')
   }
  }
 }
 document.writeln('</SELECT>')
 document.write(' <INPUT type="BUTTON" ')
 document.write('value="Select Product Type" ')
 document.writeln('onClick="selectProductCat()">')
 document.writeln('</P>')
}
function displayProductsList() {
 document.write('<P>')
 document.write('Products: ')
 document.writeln('<SELECT name="allProductsField">')
 var sortedOptions = new Array(prod.length)
```

```
      for(var i=0;i<prod.length;++i) {
       sortedOptions[i]=prod[i].name+" ("
       sortedOptions[i]+=roomName(prod[i].room)+")"
       sortedOptions[i]+="|"+i
      }
      sortedOptions.sort()
      for(var i=0;i<sortedOptions.length;++i){
       document.write('<OPTION VALUE="')
       var parts=sortedOptions[i].split("|")
       document.writeln(parts[1]+'">'+parts[0])
      }
      document.writeln('</SELECT>')
      document.write(' <INPUT type="BUTTON" ')
      document.write('value="Select Product" ')
      document.writeln('onClick="selectFromBigList()">')
      document.writeln('</P>')
     }
     function altView() {
      var field=window.document.forms[0].viewField
      var ix=field.selectedIndex
      view=field.options[ix].value
      setCookie()
     }
     function selectRoom() {
      var field=window.document.forms[0].roomField
      var ix=field.selectedIndex
      room=field.options[ix].value
      for(var i=0;i<roomCategories.length;++i) {
       if(room==roomCategories[i].room){
        cat=roomCategories[i].cat
        break
       }
      }
      setCookie()
     }
     function selectProductType() {
      var field=window.document.forms[0].catField
      var ix=field.selectedIndex
      cat=field.options[ix].value
      setCookie()
     }
     function selectProduct() {
      var field=window.document.forms[0].productField
```

```
    var ix=field.selectedIndex
    prodIX=field.options[ix].value
    writeDocument(0,prod[prodIX].image+" is loaded here.")
    writeDocument(1,prod[prodIX].desc+" is loaded here.")
}
function selectProductCat() {
    var field=window.document.forms[0].catListField
    var ix=field.selectedIndex
    var fieldValue=field.options[ix].value
    room=fieldValue.substring(0,2)
    cat=fieldValue.substring(2,4)
    setCookie()
}
function selectFromBigList() {
    var field=window.document.forms[0].allProductsField
    var ix=field.selectedIndex
    prodIX=field.options[ix].value
    writeDocument(0,prod[prodIX].image+" is loaded here.")
    writeDocument(1,prod[prodIX].desc+" is loaded here.")
}
function writeDocument(n,s) {
    var doc=parent.frames[1].frames[n].document
    doc.open()
    doc.writeln(s)
    doc.close()
}
function setCookie() {
    var newCookie = "room="+room
    window.document.cookie=newCookie
    newCookie = "cat="+cat
    window.document.cookie=newCookie
    newCookie = "view="+view
    window.document.cookie=newCookie
    window.location="catform2.htm"
}
// --></SCRIPT>
</HEAD>
<BODY bgColor="white">
<SCRIPT LANGUAGE="JavaScript"><!--
displayCatalogForm()
// --></SCRIPT>
</BODY>
</HTML>
```

Adding Multimedia Features

When you put your catalog online you want to make it interesting for the user to browse. One way that you can do that is to add multimedia features to your catalogs. High-quality graphics are a must. In addition, you can add audio and video.

> **TIP**
>
> Since audio and video can be time consuming to access over the Internet, especially for users with low-bandwidth lines, it's a good idea to implement controls that allow users to specify whether or not they want to wait for audio and video files to be loaded.

It is easy to add audio support to the product catalog developed in earlier sections of this chapter. Open `catalog3.htm` and select any product. The audio confirmation dialog box displayed in Figure 14.5 is displayed. Click OK and an audio file is played using the Navigator audio player shown in Figure 14.6. Three small changes are needed to support audio product descriptions. The `catalog3.htm` file is used to reference the `catform3.htm` file, which updates `catform2.htm` by including a reference to `playSound()` in the `selectFromBigList()` and `selectProduct()` functions. The `playSound()` function displays the confirmation dialog box, and upon positive user confirmation, loads the `a0.wav` file. This file is then played by Navigator's audio player. (Of course, a real product catalog should include a separate audio file for each product; I've set up this example for demonstration purposes only.) The audio file is identified in the updated `Product` object constructor shown in Listing 14.10. The `Product` constructor creates a sound property for each product.

FIGURE 14.5

The audio confirmation dialog box (Listing 14.9)

FIGURE 14.6

The Netscape audio
player

Listing 14.8. The multimedia catalog's top-level frame set (catalog3.htm)

```
<HTML>
<HEAD>
<TITLE>XYZ Company Catalog</TITLE>
</HEAD>
<FRAMESET ROWS="235,*" BORDER="10">
<FRAME SRC="catform3.htm">
<FRAME SRC="products.htm">
</FRAMESET>
</HTML>
```

Listing 14.9. The catalog form updated to support audio files (catform3.htm)

```
<HTML>
<HEAD>
<TITLE>XYZ Company Catalog</TITLE>
<SCRIPT LANGUAGE="JavaScript" SRC="product3.js"><!--
// --></SCRIPT>
<SCRIPT LANGUAGE="JavaScript" SRC="cookie.js"><!--
// --></SCRIPT>
<SCRIPT LANGUAGE="JavaScript"><!--
function displayCatalogForm() {
 readCookie()
 if(view=="byRoom") displayByRoom()
 else if(view=="byCat") displayByCat()
 else displayByProduct()
}
function readCookie() {
 var cookie=document.cookie
 room="li"
 cat="fu"
 view="byRoom"
 if(nameDefined(cookie,"room"))
```

```
      room=getCookieValue(cookie,"room")
   if(nameDefined(cookie,"cat"))
     cat=getCookieValue(cookie,"cat")
   if(nameDefined(cookie,"view"))
     view=getCookieValue(cookie,"view")
 }
 function displayByRoom() {
  document.writeln('<FORM>')
  displayAltView()
  displayRooms()
  displayCategories()
  displayProducts()
  document.writeln('</FORM>')
 }
 function displayByCat() {
  document.writeln('<FORM>')
  displayAltView()
  displayCatList()
  displayProducts()
  document.writeln('</FORM>')
 }
 function displayByProduct() {
  document.writeln('<FORM>')
  displayAltView()
  displayProductsList()
  document.writeln('</FORM>')
 }
 function displayAltView() {
  document.write('<P>')
  document.write('Catalog view: ')
  document.writeln('<SELECT name="viewField">')
  document.write('<OPTION VALUE="byRoom" SELECTED>By room')
  document.write('<OPTION VALUE="byCat">By product category')
  document.write('<OPTION VALUE="byProd">Alphabetical
   by product')
  document.writeln('</SELECT>')
  document.write(' <INPUT type="BUTTON" ')
  document.write('value="Select View Preference" ')
  document.writeln('onClick="altView()">')
  document.writeln('</P>')
 }
```

```
function displayRooms() {
 document.write('<P>')
 document.write('Room: ')
 document.writeln('<SELECT name="roomField">')
 for(var i=0;i<rooms.length;++i) {
  if(room==rooms[i]){
   document.write('<OPTION SELECTED')
  }else document.write('<OPTION')
  document.write(' VALUE="'+rooms[i]+'">')
  document.writeln(roomName(rooms[i]))
 }
 document.writeln('</SELECT>')
 document.write(' <INPUT type="BUTTON" value="Select Room" ')
 document.writeln('onClick="selectRoom()">')
 document.writeln('</P>')
}
function displayCategories() {
 document.write('<P>')
 document.write('Types of products: ')
 document.writeln('<SELECT name="catField">')
 for(var i=0;i<roomCategories.length;++i) {
  if(room==roomCategories[i].room) {
   if(cat==roomCategories[i].cat)
    document.write('<OPTION SELECTED')
   else document.write('<OPTION')
   document.write(' VALUE="'+roomCategories[i].cat+'">')
   document.writeln(categoryName(roomCategories[i].cat))
  }
 }
 document.writeln('</SELECT>')
 document.write(' <INPUT type="BUTTON" ')
 document.write('value="Select Product Type" ')
 document.writeln('onClick="selectProductType()">')
 document.writeln(' <B><I>The XYZ Company Catalog</B></I>')
 document.writeln('</P>')
}
function displayProducts() {
 document.write('<P>')
 document.write('Products: ')
 document.writeln('<SELECT name="productField">')
 for(var i=0;i<prod.length;++i) {
  if(room==prod[i].room) {
   if(cat==prod[i].category) {
```

```
        document.write('<OPTION VALUE="')
          document.write(i+'">')
        document.writeln(prod[i].name)
      }
    }
  }
 document.writeln('</SELECT>')
 document.write(' <INPUT type="BUTTON" ')
 document.write('value="Select Product" ')
 document.writeln('onClick="selectProduct()">')
 document.writeln('</P>')
}
function displayCatList() {
 document.write('<P>')
 document.write('Types of products: ')
 document.writeln('<SELECT name="catListField">')
 for(var i=0;i<productCategories.length;++i) {
  for(var j=0;j<roomCategories.length;++j) {
   if(productCategories[i]==roomCategories[j].cat) {
    if(cat==productCategories[i])
     document.write('<OPTION SELECTED')
    else document.write('<OPTION')
     var optionValue=roomCategories[j].room
       +productCategories[i]
     document.write(' VALUE="'+optionValue+'">')
     document.write(categoryName(productCategories[i])+" ")
      document.writeln('('+roomName(roomCategories[j].room)+')')
   }
  }
 }
 document.writeln('</SELECT>')
 document.write(' <INPUT type="BUTTON" ')
 document.write('value="Select Product Type" ')
 document.writeln('onClick="selectProductCat()">')
 document.writeln('</P>')
}
function displayProductsList() {
 document.write('<P>')
 document.write('Products: ')
 document.writeln('<SELECT name="allProductsField">')
 var sortedOptions = new Array(prod.length)
 for(var i=0;i<prod.length;++i) {
  sortedOptions[i]=prod[i].name+" ("
```

```
      sortedOptions[i]+=roomName(prod[i].room)+")"
      sortedOptions[i]+="|"+i
    }
    sortedOptions.sort()
    for(var i=0;i<sortedOptions.length;++i){
     document.write('<OPTION VALUE="')
     var parts=sortedOptions[i].split("|")
     document.writeln(parts[1]+'">'+parts[0])
    }
    document.writeln('</SELECT>')
    document.write(' <INPUT type="BUTTON" ')
    document.write('value="Select Product" ')
    document.writeln('onClick="selectFromBigList()">')
    document.writeln('</P>')
  }
  function altView() {
   var field=window.document.forms[0].viewField
   var ix=field.selectedIndex
   view=field.options[ix].value
   setCookie()
  }
  function selectRoom() {
   var field=window.document.forms[0].roomField
   var ix=field.selectedIndex
   room=field.options[ix].value
   for(var i=0;i<roomCategories.length;++i) {
    if(room==roomCategories[i].room){
     cat=roomCategories[i].cat
     break
    }
   }
   setCookie()
  }
  function selectProductType() {
   var field=window.document.forms[0].catField
   var ix=field.selectedIndex
   cat=field.options[ix].value
   setCookie()
  }
  function selectProduct() {
   var field=window.document.forms[0].productField
   var ix=field.selectedIndex
   prodIX=field.options[ix].value
```

```
    writeDocument(0,prod[prodIX].image+" is loaded here.")
    writeDocument(1,prod[prodIX].desc+" is loaded here.")
    playSound()
  }
  function selectProductCat() {
   var field=window.document.forms[0].catListField
   var ix=field.selectedIndex
   var fieldValue=field.options[ix].value
   room=fieldValue.substring(0,2)
   cat=fieldValue.substring(2,4)
   setCookie()
  }
  function selectFromBigList() {
   var field=window.document.forms[0].allProductsField
   var ix=field.selectedIndex
   prodIX=field.options[ix].value
   writeDocument(0,prod[prodIX].image+" is loaded here.")
   writeDocument(1,prod[prodIX].desc+" is loaded here.")
   playSound()
  }
  function playSound() {
   var q="Would you like to hear an audio description?"
   if(confirm(q)){
    window.location.href="a0.wav"
   }
  }
  function writeDocument(n,s) {
   var doc=parent.frames[1].frames[n].document
   doc.open()
   doc.writeln(s)
   doc.close()
  }
  function setCookie() {
   var newCookie = "room="+room
   window.document.cookie=newCookie
   newCookie = "cat="+cat
   window.document.cookie=newCookie
   newCookie = "view="+view
   window.document.cookie=newCookie
   window.location="catform3.htm"
  }
// --></SCRIPT>
</HEAD>
```

```
<BODY bgColor="white">
<SCRIPT LANGUAGE="JavaScript"><!--
displayCatalogForm()
// --></SCRIPT>
</BODY>
</HTML>
```

Listing 14.10. The updated product object (product3.js)

```
rooms = new Array("li","di","be","ki","ba")

function roomName(room) {
 if(room=="li") return "Living Room"
 if(room=="di") return "Dining Room"
 if(room=="be") return "Bed Room"
 if(room=="ki") return "Kitchen"
 if(room=="ba") return "Bath Room"
 return "Unknown"
}

productCategories = new Array("fu","ca","li","el","ac",
 "ap","cb","si","to","ba")

function categoryName(cat) {
 if(cat=="fu") return "Furniture"
 if(cat=="ca") return "Carpeting"
 if(cat=="li") return "Lighting"
 if(cat=="el") return "Electronics"
 if(cat=="ac") return "Accessories"
 if(cat=="ap") return "Appliances"
 if(cat=="cb") return "Cabinets"
 if(cat=="si") return "Sinks"
 if(cat=="to") return "Toilets"
 if(cat=="ba") return "Bath and Shower"
 return "Unknown"
}

function Product(id,name,category,room)       {
 this.id=id
 this.name=name
 this.category=category
 this.room=room
 this.image="i"+id+".gif"
```

```
this.desc="d"+id+".htm"
this.sound="a"+id+".wav"
}

function roomProductCategory(room,cat) {
this.room=room
this.cat=cat
}

var i=0
roomCategories = new Array()
roomCategories[i] = new roomProductCategory("li","fu"); ++i
roomCategories[i] = new roomProductCategory("li","ca"); ++i
roomCategories[i] = new roomProductCategory("li","li"); ++i
roomCategories[i] = new roomProductCategory("li","el"); ++i
roomCategories[i] = new roomProductCategory("li","ac"); ++i
roomCategories[i] = new roomProductCategory("di","fu"); ++i
roomCategories[i] = new roomProductCategory("di","ca"); ++i
roomCategories[i] = new roomProductCategory("di","li"); ++i
roomCategories[i] = new roomProductCategory("di","ac"); ++i
roomCategories[i] = new roomProductCategory("be","fu"); ++i
roomCategories[i] = new roomProductCategory("be","ca"); ++i
roomCategories[i] = new roomProductCategory("be","li"); ++i
roomCategories[i] = new roomProductCategory("be","el"); ++i
roomCategories[i] = new roomProductCategory("be","ac"); ++i
roomCategories[i] = new roomProductCategory("ki","ap"); ++i
roomCategories[i] = new roomProductCategory("ki","cb"); ++i
roomCategories[i] = new roomProductCategory("ki","li"); ++i
roomCategories[i] = new roomProductCategory("ki","ac"); ++i
roomCategories[i] = new roomProductCategory("ba","si"); ++i
roomCategories[i] = new roomProductCategory("ba","to"); ++i
roomCategories[i] = new roomProductCategory("ba","li"); ++i
roomCategories[i] = new roomProductCategory("ba","ba"); ++i
roomCategories[i] = new roomProductCategory("ba","ac"); ++i

var i=0
prod=new Array()

//Living room products
prod[i]=new Product(i,"Couch","fu","li"); ++i
prod[i]=new Product(i,"Sofa","fu","li"); ++i
prod[i]=new Product(i,"Arm chair","fu","li"); ++i
prod[i]=new Product(i,"Long table","fu","li"); ++i
```

```
prod[i]=new Product(i,"Side table","fu","li"); ++i
prod[i]=new Product(i,"Persian rug","ca","li"); ++i
prod[i]=new Product(i,"Cheap rug","ca","li"); ++i
prod[i]=new Product(i,"Ceiling light","li","li"); ++i
prod[i]=new Product(i,"Floor light","li","li"); ++i
prod[i]=new Product(i,"Table light","li","li"); ++i
prod[i]=new Product(i,"Big TV","el","li"); ++i
prod[i]=new Product(i,"Small TV","el","li"); ++i
prod[i]=new Product(i,"Entertainment Center","el","li"); ++i
prod[i]=new Product(i,"Stereo","el","li"); ++i
prod[i]=new Product(i,"Large painting","ac","li"); ++i
prod[i]=new Product(i,"Small painting","ac","li"); ++i
prod[i]=new Product(i,"Large fake plant","ac","li"); ++i
prod[i]=new Product(i,"Small fake plant","ac","li"); ++i
prod[i]=new Product(i,"Expensive knick knack","ac","li"); ++i
prod[i]=new Product(i,"Cheap knick knack","ac","li"); ++i

//Dining room products
prod[i]=new Product(i,"Expensive dining set","fu","di"); ++i
prod[i]=new Product(i,"Cheap dining set","fu","di"); ++i
prod[i]=new Product(i,"China cabinet","fu","di"); ++i
prod[i]=new Product(i,"Serving table","fu","di"); ++i
prod[i]=new Product(i,"Stain-proof rug","ca","di"); ++i
prod[i]=new Product(i,"Plastic floor covering","ca","di"); ++i
prod[i]=new Product(i,"Chandalier","li","di"); ++i
prod[i]=new Product(i,"Ceiling lamp","li","di"); ++i
prod[i]=new Product(i,"China set","ac","di"); ++i
prod[i]=new Product(i,"Silver set","ac","di"); ++i

//Bed room products
prod[i]=new Product(i,"King bed","fu","be"); ++i
prod[i]=new Product(i,"Queen bed","fu","be"); ++i
prod[i]=new Product(i,"Single bed","fu","be"); ++i
prod[i]=new Product(i,"In table","fu","be"); ++i
prod[i]=new Product(i,"Dresser","fu","be"); ++i
prod[i]=new Product(i,"Lamb skin carpet","ca","be"); ++i
prod[i]=new Product(i,"Bear skin carpet","ca","be"); ++i
prod[i]=new Product(i,"Ceiling lamp","li","be"); ++i
prod[i]=new Product(i,"Table lamp","li","be"); ++i
prod[i]=new Product(i,"Clock Radio","el","be"); ++i
prod[i]=new Product(i,"Electronic head board","el","be"); ++i
prod[i]=new Product(i,"Pillow set","ac","be"); ++i
prod[i]=new Product(i,"Linen set","ac","be"); ++i
```

```
prod[i]=new Product(i,"Bed spread","ac","be"); ++i

//Kitchen products
prod[i]=new Product(i,"Refrigerator","ap","ki"); ++i
prod[i]=new Product(i,"Stove - oven","ap","ki"); ++i
prod[i]=new Product(i,"Microwave oven","ap","ki"); ++i
prod[i]=new Product(i,"Toaster","ap","ki"); ++i
prod[i]=new Product(i,"Coffee maker","ap","ki"); ++i
prod[i]=new Product(i,"Dish washer","ap","ki"); ++i
prod[i]=new Product(i,"Deluxe cabinets","cb","ki"); ++i
prod[i]=new Product(i,"Standard cabinets","cb","ki"); ++i
prod[i]=new Product(i,"Deluxe counter","cb","ki"); ++i
prod[i]=new Product(i,"Standard counter","cb","ki"); ++i
prod[i]=new Product(i,"Ceiling light","li","ki"); ++i
prod[i]=new Product(i,"Counter light","li","ki"); ++i
prod[i]=new Product(i,"Cookware","ac","ki"); ++i
prod[i]=new Product(i,"Storage containers","ac","ki"); ++i
prod[i]=new Product(i,"Wall clock","ac","ki"); ++i

//Bath room products
prod[i]=new Product(i,"Deluxe sink","si","ba"); ++i
prod[i]=new Product(i,"Standard sink","si","ba"); ++i
prod[i]=new Product(i,"Deluxe toilet","to","ba"); ++i
prod[i]=new Product(i,"Standard toilet","to","ba"); ++i
prod[i]=new Product(i,"Ceiling light","li","ba"); ++i
prod[i]=new Product(i,"Wall light","li","ba"); ++i
prod[i]=new Product(i,"Deluxe bath tub","ba","ba"); ++i
prod[i]=new Product(i,"Standard bath tub","ba","ba"); ++i
prod[i]=new Product(i,"Shower stall","ba","ba"); ++i
prod[i]=new Product(i,"Wall cabinet","ac","ba"); ++i
prod[i]=new Product(i,"Towel rack","ac","ba"); ++i
prod[i]=new Product(i,"Towels","ac","ba"); ++I
```

Summary

In this chapter you learned how to use JavaScript to create a variety of catalogs. You learned how to develop catalogs without the need for CGI programs. You also learned to tailor your catalogs based on user preferences and to add multimedia features to your catalogs. In the next chapter you'll learn how to use JavaScript to implement custom site searching and navigation aids.

CHAPTER

FIFTEEN

Site Searching Tools

- Search Forms

- Search Engines

- Connecting Search Forms to Search Engines

- Creating Local Search Engines

Some of the most frequently visited Web sites are those that help you to find other Web pages. Alta Vista, Yahoo, Infoseek, and Lycos are popular search sites. In addition, many large sites, such as Microsoft's and CNN's, provide site-specific search capabilities.

With JavaScript, implementing search capabilities in your Web pages is easy. You can use JavaScript to develop a full-featured search interface to connect to existing search engines, or to implement your own browser-based search scripts.

In this chapter, you'll learn to integrate search capabilities in your Web pages. You'll learn to use JavaScript to write interfaces to search engines and to implement local search capabilities. When you finish this chapter, you'll be able to incorporate advanced search features in your Web pages.

Search Forms

Search forms are used to gather search information from a user and forward it to one or more search engines. The search engines then perform the search and forward the search results back to the user. Since the search form is what the user sees when he or she performs the search, it is important to provide an interface that is flexible, efficient, and easy to use.

JavaScript-based search forms have a major advantage over those that are implemented in HTML alone—they allow form-related events to be handled locally. This lets you develop forms that can dynamically adapt to entries the user may have made previously. These dynamic forms help users to specify search criteria more easily and efficiently. Dynamic search forms can also be used to present a more flexible and intuitive interface to the user.

To get a better feel for how JavaScript can be used to enhance a search interface, consider the search form shown in Figure 15.1. This form allows you to select a particular Web technology area of interest and then a specific topic within that area. Open the file `search.htm` (Listing 15.1) with your browser to see how this form works.

FIGURE 15.1

The search form opening
display (Listing 15.1)

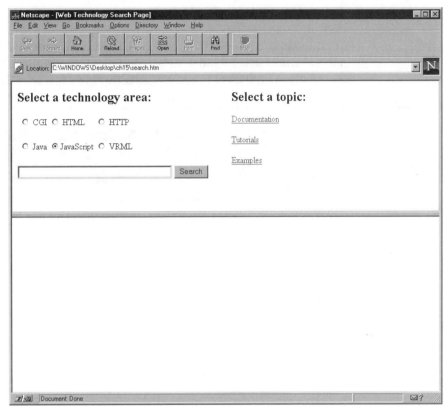

NOTE In this chapter, I've provided three different search engines for different purposes. For each example in the chapter, I'll instruct you to rename `engines-1.htm`, `engines-2.htm`, or `engines-3.htm` to simply `engines .htm` in order to run the appropriate search engine in the particular example being discussed.

When you click on a "Select a technology area" radio button, the list of topic links to the right changes to reflect the area you selected. For this example, click on the HTTP technology area and the list of topics is updated with links that are specific to HTTP—Specification, Security, and Versions—as shown in Figure 15.2. Click on the Security link; a Web search engine form is displayed, as shown in Figure 15.3. Note that the area and topic the user selected, in this case HTTP security, are automatically inserted into the search text field. Forms such as the ones shown in this example make it much easier for the user to formulate a search query. In the next section, you'll learn how to connect this form to a search engine.

FIGURE 15.2

Selecting a technology area (Listing 15.3)

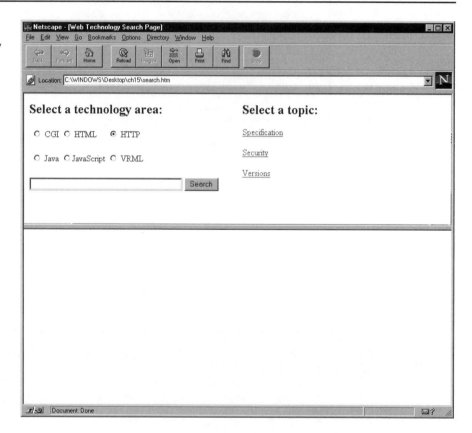

Listing 15.1 contains the `search.htm` file. This file sets up a two-frame set with `sform.htm` (Listing 15.2) loaded into the top frame. Listing 15.2 shows that `sform.htm` breaks the top frame into two colums, with `topic.htm` loaded into the left frame.

FIGURE 15.3

Selecting a search
engine (Listing 15.4)

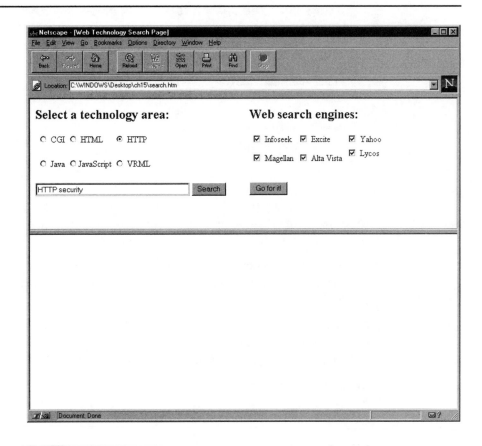

Listing 15.1. The search form's top-level frame set (search.htm)

```
<HTML>
<HEAD>
<TITLE>Web Technology Search Page</TITLE>
</HEAD>
<FRAMESET ROWS="250,*" BORDER="10">
<FRAME SRC="sform.htm">
<FRAME SRC="blank.htm">
</FRAMESET>
</HTML>
```

Listing 15.2. The search form's second-level frame set (sform.htm)

```
<HTML>
<HEAD>
<TITLE>Web Technology Search Page</TITLE>
</HEAD>
<FRAMESET COLS="*,*" BORDER="0">
<FRAME SRC="topic.htm">
<FRAME SRC="blank.htm">
</FRAMESET>
</HTML>
```

The `topic.htm` file implements the search form. It creates the radio button form shown in the upper left frame of Figure 15.1 and implements the following functions and arrays.

Topic() This function is the constructor of the search's `Topic` object. A `Topic` consists of a topic title and a string of keywords to search for that are related to this topic.

topics The `topics` array is an array of the arrays of all topics supported for each technology area. For example, `topics[0]` identifies the topics related to the CGI area, `topics[1]` identifies the topics related to HTML, and so on.

processArea() This function determines which technology area radio button is checked and invokes `displayTopics()` to display the topics related to the technology area.

displayTopics() This function creates the document shown in the upper right frame of the window. It creates a link for each topic in the `topics` array related to the technology area. The `engines.htm` file is the destination of each link. The `setSearch()` function is the onClick event handler for each link. The `setSearch()` function displays the link's search string in the text field of the frame located in the upper left of the window.

performSearch() This function is a function stub for the onClick event handler for the search string displayed in the upper left frame. This function may be implemented to provide a direct search capability. However, for this example we use the form generated by the `engines.htm` file.

Listing 15.3. Implementing the search form (topic.htm)

```
<HTML>
<HEAD>
<TITLE>Web Technologies Search Form</TITLE>
<SCRIPT LANGUAGE="JavaScript"><!--
function Topic(desc,search) {
 this.desc=desc
 this.search=search
}

topics = new Array()
topics[0] = new Array(
 new Topic("Tutorials","CGI tutorial"),
 new Topic("Documentation","CGI documentation"),
 new Topic("Examples","CGI example"),
 new Topic("Using cookies","CGI cookies")
)
topics[1] = new Array(
 new Topic("HTML 2.0","HTML 2.0"),
 new Topic("HTML 3.0","HTML 3.0"),
 new Topic("HTML 3.2","HTML 3.2"),
 new Topic("Extensions","HTML extensions"),
 new Topic("Tutorials","HTML tutorial")
)
topics[2] = new Array(
 new Topic("Specification","HTTP specification"),
 new Topic("Security","HTTP security"),
 new Topic("Versions","HTTP version")
)
topics[3] = new Array(
 new Topic("Documentation","Java documentation"),
 new Topic("Tutorials","Java tutorial"),
 new Topic("Examples","Java example"),
 new Topic("Shareware","Java shareware")
)
topics[4] = new Array(
 new Topic("Documentation","JavaScript documentation"),
 new Topic("Tutorials","JavaScript tutorial"),
 new Topic("Examples","JavaScript example")
)
topics[5] = new Array(
 new Topic("Documentation","VRML documentation"),
```

```
new Topic("Tutorials","VRML tutorial"),
new Topic("Examples","VRML example"),
new Topic("Web sites","VRML sites")
)

function processArea() {
 var thisForm=window.document.forms[0]
 var elements=thisForm.elements
 for(var i=0;i<topics.length;++i) {
  if(elements[i].checked) displayTopics(i)
 }
}

function displayTopics(n) {
 var doc=parent.frames[1].document
 doc.open()
 doc.writeln('<HTML>')
 doc.writeln('<HEAD>')
 doc.writeln('<SCRIPT LANGUAGE="JavaScript">')
 doc.writeln('function setSearch(s) {')
 doc.writeln('text=parent.frames[0].document.forms[0].srch')
 doc.writeln('text.value=s')
 doc.writeln('}')
 doc.writeln('</SCRIPT>')
 doc.writeln('</HEAD>')
 doc.writeln('<BODY BGCOLOR="white">')
 doc.writeln('<H2>Select a topic:</H2>')
 for(var i=0;i<topics[n].length;++i) {
  doc.writeln('<P><A HREF="engines.htm" ')
  doc.writeln('onClick="setSearch(\''
    +topics[n][i].search+'\')">')
  doc.writeln(topics[n][i].desc+'</A></P>')
 }
 doc.writeln('</BODY>')
 doc.writeln('</HTML>')
 doc.close()
}

function performSearch() {
}
// --></SCRIPT>
</HEAD>
```

```
<BODY BGCOLOR="white">
<FORM>
<H2>Select a technology area:</H2>
<TABLE>
<TR><TD><P>
<INPUT TYPE="RADIO" NAME="area" VALUE="cgi"
 onClick="processArea()"> CGI</P></TD>
<TD><P>
<INPUT TYPE="RADIO" NAME="area" VALUE="html"
 onClick="processArea()"> HTML</P></TD>
<TD><P>
<INPUT TYPE="RADIO" NAME="area" VALUE="http"
 onClick="processArea()"> HTTP</P></TD>
</TR>
<TR><TD><P>
<INPUT TYPE="RADIO" NAME="area" VALUE="java"
 onClick="processArea()"> Java</P></TD>
<TD><P>
<INPUT TYPE="RADIO" NAME="area" VALUE="javascript"
 CHECKED="CHECKED" onClick="processArea()">JavaScript</P>
<TD><P>
<INPUT TYPE="RADIO" NAME="area" VALUE="vrml"
 onClick="processArea()"> VRML</P></TD>
</TR>
</TABLE>
<INPUT TYPE="text" NAME="srch" SIZE="40">
<INPUT TYPE="button" NAME="search" VALUE="Search"
 onClick="performSearch()">
</FORM>
<SCRIPT LANGUAGE="JavaScript"><!--
processArea()
// --></SCRIPT>
</BODY>
</HTML>
```

Search Engines

Search engines are programs (usually CGI scripts) that perform a search and generate search results. They commonly use one or more databases to keep track of a large collection of URLs for Web pages, and the keywords the pages contain.

JavaScript scripts can make use of and enhance the capabilities provided by these CGI-based search engines. The following sections show how to set up a basic page to connect a user to some search engines, and then how to connect your scripts to the search engines.

The First Search Engine

The `engines-1.htm` file is the first of three search "engines" that you'll be creating in the examples in this chapter. You must rename this file to `engines.htm` for it to be used with the current version of our search form. This file is not in itself a search engine—in fact, this version doesn't actually perform any searching at all. Instead, it displays a handful of popular and freely available Web search engines, shown in the upper right frame of Figure 15.3. It also handles the `onClick` event of the Go for it! button using the `goSearch()` function (which is a function stub that will implemented in `engines-2.htm` and `engines-3.htm`, search engines that are introduced in later sections of this chapter).

> **NOTE** The file `engines-1.htm` we're using in this example will be the basis of the other two engines we develop later in the chapter—`engines-2.htm` will make use of the six Web search engines listed in this example to perform actual searching, and `engines-3.htm` will be adapted for use as a local search engine.

Listing 15.4. Selecting a search engine (engines-1.htm)

```
<HTML>
<HEAD>
<TITLE>Web Search Engines</TITLE>
<SCRIPT LANGUAGE="JavaScript"><!--
function goSearch() {
}
// --></SCRIPT>
</HEAD>
<BODY BGCOLOR="white">
<H2>Web search engines:</H2>
<FORM>
<TABLE>
<TR>
<TD><INPUT TYPE="CHECKBOX" CHECKED NAME="infoseek"> Infoseek
```

```
</TD>
<TD><INPUT TYPE="CHECKBOX" CHECKED NAME="excite"> Excite
</TD>
<TD><INPUT TYPE="CHECKBOX" CHECKED NAME="yahoo"> Yahoo
</TD>
</TR>
<TR>
<TD><INPUT TYPE="CHECKBOX" CHECKED NAME="magellan"> Magellan
</TD>
<TD><INPUT TYPE="CHECKBOX" CHECKED NAME="altaVista"> Alta Vista
</TD>
<TD><INPUT TYPE="CHECKBOX" CHECKED NAME="lycos"> Lycos</P>
</TD>
</TR>
</TABLE>
<P><INPUT TYPE="BUTTON" VALUE="Go for it!"
 onClick="goSearch()"></P>
</FORM>
</BODY>
</HTML>
```

Connecting Search Forms to Search Engines

In order to perform a search, you must pass the search criteria gathered from the user (via the search form) to the CGI program implementing the search engine. This search criteria is generally passed in the form of a *query string*.

A query string passes data to a CGI program via the URL used to access the CGI program. It consists of a question mark (?) followed by the data to be passed. For example, the following URL passes the string *This is a test* to my echo-query CGI program:

http://www.jaworski.com/cgi-bin/echo-query?This+is+a+test

You may have noticed in the above URL that spaces are encoded with plus signs (+) when they are passed via query strings. Other codings are used to pass special characters and binary data as described in Chapter 26, "Interfacing with CGI programs."

Listing 15.5 shows how search data can be passed to more than one search engine at the same time. It builds upon the first example shown in this chapter by adding the JavaScript necessary to implement the `goSearch()` function. First, you must rename `engines-2.htm` as `engines.htm` (in order to install that file as the new search engine for the search form introduced in the previous section). Then open `search.htm` with your browser. Finally, make sure that you are connected to the Internet, because the `engines-2.htm` file contains links to connect your search form to popular online search engines.

For this example, click on the VRML radio button and then on the Examples link. The "Web search engines" form appears in the upper right frame. Click on the Go for it! button to perform a search for the string "VRML example" using all of the six major search engines. The search results produced by these engines are provided in six separate frames at the bottom of the window (refer to Figure 15.4). You can click on the links in each of these frames to find more information on VRML examples. Wouldn't it be impressive to provide the same search capabilities in your Web pages?

Figure 15.5 shows the results of a search that uses only four search engines. Figure 15.6 shows the results of a single engine search.

FIGURE 15.4

Using all six search engines at once (Listing 15.5)

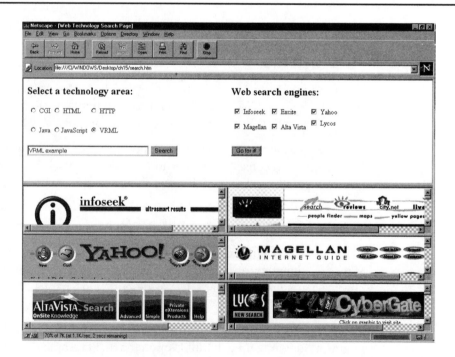

FIGURE 15.5

Using four search
engines (Listing 15.5)

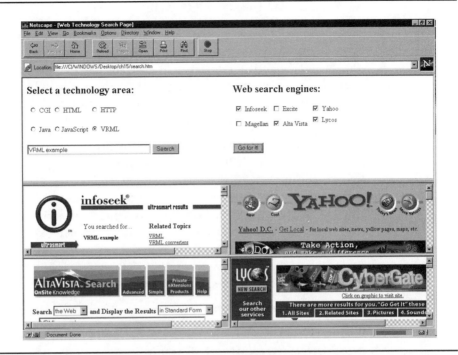

FIGURE 15.6

Using a single search
engine (Listing 15.5)

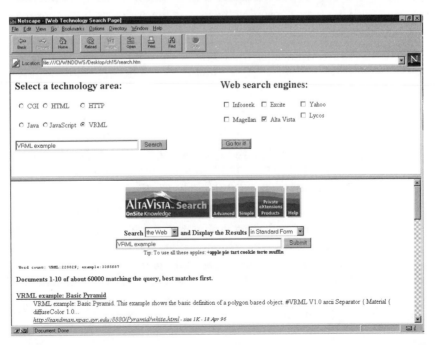

The Second Search Engine

The `engines-2.htm` search engine is more of a transmission than an engine. It takes the search string produced by the search form introduced in the previous section and converts it into a form that can be used with popular Web search engines. It then prompts these engines to perform a search of the search string and displays the results they return in separate frames. The functions implemented by `engines-2.htm` are presented in the following paragraphs.

goSearch() This function handles the `onClick` event of the Go for it! button and initiates the search. It retrieves the search string contained in the text field of the frame in the upper left corner of the window, and converts it to a URL query string using the `convertToQueryString()` function. It determines how many search sites the user selected in the "Web search engines" form, creates that many frames to store the query results, and waits two seconds before invoking `loadFrames()` to load the search results into these frames. The two-second delay is used to make sure that the new frames are created before the search is initiated. If you have a low-powered computer then you may wish to increase this delay.

convertToQueryString() This function converts spaces in the search string to plus signs (+) so that it can be passed via a query string.

numberOfSearchSites() This function determines how many Web search sites were chosen by the user in the Web search engines form.

createFrames() This function creates the required number of frames to display the search results by loading the appropriate document (from the set of documents named `frames2.htm` through `frames6.htm`) into the lower frame of the window. These files are shown in Listings 15.6 through 15.10.

loadFrames() This function uses the `loadNextFrame()` function to perform the search, and loads the results into the frames created by the `createFrames()` function. The `loadNextFrame()` function is passed the frame that the search results should be loaded into; it is also passed the index of the next search site to be considered as a candidate for searching.

loadNextFrame() This function uses a search site to perform a search and stores the results in a designated frame. The `frameObj` parameter identifies the frame in which the search results should be loaded. The `start` parameter identifies the index of the next search site to be considered as a candidate for searching. If the check box at the specified index is not checked, then subsequent check boxes are examined for the next search site to be used. This function prepares the URLs necessary to using the Infoseek, Excite, Yahoo, Magellan, Alta Vista, and

Lycos search engines, and appends the value of the `searchString` variable to these URLs. The search is initiated by setting the destination frame's location property to the search URL.

> **NOTE**
>
> The URLs of the search engines used in `loadNextFrame()` were determined by trial and error, playing with the search engines at each search site. The conventions used in these URLs are specific to each site.

Listing 15.5. Connecting to other search engines (engines-2.htm)

```
<HTML>
<HEAD>
<TITLE>Web Search Engines</TITLE>
<SCRIPT LANGUAGE="JavaScript"><!--
function goSearch() {
 searchString=parent.frames[0].document.forms[0].srch.value
 searchString=convertToQueryString(searchString)
 var n=numberOfSearchSites()
 createFrames(n)
 setTimeout("loadFrames("+n+")",2000)
}
function convertToQueryString(s) {
 var result=""
 for(var i=0;i<s.length;++i)
  if(s.charAt(i)==' ') result+="+"
  else result+=s.charAt(i)
 return result
}
function numberOfSearchSites() {
 var result=0
 var elements=window.document.forms[0].elements
 for(var i=0;i<elements.length-1;++i)
  if(elements[i].checked) ++result
 return result
}
function createFrames(n) {
 if(n>1)
  parent.parent.frames[1].location.href="frames"+n+".htm"
}
```

```
function loadFrames(n) {
 var mainFrame=parent.parent.frames[1]
 var newStart
 if(n==1) loadNextFrame(mainFrame,0)
 else if(n==2) {
  newStart=loadNextFrame(mainFrame.frames[0],0)
  loadNextFrame(mainFrame.frames[1],newStart)
 }else if(n==3) {
  newStart=loadNextFrame(mainFrame.frames[0],0)
  newStart=loadNextFrame(mainFrame.frames[1],newStart)
  loadNextFrame(mainFrame.frames[2],newStart)
 }else if(n==4) {
  newStart=loadNextFrame(mainFrame.frames[0].frames[0],0)
  newStart=loadNextFrame(mainFrame.frames[0].frames[1],newStart)
  newStart=loadNextFrame(mainFrame.frames[1].frames[0],newStart)
  loadNextFrame(mainFrame.frames[1].frames[1],newStart)
 }else if(n==5) {
  newStart=loadNextFrame(mainFrame.frames[0].frames[0],0)
  newStart=loadNextFrame(mainFrame.frames[0].frames[1],newStart)
  newStart=loadNextFrame(mainFrame.frames[1].frames[0],newStart)
  newStart=loadNextFrame(mainFrame.frames[1].frames[1],newStart)
  loadNextFrame(mainFrame.frames[2],newStart)
 }else if(n==6) {
  newStart=loadNextFrame(mainFrame.frames[0].frames[0],0)
  newStart=loadNextFrame(mainFrame.frames[0].frames[1],newStart)
  newStart=loadNextFrame(mainFrame.frames[1].frames[0],newStart)
  newStart=loadNextFrame(mainFrame.frames[1].frames[1],newStart)
  newStart=loadNextFrame(mainFrame.frames[2].frames[0],newStart)
  loadNextFrame(mainFrame.frames[2].frames[1],newStart)
 }
}
function loadNextFrame(frameObj,start) {
 var elements=window.document.forms[0].elements
 for(var i=start;i<elements.length-1;++i) {
  if(elements[i].checked){
   var searchURL="http://"
   if(elements[i].name=="infoseek")
    searchURL+="guide-p.infoseek.com/Titles?qt="
   else if(elements[i].name=="excite")
    searchURL+="www.excite.com/search.gw?search="
   else if(elements[i].name=="yahoo")
    searchURL+="search.yahoo.com/bin/search?p="
```

```
      else if(elements[i].name=="magellan")
       searchURL+="searcher.mckinley.com/searcher.cgi?query="
      else if(elements[i].name=="altaVista"){
       searchURL+="www.altavista.digital.com"
       searchURL+="/cgi-bin/query?pg=q&what=web&fmt=.&q="
      }else if(elements[i].name=="lycos")
       searchURL+="www.lycos.com/cgi-bin/pursuit?query="
      searchURL+=searchString
      frameObj.location.href=searchURL
      return (i+1)
   }
 }
 return start
}
// --></SCRIPT>
</HEAD>
<BODY BGCOLOR="white">
<H2>Web search engines:</H2>
<FORM>
<TABLE>
<TR>
<TD><INPUT TYPE="CHECKBOX" CHECKED NAME="infoseek"> Infoseek
</TD>
<TD><INPUT TYPE="CHECKBOX" CHECKED NAME="excite"> Excite
</TD>
<TD><INPUT TYPE="CHECKBOX" CHECKED NAME="yahoo"> Yahoo
</TD>
</TR>
<TR>
<TD><INPUT TYPE="CHECKBOX" CHECKED NAME="magellan"> Magellan
</TD>
<TD><INPUT TYPE="CHECKBOX" CHECKED NAME="altaVista"> Alta Vista
</TD>
<TD><INPUT TYPE="CHECKBOX" CHECKED NAME="lycos"> Lycos</P>
</TD>
</TR>
</TABLE>
<P><INPUT TYPE="BUTTON" VALUE="Go for it!"
 onClick="goSearch()"></P>
</FORM>
</BODY>
</HTML>
```

The following `frames*.htm` files are used by the `engines-2.htm` file to create frames to display the results of the Web search engines. The `double.htm` file splits a frame into a two-column frame set.

Listing 15.6. Displaying the results of two search engines (frames2.htm)

```
<HTML>
<FRAMESET ROWS="*,*" BORDER="5">
<FRAME SRC="blank.htm">
<FRAME SRC="blank.htm">
</FRAMESET>
</HTML>
```

Listing 15.7. Displaying the results of three search engines (frames3.htm)

```
<HTML>
<FRAMESET ROWS="*,*,*" BORDER="5">
<FRAME SRC="blank.htm">
<FRAME SRC="blank.htm">
<FRAME SRC="blank.htm">
</FRAMESET>
</HTML>
```

Listing 15.8. Displaying the results of four search engines (frames4.htm)

```
<HTML>
<FRAMESET ROWS="*,*" BORDER="5">
<FRAME SRC="double.htm">
<FRAME SRC="double.htm">
</FRAMESET>
</HTML>
```

Listing 15.9. Displaying the results of five search engines (frames5.htm)

```
<HTML>
<FRAMESET ROWS="*,*,*" BORDER="5">
<FRAME SRC="double.htm">
```

```
<FRAME SRC="double.htm">
<FRAME SRC="blank.htm">
</FRAMESET>
</HTML>
```

Listing 15.10. Displaying the results of six search engines (frames6.htm)

```
<HTML>
<FRAMESET ROWS="*,*,*" BORDER="5">
<FRAME SRC="double.htm">
<FRAME SRC="double.htm">
<FRAME SRC="double.htm">
</FRAMESET>
</HTML>
```

Listing 15.11. Creating two columns (double.htm)

```
<HTML>
<FRAMESET COLS="*,*" BORDER="5">
<FRAME SRC="blank.htm">
<FRAME SRC="blank.htm">
</FRAMESET>
</HTML>
```

Local Search Engines

A local search engine is one that implements search algorithms on the browser instead of using a server-based CGI program. The main advantage of local search engines is that they take the processing load off of your server and put it on the browser. Their main disadvantage is that they are downloaded to the browser and are therefore limited in the amount of search data that they can contain. Local search engines may be impractical for searching large Web sites, such as those of Microsoft, IBM, and Sun, but they may be the perfect solution for searching the Web sites of small to medium-size companies. Local search engines may also be combined with server-based search engines to take some of the processing load off the server-based search engines.

Keyword Search Scripts

For small to medium-size Web sites, simple *keyword search scripts* may be used as local search engines. These scripts present a selection list of terms (keywords) that categorize or describe Web pages that you think may be of interest to the user. The keywords you provide should be categories that you think the page's topics might fall into, or words or phrases that you think users might use to describe the page's content. For example, for a document about server-side Web programming, you might list the keywords *CGI, LiveWire, Perl* as categories, and/or *programming, client/server*, and so on as descriptions.

The advantages of keyword scripts are that they are small, user-friendly, and easy to develop. Their main disadvantage is that they become unwieldy when the number of keywords used becomes large.

Keyword search scripts can be created in such a way that when the user clicks on a keyword, the URLs for relevant Web pages are displayed. Of course, you can also create a script that first offers topic or category keywords (as you first saw in search.htm at the beginning of the chapter), which would link to more-detailed lists of keywords that are linked to specific URLs. This latter approach is the one we've been building up to throughout the chapter, and is the approach I'll be illustrating with the following listing.

Listing 15.12 provides an example of a local search engine that provides lists of keywords to choose from in various categories *and* at various levels of focus (for documents of interest to the entire company, to a company division, or to a single department). To run this example, rename engines-3.htm to engines.htm to use it with the search form developed in the first section of this chapter. After renaming it, open search.htm and, for this example, try the following keyword searches:

1. Click on the Java radio button in the "Select a technology area" frame, then click the Documentation link in the "Select a topic" frame.

2. Scroll down in the upper panel to see the choices offered by the "Search depth" form.

3. Choose the Department button to perform a department-level search, then click on the Go for it! button. The search results are shown in Figure 15.7.

FIGURE 15.7

Searching for documents
related to Java at the
department level
(Listing 15.12)

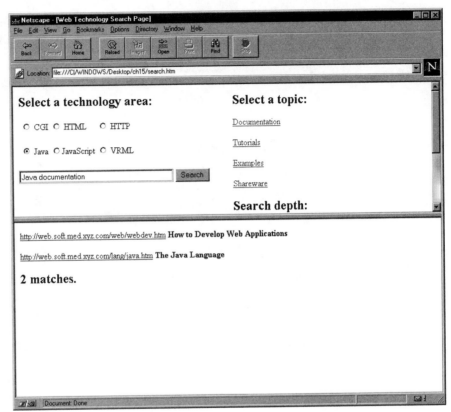

The "Search depth" form in this example provides local search capabilities at different levels, in this case at department, division, and sector levels. I chose these levels to reflect the differences in scope you might want to address within a company's organization. In this example, the company is considered to be comprised of sectors, which are made up of divisions, which consist of departments. Documents that are intended for readership at the sector level are for the use of all divisions and departments within the sector. Other documents may be intended for both the division and sector levels, and still others may be of interest only within a department.

When you perform a similar search for JavaScript documentation at the division level, you see the results shown in Figure 15.8. Searching for VRML tutorials at the Sector level produces the result shown in Figure 15.9.

FIGURE 15.8

Searching for documents relating to JavaScript at the division level (Listing 15.12)

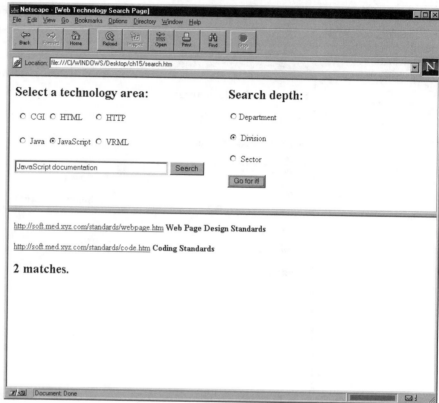

The Third Search Engine

The `engines-3.htm` file implements the local search engine using the following functions. Note that the JavaScript code it includes is contained in `db.js`.

goSearch() This function handles the `onClick` event of the Go for it! button and initiates the search. It retrieves the search string contained in the text field of the frame in the upper left corner of the window, and converts it to a URL query string using the `convertToQueryString()` function. It then invokes `performSearch()` to perform the search and `listURLs()` to display the search results.

convertToQueryString() This function converts spaces in the search string to plus signs (+) so that it can be passed via a query string.

FIGURE 15.9

Searching for documents
relating to VRML at the
sector level (Listing 15.12)

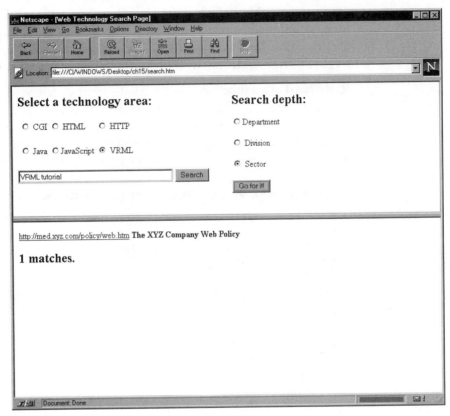

performSearch() This function searches the search database for each word in
the search string. The `buildHitList()` function builds a list of candidate URLs,
referred to as a *hit list*. The `updateSearch()` function updates the `hitList`
array based on the search for each word.

buildHitList() This function creates a list of all URLs that are candidates for the
search. This `hitList` is implemented as indices into the `deptURLs`, `divURLs`, or
`sectURLs` arrays defined in `db.js`. The `scope` variable is set to 0, 1, or 2 by the
`onClick` event handlers of the Department, Division, and Sector radio buttons.

updateSearch() This function performs the central search processing. It creates
a `mask` array the same size as `hitList`, setting the default search value to `false`.
It then finds the search word identified by the `s` variable in the `dictionary` array
(defined in `db.js`). It sets the values of the `mask` array to `true` depending on

whether the value of s is contained in a document in the list of URLs specified by the scope variable. Refer to the description of the db array (defined in db.js) for more information on how this is accomplished. The values of the elements of the mask array are then logically *AND*ed with the values of the elements of the hitList array to identify which URLs are still search candidates.

listURLs() This function uses the hitList array to display the URLs and their descriptions in the lower frame of the window. The urlSet variable is assigned the deptURLs, divURLs, or sectURLs array depending upon the value of scope. It then uses urlSet and the urlDescs array (defined in db.js) to display and describe the URLs that have met the search criteria.

Listing 15.12. A local search engine (engines-3.htm)

```
<HTML>
<HEAD>
<TITLE>Local Search Engine</TITLE>
<SCRIPT LANGUAGE="JavaScript" SRC="db.js"><!--
// --></SCRIPT>
<SCRIPT LANGUAGE="JavaScript"><!--
scope=0
function goSearch() {
 searchString=parent.frames[0].document.forms[0].srch.value
 searchString=convertToQueryString(searchString)
 performSearch()
 listURLs()
}
function convertToQueryString(s) {
 var result=""
 for(var i=0;i<s.length;++i)
  if(s.charAt(i)==' ') result+="+"
  else result+=s.charAt(i)
 return result
}
function performSearch() {
 strings=searchString.split("+")
 buildHitList()
 for(var i=0;i<strings.length;++i)
  updateSearch(strings[i])
}
function buildHitList() {
 if(scope==0) hitList = new Array(deptURLs.length)
```

```
   else if(scope==1) hitList = new Array(divURLs.length)
   else if(scope==2) hitList = new Array(sectURLs.length)
   for(var i=0;i<hitList.length;++i) hitList[i]=true
}
function updateSearch(s) {
 var mask = new Array(hitList.length)
 for(var i=0;i<mask.length;++i) mask[i]=false
 for(var i=0;i<dictionary.length;++i) {
  if(dictionary[i]==s) {
   for(var j=0;j<db[i][scope].length;++j) {
     mask[db[i][scope][j]]=true
   }
  }
 }
 for(var i=0;i<hitList.length;++i)
  hitList[i]=hitList[i] && mask[i]
}
function listURLs() {
 doc=parent.parent.frames[1].document
 doc.open()
 var hitCount=0
 var urlSet = deptURLs
 if(scope==1) urlSet=divURLs
 else if(scope==2) urlSet=sectURLs
 doc.writeln("<HTML><BODY BGCOLOR='white'>")
 for(var i=0;i<hitList.length;++i) {
  if(hitList[i]) {
   ++hitCount
   doc.writeln("<P>"+urlSet[i].link(urlSet[i])+" ")
   doc.writeln("<B>"+urlDescs[scope][i]+"</B></P>")
  }
 }
 doc.writeln("<H2>"+hitCount+" matches.</H2>")
 doc.writeln("</BODY></HTML>")
 doc.close()
}
// --></SCRIPT>
</HEAD>
<BODY BGCOLOR="white">
<H2>Search depth:</H2>
<FORM>
<P><INPUT TYPE="RADIO" CHECKED NAME="depth" VALUE="dept"
```

```
  onClick="scope=0">Department
</P><P><INPUT TYPE="RADIO" NAME="depth" VALUE="div"
  onClick="scope=1"> Division
</P><P><INPUT TYPE="RADIO" NAME="depth" VALUE="sect"
  onClick="scope=2"> Sector
</P>
<P><INPUT TYPE="BUTTON" VALUE="Go for it!"
  onClick="goSearch()"></P>
</FORM>
</BODY>
</HTML>
```

The db.js file contains the search database used by engines-3.htm. It consists of the following arrays.

dictionary   This array contains all of the keywords that are supported by the search engine. The list presented here is small. Most search engines would have a list containing between 100 and 1,000 words.

deptURLs   This array identifies the department-level URLs that are covered by the search engine. My script lists only a few, for example purposes. A list of hundreds of URLs would be more normal for a real application, and would still be manageable by most local search engines.

divURLs   This array identifies the division-level URLs that are covered by the search engine.

sectURLs   This array identifies the sector-level URLs that are covered by the search engine.

urlDescs   This array provides a description of the department, division, and sector URLs. It is an array of arrays of descriptions that can be indexed by the scope variable (see engines-3.htm) to provide department, division, or sector URL descriptions.

db   This array is the heart of the search database. Each element of db contains information on a specific word in the dictionary array. For example, db[0] contains info pertaining to the keyword *CGI*, db[1] contains info pertaining to the keyword *Tutorial*, and db[18] contains info pertaining to the keyword *Sites*. In addition, every db[n] is itself a three-element array, for it contains the aforementioned information at the department, division, and sector levels respectively. For example, in the listing below, db[5][0] is an array containing the indices for the HTML keyword for department-level URLs. These URLs are deptURLs[0], deptURLs[1], deptURLs[2], deptURLs[5], deptURLs[6], and deptURLs[8]. Similarly, db[5][1] is an array containing the indices for the HTML keyword for division-level URLs. These URLs are divURLs[0], divURLs[1], divURLs[3], divURLs[4], divURLs[5] and divURLs[6].

Listing 15.13. The search database (db.js)

```
dictionary = new Array(
 "CGI",
 "tutorial",
 "documentation",
 "example",
 "cookies",
 "HTML",
 "2.0",
 "3.0",
 "3.2",
 "extensions",
 "HTTP",
 "specification",
 "security",
 "version",
 "Java",
 "shareware",
 "JavaScript",
 "VRML",
 "sites"
)

deptURLs = new Array(
 "http://web.soft.med.xyz.com/web/webdev.htm",
 "http://web.soft.med.xyz.com/web/webtut.htm",
 "http://web.soft.med.xyz.com/web/examples.htm",
 "http://web.soft.med.xyz.com/spec/http.htm",
 "http://web.soft.med.xyz.com/spec/vrml.htm",
 "http://web.soft.med.xyz.com/lang/java.htm",
 "http://web.soft.med.xyz.com/lang/javascript.htm",
 "http://web.soft.med.xyz.com/lang/vrml.htm",
 "http://web.soft.med.xyz.com/lang/html.htm"
)

divURLs = new Array(
 "http://soft.med.xyz.com/standards/webpage.htm",
 "http://soft.med.xyz.com/standards/code.htm",
```

```
   "http://soft.med.xyz.com/standards/http.htm",
   "http://soft.med.xyz.com/tutorials/html.htm",
   "http://soft.med.xyz.com/tutorials/cgi.htm",
   "http://soft.med.xyz.com/tutorials/java.htm",
   "http://soft.med.xyz.com/tutorials/javascript.htm",
   "http://soft.med.xyz.com/tutorials/vrml.htm"
  )

sectURLs = new Array(
  "http://med.xyz.com/policy/web.htm",
  "http://med.xyz.com/policy/whatsnew.htm"
  )

urlDescs = new Array(
  new Array(
   "How to Develop Web Applications",
   "A Web Tutorial",
   "Examples of Web Application Development",
   "The HTTP Specification",
   "The VRML Specification",
   "The Java Language",
   "The JavaScript Language",
   "The VRML Language",
   "The HTML Language"
   ),
  new Array(
   "Web Page Design Standards",
   "Coding Standards",
   "The HTTP Specification",
   "An HTML Tutorial",
   "A CGI Tutorial",
   "A Java Tutorial",
   "A JavaScript Tutorial",
   "A VRML Tutorial"
   ),
  new Array(
   "The XYZ Company Web Policy",
   "What's New at XYZ?"
   )
  )
```

```
db = new Array(dictionary.length)
db[0]=new Array(
 new Array(0,1,2),
 new Array(0,1,4),
 new Array()
)
db[1]=new Array(
 new Array(1),
 new Array(3,4,5,6,7),
 new Array(1)
)
db[2]=new Array(
 new Array(0,3,4,5,6,7,8),
 new Array(0,1,2),
 new Array(1)
)
db[3]=new Array(
 new Array(2),
 new Array(3,4,5,6,7),
 new Array()
)
db[4]=new Array(
 new Array(0,3),
 new Array(1,2,4),
 new Array()
)
db[5]=new Array(
 new Array(0,1,2,5,6,8),
 new Array(0,1,3,4,5,6),
 new Array(0,1)
)
db[6]=new Array(
 new Array(0,1,2,8),
 new Array(0,1,3),
 new Array(0)
)
db[7]=new Array(
 new Array(8),
 new Array(0),
 new Array(0)
)
```

```
db[8]=new Array(
 new Array(0,8),
 new Array(0,3),
 new Array(0,1)
)
db[9]=new Array(
 new Array(0,1,8),
 new Array(0,3),
 new Array(0,1)
)
db[10]=new Array(
 new Array(3),
 new Array(2),
 new Array()
)
db[11]=new Array(
 new Array(0,3,4),
 new Array(0,1,2),
 new Array()
)
db[12]=new Array(
 new Array(),
 new Array(0,1,2,4),
 new Array(0,1)
)
db[13]=new Array(
 new Array(3,4),
 new Array(0,1,2),
 new Array(0,1)
)
db[14]=new Array(
 new Array(0,1,2,5),
 new Array(0,1,5),
 new Array(0,1)
)
db[15]=new Array(
 new Array(2),
 new Array(4,5),
 new Array()
)
```

```
db[16]=new Array(
 new Array(0,1,2,6),
 new Array(0,1,6),
 new Array(0,1)
)
db[17]=new Array(
 new Array(4,7),
 new Array(7),
 new Array(1)
)
db[18]=new Array(
 new Array(7),
 new Array(7),
 new Array(1)
)
```

Summary

In this chapter you learned how to develop and integrate JavaScript-based search capabilities in your Web pages. In the next chapter you'll have a little fun. You'll learn how to develop some interesting games using JavaScript.

CHAPTER
SIXTEEN

16

Game Programming

- Poker Machine

- Board Game

You've worked hard over the last 15 chapters to learn the JavaScript language and many of its applications. In this chapter, you'll have some fun as you learn more JavaScript game programming. First, you'll develop a poker machine that will let you play poker against your browser. Then, you'll develop a board game that I call "Web Walk" that will test your knowledge of the Web. Of course, the chapter isn't only fun and games—by programming these entertaining projects, you'll learn some very useful skills, including how to use JavaScript to build appealing user interfaces, to work with images, and to respond to a variety of user interface events. When you finish this chapter, you'll be able to develop your own games in JavaScript.

Poker Machine

The first game that you'll develop is a JavaScript version of a Vegas-style poker machine. In this game, you place an initial bet of one dollar and are dealt five cards which you use to try to form a poker hand. Refer to Table 6.1 for a description and ranking of possible poker hands.

TABLE 16.1   Ranking of poker hands

Rank	Hand	Description
1	Royal flush	10 through Ace of the same suit
2	Straight flush	5 consecutive cards of the same suit
3	4 of a kind	4 cards of the same rank
4	Full house	3 cards of one rank and two cards of another
5	Flush	5 cards of the same suit
6	Straight	5 consecutive cards
7	3 of a kind	3 cards of the same rank
8	2 pair	2 cards of the same rank and 2 cards of another rank
9	1 pair	2 cards of the same rank
10	Everything else	

After receiving your five cards, you are allowed to discard any unwanted cards and receive an equal number of replacement cards in return. (You discard a card by clicking on it.) Once you have been dealt your replacement cards, you will receive a payoff based on the value of your hand. Table 16.2 summarizes the payoff algorithm.

TABLE 16.2   The payoff algorithm

Hand	Payoff (Dollars)
Royal flush	1,000
Straight flush	500
4 of a kind	250
Full house	100
Flush	50
Straight	25
3 of a kind	10
2 pair	5
1 pair of Jacks or higher	1

To play this game, open `poker.htm`. The program will display the screen shown in Figure 16.1 until it loads all of the card images. It will then deal you a five-card hand, as shown in Figure 16.2. You are also given $100.00 dollars to start with—the "You have $" text box displays your current budget for the game. The amount is updated after each hand. (Each hand costs $1.00 to play.)

- If you're happy with the hand you were dealt, click on the Continue button to play the next hand.

- Otherwise, click on any cards that you want to discard—they will be turned over, as shown in Figure 16.3—and then click on the Continue button. The cards you indicated as discards will be replaced, and you will be told of your winnings, as shown in Figure 16.4. Click on the Continue button to play another hand.

FIGURE 16.1

Poker machine being
loaded (Listing 16.1)

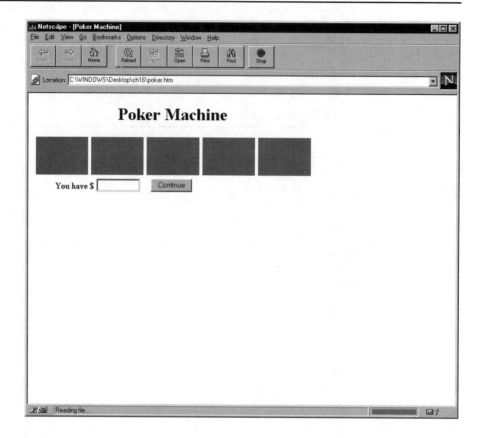

Listing 16.1 shows the source code of poker.htm. It is mostly JavaScript except for the HTML in the document body that creates the table used to display the card images. Temporary green images (turned-over cards) are initially loaded and displayed, as shown in Figure 16.1, until all 52 cards have been loaded. The script in the document body invokes startGame() to begin play. The arrays and functions defined in the document head are described in the following paragraphs.

cardImages This array contains the images to be displayed for each card. They are loaded from the files card0.gif through card51.gif.

deck This array is used to simulate a deck of cards. They are identified numerically as shown in Table 16.3.

FIGURE 16.2

Poker machine initial
deal (Listing 16.1)

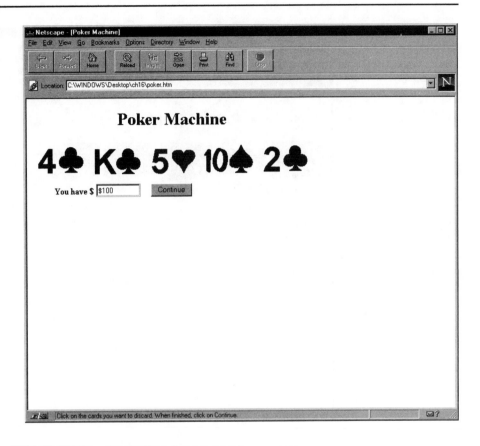

TABLE 16.3   Numerical coding of card values

Value range	Description
0 through 12	Ace through King of Spades
13 through 25	Ace through King of Clubs
26 through 38	Ace through King of Hearts
39 through 51	Ace through King of Diamonds

FIGURE 16.3

Selecting cards to
discard (Listing 16.1)

cards This array contains the cards that are initially dealt to the user.

replacements This array contains replacement cards for those cards that the user discards.

rank This array identifies the numerical ranking of each card in the `cards` array. Values range from 1 (Ace) through 13 (King).

suit This array identifies the suit of each card in `cards`. Suits are 0 (Spades), 1 (Clubs), 2 (Hearts), and 3 (Diamonds).

startGame() This function is invoked to begin play of the game. It sets the program `state` to load, gives the user a budget of $100, loads the card images, and sets a timeout to check for the completion of image loading.

FIGURE 16.4

A winning hand
(Listing 16.1)

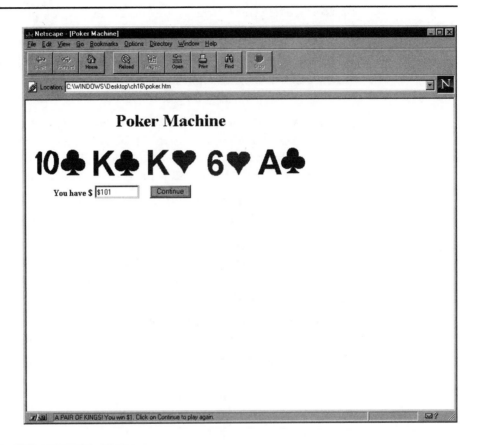

checkImageLoading() Since there are so many GIF images used in this program, it would probably take a significant amount of time for them to be loaded over a low-speed modem line. This function repeatedly checks (through timeouts) to determine if all card images have been loaded. The `play()` method is invoked when all images have been loaded.

TIP

Whenever you require images to be loaded before the main part of a script begins, use timeouts to check for the completion of image loading.

loadImages() This function performs the loading of the card images.

play() This function is invoked when all images have been loaded. It sets the program `state` to *deal*, shuffles the deck, and deals a hand to the user.

shuffleDeck() This function shuffles the deck array by switching the 52 cards to random positions within the deck.

dealCards() This function assigns five cards from the deck to the `cards` array and five to the `replacements` array. It then displays the cards to the user, identifies how much money the user has available, and displays a help message in the window's status bar. It then sets the program `state` to *draw*.

displayCards() This function is used by `dealCards()` to display the value of the cards array to the user.

processCard() This function handles the event that occurs when the user clicks on a card. It checks to make sure the program is in the *draw* `state`, and if so, flips the designated card over(flips it face-down or face-up depending on its current display status).

statusChange() This function handles the `onChange` event associated with the `status` text field by preventing the user from modifying the field's value.

continueClicked() This function handles the clicking of the Continue button.

- If the `state` is *draw* then the `state` is changed to *payoff*; replacement cards are displayed to the user; and the `showPayoff()` function is invoked to compute a new total based on how much the user won or lost. Since users bet $1.00 per hand, they can not lose more than a dollar at a time.

- If the `state` is *payoff* then a new round of play is initiated.

showPayoff() This function checks to see how much the user won or lost by invoking functions that evaluate the hand. The user's budget is updated by this amount.

compare() This function is used for numerical comparison by the `sort()` method of the `array` object.

evaluateHand() This function generates the `rank` and `suit` arrays from the `cards` array and then sorts the `rank` array.

isRoyalFlush() This function checks a hand to see if it is a Royal Flush.

sameSuit() This function checks a hand to see if all the cards are the same suit.

straight() This function checks a hand to see if it is a Straight. It checks for both Ace low and Ace high.

straightCheck() This function is used by `straight()` to check a hand to see if it is a Straight.

isStraightFlush() This function checks a hand to see if it is a Straight Flush.

isFlush() This function checks a hand to see if it is a Flush.

isStraight() This function checks a hand to see if it is a Straight.

isFourOfAKind() This function checks a hand to see if it contains four of a kind.

matches() This function returns the number of cards in a hand that are of the same rank.

isThreeOfAKind() This function checks a hand to see if it contains three of a kind.

isFullHouse() This function checks a hand to see if it is a Full House.

isTwoPair() This function checks a hand to see if it contains two pairs.

isJacksOrBetter() This function checks a hand to see if it contains a pair of Jacks or higher.

jacksOrBetterPairName() If the hand contains a pair of Aces, Kings, Queens, or Jacks, this function returns the name of the highest pair contained in the hand.

Listing 16.1. A poker machine (poker.htm)

```
<HTML>
<HEAD>
<TITLE>Poker Machine</TITLE>
<SCRIPT LANGUAGE="JavaScript"><!--

cardImages=new Array(52)
deck=new Array(52)
cards = new Array(5)
replacements = new Array(5)
rank = new Array(5)
suit = new Array(5)

function startGame() {
```

```
  state="load"
  budget=100
  loadImages()
  setTimeout("checkImageLoading()",1000)
 }
 function checkImageLoading() {
  var allLoaded=false
  for(var i=0;i<52;++i){
   if(!cardImages[i].complete){
    setTimeout("checkImageLoading()",1000)
    break
   }else if(i==51) play()
  }
 }
 function loadImages() {
  blankCard = new Image()
  blankCard.src="blank.gif"
  for(var i=0;i<52;++i) {
   cardImages[i]=new Image()
   cardImages[i].src="card"+i+".gif"
  }
 }
 function play() {
  state="deal"
  shuffleDeck()
  dealCards()
 }
 function shuffleDeck() {
  for(var i=0;i<52;++i) deck[i]=i
  for(var i=0;i<52;++i) {
   var temp=deck[i]
   var rand=Math.round(Math.random()*51)
   deck[i]=deck[rand]
   deck[rand]=temp
  }
 }
 function dealCards() {
  for(var i=0;i<5;++i){
   cards[i]=deck[i]
   replacements[i]=deck[5+i]
  }
  displayCards()
```

```
    window.document.forms[0].status.value="$"+budget
    var msg="Click on the cards you want to discard. "
    msg+="When finished, click on Continue."
    window.defaultStatus=msg
    state="draw"
}
function displayCards() {
 for(var i=0;i<5;++i)
  window.document.images[i].src=cardImages[cards[i]].src
}
function processCard(n) {
 if(state=="draw") {
  var img=window.document.images[n]
  if(img.src!=cardImages[cards[n]].src)
   img.src=cardImages[cards[n]].src
  else img.src="blank.gif"
 }
}
function statusChange() {
 alert("Are you cheating?")
 window.document.forms[0].status.value="$"+budget
}
function continueClicked() {
 if(state=="draw") {
  state="payoff"
  for(var i=0;i<5;++i) {
   var img=window.document.images[i]
   if(img.src!=cardImages[cards[i]].src) {
    cards[i]=replacements[i]
    img.src=cardImages[cards[i]].src
   }
  }
  showPayoff()
 }else if(state=="payoff") play()
}
function showPayoff() {
 var payoff=-1
 evaluateHand()
 if(isRoyalFlush()) payoff=1000
 else if(isStraightFlush()) payoff=500
 else if(isFourOfAKind()) payoff=250
 else if(isFullHouse()) payoff=100
```

```
   else if(isFlush()) payoff=50
   else if(isStraight()) payoff=25
   else if(isThreeOfAKind()) payoff=10
   else if(isTwoPair()) payoff=5
   else if(isJacksOrBetter()) payoff=1
   else msg="You lose $1."
   window.defaultStatus=msg+" Click on Continue to play again."
   budget+=payoff
   window.document.forms[0].status.value="$"+budget
}
function compare(a,b) {
 return a-b
}
function evaluateHand() {
 for(var i=0;i<5;++i) {
  rank[i]=cards[i]%13+1
  suit[i]=Math.floor(cards[i]/13)
 }
 rank=rank.sort(compare)
}
function isRoyalFlush() {
 if(sameSuit() && straight()) {
  if(rank[0]==1 && rank[1]==10) {
   msg="A ROYAL FLUSH! You win $1000."
   return true
  }
 }
 return false
}
function sameSuit() {
 if(suit[0]==suit[1] && suit[0]==suit[2]
  && suit[0]==suit[3] && suit[0]==suit[4]) return true
 return false
}
function straight() {
 var aceHi = new Array(5)
 for(var i=0;i<5;++i) {
  aceHi[i]=rank[i]
  if(aceHi[i]==1) aceHi[i]=14
 }
 if(straightCheck(rank)) return true
 if(straightCheck(aceHi.sort(compare))) return true
```

```
 return false
}
function straightCheck(a) {
 for(var i=0;i<4;++i)
  if(a[i]+1!=a[i+1]) return false
 return true
}
function isStraightFlush()      {
 if(sameSuit() && straight()) {
  msg="A STRAIGHT FLUSH! You win $500."
  return true
 }
 return false
}
function isFlush()         {
 if(sameSuit()) {
  msg="A FLUSH! You win $50."
  return true
 }
 return false
}
function isStraight()     {
 if(straight()) {
  msg="A STRAIGHT! You win $25."
  return true
 }
 return false
}
function isFourOfAKind() {
 for(var i=0;i<2;++i) {
  if(matches(rank[i])==4) {
   msg="FOUR OF A KIND! You win $250."
   return true
  }
 }
 return false
}
function matches(n) {
 var count=0
 for(var i=0;i<5;++i)
  if(rank[i]==n) ++count
```

```
   return count
  }
  function isThreeOfAKind() {
   for(var i=0;i<3;++i) {
    if(matches(rank[i])==3) {
     msg="THREE OF A KIND! You win $10."
     return true
    }
   }
   return false
  }
  function isFullHouse() {
   var matched3 = false
   var matched2 = false
   for(var i=0;i<4;++i) {
    if(matches(rank[i])==3) matched3=true
    else if(matches(rank[i])==2) matched2=true
   }
   if(matched3 && matched2) {
     msg="A FULL HOUSE! You win $100."
     return true
   }
   return false
  }
  function isTwoPair() {
   var count = 0
   for(var i=0;i<5;++i)
    if(matches(rank[i])==2) ++count
   if(count==4) {
     msg="TWO PAIR! You win $5."
     return true
   }
   return false
  }
  function isJacksOrBetter() {
   for(var i=0;i<5;++i) {
    if(matches(rank[i])==2){
     if(rank[i]==1 || rank[i]>10){
      msg="A PAIR OF "
      msg+=jacksOrBetterPairName(rank[i])
      msg+="! You win $1."
```

```
   return true
  }
 }
}
 return false
}
function jacksOrBetterPairName(n) {
 if(n==1) return "ACES"
 if(n==11) return "JACKS"
 if(n==12) return "QUEENS"
 if(n==13) return "KINGS"
 return ""
}
// --></SCRIPT>
</HEAD>
<BODY BGCOLOR="white">
<TABLE>
<TR>
<TD COLSPAN="5">
<H1 ALIGN="CENTER">Poker Machine</H1></TD>
</TR>
<TR>
<TD><A HREF="javascript:void(0)" onClick="processCard(0)">
<IMG SRC="blank.gif" BORDER="0"></A></TD>
<TD><A HREF="javascript:void(0)" onClick="processCard(1)">
<IMG SRC="blank.gif" BORDER="0"></A></TD>
<TD><A HREF="javascript:void(0)" onClick="processCard(2)">
<IMG SRC="blank.gif" BORDER="0"></A></TD>
<TD><A HREF="javascript:void(0)" onClick="processCard(3)">
<IMG SRC="blank.gif" BORDER="0"></A></TD>
<TD><A HREF="javascript:void(0)" onClick="processCard(4)">
<IMG SRC="blank.gif" BORDER="0"></A></TD>
</TR>
<TR>
<TD ALIGN="RIGHT" COLSPAN="2">
<FORM>
<B>You have $</B>
<INPUT TYPE="TEXT" NAME="status" VALUE="" SIZE="10"
onChange="statusChange()">
</FORM>
</TD>
```

```
<TD ALIGN="CENTER">
<FORM>
<INPUT TYPE="BUTTON" NAME="continue" VALUE="Continue"
onClick="continueClicked()">
</FORM>
</TD>
<TD>
</TD>
<TD>
</TD>
</TR>
</TABLE>
<SCRIPT LANGUAGE="JavaScript"><!--
startGame()
// --></SCRIPT>
</BODY>
</HTML>
```

A Board Game: "Web Walk"

Board games, such as Parker Brothers' *Monopoly*, Milton Bradley's *Life*, and the traditional *Backgammon*, have been popular for a long time. They are easy to learn, present a variety of interesting situations, and include an element of risk. In this section, you'll learn how to create a simple JavaScript board game that is based on a simple "advance around the board" concept, with multiple-choice questions about the World Wide Web. I call the game *Web Walk*, and though it will probably never be as popular as *Backgammon*, it should be entertaining.

Web Walk is played like *Life*. To see how it's played, open `webwalk.htm`. You start off at a fixed starting point and move across a path to a fixed destination. The path consists of marked squares.

You begin the game by clicking on the Start square shown in Figure 16.5. This generates a random number, between 1 and 3, telling you how many squares you must move, as shown in Figure 16.6. You then move by clicking on the squares in your chosen path (refer to Figure 16.7). Footprints mark your move.

When you click on the last square of your move, you will either be told to move again (Figure 16.8) or a question will appear in the right side of the window (Figure 16.9). This is determined by the type of square you have landed on. If the

FIGURE 16.5

The opening screen of
Web Walk (Listing 16.3)

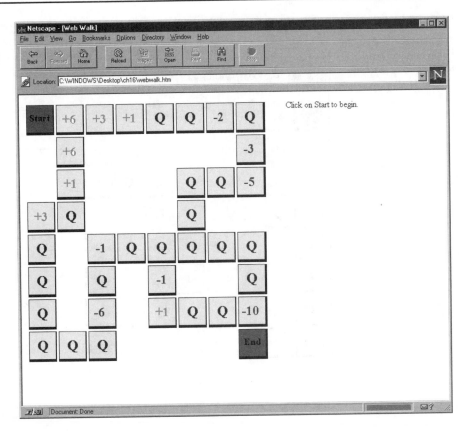

square is labeled with an integer, then you will be told to move the indicated number of squares forward or backward. If you land on a square that is labeled with a Q, then you will be asked a question. If you answer the question correctly (Figure 16.10), you will be told to move forward either 1, 2, or 3 squares. If you answer the question incorrectly, you will be told to move backward 1, 2, or 3 squares.

The object of the game is to get to the End square, as shown in Figure 16.11. To get there, you must correctly answer the questions along the way.

Web Walk is infinitely tailorable—feel free to substitute your own questions and adapt the game to your needs.

The webwalk.htm file sets up a two-frame set: the left frame runs the JavaScript code in ww.htm and the right frame is used to display messages and questions.

FIGURE 16.6

The message in the right frame tells you how many squares to move. (Listing 16.3)

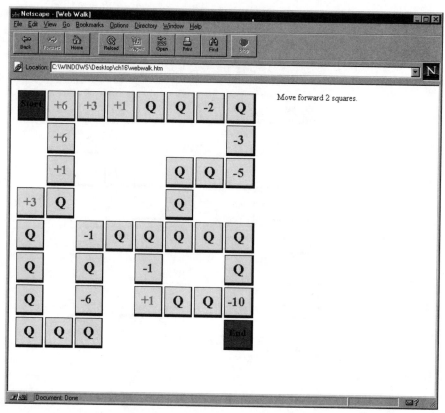

Listing 16.2. The Web Walk top-level frame set (webwalk.htm)

```
<HTML>
<HEAD>
<TITLE>Web Walk</TITLE>
<FRAMESET COLS="500,*" BORDER="0">
<FRAME SRC="ww.htm">
<FRAME SRC="blank.htm">
</FRAMESET>
</HTML>
```

The ww.htm file is very long. It contains the code to implement the game plus all of the questions and answers displayed in the right frame set. To understand how ww.htm works, start with the document body. A long table is used to display the

FIGURE 16.7

Footprints mark your
move. (Listing 16.3)

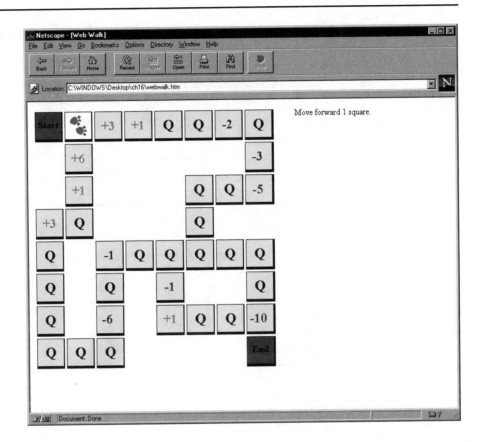

game board, and the loadImages() function is used to load cached copies of the
images displayed in the game. The startGame() function is invoked to handle
the document's onLoad event. The checkAnswers() function is invoked to handle the onFocus event. This occurs when the user has answered a question that is
displayed in the right frame of the window. The data and functions defined in the
document head are presented in the following paragraphs.

state This variable is used to identify the current state of the program's loading
and interaction with the user.

boardLayout This array identifies the design of the board's layout. It consists
of eight array elements that are used to described the elements of each row of the
board table. Table 16.4 describes the values used to identify board elements.

FIGURE 16.8

A new message appears when you finish your move on a numbered square. (Listing 16.3)

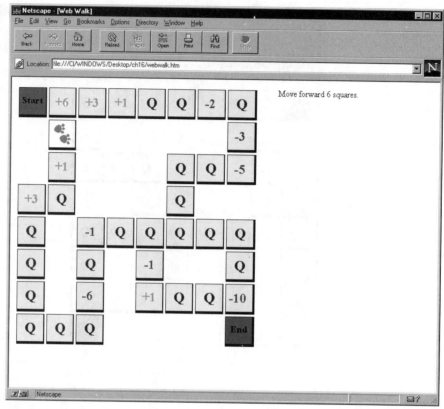

TABLE 16.4: Board layout description

Value	Board element
	None (blank area of board)
s	Starting square
e	Ending square
q	Question square
an integer	Square that specifies a forward (positive integer) or backward (negative integer) movement

FIGURE 16.9

A question appears
when you land on a
square labeled Q.
(Listing 16.3)

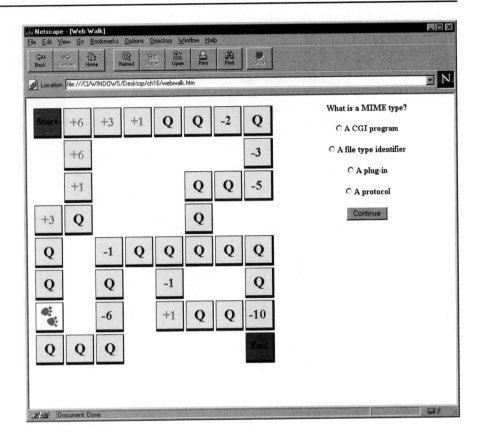

Move() This function is the constructor for the Move object type. A Move object
identifies whether a user may move from one square to another.

validMoves An array that identifies all permitted square-to-square moves.

loadImages() This function loads all images that are required to be cached so
that they may be displayed during the course of the play of the game.

startGame() This function handles the event associated with the document
loading, initializes the main program variables, and sends a start message to
the user. The position variable identifies the square (0 to 63) that the user is
currently occupying. The direction variable identifies whether the user is
moving forward (F) or backward (B). The stepsToMove variable identifies
how many more squares the user must move until that move is completed.

FIGURE 16.10

Answer the question correctly to move forward. (Listing 16.3)

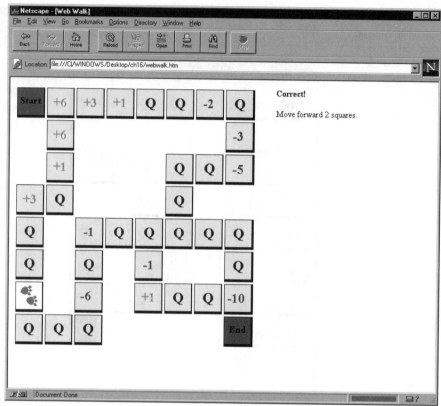

msg() This function displays a message in the right frame of the window.

square() This function handles the event that occurs when the user clicks on a square. It stores the index of the clicked square using the nextPos variable. It checks to see if the user clicked on the Start square. If the state is start, then the state is set to *move* and the user is given a random (from 1 through 3) number of squares to move.

If the state is already *move* when this function is invoked, then canMove() is invoked to determine whether it is permitted to move to the square that was clicked. If it is permitted, then the destination square is checked to see if it is the End square (and if so, the user is moved to that square, congratulated, and the game is ended). If the destination square is not the End square, the user is moved to the square

FIGURE 16.11

Work your way to the
End square to win.
(Listing 16.3)

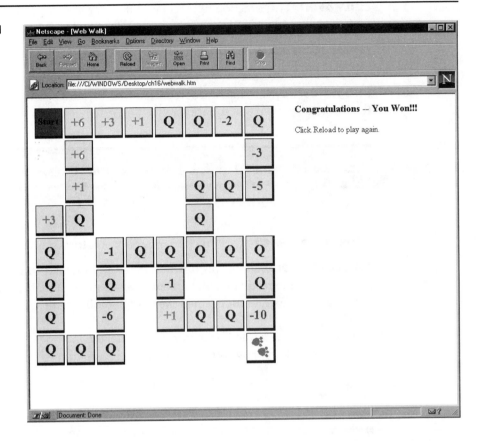

and the `state` is set to *wait*, which prevents the user from clicking on other squares while the move is being processed. The `restoreCurrentPosition()` function is invoked to clear previous footprints. The `showMovement()` function is invoked to display new footprints. The `processMovement()` function is invoked to determine how the new position will affect what the user must do.

board() This function returns the value of the `boardLayout` array for a single-value (0 to 63) index.

steps() This returns a random integer value of 1, 2, or 3.

move() This function creates a text string that identifies how many more steps the user must move.

canMove() This function returns `true` if a user is permitted to move to a specified square and `false` if they are not permitted to do so.

restoreCurrentPosition() This function displays the image of the square that was present before the user moved onto that square.

imagePosition() This function determines the index in the `images` array of the image displayed at a square.

I've included a fix in the `imagePosition()` function to address a Navigator bug that sometimes causes the length of the images array to be doubled.

showMovement() This function moves the footprints image onto a square.

processMovement() This function determines what processing should be performed as the result of a movement onto a square. If there are no more squares to move in the current move, then the two possibilites are as follows:

- The user has landed on a number square: the method automatically moves the user that many squares forward or backward.

- The user has landed on a Q square: `askQuestion()` is invoked to ask the user a question.

winner() This function notifies the user that the game has been successfully completed.

Question() This function is the constructor of the `Question` object (which was introduced in Chapter 8).

askQuestion() This function displays a question to the user in the right frame of the window. Note that the `onClick` event of the question's Continue button causes the left window to come into focus. This allows the event to be handled in the left frame of the window.

checkAnswers() This function is invoked to handle the `onFocus` event of the left frame of the window. This event is generated as the result of the user clicking on the Continue button that appears when a question is displayed in the right frame. This little trick allows events to be propagated from one frame to another. The `checkAnswers()` function checks to see if the user answered the question correctly, and invokes `correct()` or `incorrect()` depending on the result.

correct() This function causes the user to move 1, 2, or 3 steps forward as the result of answering a question correctly.

incorrect() This function causes the user to move 1, 2, or 3 steps backward as the result of answering a question incorrectly.

qa This array is used to store the `Question` objects used in the game. (Refer to Chapter 8.)

Listing 16.3. The Web Walk implementation (ww.htm)

```
<HTML>
<HEAD>
<TITLE>Web Walk</TITLE>
<SCRIPT LANGUAGE="JavaScript"><!--
state="load"
boardLayout = new Array(
 new Array("s","6","3","1","q","q","-2","q"),
 new Array("","6","","","","","","-3"),
 new Array("","1","","","","q","q","-5"),
 new Array("3","q","","","","q","",""),
 new Array("q","","-1","q","q","q","q","q"),
 new Array("q","","q","","-1","","","q"),
 new Array("q","","-6","","1","q","q","-10"),
 new Array("q","q","q","","","","","e"))

function Move(p1,p2) {
 this.from=p1
 this.to=p2
}

validMoves=new Array(
 new Move(0,1), new Move(1,2), new Move(1,9),
 new Move(2,3), new Move(3,4), new Move(4,5),
 new Move(5,6), new Move(6,7), new Move(7,15),
 new Move(9,17), new Move(15,23), new Move(17,25),
 new Move(21,29), new Move(22,21), new Move(23,22),
 new Move(24,32), new Move(25,24), new Move(29,37),
 new Move(32,40), new Move(34,35), new Move(35,36),
 new Move(36,37), new Move(36,44), new Move(37,38),
 new Move(38,39), new Move(39,47), new Move(40,48),
 new Move(42,34), new Move(44,52), new Move(47,55),
 new Move(48,56), new Move(50,42), new Move(52,53),
```

```
  new Move(53,54), new Move(54,55), new Move(55,63),
  new Move(56,57), new Move(57,58), new Move(58,50)
)

function loadImages() {
 questionGIF=new Image(); questionGIF.src="question.gif"
 feetGIF=new Image(); feetGIF.src="feet.gif"
 plus1GIF=new Image(); plus1GIF.src="plus1.gif"
 plus3GIF=new Image(); plus3GIF.src="plus3.gif"
 plus6GIF=new Image(); plus6GIF.src="plus6.gif"
 minus1GIF=new Image(); minus1GIF.src="minus1.gif"
 minus2GIF=new Image(); minus2GIF.src="minus2.gif"
 minus3GIF=new Image(); minus3GIF.src="minus3.gif"
 minus5GIF=new Image(); minus5GIF.src="minus5.gif"
 minus6GIF=new Image(); minus6GIF.src="minus6.gif"
 minus10GIF=new Image(); minus10GIF.src="minus10.gif"
}
function startGame() {
 state="start"
 position=0
 direction="F"
 stepsToMove=0
 msg("Click on Start to begin.")
}
function msg(s) {
 var doc=parent.frames[1].document
 doc.open()
 doc.writeln('<BODY BGCOLOR="white">')
 doc.writeln(s)
 doc.writeln('</BODY>')
 doc.close()
}
function square(n) {
 nextPos=parseInt(n)
 if(board(nextPos)=="s"){
  if(state=="start") {
   state="move"
   stepsToMove=steps()
   msg(move())
  }else alert("Game is already started.")
 }else if(state=="move"){
  if(canMove(nextPos)){
```

```
    if(board(nextPos)=="e") {
      state="end"
      restoreCurrentPosition()
       showMovement(nextPos)
      winner()
     }else{
      state="wait"
      restoreCurrentPosition()
       showMovement(nextPos)
       processMovement(nextPos)
     }
   }else msg("Can't move there!")
 }
}
function board(n) {
 return boardLayout[Math.floor(n/8)][n%8]
}
function steps() {
 return Math.round((Math.random()*2)+1)
}
function move() {
 var squares=" squares."
 if(stepsToMove==1) squares=" square."
 var dir=" forward "
 if(direction=="B") dir=" backward "
 return "Move"+dir+stepsToMove+squares
}
function canMove(n) {
 for(var i=0;i<validMoves.length;++i){
  if(direction=="F" && validMoves[i].from==position &&
   validMoves[i].to==n) return true
  if(direction=="B" && validMoves[i].from==n &&
   validMoves[i].to==position) return true
 }
 return false
}
function restoreCurrentPosition() {
 var sq=board(position)
 var imgPos=imagePosition(position)
 var oldImage=questionGIF
 if(sq=="s") return
 else if(sq=="1") oldImage=plus1GIF
```

```
          else if(sq=="3") oldImage=plus3GIF
          else if(sq=="6") oldImage=plus6GIF
          else if(sq=="-1") oldImage=minus1GIF
          else if(sq=="-2") oldImage=minus2GIF
          else if(sq=="-3") oldImage=minus3GIF
          else if(sq=="-5") oldImage=minus5GIF
          else if(sq=="-6") oldImage=minus6GIF
          else if(sq=="-10") oldImage=minus10GIF
          window.document.images[imgPos].src=oldImage.src
        }
        function imagePosition(n) {
         imageCount=0
         for(var i=0;i<n;++i)
          if(board(i)!="") ++imageCount
         var len=window.document.images.length
         // Fixes bug in Navigator 3.0
         if(len>38) imageCount+=Math.floor(len/2)
         return imageCount
        }
        function showMovement(n) {
         var imgPos=imagePosition(n)
         window.document.images[imgPos].src=feetGIF.src
        }
        function processMovement(n) {
         position=n
         --stepsToMove
         if(stepsToMove==0){
          var sq=board(position)
          var num=0
          if(sq=="q") askQuestion()
          else{
           num=parseInt(sq)
           if(num<0) direction="B"
           else direction="F"
           stepsToMove=Math.abs(num)
           state="move"
           msg(move())
          }
         }else{
          state="move"
          msg(move())
         }
        }
```

```
function winner() {
 var doc=parent.frames[1].document
 doc.open()
 doc.writeln('<BODY BGCOLOR="white">')
 doc.writeln('<H3>Congratulations -- You Won!!!</H3>')
 doc.writeln('Click Reload to play again.')
 doc.writeln('</BODY>')
 doc.close()
}
function Question() {
 this.question=Question.arguments[0]
 var n=Question.arguments.length
 this.answers = new Array(n-2)
 for(var i=1; i<n-1; ++i)
  this.answers[i-1]=Question.arguments[i]
 this.correctAnswer=Question.arguments[n-1]
}
function askQuestion() {
 rnd=Math.round(Math.random()*(qa.length-1))
 var doc=parent.frames[1].document
 doc.open()
 doc.writeln('<HTML>')
 doc.writeln('<BODY BGCOLOR="white">')
 doc.writeln("<H4 ALIGN='CENTER'>"+qa[rnd].question+"</H4>")
 doc.writeln('<FORM NAME="answerForm">')
 for(var ii=0;ii<qa[rnd].answers.length;++ii) {
  doc.writeln('<H4 ALIGN="CENTER">')
  doc.write('<INPUT TYPE="RADIO" NAME="answer">')
  doc.writeln(qa[rnd].answers[ii])
  if(ii+1==qa[rnd].answers.length) {
   doc.write('<BR><BR><INPUT TYPE="BUTTON"')
   doc.writeln('NAME="continue" VALUE="Continue" ')
   doc.writeln(' onClick="parent.frames[0].focus()">')
  }
  doc.writeln('</H4>')
 }
 doc.writeln('</FORM>')
 doc.writeln('</BODY></HTML>')
 doc.close()
}
function checkAnswers() {
 if(state!="wait") return
```

```
    var numAnswers=qa[rnd].answers.length
    var correctAnswer=qa[rnd].correctAnswer
    var doc=parent.frames[1].document
    for(var jj=0;jj<numAnswers;++jj) {
     if(doc.answerForm.elements[jj].checked) {
      if(jj==correctAnswer){
       correct()
        break
      }else{
        incorrect()
        break
      }
     }
     if(jj==numAnswers){
      incorrect()
      break
     }
    }
}
function correct() {
 var num=steps()
 direction="F"
 stepsToMove=num
 state="move"
 msg("<H4>Correct!</H4>"+move())
}
function incorrect() {
 var num=steps()
 direction="B"
 stepsToMove=num
 state="move"
 msg("<H4>Incorrect.</H4>"+move())
}

//Questions
qa = new Array()

qa[0] = new Question("Who created the Web?",
 "Marc Andreessen",
 "James Gosling",
 "Tim Berners-Lee",
 "Bill Gates",
 2)
```

```
qa[1] = new Question("Who invented HTML?",
 "Marc Andreessen",
 "James Gosling",
 "Tim Berners-Lee",
 "Bill Gates",
 2)
qa[2] = new Question("Who is the creator of Mosaic?",
 "Marc Andreessen",
 "James Gosling",
 "Tim Berners-Lee",
 "Bill Gates",
 0)
qa[3] = new Question("What is Mosaic?",
 "A mark-up language",
 "A Web browser",
 "A Web server",
 "A protocol",
 1)
qa[4] = new Question("What is Lynx?",
 "A mark-up language",
 "A Web browser",
 "A Web server",
 "A protocol",
 1)
qa[5] = new Question("What company developed Java?",
 "Microsoft",
 "Sun Microsystems",
 "Netscape",
 "IBM",
 1)
```

NOTE In the interest of saving pages, we'll skip the remaining questions for now. The file on the CD includes all 22 questions for this game (ww.htm).

```
// --></SCRIPT>
</HEAD>
<BODY BGCOLOR="white" onLoad="startGame()"
 onFocus="checkAnswers()">
<TABLE BGCOLOR="black">
```

```
<TR>
<TD><A HREF="javascript:void(0)" onClick="square(0)">
<IMG SRC="start.gif" BORDER="0"></A></TD>
<TD><A HREF="javascript:void(0)" onClick="square(1)">
<IMG SRC="plus6.gif" BORDER="0"></A></TD>
<TD><A HREF="javascript:void(0)" onClick="square(2)">
<IMG SRC="plus3.gif" BORDER="0"></A></TD>
<TD><A HREF="javascript:void(0)" onClick="square(3)">
<IMG SRC="plus1.gif" BORDER="0"></A></TD>
<TD><A HREF="javascript:void(0)" onClick="square(4)">
<IMG SRC="question.gif" BORDER="0"></A></TD>
<TD><A HREF="javascript:void(0)" onClick="square(5)">
<IMG SRC="question.gif" BORDER="0"></A></TD>
<TD><A HREF="javascript:void(0)" onClick="square(6)">
<IMG SRC="minus2.gif" BORDER="0"></A></TD>
<TD><A HREF="javascript:void(0)" onClick="square(7)">
<IMG SRC="question.gif" BORDER="0"></A></TD>
</TR>
<TR>
<TD> </TD>
<TD><A HREF="javascript:void(0)" onClick="square(9)">
<IMG SRC="plus6.gif" BORDER="0"></A></TD>
<TD> </TD><TD> </TD><TD> </TD><TD> </TD><TD> </TD>
<TD><A HREF="javascript:void(0)" onClick="square(15)">
<IMG SRC="minus3.gif" BORDER="0"></A></TD>
</TR>
<TR>
<TD> </TD>
<TD><A HREF="javascript:void(0)" onClick="square(17)">
<IMG SRC="plus1.gif" BORDER="0"></A></TD>
<TD> </TD><TD> </TD><TD> </TD>
<TD><A HREF="javascript:void(0)" onClick="square(21)">
<IMG SRC="question.gif" BORDER="0"></A></TD>
<TD><A HREF="javascript:void(0)" onClick="square(22)">
<IMG SRC="question.gif" BORDER="0"></A></TD>
<TD><A HREF="javascript:void(0)" onClick="square(23)">
<IMG SRC="minus5.gif" BORDER="0"></A></TD>
</TR>
<TR>
<TD><A HREF="javascript:void(0)" onClick="square(24)">
<IMG SRC="plus3.gif" BORDER="0"></A></TD>
<TD><A HREF="javascript:void(0)" onClick="square(25)">
```

```
<IMG SRC="question.gif" BORDER="0"></A></TD>
<TD> </TD><TD> </TD><TD> </TD>
<TD><A HREF="javascript:void(0)" onClick="square(29)">
<IMG SRC="question.gif" BORDER="0"></A></TD>
<TD> </TD><TD> </TD>
</TR>
<TR>
<TD><A HREF="javascript:void(0)" onClick="square(32)">
<IMG SRC="question.gif" BORDER="0"></A></TD>
<TD> </TD>
<TD><A HREF="javascript:void(0)" onClick="square(34)">
<IMG SRC="minus1.gif" BORDER="0"></A></TD>
<TD><A HREF="javascript:void(0)" onClick="square(35)">
<IMG SRC="question.gif" BORDER="0"></A></TD>
<TD><A HREF="javascript:void(0)" onClick="square(36)">
<IMG SRC="question.gif" BORDER="0"></A></TD>
<TD><A HREF="javascript:void(0)" onClick="square(37)">
<IMG SRC="question.gif" BORDER="0"></A></TD>
<TD><A HREF="javascript:void(0)" onClick="square(38)">
<IMG SRC="question.gif" BORDER="0"></A></TD>
<TD><A HREF="javascript:void(0)" onClick="square(39)">
<IMG SRC="question.gif" BORDER="0"></A></TD>
</TR>
<TR>
<TD><A HREF="javascript:void(0)" onClick="square(40)">
<IMG SRC="question.gif" BORDER="0"></A></TD>
<TD> </TD>
<TD><A HREF="javascript:void(0)" onClick="square(42)">
<IMG SRC="question.gif" BORDER="0"></A></TD>
<TD> </TD>
<TD><A HREF="javascript:void(0)" onClick="square(44)">
<IMG SRC="minus1.gif" BORDER="0"></A></TD>
<TD> </TD><TD> </TD>
<TD><A HREF="javascript:void(0)" onClick="square(47)">
<IMG SRC="question.gif" BORDER="0"></A></TD>
</TR>
<TR>
<TD><A HREF="javascript:void(0)" onClick="square(48)">
<IMG SRC="question.gif" BORDER="0"></A></TD>
<TD> </TD>
<TD><A HREF="javascript:void(0)" onClick="square(50)">
<IMG SRC="minus6.gif" BORDER="0"></A></TD>
<TD> </TD>
```

```
<TD><A HREF="javascript:void(0)" onClick="square(52)">
<IMG SRC="plus1.gif" BORDER="0"></A></TD>
<TD><A HREF="javascript:void(0)" onClick="square(53)">
<IMG SRC="question.gif" BORDER="0"></A></TD>
<TD><A HREF="javascript:void(0)" onClick="square(54)">
<IMG SRC="question.gif" BORDER="0"></A></TD>
<TD><A HREF="javascript:void(0)" onClick="square(55)">
<IMG SRC="minus10.gif" BORDER="0"></A></TD>
</TR>
<TR>
<TD><A HREF="javascript:void(0)" onClick="square(56)">
<IMG SRC="question.gif" BORDER="0"></A></TD>
<TD><A HREF="javascript:void(0)" onClick="square(57)">
<IMG SRC="question.gif" BORDER="0"></A></TD>
<TD><A HREF="javascript:void(0)" onClick="square(58)">
<IMG SRC="question.gif" BORDER="0"></A></TD>
<TD> </TD><TD> </TD><TD> </TD><TD> </TD>
<TD><A HREF="javascript:void(0)" onClick="square(63)">
<IMG SRC="end.gif" BORDER="0"></A></TD>
</TR>
</TABLE>
<SCRIPT LANGUAGE="JavaScript"><!--
loadImages()
// --></SCRIPT>
</BODY>
</HTML>
```

Summary

In this chapter you learned to program JavaScript games. You created a poker game which lets you play against your browser—good luck collecting your winnings! You also developed the Web Walk board game, a game that can be easily tailored to a variety of subjects.

This chapter was the last chapter in Part 3. In Part 4, you'll learn to interface JavaScript with its namesake—the Java programming language. You'll learn how to load, interact with, and control Java applets using JavaScript scripts. You'll also learn how Java applets can access JavaScript objects and methods.

PART IV

Integrating Java and JavaScript

Introduction to Java

- **What Is Java?**

- **Java vs. JavaScript**

- **The Java Development Kit**

- **Learning Java**

- **The Java API**

- **Programs vs. Applets**

Java is a very powerful and popular language that supports the development of Web-based applications. It provides a number of capabilities that complement those provided by JavaScript. In this chapter, you'll learn the similarities and differences between Java and JavaScript and learn how to develop simple Java programs and applets. When you finish this chapter, you'll have a basic working knowledge of Java and you'll be able to work the examples in Chapters 18 and 19.

What Is Java?

The rapid growth in the popularity of the Java language is nothing short of a phenomenon. In less than a year, Java went from a relatively unknown alpha version to an incredibly successful Version 1.0 release. Java has since been endorsed by every major computer hardware and software vendor. Its remarkable success is summed up by the fact that Microsoft, its chief rival, not only supports Java with Internet Explorer, but also sells J++, a popular Java development environment. In this section we'll explore various aspects of Java.

Java Is Platform-Independent

Java's phenomenal success is due to the fact that it provides the capability to develop compiled software that runs, without modification, on a large variety of operating system platforms—including Microsoft Windows, Apple Macintosh, IBM OS/2, Linux, and several varieties of Unix. In addition, and perhaps more importantly, specially designed Java programs known as *applets* run in the context of Java-enabled Web browsers, such as Netscape Navigator and Microsoft Internet Explorer.

NOTE   Java is distributed by JavaSoft, a subsidiary of Sun Microsystems, as the Java Development Kit (JDK), a complete set of tools for developing Java applications. The latest version of the JDK can be obtained from JavaSoft via its Web site; browse the URL *http://www.javasoft.com* and follow the appropriate links. A copy of JDK 1.1.1 is included on the CD that comes with this book.

The Java Virtual Machine is the key to Java's platform-independence. The Java Virtual Machine (JVM) provides a machine-independent and operating system-independent platform for the execution of Java code. The JVM is a program that runs on your host operating system (OS) or is embedded in a browser. The JVM executes Java programs that are compiled into the JVM byte code. This byte code is the native machine language of the JVM and does not vary between JVM implementations.

When Java is ported to a new platform, be it an OS or a browser, the JVM itself is ported, yet its interface to compiled Java programs remains the same. The code required to port the JVM to the host OS or browser varies from system to system. In addition to the JVM, this code is required to port the Java Application Programming Interface (API). The Java API is a common set of software packages that is supported by all Java implementations. Much of the API is itself written in Java and runs on the JVM. However, some parts of the API, such as the windowing and networking software, is written in C++. The JVM, together with the additional software required to support the Java API, is referred to as the *Java runtime system*.

Java Is Object-Oriented

Java is an object-oriented language, and provides all of the benefits of object-oriented programming: classification, inheritance, object composition, encapsulation, and polymorphism. Java supports single inheritance, but not multiple inheritance; however, it provides the interface construct which can be used to obtain the benefits of multiple inheritance without having to deal with any of its drawbacks.

TIP   Refer to Chapter 5, "Objects in JavaScript," for a complete discussion of object-oriented programming concepts.

Java Is Familiar

One of the most striking characteristics of Java, at least from a programmer's perspective, is its familiarity. Java is based on C++ and retains much of its syntax. This makes the language very easy to learn for C++ programmers. Since JavaScript is also based on both C++ and Java, Java's syntax will be easy for you to learn. However, since Java is a full object-*oriented* language (as opposed to an object-*based* language, like JavaScript), you will have to learn some additional programming constructs.

Appendix C, "Java Reference," provides a reference manual for the Java language and API.

Java Is Simpler and More Reliable

Although Java is based on C++, it is simpler and easier to use. This is because the designers of Java eliminated many of the complex and dangerous features of C++. By doing so, Java's fathers also increased its overall reliability, making it an attractive language for mission-critical applications.

The Java API Supports Window and Network Programming

Another attractive feature of Java is the extensive API that comes standard with the JDK. The API provides portable libraries for the development of window and network-based programs. The same API is used to develop console-based programs; windowed programs; network clients and servers; applets; and fully distributed Web-based applications. It also supports the development of multi-threaded programs.

Java Supports Executable Web Content

The capability to develop applets for use in Web applications is one of the most attractive features provided by Java. Applets are programs that execute in the context of a browser window; thus they allow executable content to be embedded in a Web page. This enables Web pages to be more dynamic and interactive and greatly increases the number and types of Web applications that can be supported.

Chapter 1 introduced applets within the context of a general introduction to client- and server-side Web programming technologies. Chapter 5 discussed some of Java's object-oriented programming features.

Java Is Secure

The power and flexibility provided by applets requires iron-clad security on the part of the Java runtime system. This high level of security is required to prevent malicious applets from disclosing or damaging the information stored on the user's computer. Java provides several levels of security protection:

- At the language level, Java has eliminated dangerous programming features such as pointers, memory allocation and deallocation operators, and automatic type conversion.

- At the compiler level, the Java compiler performs extensive checks that prevent errors and ensure that the compiled code does not contain any inconsistencies that could allow objects to be accessed in ways other than explicitly allowed.

- At the runtime level, the Java runtime system prevents applets from performing actions that could result in damage to or disclosure of information stored on your computer.

Java Is Free

Finally, if none of the above features are compelling enough to go with Java, Sun gives the JDK away for free—it is publicly available at JavaSoft's Web site.

Java vs. JavaScript

Although Java and JavaScript have similar names, there are a number of significant differences between the two languages. These differences do not make one language superior to the other—the features of both languages are well-suited to their respective programming niches. For example, JavaScript is designed to supplement the capabilities of HTML with scripts that are capable of responding to Web page events. As such, it has complete access to all aspects of the browser window. Java is designed to implement executable content that can be embedded in Web pages. For this purpose, it is endowed with much more powerful programming capabilities. However, these capabilities are confined to a limited area of the browser window.

Java and JavaScript complement each other well. Java is the industrial-strength programming language for developing advanced Web objects. JavaScript is the essential glue that combines HTML, Java applets, plug-ins, server-side programs, and other Web components into fully integrated Web applications. While Java's forte is in Web component development, JavaScript excels at component integration. The following subsections identify the differences between these two languages and shows how these differences enable each language to achieve its respective Web programming goals.

Compiled vs. Interpreted

The most obvious difference between Java and JavaScript is that Java is compiled and JavaScript is interpreted. As you would expect, there is a good reason for this difference.

Java is intended to be used to develop secure, high-performance Web applications. The JVM executes compiled byte code rather than interpreting source Java statements. The byte code instruction set is designed for quick and efficient execution, allowing Java to achieve performance comparable to native code compilers.

JavaScript, on the other hand, is intended to create scripts that can be embedded in HTML documents. These scripts control the way the documents are laid out and define functions to handle user events. JavaScript can be viewed as an extension to HTML that provides additional capabilities for browser and document control. From this perspective, it is important that JavaScript be included in HTML as source code—so the browser can inspect the code. This is the reason why it is an interpreted language instead of a compiled language, like Java.

Although compiled JavaScript scripts would be inappropriate for Web page development, there is no reason why server-side scripts should not be compiled. In Chapter 27, you'll learn how Netscape's LiveWire tools provide a unique approach to integrating server-side scripts with Web pages.

Object-Oriented vs. Object-Based

Java and JavaScript differ in the degree to which they support object-oriented programming. Java is fully-committed to object-oriented programming and supports all object-oriented programming features except multiple inheritance. Even so, Java's use of single inheritance combined with its interface construct provides the benefits of multiple inheritance while retaining the simple class structure that is characteristic of single-inheritance. Java's commitment to object-oriented programming stems from the fact that it was originally intended to be used to develop software for consumer electronic devices. Full support of object-oriented programming is integral to the development of the simple and reliable software components that characterize these devices.

JavaScript does not share Java's commitment to object-oriented programming. JavaScript's approach is to take what's most useful from object-oriented programming and discard everything else. For example, JavaScript supports object types, instantiation, composition, re-use, and polymorphism, but it does not support classification and inheritance.

The reasons for JavaScript's pick-and-choose attitude towards object-oriented programming are based on the nature of the objects which JavaScript is compelled to support. Objects, such as windows, frames, documents, forms, and so on, are the reason for JavaScript's existence. These objects are accessed more effectively using the Navigator object hierarchy, introduced in Chapter 5, than using a pure object-oriented approach.

Strongly Typed vs. Loosely Typed

JavaScript is a *loosely typed* language, and Java is *strongly typed*. A *loosely typed* language is one in which data of one type is automatically converted to another type during the runtime execution of a program or script. A *strongly typed* language, on the other hand, is one that, instead of converting data types, flags inappropriate type conversions as errors. Strongly typed languages flag type-conversion errors during program compilation, loading, and execution.

The difference between loosely and strongly typed is suggestive of the ways in which each language is intended to be used.

Java focuses on the development of software that is secure and reliable. Strong typing is absolutely essential to achieving each of these goals. The ability to restrict operations on objects to only those that are explicitly defined is basic to Java's security approach. This control is needed to ensure that objects are not accessed in ways that circumvent the security checks imposed by the JVM.

Strong typing is also important to developing reliable software. Software reliability studies have repeatedly shown that automatic type conversion is a contributing factor in many common programming errors.

JavaScript's decision to go with loose typing can be viewed as a trade-off between expediency and reliability. This is characteristic of most scripting languages. By not enforcing strong typing, a scripting language confers more power and responsibility on the programmer. It says, "I'm going to permit you to perform this operation. It may be dangerous, but I trust your judgment."

JavaScript's support of loose typing is consistent with its role as a Web scripting language. Rather than forcing you to clutter your scripts with the extra code needed to perform explicit type conversion, it automatically performs these conversions for you. This reduces the overall size of your scripts and lets you focus on the pertinent aspects of your Web application.

Browser Window vs. Full Browser Interaction

Perhaps the most important differences between Java and JavaScript lie in their different capabilities for interacting with the user, the browser, and the rest of the Web. These differences determine what applications can be supported by each language.

Java applets are intended to be *embedded* in Web pages, and their capabilities reflect this intent. Applets are assigned a limited area of the browser window in which they are allowed to interact with the user. Applets are not allowed to display information in other areas of the browser window or to respond to events that occur as the result of actions taken with respect to other window areas. This precludes Java from providing the controls for Web page layout and event-handling support that we have seen are possible with JavaScript. Although *LiveConnect* (Chapter 19) provides applets with access to Navigator and plug-in methods, an applet is limited, for security reasons, from communicating with Internet hosts other than the one from which it was loaded. This prevents evil programmers from creating applets that could spy on a user's computer and send information to other hosts on the Internet.

JavaScript scripts are not employed in the same manner as Java applets. JavaScript scripts are not confined to a limited area of the browser window; rather, they are allowed to control the display of an entire Web page, to handle all events that occur with respect to a window, and to interact with other frames and windows. These total Web-page control capabilities enable JavaScript to carry out its role of being the glue that integrates HTML, Java, plug-ins, and server-side scripts into complete Web applications.

Even though JavaScript has considerably more latitude than Java in Web page control, it is faced with similar security restrictions. Navigator prevents scripts that are loaded from one server from accessing the properties of documents that are loaded from other servers. This restriction prevents a script from accessing sensitive data entered in another frame or window and sending it to an arbitrary Internet host.

The Java Development Kit

In order to work the examples in this and later chapters, you will need to obtain and install a copy of the Java Development Kit on your computer. The latest version of the JDK may be obtained by following the appropriate links from the JavaSoft home page *http://www.javasoft.com*. Figure 17.1 shows the JavaSoft home page. It contains a number of useful links which you can follow to learn more about Java. The JDK is free to download, but make sure that you read and agree with Sun's license agreement before downloading the JDK.

NOTE The examples in this book assume that you install the JDK in the directory `c:\jdk1.1.1` of your hard disk. I recommend that you install the JDK in this directory in order to avoid any problems in completing the examples.

FIGURE 17.1

The JavaSoft Home Page

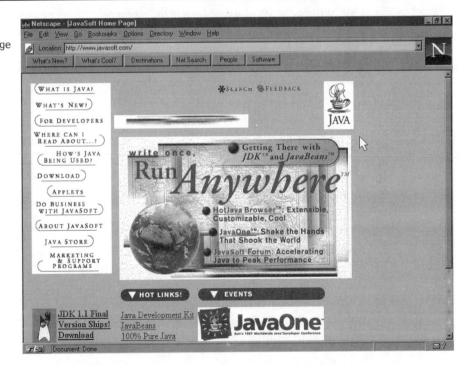

Learning Java

Besides giving the JDK away for free, Sun wanted to make sure that you would be able to use it. They have included an extensive online tutorial at their Web site. I highly recommend that you take this tutorial if you intend to program in Java. Although Java is simple and easy to use, a complete introduction to Java is beyond the scope of this book. We get you started in this chapter, by showing you how to develop a Java console program, a window program, and an applet. Later chapters show you how to use applets in your Web pages. For those of you who already know Java or are adept at learning new languages, you may find everything you need concerning Java in Appendix C of this book, which is a short reference manual for the Java language.

The Java API

One of the benefits of using Java is that it comes with an extensive application programming interface. This API provides access to all of the objects and methods that you need to develop sophisticated window and network programs and Java applets. Sun provides excellent documentation for the Java API at its Web site. This documentation can be viewed online or downloaded to your computer.

Programs vs. Applets

Java is a general-purpose software development language. You can use it to create Web applets which run in the context of a Web browser. But Java can also be used to develop stand-alone console and window programs that run independently of a browser and the Web. The term *console program* refers to text mode programs, such as DOS and Unix command-line programs, that do not use a windowing system, such as Microsoft Windows or the X Window System. Java *window programs* are distinguished from Microsoft Windows programs in that they can execute on Microsoft Windows (95 or NT), X Window System, Motif, and the Macintosh windowing system. In this section, you'll learn how to develop all three types of Java programs. In addition, later chapters will focus more on applets in particular.

Java is an easy programming language to learn—especially if you've already programmed in JavaScript. Start by browsing Sun's online Java tutorial or the

Java reference included in Appendix C to get a feel for the language and how it compares to JavaScript. You will find that Java's syntax is very similar to JavaScript's, but of course there are some differences between the two languages. In order to get you up and programming in Java, I'll list the most important differences here and then illustrate them in the programming examples covered in the following subsections.

Classes Java programs are built from *classes*. Classes are analogous to object types in JavaScript. They define *variables* (also called *fields*) and methods which correspond to JavaScript's properties and methods.

Packages Related classes are organized into *packages*. When you write a Java program, you can access previously defined classes by *importing* them into your program.

The *main()* Method The main() method is the first method that is executed when you run a stand-alone Java program.

Keywords Java uses keywords, like public and static, to identify additional properties of variables.

An Example Console Program

The traditional first program in any language displays the text *Hello World!*, with the objective being to create a small program that produces a visible result. In keeping with this tradition, Listing 17.1 shows the simplest possible Java program— a program that you'll soon create. Open an MS-DOS window and compile the program using the Java compiler as follows:

```
javac ConsolePrg.java
```

Then run the program using the following command line:

```
java ConsolePrg
```

It will display the text *Hello World!* to the console window.

Listing 17.1. A Java console program (ConsolePrg.java)

```
import java.lang.System;

class ConsolePrg {
 public static void main (String args[]) {
  System.out.println("Hello World!");
 }
}
```

Now that you are a Java programmer, let's review the program's source code. It begins with an `import` statement which imports the `System` class from the `java.lang` package into your program. By importing it, we make it available for use in your program.

Following the `import` statement is the declaration of the `ConsolePrg` class. This class declaration ends with the last closing brace (`}`).

Within the `ConsolePrg` class, we define the `main()` method. This method is declared as `public`, `static`, and `void`. The `public` keyword identifies it as publicly accessible. The `static` keyword specifies that `main()` is used with the `ConsolePrg` class as a whole, rather than with an instance of the class. The `void` keyword identifies `main()` as not returning a value.

The one and only statement within `main()` prints the text *Hello World!* on the console window. It invokes the `println()` method for the `out` variable of the `System` class. The `println()` method is similar to the JavaScript `writeln()` method. The `System.out` variable identifies the console as the object to which the output is to be displayed. It is a standard variable provided by the `System` class.

NOTE In practice, `java.lang.System` is always imported, by default, regardless of whether it is identified in an import statement. The import statement was included in this example only so that we could cover it in the context of the first program.

An Example Windows Program

Now that you are a Java programmer and understand a little about Java programs, let's write a window-based version of the Hello World! program. It will quickly get you up to speed writing stand-alone Java window programs.

Compile `WindowsPrg.java` using the following statement:

```
javac WindowsPrg.java
```

and then run it using

```
java WindowsPrg
```

It displays the window shown in Figure 17.2. Now we're making progress! When you've finished marveling at your creation, you can close it by clicking on the x in the upper right corner of the program's title bar.

FIGURE 17.2

A Java window program

The program begins by importing `java.awt.*;`. This tells the Java compiler to import all classes in the `java.awt` package. This package contains the classes used for window program development.

The class `WindowsPrg` is declared as a `public` class that `extends` the `Frame` class. The `Frame` class is a class of the `java.awt` package that defines the main window of an application program. Four methods are declared for the `WindowsPrg` class, as follows.

main() The `main()` method is the first method to be executed when the `WindowsPrg` program is run. It creates an object of the `WindowsPrg` class and assigns it to the `program` variable. The `program` variable is declared as an object of the `WindowsPrg` class.

WindowsPrg() This is the constructor for the `WindowsPrg` class. Like all constructors, it does not specify a return value. It invokes the `super()` method to set the window's title bar to the text `"A Java Windows Program"`. The `super()` method is a way of calling the constructor of `WindowsPrg`'s parent class (`Frame`). The `Frame()` constructor takes a string as a parameter and displays it as the document's title. You may want to look up the description of the `Frame` class in the Java API.

WindowsPrg() then invokes the `pack()` method to pack the contents of the window. This is a standard method that is called when a window is constructed to place and organize any window components within the window. The window is then resized to 500 pixels by 250 pixels using the `resize()` method, and the window is displayed using the `show()` method. The `pack()`, `resize()`, and `show()` methods are inherited from the `Frame` class by `WindowsPrg`.

paint0 The `paint()` method is the method that is called to draw a window when it is initially displayed or needs to be redrawn. It takes a `Graphics` object as a parameter. The `Graphics` object is where the screen updates are drawn. The first statement invokes the `setFont()` method of the `Graphics` class to set the drawing font to 48-point, bold and italic Times Roman. The `Font()` constructor is used to create this font. The second statement invokes the `setColor()` method to set the drawing color to red. The `Color` class provides a set of color constants. The third statement invokes the `drawString()` method to draw the text "Hello World!" on the screen at the offset (100,125) within the `Graphics` object.

handleEvent0 The `handleEvent()` method returns a `boolean` value that indicates whether or not it has handled an event. It is invoked to handle events that occur in a `WindowsPrg` object. The `Event` class defines events that are handled by window programs. An `if` statement is used to see if the event passed as an argument to `handleEvent()` is the `WINDOW_DESTROY` event. This event occurs when you try to close a window. If the event is a `WINDOW_DESTROY` event, the `exit()` method of the `System` class is invoked to cause the program to terminate. A `true` value is returned to indicate that the event was handled. Otherwise, a `false` value is returned.

> **NOTE** Listing 17.2 is written using the Java 1.02 API so that it will run under the JDK 1.02, 1.1, or 1.1.1. When you compile it, you will be warned that you are using a deprecated (meaning soon to be phased out) API call. You can safely ignore this warning.

Listing 17.2. A Java window program (WindowsPrg.java)

```java
import java.awt.*;

public class WindowsPrg extends Frame {
 public static void main(String args[]){
  WindowsPrg program = new WindowsPrg();
 }
 public WindowsPrg() {
  super("A Java Windows Program");
  pack();
  resize(500,250);
  show();
 }
```

```
public void paint(Graphics g) {
 g.setFont(new Font("TimesRoman",Font.BOLD+Font.ITALIC,48));
 g.setColor(Color.red);
 g.drawString("Hello World!",100,125);
}
public boolean handleEvent(Event event) {
 if(event.id==Event.WINDOW_DESTROY){
  System.exit(0);
  return true;
 }else return false;
}
}
```

An Example Applet

Now that you can develop Java window programs, let's learn how to create an applet. Remember, applets execute in the context of a browser window. This means that you have to develop and compile the applet and then create an HTML document that displays the applet as part of a Web page. Listing 17.3 contains the source code of an applet I've named *WebApp*. Compile it using the following statement:

```
javac WebApp.java
```

This creates the WebApp.class file, which is the compiled applet code.

Listing 17.3. A Java applet (WebApp.java)

```
import java.awt.*;
import java.applet.*;

public class WebApp extends Applet {
 public void paint(Graphics g) {
  g.setFont(new Font("TimesRoman",Font.BOLD+Font.ITALIC,48));
  g.setColor(Color.red);
  g.drawString("Hello World!",50,100);
 }
}
```

The web.htm file shown in Listing 17.4 contains an HTML document that inserts the applet as part of a Web page. Open web.htm with your browser. Figure 17.3 shows the Web page that is displayed. The gray area of the Web page is the applet's display area. I purposely set the document's background to white so that the applet would stand out.

Listing 17.4. An HTML file that displays a Java applet (web.htm)

```
<HTML>
<HEAD>
<TITLE>A Java Applet</TITLE>
</HEAD>
<BODY BGCOLOR="white">
<APPLET CODE="WebApp.class" WIDTH=400 HEIGHT=200>
[WebApp applet]
</APPLET>
</BODY>
</HTML>
```

FIGURE 17.3

A Java applet

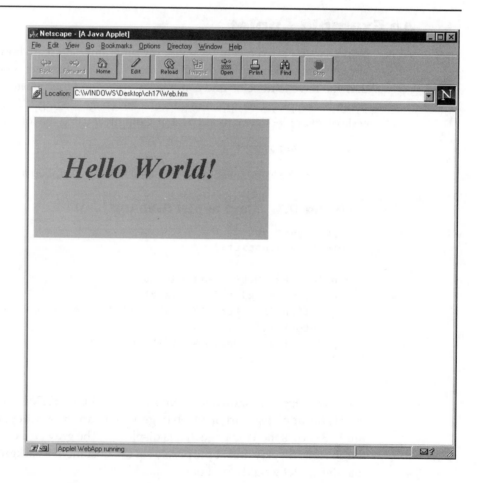

The `<applet>` tag shown in Listing 17.4 contains three attributes: `CODE`, `WIDTH`, and `HEIGHT`. The `CODE` attribute identifies the Java byte code file of the applet to be loaded. The `WIDTH` and `HEIGHT` attributes identify the dimensions of the applet's display area. Any text between the `<applet>` and `</applet>` tags is displayed by browsers that are not capable of or configured to handle applets. A non-Java-capable browser would display the phrase *[WebApp applet]* in place of the applet.

The applet's code will be easy to follow since you've used the same methods you used in the window programming example. In fact, applets use many of the standard `java.awt` window classes. The classes of the `java.applet` package are imported in addition to the `java.awt` classes. The `WebApp` class is declared as a class that `extends` the `Applet` class. The `Applet` class is the common ancestor of all applet classes in the Java class hierarchy.

The `WebApp` class does not define a `main()` method. This is because it is not a stand-alone program. It defines the `paint()` method to draw the `Graphics` object of the applet display area. The `paint()` method works in the same way as for window programs. The three statements contained in the `paint()` method are identical to those of the window program presented in the previous section except that the text is drawn at location (50,100) instead of (100,125).

Summary

In this chapter, you were introduced to Java and learned about the capabilities that it provides. You covered the similarities and differences between Java and JavaScript, and learned how to develop simple Java programs and applets. In the next chapter, you'll learn how to use JavaScript to communicate with a Java applet and how to invoke JavaScript functions from within an applet.

Communicating with Applets

- ■ Accessing Java Methods from within JavaScript

- ■ Accessing Applets from within JavaScript

- ■ Using JavaScript in an Applet

- ■ Reading Values Entered in a Form

In the previous chapter, you were introduced to Java and learned how to develop a simple Java program and an applet. These simple examples do not do justice to the tremendous capabilities provided by Java, yet they are starting points from which you can begin learning about Java. A complete introduction to Java would require an entire book in itself. In this chapter, you'll learn how to use Netscape Navigator's LiveConnect feature to enable communication between JavaScript scripts and Java applets. You'll also learn how to use LiveConnect to invoke JavaScript functions from within applets. By the time you finish this chapter, you'll be able to create Web applications that use the JavaScript-to-Java communication capabilities of LiveConnect.

Accessing Java Methods from within JavaScript

One of the easiest ways to use Java in JavaScript is to invoke Java methods directly in your scripts. For example, consider the following Java statement, which displays the text *Hello World!* to the Java console window:

```
java.lang.System.out.println("Hello World!")
```

You can execute this statement directly from within a JavaScript script, as shown in Listing 18.1. To see how this script works, open `console.htm` with your Web browser. It will display the Web page shown in Figure 18.1. To view the Java console window, select Show Java Console from the Options pull-down menu. The window shown in Figure 18.2 will be displayed.

Listing 18.1. Calling Java methods (console.htm)

```
<HTML>
<HEAD>
<TITLE>Calling Java Methods</TITLE>
</HEAD>
<BODY>
<P>This script writes the text, <EM>Hello World!</EM>
 to the Java console window.</P>
<SCRIPT LANGUAGE="JavaScript"><!--
java.lang.System.out.println("Hello World!")
// --></SCRIPT>
</BODY>
</HTML>
```

FIGURE 18.1

The browser window
(Listing 18.1)

FIGURE 18.1

The browser window
(Listing 18.1)

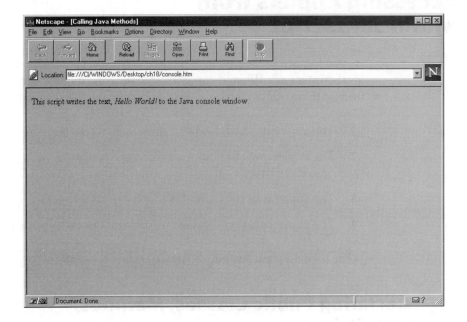

FIGURE 18.2

The Java console
window (Listing 18.1)

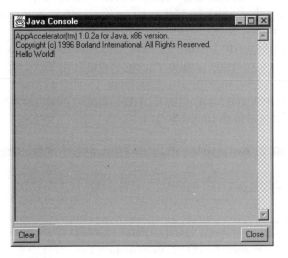

Accessing Applets from within JavaScript

As you learned in the previous section, accessing Java methods from within JavaScript is easy. When it comes to accessing the methods and variables of *applets* from within your Javascript scripts, however, the following steps must be taken:

1. The applet methods and variables must be declared as `public`.

2. The applet must be compiled using the Netscape `java_version` file in your CLASSPATH.

3. The applet must be loaded before it can be accessed.

4. The applet must be accessed using JavaScript's `applet` object.

The following subsections describe each of these steps.

Declaring Public Classes, Methods, and Variables

In order to access a method or variable used by an applet, the method or variable must be declared as `public` and must be declared as part of a `public` class. In practice, this is easy to accomplish—you use the `public` keyword in the class, method, or variable declaration. Listing 18.2 provides an example of an applet that displays a text string within its applet window. The `setText()` method is declared as `public`, making it accessible to JavaScript code. This method is used to change the text that is displayed by the applet. Note that the `FancyText` sub-class of applet is also declared as `public`.

Listing 18.2. An applet that displays text (FancyText.java)

```
import java.applet.*;
import java.awt.*;

public class FancyText extends Applet {
 String text="I like Java!";
 Font font = new Font("TimesRoman",Font.BOLD+Font.ITALIC,36);
 public void paint(Graphics g) {
  g.setFont(font);
  g.drawString(text,30,30);
 }
```

```
public void setText(String s) {
 text=s;
 repaint();
}
}
```

Placing the Netscape java_*version* File in Your *CLASSPATH*

In order to use LiveConnect, the appropriate LiveConnect classes must be made available to your applet. These classes are defined in the `java_version` file, where *version* refers to the version of Navigator that you are using. For example, if your browser is Navigator 3.0, then `java_30` is the file to use. Since my browser is Navigator 3.01, I use `java_301` instead of `java_30`.

To use the `java_version` file, you must put it in your CLASSPATH, an environment variable used by the programs of the JDK. I set my CLASSPATH by adding the following line to my AUTOEXEC.BAT file:

```
set CLASSPATH=.;c:\jdk1.1.1;c:\java\lib\classes.zip;
➡ c:\Progra~1\Netscape\Navigator\Program\Java\classes\java_301
```

Loading an Applet

An applet must be completely loaded before you can access its variables and methods. Although there is no `onLoad` event defined for the `applet` object, you can use the `window` object's `onLoad` event handler by specifying it in a document's `<body>` tag.

Consider the example shown in Listing 18.3. This example loads the applet shown in Listing 18.2. The `onLoad` event handler invokes the `accessApplet()` function after the document (and therefore the applet) has been loaded. We'll complete the discussion of Listing 18.3 after we cover the `applet` object in the next section.

Listing 18.3. Loading and accessing an applet (use-app1.htm)

```
<HTML>
<HEAD>
<TITLE>Accessing Applets</TITLE>
<SCRIPT LANGUAGE="JavaScript"><!--
function accessApplet() {
 setTimeout("changeText('I like JavaScript!')",2000)
```

```
    setTimeout("changeText('I like LiveConnect!')",4000)
}
function changeText(s) {
 window.document.fancyText.setText(s)
}
// --></SCRIPT>
</HEAD>
<BODY onLoad="accessApplet()">
<APPLET CODE="FancyText.class" NAME="fancyText"
 WIDTH=400 HEIGHT=300>
[The FancyText Applet]
</APPLET>
</BODY>
</HTML>
```

Using the *applet* Object

The `applet` object is provided by JavaScript to enable JavaScript code to access Java variables and methods. This object has a single property—the `name` property—and no methods or event handlers. The `name` property is used to access the `name` attribute of the `<applet>` tag.

The `applet` object is a property of the `document` object. Individual applets can be accessed by name. For example, in the `changeText()` function of Listing 18.3, the following statement,

```
window.document.fancyText.setText(s)
```

is used to invoke the `setText()` method of the applet named *fancyText*.

The `applets` array is also a property of the `document` object. This array provides access to all applets that are defined for a particular document.

My FancyText Example

Listings 18.2 and 18.3 provide a complete example of how JavaScript code is able to access a Java applet. To run this example, make sure that your CLASSPATH includes the `java_version` file that is appropriate to your browser, and compile `FancyText.java` with your Java compiler. This will produce the `FancyText.class` byte-code file.

`FancyText.class` is loaded via the `<applet>` tag shown in Listing 18.3. The applet is named *fancyText*. When the `use-appl.htm` file is loaded, the `onLoad` event handler of the `<body>` tag invokes the `accessApplet()` function. This function sets two timeouts. The first timeout invokes `changeText()` after two seconds, passing it the *I like JavaScript!* string. The second timeout invokes `changeText()` after four seconds, passing it the *I like LiveConnect!* string.

The `changeText()` function invokes the `setText()` method of the `FancyText` class defined in Listing 18.2. It uses `setText()` to change the text displayed by the applet.

To see the effect of using the JavaScript of Listing 18.3 with the Java of Listing 18.2, open `use-app1.htm` with your browser. Your browser will initially display the text shown in Figure 18.3. After two seconds, your browser will display the text shown in Figure 18.4. After two more seconds, your browser will display the text shown in Figure 18.5.

FIGURE 18.3

Initial text display (Listing 18.3)

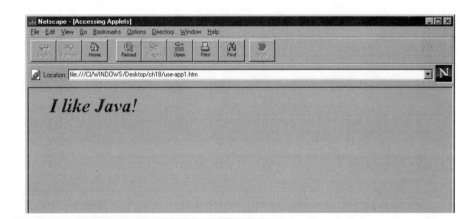

FIGURE 18.4

The display after two seconds (Listing 18.3)

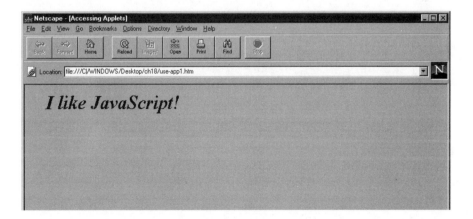

FIGURE 18.5

The display after four
seconds (Listing 18.3)

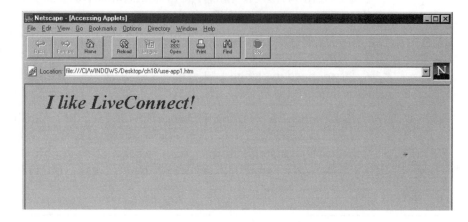

Using JavaScript in an Applet

So far you have learned how to access and control Java applets from within Java-Script. But what if you want to do the converse, that is, access JavaScript objects and functions from within an applet? LiveConnect provides an interface between Java and JavaScript that allows you to do this. However, as with JavaScript-to-Java communication, there are a few steps involved:

1. Use the MAYSCRIPT attribute of the <applet> tag to permit an applet to access a script.

2. Import the netscape.javascript package in your applet.

3. Create a handle to a JavaScript window using the JSObject class and the getWindow() method.

4. Use the getMember() method of the JSObject class to obtain access to JavaScript objects.

5. Use the eval() method of the JSObject class to invoke JavaScript methods.

These steps are covered in the following subsections.

Using the *MAYSCRIPT* Attribute

For an applet to be able to access a JavaScript object or function, the applet must be given explicit permission to do so. This prevents the applet from modifying other areas of a Web page without the Web page designer knowing about it. The MAYSCRIPT attribute must be placed in the `<applet>` tag to allow an applet to access JavaScript. If an applet tries to access JavaScript without the MAYSCRIPT attribute being specified, then the applet will generate an exception, display an error message, and stop running. In Listing 18.4, the ReadForm applet is loaded and given permission to access JavaScript objects and functions.

Listing 18.4. Accessing JavaScript from an applet (use-app2.htm).

```
<HTML>
<HEAD>
<TITLE>Accessing JavaScript from an applet</TITLE>
</HEAD>
<BODY>
<FORM NAME="textForm">
<P>Enter some text and then click Display Text:
 <INPUT TYPE="text" NAME="textField" SIZE="20"></P>
</FORM>
<APPLET CODE="ReadForm.class" WIDTH=400 HEIGHT=100 NAME="readApp"
 MAYSCRIPT>
[The ReadForm Applet]
</APPLET>
</BODY>
</HTML>
```

Importing *netscape.javascript*

In order for an applet to access JavaScript objects and functions, it must import the JSObject and JSException classes of the netscape.javascript package. The import statements shown in Listing 18.5 may be used to import these classes. You only need to import JSException if you plan to handle this exception within your applet. The use of JSObject in Java-to-JavaScript communication is covered in the following sections.

WARNING In some cases, importing netscape.javascript.*; may lead to a compilation error. To avoid this problem, import JSObject and JSException via separate import statements as shown in Listing 18.5.

Listing 18.5. Reading a JavaScript form (ReadForm.java)

```java
import java.applet.*;
import java.awt.*;
import netscape.javascript.JSObject;
import netscape.javascript.JSException;

public class ReadForm extends Applet {
 String text="Enter some text for me to display!";
 Font font = new Font("TimesRoman",Font.BOLD+Font.ITALIC,24);
 JSObject win, doc, form, textField;
 public void init() {
  win = JSObject.getWindow(this);
  doc = (JSObject) win.getMember("document");
  form = (JSObject) doc.getMember("textForm");
  textField = (JSObject) form.getMember("textField");
  setLayout(new BorderLayout());
  Panel buttons = new Panel();
  buttons.add(new Button("Display Text"));
  add("South",buttons);
 }
 public void paint(Graphics g) {
  g.setFont(font);
  g.drawString(text,30,30);
 }
 public boolean handleEvent(Event event) {
  if(event.target instanceof Button &&
    event.id==Event.ACTION_EVENT) {
    text= (String) textField.getMember("value");
    win.eval("alert(\"This alert comes from Java!\")");
    repaint();
    return true;
  }
  return false;
 }
}
```

Creating a Handle to a
JavaScript Window

When accessing JavaScript methods and functions from within Java, one of the first things that you'll want to do is to gain access to the JavaScript window object associated with the window in which the applet is loaded. By doing so, you'll be able to access other objects (`document`, `form`, `image`) that are created in the Navigator instance hierarchy.

To access the JavaScript `window` object, declare a variable of type `JSObject` and use the `getWindow()` method of the `JSObject` class to assign the `window` object to the variable. For example, in Listing 18.5 the `win` variable is declared as class `JSObject`. The first statement in the `init()` method of the `ReadForm` class assigns the `window` object to the `win` variable. The `this` parameter that is passed to the `getWindow()` method causes `getWindow()` to return the `window` object associated with the window containing the applet.

Using *getMember()*

The `getMember()` method of the `JSObject` class is used to access objects and values that are properties of a `JSObject` object. This method takes a `String` argument that identifies the object or value to be accessed. For example, in the `init()` method of Listing 18.5, the following lines of code use `getMember()` to access objects that are properties of other JavaScript objects:

```
doc = (JSObject) win.getMember("document");
form = (JSObject) doc.getMember("textForm");
textField = (JSObject) form.getMember("textField");
```

- The first statement invokes `getMember()` for the `win` variable used to reference the current document window. The `"document"` string is passed as an argument. `getMember()` returns the JavaScript object corresponding to `window.document` and assigns it to the `doc` variable. The `doc`, `form`, and `textField` variables are all declared as class `JSObject` in the beginning of the definition of the `ReadForm` class.

- In the second statement, `getMember()` is invoked for `doc` and returns the JavaScript object corresponding to `window.document.textForm`. This object is the form defined in Listing 18.4. It is assigned to the `form` variable.

- The third statement invokes `getMember()` for the `form` variable. `getMember()` returns the JavaScript object `window.document.textForm.textField`. This object is assigned to the `textField` variable.

In the `handleEvent()` method of Listing 18.5, the following statement is used to retrieve the value of an HTML text field and assign it to the Java `text` variable:

```
text= (String) textField.getMember("value");
```

Notice that in this statement, the value returned by `getMember()` is coerced into a value of the `String` class via the `(String)` type cast operator.

Using *eval()*

The `eval()` method of the `JSObject` class is used to invoke a method of a JavaScript object and make the value returned by the method available to a Java variable. It is used in the `handleEvent()` method of Listing 18.5 to display the alert dialog box:

```
win.eval("alert(\"This alert comes from Java!\")");
```

Note that double quotes should be replaced by their escape character sequence `\"` when used as arguments to a method that is being evaluated.

Reading Values Entered in a Form

Now that you've covered the basics of Java-to-JavaScript communication, let's walk through the example provided by Listings 18.4 and 18.5.

Open `use-app2.htm` with your browser. It displays the Web page shown in Figure 18.6. Type *Hello JavaScript!* in the form's text field and click on the Display Text button. The Java applet generates the alert dialog box shown in Figure 18.7. After you've clicked OK, the applet uses JavaScript to read the text you typed into the HTML form and displays it in the applet area of the window, as shown in Figure 18.8. This small example shows how Java, JavaScript, and HTML can communicate to produce an interesting Web page effect.

The HTML file shown earlier in Listing 18.4 combines a simple form with the `ReadForm` applet. No JavaScript code is used in the file. The applet shown in Listing 18.5 accesses the HTML form via the JavaScript objects that are automatically created by Navigator. Note that the `win`, `doc`, `form`, and `textField` variables are declared as class `JSObject`. These variables are used with the getWindow() and getMember() methods to provide access to the text field of the form. The handleEvent() method handles the clicking of the Display Text button and uses the eval() method to display the JavaScript alert dialog box.

FIGURE 18.6

Accessing JavaScript from an applet (use-app2.htm)

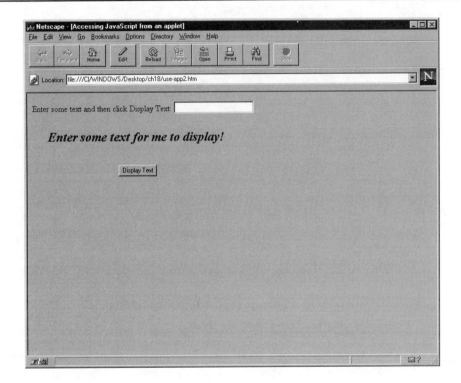

FIGURE 18.7

Java generates a JavaScript alert dialog box. (use-app2.htm)

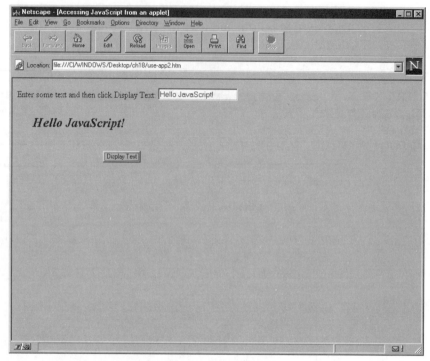

FIGURE 18.8

Java uses JavaScript to read the HTML form and displays its value in the applet window area. (use-app2.htm).

Other *JSObject* Methods

The JSObject class provides other methods besides getWindow(), getMember(), and eval(). Table 18.1 contains a complete list of the JSObject methods.

TABLE 18.1   Methods of the JSObject class

Method	Description
call(*String, Object[]*)	Invokes the JavaScript method specified by *String* and passes it the arguments specified in *Object[]*.
eval(*String*)	Invokes the JavaScript method specified by *String*.
finalize()	Decrements the reference count on a JavaScript object.
getMember(*String*)	Returns the object or value specified by *String*.

TABLE 18.1 Methods of the JSObject class (continued)

Method	Description
getSlot(*int*)	Returns the object array element specified by *int*.
getWindow(*Applet*)	Returns the window containing the specified *Applet*.
removeMember(*String*)	Removes the object specified by *String*.
setMember(*String*, *Object*)	Sets the object specified by *String* to the value specified by *Object*.
setSlot(*int*,*Object*)	Sets the value of the object array element specified by *int* to the value specified by *Object*.
toString()	Converts the JSObject to a String value.

Summary

In this chapter, you learned how to use Netscape Navigator's LiveConnect feature to support communication between JavaScript scripts and Java applets. You also learned how to access JavaScript objects and invoke JavaScript functions from within Java applets. In the next chapter, you'll learn how to use these capabilities to develop combined JavaScript+Java applications.

CHAPTER

NINETEEN

19

Developing Combined Applications with LiveConnect

- A JavaScript Jukebox

- GraphIt!

In Chapter 18, you learned how to use LiveConnect to communicate between JavaScript scripts and Java applets. The examples you studied illustrated the basic steps involved in script-to-applet communication. In this chapter, you'll study two more examples of combined JavaScript and Java applications. These examples are a little more advanced, and they demonstrate the benefits of integrating JavaScript and Java. When you finish this chapter, you'll have a better and more complete understanding of how you can use LiveConnect in your Web pages.

A JavaScript Jukebox

The first example of this section shows how Java can be used to bring sound to your Web pages without the need for a plug-in or Netscape's audio player. Live-Connect makes this capability available to your JavaScript code. The example also shows how to handle JavaScript events with Java code.

The capability to play sounds as users interact with your Web pages greatly enhances the attractiveness and effectiveness of your user interface. By using Java's audio capabilities you don't need to worry whether your user has an audio plug-in or whether they will have to bear with the distracting audio player provided by Netscape. As long as your sound files are in the Sun .au format, you can use Java to play sounds ranging from short audio clips to complete songs.

To see Java in action, open jukebox.htm (Listing 19.1) with your browser. When the document is loaded, you will hear the word "Hi" and your browser display will look like that shown in Figure 19.1.

NOTE   You must have a working sound card to hear the audio sounds played in this example. You must also have Sun's Java Development Kit installed in the C:\jdk1.1.1 directory of your computer. This example uses the audio files provided with the JDK. If you have Java installed in a different directory, you can modify the base path where the code looks for these audio files.

FIGURE 19.1

The Jukebox initial display (jukebox.htm)

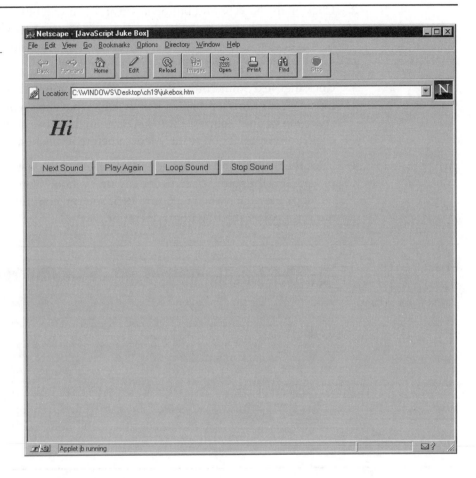

You're probably not going to dump your audio CD player as the result of running jukebox.htm, but you should realize the potential benefit that this simple example can have on your Web pages. It shows how simple sounds can be associated with user interface events. These sounds can be played by all users who have a sound card and Navigator.

Once the display is running, you can check out its features by clicking the various buttons, as follows:

1. Click on the Next Sound button and you will hear a beep; also, your browser display will be updated as shown in Figure 19.2. Click the Play Again button and the beep sound will be replayed.

2. Click on the Next Sound button again and you will hear chirping. Your browser display will look like that shown in Figure 19.3. Click the Loop Sound button and your browser will chirp along continuously. When you have heard enough, click the Stop Sound button.

3. Click the Next Sound button another time and you will hear some "space music". Your browser display will look like that shown in Figure 19.4. The space music audio clip is a little longer than the other audio clips. You can click Stop Sound if you want to stop it before it finishes.

4. Click the Next Sound button one more time and the last audio clip is played. It is the sound of someone saying "yahoo!" Your browser's display will look like that shown in Figure 19.5. You can continue to use the jukebox buttons to experiment with its operation.

FIGURE 19.2

The beep sound is played. (jukebox.htm)

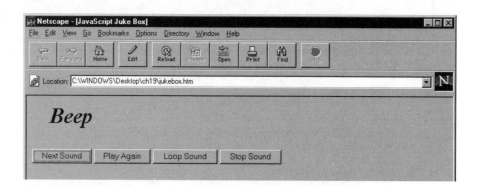

FIGURE 19.3

The chirping sound is played. (jukebox.htm)

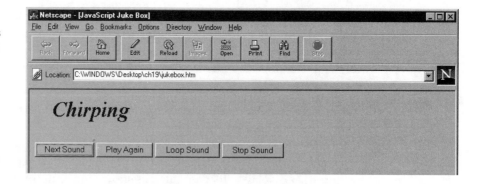

FIGURE 19.4

Space music is played.
(jukebox.htm)

FIGURE 19.5

The yahoo sound is
played. (jukebox.htm)

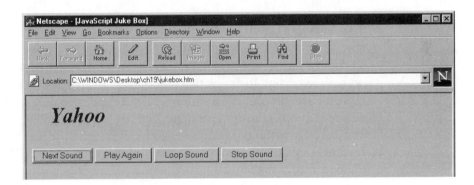

If you examine Listing 19.1 you will see that the only place where JavaScript code was used was in the event-handling code attributes for the various buttons' `onClick` events. This JavaScript code handled the events by invoking the `nextSound()`, `playSound()`, `loopSound()`, and `stopSound()` methods of the applet's JukeBox class. In effect, the JavaScript code redirected the events so that they could be handled in the applet. This technique lets you use HTML form elements to control the operation of Java applets.

Listing 19.1. A Jukebox form (jukebox.htm)

```
<HTML>
<HEAD>
<TITLE>JavaScript Juke Box</TITLE>
</HEAD>
<BODY>
```

```
<APPLET CODE="JukeBox.class" NAME="jb" WIDTH=300 HEIGHT=50>
[JukeBox applet]
</APPLET>
<FORM>
<INPUT TYPE="button" VALUE="Next Sound"
 onClick="window.document.jb.nextSound()">
<INPUT TYPE="button" VALUE="Play Again"
 onClick="window.document.jb.playSound()">
<INPUT TYPE="button" VALUE="Loop Sound"
 onClick="window.document.jb.loopSound()">
<INPUT TYPE="button" VALUE="Stop Sound"
 onClick="window.document.jb.stopSound()">
</FORM>
</BODY>
</HTML>
```

The *Sound* Class The JukeBox applet shown in Listing 19.2 creates the Sound class as a way of associating a title with an AudioClip object. AudioClip is not a class; it is an *interface*. Java interfaces are used to specify how objects are to be used without restricting their position in the class hierarchy. (Consult Appendix C for more information on Java interfaces.) The Sound class defines the setSound(), play(), stop(), loop(), and getTitle() methods. The play(), stop(), and loop() methods operate as their names imply. The setSound() method is used to associate a Sound object with a particular audio clip. The getTitle() method returns the title associated with a Sound object.

The *JukeBox* Class variables The JukeBox class assigns the URL of the Java Development Kit's demo files to the base variable. If your /jdk1.1.1/demo directory is located elsewhere on your computer then you will have to modify this URL. The loc array contains the offsets to the base URL where the specific sound files are located. The sounds array creates the five Sound objects used in this example. The sound variable is used to store the currently selected Sound object. The currentSound variable contains the index in the sounds array of the current sound.

init() This method loads and assigns the audio clips associated with each Sound object specified in the sounds array.

start() This method starts the applet by playing the default "Hi" sound clip.

paint() This method displays the title of the sound in the applet window area.

nextSound() This method stops the currently playing sound and plays the next sound in the sounds array, using repaint() to display the sound's title.

playSound0 This method plays the current sound again.

stopSound0 This method stops the playing of the current sound.

loopSound0 This method plays the current sound in a continuous looping fashion.

Listing 19.2. The Java behind the Jukebox (JukeBox.java)

```java
import java.applet.*;
import java.awt.*;
import java.net.*;

class Sound {
 String title;
 AudioClip audio;
 public Sound(String title) {
  this.title=title;
 }
 public void setSound(AudioClip audioClip) {
  audio = audioClip;
 }
 public void play() {
  audio.play();
 }
 public void stop() {
  audio.stop();
 }
 public void loop() {
  audio.loop();
 }
 public String getTitle() {
  return title;
 }
}

public class JukeBox extends Applet {
 String loc[] = {"JumpingBox/sounds/cannot.be.completed.au",
  "Animator/audio/spacemusic.au",
  "TicTacToe/audio/yahoo1.au",
  "ImageMap/audio/hi.au",
  "TicTacToe/audio/beep.au"};
 String base="file:///C|/jdk1.1.1/demo/";
 Sound sounds[] = {
```

```
    new Sound("Chirping"),
    new Sound("Space Music"),
    new Sound("Yahoo"),
    new Sound("Hi"),
    new Sound("Beep"),
  };
  Sound sound;
  int currentSound=3;

  public void init() {
   for(int i=0;i<sounds.length;++i) {
    try {
     sounds[i].setSound(getAudioClip(new URL(base+loc[i])));
     }catch(MalformedURLException ex) {
     }
    }
  }
  public void start() {
   sound = sounds[currentSound];
   sound.play();
  }
  public void paint(Graphics g) {
   g.setFont(new Font("TimesRoman",Font.BOLD+Font.ITALIC,36));
   g.drawString(sounds[currentSound].getTitle(),30,30);
  }
  public void nextSound() {
   sound.stop();
   ++currentSound;
   currentSound %= sounds.length;
   sound = sounds[currentSound];
   repaint();
   sound.play();
  }
  public void playSound() {
   sound.play();
  }
  public void stopSound() {
   sound.stop();
  }
  public void loopSound() {
   sound.loop();
  }
}
```

GraphIt!

JavaScript and Java provide complementary capabilities for Web page development:

- JavaScript provides a way to control the entire browser window.

- Java provides a capability to execute advanced programs within a limited area of the browser window.

- LiveConnect provides the capability to link events that occur in the larger JavaScript-controlled window area to the Java methods that control the applet's operation.

The example presented in this section shows how JavaScript can easily interface with and make use of Java components. This example creates a Web application called *GraphIt!* that allows a user to specify points to be plotted on a graph. The user types the coordinates of individual points he or she wishes to have included on the graph, and the applet draws line segments to connect the points. It connects points according to their X coordinates, starting with the leftmost point and moving to the right. If two points have the same X coordinate, the applet connects to the lower point before drawing a line to the higher one. The user can also direct GraphIt! to remove a point from the graph, and the applet redraws to show the new result.

The GraphIt! example illustrates the symbiosis between JavaScript and Java. The applet designer, on the one hand, is free to design the applet without having to develop an explicit control interface; all he or she has to do is provide methods for adding and deleting points of the graph. The Web page designer, on the other hand, is able to use the applet without having to figure out the details of its operation; all she or he has to do is learn how to use the methods for adding and deleting points.

To see how the example works, open `graph.htm` (Listing 19.3) with your browser. The Web page displayed by your browser should look like Figure 19.6. The drawing area shows the intersection of the x and y axes. Initially, the drawing area extends to plus and minus 1 in each axis direction.

1. For the first point on the graph, enter **2** in the X-Coordinate text field and **1** in the Y-coordinate text field to indicate the point (2,1), and click on the Add Point button. Because the graph contains only one point so far, no line is displayed, but the drawing area is automatically rescaled to accommodate this point. Refer to Figure 19.7.

FIGURE 19.6

Top: The initial graph display
Bottom: The display after the user has entered a few points to be graphed (graph.htm)

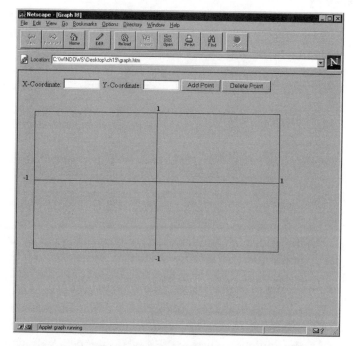

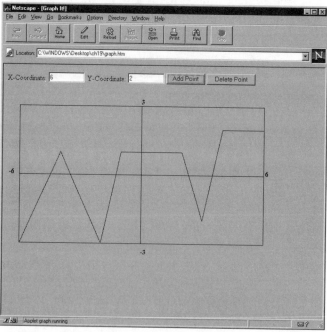

FIGURE 19.7

When you add a first
point (2,1), the drawing
area automatically
rescales to include the
point. (graph.htm)

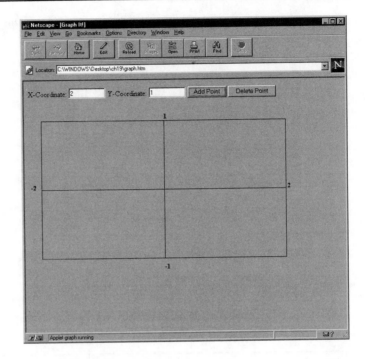

2. Now add a second point (–2,–3) by entering –2 and –3 in the text fields, and click on Add Point. Notice how the drawing area is rescaled again to accommodate the greater value along the Y axis. Also, a line is drawn connecting the two points, as shown in Figure 19.8.

3. Add a third point (–1,1), as shown in Figure 19.9. Note how the graph is automatically updated to include this point. Since it connects the points in left-to-right, bottom-to-top order, it connects the point (–2,3) to (-1,1) and then connects (–1,1) to (2,1).

4. Now add the following points, one at a time: (3,–2), (4,2), (–4,1), (–6,–3), and (6,2). Your browser should look like that shown in Figure 19.10.

5. To see how the Delete Point feature works, delete the point (3,–2) by entering the coordinates in the text fields and clicking on the Delete Point button. The results are shown in Figure 19.11. Compare this to the graph shown in Figure 19.10; notice how the graph was redrawn to eliminate the deleted point.

FIGURE 19.8

The drawing area is
rescaled again after
adding (2,1) and (−2,−3),
and the graph begins to
take shape, with a line
drawn to connect the
two points. (graph.htm)

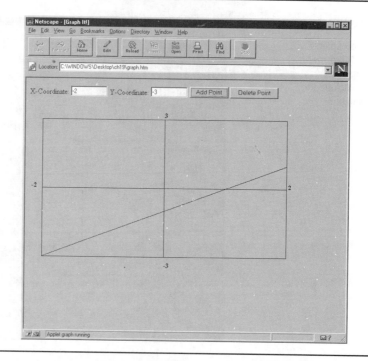

FIGURE 19.9

The graph now connects
all three points the user
has entered: (2,1), (−2,−3),
and (−1,1). (graph.htm)

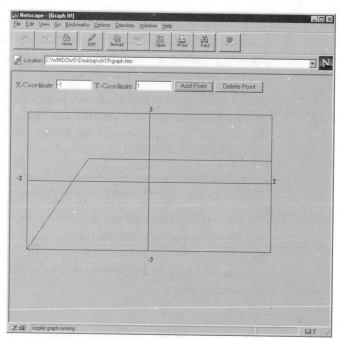

FIGURE 19.10

The graph connecting
(2,1), (−2,−3), (−1,1),
(3,−2), (4,2), (−4,1),
(-6,-3), and (6,2)
(graph.htm)

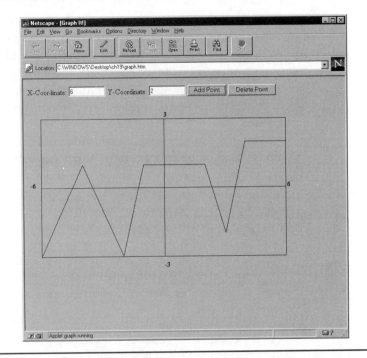

FIGURE 19.11

The graph after deleting
(3,−2) (graph.htm)

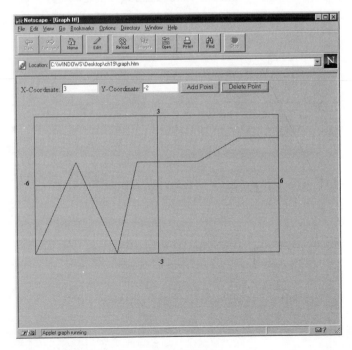

The `graph.htm` file is shown in Listing 19.3. It creates a simple form for specifying the points that are to be added and deleted from a graph. The `addPoint()` and `deletePoint()` functions handle the onClick events associated with the Add Point and Delete Point buttons. The `addPoint()` function reads the x and y coordinates entered by the user, converts them to floating point, and passes them to the `addPoint()` method of the `GraphApp` class. The `deletePoint()` function interfaces with the `deletePoint()` method of the `GraphApp` class in a similar manner.

Listing 19.3. A graph control form (graph.htm)

```html
<HTML>
<HEAD>
<TITLE>Graph It!</TITLE>
<SCRIPT LANGUAGE="JavaScript"><!--
function addPoint() {
 var x=parseFloat(window.document.xy.x.value)
 var y=parseFloat(window.document.xy.y.value)
 window.document.graph.addPoint(x,y)
}
function deletePoint() {
 var x=parseFloat(window.document.xy.x.value)
 var y=parseFloat(window.document.xy.y.value)
 window.document.graph.deletePoint(x,y)
}
// --></SCRIPT>
</HEAD>
<BODY>
<FORM NAME="xy">
X-Coordinate: <INPUT TYPE="text" NAME="x" SIZE="10">
Y-Coordinate: <INPUT TYPE="text" NAME="y" SIZE="10">
<INPUT TYPE="button" VALUE="Add Point"
 onClick="addPoint()">
<INPUT TYPE="button" VALUE="Delete Point"
 onClick="deletePoint()">
</FORM>
<APPLET CODE="GraphApp.class" NAME="graph" WIDTH=650 HEIGHT=400>
[Graph applet]
</APPLET>
</BODY>
</HTML>
```

The `GraphApp.java` file, shown in Listing 19.4, defines three classes: `Float-Point`, `PointSet`, and `GraphApp`. The first one, `FloatPoint`, is used for storing two-dimensional floating-point coordinates. The second class, `PointSet`, is used for manipulating and graphing sets of points. I'll present this class's functions below. The third class, `GraphApp`, implements the basic applet code. It creates an object of class `PointSet` and uses `addPoint()` and `deletePoint()` for adding and deleting points to the `PointSet` object. The `paint()` method invokes the `displayGraph()` method of the `PointSet` class to draw the graph.

The variables and functions of the `PointSet` class are as follows:

v This variable is assigned a `Vector` object that is used to store the points added by the user.

xUL and yUL These variables specify the location of the upper left corner of the graph with respect to upper left corner of the applet window.

width and height These variables identify the dimensions of the graph in pixels.

xOrig and yOrig These variables identify the location of the point (0,0) on the graph.

numPoints This variable identifies the number of points in the graph.

xMin, xMax, yMin, and yMax These variables identify the minimum and maximum coordinates of the points to be included in the graph. These values are used to rescale the graph to automatically accommodate newly added points.

xDelta and yDelta These variables identify the range of points that are to be included along each axis. (Note that the x and y axes are not of the same scale.)

add() This method adds a point to v.

delete() This method deletes a point from v.

displayGraph() This method invokes the following five methods to display the graph.

- `updateGraphParameters()`   This method sets the values of xUL, yUL, width, height, xOrig, and yOrig. It then calculates the values of xMax, yMax, xMin, yMin, xDelta, and yDelta based upon the points entered by the user.

- `drawGraphBox()`   This method draws the drawing area—the rectangle surrounding the graph area.

- `drawAxes()` This method draws the x and y axes.

- `labelAxes()` This method displays the values of the x and y axes at their intersections with the graph boundary.

- `drawPoints()` This method invokes sortPoints() to sort v and then creates the vTrans vector to translate the absolute coordinates to points within the Graphics object on which the graph is to be displayed. It then draws a line between consecutive points of the vTrans vector.

sortPoints() This method sorts the points contained in the v `Vector` object from left to right and bottom to top.

Listing 19.4. The graphing applet (GraphApp.java)

```java
import java.applet.*;
import java.awt.*;
import java.util.*;

class FloatPoint {
 public float x;
 public float y;
 public FloatPoint(float x,float y) {
  this.x=x;
  this.y=y;
 }
 public String xVal() {
  return String.valueOf(x);
 }
 public String yVal() {
  return String.valueOf(y);
 }
}

class PointSet {
 Vector v = new Vector();
 int xUL, yUL, width, height, xOrig, yOrig, numPoints;
 float xMin, xMax, yMin, yMax, xDelta, yDelta;
 public void add(FloatPoint p) {
  for(int i=0;i<v.size();++i) {
   FloatPoint q=(FloatPoint) v.elementAt(i);
   if(q.x==p.x && q.y==p.y) return;
  }
```

```
  v.addElement(p);
}
public void delete(FloatPoint p) {
 for(int i=0;i<v.size();++i) {
  FloatPoint q=(FloatPoint) v.elementAt(i);
  if(q.x==p.x && q.y==p.y){
   v.removeElementAt(i);
    break;
  }
 }
}
public void displayGraph(Graphics g) {
 updateGraphParameters();
 drawGraphBox(g);
 drawAxes(g);
 labelAxes(g);
 drawPoints(g);
}
public void updateGraphParameters() {
 xUL=30;
 yUL=30;
 width=550;
 height=300;
 xOrig=xUL+(width/2);
 yOrig=yUL+(height/2);
 numPoints=v.size();
 if(numPoints==0){
  xMax=1;
  yMax=1;
 }else if(numPoints==1){
  FloatPoint p=(FloatPoint) v.firstElement();
  xMax=Math.abs(p.x);
  yMax=Math.abs(p.y);
 }else{
  FloatPoint p=(FloatPoint) v.firstElement();
  xMax=Math.abs(p.x);
  yMax=Math.abs(p.y);
  for(int i=0;i<numPoints;++i) {
    p=(FloatPoint) v.elementAt(i);
    if(Math.abs(p.x)>xMax) xMax=Math.abs(p.x);
    if(Math.abs(p.y)>yMax) yMax=Math.abs(p.y);
  }
 }
```

```
  xDelta=xMax*2;
  yDelta=yMax*2;
  xMin=-xMax;
  yMin=-yMax;
 }
 public void drawGraphBox(Graphics g) {
  g.drawRect(xUL-1,yUL-1,width+2,height+2);
 }
 public void drawAxes(Graphics g) {
  g.drawLine(xUL,yOrig,xUL+width,yOrig);
  g.drawLine(xOrig,yUL,xOrig,yUL+height);
 }
 public void labelAxes(Graphics g) {
  g.setFont(new Font("TimesRoman",Font.BOLD,14));
  int offset1=5;
  int offset2=25;
  g.drawString(String.valueOf(xMin),xUL-offset2,yOrig);
  g.drawString(String.valueOf(xMax),xUL+width+offset1,yOrig);
  g.drawString(String.valueOf(yMax),xOrig,yUL-offset1);
  g.drawString(String.valueOf(yMin),xOrig,yUL+height+offset2);
 }
 public void drawPoints(Graphics g) {
  sortPoints();
  Vector vTrans = new Vector();
  for(int i=0;i<numPoints;++i) {
   FloatPoint p = (FloatPoint) v.elementAt(i);
   int xTrans=xOrig;
   int yTrans=yOrig;
   xTrans+=Math.round(((float)width/2.0)*(p.x/xMax));
   yTrans-=Math.round(((float)height/2.0)*(p.y/yMax));
   vTrans.addElement(new Point(xTrans,yTrans));
  }
  for(int i=0;i<numPoints-1;++i) {
   Point p1=(Point) vTrans.elementAt(i);
   Point p2=(Point) vTrans.elementAt(i+1);
   g.drawLine(p1.x,p1.y,p2.x,p2.y);
  }
 }
 public void sortPoints() {
  boolean again=true;
  while (again) {
   again=false;
   for(int i=0;i<numPoints-1;++i) {
```

```
      FloatPoint p1=(FloatPoint) v.elementAt(i);
      FloatPoint p2=(FloatPoint) v.elementAt(i+1);
      if(p2.x<p1.x || (p2.x==p1.x && p2.y<p1.y)){
       v.setElementAt(p2,i);
       v.setElementAt(p1,i+1);
       again=true;
      }
    }
   }
  }
}

public class GraphApp extends Applet {
 PointSet ps=new PointSet();
 public void paint(Graphics g) {
  ps.displayGraph(g);
 }
 public void addPoint(float x,float y) {
  FloatPoint p=new FloatPoint(x,y);
  ps.add(p);
  repaint();
 }
 public void deletePoint(float x,float y) {
  FloatPoint p=new FloatPoint(x,y);
  ps.delete(p);
  repaint();
 }
}
```

Summary

In this chapter, you studied two examples of integrating JavaScript and Java applications using LiveConnect. The jukebox example showed how Java can be used to bring sound to your Web pages without the need for a plug-in or Netscape's audio player. It also showed how JavaScript events can be handled by Java code. The GraphIt! example showed how JavaScript can easily interface with and make use of Java components, and illustrated the symbiosis between JavaScript and Java. This is the last chapter in Part 4. Part 5 will continue with LiveConnect but will focus on using plug-ins with JavaScript.

PART V

Working with Plug-Ins

CHAPTER

TWENTY

20

How Plug-Ins Work

- **Popular Plug-Ins**

- **Plug-In Resources**

- **Plug-Ins in Action**

- **The Interface between Navigator and Plug-Ins**

Plug-ins are one of the most exciting developments in browser technology. They provide the capability to extend your browser in a variety of ways. You can use a plug-in to listen to a radio broadcast, to watch a video, or to remotely control another computer. The potential applications for plug-ins are limitless. In this chapter, you'll learn all about plug-ins—how they work, how they are used, and how they interface with Navigator. You'll also see some examples of popular plug-ins. When you finish this chapter, you'll have a good understanding of how plug-ins work and how to use them in your Web applications.

Popular Plug-Ins

Since Netscape first introduced them, a large variety of attractive and useful plug-ins have been developed. They range from inline viewers, such as the Adobe Acrobat Viewer, to complete browser-embedded applications, such as SCIENCE.ORG's transferRNA. The Netscape Plug-In page provides links to many exciting and useful plug-ins (refer to Figure 20.1). It is located at the following URL:

http://home.netscape.com/comprod/products/navigator/version_2.0 /plugins/index.html

The following subsections cover a few of the most popular browser plug-ins.

LiveAudio

Netscape's LiveAudio plug-in comes standard with Netscape. It plays audio files in WAV, AU, AIFF, and MIDI formats. LiveAudio is LiveConnect-capable and may be accessed from JavaScript. Figure 20.2 shows the LiveAudio player. LiveAudio differs from other plug-ins in that it uses a separate window that is independent of Navigator.

FIGURE 20.1

The Netscape
Plug-In guide

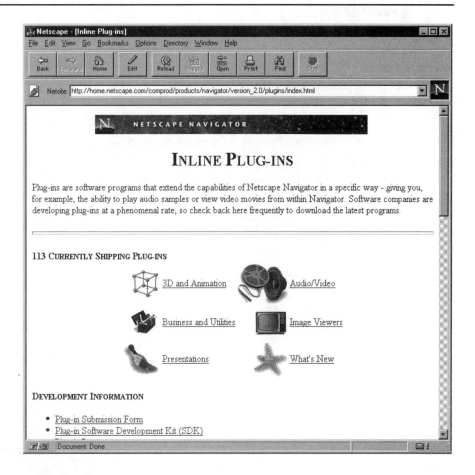

FIGURE 20.2

Netscape's
LiveAudio player

Live3D

Live3D is a LiveConnect-capable Virtual Reality Modeling Language (VRML) plug-in that was built by Netscape and comes with Navigator 3.0. It is an excellent viewer for displaying the three-dimensional worlds of VRML. Figure 20.3 shows a Live3D display.

FIGURE 20.3

Netscape's Live3D plug-in

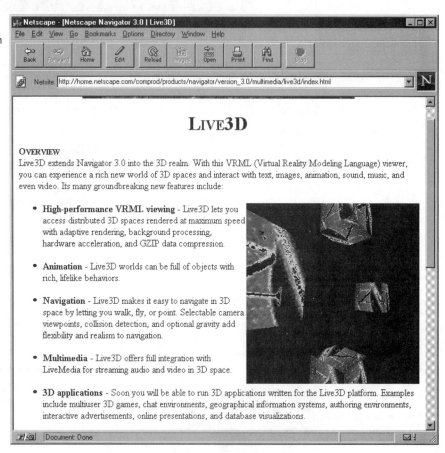

Media Player

The Netscape Media Player is a new Navigator plug-in that plays streaming audio and synchronized multimedia. It is used in conjunction with the Netscape Media Server. It is LiveConnect-capable and can be accessed from JavaScript. Figure 20.4 shows how it is displayed by Navigator. It is available from Netscape's home page at the following URL:

http://home.netscape.com

FIGURE 20.4

The Netscape
Media Player

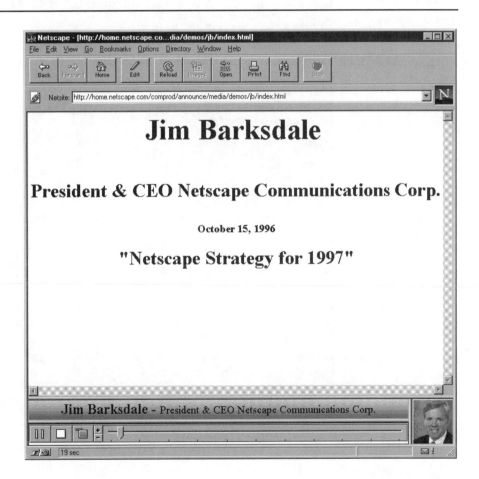

QuickTime

The QuickTime plug-in displays QuickTime video files in an area of a browser window, as shown in Figure 20.5. The QuickTime plug-in was developed by Apple and is available at the following URL:

http://www.quickTime.apple.com/sw/

FIGURE 20.5

Apple's QuickTime
video player

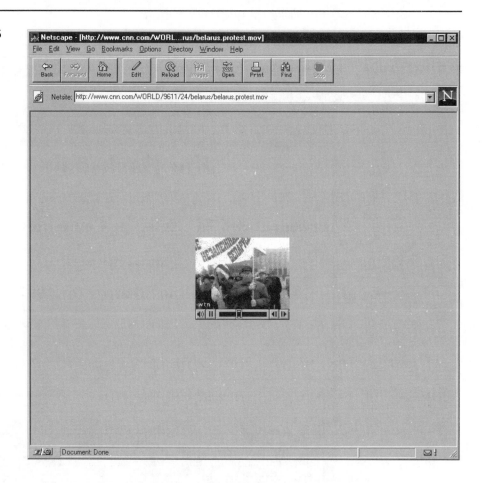

LiveVideo

The Netscape LiveVideo plug-in is LiveConnect-capable and can be accessed from JavaScript. It is used to display videos that are in the Windows AVI format. Figure 20.6 provides a sample browser display.

FIGURE 20.6

Netscape's LiveVideo player

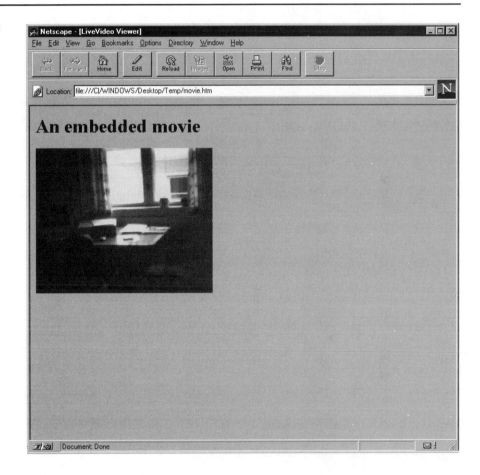

Adobe Acrobat

Adobe's Acrobat plug-in allows you to display documents that are in Adobe's Portable Document Format (PDF). PDF files are becoming a standard for distributing documents in electronic form. Figure 20.7 shows how the Acrobat plug-in appears in the Navigator window. It is available from Adobe's home page at the following URL:

> *http://www.adobe.com*

FIGURE 20.7

Adobe's Acrobat plug-in

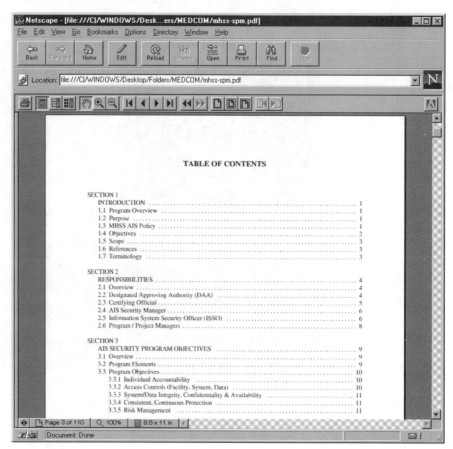

Pointcast

The Pointcast Network plug-in allows up-to-the-minute news, weather, sports, and other information to be broadcast to your browser as shown in Figure 20.8. It is available from the Pointcast home page at the following URL:

http://www.pointcast.com

FIGURE 20.8

The Pointcast
Network plug-in

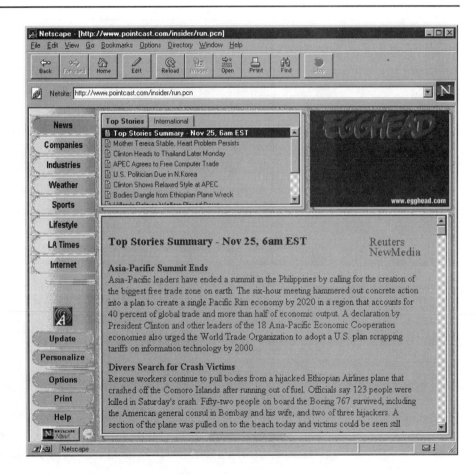

Macromedia Shockwave

The Macromedia Shockwave plug-in displays animations, movies, and other multimedia presentations that are produced by the Macromedia Director. Figure 20.9 shows how Shockwave displays a multimedia presentation. It is available from the Macromedia home page at the following URL:

http://www.macromedia.com

FIGURE 20.9

Macromedia's
Shockwave plug-in
makes this game work.

NCompass ScriptActive

The NCompass ScriptActive plug-in allows ActiveX-based applications to be displayed via Netscape Navigator as shown in Figure 20.10. It is available from the NCompass Labs home page at the following URL:

http://www.ncompasslabs.com

FIGURE 20.10

The NCompass ScriptActive plug-in

Corel CMX Viewer

The Corel CMX Viewer allows vector-based graphics files created by CorelDRAW to be displayed in a Web page as shown in Figure 20.11. It is available from the following URL:

http://www.corel.com/corelcmx/

FIGURE 20.11

The Corel CMX Viewer

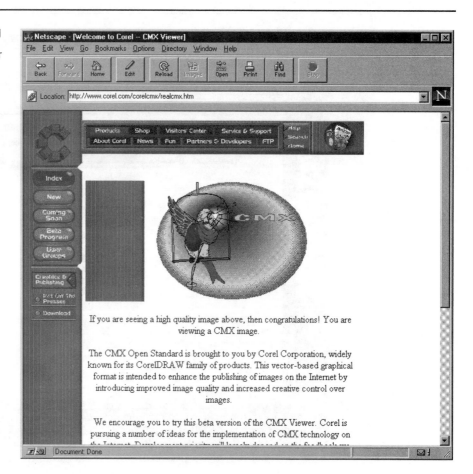

Plug-In Resources

The plug-ins covered in the previous sections are some of the most useful and popular ones that are available. However, they are only a small sample of what's available in plug-in technology. To find more information about what plug-ins are available for different applications, consult the BrowserWatch - Plug-In Plaza! Web page (Figure 20.12) at the following URL:

http://browserwatch.iworld.com/plug-in.html

FIGURE 20.12

BrowserWatch's
Plug-In Plaza!

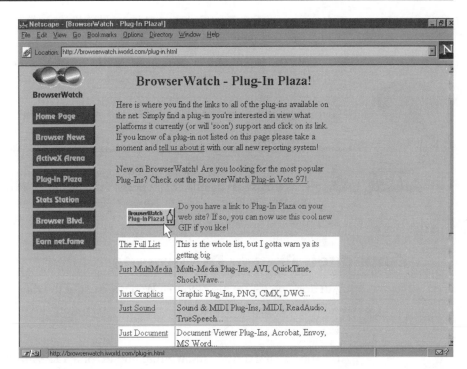

Plug-Ins in Action

Plug-ins are independently developed software components that execute in the context of a browser window. They are compiled in the native executable code format of the operating system and computer in which they are run. Plug-ins are installed for use with Navigator by placing them in Navigator's `Plugins` directory and registering them for use with documents of a particular MIME type.

Plug-ins provide the capability to view documents of different MIME types. The documents can be viewed in *embedded mode* or in *full-page mode*. When a plug-in operates in embedded mode, it is assigned a dedicated part of a loaded HTML document in which to display information to the user and to respond to user-generated events, such as mouse and keyboard actions. When a plug-in operates in full-page mode, it is not displayed as part of a larger HTML document. Instead, it is given an entire browser window in which to operate.

Whether a plug-in document is viewed in embedded mode or full-page mode depends on how it is included in a document:

- If a plug-in document is inserted in an HTML document using the ⟨embed⟩ tag then it is viewed in embedded mode.

- If a plug-in document is referenced as part of a URL, then it is displayed in full-page mode.

The following sections describe the uses of embedded and full-page mode.

> **WARNING**   Plug-ins, unlike HTML, JavaScript, and Java, are platform dependent. This means that some plug-ins do not exist for users of certain operating systems. Most plug-ins, however, support Windows and Macintosh platforms.

Embedded Plug-In Documents

Plug-in documents are inserted in a Web page using the ⟨embed⟩ tag. The syntax of the ⟨embed⟩ tag is as follows:

```
<embed attributes>
```

An ⟨embed⟩ tag must contain either an SRC or a TYPE attribute. The SRC attribute, which identifies the document to be viewed by the plug-in, is used more often than the TYPE attribute. The TYPE attribute is used by plug-ins that aren't principally used as viewers, but rather are used to create browser-based applications that are not necessarily document-specific, as discussed in the section "Plug-Ins as Embedded Applications" later in this chapter.

There are numerous other embed attributes that can be included in addition to the SRC and TYPE attributes. For example, other important and frequently used attributes are the NAME attribute and the HEIGHT and WIDTH attributes. The NAME attribute is used in JavaScript to access the plug-in object by name. The HEIGHT and WIDTH attributes are used to specify the location of the window area that is assigned to the plug-in. All the attributes of the ⟨embed⟩ tag are summarized in Table 20.1.

TABLE 20.1 The attributes of the `<embed>` tag

Attribute	Description
HEIGHT	Specifies the vertical dimension of the plug-in area.
HIDDEN	Specifies whether the plug-in is to be hidden or visible.
NAME	Associates a name with the plug-in instance.
PALETTE	Specifies the mode of the plug-in's color palette.
PLUGINSPAGE	Specifies a URL containing instructions for installing the plug-in. This helps you to assist the user in installing a plug-in needed for a particular MIME type. (You'll learn how to use this attribute in Chapter 22.)
SRC	Specifies the document to be displayed by the plug-in.
TYPE	Specifies the MIME type associated with the plug-in.
WIDTH	Specifies the horizontal dimension of the plug-in area.
UNITS	Specifies the units of measurement associated with the HEIGHT and WIDTH attributes. The default is pixels.

Plug-ins are free to define additional attributes beside those listed in Table 20.1. The values of these plug-in-specific attributes are automatically passed to the plug-in by Navigator.

How the *SRC* Attribute Is Processed

When an `<embed>` tag contains an SRC attribute, the value of the attribute is a URL that identifies the location of a document to be viewed by a plug-in. For example, consider the following `<embed>` tag.

```
<embed SRC="movie.avi">
```

When your browser loads an HTML file containing the above tag, it asks the Web server at the document's location what the document's MIME type is. When your browser receives the MIME type information from the Web server, it checks in its MIME type table to see if there is a plug-in associated with that MIME type. If a registered plug-in is found, then the plug-in is loaded into memory and a specific instance of the plug-in is created.

After a plug-in instance is created, the document identified by the SRC attribute is retrieved from its Web server by your browser. The contents of this document are then passed to the plug-in as a data stream. The plug-in reads the data stream and processes and displays the data in accordance with its MIME type. The plug-in is free to interact with the user via its allocated window area. It may access other network resources by instructing the browser to get information at a specific URL or to post information to a URL.

When the page containing a plug-in document is no longer displayed in a browser window, the plug-in instance associated with the document is deleted. When all instances of a plug-in have been deleted, the plug-in is removed from memory.

Plug-In Documents Referenced as URLs

When a plug-in document is to be displayed in full-page mode, it is not referenced using an <embed> tag. Instead, it is referenced directly via a URL. For example, consider the following link:

```
<A HREF="manual.pdf">Link to a plug-in document.</A>
```

When you click on the above link, your browser attempts to load the manual.pdf document. First, it queries the Web server at the document's location to determine the document's MIME type. It then processes the MIME type information in the same way that it would for embedded plug-in documents. It looks in its table of registered MIME types to determine what plug-in (if any) is registered for that MIME type. If a registered plug-in is found, then the plug-in is loaded into memory and an instance of that plug-in is created.

The plug-in instance is given an entire Navigator window in which to interact with the user. This is the only difference between the ways that full-page and embedded plug-ins are handled. The plug-in instance is deleted either as the result of its window being closed or as the result of a different document being loaded into its window. The plug-in is removed from memory when all of its instances are deleted.

Plug-Ins as Embedded Applications

Back in the early days of the Web, separate helper programs, referred to as *external viewers*, were launched by a browser to display documents of those MIME types that could not be handled by the browser. These ancestors of modern plug-ins were cumbersome to install and work with.

Plug-ins were originally developed as *inline viewers*. This means they were used to integrate external viewers into the browser application. Most plug-ins still serve this purpose—they display plug-in documents in embedded or full-page mode. However, a new breed of plug-in is becoming popular: embedded *applications* that execute in the context of a browser window. These embedded applications might or might not display documents—their main purpose is to perform a service that is independent of a particular document. Figure 20.13 shows a plug-in developed by the folks at SCIENCE.ORG that is used to transfer files from one user to another.

FIGURE 20.13

SCIENCE.ORG's transfer-RNA, a file transfer plug-in

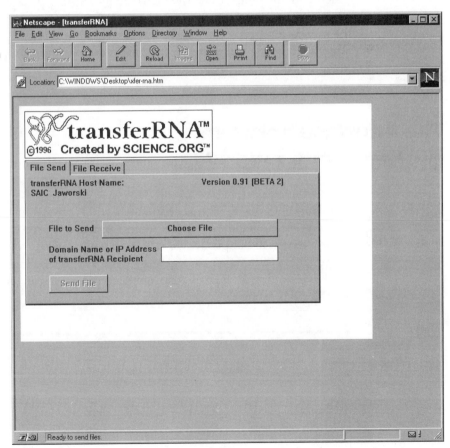

You may wonder how these plug-ins work if they aren't associated with a document of a specific MIME type. The answer is that they *are* associated with a MIME type, but not with a specific *document* of that MIME type.

Embedded application plug-ins are identified using the TYPE attribute of an <embed> tag as opposed to the SRC attribute. Consider the following example.

```
<embed TYPE="application/x-transferRNA" HEIGHT="390" WIDTH="600"
➥ ShowRecvPage="0">
```

The above <embed> tag may be used to include the transferRNA plug-in in your Web page. When your browser encounters the above <embed> tag in a document, it uses the TYPE attribute to determine what MIME type is associated with the plug-in, and then looks in its MIME type table to see what plug-in (if any) is registered for that MIME type. (In this case, the plug-in is the transferRNA plug-in. Note that in this case the MIME type was named after the plug-in.) Your browser then loads the transferRNA plug-in, as shown in Figure 20.13.

The Interface between Navigator and Plug-Ins

Navigator and plug-ins communicate with each other through the plug-in API. This API consists of plug-in methods and Netscape methods. The plug-in methods are implemented by the plug-in and are invoked by Navigator. Netscape methods are implemented by Navigator and are invoked by a plug-in. Plug-in methods are named beginning with *NPP_*. Navigator methods are named beginning with *NPN_*. The methods of the plug-in API are summarized in Tables 20.2 and 20.3.

NOTE   The plug-in API is implemented in C++.

T A B L E 2 0 . 2 Plug-in methods

Method	Description
NPP_Destroy()	Deletes a plug-in instance.
NPP_DestroyStream()	Informs a plug-in instance that a stream is to be deleted.
NPP_GetJavaClass()	Returns the Java class associated with the plug-in.
NPP_HandleEvent()	Delivers an event to a plug-in instance.
NPP_Initialize()	Initializes a plug-in.
NPP_New()	Creates a new instance of a plug-in.
NPP_NewStream()	Notifies a plug-in instance that a new data stream has been created.
NPP_Print()	Requests a print operation of a plug-in instance.
NPP_SetValue()	Used to identify windowless plug-ins.
NPP_SetWindow()	Informs a plug-in instance of the window that is assigned to it.
NPP_Shutdown()	Used to remove a plug-in from memory.
NPP_StreamAsFile()	Informs a plug-in instance of a file name by which a stream may be accessed.
NPP_URLNotify()	Notifies a plug-in instance that a URL request has been completed.
NPP_Write()	Delivers data from a stream to a plug-in instance.
NPP_WriteReady()	Returns the maximum number of bytes that a plug-in instance will accept from an NPP_Write() call.

T A B L E 2 0 . 3 Navigator methods

Method	Description
NPN_DestroyStream()	Closes and deletes a stream.
NPN_ForceRedraw()	Causes window to be redrawn.
NPN_GetJavaEnv()	Returns the Java execution environment associated with the plug-in instance.

TABLE 20.3 Navigator methods (continued)

Method	Description
NPN_GetJavaPeer()	Returns the Java object associated with the plug-in instance.
NPN_GetURL()	Creates a new stream associated with a specified URL.
NPN_GetURLNotify()	Creates a new stream associated with a specified URL and notifies the plug-in instance of the completion of the request.
NPN_GetValue()	Returns information about a plug-in.
NPN_InvalidateRect()	Causes repainting of a rectangular area.
NPN_InvalidateRegion()	Causes repainting of a display region.
NPN_MemAlloc()	Allocates memory for use by the plug-in instance.
NPN_MemFlush()	Frees memory for use by the plug-in instance.
NPN_MemFree()	De-allocates memory used by the plug-in instance.
NPN_NewStream()	Creates a stream for communication between the plug-in instance and Navigator.
NPN_PostURL()	Causes data to be posted to a URL.
NPN_PostURLNotify()	Causes data to be posted to a URL and notifies the plug-in instance of the completion of the post operation.
NPN_RequestRead()	Requests data to be read from a stream.
NPN_SetValue()	Sets information about a plug-in.
NPN_Status()	Displays a status message.
NPN_UserAgent()	Returns the browser's user agent identifier.
NPN_Version()	Returns the version of the plug-in API.
NPN_Write()	Writes data to a stream read by Navigator.

Summary

In this chapter, you were introduced to browser plug-ins. You learned how they work, how they are used in Web pages, and how they interface with Navigator. You also covered some examples of popular plug-ins. In the next chapter, you'll learn how to access plug-ins from within JavaScript.

CHAPTER

TWENTY-ONE

21

Accessing Plug-Ins
with JavaScript

- Working with MIME Types

- Determining Installed Plug-Ins

- How Help ➤ About Plug-ins Works

- Detecting Plug-Ins

- Accessing Plug-Ins from within JavaScript

In Chapters 19 and 20, you learned how to take advantage of LiveConnect's features that enable communication between JavaScript scripts and Java applets. LiveConnect also supports communication between Java and plug-ins, and therefore between JavaScript and plug-ins. This allows you to use scripts to control audio and video players, specialized graphics viewers, and embedded applications, such as calendar and scheduling tools. In this chapter, you'll learn to use JavaScript to detect available plug-ins and determine the MIME types they support. You'll also learn how to communicate with plug-ins and control their behavior from JavaScript. By the time you've finished this chapter you'll be able to integrate plug-ins with your JavaScript applications.

Working with MIME Types

MIME types are fundamental to the operation of the Web. Browsers use MIME types to determine how to display files that are retrieved from Web servers. Similarly, in order to use a plug-in, it must be associated with a MIME type. The `mimeTypes` array, a property of the `navigator` object, describes all of the MIME types that are known to the browser.

The elements of the `mimeTypes` array are `mimeTypes` objects. Table 21.1 summarizes the properties of the `mimeTypes` object. These properties describe the MIME type and identify the plug-in that is installed and enabled to handle the MIME type. The `mimeTypes` object has no methods and is not associated with any events.

> **NOTE** The `plugins` object is covered in the next section.

TABLE 21.1 Properties of the `mimeTypes` object

Property	Description
type	The name of the MIME type.
description	A description of the MIME type.
enabledPlugin	The `plugins` object that is enabled to handle the MIME type. If no enabled plug-in is associated with the MIME type, then this value is `null`.
suffixes	A comma-separated list of the file extensions associated with the MIME type.

Listing 21.1 shows how the `mimeTypes` array is used. Open `mime.htm` with your browser. It will display a list of the MIME types that your browser is familiar with. Figure 21.1 shows the MIME types that my browser displayed. Your browser may display a different list depending on the plug-ins you've installed.

FIGURE 21.1

Displaying the MIME types that are familiar to your browser (Listing 21.1)

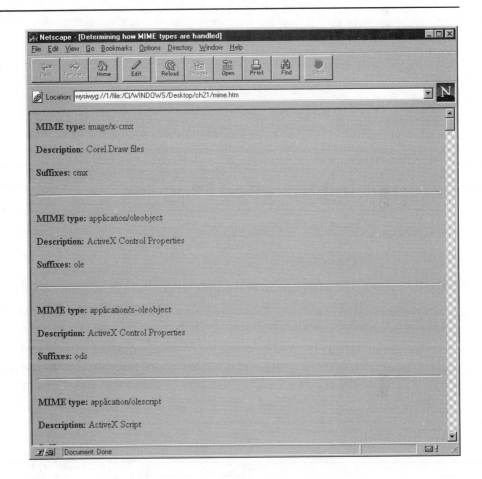

Listing 21.1. Using the mimeTypes object (mime.htm)

```
<HTML>
<HEAD>
<TITLE>Determining how MIME types are handled</TITLE>
</HEAD>
<BODY>
<SCRIPT LANGUAGE="JavaScript"><!--
m=navigator.mimeTypes
```

```
for(var i=0;i<m.length;++i){
 with(document){
  writeln('<P><B>MIME type: </B>'+m[i].type+'</P>')
  writeln('<P><B>Description: </B>'+m[i].description+'</P>')
  writeln('<P><B>Suffixes: </B>'+m[i].suffixes+'</P>')
  writeln('<HR>')
 }
}
// --></SCRIPT>
</BODY>
</HTML>
```

The script shown in Listing 21.1 iterates through the `mimeTypes` array and displays each `mimeTypes` object's `type`, `description`, and `suffixes` properties.

Determining Installed Plug-Ins

One of the first things that you'll want to do in order to use plug-ins is to determine which plug-ins are installed for a browser. JavaScript provides the `plugins` array for that purpose.

The `plugins` array is a property of the `navigator` object. It contains an entry for each plug-in that is installed for a browser. Each element of the array is a `plugins` object.

The `plugins` object has the five properties described in Table 21.2. It does not have any methods, and is not associated with any events. It does provide the capability to completely describe all plug-ins installed for a particular browser.

TABLE 21.2   Properties of the `plugins` object

Property	Description
name	The name of the plug-in.
filename	The name of the file from which the plug-in is loaded.
description	The description of the plug-in provided by the plug-in's developer.
length	The number of MIME types supported by the plug-in.
[]	An array of the MIME types supported by the plug-in. Each element is a `mimeTypes` object.

Each `plugins` object is also an array, of `mimeTypes` objects. This is confusing, so I'll summarize here how the `plugins` array and `plugins` object fit into the `navigator` object hierarchy:

- The `plugins` array is a property of the `navigator` object.

- Each element of the `plugins` array is a `plugins` object.

- The `plugins` object has five properties.

- One of those properties is an array of `mimeTypes` objects.

- The elements of this array are accessed by indexing the `plugins` object.

To clarify how the `plugins` array and the `plugins` object are used in a script, open `plugins.htm` (Listing 21.2) with your browser. Your browser will display a Web page similar to the one shown in Figure 21.2. As you can see, the information provided by the `plugins` object is very comprehensive.

Listing 21.2. Displaying plug-in information (plugins.htm)

```
<HTML>
<HEAD>
<TITLE>Determining Installed Plug-ins</TITLE>
</HEAD>
<BODY>
<SCRIPT LANGUAGE="JavaScript"><!--
p=navigator.plugins
for(var i=0;i<p.length;++i){
 with(document){
  writeln('<P><B>Plugin: </B>'+p[i].name+'</P>')
  writeln('<P><B>File name: </B>'+p[i].filename+'</P>')
  writeln('<P><B>Description: </B>'+p[i].description+'</P>')
  writeln('<P><B>MIME Types: </B>')
  for(var j=0;j<p[i].length;++j)
   writeln(p[i][j].type+'</BR>')
  writeln('</P><HR>')
 }
}
// --></SCRIPT>
</BODY>
</HTML>
```

FIGURE 21.2

Displaying plug-in information (Listing 21.2)

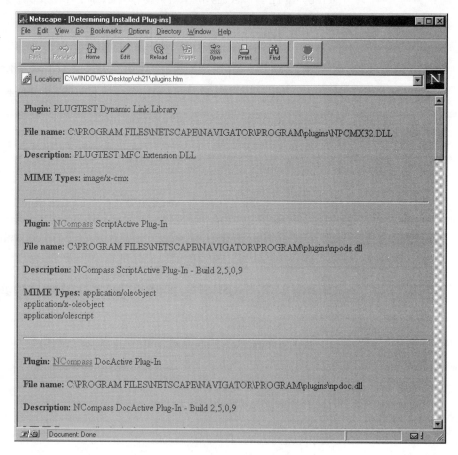

Listing 21.2 shows the contents of plugins.htm. A single script is included in the document's body. This script uses the p variable to refer to the plugins array. It then loops through each element of the plugins array and displays the name, filename, and description properties of the plugins objects. The length property is used to determine how many MIME types are supported by the plugins object. The type property of each of the mimeTypes objects referenced by each plugins object is printed.

NOTE The way that Netscape designed the `plugins` object is very messy. Instead of defining each `plugins` object as array of `mimeTypes` objects, it would have been much cleaner to have given the `plugins` object a `mime-Types` property that would consist of an array of `mimeTypes` objects.

How Help ➤ About Plug-ins Works

When you select About Plug-ins from the Navigator Help menu, your browser displays a description of all plug-ins supported by your browser, in the format shown in Figure 21.3. If you select Document Source from the View menu, you'll see the HTML file shown in Listing 21.3. This file provides a good example of how the `plugins` and `mimeTypes` objects can be used together to list and describe all of the `plugins` known to a browser.

Listing 21.3. The About Plug-ins script (about.htm)

```
<HTML>
<HEAD>
<TITLE>About Plug-ins</TITLE>
</HEAD>
<BODY>
<SCRIPT language="javascript">

<!-- JavaScript to enumerate and display all installed
  plug-ins -->

numPlugins = navigator.plugins.length;

if (numPlugins > 0)
  document.writeln("<b><font size=+3>Installed plug-ins
    </font></b><br>");
else
  document.writeln("<b><font size=+2>No plug-ins are
    installed.</font></b><br>");
  document.writeln("For more information on Netscape
    plug-ins, <A HREF=http://home.netscape.com/comprod/
    products/navigator/version_2.0/plugins/index.html>
    click here</A>.<p><hr>");

for (i = 0; i < numPlugins; i++)
{
```

```
plugin = navigator.plugins[i];

document.write("<center><font size=+1><b>");
document.write(plugin.name);
document.writeln("</b></font></center><br>");

document.writeln("<dl>");
document.writeln("<dd>File name:");
document.write(plugin.filename);
document.write("<dd><br>");
document.write(plugin.description);
document.writeln("</dl>");
document.writeln("<p>");

document.writeln("<table width=100% border=2 cellpadding=5>");
document.writeln("<tr>");
document.writeln("<th width=20%><font size=-1>Mime Type</font>
</th>");
document.writeln("<th width=50%><font size=-1>Description
</font></th>");
document.writeln("<th width=20%><font size=-1>Suffixes</font>
</th>");
document.writeln("<th><font size=-1>Enabled</th>");
document.writeln("</tr>");
numTypes = plugin.length;
for (j = 0; j < numTypes; j++)
{
 mimetype = plugin[j];

 if (mimetype)
 {
  enabled = "No";
  enabledPlugin = mimetype.enabledPlugin;
  if (enabledPlugin && (enabledPlugin.name == plugin.name))
   enabled = "Yes";

  document.writeln("<tr align=center>");
  document.writeln("<td>");
  document.write(mimetype.type);
  document.writeln("</td>");
  document.writeln("<td>");
  document.write(mimetype.description);
  document.writeln("</td>");
  document.writeln("<td>");
  document.write(mimetype.suffixes);
```

```
   document.writeln("</td>");
   document.writeln("<td>");
   document.writeln(enabled);
   document.writeln("</td>");
   document.writeln("</tr>");
  }
 }

 document.write("</table>");
 document.write("<p><hr><p>");
}


</SCRIPT>
</BODY>
</HTML>
```

FIGURE 21.3

The About Plug-ins
Display (Listing 21.3)

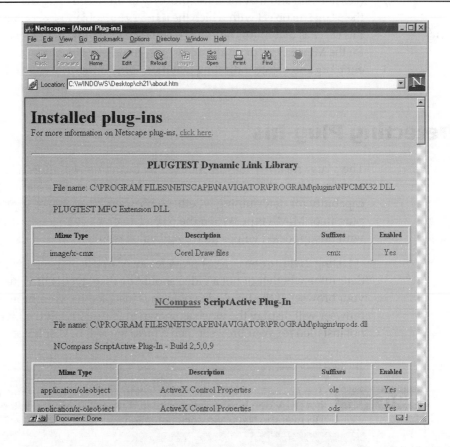

The `about.htm` file contains a single script in the document body. The `numPlugins` variable is set to the number of `plugins` objects contained in the `plugins` array. After displaying header information, the script loops through the `plugins` array and displays the `name`, `filename`, and `description` properties of each `plugins` object. The script then constructs a table to describe the `mimeTypes` objects associated with each `plugins` object. The table lists the `type`, `description`, and `suffixes` properties, and contains a fourth column that identifies whether an enabled plug-in exists for the MIME type.

The `numTypes` property is set to the `length` property of each `plugins` object. The script then loops through the array of `mimeTypes` objects of each `plugins` object and displays the table data. The `enabledPlugin` variable is set to the value of the `mimeTypes` object's `enabledPlugin` property.

The `if` statement that follows this assignment checks if `enabledPlugin` is *true* (i.e., not *null*) and that the `name` property of `enabledPlugin` is the same as that of the `plugins` object with which the `mimeTypes` object is associated. The reason for this check is that `enabledPlugin` could be *null*, indicating that no plug-in is enabled for the MIME type, or `enabledPlugin` could have its `name` property set to a different `plugins` object, indicating that the another plug-in is enabled for the MIME type.

Detecting Plug-Ins

The `plugins` array may be indexed by the name of a plug-in, and the `mimeTypes` array may be indexed by the name of a MIME type. This feature provides a handy capability for determining whether a browser is capable of supporting a particular plug-in or MIME type. When the `plugins` or `mimeTypes` arrays are accessed with unsupported values then a *null* value results.

Listing 21.4 (`detect.htm`) provides an example of using the above features to determine whether or not a video should be displayed. Open `detect.htm` with your browser. If the LiveVideo plug-in is installed for your browser then your browser will display the video as shown in Figure 21.4. If the LiveVideo plug-in is not installed for your browser then a message will be displayed in lieu of the video.

NOTE   The AUTOSTART attribute can be set to TRUE or FALSE to specify whether or not LiveVideo is to automatically start playing the video. In the next chapter, I'll cover the Netscape documentation for LiveVideo and LiveAudio.

FIGURE 21.4

The video is displayed.
(Listing 21.4)

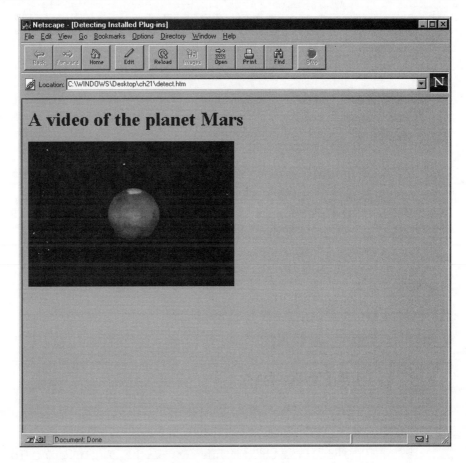

Listing 21.4. Determining whether the LiveVideo plug-in is installed (detect.htm)

```
<HTML>
<HEAD>
<TITLE>Detecting Installed Plug-ins</TITLE>
</HEAD>
<BODY>
<H1>A video of the planet Mars</H1>
<SCRIPT LANGUAGE="JavaScript"><!--
plugins=navigator.plugins
```

```
if(plugins["NPAVI32 Dynamic Link Library"]){
  document.write('<EMBED SRC="mars.avi" AUTOSTART="TRUE"')
  document.writeln('WIDTH="350" HEIGHT="240">')
}else{
  document.write('Sorry. Your browser does not have ')
  document.writeln('LiveVideo installed.')
}
// --></SCRIPT>
</BODY>
</HTML>
```

NOTE If your browser does not support LiveVideo, you should upgrade to a version that does. If you are using a non-Windows OS then you'll have to follow along with the book. The reason I use LiveVideo and AVI files in this chapter and Chapter 22 is that LiveVideo provides full support of LiveConnect and therefore allows plug-in methods to be accessed from JavaScript.

Accessing Plug-Ins from within JavaScript

With LiveConnect, accessing plug-ins is easy—you use the embeds array. The embeds array is a property of the document object. The embeds array contains an entry for each of the document's <embed> tags. Each element of the embeds array is a plugin object.

The plugin object is different from the plugins object. The plugins objects, on the one hand, are elements of the plugins array, which is a property of the navigator object. The plugin objects, on the other hand, are elements of the embeds array, which is a property of the document object. Further, whereas the plugins object *describes* a plug-in, the plugin object *provides access* to the properties and methods of a plug-in.

Each plugin object is also a property of the document object. If an <embed> tag contains a name attribute, then the plugin object can be accessed by its name.

Listing 21.5 (access.htm) provides an example of how the plugin object may be used to access and control a plug-in. Open access.htm with your browser.

After a few seconds, your browser loads and plays a Mars video, as shown in Figure 21.5. This is the same video as shown in Figure 21.4 except for one difference: this time you are controlling it from within JavaScript. Click the Start button and the video is rewound to the beginning, as shown in Figure 21.6. Click the Play button and the video begins playing again. Click the Stop button to freeze the video on a particular frame. Use the Frame Forward and Frame Backward buttons to advance or rewind the video one frame at a time. Click the End button to go to the last frame of the video, as shown in Figure 21.7.

FIGURE 21.5

The video automatically plays when the page loads. (Listing 21.5)

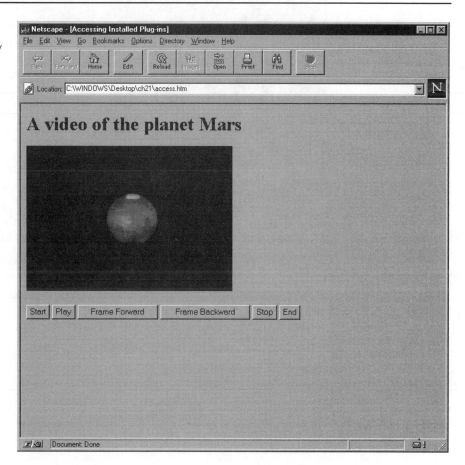

FIGURE 21.6

Clicking the Start button
rewinds the video to the
beginning. (Listing 21.5)

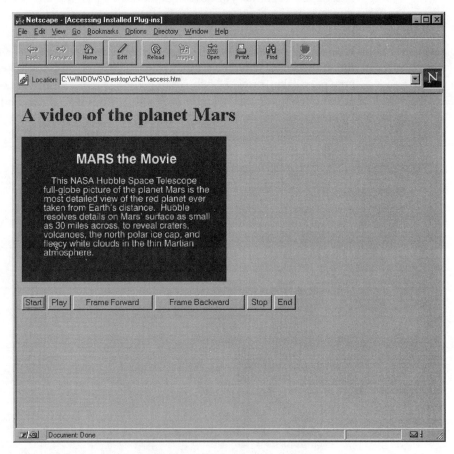

Listing 21.5. Accessing a plug-in (access.htm)

```
<HTML>
<HEAD>
<TITLE>Accessing Installed Plug-ins</TITLE>
<SCRIPT LANGUAGE="JavaScript"><!--
function playVideo() {
 window.document.mars.play()
}
function stopVideo() {
 window.document.mars2.stop()
}
```

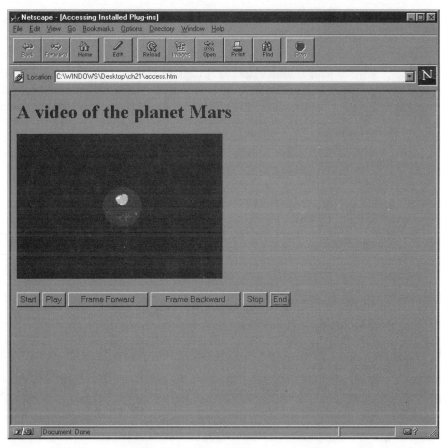

```
function rewindVideo() {
 window.document.mars.rewind()
}
function forwardVideo() {
 window.document.mars.forward()
}
function forward() {
 window.document.mars.frameBack()
}
function back() {
 window.document.mars.frameForward()
}
```

```
// --></SCRIPT>
</HEAD>
<BODY>
<H1>A video of the planet Mars</H1>
<SCRIPT LANGUAGE="JavaScript"><!--
plugins=navigator.plugins
if(plugins["NPAVI32 Dynamic Link Library"]){
  document.write('<EMBED SRC="mars.avi" NAME="mars" ')
  document.writeln('AUTOSTART="TRUE" WIDTH="350" HEIGHT="240">')
}else{
  document.write('Sorry. Your browser does not have ')
  document.writeln('LiveVideo installed.')
}
// --></SCRIPT>
<FORM>
<INPUT TYPE="BUTTON" VALUE="Start" onClick="rewindVideo()">
<INPUT TYPE="BUTTON" VALUE="Play" onClick="playVideo()">
<INPUT TYPE="BUTTON" VALUE="Frame Forward" onClick="forward()">
<INPUT TYPE="BUTTON" VALUE="Frame Backward" onClick="back()">
<INPUT TYPE="BUTTON" VALUE="Stop" onClick="stopVideo()">
<INPUT TYPE="BUTTON" VALUE="End" onClick="forwardVideo()">
</FORM>
</BODY>
</HTML>
```

Listing 21.5 shows how easy it is to access and control a plug-in from JavaScript. The onClick event handlers of the form's buttons are JavaScript functions that invoke the methods of the LiveVideo plug-in.

NOTE

Note that the frameBack() and frameForward() methods of the Live-Video plug-in work in an opposite manner than you might expect—frame-Back() causes the video to move forward, and frameForward() causes the video to move back.

The script in the document body is similar to the one used in Listing 21.4. The only difference is that the <embed> tag is given a name attribute.

Summary

In this chapter, you learned how to use JavaScript to work with plug-ins. You learned how to use the `plugins` and `mimetypes` objects to detect available plug-ins and determine the MIME types associated with these plug-ins. You also learned how to use LiveConnect to communicate with plug-ins and control their behavior. In the next chapter, you'll learn how to use LiveConnect to integrate JavaScript and plug-ins in your Web applications.

CHAPTER

TWENTY-TWO

22

Advanced Use of Plug-Ins

- Netscape's Plug-In Documentation

- LiveVideo and LiveAudio

- The `netscape.plugin.Plugin` class

- Listing Plug-In Methods

- Synchronizing Multiple Plug-Ins

- Assisting Users in Installing Plug-Ins

- Developing Your Own Plug-Ins

In the last chapter, you learned how to use JavaScript to access and control the LiveVideo plug-in. You now have a basic understanding of how to combine JavaScript and plug-ins in your Web applications. In this chapter, you'll learn some additional techniques for accessing plug-ins from JavaScript. You'll learn how to determine what methods are available, and how to synchronize multiple plug-ins. You'll also learn how to assist users in installing plug-ins. Finally, we'll point you to information that you'll need if you decide to develop your own plug-ins.

Netscape's Plug-In Documentation

When you worked the last LiveVideo example of Chapter 21 you were probably wondering how I was able to determine what methods were supported by the LiveVideo plug-in. Part of the answer is that Netscape provides plug-in documentation at its Web site. This documentation includes the description of the `netscape.plugin.Plugin` Java class, which defines the minimal set of functions to be implemented by any LiveConnect-capable plug-in (and therefore the LiveVideo plug-in).

The other part of the answer is that LiveConnect lists all of the properties and methods of a plug-in as properties of whichever `plugin` object is associated with the plug-in. This lets you use the `for in` statement to list all of the plug-in's properties and methods.

The following subsections summarize the plug-in documentation provided by Netscape for LiveVideo and LiveAudio. Subsequent subsections describe the `netscape.plugin.Plugin` class and show how to use the `for in` statement to list all of a plug-in's properties and methods.

LiveVideo

You've already used LiveVideo in Chapter 21 and are familiar with most of its methods. LiveVideo plays video files that are in the AVI format. Although it is LiveConnect-capable, it is currently supported only on the Windows 95 and Windows NT operating system platforms.

In this section, I'll summarize the LiveVideo documentation provided by JavaScript. In the later section, "Listing Plug-In Methods," you'll learn how to list all of the properties of a plug-in.

The LiveVideo plug-in supports three application-specific attributes: AUTOSTART, LOOP, and ALIGN. The AUTOSTART and LOOP attributes take on the values of *TRUE* or *FALSE*. Their default values are *FALSE*. The AUTOSTART attribute determines whether the plug-in should automatically play the movie when the page is loaded. The LOOP attribute determines whether the video should be played in a continuous loop. The ALIGN attribute controls text alignment around the video display area. It is used in the same way as the <img> tag.

The LiveVideo documentation identifies four methods that may be used with the LiveVideo plug-in. These methods are described in Table 22.1. You'll learn additional methods in the section "Listing Plug-In Methods" later in this chapter.

TABLE 22.1 Documented LiveVideo plug-in methods

Method	Description
play()	Plays the video starting at the current frame
stop()	Stops playing the video at the current frame
rewind()	Sets the current frame to the first frame of the video
seek(n)	Sets the current frame to the frame specified by n

LiveAudio

LiveAudio is a very powerful LiveConnect-capable audio player that is capable of playing audio files that are in the WAV, AIFF, AU, and MIDI format. You've used the Netscape LiveAudio plug-in in examples of previous chapters. You probably thought that it was awkward to work with. It *is* awkward to work with, at least in its default configuration. However, LiveAudio provides a number of configuration options which can be used to tailor the way it appears and behaves.

Table 22.2 describes attributes that can be used with the LiveAudio plug-in. They can be used to hide or change the appearances of the audio player or to customize the way that an audio file is played.

TABLE 22.2 Attributes of the LiveAudio plug-in

Attribute	Description
ALIGN	Controls the way text is displayed around the audio player's controls. It is used in the same manner as the `<img>` tag.
AUTOSTART	When set to *TRUE* the audio player begins playing the audio file when the Web page is loaded. It is set to *FALSE* by default.
CONTROLS	May be set to CONSOLE, SMALLCONSOLE, PLAYBUTTON, PAUSEBUTTON, STOPBUTTON, or VOLUMELEVER to identify what type of audio control is to be displayed.
ENDTIME	Takes a *minutes:seconds* value that identifies where in the audio file the playback is to end.
HIDDEN	When set to *TRUE* this attribute causes the audio controls to be hidden.
LOOP	Takes the values *TRUE, FALSE,* or an integer. If set to *TRUE* it causes the audio file to be played in a continuous looping fashion. If set to *FALSE* it turns off looping. If an integer value is supplied then the audio file is repeatedly played the specified number of times.
MASTERSOUND	This attribute is used with the name attribute to identify which file contains the actual file to be played.
NAME	Rather than naming the plug-in so that it can be accessed from JavaScript, this attribute is used to name a group of controls that apply to a single sound.
STARTTIME	Takes a *minutes:seconds* value that identifies where in the audio file the playback is to start.
VOLUME	Uses the values 0 to 100 to specify the percentage of the volume setting at which the audio file is to be played.

You'll learn how to use the attributes of Table 22.2 in Chapter 24, where you'll learn how to use the `layer` object to implement multimedia applications.

Table 22.3 identifies LiveAudio methods provided for use by JavaScript. These methods provide all of the capabilities needed to implement custom audio controls.

TABLE 22.3 Methods of the LiveAudio plug-in

Method	Description
end_time(*n*)	Sets the end time *n* in seconds
fade_from_to(*v1*,*v2*)	Fades the volume level from *v1* to *v2*
fade_to(*v*)	Fades the volume level to *v*
GetVolume()	Gets the current volume level
IsPaused()	Returns true if the audio player is currently paused
IsPlaying()	Returns true if the audio player is currently playing
IsReady()	Returns true if the audio player has been loaded
pause()	Causes the audio player to pause
play()	Causes the audio player to start playing
play(*n*,*url*)	Causes the audio player to start playing the first *n* seconds of the file located at the specified URL
setvol(*v*)	Sets the volume to the specified level
start_at_beginning()	Sets the start time to the beginning of the file
start_time(*n*)	Sets the start time to the specified number of seconds
stop()	Stops the playing of the audio file
stop_at_end()	Sets the end time to the end of the file

NOTE Volume levels in LiveAudio methods are expressed as an integer in the range of 0 to 100.

The *netscape.plugin.Plugin* class

The interface to LiveConnect-capable plug-ins is specified by the `netscape` `.plugin.Plugin` class. LiveConnect-capable plug-ins are subclasses of this class and add methods to it to enable the plug-ins to be accessed from Java and JavaScript. The `netscape.plugin.Plugin` class is of primary interest to plug-in developers, but as you'll see in the next section, it is good for you to know which methods it defines. This knowledge will help you to identify which methods are inherited from the Plugin class and which are specific to a particular plug-in. The methods of the `netscape.plugin.Plugin` class are described in Table 22.4.

TABLE 22.4 Methods of the `netscape.plugin.Plugin` class

Method	Description
Plugin()	The class constructor
destroy()	Automatically invoked when the plug-in is destroyed
getPeer()	Returns the native object corresponding to the plug-in instance
getWindow()	Returns the JavaScript window in which the plug-in displays its results
init()	Automatically invoked to initialize a plug-in
isActive()	Determines whether the plug-in is active

Listing Plug-In Methods

The publicly accessible properties and methods of LiveConnect-capable plug-ins are accessible as the properties of `plugin` objects. This lets you use the `for in` statement to find all of the undocumented features of a plug-in. Listing 22.1 (`listprop.htm`) illustrates this technique. When you open `listprop.htm` with your browser, it displays a Web page like that shown in Figure 22.1. Since I did not use the `WIDTH` and `HEIGHT` attributes in the `<embed>` tag, the video player display (the dark box at the top of the Web page) is minimized. This is fine since for our purposes we are more interested in LiveVideo's properties and methods than in watching the video.

FIGURE 22.1

The properties of the LiveVideo `plugin` object (Listing 22.1)

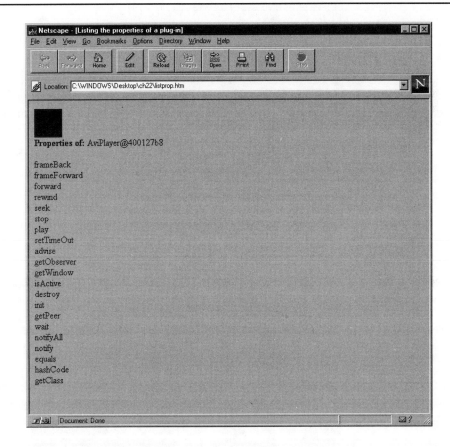

Listing 22.1. Listing plug-in properties (listprop.htm)

```
<HTML>
<HEAD>
<TITLE>Listing the properties of a plug-in</TITLE>
<SCRIPT LANGUAGE="JavaScript"><!--
function listProperties(obj) {
 document.writeln("<B>Properties of: </B>"+obj+"<BR>")
 for(var p in obj)
  document.writeln(p+"<BR>")
}
// --></SCRIPT>
</HEAD>
<BODY>
<EMBED SRC="Mars.avi"><BR>
```

```
<SCRIPT LANGUAGE="JavaScript"><!--
listProperties(document.embeds[0])
// --></SCRIPT>
</BODY>
</HTML>
```

listprop.htm uses an `<embed>` tag to display the Mars.avi file. The script in the document's body invokes the listProperties() function with the Live-Video plugin object passed as an argument.

listProperties() uses the for in statement to loop through and display the properties of the obj parameter.

listprop.htm may be easily adapted to display the properties of other plug-ins. Listing 22.2 shows the listaud.htm file which lists the properties of the LiveAudio plug-in. Figure 22.2 shows the Web page it displays.

FIGURE 22.2

The properties of the LiveAudio plug-in object (Listing 22.2)

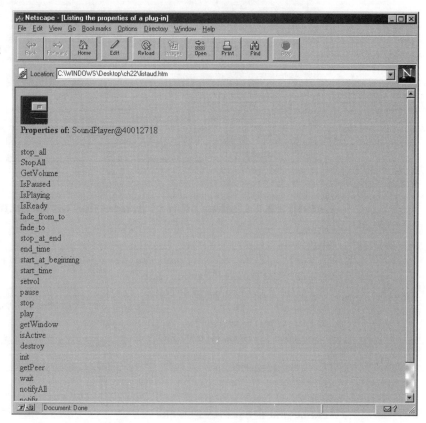

Listing 22.2. Tailoring listprop.htm (listaud.htm)

```
<HTML>
<HEAD>
<TITLE>Listing the properties of a plug-in</TITLE>
<SCRIPT LANGUAGE="JavaScript"><!--
function listProperties(obj) {
  document.writeln("<B>Properties of: </B>"+obj+"<BR>")
  for(var p in obj)
    document.writeln(p+"<BR>")
}
// --></SCRIPT>
</HEAD>
<BODY>
<EMBED SRC="test.wav"><BR>
<SCRIPT LANGUAGE="JavaScript"><!--
listProperties(document.embeds[0])
// --></SCRIPT>
</BODY>
</HTML>
```

Synchronizing Multiple Plug-Ins

In some multimedia applications you may wish to use two or more plug-ins. For example, the `Mars.avi` video that you used in this chapter and the previous chapter was converted from a NASA MPEG video, and it does not contain any sound. If you're creating a multimedia application that uses the `Mars.avi` video, you may want to add an audio file to provide a narration for the video.

When using two or more plug-ins on the same Web page you may need to synchronize the plug-ins so that they start and stop together and display the correct information at the right time.

In general, most plug-ins do not provide synchronization primitives. To ensure that your plug-ins operate in tandem you can provide synchronization at the user interface level. Listing 22.3 (`synchro.htm`) provides a simple example of this type of synchronization.

Open `synchro.htm` with your browser. It displays the Web page shown in Figure 22.3. Click the Play button, and the video and audio files are played simultaneously. Click the Stop button, and the video and audio players stop at the same time. Click Play again, and they both play where they left off. The Start button "rewinds" the video and audio files, and the End button displays the last frame of the video file and stops the audio file.

FIGURE 22.3

The initial script display (Listing 22.3)

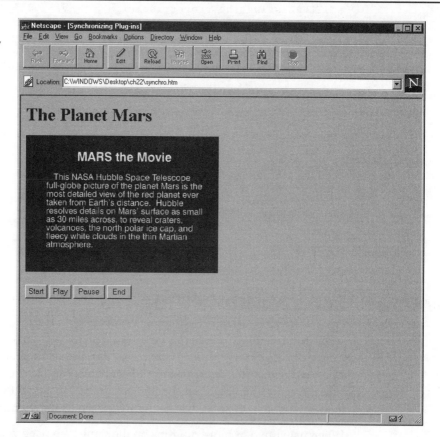

Listing 22.3. Synchronizing two plug-ins (synchro.htm)

```
<HTML>
<HEAD>
<TITLE>Synchronizing Plug-ins</TITLE>
<SCRIPT LANGUAGE="JavaScript"><!--
function play() {
 window.document.embeds[0].play()
 window.document.embeds[1].play()
}
function stop() {
 window.document.embeds[0].stop()
```

```
  window.document.embeds[1].pause()
}
function start() {
  window.document.embeds[0].rewind()
  window.document.embeds[1].stop()
}
function end() {
  window.document.embeds[0].forward()
  window.document.embeds[1].stop()
}
// --></SCRIPT>
</HEAD>
<BODY onLoad="start()">
<H1>The Planet Mars</H1>
<EMBED SRC="mars.avi" NAME="video" AUTOSTART="TRUE"
 WIDTH="350" HEIGHT="240">
<EMBED SRC="mars.wav" HIDDEN="TRUE">
<FORM>
<INPUT TYPE="BUTTON" VALUE="Start" onClick="start()">
<INPUT TYPE="BUTTON" VALUE="Play" onClick="play()">
<INPUT TYPE="BUTTON" VALUE="Pause" onClick="stop()">
<INPUT TYPE="BUTTON" VALUE=" End " onClick="end()">
</FORM>
</BODY>
</HTML>
```

Listing 22.3 shows how the two plug-ins are synchronized. The document body loads the LiveVideo plug-in to display the mars.avi file. It then loads the LiveAudio plug-in to play the mars.wav file. The <body> tag's onClick event handler invokes the start() function to ensure that both files are rewound upon document loading. The four functions in the document header are used as follows.

play() This function invokes the play() method of both plug-ins to cause the plug-ins to begin playing at the same time. It handles the clicking of the Play button.

stop() This function invokes the stop() method of the LiveVideo plug-in and the pause() method of the LiveAudio plug-in to cause both plug-ins to stop playing at the current position within their respective files. It handles the clicking of the Stop button.

start() This function invokes the rewind() method of the LiveVideo plug-in and the stop() method of the LiveAudio plug-in to cause both plug-ins to rewind their respective files to their initial position. It handles the clicking of the Start button.

end() This function invokes the `forward()` method of the LiveVideo plug-in and the `stop()` method of the LiveAudio plug-in. This causes the LiveVideo plug-in to display its last frame and the LiveAudio plug-in to restart. The `end()` function handles the clicking of the End button.

Assisting Users in Installing Plug-Ins

Navigator provides a special feature to assist the user in installing plug-ins that may be required by a script. When a user displays a page that requires a new plug-in to be installed, it displays a plug-in icon in place of the plug-in and launches a dialog box that provides the user with two buttons: *Get the Plugin* and *Cancel*.

- If the user clicks *Get the Plugin*, then Navigator opens the URL specified by the `PLUGINSPAGE` attribute of the plug-in's `<embed>` tag. The designated URL should contain instructions on how to download and install the plug-in. (If the `PLUGINSPAGE` attribute is not supplied, then the Netscape plug-ins page is loaded.)

- If the user clicks the *Cancel* button instead of the *Get the Plugin* button, then the assisted plug-in installation process is aborted. If the user changes their mind then they can click the plug-in icon again and the dialog box will be redisplayed.

Listing 22.4 (`assist.htm`) shows how assisted plug-in installation is implemented. It contains an `<embed>` tag with the `SRC` attribute set to `test.ijk` and the `PLUGINSPAGE` attribute set to the following URL:

http://www.jaworski.com/javascript/install.htm

I've configured my Web server to return a MIME type of *application/x-ijk* for files with the `.ijk` suffix.

Listing 22.4. Assisted plug-in installation (assist.htm)

```
<HTML>
<HEAD>
<TITLE>Assisted Plug-In Installation</TITLE>
</HEAD>
<BODY>
<H1>This page uses the ijk plugin</H1>
<EMBED SRC="test.ijk"
```

```
PLUGINSPAGE="http://www.jaworski.com/javascript/install.htm">
</BODY>
</HTML>
```

In order to see how it works, you'll have to load it from my Web server. (If you load it from your local file system the correct MIME type will not be returned.) Open *http://www.jaworski.com/javascript/assist.htm* with your browser. It will display the Web file shown in Figure 22.4. Note how the plug-in object is displayed in the left corner of the window.

Immediately after the Web page shown in Figure 22.4 is loaded, the dialog box shown in Figure 22.5 is displayed. This dialog box gives you the option of obtaining and installing the plug-in. Click *Get the Plugin* and the Web page shown in Figure 22.6 (Listing 22.5) is loaded and displayed. This Web page would be used to provide instructions on downloading and installing the plug-in.

FIGURE 22.4

The plug-in object
(Listing 22.4)

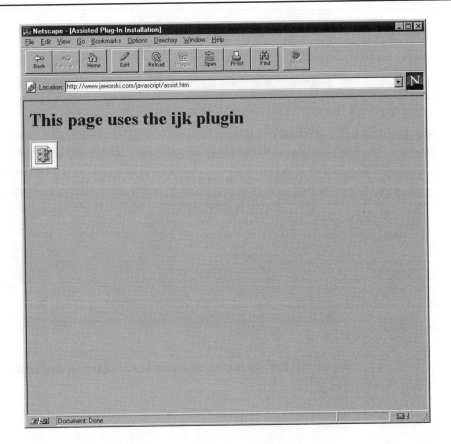

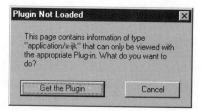

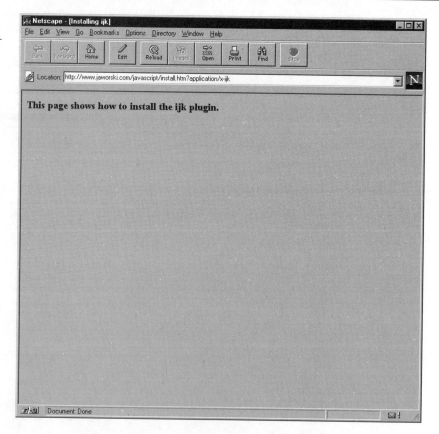

Listing 22.5. The installation instructions (install.htm)

```
<HTML>
<HEAD>
<TITLE>Installing ijk</TITLE>
```

```
</HEAD>
<BODY>
<H3>This page shows how to install the ijk plugin.</H3>
</BODY>
</HTML>
```

Developing Your Own Plug-Ins

There are over a hundred Navigator plug-ins currently available. In almost all cases, therefore, you'll be able to use an available plug-in for your Web application development. However, there may come a time when you'll need to develop your own plug-ins. Fortunately, all the information you'll need for this task is available online in the documentation section of the Netscape library. You can access the library at the following URL:

http://developer.netscape.com/library/documentation/index.html

The documents described in Table 22.5 will help you get started in developing your plug-in. Links to these documents may be found on the *Mastering JavaScript* home page at *http://www.jaworski.com/javascript/*.

TABLE 22.5 Documentation available for developing your own plug-ins

Document	Description
LiveConnect/Plug-In Developer's Guide	The complete guide to writing Navigator plug-ins. It describes the user's and programmer's view of plug-ins, documents the Plug-In API, and identifies the steps involved in creating a plug-in.
LiveConnecting Plug-Ins with Java	This document shows how to interface plug-ins with Java. It covers calling Java methods from plug-ins and calling plug-in methods from Java.
The Java Runtime Interface (JRI)	The JRI provides a standard interface to Java services. This document describes the JRI and shows how to use it to develop applets and plug-ins independent of the particular Java version used by Navigator.
LiveConnect Communication	This is a section of the *JavaScript Guide* that shows how to use LiveConnect to interface JavaScript with Java and plug-ins.
Using LiveConnect	A summary description of LiveConnect.

If you are going to be developing your own plug-in, you'll also need a version of the LiveConnect/Plug-In software development kit (SDK) for the particular OS platform on which your plug-in will run. Versions of the SDK are available for Macintosh, OS/2 Warp, Windows, and Unix platforms. The SDK provides the header files, common source code and binary files, and tools that you'll need to develop a plug-in. It also provides a lot of useful examples. Links to the SDK can be found in the *LiveConnect/Plug-In Developer's Guide*.

Summary

In this chapter, you learned some additional techniques for accessing plug-ins from JavaScript. You learned how to use the `for in` statement to determine what plug-in methods are available for a particular plug-in. You learned how to work with multiple plug-ins and various approaches to synchronizing plug-ins. You also learned how to assist users in installing plug-ins.

This is the last chapter of Part 5. In the next part, you'll learn about the newest features of Navigator 4.0 that are accessible to JavaScript.

PART VI

Advanced Applications

CHAPTER

TWENTY-THREE

23

JavaScript Style Sheets

- What Are Style Sheets?

- JavaScript Style Sheets versus Cascading Style Sheets

- Defining Style Sheets

- Using the `<LINK>` Tag to Include Styles

- Using Multiple Style Sheets

One of the most exciting capabilities provided with HTML 3.2 is the capability to specify the *style* in which different HTML elements are formatted and displayed. Before the advent of style sheets, Web page authors were confined to using the standard formatting provided by individual HTML elements. Headings, paragraphs, lists, and other text elements provided little variety or flexibility in the way that they were presented. Style sheets changed all that—now Web authors can control the color, font, margins, and many other aspects of individual HTML elements. This powerful new capability results in Web pages that are livelier, more colorful, and more closely tailored to their target audience. This means that you can create, on the one hand, more stirring pages for those who want to be moved, and, on the other hand, more tightly organized pages for those who admire standardization.

In this chapter, you'll be introduced to style sheets. You'll learn the differences between JavaScript style sheets and the "Cascading Style Sheets" that have been developed by the World Wide Web Consortium. You'll cover the tags, properties, and attributes used with JavaScript style sheets, and learn how to work with both internally and externally defined styles. When you finish this chapter, you'll be able to take advantage of JavaScript style sheets to add both flair and consistency to your Web applications.

What Are Style Sheets?

Style sheets provide the capability to control the way in which HTML elements, such as headings, paragraphs, and lists are laid out and displayed. They enable Web page designers to use standard HTML elements in a limitless variety of new ways. For example, before style sheets were developed, Web authors had six heading levels to work with. These headings could be right-justified, left-justified, or centered. They could be made to use a different size font or display style, but not much more. With style sheets, you can specify that different-level headings be displayed with different colors, font styles, font sizes, and more. You can also specify the way that headings are laid out—the spacing before and after the heading and the margins used with the heading. You can collect styles for certain types of projects and save them in style *sheets*. With style sheets, you have complete flexibility and control in the way that the pages of your Web applications are presented.

You may wonder what possible uses you can make of all this flexibility. Well, if you develop Web pages for a number of different audiences, then style sheets are an absolute must. You can create a standard company style sheet to lay out the pages that you develop at work, a style sheet to lay out documents that are unique to your department at school, a style sheet to create your own casual looking personal Web pages, and a style sheet of really outrageous styles for the Web pages that you develop for your friends, kids, or hobbies.

Within an organization, different styles can be used for different departments (engineering vs. marketing), different types of documents (product descriptions vs. design specifications), or for different types of information (company sensitive vs. freely distributable).

JavaScript Style Sheets versus Cascading Style Sheets

Much of the underlying technology of the Web, including HTML, Web browsers, and Web servers, was developed at the CERN physics laboratory in Geneva, Switzerland. For a bunch of scientists, they sure turn out some amazing internetworking technologies. Style sheets are another development of CERN. In 1994, work on HTML style sheets was initiated, and in December 1996, a specification called Cascading Style Sheets was proposed. The style sheets are referred to as *cascading* because the specification allows for multiple levels of styles to be applied to a single document where the output of some styles are the input of others.

The Cascading Style Sheets, referred to by their acronym CSS1, are a natural outgrowth of CERN's involvement in the development of HTML 3.2. HTML 3.2 and CSS1 are implemented by several browsers, including Netscape Navigator 4.0, Internet Explorer 3.0 and 4.0, and HotJava 1.0. In addition to supporting CSS1, Netscape Navigator 4.0 also supports a JavaScript-based approach to style sheets, referred to as JavaScript style sheets, or JSS for short. JavaScript style sheets support the styles provided by CSS1 and have the advantage of making these styles available as JavaScript *properties*. This advantage enables style properties to be created, read, and updated via JavaScript scripts. You can think of JavaScript style sheets as CSS1 style properties that have become JavaScript-enabled.

Being a JavaScript programmer, you will find JSS more intuitive and easier to use than CSS. You will also appreciate the capability to work with style properties within scripts. However, the advantages of JSS are offset by the fact that only Navigator 4.0 supports JSS. This means that only users with Navigator 4.0 (and beyond) will be able to view the fancy styles that you specify with JSS. All other users will view your Web pages using the default HTML style. This tradeoff is not all that bad, really—with JSS you can still appeal to the majority of Web users, because its fallback mode for those users who do not take advantage of Navigator 4.0's browsing capabilities is still as appealing as it always was.

NOTE The remainder of this chapter describes JavaScript style sheets. For a complete treatment of Cascading Style Sheets, refer to the W3C CSS1 proposal. It is available at the URL *http://www.w3.org/pub/WWW/TR/REC-CSS1*.

An Introductory Example

To give you a better feel for how style sheets work, we'll start off with a simple example. Listing 23.1 contains a document that displays a few headings and paragraphs in different colors. Figure 23.1 provides a black-and-white representation of the Web page that is displayed by Navigator 4.0.

FIGURE 23.1

A simple introduction to JavaScript style sheets

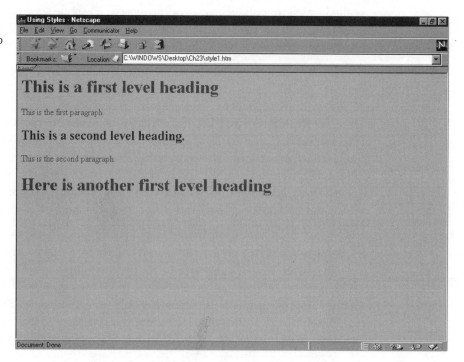

Listing 23.1. An introductory style sheet example (style1.htm)

```
<HTML>
<HEAD>
<TITLE>Using Styles</TITLE>
<STYLE TYPE="text/javascript">
document.tags.BODY.backgroundColor = "cyan";
document.tags.H1.color="red";
document.tags.H2.color="blue";
document.tags.P.color="green";
</STYLE>
</HEAD>
<BODY>
<H1>This is a first level heading</H1>
<P>This is the first paragraph.</P>
<H2>This is a second level heading.</H2>
<P>This is the second paragraph.</P>
<H1>Here is another first level heading</H1>
</BODY>
</HTML>
```

Open style1.htm with your browser (Navigator 4.0 or better) to see how the document is displayed. You'll probably be aghast at the awful color scheme that I've chosen—style sheets make it as easy to convey a lack of a sense of style as easily as a well-developed sense of style. But please bear with me. Your document background color should be set to cyan. The first and last headings in the document are level-1 headings that are displayed in red. In the middle of the document is a level-2 heading that is displayed in blue. The document contains two one-line paragraphs that are displayed in green.

If you look at Listing 23.1, you'll see that except for the <STYLE> element in the document head, the rest of the document appears to be just regular HTML. That's the power of style sheets—you can change the formatting and display of an entire document by just changing the style of the document. In the case of style1.htm, all you had to do was add the <STYLE> element to change a very normal looking HTML document into a very unusual looking one.

The <STYLE> tags shown in Listing 23.1 are surrounding tags. They surround four JavaScript statements which assign color values to different subproperties of the document.tags property. The <STYLE> tag uses the TYPE attribute to determine what type of style sheet is in effect. The text/javascript value is used to identify a JavaScript style sheet. The text/css value would be used to identify a Cascading Style Sheet.

> **NOTE**
> The `tags` property always applies to the current document. You do not need to explicitly reference the `document` object.

Defining Style Sheets

As you saw in the previous example, using JavaScript style sheets is easy. You write your HTML documents using traditional HTML tags and then define a style sheet to specify the style changes to be used with selected HTML elements. This is the preferred way to use style sheets, although a number of usage options are provided.

JavaScript style sheets, like Cascading Style Sheets, may be defined in any of the following ways:

- The `<STYLE>` tag may be used to define styles in the document head.
- The `<LINK>` tag may be used to refer to a style sheet that is in a separate, external document.
- The `<SPAN>` tag may be used to surround text to which a particular style is to be applied.

The following sections show how to use each of the above mechanisms to define and use JavaScript styles within your documents.

The `<STYLE>` Tag

You've already learned to use the `<STYLE>` tag in the first example of this chapter:

- You put `<STYLE>` and `</STYLE>` tags in a document's header.
- You set the TYPE attribute to `text/javascript`.
- You place JavaScript statements which define styles between the `<STYLE>` tags.

The `<STYLE>` tag is very easy to use. The hard part is figuring out what kind of styles you want to define.

The styles used in Listing 23.1 showed how the styles associated with individual HTML elements can be defined. Basically, you redefined all level 1 and 2 headings and paragraphs to use certain colors. The statements that are included between the <STYLE> tags may be used to provide much more power and flexibility in the way that styles are defined. For example, you can use JavaScript statements to:

- Specify the style and size of fonts to be used with specific HTML elements.
- Specify the way that text is to be aligned (vertically and horizontally), indented, capitalized, and decorated (underline, overline, blink, and strikethrough).
- Specify foreground and background colors and the use of background images.
- Identify the margins, borders, padding, and alignment to be used to lay out block-formatted HTML elements.
- Define classes of styles and specify which HTML elements belong to each class.
- Define exceptions to a style or class of styles.
- Insert comments that document your style definitions.

While the above list may seem daunting, don't worry; we're going to cover each of the above capabilities, one at a time, in the following sections.

Inserting Comments

JavaScript comments /* */ and // can be used to document your style sheets.

The *tags* Property

The tags property is a property of the document object that allows you to define the style for individual HTML tags. You used the tags property in Listing 23.1 to redefined the styles of level 1 and 2 headings and paragraphs. The tags property is typically set in an assignment statement as follows:

```
tags.tagID.property = value;
```

where *tagID* is the HTML tag that you want to define (e.g., BODY, H1, P, etc.), *property* is the style property that you want to change (e.g., color, fontStyle, etc.), and *value* is the value that you want to change the property to (e.g., red, italic, small-caps, etc.). In subsequent sections of this chapter, you'll learn more about the properties and values that can be specified.

The *ids* Property and *ID* Attribute

While the tags property is used to redefine all instances of a particular HTML tag, the ids property is used to create specific exceptions to a style definition. For example, you can create an ID to specify that a particular HTML element is to be displayed in red. The ids property is typically set in an assignment statement as follows:

```
ids.ID.property = value;
```

where *ID* is the name of the ID that you want to define. The ID is then used as an attribute value, as shown in Listing 23.2.

Listing 23.2. Using the ids property and ID attribute (ids.htm)

```
<HTML>
<HEAD>
<TITLE>Using the ids property and ID attribute</TITLE>
<STYLE TYPE="text/javascript">
tags.BODY.backgroundColor="white";
tags.P.color="blue";
ids.WARNING.color="red";
</STYLE>
</HEAD>
<BODY>
<P>This is the first paragraph.
It uses the redefined paragraph style.</P>
<P ID="WARNING">This is the second paragraph.
It has its ID attribute set to WARNING.</P>
<P>This is the third paragraph.
It uses the redefined paragraph style.</P>
<H1>This is a normal H1 heading.</H1>
<H1 ID="WARNING">This H1 heading uses the WARNING ID.</H1>
</BODY>
</HTML>
```

The tags property is used to define styles for the <BODY> and <P> tags. The ids property is used to define an ID, named WARNING, that is used in the second paragraph and the last heading. This causes the second paragraph and last heading to be displayed in red, as shown in Figure 23.2.

In general, you use the `ids` property to define an ID. Then set the `ID` attribute of an HTML tag to the ID that you've defined. By using IDs, you can create specific exceptions to the styles that you define using the `tags` and `classes` properties (covered later in this chapter).

FIGURE 23.2

How the `ids` property
and `ID` attribute are used

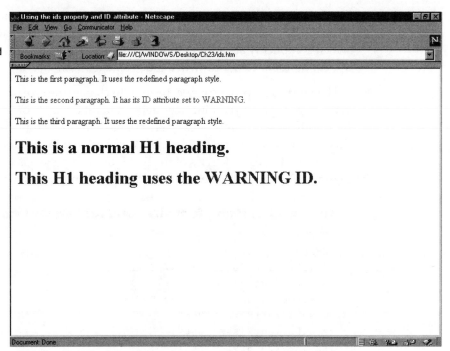

Setting Font Properties

The `fontStyle` and `fontSize` properties of an HTML element may be specified as part of the element's style definition. For example,

```
<STYLE TYPE="text/javascript">
tags.H1.fontStyle="italic";
tags.H1.fontSize="smaller";
</STYLE>
```

The `fontStyle` property may be assigned the following values:

- `normal`
- `italic`
- `oblique`
- `small-caps`

The `italic` and `oblique` values may be combined with `small-caps`. Use of the `oblique` style causes text to be slanted (which is different from an italic font, which is explicitly *designed* to look slanted). Use of `small-caps` causes text to appear in upper case, but with a much smaller font.

The `fontSize` property may be used to change the size of the font in which text is displayed. Displayed font sizes depend upon the table of font sizes that is used by your browser. Your browser may not have the exact font size that you specify; if this is the case, it will try to find the one closest to it in the table. Listing 23.3 shows how the font sizes and styles of the first four heading levels may be redefined. Figure 23.3 shows how the new headings are displayed by a browser.

Listing 23.3. Using font sizes and font styles (fonstyle.htm)

```
<HTML>
<HEAD>
<TITLE>Using Font Sizes</TITLE>
<STYLE TYPE="text/javascript">
tags.BODY.backgroundColor="white";
tags.H1.fontSize="10pt";
tags.H2.fontSize="20pt";
tags.H2.fontStyle="italic";
tags.H3.fontSize="30pt";
tags.H4.fontSize="40pt";
tags.H4.fontStyle="italic";
</STYLE>
</HEAD>
<BODY>
<H1>A level 1 heading</H1>
<H2>A level 2 heading</H2>
<H3>A level 3 heading</H3>
<H4>A level 4 heading</H4>
</BODY>
</HTML>
```

FIGURE 23.3

Redefining the first four
heading levels using font
sizes and font styles

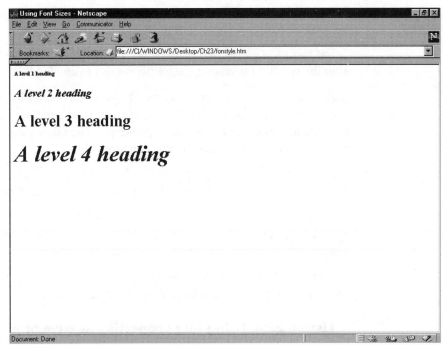

FIGURE 23.3

Redefining the first four
heading levels using font
sizes and font styles

Setting Text Properties

You can define a number of properties that govern the display of text within an
HTML element:

- `lineHeight` controls the spacing between lines of text.

- `textAlign` specifies the horizontal alignment of text within an HTML
  element.

- `verticalAlign` specifies the vertical alignment of text within an HTML
  element.

- `textTransform` specifies the case to be used for text within an HTML
  element.

- `textDecoration` specifies how text is to be adorned using underlining,
  overlining, blinking and strike-through.

The lineHeight property is set to a number such as 1.5 for space and a half, 2 for double spacing, 3 for triple spacing, etc., that identifies the line spacing to be used between adjacent lines of text.

The textAlign property can be set to left, right, center, or justify to alter the way that text is aligned with respect to an HTML element.

The verticalAlign property may be set to the values baseline, sub, super, top, text-top, middle, bottom, and text-bottom. The sub and super values are used to create subscripts and superscripts. The other values are similar to the HTML attribute values used to align images.

The textTransform property may be set to uppercase, lowercase, capitalize, or none. The none value turns off capitalization.

The textDecoration property may be set to the values none, underline, overline, line-through, or blink. The none value turns off any previously assigned decorations. The overline value is not currently supported.

Listing 23.4 provides an example of using text properties. Figure 23.4 shows how these properties are reflected in a browser's display.

Listing 23.4. Using text properties (textyle.htm)

```
<HTML>
<HEAD>
<TITLE>Using Text Properties</TITLE>
<STYLE TYPE="text/javascript">
tags.BODY.backgroundColor="white";
ids.HALF.lineHeight=.5;
ids.ONEPT5.lineHeight=1.5;
ids.ONEPT5.textAlign="center";
ids.ONEPT5.textTransform="uppercase";
ids.ONEPT5.textDecoration="blink";
ids.DOUBLE.lineHeight=2;
ids.DOUBLE.textTransform="lowercase";
ids.DOUBLE.textDecoration="underline";
ids.TRIPLE.lineHeight=3;
ids.TRIPLE.textTransform="capitalize";
ids.TRIPLE.textDecoration="line-through";
</STYLE>
</HEAD>
<BODY>
<P>This is paragraph 1.</P>
<P ID="HALF">This is paragraph 2.</P>
```

```
<P ID="ONEPT5">This is paragraph 3.</P>
<P ID="DOUBLE">This is paragraph 4.</P>
<P ID="TRIPLE">This is paragraph 5.</P>
</BODY>
</HTML>
```

FIGURE 23.4

Changing paragraph
formats using text styles

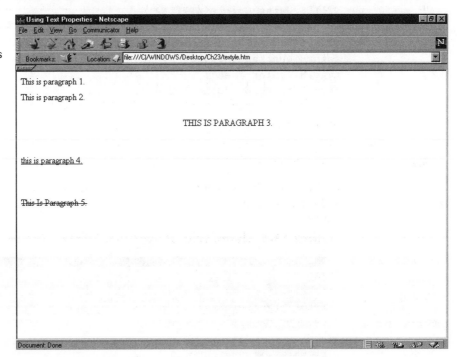

Using Colors and Background Images

You are already familiar with using the `color` and `backgroundColor` properties
from previous examples. The `color` property is used to set the text foreground
color and the `backgroundColor` property is used to set the color of the background occupied by an HTML element. The RGB values of custom colors may be
specified using the `rgb()` function. For example, a color with a 50 red value, 100
green value, and 150 blue value may be specified using `rgb(50,100,150)`. Listing 23.5 shows how background and foreground colors can be specified using the
`backgroundColor` and `color` properties. Figure 23.5 shows a black-and-white
version of the Web page displayed by Listing 23.5. If it were in color, it would show
a white document background, a level 1 heading with red foreground and yellow

background colors, and a paragraph with white foreground and blue background colors. Note that the heading is displayed using a paragraph-like font style.

Listing 23.5. Using background and foregrounds (colors.htm)

```
<HTML>
<HEAD>
<TITLE>Using Colors</TITLE>
<STYLE TYPE="text/javascript">
tags.BODY.backgroundColor="white";
tags.H1.backgroundColor="yellow";
tags.H1.color="red";
tags.P.backgroundColor="blue";
tags.P.color="white";
</STYLE>
</HEAD>
<BODY>
<H1>This is a level 1 heading.</H1>
<P>This is a paragraph.</P>
</BODY>
</HTML>
```

FIGURE 23.5

Background and foreground colors may be set using color properties.

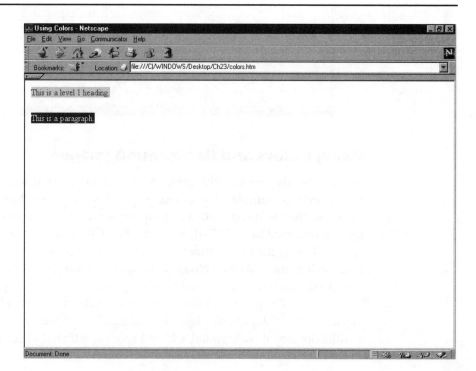

678

The `backgroundImage` property may be used to identify a background image to be used with an HTML element. The property takes a URL as its value. Background images are typically used with the document as a whole, by assigning an image to the `<BODY>` tag. However, JavaScript style sheets allow background images to be assigned to block-formatted elements. Block-formatted elements are covered in the next section.

Laying Out Block-Formatted Elements

Block-formatted elements are HTML elements that begin on a new line. Examples are headings, paragraphs, and lists. The margins, border, and padding of block-formatted elements can be defined by JavaScript style sheets.

Margins are defined using the `marginsRight`, `marginsLeft`, `marginsTop`, and `marginsBottom` properties. The `margins()` method sets all four margins at the same time. It takes four arguments that can be used to set the top, right, bottom, and left margins as follows:

```
margins(top, right, bottom, left)
```

The width of the border around a block element is set using the `borderLeft-Width`, `borderRightWidth`, `borderTopWidth`, and `borderBottomWidth` properties. The `borderWidths()` method can be used in the same manner as the `margins()` method to set the width of all four borders at once. The `borderStyle` property sets the style of the border to `solid`, 3D, or `none`.

The padding between a block element and its border is set using the `padding-Right`, `paddingLeft`, `paddingTop`, and `paddingBottom` properties. The `paddings()` method sets all four paddings.

The `width` and `height` properties specify the dimensions to be used in laying out block elements. If the `width` and `height` properties are set to `auto`, then any replacement for the block element, such as a loaded image, will cause the block to be automatically resized. If the properties are not set to `auto`, then the replacement will be resized to fit the block. The `align` property may be set to `left`, `right`, or `none`. It is used in the same manner as the `ALIGN` attribute of the image tag. The `clear` property may be set to `left`, `right`, `none`, or `both`. It is used in the same manner as the `CLEAR` attribute of the break tag.

Listing 23.6 provides an example of block formatting. Figure 23.6 shows how the block formatting attributes affect the margins, border, and padding of paragraphs.

Listing 23.6. Using block formatting properties (blocks.htm)

```
<HTML>
<HEAD>
<TITLE>Formatting Block Properties</TITLE>
<STYLE TYPE="text/javascript">
tags.BODY.backgroundColor="white";
tags.P.marginLeft=10;
tags.P.borderLeftWidth=1;
tags.P.borderStyle="solid";
tags.P.backgroundColor="cyan";
ids.para2.marginLeft=50;
ids.para2.paddingLeft=10;
ids.para2.paddingTop=15;
ids.para2.paddingBottom=0;
</STYLE>
</HEAD>
<BODY>
<P>This is a paragraph.</P>
<P ID="para2">This is another paragraph.</P>
</BODY>
</HTML>
```

FIGURE 23.6

Block formatting properties can be used to change the margins, border, and padding of block elements.

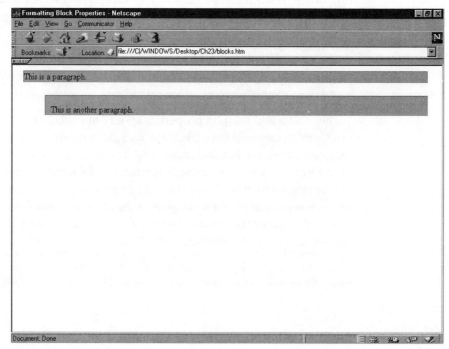

680

Using Measurement Units

JavaScript style sheets support the measurement units defined in Section 6.1 of the Cascading Style Sheets proposal (*http://www.w3.org/pub/WWW/TR/REC-CSS1*). These measurement units are used to specify font sizes, margins, and other element properties. They are organized into three categories:

- *Absolute units.* These units specify the actual magnitude of a property. For example, "14pt" may be used to identify a 14-point font.

- *Relative units.* These units specify the magnitude of a property relative to the element being defined. For example, "5em" may be used to identify a 5-em margin. (An em is a real unit of measure: it's defined as the width of the capital letter M; obviously, this unit changes from one font to another.)

- *Proportional units.* These units specify the size of a property in proportion to the element being defined. For example, "50%" may be used to reduce the font size of a heading by half.

Listing 23.7 shows how absolute, relative, and proportional units may be used in JavaScript style sheets. Figure 23.7 shows how the document of Listing 23.7 is displayed.

Listing 23.7. Using measurement units (units.htm)

```
<HTML>
<HEAD>
<TITLE>Measurement Units</TITLE>
<STYLE TYPE="text/javascript">
tags.BODY.backgroundColor="white";
tags.H1.fontSize="15%";
tags.P.marginLeft="5em";
ids.para2.fontSize="36pt";
</STYLE>
</HEAD>
<BODY>
<H1>This level 1 heading is reduced to 15%.</H1>
<P>This is a normal paragraph with a 5 em margin.</P>
<P ID="para2">This paragraph uses a 36 point font and
has a 5 em margin.</P>
</BODY>
</HTML>
```

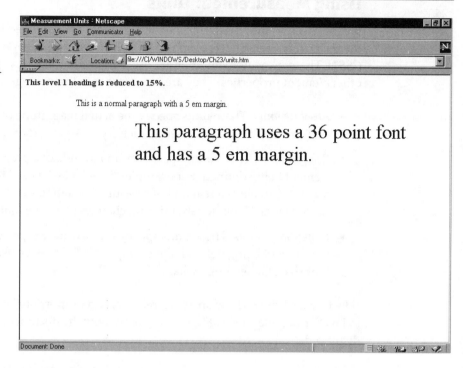

FIGURE 23.7

CSS measurement
units may be used in
JavaScript style sheets.

Using Classes

JavaScript style sheets can be used to define classes of styles which can be applied to different parts of a document. For example, you can define a class for marking company-sensitive data within a document, for highlighting important text, or for inserting revisions into a document. Classes are defined using the `classes` property. They are typically defined in assignment statements using the following syntax:

```
classes.className.tag.property = value;
```

where `className` and `tag` are the name of the class and tag being defined. The `all` keyword may be used to apply the property to all HTML tags.

Classes are applied to HTML elements by setting their `CLASS` attribute. Listing 23.8 shows how this is done. Figure 23.8 shows how the document described by Listing 23.8 is displayed.

FIGURE 23.8

Classes add power and
flexibility to JavaScript
style sheets.

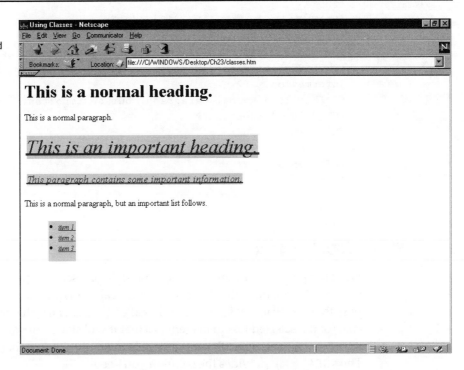

Listing 23.8. Using classes to define important text (classes.htm)

```
<HTML>
<HEAD>
<TITLE>Using Classes</TITLE>
<STYLE TYPE="text/javascript">
tags.BODY.backgroundColor="white";
classes.important.H1.fontSize="36pt";
classes.important.P.fontSize="18pt";
classes.important.UL.fontSize="12pt";
classes.important.all.textDecoration="underline";
classes.important.all.fontStyle="italic";
classes.important.all.textDecoration="underline";
classes.important.all.color="red";
classes.important.all.backgroundColor="yellow";
</STYLE>
</HEAD>
```

```
<BODY>
<H1>This is a normal heading.</H1>
<P>This is a normal paragraph.</P>
<H1 CLASS="important">This is an important heading.</H1>
<P CLASS="important">This paragraph contains some important
information.</P>
<P>This is a normal paragraph, but an important list follows.</P>
<UL CLASS="important">
<LI>item 1
<LI>item 2
<LI>item 3
</UL>
</BODY>
</HTML>
```

The <SPAN> Tag

What happens if you want to change the style of a selected portion of text and do not want to redefine other logical and physical formatting tags? For example, suppose that you want to develop a style, called highlight, that merely changes the color of the selected text to magenta so that it will stand out. You could redefine the <EM> tag, but you still want to be able to emphasize text that is highlighted. The <SPAN> tag provides the solution you need.

The <SPAN> tag is used to apply styles to *selected* text. Use the <SPAN> and </SPAN> tags to surround the text to which the style is to be applied. You can then use the CLASS and ID attributes to apply a style to the text.

For example, consider Listing 23.9. It defines a highlight style that changes the text foreground color to magenta. Highlighted text is selected by the <SPAN> tags and the ID attribute of the <SPAN> tag is set to highlight. Use of the <SPAN> tags does not conflict with the <EM> tag. Figure 23.9 shows how the document of Listing 23.9 is displayed.

Listing 23.9. Using the <SPAN> tag to change the style of selected text (span.htm)

```
<HTML>
<HEAD>
<TITLE>Using the SPAN tag</TITLE>
<STYLE TYPE="text/javascript">
```

```
tags.BODY.backgroundColor="white";
tags.P.fontSize="36pt";
tags.P.marginLeft="5em";
tags.P.marginRight="5em";
tags.P.marginTop="1em";
ids.highlight.color="magenta";
</STYLE>
</HEAD>
<BODY>
<P>This paragraph contains some
<SPAN ID="highlight">highlighted</SPAN> text.</P>
<P>This paragraph contains some
<SPAN ID="highlight">highlighted and <EM>emphasized</EM></SPAN>
text.</P>
</BODY>
</HTML>
```

FIGURE 23.9

The <SPAN> tag allows styles to be applied to selected text.

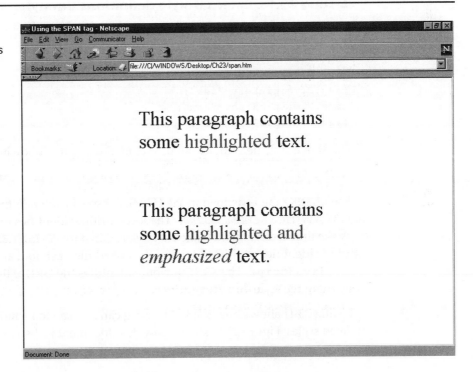

Using the *<LINK>* Tag to Include Styles

Now that you are familiar with JavaScript styles, you're probably wondering whether you have to reenter your favorite style definitions in the documents that use those styles. The answer is no—you can use the <LINK> tag to use styles that are defined in external files. This means that you can define your styles once and then reuse them over and over again. It also means that you can update the styles used for multiple documents by changing a single file.

An external style file defines styles using the tags, classes, and ids properties. JavaScript style assignments are inserted into the file without the surrounding <STYLE> tags. For example, Listing 23.10 contains style definitions for the document body and paragraph tags.

Listing 23.10. External style definitions (favstyle)

```
tags.BODY.backgroundColor="blue";
tags.P.fontSize="24pt";
tags.P.fontStyle="italic";
tags.P.color="white";
tags.P.marginLeft="5em";
tags.P.marginRight="5em";
tags.P.marginTop="5em";
```

The above style definitions can be included using the following <LINK> tag:

```
<LINK REL=STYLESHEET TYPE="text/JavaScript" HREF="favstyle">
```

The <LINK> tag is defined in the HTML 3.2 specification (*http://www.w3.org /pub/WWW/TR/REC-html32.html*). The REL attribute identifies the relationship with the linked document. It should always be set to STYLESHEET. The TYPE attribute identifies the MIME type of the linked file. It should always be set to text/JavaScript. The HREF attribute identifies the URL of the external file containing the style definitions.

Listing 23.11 shows how the <LINK> tag can be used to include externally defined styles. Figure 23.10 shows how this document is displayed.

Listing 23.11. Using the <LINK> tag (usestyle.htm)

```
<HTML>
<HEAD>
<TITLE>Using the LINK tag</TITLE>
<LINK REL=STYLESHEET TYPE="text/JavaScript" HREF="favstyle">
</HEAD>
<BODY>
<P>This paragraph uses the style sheet that is contained in
the favstyle file. You can modify favstyle to update the styles
used for all of your favorite documents.</P>
</BODY>
</HTML>
```

FIGURE 23.10

The <LINK> tag allows externally defined styles to be included in a document.

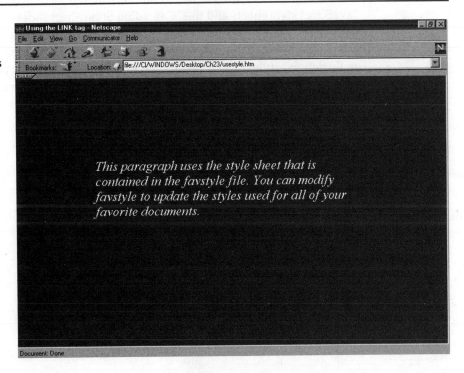

Using Multiple Style Sheets

Multiple JavaScript style sheets can be used in a single document. Externally defined style sheets can also be combined with internally defined style sheets. The internally defined styles take precedence over the externally defined styles. Later referenced external styles take precedence over earlier referenced external styles.

Summary

In this chapter, you were introduced to style sheets and covered several examples of their application. You learned about the differences between Netscape's JavaScript style sheets and the "Cascading Style Sheets" developed by the World Wide Web Consortium. You covered the tags, properties, and attributes used with JavaScript style sheets, and learned how to work with both internally and externally defined styles. You probably can't wait to use style sheets to spice up your own Web applications. In the next chapter, you'll learn to use another important capability provided by JavaScript 1.2—*layers*. You'll learn how to use layers to create multiple levels of multimedia overlays that will add a new dimension to your applications' appearance and appeal.

CHAPTER
TWENTY-FOUR

24

Layers and Multimedia Applications

- Using Layers

- Working with Audio

- Performing Animation

- Using Video

Multimedia features, such as audio, video, and animation, can add to the effectiveness and appeal of your Web pages. You learned how to work with multimedia features in Part 5 when you studied plug-ins. The introduction of *layers* with Navigator 4.0 adds to the multimedia capabilities provided by plug-ins. Layers can be used to move and control the display of different objects within a Web page. JavaScript 1.2 provides access to layers and allows you to manipulate the positioning and display of layers during a script's execution.

In this chapter, you'll learn how to use the <LAYER> tags to integrate multimedia capabilities in your Web applications. You'll cover the JavaScript layer object and learn how to use its properties and methods to enhance animations, create slide shows, and increase the effectiveness of videos. When you finish this chapter, you'll be able to use layers to augment the multimedia features of your Web applications.

Using Layers

Layers are one of the most attractive capabilities introduced with Navigator 4.0. They allow you to organize your documents into multiple levels of opaque or transparent sections that can be overlaid, moved, or selectively displayed. Each layer is able to contain HTML content; thus each layer can include other layers, Java applets, forms, and plug-ins. Layers can be combined to produce the effect of multiple documents being dynamically integrated within a single window. When used to create multimedia effects, layers can be used to create PowerPoint-like slide shows, perform advanced animation, or add new dimensions to the ways that plug-ins are displayed.

The Layer Tags

The <LAYER> and <ILAYER> tags are used to define layers. The <LAYER> tag is used to define a fixed position layer, while the <ILAYER> tag is used to define a layer that is formatted as part of the document's natural flow. Both tags are surrounding tags and are used as follows:

```
<LAYER attributes>
HTML tags included within layer
</LAYER>
```

or

```
<ILAYER attributes>
HTML tags included within layer
</ILAYER>
```

The <LAYER> and <ILAYER> tags use the same attributes, as described in Table 24.1. All of these attributes are optional.

Layers are ordered according to a *stacking* order. This means that layers are stacked over each other like a deck of cards. This order is called a *z-order*. The Z-INDEX, ABOVE, and BELOW attributes are used to create this ordering. Only one of these three attributes can be used for a given layer definition. The Z-INDEX attribute is used to identify a layer's position within the ordering: layers with higher Z-INDEX attribute values are stacked above those with lower values. The ABOVE attribute identifies the layer (by name) that is immediately above the layer being defined. The BELOW attribute identifies the layer (by name) that is immediately below the layer being defined.

A layer is either transparent or opaque. A layer is opaque if its BACKGROUND or BGCOLOR attributes are specified; otherwise it is transparent. The VISIBILITY attribute is set to hide, show, or inherited. The show value causes a layer to be displayed. The hide value causes a layer to be hidden. The inherited value causes the visibility of a layer to be that of its parent (i.e., an outer layer in which it is enclosed). If a layer has no parent, then setting its visibility to inherited is the same as setting it to show.

The SRC attribute loads the content of a layer from the document specified by a URL. The HTML elements contained in the file should be those that can appear within a document's body.

TABLE 24.1 Attributes of the <LAYER> and <ILAYER> tags

Attribute	Description
ABOVE	Identifies the layer that is positioned immediately above the layer being defined.
BACKGROUND	Specifies the background image to be used with the layer.
BELOW	Identifies the layer that is positioned immediately below the layer being defined.
BGCOLOR	Specifies the background color to be used with the layer.

TABLE 24.1 Attributes of the `<LAYER>` and `<ILAYER>` tags (continued)

Attribute	Description
CLIP	Identifies the clipping rectangle of the layer. This attribute takes four comma-separated arguments of the form `CLIP` = *left*, *top*, *right*, *bottom*. These arguments identify the number of pixels from each side that should be clipped when the layer is displayed. The clipping rectangle can also be specified as two numbers `CLIP` = *right*, *bottom*. In this option, the left and top values are assumed to be 0.
LEFT	Identifies the horizontal distance from the left side of the window (`<LAYER>` tag) or from its normal positioning (`<ILAYER>` tag) where the layer is to be displayed.
NAME	Identified the window's name.
SRC	Specifies a URL from which the contents of the layer should be loaded.
TOP	Identifies the vertical distance from the top of the window (`<LAYER>` tag) or from its normal positioning (`<ILAYER>` tag) where the layer is to be displayed.
VISIBILITY	Identifies whether the layer is to be displayed.
WIDTH	Determines the width of the layer's display.
Z-INDEX	Specifies a positive integer that is used to determine how the layer is positioned with respect to other layers.

Windowed Elements

Forms, plug-ins, and applets are referred to as *windowed* elements. Windowed elements are always displayed, regardless of whether they are in a non-visible layer. In addition, windowed elements disappear if any part of the element is moved outside the visible area of a window. In comparison, *windowless* plug-ins are specially designed so that they can be hidden in non-visible layers.

The *layers* Array and *layer* Object

JavaScript provides access to layers via the `layers` array and the `layer` object. The `layers` array is a property of the `document` object that contains an entry for every layer defined within the document. The `layers` array does *not* contain entries for layers that are defined *within* layers; these layers can be accessed via a second-level or third-level `layers` array. For example, the second sublayer of the fourth layer of a document can be referenced as `document.layers[3].layers[1]`. The name of a layer can also be used as its index into the `layers` array.

The `layer` object is a property of the `document` object that is used to provide access to the attributes of an individual layer. Layers can be accessed by name or via the `layers` array. The properties of the `layer` object mimic the attributes of the `<LAYER>` tag. These properties include `above`, `background`, `below`, `bgColor`, `clip`, `left`, `name`, `src`, `top`, `visibility`, `width`, and `zIndex`. The `clip` property has `top`, `left`, `right`, `bottom`, `width`, and `height` properties.

In addition, the layer object also has the `height`, `layers`, `parentLayer`, `siblingAbove`, and `siblingBelow` properties. The `parentLayer` property is used to identify the layer in which a layer is nested. The `siblingAbove` and `siblingBelow` properties identify layers above or below a layer that share the same parent.

The methods of the `layer` object are described in Table 24.2.

TABLE 24.2   Methods of the `layer` object

Method	Description
`moveAbove`(*layer*)	Move the layer above the identified layer.
`moveBelow`(*layer*)	Move the layer below the identified layer.
`moveTo`(*x,y*)	Move the layer to the specified position.
`offset`(*x,y*)	Move the window x pixels to the right and y units to the bottom.
`resize`(*width, height*)	Resize the window to the specified dimensions.

A Slide Show Example

We've talked about layers long enough—it's time to get busy using them in an example. Listing 24.1 shows how layers can be used to create a slide show-like presentation. While this script won't knock PowerPoint off of the software charts, it does illustrate how JavaScript and layers can be combined to produce some interesting effects.

Open `slidshow.htm` with your browser, and it displays the browser window shown in Figure 24.1. This window shows the first slide of a five-slide presentation about layers. The slide show is controlled by four buttons—First Slide, Previous Slide, Next Slide, and Last Slide. Click the Next Slide button and your browser displays the slide shown in Figure 24.2. You can quickly move to the last slide of the briefing by clicking the Last Slide button, or the previous slide by clicking the Previous Slide button. Play around with the script until you become familiar with its operation.

FIGURE 24.1

The slide show
opening display

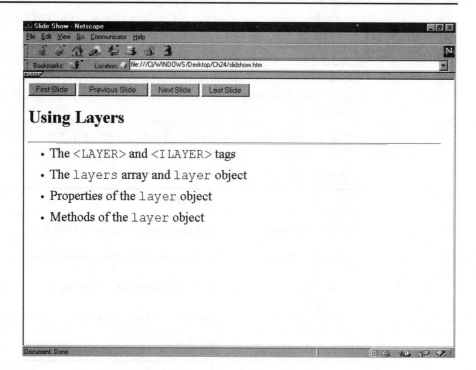

Listing 24.1. A layer-based slide show (slidshow.htm)

```
<HTML>
<HEAD>
<TITLE>Slide Show</TITLE>
</HEAD>
<SCRIPT LANGUAGE="JavaScript"><!--
function hideAll(){
 for(var i=0;i<document.layers.length;++i)
  document.layers[i].visibility="hide"
}
```

FIGURE 24.2

Clicking the Next Slide button causes the next slide in the briefing to be displayed.

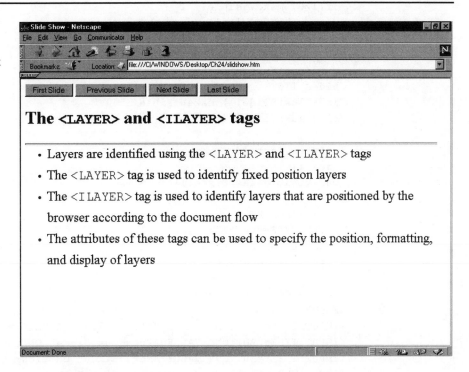

```
function getCurrent(){
 for(var i=0;i<document.layers.length;++i)
  if(document.layers[i].visibility!="hide") return i
 return 0
}
function makeVisible(i){
 document.layers[i].visibility="inherit"
}
function lastSlide(){
 return document.layers.length-1
}
function first(){
 hideAll()
 makeVisible(0)
}
function prev(){
 var i=getCurrent()
 hideAll()
```

```
 if(i>0) makeVisible(i-1)
 else makeVisible(i)
}
function next(){
 var i=getCurrent()
 hideAll()
 if(i<lastSlide()) makeVisible(i+1)
 else makeVisible(i)
}
function last(){
 hideAll()
 makeVisible(lastSlide())
}
// --></SCRIPT>
<STYLE TYPE="text/javascript">
 tags.UL.fontSize="24pt"
 tags.UL.lineHeight=2
</STYLE>
<BODY BGCOLOR="white">
<FORM>
<INPUT TYPE="BUTTON" VALUE="First Slide" ONCLICK="first()">
<INPUT TYPE="BUTTON" VALUE="Previous Slide" ONCLICK="prev()">
<INPUT TYPE="BUTTON" VALUE="Next Slide" ONCLICK="next()">
<INPUT TYPE="BUTTON" VALUE="Last Slide" ONCLICK="last()">
</FORM>
<LAYER NAME="slide0" BGCOLOR="white" VISIBILITY="SHOW">
<H1>Using Layers</H1>
<HR>
<UL>
<LI>The <CODE>&ltLAYER&gt</CODE> and
<CODE>&ltILAYER&gt</CODE> tags
<LI>The <CODE>layers</CODE> array and <CODE>layer</CODE> object
<LI>Properties of the <CODE>layer</CODE> object
<LI>Methods of the <CODE>layer</CODE> object
</UL>
</LAYER>
<LAYER NAME="slide1" BGCOLOR="white" VISIBILITY="HIDE">
<H1>The <CODE>&ltLAYER&gt</CODE> and
<CODE>&ltILAYER&gt</CODE> tags</H1>
<HR>
<UL>
<LI>Layers are identified using the
```

```
<CODE>&ltLAYER&gt</CODE> and
<CODE>&ltILAYER&gt</CODE> tags
<LI>The <CODE>&ltLAYER&gt</CODE> tag is used to identify
fixed position layers
<LI>The <CODE>&ltILAYER&gt</CODE> tag is used to identify
layers that are positioned by the browser according to
the document flow
<LI>The attributes of these tags can be used to specify
the position, formatting, and display of layers
</UL>
</LAYER>
<LAYER NAME="slide2" BGCOLOR="white" VISIBILITY="HIDE">
<H1>The <CODE>layers</CODE> array and <CODE>layer</CODE>
object</H1>
<HR>
<UL>
<LI>Access to layers from JavaScript is provided by the
<CODE>layers</CODE> array and <CODE>layer</CODE> object
<LI>The <CODE>layers</CODE> array identifies all layers
in a document
<LI>The <CODE>layer</CODE> object provides access to the
attributes of an individual object
</UL>
</LAYER>
<LAYER NAME="slide3" BGCOLOR="white" VISIBILITY="HIDE">
<H1>Properties of the <CODE>layer</CODE> object</H1>
<HR>
<UL>
<LI>The properties of the <CODE>layer</CODE> object
correspond to the attributes of the
<CODE>&ltLAYER&gt</CODE> and <CODE>&ltILAYER&gt</CODE>
tags
<LI>These properties may be used to change the location
and visibility of a layer
</UL>
</LAYER>
<LAYER NAME="slide4" BGCOLOR="white" VISIBILITY="HIDE">
<H1>Methods of the <CODE>layer</CODE> object</H1>
<HR>
<UL>
<LI><CODE>offset(x, y)</CODE>
<LI><CODE>moveTo(x, y)</CODE>
```

```
<LI><CODE>resize(width, height)</CODE>
<LI><CODE>moveAbove(layer)</CODE>
<LI><CODE>moveBelow(layer)</CODE>
</UL>
</LAYER>
</BODY>
</HTML>
```

The slide show script makes extensive use of layers. Five layers, named slide0 through slide4, are defined in the document body. The layers all have a white background color, but only the first slide is initially visible. Each layer contains an HTML description of its associated slide's contents. A simple four-button form is included at the top of the document body. These buttons invoke the first(), prev(), next(), and last() methods to move between slides.

The <STYLE> tags in the document head are used to change the list items of each slide to a larger font (24 point) and to display them using double-spacing.

The script in the document head defines eight methods, whose descriptions follow.

hideAll() The hideAll() method loops through all layers defined in the current document, and sets their visibility property to hide.

getCurrent() The getCurrent() method loops through all layers defined in the current document and returns the index of the layer whose visibility is *not* set to hide.

makeVisible() The makeVisible() method sets the visibility of a specified layer to inherit. This causes the layer to inherit the visibility of the overall document and therefore be displayed.

lastSlide() The lastSlide() method returns the index of the last layer in the layers array.

first() The first() method hides all layers using the hideAll() method, and then invokes the makeVisible() method to display the first slide in the slide show.

prev() The prev() method invokes getCurrent() to get the index of the currently visible layer and then hides all layers using the hideAll() method. If the current slide is not the first slide then the makeVisible() method is invoked to display the previous slide in the slide show.

next0 The next() method invokes getCurrent() to get the index of the currently visible layer, and then hides all layers using the hideAll() method. If the current slide is not the last slide, then the makeVisible() method is invoked to display the next slide in the slide show.

last0 The last() method hides all layers using the hideAll() method, and then invokes the lastSlide() and makeVisible() methods to display the last slide in the slide show.

Working with Audio

The topic of this chapter is multimedia, so let's look at how we can integrate multimedia features with layers. The slide show example of the previous section is a good place to start. Listing 24.2 shows how we can add an audio narrative to each slide. Open audiosho.htm with your browser, and you'll hear me providing a slide-by-slide commentary.

Listing 24.2. An audio-enhanced slide show (audiosho.htm)

```
<HTML>
<HEAD>
<TITLE>Slide Show with Audio</TITLE>
</HEAD>
<SCRIPT LANGUAGE="JavaScript"><!--
function hideAll(){
 for(var i=0;i<document.layers.length;++i){
  document.layers[i].visibility="hide"
  document.embeds[i].stop()
 }
}
function getCurrent(){
 for(var i=0;i<document.layers.length;++i)
  if(document.layers[i].visibility!="hide") return i
 return 0
}
function makeVisible(i){
 document.layers[i].visibility="inherit"
 document.embeds[i].play()
}
```

```
function lastSlide(){
 return document.layers.length-1
}
function first(){
 hideAll()
 makeVisible(0)
}
function prev(){
 var i=getCurrent()
 hideAll()
 if(i>0) makeVisible(i-1)
 else makeVisible(i)
}
function next(){
 var i=getCurrent()
 hideAll()
 if(i<lastSlide()) makeVisible(i+1)
 else makeVisible(i)
}
function last(){
 hideAll()
 makeVisible(lastSlide())
}
// --></SCRIPT>
<STYLE TYPE="text/javascript">
 tags.UL.fontSize="24pt"
 tags.UL.lineHeight=2
</STYLE>
<BODY BGCOLOR="white">
<FORM>
<INPUT TYPE="BUTTON" VALUE="First Slide" ONCLICK="first()">
<INPUT TYPE="BUTTON" VALUE="Previous Slide" ONCLICK="prev()">
<INPUT TYPE="BUTTON" VALUE="Next Slide" ONCLICK="next()">
<INPUT TYPE="BUTTON" VALUE="Last Slide" ONCLICK="last()">
</FORM>
<LAYER NAME="slide0" BGCOLOR="white" VISIBILITY="SHOW">
<H1>Using Layers</H1>
<HR>
<UL>
<LI>The <CODE>&ltLAYER&gt</CODE> and
<CODE>&ltILAYER&gt</CODE> tags
```

```
<LI>The <CODE>layers</CODE> array and <CODE>layer</CODE> object
<LI>Properties of the <CODE>layer</CODE> object
<LI>Methods of the <CODE>layer</CODE> object
</UL>
</LAYER>
<LAYER NAME="slide1" BGCOLOR="white" VISIBILITY="HIDE">
<H1>The <CODE>&ltLAYER&gt</CODE> and
<CODE>&ltILAYER&gt</CODE> tags</H1>
<HR>
<UL>
<LI>Layers are identified using the
<CODE>&ltLAYER&gt</CODE> and
<CODE>&ltILAYER&gt</CODE> tags
<LI>The <CODE>&ltLAYER&gt</CODE> tag is used to identify
fixed position layers
<LI>The <CODE>&ltILAYER&gt</CODE> tag is used to identify
layers that are positioned by the browser according to
the document flow
<LI>The attributes of these tags can be used to specify
the position, formatting, and display of layers
</UL>
</LAYER>
<LAYER NAME="slide2" BGCOLOR="white" VISIBILITY="HIDE">
<H1>The <CODE>layers</CODE> array and <CODE>layer</CODE>
object</H1>
<HR>
<UL>
<LI>Access to layers from JavaScript is provided by the
<CODE>layers</CODE> array and <CODE>layer</CODE> object
<LI>The <CODE>layers</CODE> array identifies all layers
in a document
<LI>The <CODE>layer</CODE> object provides access to the
attributes of an individual object
</UL>
</LAYER>
<LAYER NAME="slide3" BGCOLOR="white" VISIBILITY="HIDE">
<H1>Properties of the <CODE>layer</CODE> object</H1>
<HR>
<UL>
<LI>The properties of the <CODE>layer</CODE> object
correspond to the attributes of the
```

```
<CODE>&ltLAYER&gt</CODE> and <CODE>&ltILAYER&gt</CODE>
tags
<LI>These properties may be used to change the location
and visibility of a layer
</UL>
</LAYER>
<LAYER NAME="slide4" BGCOLOR="white" VISIBILITY="HIDE">
<H1>Methods of the <CODE>layer</CODE> object</H1>
<HR>
<UL>
<LI><CODE>offset(x, y)</CODE>
<LI><CODE>moveTo(x, y)</CODE>
<LI><CODE>resize(width, height)</CODE>
<LI><CODE>moveAbove(layer)</CODE>
<LI><CODE>moveBelow(layer)</CODE>
</UL>
</LAYER>
<EMBED SRC="slide0.wav" HIDDEN="true" AUTOSTART="true">
<EMBED SRC="slide1.wav" HIDDEN="true" AUTOSTART="false">
<EMBED SRC="slide2.wav" HIDDEN="true" AUTOSTART="false">
<EMBED SRC="slide3.wav" HIDDEN="true" AUTOSTART="false">
<EMBED SRC="slide4.wav" HIDDEN="true" AUTOSTART="false">
</BODY>
</HTML>
```

The inclusion of audio narration can make a presentation more interesting and effective. You can record .wav files using a microphone with your computer's sound board. I recorded the files slide0.wav through slide4.wav using the built-in microphone that came with my computer. These files are included at the bottom of the document's body using <EMBED> tags. Their HIDDEN attributes are set to true in order to hide the plug-in's toolbar. The AUTOSTART attribute of the first sound file is set to true so that it starts playing when the document is loaded. The AUTOSTART attributes of the other files are set to false so that they remain silent until they are explicitly played.

The only other changes required to implement the audio narration are in the hideAll() and makeVisible() methods. The hideAll() method is modified to stop the playing of all plug-ins by invoking the stop() method for each element of the embeds array. The makeVisible() method is updated to invoke the play() method for the plug-in corresponding to the layer being displayed.

Performing Animation

As you have probably surmised, layers can be used to extend JavaScript's animation capabilities. Two different types of animation can be supported by combining JavaScript and layers:

- You can create a stack of layers that contain the slides of an image's animation, and then flip through the slides to cause the animation effect.

- You can place an animated image in a layer and then move the layer around the screen to further increase the image's animation effect.

Listing 24.3 provides an example of the second kind of animation. Open `anilayer.htm` with your browser and you'll see an animated image of an airplane fly from the bottom of your screen to the top of your screen. The page includes sound effects of the plane's engine. The plane flies between a set of clouds as shown in Figure 24.3. Some of the clouds are displayed in front of the plane and others are displayed in back of the plane. The plane then flies behind the heading as shown in Figure 24.4. You can let the animation run to observe its behavior. It loops to repeat itself over time.

FIGURE 24.3

The plane is able to fly between the clouds.

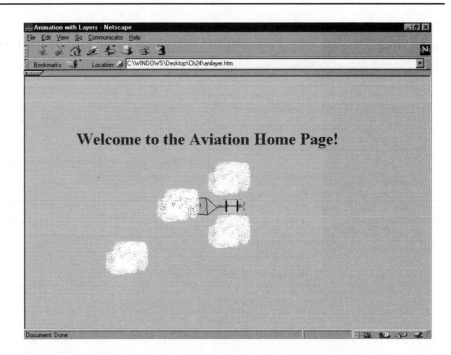

FIGURE 24.4

The plane flies over the heading.

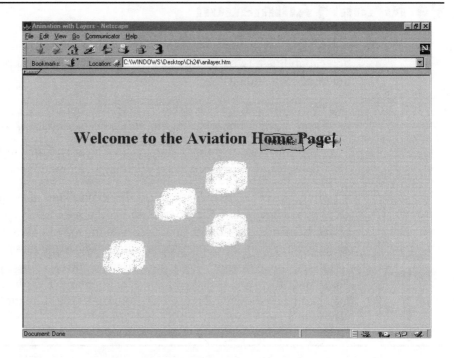

Listing 24.3. Using layers to support animation (anilayer.htm)

```
<HTML>
<HEAD>
<TITLE>Animation with Layers</TITLE>
</HEAD>
<SCRIPT LANGUAGE="JavaScript"><!--
function fly() {
 var plane=window.document.layers["plane"]
 if(plane.top<10) plane.moveTo(0,400)
 else plane.offset(8,-5)
 setTimeout("fly()", 10);
}
// --></SCRIPT>
<STYLE TYPE="text/javascript">
tags.H1.color="yellow"
</STYLE>
<BODY BGCOLOR="blue" ONLOAD="fly()">
```

```
<LAYER NAME="heading" VISIBILITY="SHOW" LEFT=100 TOP=100>
<H1>Welcome to the Aviation Home Page!</H1>
</LAYER>
<LAYER NAME="plane" VISIBILITY="SHOW" ABOVE="heading"
 LEFT=0 TOP=400>
<IMG SRC="plane.gif">
</LAYER>
<LAYER NAME="cloud1" VISIBILITY="SHOW" BELOW="plane"
 LEFT=150 TOP=300>
<IMG SRC="cloud.gif">
</LAYER>
<LAYER NAME="cloud2" VISIBILITY="SHOW" BELOW="cloud1"
 LEFT=250 TOP=200>
<IMG SRC="cloud.gif">
</LAYER>
<LAYER NAME="cloud3" VISIBILITY="SHOW" ABOVE="plane"
 LEFT=350 TOP=150>
<IMG SRC="cloud.gif">
</LAYER>
<LAYER NAME="cloud4" VISIBILITY="SHOW" ABOVE="cloud3"
 LEFT=350 TOP=250>
<IMG SRC="cloud.gif">
</LAYER>
<EMBED SRC="plane.wav" HIDDEN="true" AUTOSTART="true"
 LOOP="true">
</BODY>
</HTML>
```

The anilayer.htm file defines six layers in the document body—heading, plane, and cloud1 through cloud4. The heading layer displays the welcome message heading. It is positioned at (100,100). The plane layer displays the airplane, initially at (0,400). The heading layer is identified as being above the plane layer. The cloud1 layer displays a cloud at (150,300) and specifies the plane layer as being below it. The cloud2 layer displays a cloud at (250,200) above the cloud1 layer. The cloud3 layer displays a cloud below the plane layer and the cloud4 layer displays a cloud below the cloud3 layer. All four clouds display the same image. The ordering of the layers is what causes the plane to fly in front of some objects and behind others.

The flying of the airplane is initiated when the document is loaded. The onLoad event is handled by invoking the fly() method. This method checks to see if the plane is within 10 pixels of the top of the window, and if so, moves the plane back to its original position. Otherwise, the position of the plane is moved 8 pixels to the right and 5 pixels up the page. The `setTimeout()` method is used to invoke the `fly()` method after 10 milliseconds have transpired. This repeated calling of `fly()` causes the plane to move across the page.

Using Video

When we think of multimedia, we generally think of audio, video, and animation combined. As you have seen from previous examples of this chapter, audio and animation capabilities can easily be added to your documents through the use of layers. Video is also easy to work with, but has some drawbacks that must be considered:

- Video files are huge by Web standards—on the order of megabytes. This means that users will have to wait to download any video files that you insert in your Web documents. Audio and image files are usually less than a megabyte in size.

- Because of their large size, video dimensions are usually kept small—not much larger than a postage stamp. Videos are usually very short, too. Finding a video lasting longer than a minute or two is unusual on the Web. The small dimensions of videos and their short length tend to limit the effectiveness of videos in enhancing the information presented on your Web pages.

Despite the limitations identified above, videos can be used to contribute to your Web pages' appeal and effectiveness. Listing 24.4 provides an example that combines videos with layers to create a Web page whose purpose is unmistakable.

Open `videolay.htm` with your browser. A video of a moving boat is loaded and displayed. The video is then moved to different positions around the heading at three-second intervals. A looping audio message is also included with the Web page. While this page (see Figure 24.5) is far from subtle, it does illustrate the techniques of combining video, layers, and audio to create multimedia effects.

FIGURE 24.5

The boat video is moved around the heading.

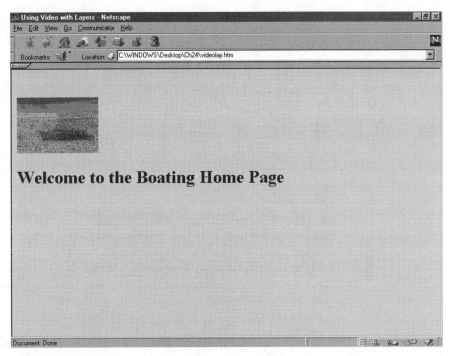

Listing 24.4. Using video with layers (videolay.htm)

```
<HTML>
<HEAD>
<TITLE>Using Video with Layers</TITLE>
</HEAD>
<SCRIPT LANGUAGE="JavaScript"><!--
state=0
function sail() {
 var video=window.document.layers["video"]
 switch(state){
 case 0:
  state=1
  break
 case 1:
  state=2
  video.moveTo(10,230)
  break
```

```
     case 2:
      state=3
      video.moveTo(510,140)
      break
     case 3:
      state=1
      video.moveTo(10,50)
     }
     setTimeout("sail()", 3000);
    }
    // --></SCRIPT>
    <STYLE TYPE="text/javascript">
    tags.H1.color="blue"
    </STYLE>
    <BODY BGCOLOR="yellow" ONLOAD="sail()">
    <LAYER NAME="heading" VISIBILITY="SHOW" LEFT=10 TOP=175>
    <H1>Welcome to the Boating Home Page</H1>
    </LAYER>
    <LAYER NAME="video" VISIBILITY="SHOW" ABOVE="heading"
     LEFT=10 TOP=50>
    <EMBED SRC="boat.avi" AUTOSTART="true" WIDTH=150 HEIGHT=100
     LOOP="true">
    </LAYER>
    <EMBED SRC="boat.wav" AUTOSTART="true"
     HIDDEN="true" LOOP="true">
    </BODY>
    </HTML>
```

The videolay.htm file defines two layers. The first is used to hold the document heading and the second is used to display the video. The video is automatically started and is set in loop mode. An audio file is embedded at the end of the document. This file repeatedly plays the welcome message.

The loading of the document invokes the sail() method. This method moves the video layer to different positions around the heading layer, depending upon the value of the state variable. The state variable is initially set to 0. When the sail() method is first invoked, it does not move the video; it just sets state to 1. From then on, state is changed from 1 to 2 to 3, and back to 1 again, and the video is moved to different locations within the Web page. The setTimeout() method is used to repeatedly invoke sail() every three seconds.

Summary

In this chapter, you learned how to use layers to integrate multimedia capabilities in your Web applications. You covered the JavaScript `layer` object and learned how to use its properties and methods to create animations, develop slide shows, and increase the effectiveness of videos. In the next chapter, "VRML and Live3D," you'll learn how to combine JavaScript and VRML to further enhance your Web applications.

CHAPTER TWENTY-FIVE

VRML and Live3D

- An Overview of the VRML Language

- A Simple VRML Example

- Using VRML Links

- Using JavaScript to Generate VRML

- Scripting and VRML 2.0

In Chapter 24 you learned how to use layers to integrate multimedia capabilities in your JavaScript applications. These capabilities increase the attractiveness and effectiveness of your Web pages. VRML, like multimedia, is another hot technology for enhancing Web applications. VRML (Virtual Reality Modeling Language) lets you create three-dimensional worlds that can be explored via a browser plug-in. You can embed a virtual world in your Web pages to increase their attractiveness and to allow users to explore a 3-D representation of your company, school, products, or even ideas. Some VRML applications even allow multiple users to interact with each other within the virtual world.

In this chapter, you'll be introduced to VRML and learn how to develop simple virtual-reality applications. You'll learn how to link worlds and how to dynamically generate VRML from JavaScript. You'll also learn about the scripting capabilities introduced with VRML 2.0. When you finish this chapter, you'll be knowledgeable enough about using VRML that you'll be able to include it in your Web applications.

Introduction to VRML

The Virtual Reality Modeling Language (VRML) is used to create 3-D virtual worlds that are viewed over the Web or an intranet using a VRML browser or plug-in. There are two versions of VRML currently available. VRML 1.0 supports the creation of virtual worlds, but does not provide many interactive simulation features. (It does, however, support hyperlinks to and from HTML documents.) VRML 2.0 adds much more user interaction support, animation capabilities, and language-specific hooks for using JavaScript.

The best way to get a feel for what VRML is all about is to look at a few examples. My favorite VRML world is at the *Popular Mechanics* magazine Web site:

http://popularmechanics.com/vrml/VRML.html

This world consists of several platforms in space, as shown in Figure 25.1. It also contains moving objects, such as asteroids and cars.

FIGURE 25.1

The Popular Mechanics world is fun to explore.

Silicon Graphics has taken the jack-in-the-box to new levels with its world at the following URL:

http://vrml.sgi.com/worlds/vrml2/jackbox/jackbox.wrl

The jack-in-the-box shown in Figure 25.2 opens when clicked—inside there is a planet for you to explore.

Numerous other worlds are available for your viewing over the Web. A good starting point for entering these worlds is the Yahoo Web site:

http://www.yahoo.com/Computers_and_Internet/Internet/World_Wide_Web /Virtual_Reality_Modeling_Language__VRML_/

From here you can follow links that will take you to VRML worlds and provide more information on how these worlds are created.

FIGURE 25.2

The Silicon Graphics jack-in-the-box pops open to reveal a new world inside.

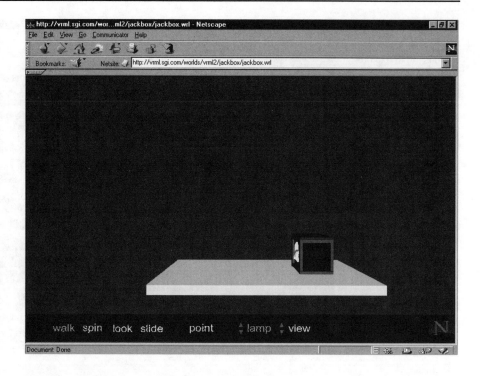

An Overview of the VRML Language

VRML, unlike HTML, is complex and difficult to learn. A complete introduction to VRML is a book in itself. In this chapter you'll learn enough VRML to create simple worlds. More importantly, you'll learn how to integrate the use of JavaScript and VRML.

VRML and HTML do not have a similar syntax. VRML documents are referred to as *worlds*, and traditionally end with the .wrl extension. Their MIME type is x-world/x-vrml. Worlds are written in ASCII text and are composed of 3-D objects that are referred to as *nodes*. Nodes have *characteristics*, such as their object type or shape, shape parameters, name (node names are not necessarily unique), and *child nodes*. Child nodes are nodes which are assembled into composite nodes, which are referred to as group nodes.

Nodes are organized into *scene graphs* which define a structure and ordering for nodes. Scene graphs also maintain state information. This allows earlier existing nodes to have an effect on later existing nodes. Some capabilities are also provided to isolate nodes (i.e., to limit these effects).

History of VRML

VRML, like all Web technologies, is of recent vintage. It was created in 1994 by Gavin Bell, Mark Pesce, and others based on a subset of the Open Inventor File Format from Silicon Graphics, Inc. The VRML 1.0 specification has been revised since then. Its latest version can be found at the VRML Architecture Group Web site:

> *http://vag.vrml.org*

VRML 1.0 provides the capability to create 3-D worlds that can be navigated by VRML browsers and plug-ins. The worlds created by VRML 1.0 are described as *static*, in that there is limited interaction between the user and the world.

As the VRML 1.0 specification was published, work was underway to create VRML worlds that supported greater interaction between the user and the world and also that allowed interaction between multiple users. The VRML 2.0 specification was completed in August 1996. VRML 2.0 builds upon the features of VRML 1.0 and adds event-based interaction, animation, scripting, and prototyping capabilities. You'll learn about these capabilities later in this chapter. The scripting capability supports JavaScript and Java. (The JavaScript-based scripting is covered in Appendix D of the specification.) The VRML 2.0 specification is also available at the URL mentioned above: *http://vag.vrml.org*.

For more information on VRML itself, an excellent starting point is the VRML Repository at:

> *http://www.sdsc.edu/vrml/*

You can find some very helpful tutorials at The Virtual Reality Universe site, at the following URL:

> *http://www.vruniverse.com/tutorial.shtml*

The best overall reference documents for VRML are the Version 1.0 and 2.0 specifications themselves, available at *http://vag.vrml.org*.

> **NOTE**
>
> To keep the discussion as simple as possible, we'll stick to VRML 1.0 for most of this chapter. It is much easier to learn VRML 1.0 before tackling VRML 2.0.

A Simple VRML Example

Listing 25.1 shows a simple VRML file. This file, `shapes.wrl`, describes a simple VRML world consisting of a red cube, a green sphere, and a blue cone. Figure 25.3 shows how this world is displayed by Navigator 4.0's Live3D plug-in. Make sure that you have Live3D installed, and then open `shapes.wrl` with your browser. Once the world is open, you can then use Live3D's navigation controls to move around the world. Click inside the world to select it, and then use your arrow keys to move within it. Try to move between the objects to get the full 3-D effect, as shown in Figure 25.4. Experiment with some of the other navigational controls provided by Live3D:

- *walk*—Allows you to use the mouse and arrow keys to walk around (i.e., move) within the world.

- *spin*—Allows you to spin the world around your current location. Click the left mouse button and drag to spin the world.

- *look*—Allows you to turn your head within the world. Click the left mouse button and drag to look.

- *slide*—Similar to *look*, *slide* moves the world left, right, up and down with respect to your current position.

- *point*—Allows you to click a point within the world and be moved to that point.

- *lamp*—Increases or decreases the lighting within the world.

- *view*—Moves between viewpoints in the virtual world. In the case of `shapes.wrl`, *view* moves you to the starting viewpoint.

Take a few minutes to get comfortable moving around in this world before you go on to learn how it is created.

FIGURE 25.3

VRML worlds are
created from simple
geometrical shapes.
(shapes.wrl)

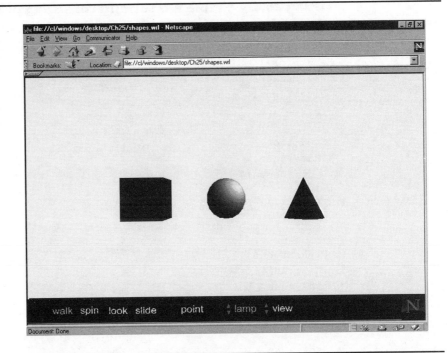

FIGURE 25.4

Moving between objects
accentuates their 3-D
effects. (shapes.wrl)

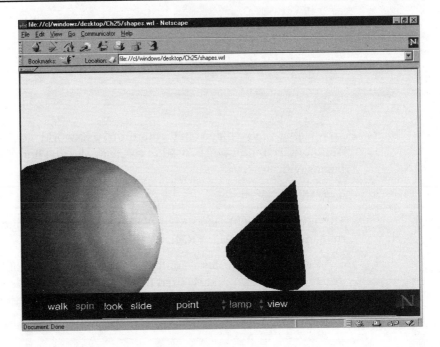

Listing 25.1. A simple VRML world consisting of basic geometric nodes (shapes.wrl)

```
#VRML V1.0 ascii
Separator {
 DEF BackgroundImage Info { string "white.gif" }
 DirectionalLight {
  direction -1 -1 -1
 }
 Separator {
  Material {
   diffuseColor 1 0 0
  }
  Translation { translation -4 0 0 }
  Cube {}
 }
 Separator {
  Material {
   diffuseColor 0 1 0
  }
  Sphere {}
 }
 Separator {
  Material {
   diffuseColor 0 0 1
  }
  Translation { translation 4 0 0 }
  Cone {}
 }
}
```

Now that you've played in the `shapes.wrl` world, you are probably wondering about the funny syntax used to create it. The first line of any VRML 1.0 file begins with:

```
#VRML V1.0 ascii
```

This identifies the file as VRML 1.0. VRML files ignore whitespace characters in the same way as HTML. VRML is case-sensitive.

A VRML 1.0 file creates a single scene graph consisting of VRML nodes. The `Separator { … }` node is used to group other nodes into a single group node. The second line of the file starts a group node which includes all subsequent nodes in the file.

The third line of the file consists of an information node definition. The DEF keyword indicates a definition. The BackgroundImage name is associated with the string "white.gif". This causes the white.gif file to be used as the world's background image. (The default background color of a world is black.)

The following lines define the world's lighting source using the Directional-Light node.

```
DirectionalLight {
  direction -1 -1 -1
  }
```

The direction field of the light is given by the three coordinates -1 -1 -1. These coordinates define a light source along the line from (0,0,0) to (-1,-1,-1). It is a good idea to always define a lighting source. Otherwise, your world may be displayed in total darkness.

> **NOTE**
>
> A Cartesian coordinate system is used within VRML worlds, with the X axis increasing from left to right, the Y axis increasing from bottom to top, and the Z axis increasing in a line moving from the display to the user. These axes may be changed.

A Separator node is used to group the nodes of the red cube, as follows:

```
Separator {
  Material {
   diffuseColor 1 0 0
   }
  Translation { translation -4 0 0 }
  Cube {}
  }
```

Within the Separator node, the Material node, also referred to as a *property*, specifies the color of the cube by setting its diffuseColor field to 1 0 0. The first number specifies the red color intensity, the second number specifies the green color intensity, and the third number specifies the blue color intensity. Diffuse color is color that changes based on the position of an object with respect to a light source.

A `Translation` node is used to position an object within 3-space. The coordinates -4 0 0 specify that the cube should be placed four units to the left of the center of the space.

A `Cube` node specifies that the shape of the object is to be a cube.

Another `Separator` node is used to group the nodes of the green sphere, as follows:

```
Separator {
  Material {
   diffuseColor 0 1 0
  }
  Sphere {}
}
```

Notice that in this group the `diffuseColor` field of the material node is set to green and that the `Sphere` node replaces the `Cube` node. Since no translation node is specified, the sphere is placed in the center of the world.

Finally, a `Separator` node is used to group the nodes of the blue cone, as follows:

```
Separator {
  Material {
   diffuseColor 0 0 1
  }
  Translation { translation 4 0 0 }
  Cone {}
}
```

The `diffuseColor` field of the `Material` node is set to blue. The `Translation` node moves the cone four units to the right of the world's center. The `Cone` node is used to specify the object's shape.

TIP

Remember, at this point I'm providing just enough VRML for you to be able to work a few simple examples. The focus of this chapter is less on VRML itself than on JavaScript's relationship to VRML; in the remaining sections you'll see how to link VRML worlds using JavaScript, and how to dynamically generate VRML from JavaScript. To go further in your study of VRML itself, you should read through the VRML 1.0 and 2.0 specifications.

Using VRML Links

One of the nicer features incorporated into VRML 1.0 is the capability to link VRML worlds together via URLs. These links can be associated with 3-D objects. When a user is navigating a world, a text description of a link appears as the mouse is moved over the linked objects. Clicking on the object causes the world at the link's destination to be loaded.

The example shown in Listing 25.2 illustrates the use of VRML links. It also shows how VRML worlds may be embedded in an HTML document. Open `links.htm` with your browser. Move around in the embedded VRML world. Note how text pops up when you move the cursor over linked objects, as shown in Figure 25.5. Click on the blue cone and the world shown in Figure 25.6 is loaded. Note that this world contains a link back to the original HTML document. Click on this link to return to `links.htm`.

FIGURE 25.5

VRML links are displayed when the cursor is placed over 3-D objects. (urls.wrl)

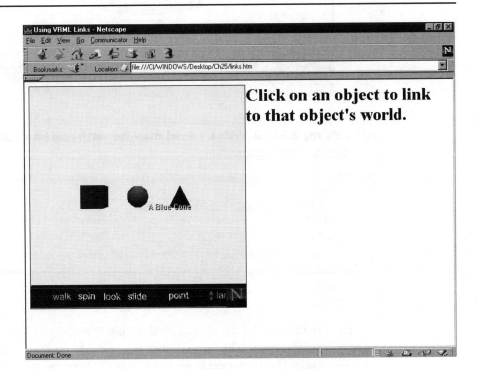

FIGURE 25.6

A new world is loaded
when the VRML link is
clicked. Moving the
mouse pointer to the
object displays a return
link to the original HTML
document. (cone.wrl)

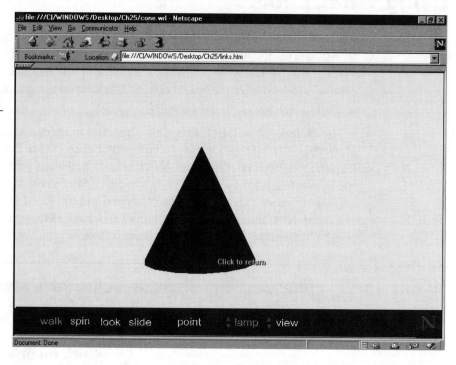

Listing 25.2. A VRML world may be embedded in an HTML document. (links.htm)

```
<HTML>
<HEAD>
<TITLE>Using VRML Links</TITLE>
</HEAD>
<BODY>
<EMBED SRC="urls.wrl" HEIGHT=400 WIDTH=400 ALIGN="LEFT">
<H1>Click on an object to link to that object's world.</H1>
</BODY>
</HTML>
```

The links.htm file uses the <EMBEDS> tag to embed the Live3D plug-in within the HTML document. The dimensions of the plug-in window are set to 400 pixels by 400 pixels. The alignment is set to LEFT so that text can be displayed to the right of the plug-in. The embedded VRML file is urls.wrl. This file is shown in Listing 25.3.

Listing 25.3. Adding links to VRML objects (urls.wrl)

```
#VRML V1.0 ascii
Separator {
 DEF BackgroundImage Info { string "white.gif" }
 DirectionalLight {
     on          TRUE
     intensity   0.6
     color       1 1 1
     direction   0 -1 -1
 }
 Separator {
  WWWAnchor {
   name "cube.wrl"
   description "A Red Cube"
   Translation { translation -4 0 0 }
   Material { diffuseColor 1 0 0 }
   Cube {}
  }
 }
 Separator {
  WWWAnchor {
   name "sphere.wrl"
   description "A Green Sphere"
   Material { diffuseColor 0 1 0 }
   Sphere {}
  }
 }
 Separator {
  WWWAnchor {
   name "cone.wrl"
   description "A Blue Cone"
   Material { diffuseColor 0 0 1 }
   Translation { translation 4 0 0 }
   Cone {}
  }
 }
}
```

The urls.wrl file is based on the shapes.wrl file that you studied earlier in the chapter. You'll notice that the DirectionalLight field has been modified to include three more fields. The on field is set to TRUE to indicate that the light is on. The intensity field is set to 0.6 to reduce the light's intensity to 60% of the maximum. The color is set to 1 1 1 to change the lighting color to white. The light's direction is set to 0 -1 -1 to specify that the light arrive from the front and top.

The only other difference between urls.wrl and shapes.wrl are the WWWAnchor nodes which group the geometrical shapes into link anchors. The name field of the WWWAnchor node is set to the destination of the link. The description field specifies the text that is to be displayed when the user moves the cursor onto the object.

Listings 25.4 through 25.6 show the VRML files that are loaded when the user clicks on the objects of urls.wrl. Note that each of these files contains a link back to the links.htm file.

Listing 25.4. The red cube world (cube.wrl)

```
#VRML V1.0 ascii
Separator {
 DEF BackgroundImage Info { string "white.gif" }
 DirectionalLight {
    on          TRUE
    intensity   0.6
    color       1 1 1
    direction   0 -1 -1
 }
 Separator {
  WWWAnchor {
   name "links.htm"
   description "Click to return"
   Translation { translation -4 0 0 }
   Material {
    emissiveColor 1 0 0
    diffuseColor 1 0 0
   }
   Cube {}
  }
 }
}
```

Listing 25.5. The green sphere world (sphere.wrl)

```
#VRML V1.0 ascii
Separator {
 DEF BackgroundImage Info { string "white.gif" }
 DirectionalLight {
    on          TRUE
    intensity   0.6
    color       1 1 1
```

```
     direction    0 -1 -1
 }
Separator {
 WWWAnchor {
  name "links.htm"
  description "Click to return"
  Material { diffuseColor 0 1 0 }
  Sphere {}
 }
 }
}
```

Listing 25.6. The blue cone world (cone.wrl)

```
#VRML V1.0 ascii
Separator {
 DEF BackgroundImage Info { string "white.gif" }
 DirectionalLight {
     on          TRUE
     intensity   0.6
     color       1 1 1
     direction   0 -1 -1
 }
 Separator {
  WWWAnchor {
   name "links.htm"
   description "Click to return"
   Material {
    diffuseColor 0 0 1
   }
   Translation { translation 4 0 0 }
   Cone {}
  }
 }
}
```

Using JavaScript to Generate VRML

In the previous section, you learned how to embed VRML worlds in HTML documents. The VRML files that you've been working with are simple files that were built by hand. For more complex VRML applications you will probably want to use a *world-building tool*. You can find links to several of these tools on the Yahoo VRML pages, which can be found at the following URL:

*http://www.yahoo.com/Computers_and_Internet/Internet/World_Wide_Web
/Virtual_Reality_Modeling_Language__VRML_/*

In addition to using world-building tools, VRML may also be dynamically generated using JavaScript. Of course, you have to write the JavaScript that creates the VRML. Listing 25.7 provides a simple example of how this can be accomplished. Open `generate.htm` with your browser. It displays a two-frame document. At first, the upper frame displays the empty world specified by `blank.wrl` (Listing 25.8). The bottom frame contains the HTML/JavaScript file shown in Listing 25.9. This frame allows different types of VRML objects to be dynamically created in the upper frame. For example, select the Cone and Green radio buttons and click on the Generate VRML button. The upper frame is updated to display a green cone, as shown in Figure 25.7.

FIGURE 25.7

Making your selection in the bottom frame (generate.htm) tells JavaScript to generate a VRML object in the top frame.

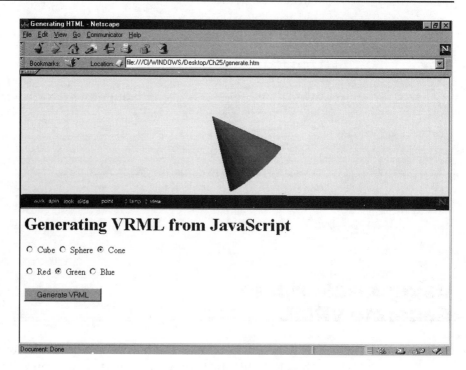

Listing 25.7. Setting up the frame set of Figure 25.7 (generate.htm)

```
<HTML>
<HEAD>
<TITLE>Generating HTML</TITLE>
</HEAD>
<FRAMESET ROWS="*,*" BORDER=0>
<FRAME NAME="VRML" SRC="blank.wrl">
<FRAME NAME="controls" SRC="controls.htm">
</FRAMESET>
</HTML>
```

Listing 25.8. An empty world (blank.wrl)

```
#VRML V1.0 ascii
Separator {
 DEF BackgroundImage Info { string "white.gif" }
 DirectionalLight {
    on          TRUE
    intensity   0.6
    color       1 1 1
    direction   0 -1 -1
 }
}
```

Listing 25.9. The VRML-generating code (controls.htm)

```
<HTML>
<HEAD>
<TITLE>VRML Generator</TITLE>
<SCRIPT LANGUAGE="JavaScript"> <!--
function generateVRML() {
 var formRef=window.document.forms[0]
 var newShape="cone"
 var newColor="blue"
 if(formRef.elements[0].checked) newShape="cube"
 else if(formRef.elements[1].checked) newShape="sphere"
 if(formRef.elements[3].checked) newColor="red"
 else if(formRef.elements[4].checked) newColor="green"
 var doc=parent.frames[0].document
 with(doc) {
  open("x-world/x-vrml")
  writeln("")
  writeln("#VRML V1.0 ascii")
  writeln("Separator {")
```

```
        writeln('DEF BackgroundImage Info { string "white.gif" }')
        writeln("DirectionalLight {")
        writeln("on TRUE")
        writeln("intensity 0.6")
        writeln("color 1 1 1")
        writeln("direction 0 -1 -1")
        writeln("}")
        writeln("Separator {")
        writeln("Material {")
        if(newColor=="red") writeln("diffuseColor 1 0 0")
        else if(newColor=="green") writeln("diffuseColor 0 1 0")
        else writeln("diffuseColor 0 0 1")
        writeln("}")
        writeln("Translation { translation 0 0 -10}")
        writeln("Rotation { rotation 0 0 1 .7 }")
        writeln("Rotation { rotation 0 1 0 .7 }")
        if(newShape=="cube") writeln("Cube {}")
        else if(newShape=="sphere") writeln("Sphere {}")
        else writeln("Cone {}")
        writeln("}")
        writeln("}")
        close()
    }
}
// --> </SCRIPT>
</HEAD>
<BODY>
<H1>Generating VRML from JavaScript</H1>
<FORM>
<P><INPUT TYPE="RADIO" NAME="shape" VALUE="cube" CHECKED>
Cube
<INPUT TYPE="RADIO" NAME="shape" VALUE="sphere">
Sphere
<INPUT TYPE="RADIO" NAME="shape" VALUE="cone">
Cone</P><P>
<INPUT TYPE="RADIO" NAME="color" VALUE="red" CHECKED>
Red
<INPUT TYPE="RADIO" NAME="color" VALUE="green">
Green
<INPUT TYPE="RADIO" NAME="color" VALUE="blue">
Blue</P>
<INPUT TYPE="BUTTON" VALUE="Generate VRML"
 ONCLICK="generateVRML()">
```

```
</FORM>
</BODY>
</HTML>
```

The `controls.htm` file provides two groups of radio buttons—one to select the object's shape and another to select the object's color. The `onClick` event handler of the Generate VRML button is the `generateVRML()` function. This function checks to see which radio buttons were selected and sets the `newShape` and `newColor` variables accordingly. The document in the top frame is opened and its MIME type is set to `x-world/x-vrml`. A series of `writeln()` method invocations are used to write the VRML code corresponding to the selected object. The `close()` method closes the document and causes the top frame to be updated.

Scripting and VRML 2.0

While the previous example shows how JavaScript can be used to generate VRML, an even tighter coupling of JavaScript and VRML is supported by VRML 2.0. This version of VRML extends VRML 1.0 by providing greater interaction via an event-based model. In VRML 2.0, events are created by `Sensor` nodes as the result of user actions, the passage of time, or the processing of previously generated events. These events are propagated to other nodes via *routes*. Routes connect the output events of source nodes with the input events of destination nodes. The destination nodes may generate other events as the result of processing incoming events.

The processing of events is accomplished using VRML `Script` nodes. Script nodes define input and output events via their `eventIn` and `eventOut` fields. Code is attached to `Script` nodes via their `url` field. Although VRML browsers are not required to support any specific scripting language, the VRML 2.0 specification contains appendices that cover both JavaScript and Java scripting. JavaScript scripting is covered in the VRML specification's Appendix D.

Summary

In this chapter, you were introduced to VRML and learned how to include it in your Web applications. You learned how to work with VRML links and how to dynamically generate VRML from JavaScript. You were also introduced to VRML 2.0 scripting. This chapter concludes Part 6. In Part 7 you'll learn all about server-side Web programming using JavaScript.

PART VII

Server Programming

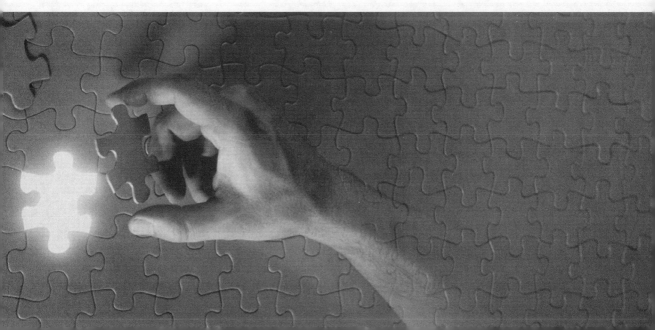

CHAPTER

TWENTY-SIX

26

Interfacing JavaScript with CGI Programs

The Common Gateway Interface (CGI) is the standard for communication between Web servers and server-side Web programs. Netscape, Microsoft, and most other Web servers support the Common Gateway Interface; thus, for the most part, Web application designers can develop server-side programs that will work regardless of the particular type of Web server used at a Web site. If you want to write a server-side program that will have the greatest portability, then develop it as a CGI program.

In this chapter, you'll learn how CGI programs work, and we'll cover the types of Web applications in which CGI programs are used. On the one hand, you'll learn how to interface JavaScript scripts with CGI scripts, and on the other hand you'll learn how to use CGI programs to generate JavaScript code. When you finish this chapter, you'll know how to combine JavaScript scripts with CGI programs in your Web applications.

When to Use CGI Programs

In previous chapters we stressed the need to perform as much processing as possible on the browser, rather than on the server, to conserve precious communication bandwidth and server-processing resources. Any processing that is performed locally reduces the load on your Web server.

However, for some Web applications, server-side processing is absolutely essential. These applications include any that collect and store data about multiple users (for example, online registration forms and customer surveys), and applications that require significant database support (for example, large catalogs and search engines).

CGI programs provide the interface between Web browsers and online databases. They also provide gateways to other online services, such as Gopher and WAIS (though, admittedly, the popularity of these services has declined with the rise of the World Wide Web). Any Web application that requires server-side storage or access to non-Web resources is a potential candidate for the use of a CGI program.

How CGI Programs Work

CGI programs (also referred to as CGI scripts) are the external programs I was talking about when I said that the CGI is a standard interface for communication between Web servers and external programs. The CGI specification identifies how data is to be passed from a Web server to a CGI program, and back from the CGI program to the Web server.

NOTE Refer to Chapter 1 for a general overview of CGI programs. Refer to Chapter 7 for a discussion and examples of using CGI programs with forms.

The following points summarize how the CGI works:

- A browser requests a CGI program by specifying the CGI program's URL. The request arises as the result of the user submitting a form or clicking on a link. (The browser may append to the URL a query string or extra path information.)

- When a Web server receives a URL request, it determines whether the URL refers to a CGI program. Most Web servers identify CGI programs by the path in which they are located or by their filename extension. For example, all files in the path `/cgi-bin/` or with the extensions `.cgi` or `.pl` could be considered CGI programs.

- When a Web server identifies a request for a CGI program, it executes the CGI program as a separate process and passes any data included in the URL to the program.

- The CGI program performs its processing and then returns its output to the Web server. The conventions defined by the CGI specification determine how CGI programs receive data from and return data to Web servers. These conventions are described in the following sections.

The overall process is depicted in Figure 26.1.

FIGURE 26.1

Web servers communi-
cate with external
programs using the
conventions of the CGI.

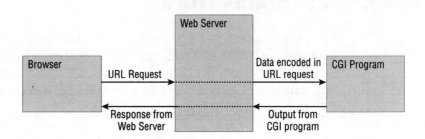

Getting Data from the Web Server

When a CGI program is executed, one of its first tasks is to determine what data
was passed to it by the Web server. This data may be passed in the following ways:

- Command-line arguments

- Environment variables

- The program's standard input stream

Command-line arguments and the standard input stream are supported by
almost all programming languages. Environment variables are less commonly
used outside of Web applications. The following subsections describe when and
how CGI programs receive data via each of these mechanisms.

Command-Line Arguments

Command-line arguments are parameters that are passed to programs via the command line that is used to execute the program. For example, the following command
line executes the `search` program and passes it the string `news` as an argument.

```
search news
```

HTTP `ISINDEX` queries are the means of passing data to CGI programs as
command-line arguments. CGI programs read the command-line arguments via
the mechanisms provided by the programming language in which they are written. For example, the C programming language provides the `argc` and `argv` variables for accessing command-line arguments. The Perl programming language
provides the `@ARGV` array for the same purpose.

Environment Variables

Environment variables are the primary mechanism by which Web servers communicate with CGI programs. All CGI programs can receive data from Web servers via environment variables.

Environment variables are variables which are external to a program's execution. They are used to define the environment in which a program executes. Table 26.1 identifies the environment variables defined by CGI version 1.1. The most important of these variables are CONTENT_LENGTH, which identifies the number of bytes that are passed via standard input, and PATH_INFO and QUERY_STRING, which identify data that is passed via extra path information or a query string.

TABLE 26.1 Environment variables used by the CGI

Environment Variable	Description
AUTH_TYPE	The authentication scheme used to validate the user requesting access to a Web page.
CONTENT_LENGTH	The number of characters that have been passed via standard input.
CONTENT_TYPE	The MIME type associated with the data available via standard input.
GATEWAY_INTERFACE	The version of the CGI specification supported by the server.
HTTP_*	The contents of the various HTTP headers received by the Web server. "HTTP_" is prepended to the name of the header. For example, the ACCEPT header is represented by the HTTP_ACCEPT environment variable and the USER_AGENT header is represented by the HTTP_USER_AGENT variable.
PATH_INFO	The extra path information added to the URL of the CGI program.
PATH_TRANSLATED	The full path name that was translated from the URL by the Web server.
QUERY_STRING	The query string portion of the URL.
REMOTE_ADDR	The IP address of the host associated with the requesting browser.
REMOTE_HOST	The name of the host associated with the requesting browser.
REMOTE_IDENT	The verified name of the host associated with the requesting browser.

TABLE 26.1 Environment variables used by the CGI (continued)

Environment Variable	Description
REMOTE_USER	The name of the user associated with the requesting browser.
REQUEST_METHOD	The method associated with the browser request: GET, POST, HEAD, etc.
SCRIPT_NAME	The path and name of the CGI program.
SERVER_NAME	The name of the Web server host.
SERVER_PORT	The HTTP port number (usually 80) used by the Web server.
SERVER_PROTOCOL	The name and version of the protocol used by the requesting browser to submit the request.
SERVER_SOFTWARE	The name and version number of the Web server software.

The environment variables shown in Table 26.1 are available to all CGI programs regardless of whether the CGI program was executed as the result of an ISINDEX query, a form submission, or the clicking of a hyperlink.

Many programming languages provide special mechanisms for accessing environment variables. For example, Perl provides the $ENV array and C provides the getenv() library function. Since the capability to read environment variables is important for any non-trivial CGI programs, it should be a primary consideration when selecting a CGI programming language.

> **TIP**
>
> Some Web servers, such as Netscape servers, define server-specific environment variables in addition to those defined by the CGI. If you want your CGI programs to be portable between Web servers, you should not use these server-specific environment variables.

Reading Query String Data   When data is passed to a CGI program via the QUERY_STRING environment variable the data is encoded using the following conventions. These coding conventions are referred to as *URL coding*.

- Spaces are replaced by plus (+) signs.

- Other characters may be replaced by character codes of the form %*xx* (with the *xx* being replaced by two hexadecimal digits corresponding to the character's ASCII value). For example, %2a is used to encode a plus sign.

CGI programs must decode the data passed via the QUERY_STRING variable. This is accomplished by replacing plus signs with spaces, and sequences of the form %*xx* with their character equivalent. This decoding is known as *URL decoding*.

> **NOTE** JavaScript provides the escape() and unescape() functions to support URL encoding and decoding. The escape() function takes a single string parameter and returns a URL-encoded version of the string. The unescape() function takes a single string parameter and returns the URL-decoded version of the string.

Form Data Coding   In addition to query string encoding, other application specific codings may be used. For example, form data is encoded as a sequence of *name*=*value* pairs, separated by ampersands (the & symbol), with *name* being replaced by the form field's name attribute and *value* being replaced by the field's value when submitted by the user. Any equals signs or ampersands appearing in the data are encoded using the %*xx* hexadecimal coding scheme covered in the previous section.

When the form uses the GET method, form data is passed to CGI programs via the QUERY_STRING environment variable. When the form uses the POST method, form data is passed to the CGI programs via standard input. The use of standard input is covered in a later section of this chapter.

CGI programs should decode form data by using the ampersands to separate the query string into *name*=*value* pairs, using the equals signs to separate the *name* and *value* portions, and then decoding the name and value portions using the URL decoding conventions.

> **NOTE** If a query string does not have data in the form of *name*=*value* pairs, then most Web servers assume that the requested URL is an ISINDEX query, and pass the query string as a command-line argument.

Reading Extra Path Data Extra path information is data that is added to a URL as additional path information following the path to the CGI program. The extra path information is passed to a CGI program using the PATH_INFO environment variable. For example, in the following URL,

http://www.jaworski.com/cgi-bin/echo-query/extra/path/info

the path */extra/path/info* that follows *echo-query* would be passed to the echo-query program via PATH_INFO as "/extra/path/info". Extra path information is an easy way to send fixed information to CGI programs. It is usually used with non-form URLs.

> **TIP**
>
> If you intend to use extra path information to send data to CGI programs, you should use URL-coding to ensure that the data is correctly processed by Web browsers and servers.

The Standard Input and Output Streams

Standard input refers to the keyboard input received by character-mode programs, such as nongraphical DOS programs and UNIX and Windows NT command-line programs. Relatedly, *standard output* refers to the visible output produced by these programs: characters that are displayed on the console monitor (in this context, this would normally be the *server's* console, not the user's).

In addition to treating users' input and output in standard ways, most operating systems have the capability of allowing command-line programs to run in an environment where the user's keyboard and display monitor can be *simulated*. This means that input other than the user's keyboard input (for instance, a query string or extra path information in a URL, or data from a browser form) can be *redirected* to a program *as* standard input, and the program can process the data regardless of the fact that the data came from some source other than the standard source (keyboard input). Similarly, a program's output can be redirected by a server to the user's browser as though it were standard output to the server's own console display. Web servers make use of this redirection capability to process posted form data, as shown in Figure 26.2.

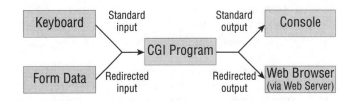

FIGURE 26.2

Web servers redirect the standard input and output streams of CGI programs to support browser/CGI program communication.

When the POST method is used to submit a form, the form's data is sent by the Web server to a CGI program as standard input to the CGI program. When a Web server creates a process to execute a CGI program, it redirects the form's data to the standard input stream of the CGI program. This data appears to a CGI program as if it were typed by a user at a keyboard. (*Note:* The amount of data that can be redirected in this manner is subject to limitation. You can use the CONTENT_LENGTH environment variable to identify the number of bytes to be made available via standard input.)

The output of the CGI program is returned to the Web server so that it can be redirected to the user's browser. By redirecting standard input and output, the Web server allows CGI programs to be designed using the simple character-stream approach common to DOS and UNIX programs. Almost all programming languages provide capabilities to read data from the standard input stream and write data to the standard output stream.

Sending Data Back to the Web Server

A CGI program returns data to the requesting browser via the Web server. In all cases, it returns the data by writing it to the standard output stream. The output of the CGI program must begin with a header line, followed by a blank line, and then by the data to be displayed by the browser. The header line usually consists of a Content-type header that specifies the MIME type of the data returned by the CGI program. In most cases, the MIME type will be text/html, as shown in the following example.

```
Content type: text/html

<HTML>
<HEAD>
```

```
<TITLE>CGI Results</TITLE>
</HEAD>
<BODY>
<H1>It worked!</H1>
</BODY>
</HTML>
```

The header line does not have to be a `Content-type` header; a CGI program can instead return a `Location` header that specifies the name of a URL to be loaded. For example, consider the following program output. The `Location` header specifies that the `results.htm` file that is located at the partial URL `/javascript/results.htm` is to be returned as the result of the CGI program's execution.

```
Location: /javascript/results.htm
blank line
```

> **TIP**
>
> When using a `Location` header be sure to follow it by a single blank line, even if the header is the entirety of your script.

Using Non-Parsed Header Programs

As mentioned in the previous section, CGI programs normally return data to the requesting browser via the Web server, which takes care of providing all of the required HTTP headers. It is possible, however, for CGI programs to bypass the Web server and return data directly to the requesting browser. Of course, when you do this, your CGI program is then responsible for providing all of the required headers.

CGI programs that bypass the Web server and return data directly to Web browsers are referred to as *nonparsed header programs*. Most Web servers require nonparsed header CGI programs to begin with the characters nph- (nph followed by a hyphen) to help servers differentiate between regular CGI programs and nonparsed header programs.

When should you use nonparsed header programs? The answer is almost never. By going through the Web server, your CGI programs can be designed much simpler and easier. The only time it makes sense to bypass the Web server is when your CGI program returns a large amount of data and you don't want the server to delay transmission of the data to the browser.

The General Design of a CGI Program

Now that you've learned how CGI programs receive data from and return data to Web servers, we'll cover the general design of typical CGI programs.

Most CGI programs are *transaction oriented*. They receive input data from a browser, perform processing based on the data received from the browser, and return the results of the processing to the browser. The way that a CGI program reads and processes its data depends on the way that it is requested by a browser.

ISINDEX Queries

The CGI program looks for input data by checking its command-line arguments.

- If it does not have any data, then it returns a Web page containing an ISINDEX tag to the requesting browser. This allows the user to submit data to the CGI program.

- If the CGI program does receive data in its command-line arguments, then it decodes the data using URL decoding, processes the ISINDEX query, and sends the results of the query to the requesting browser.

Form Processing

CGI programs that process form data access the form data in different ways depending on whether the form is submitted using the GET or POST method.

- If the form is submitted via the GET method then the form data is read from the QUERY_STRING variable.

- If the form is submitted via the POST method then the form data is read from the standard input stream.

When the form data has been read, it is decoded and processed. The data returned by the CGI program can consist of other forms, other Web pages, or files of other MIME types.

Server-Side Image Map Queries

CGI programs that process image-map queries read the coordinates of the user's click from the QUERY_STRING environment variable. These programs perform their processing based on the coordinates of the click and a map file. The map file associates image regions with URLs.

The particular map file to be used can be specified as extra path information. The image-map program returns the URL associated with the coordinates of the user's click.

Hyperlinks

Some CGI programs may be invoked as the result of the user clicking on a hyperlink. Data may be passed to the CGI program via a query string or extra path information contained in the URL. The CGI program uses command-line arguments and environment variables to access this data. It performs its processing and then returns its output to the browser.

A Shell Script Example

By now, you are probably anxious to see an example of a CGI program. Listing 26.1 provides a CGI script written in the Linux shell programming language. Don't worry if you don't understand Linux shell programming, the script only uses the echo command and the inout program. The first line of the script identifies the file as a shell script. The second line writes the Content-type header to standard output. The third line writes the required blank line to standard output. Subsequent lines write an HTML document to standard output.

The first part of the document identifies the command-line arguments that are passed to the CGI program. The $# variable identifies the number of command-line arguments and the $* variable identifies the values of these arguments.

Listing 26.1. The echo-query Script (echo-query)

```sh
#!/bin/sh
echo Content-type: text/html
echo
echo "<HTML>"
echo "<HEAD>"
echo "<TITLE>Echo CGI Request</TITLE>"
echo "</HEAD>"
echo "<BODY>"
echo "<H1>CGI Request</H1>"
echo "<H2>Command-line Arguments</H2>"
echo "<P>Number of command-line arguments: $#</P>"
echo "<P>Command-line arguments: "$*"</P>"
echo "<H2>Environment Variables</H2>"
echo "<PRE>"
echo AUTH_TYPE = $AUTH_TYPE
echo CONTENT_LENGTH = $CONTENT_LENGTH
echo CONTENT_TYPE = $CONTENT_TYPE
echo GATEWAY_INTERFACE = $GATEWAY_INTERFACE
echo HTTP_ACCEPT = "$HTTP_ACCEPT"
echo HTTP_USER_AGENT = "$HTTP_USER_AGENT"
echo PATH_INFO = "$PATH_INFO"
echo PATH_TRANSLATED = "$PATH_TRANSLATED"
echo QUERY_STRING = "$QUERY_STRING"
echo REMOTE_ADDR = $REMOTE_ADDR
echo REMOTE_HOST = $REMOTE_HOST
echo REMOTE_IDENT = $REMOTE_IDENT
echo REMOTE_USER = $REMOTE_USER
echo REQUEST_METHOD = $REQUEST_METHOD
echo SCRIPT_NAME = "$SCRIPT_NAME"
echo SERVER_NAME = $SERVER_NAME
echo SERVER_PORT = $SERVER_PORT
echo SERVER_PROTOCOL = $SERVER_PROTOCOL
echo SERVER_SOFTWARE = $SERVER_SOFTWARE
echo "</PRE>"
echo "<H2>Standard Input</H2>"
inout $CONTENT_LENGTH
echo "</BODY>"
echo "</HTML>"
```

The second part of the returned document identifies the environment variables that are passed to the CGI program. These variables are referenced by prepending a $ to the name of the environment variable.

The last part of the returned document identifies the data that is sent to the CGI program via the standard input stream. The `inout` program is invoked to read `CONTENT_LENGTH` characters from standard input and write them to standard output.

NOTE

The `echo-query` program shown in Listing 26.1 is accessible via the URL *http://www.jaworski.com/cgi-bin/echo-query*.

In order to use the `echo-query` script, you need to create an HTML document to access the script's URL. Listing 26.2 provides such a document. It contains a link to `echo-query` with both extra path information and a query string appended.

Open `cgi-test.htm` with your browser. Figure 26.3 shows the Web page that is displayed. Click on the link to the CGI program. Figure 26.4 shows the Web page that is returned. Note the value of the `QUERY_STRING` and `PATH_INFO` variables.

TIP

The `echo-query` script is a useful tool for testing your links in order to see how the data they encode is passed to a CGI program.

Listing 26.2. Accessing the echo-query Script (cgi-test.htm)

```
<HTML>
<HEAD>
<TITLE>CGI Test</TITLE>
</HEAD>
<BODY>
<A HREF=
 "http://www.jaworski.com/cgi-bin/echo-query/extra/path
➥/info?f1=v1&f2=v2">
Click here to access echo-query</A>
</BODY>
</HTML>
```

FIGURE 26.3

The Web page generated by `cgi-test.htm` (Listing 26.2)

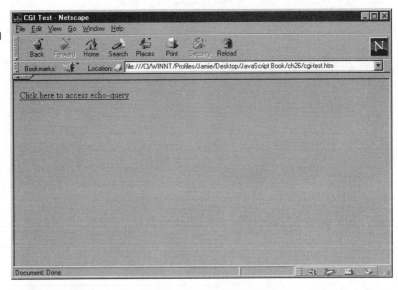

FIGURE 26.4

The results returned by `echo-query` (Listing 26.2)

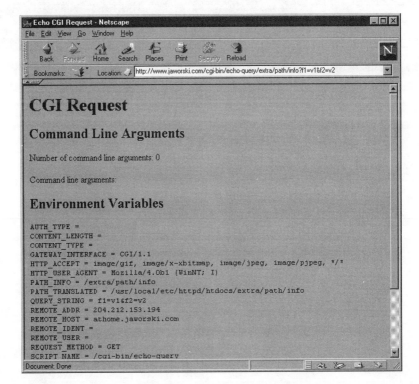

Interfacing JavaScript Scripts with CGI Scripts

JavaScript scripts can make use of CGI programs to access online databases, Internet services, or perform other types of server-side processing. The interface between a JavaScript script and a CGI program is through the CGI program's URL. Scripts can use the URL to invoke a CGI program and pass data to it as a query string or extra path information. If a CGI program is accessed via an HTML form, then the form's data can be used to control the CGI program's behavior.

The js2cgi.htm file, shown in Listing 26.3, demonstrates how CGI programs can be accessed via JavaScript. Open js2cgi.htm with your browser. It generates the HTML form shown in Figure 26.5. Fill out the form and click on the Submit button. Your form data is sent to the add2db.pl CGI program at the URL *http://www.jaworski.com/cgi-bin/add2db.pl* and the Web page shown in Figure 26.6 is displayed.

FIGURE 26.5

Using JavaScript to process a form's data and send it to a CGI program (Listing 26.3)

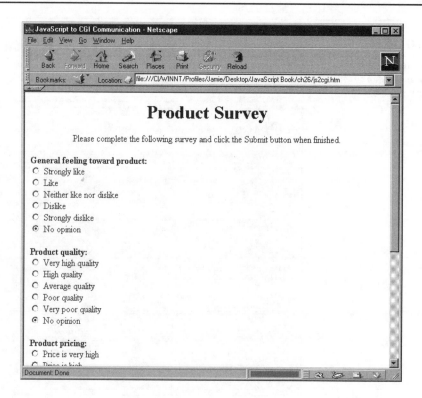

FIGURE 26.6

FIGURE 26.6

The survey results are displayed using JavaScript generated by a CGI program. (Listing 26.5)

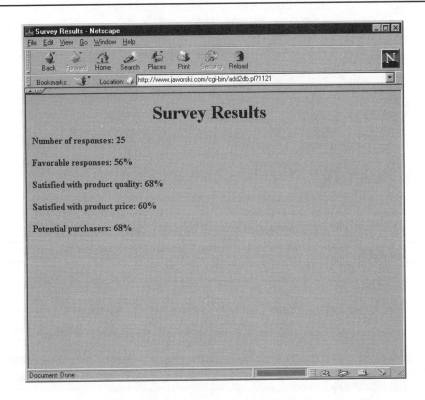

The js2cgi.htm file consists of an HTML form with four sets of radio buttons. The user clicks on the radio buttons to fill out the product survey. The sendToCGI() function handles the onClick event of the Submit button by determining which buttons were selected and creating a four-character text string (stored in the results variable) that summarizes the form's data. For example, suppose a user selected the third value of the first set of radio buttons, the fourth value of the second set, the first value of the third set and the last value of the last set. The value of the results variable would be *2305*.

The value of the results variable is appended to the URL of the CGI program as a query string, and the href property of the current window's location object is set to the URL. This causes the URL of the CGI program to be requested.

Listing 26.3. Interfacing JavaScript with a CGI program (js2cgi.htm)

```
<HTML>
<HEAD>
<TITLE>JavaScript to CGI Communication</TITLE>
```

```
<SCRIPT LANGUAGE="JavaScript"><!--
function sendToCGI() {
 results=""
 survey=window.document.survey
 for(var i=0;i<survey.length-1;++i)
  if(survey.elements[i].checked)
   results+=i%6
 window.location.href=
  "http://www.jaworski.com/cgi-bin/add2db.pl?"+results
}
// --></SCRIPT>
</HEAD>
<BODY BGCOLOR="white"">
<H1 ALIGN="CENTER">Product Survey</H1>
<P ALIGN="CENTER">Please complete the following survey and
click the Submit button when finished.</P>
<FORM NAME="survey">
<P><B>General feeling toward product:</B><BR>
<INPUT TYPE="radio" NAME="g1"> Strongly like<BR>
<INPUT TYPE="radio" NAME="g1"> Like<BR>
<INPUT TYPE="radio" NAME="g1"> Neither like nor dislike<BR>
<INPUT TYPE="radio" NAME="g1"> Dislike<BR>
<INPUT TYPE="radio" NAME="g1"> Strongly dislike<BR>
<INPUT TYPE="radio" NAME="g1" CHECKED> No opinion<BR>
</P>
<P><B>Product quality:</B><BR>
<INPUT TYPE="radio" NAME="g2"> Very high quality<BR>
<INPUT TYPE="radio" NAME="g2"> High quality<BR>
<INPUT TYPE="radio" NAME="g2"> Average quality<BR>
<INPUT TYPE="radio" NAME="g2"> Poor quality<BR>
<INPUT TYPE="radio" NAME="g2"> Very poor quality<BR>
<INPUT TYPE="radio" NAME="g2" CHECKED> No opinion<BR>
</P>
<P><B>Product pricing:</B><BR>
<INPUT TYPE="radio" NAME="g3"> Price is very high<BR>
<INPUT TYPE="radio" NAME="g3"> Price is high<BR>
<INPUT TYPE="radio" NAME="g3"> Price is about right<BR>
<INPUT TYPE="radio" NAME="g3"> Price is low<BR>
<INPUT TYPE="radio" NAME="g3"> Price is very low<BR>
<INPUT TYPE="radio" NAME="g3" CHECKED> No opinion<BR>
</P>
<P><B>Purchase plans:</B><BR>
```

```
<INPUT TYPE="radio" NAME="g4"> Plan to purchase<BR>
<INPUT TYPE="radio" NAME="g4"> May purchase<BR>
<INPUT TYPE="radio" NAME="g4"> May purchase if price is
  lowered<BR>
<INPUT TYPE="radio" NAME="g4"> May purchase if quality is
  improved<BR>
<INPUT TYPE="radio" NAME="g4"> Do not plan to purchase<BR>
<INPUT TYPE="radio" NAME="g4" CHECKED> No opinion<BR>
</P>
</TABLE>
<INPUT TYPE="BUTTON" VALUE="Submit"
  onClick="sendToCGI()">
</FORM>
</BODY>
</HTML>
```

When my Web server receives the URL request for add2db.pl, it executes the Perl script shown in Listing 26.4. Since the query string passed by js2cgi.htm is a single value and not a *name=value* pair, my Web server assumes that the request is an ISINDEX query and passes the data contained in the URL's query string as a command-line argument.

The add2db.pl script works as follows. The first line identifies the location of the Perl interpreter. The second line opens the file db.txt with append access. This means that anything written to db.txt will be appended to the end of the file. The third line writes the value of the command-line argument to the db.txt file. This value is the four-character form processing result that was appended to the URL of add2db.pl. The fourth line writes a new line character to db.txt. The fifth line closes the db.txt file, and the last line returns the file located at *http://www.jaworski.com/javascript/results.htm* as the result of the CGI program's processing. Figure 26.6 shows how results.htm is displayed.

Listing 26.4. A Perl program that stores the form data on the server (add2db.pl)

```
#!/usr/bin/perl
open (OUTPUT, ">>db.txt");
print OUTPUT @ARGV;
print OUTPUT "\n";
close (OUTPUT);
print "Location: /javascript/results.htm\n\n";
```

Returning JavaScript from CGI Programs

One of the more powerful techniques of integrating client-side JavaScript scripts with CGI programs is to use CGI programs to return JavaScript code. In doing so, your Web applications become more dynamic and efficient by allowing browsers to perform some of the CGI program's processing. Instead of responding with a static Web page, your CGI programs are able to perform the minimum amount of server-side processing and return a JavaScript script that completes the application processing on the browser.

The following example shows how CGI programs can be used to return JavaScript code. This example builds on the add2db.pl example of the previous section.

In the last line of Listing 26.4 the results.htm file is returned to complete the processing of add2db.pl. Listing 26.5 shows the contents of results.htm. It contains two scripts in the document head. The first script includes JavaScript code from the URL *http://www.jaworski.com/cgi-bin/getdb*. But this is the URL of a CGI program. Listing 26.6 shows the source code of getdb.

Since the output of getdb is crucial to the operation of results.htm, we'll examine the operation of getdb before continuing with the discussion of results.htm. The file getdb is a Perl script that summarizes the data contained in db.txt and returns its results as a JavaScript array. Recall that each line of db.txt is a four-digit value that describes the data entered into the form shown in Listing 26.3. The getdb script reads through db.txt and counts how many times radio buttons 1 through 6 are selected for survey topics 1 through 4. This results in a 24-value array. A 25th value is added that identifies the number of lines in db.txt.

getdb performs its processing as follows:

line 1 Identifies the location of the Perl interpreter. Note that the .pl extension was not used with getdb—it was left off in order to prevent the browser from expecting a file of a different MIME type.

line 2 Identifies the MIME type of the data returned by getdb as application/x-javascript. Note that a blank line follows the Content header.

line 3 Returns the beginning of a JavaScript array definition that is assigned to variable r.

lines 4–6 Opens db.txt for input. Initializes the @totals array to 0. Sets $num to 0.

lines 7–15 Loops through db.txt and reads each line. $num counts the number of lines read. $totals[6*$i+$n] counts the number of times radio button $n is selected for topic $i.

lines 16–19 Prints the values of $totals to the JavaScript output.

lines 20–21 Adds the number of lines in db.txt as the 25th value of the r array.

Getting back to results.htm, the second script contains two functions, displayResults() and writeResult(). The first of these, displayResults(), performs further processing on the r array to summarize and display the results of the survey. It sets n to r[24] which is the number of lines in db.txt. It then calculates the percentage of favorable responses, the percentage of responses in which the product quality and price were acceptable, and the percentage of respondents who are potential purchasers. These results are then displayed using the writeResults() function.

Listing 26.5. Displaying the results of the product survey (results.htm)

```
<HTML>
<HEAD>
<TITLE>Survey Results</TITLE>
<SCRIPT LANGUAGE="JavaScript"
 SRC="http://www.jaworski.com/cgi-bin/getdb"><!--
// --></SCRIPT>
<SCRIPT LANGUAGE="JavaScript"><!--
function displayResults() {
 var n=r[24]
 var favorable=(r[0]+r[1])/n
 favorable=Math.round(favorable*100)
 var quality=(r[6]+r[7]+r[8])/n
 quality=Math.round(quality*100)
 var price=(r[14]+r[15]+r[16])/n
 price=Math.round(price*100)
 var purchase=(n-r[22])/n
 purchase=Math.round(purchase*100)
 document.write("<P><B>Number of responses: "+n+"</B></P>")
 writeResult("Favorable responses: ",favorable)
 writeResult("Satisfied with product quality: ",quality)
```

```
writeResult("Satisfied with product price: ",price)
writeResult("Potential purchasers: ",purchase)
}
function writeResult(s,n) {
 document.write("<P><B>"+s+n+"%</B></P>")
}
// --></SCRIPT>
</HEAD>
<BODY>
<H1 ALIGN="CENTER">Survey Results</H1>
<SCRIPT LANGUAGE="JavaScript"><!--
displayResults()
// --></SCRIPT>
</BODY>
</HTML>
```

Listing 26.6. A CGI that returns its results as JavaScript (getdb)

```
#!/usr/bin/perl
print "Content-type: application/x-javascript\n\n";
print "r= new Array(";
open (INPUT,"db.txt");
@totals=(0,0,0,0,0,0,0,0,0,0,0,0,0,0,0,0,0,0,0,0,0,0,0,0);
$num=0;
while(<INPUT>) {
 $num++;
 chop;
 $line=$_;
 for($i=0;$i<4;$i++){
  $n=substr($line,$i,1);
  $totals[6*$i+$n]++;
 }
}
for($i=0;$i<24;$i++){
 print $totals[$i];
 print ",";
}
print $num;
print ")\n";
```

Summary

In this chapter, you learned how CGI programs work and saw the types of Web applications in which CGI programs are used. You learned how to interface JavaScript scripts with CGI scripts and how to use CGI programs to generate JavaScript code. In the next chapter, you'll learn how to use LiveWire with JavaScript to develop integrated server-side Web applications for client/server systems.

CHAPTER

TWENTY-SEVEN

27

Working with LiveWire

- The LiveWire Toolset

- The LiveWire Compiler

- Site Manager

- Application Manager

- Server-Side JavaScript Programming

- Server-Side Objects

- State Maintenance

- Server Functions

In the previous chapter, you learned how to develop server-side Web programs using the CGI and how to use interface client-side JavaScript scripts with CGI programs. In this chapter, you'll learn how to use LiveWire to create Web applications that eliminate the need for CGI programs. You'll learn how to use JavaScript 's server programming capabilities to process data received from browsers and to dynamically return new Web pages to browsers. You'll also learn how to combine client- and server-side JavaScript to develop server-based Web applications that maximize the use of browser programming capabilities.

The LiveWire Toolset

In the previous chapter, you learned how to write server-side programs that communicate with Web servers using the CGI. You might have been thinking, "Oh great! Now I have to learn Perl or some other server scripting language." You may have been a little perturbed at the thought of having to develop your server-side programs independent of your HTML and JavaScript files. If you were, then you would have had a legitimate gripe—there *ought* to be a way to develop all parts of a Web application in an integrated fashion. LiveWire is an answer to that need.

LiveWire is a Web application development environment that works with Netscape FastTrack and Enterprise servers. It provides the solution to the problem of developing both browser and server-side parts of Web applications using a common language and an integrated development environment. It allows JavaScript to be used to write server-side scripts that eliminate the need for CGI programs. These scripts are developed, integrated, and maintained with the HTML and client-side JavaScript displayed by the browser.

Browser and server elements of Web applications are compiled into .web files that are used by Netscape servers to handle browser requests. The compilation process integrates HTML and client- and server-side JavaScript into a single application file, and eliminates the need to separately develop and manage browser and server elements of the same Web application.

LiveWire consists of the following three tools:

- *Netscape Navigator 3.01 Gold.* You can use this to edit and display Web applications written in HTML and JavaScript. The newer Navigator 4 and Composer components of Netscape Communicator may be used instead of the older Navigator 3.01 Gold. Other editors may also be used.

- *Site Manager and the LiveWire Compiler.* Site Manager provides a graphical tool for developing, deploying, and managing a Web site. It also provides the capability to compile Web applications from within the graphical environment. The LiveWire Compiler may also be used in a command-line mode external to Site Manager.

- *LiveWire Server Extension (includes Application Manager).* This extension allows Netscape servers to support application objects that can be accessed from server-side JavaScript scripts. The *Application Manager* tool is used to make Web applications available to Netscape servers.

Figure 27.1 summarizes how these tools interact to develop and manage Web applications. Navigator Gold or Composer is used to edit HTML files containing client- or server-side JavaScript. These files are managed by Site Manager and are compiled into integrated Web applications. Application Manager is used to install Web applications on Netscape servers and to manage the applications that have been installed. Finally, Navigator or other browsers are used to view and interact with the installed applications.

NOTE A fuller version of LiveWire, *LiveWire Pro*, adds a Structured Query Language (SQL) database and a database report generator to the capabilities provided by LiveWire. Chapter 28 covers LiveWire Pro.

To run LiveWire, you'll need access to a FastTrack or Enterprise server. Like most Netscape products, LiveWire runs on a variety of OS platforms, including Windows 95. I prefer Windows NT 4.0 because of the additional security and greater stability that it provides. LiveWire and Netscape servers may be downloaded from Netscape's Web site at *http://home.netscape.com*. These products are easy to install and come with excellent documentation.

FIGURE 27.1

The LiveWire tools
are used to develop
and manage Web appli-
cations that integrate
browser and server pro-
gramming capabilities.

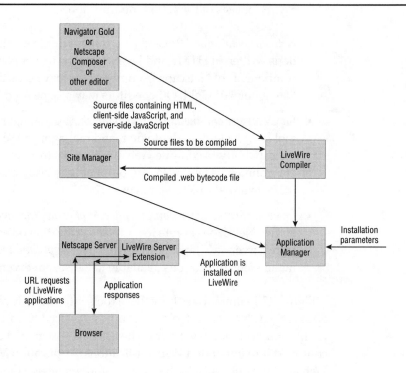

A Simple LiveWire
Example: *"simple"*

In order to quickly get you up to speed using LiveWire, we'll start with a simple example. In this example, you'll be exposed to server-side JavaScript and learn how to use the LiveWire tools to compile a Web application and install it on your Web server. The example will provide you with an overview of how LiveWire is used. Later sections of this chapter will fill in the details.

The example application presents you with the Web page shown in Figure 27.2. It displays a *Hello From LiveWire!* message followed by information about your browser and Web server. This is a very simple application, but it illustrates concepts and approaches common to all LiveWire applications.

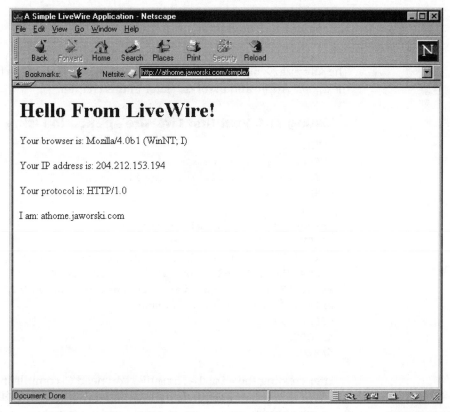

FIGURE 27.2

A simple application that shows how to use LiveWire. (Listing 27.1)

Building the Example Application

Building the example *simple* application involves the following steps:

1. Enter the source code found in the file `simple.htm`.

2. Compile `simple.htm` using Site Manager or the LiveWire compiler.

3. Move the compiled application file to the Web server.

4. Install the application using Application Manager.

Listing 27.1 contains the source HTML and JavaScript code for the *simple* application. This code can be entered into `simple.htm` using Netscape Composer, Navigator Gold, or your favorite editor.

You probably have a few questions on how `simple.htm` works. Hang in there. The `<server>` tag and the enclosed JavaScript is covered in the section "How the *Simple* Application Works," later in this chapter.

Listing 27.1. Your first LiveWire application (simple.htm)

```
<HTML>
<HEAD>
<TITLE>A Simple LiveWire Application</TITLE>
</HEAD>
<BODY>
<H1>Hello From LiveWire!</H1>
<SERVER>
write("Your browser is: "+request.agent+"<P>")
write("Your IP address is: "+request.ip+"<P>")
write("Your protocol is: "+request.protocol+"<P>")
write("I am: "+server.hostname)
</SERVER>
</BODY>
</HTML>
```

After creating the `simple.htm` file, you need to compile it. You can use the LiveWire compiler directly via the command line, or indirectly via Site Manager. To use the LiveWire compiler directly, enter the following at the command-line prompt while in the directory in which `simple.htm` is located:

```
lwcomp -v -o simple.web simple.htm
```

The above command produces the following output:

```
C:\jscript\Ch27\Live1>lwcomp -v -o simple.web simple.htm
Livewire Compiler Version 14.4
Copyright (C) Netscape Communications Corporation 1996
All rights reserved
Reading file simple.htm
Compiling file simple.htm
Writing .web file

C:\jscript\Ch27\Live1>
```

If you prefer to use Site Manager, click on the directory in which `simple.htm` is located and select *Manage* from the Site menu to put the directory under management (refer to Figure 27.3). Select *Build application* from the Site menu to compile `simple.htm` as shown in Figure 27.4. Make sure that you use `simple` as the name of your application. Figure 27.5 shows the output produced by the compiler.

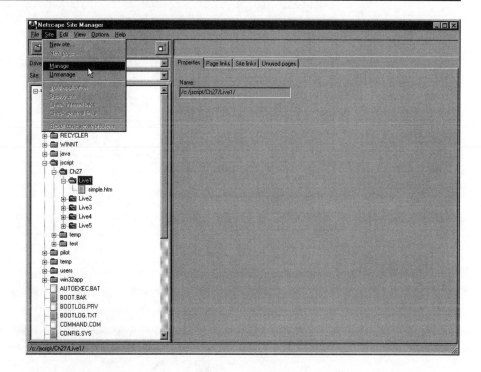

Having compiled the *simple* application, it is now necessary to move the `simple.web` file to your Web server. If your Web server is on the same machine, you can copy the file to a directory under your server's root directory. If your server is on a different machine, you can use FTP to move the file. You can also use Site Manager's *Deploy site* command, as shown in Figure 27.6. To use this command you must set the site deployment area (in the Properties tab on the right side of the Site Manager window) to the location where the application is to be deployed (copied for operational use).

FIGURE 27.4

Using Site Manager
to compile a Web
application

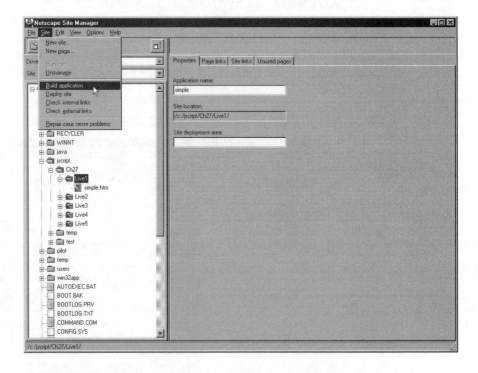

FIGURE 27.5

The output produced
from compiling the
simple application

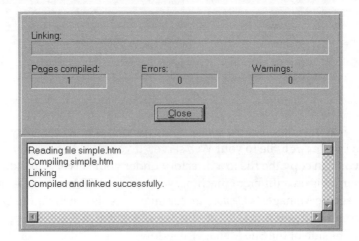

FIGURE 27.6

Site Manager's Deploy
site command automates
the process of moving
application files to a Web
server.

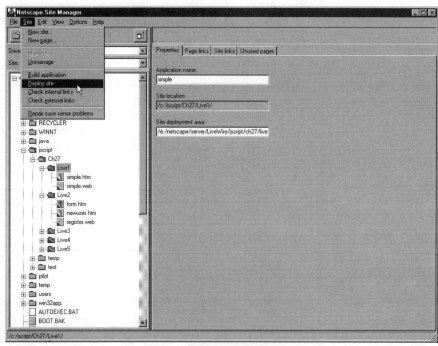

Make sure that you put the `simple.web` file under Site Manager management before you use the *Deploy site* command.

Once you've moved the `simple.web` file to your Web server, you must install the *simple* application using Application Manager. Open Application Manager and click on the Add link. Figure 27.7 shows the Application Manager Add Application form. Set the fields of this form as shown in Table 27.1 and click on the Enter button. Application Manager displays the output shown in Figure 27.8.

TABLE 27.1 Filling out the Add Application form

Field	Value
Name	**simple**
Web File Path	*(Type the full path to the `simple.web` file's location on your Web server)*
Default Page	**simple.htm**
Initial Page	*(Leave blank)*
Maximum Database Connections	**0**
External Libraries	*(Leave blank)*
Client Object Maintenance	**client-cookie**

FIGURE 27.7

The Application Manager Add Application form

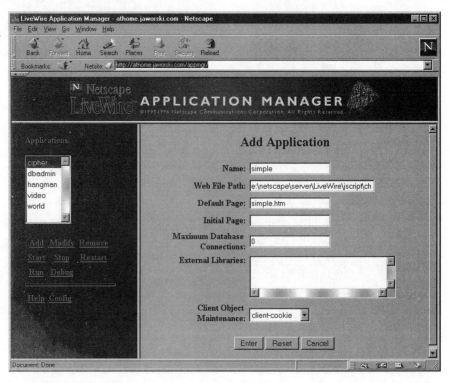

FIGURE 27.8

The output produced by Application Manager after adding the *simple* application.

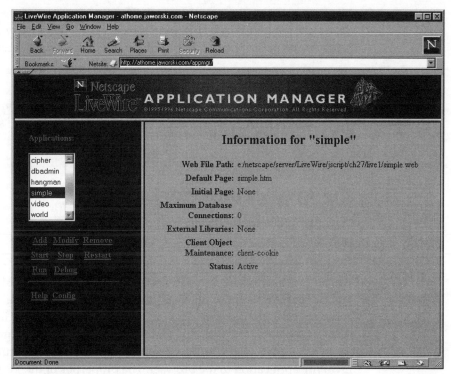

One more step to go. In the left frame of the Application Manager window, click on the Start link. This starts the *simple* application. It is now ready to run.

Running the Application

You can run the *simple* application in two ways.

- In the left frame of the Application Manager window, click on the Run link. This launches Navigator and opens the link at *http://your.server.com/simple/* where your Web server's host name is substituted for *your.server.com*.

- *Or,* use your browser to open the URL *http://your.server.com/simple/* as described in step 1 above.

When you access the application's URL, your Web server first checks with LiveWire to determine whether the URL refers to a LiveWire application. If it does, then the LiveWire application is executed. Otherwise, your Web server looks for the path specified in the URL in the server's document directory.

TIP
Make sure that you don't name your application with the same name as a path in your server's document directory. If you do, the documents in your server's document directory will become inaccessible.

How the Application Works

Now that you have the *simple* application up and running, let's take a look at how it works.

The first thing that you probably noticed is the use of the `<server>` tags. As you might have guessed, the `<server>` tags enclose server-side JavaScript statements. These statements generate HTML and client-side JavaScript that is sent to and displayed by browsers. The `write()` function operates in the same way as it does in client-side JavaScript. However, instead of generating HTML to be displayed to a document window, it generates HTML that is returned from the LiveWire application to the browser. The properties of the `request` and `server` objects are written to the document displayed by the browser. These objects are described later in this chapter.

Figure 27.9 shows the source document displayed by my browser when it accesses the *simple* application. Note the HTML that was generated by the server-side JavaScript.

The LiveWire Compiler

The LiveWire compiler translates files containing HTML, client-side JavaScript, and server-side JavaScript into bytecode-executable files with the `.web` extension. These files are installed as part of the LiveWire server extension by Application Manager. The `.web` files are in a format that can be executed by the LiveWire server extension. Figure 27.10 summarizes the compiler's role in the development of LiveWire applications.

FIGURE 27.9

The source document displayed by your browser is generated by the *simple* application.

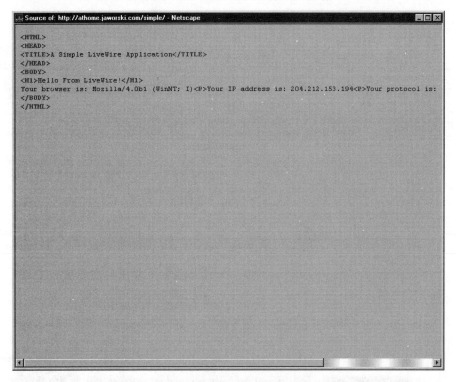

FIGURE 27.10

The LiveWire compiler translates source HTML and JavaScript files into LiveWire applications.

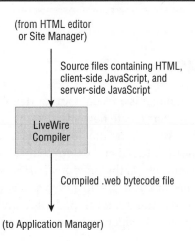

The compiler command-line syntax is as follows:

```
lwcomp [options] HTML_files [JavaScript_files]
```

The HTML and JavaScript files are the source files used in the application. The compiler options are described in Table 27.2. Spaces should be used to separate options and files. The -o option should be the last option that is specified.

TABLE 27.2 LiveWire compiler command-line options

Option	Description
-c	Checks syntax without generating a .web file
-d	Displays the JavaScript statements that are generated
-o *outfile*	Identifies the .web file to which the output should be written. (*NOTE:* If you're using more than one option from this table, be sure to put this option last.)
-v	Requests verbose output
-?	Causes compiler help information to be displayed

TIP

The -v option is especially useful; I use it all the time to get more information about the compilation results.

Site Manager

Site Manager is a visual tool for developing and managing Web sites. It helps Webmasters create new sites using a set of site templates. It provides a graphical tool for organizing the documents contained in a Web site, and checks and maintains site-internal and external links. Site Manager lets you compile LiveWire applications via the *Build application* menu option. It also lets you quickly deploy the files of a Web site to a Web server (using the *Deploy site* menu option). While you can certainly develop, deploy, and maintain Web sites without Site Manager, using Site Manager makes it a whole lot easier.

Site Manager provides extensive online help via the Help menu. If you want to learn how to use Site Manager, this is the best place to start.

Application Manager

Application Manager is a browser-based tool for managing LiveWire applications. (In fact, Application Manager is itself a LiveWire application.) It provides a set of links and forms that allow you to:

- Add new LiveWire applications to the LiveWire server extension.
- Modify existing applications.
- Start, stop, and restart applications.
- Run and debug applications.
- Also, you can use it to remotely manage Netscape Web servers from anywhere on the Web.

To start Application Manager, open your browser to the following URL:

http://your.server.com/appmgr/

(but replace the host name *your.server.com* by the host name of your Web server).

Make sure that you use your server's access-control features to prevent the world at large from running Application Manager on your server.

To use Application Manager, just click on the appropriate link in the left frame of the Application Manager window. Application Manager provides online help via the Help link.

When adding or modifying a LiveWire application, Application Manager prompts you for some basic information about your application using the HTML form shown in Figure 27.11. Table 27.3 explains how to fill out each of the fields in the Add Application form.

FIGURE 27.11

The Application Manager's Add Application form for information about the application to be installed

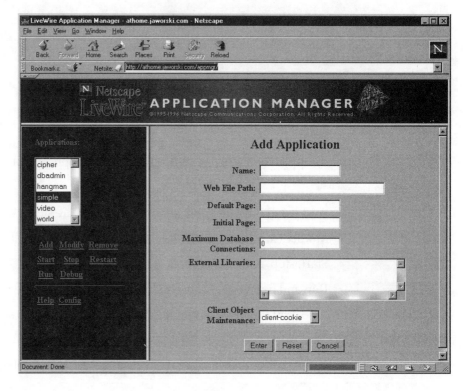

TABLE 27.3 Filling out the Add Application form

Field	How to fill out
Name	Identify the name of your application. If your application's name is *app-name* and your Web server's address is *your.server.com* then the URL of your application is *http://your.server.com/appname*.
Web File Path	Enter the full path to the `.web` file to be used in the application. Use the path naming conventions of your local operating system.
Default Page	Identify the Web page to be loaded for an application if no other page has been specified. The first time a user runs the application, the Initial Page (identified in the next field) is served before the Default Page.
Initial Page	Identify the Web page that LiveWire serves when a user first runs an application. This page is used to perform any required initialization. The Default Page (identified in the previous field) is served after the Initial Page has been processed.

TABLE 27.3   Filling out the Add Application form (continued)

Field	How to fill out
Maximum Database Connections	Enter the maximum number of database connections allowed by your database server license. This field only applies to Windows NT versions of LiveWire Pro.
External Libraries	If your application needs to access any external functions written in C, C++, or other programming languages, then enter the location of the external libraries here. The development of external libraries is platform-specific. Windows platforms use dynamic link libraries. Unix platforms use shared objects. Consult your LiveWire documentation for more information.
Client Object Maintenance	Select client-cookie, client-url, server-ip, server-cookie, or server-url. See the section "State Maintenance" later in this chapter for more information on the meaning of each of these options.

NOTE   The Default Page, Initial Page, and External Libraries fields are optional.

TIP   Remember to use Application Manager's Restart link to restart any applications that have been modified or recompiled. You must restart an application for any changes to take effect.

NOTE   On Unix systems, you must stop and restart your Web server when new applications are added.

Server-Side JavaScript Programming

Server-side JavaScript programs are developed as LiveWire applications. The same steps used to develop the *simple* application earlier in this chapter are used in all LiveWire applications. The only differences between the *simple* application and other LiveWire applications are the contents of their source files and their Application Manager installation parameters. With this in mind, learning server-side JavaScript programming consists of the following:

1. Learning to create source files using HTML, client-side JavaScript, and server-side JavaScript. (You already know how to use HTML and client-side JavaScript. The rest of this chapter shows you how to use server-side JavaScript.)

2. Learning to use the LiveWire compiler to compile source files into .web files. (You already know how to do this, and you'll get more experience in subsequent examples.)

3. Learning to use Application Manager to install compiled applications. (You already know how to use Application Manager. The section entitled "State Maintenance," later in this chapter, explains how to use the client object state maintenance feature of LiveWire.)

Server-side JavaScript is included in LiveWire source files in three different ways:

- By enclosing the JavaScript statements within `<server>` tags.
- By surrounding the JavaScript statements with backquotes (`` ` ``) or (\Q).
- By putting the JavaScript statements in a `.js` file.

You already learned how to use the `<server>` tags with the *simple* application earlier in this chapter. The `<server>` tags are the most common way of using server-side JavaScript. Use the `write()` function within the `<server>` tags to generate HTML that will be sent to the browser.

Back quotes (`` ` ``) are used within an HTML tag to specify attributes or attribute values based on the value of JavaScript expressions. For example, suppose the value of the `imageName` variable is *image10.gif*. The following image tags are equivalent.

```
<img src="image10.gif">


<img src=\QimageName\Q>


<img src=`imageName`>
```

NOTE LiveWire automatically surrounds back-quoted expressions with double quotes when generating HTML.

JavaScript (.js) source files are used in the same way for server-side JavaScript as for client-side JavaScript. However, server-side .js files do not need to be referenced via an SRC attribute to be included in an application. Simply reference the .js file in the LiveWire compiler command line, or include the file in the site being compiled by Site Manager.

Within the <server> tags, back quotes, and .js files, server-side JavaScript scripts are written in the same way as client-side JavaScript scripts. The language syntax remains the same. The only difference is in the objects, methods, properties, and functions available on the server. The following sections introduce these new language elements, beginning with server-side objects.

Server-Side Objects

LiveWire provides four objects that are at the heart of any server-side JavaScript application: request, client, project, and server. These objects are referred to as the *LiveWire object framework*, and are used to simplify the process of application development. After having experimented with writing CGI programs in the previous chapter, you'll appreciate the features provided by these objects. Figure 27.12 summarizes how the LiveWire object framework is used to develop server-based applications.

The properties of the request object provide basic information about the browser requesting the URL of a LiveWire application. Its properties also provide easy access to the information contained in a URL request, such as form data, image map coordinates, and data that is included in a query string. You can also define additional request properties for use in your application. A request object only exists until the application finishes responding to the request.

The client object maintains information about an individual browser across browser requests. The properties of the client object are application-specific and are maintained using the client object maintenance mechanism specified when an application is installed via Application Manager. LiveWire maintains client information in a near-transparent manner—you don't have to worry (very much)

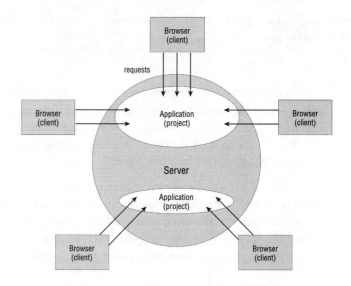

FIGURE 27.12

The LiveWire object framework simplifies the development of server-based applications.

about programming cookies or encoding data in URLs to maintain `client` properties. A `client` object exists for a predefined duration; the default is 10 minutes.

The `project` object maintains information that is common to all clients that access an application. This information is stored using application-specific properties of the `project` object. The `project` object exists until the application is stopped or restarted.

The `server` object maintains information that is common to all projects that are running on a server. The `server` object exists until the server is stopped or restarted.

The following subsections explain how to use each of the objects of the LiveWire object framework.

The *request* Object

The `request` object encapsulates a browser's request of an application URL. Unique `request` objects are created for each instance of a URL request. All `request` objects have the four predefined properties described in Table 27.4. A `request` object also contains properties that provide access to data sent by the browser to the application. These properties contain the values of form fields, image map clicks, and query string data encoded in URLs. Table 27.5 summarizes the `request` properties that are created for URL requests. These properties greatly simplify the processing of browser data. All the overhead of parsing query strings, common to CGI programs, is automatically handled by LiveWire.

TABLE 27.4   Predefined `request` properties

Property	Description
`agent`	The name and version of the browser making the URL request.
`ip`	The IP address of the host from which the request is made.
`method`	The HTTP method used with the request.
`protocol`	The version of the HTTP protocol used by the requesting browser.

TABLE 27.5   Properties that are created for URL requests

Request Type	Properties that are created
Form submission (`GET` or `POST`)	The form elements are given properties of the form `request .name` where `name` is the name of the form element. For example, if a form has text fields named `address` and `city` then the properties `request.address` and `request.city` are created to provide access to the data submitted in these fields.
Server-side image map click	The properties `request.imageX` and `request.imageY` are created to provide access to the coordinates of the mouse click.
Link with appended query string	If the query string contains *name=value* pairs of the form `?name1=value1& ... namen=valuen` then the `request` properties `request.name1` through `request.namen` are created with values *value1* through *valuen*.

> **NOTE**   The *file upload* form element cannot be used in LiveWire applications.

The *simple* application earlier in the chapter showed how to use the predefined `request` properties. The following sections provide examples of server-side scripts that show how to access data that is sent by browsers in URL requests.

Form Example

Listing 27.2 shows the contents of the `form.htm` file. This file contains a simple HTML form with the `newuser.htm` file specified as the `ACTION` attribute of the form. The form is used to get the first name, last name, and e-mail address of a user in order to register the user at the Web site.

Listing 27.3 shows the contents of `newuser.htm`. This file contains server-side JavaScript that displays the values of the `firstName`, `lastName`, and `email` fields that are received when the form of Listing 27.2 is submitted.

To see how `form.htm` and `newuser.htm` work together as part of a LiveWire application, use the following statement to compile the files into an application file named `register.web`.

```
lwcomp -v -o register.web form.htm newuser.htm
```

Now move `register.web` to a directory on your Web server. Use Application Manager to add the application to LiveWire. Then set the application name to `register` and the default page to `form.htm`. Next, start the application by clicking on the Start LiveWire link. Finally, click Run to run the `register` application. It will generate a Web page, as shown in Figure 27.13. Fill out the registration form and click on Submit Registration. This will result in a Web page similar to the one shown in Figure 27.14. (Note how the values you entered in the form are displayed by the server script contained in `newuser.htm`.)

Listing 27.2. A registration form (form.htm)

```
<HTML>
<HEAD>
<TITLE>Registration Form</TITLE>
</HEAD>
<BODY>
<H1>Please Register</H1>
<FORM NAME="registration" ACTION="newuser.htm">
Firt Name: <INPUT TYPE="text" NAME="firstName">
Last Name: <INPUT TYPE="text" NAME="lastName"><P>
E-Mail Address: <INPUT TYPE="text" NAME="email" SIZE="50"><P>
<INPUT TYPE="SUBMIT" VALUE="Submit Registration">
</FORM>
</BODY>
</HTML>
```

Listing 27.3. Displaying submitted form data (newuser.htm)

```
<HTML>
<HEAD>
<TITLE>Thank You</TITLE>
</HEAD>
<BODY>
<H1>Thanks for registering</H1>
<P>Your registration information is as follows:</P>
<P><SERVER>
write(request.firstName+" "+request.lastName+"<BR>")
write(request.email)
</SERVER></P>
</BODY>
</HTML>
```

FIGURE 27.13

A registration form that is used to send sample form data to a server-side script (Listing 27.2)

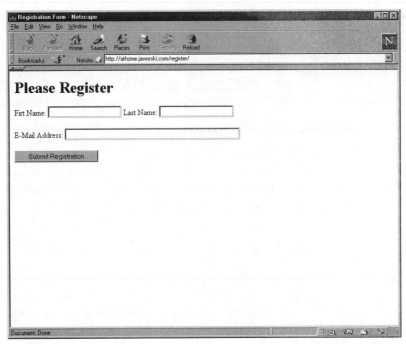

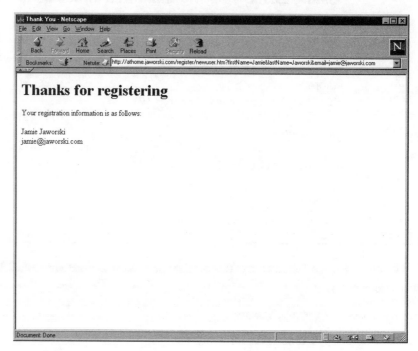

FIGURE 27.14

A server-side script that displays the form data it receives from the browser (Listing 27.3)

Image Map Example

Listing 27.4 shows the contents of the `map.htm` file. This file displays a simple server-side image map. The coordinates of the user's clicks are sent to the file `disp-xy.htm`, shown in Listing 27.5. The files, `map.htm` and `disp-xy.htm`, work together as part of a LiveWire application. Compile these files using the following command:

```
lwcomp -v -o imagemap.web map.htm disp-xy.htm
```

Move `imagemap.web` and `shapes.gif` to a directory on your Web server. Use Application Manager to add the application to LiveWire. Then set the application name to `imagemap` and the default page to `map.htm`. Now start and run the `imagemap` application. It will generate a Web page, as shown in Figure 27.15. Click on the image. This will result in a Web page similar to the one shown in Figure 27.16. (Note how the values of your click are displayed by the server script contained in `disp-xy.htm`.)

Listing 27.4. A simple image map (map.htm)

```
<HTML>
<HEAD>
<TITLE>Using Image Maps</TITLE>
</HEAD>
<BODY>
<H1>Using Image Maps</H1>
<A HREF="disp-xy.htm">
<IMG SRC="shapes.gif" ISMAP="ISMAP">
</A>
</BODY>
</HTML>
```

FIGURE 27.15

The image map is used to send the coordinates of your click to a server-side script. (Listing 27.4)

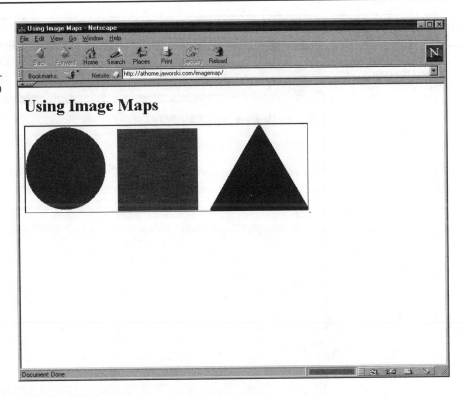

Listing 27.5. Displaying image map coordinates (disp-xy.htm)

```
<HTML>
<HEAD>
<TITLE>Image Map Processing</TITLE>
</HEAD>
<BODY>
<H1>You clicked at
<SERVER>
write("("+request.imageX+","+request.imageY+")")
</SERVER>
.<H1>
</BODY>
</HTML>
```

FIGURE 27.16

The server-side script displays the coordinates of your click. (Listing 27.5)

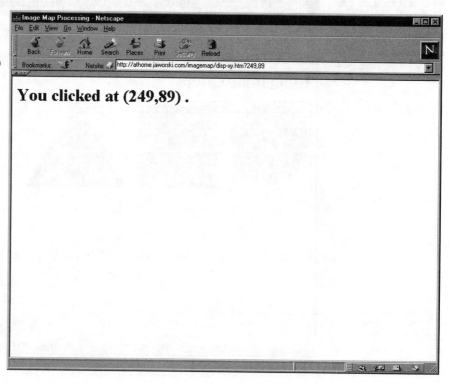

Custom URL Example

Listing 27.6 shows the contents of the `qstring.htm` file. This file displays a link with an attached query string. When the user clicks on this link the query string is forwarded to the file `disp-qs.htm`, shown in Listing 27.7. The files `qstring.htm` and `disp-qs.htm` work together as part of a LiveWire application. Compile these files using

```
lwcomp -v -o querystring.web qstring.htm disp-qs.htm
```

Move `querystring.web` to a directory on your Web server. Use Application Manager to add the application to LiveWire. Then set the application name to `querystring` and the default page to `qstring.htm`. Now start and run the `querystring` application. It will generate a Web page, as shown in Figure 27.17. Click on the link. This will result in a Web page similar to the one shown in Figure 27.18. (Note how the query string values are displayed by the server script contained in `disp-qs.htm`.)

Listing 27.6. A link with a query string (qstring.htm)

```
<HTML>
<HEAD>
<TITLE>Query String Test</TITLE>
</HEAD>
<BODY>
<A HREF="disp-qs.htm?var1=LiveWire&var2=is&var3=great">
disp-qs.htm?var1=LiveWire&var2=is&var3=great
</A>
</BODY>
</HTML>
```

Listing 27.7. Displaying query string values (disp-qs.htm)

```
<HTML>
<HEAD>
<TITLE>Query String Results</TITLE>
</HEAD>
<BODY>
<P>The method associated with the URL is:
<B><SERVER>write(request.method)</SERVER></B></P>
<P>The value of var1 is:
<B><SERVER>write(request.var1)</SERVER></B></P>
<P>The value of var2 is:
<B><SERVER>write(request.var2)</SERVER></B></P>
```

```
<P>The value of var3 is:
<B><SERVER>write(request.var3)</SERVER></B></P>
</BODY>
</HTML>
```

FIGURE 27.17

The link is used to send a query string to a server-side script. (Listing 27.6)

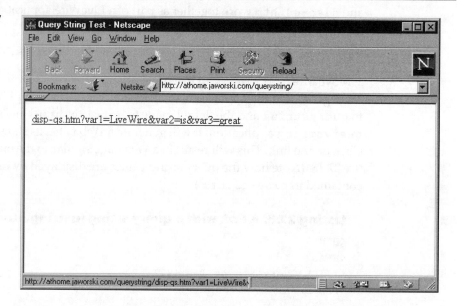

FIGURE 27.18

The server-side script displays the query string values. (Listing 27.7)

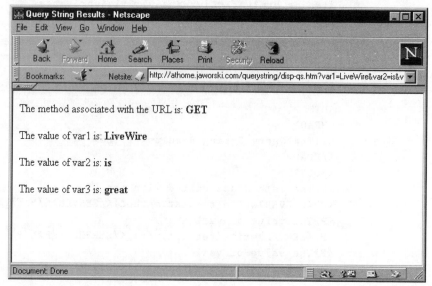

The *client* Object

The `client` object provides the capability to maintain client-specific information across multiple browser requests. This allows you to keep track of the application state of individual clients. For example, the `client.id` property could be defined to assign a unique ID to the client for the duration of a browser session. As another example, consider an online sales application. The `client.selections` array could be used to keep track of the products a user selected for purchase.

The `client` object does not have any predefined properties. Client properties are created by the application by assigning a value to the property. For example, the following statement creates the `client.id` property and assigns it the value of the `nextID()` function.

```
client.id = nextID()
```

By default, `client` objects expire and cease to exist after 10 minutes. This default expiration time can be changed using the `expiration()` method. This method takes as a parameter the number of seconds that a client is allowed to exist before it expires. For example, the following statement extends the lifetime of a client object to an hour.

```
client.expiration(3600)
```

The `destroy()` method can be used to destroy a `client` object immediately. Use this method to destroy a `client` object's property values. Use `expiration(0)` to remove all client property information stored on a user's browser.

> **NOTE** Client expiration does not apply if the client-url approach is used to maintain client data. See the section "State Maintenance" later in this chapter for more information.

The *project* Object

The `project` object allows properties to be specified that apply to an entire application. These properties are accessible to all clients that use the application. For example, a `project.counter` can be defined to count the number of times an application has been accessed. As another example, consider a `project.nextID` property that is used to assign user IDs to individual clients.

The `project` object does not have any predefined properties. Application-specific properties are created in the same way that they are with the `client` object. The `project` object exists until the application is stopped or restarted.

Since the `project` object is shared among multiple clients, a special mechanism, referred to as *locking*, is implemented to prevent one client from interfering with the processing of another.

The `lock()` method is used to lock the `project` object. When the `project` object is locked, only the script instance that invoked the `lock()` method is able to modify any properties of the `project` object. (A *script instance* is a script that is executing in response to a browser request.) All other script instances attempting to modify `project` properties must wait until the lock is released. The `unlock()` method is used to release a lock on the `project` object. Since other script instances may be waiting for a project to be unlocked, it is important to minimize the code that is executed between invoking `lock()` and `unlock()`.

NOTE LiveWire automatically prevents a `project` property from being modified (by another script) when a script reads or writes a `project` property. Locking is used to prevent any modifications between reads and writes.

The *server* Object

The `server` object is used to store information that is common to all applications supported by a server. The `server` object has the predefined properties shown in Table 27.6. In addition to these properties, application-specific properties may be defined in the same way as with the `client` and `project` objects. For example, the `server.nextUserID` property may be used to assign a user ID for each user that accesses applications on a server.

The `server lock()` and `unlock()` methods support `server` object locking in the same manner as for the `project` object. The `server` object exists until the server is stopped or restarted.

TABLE 27.6   The predefined properties of the `server` object

Property	Description
`hostname`	The name of the host and protocol port used by the server
`host`	The name of the host on which the server runs
`protocol`	The protocol used by the server (*http:*)
`port`	The protocol port used by the server

File Input and Output

Since all objects of the LiveWire object framework expire at some point in time, it is important to maintain permanent copies of critical application information. The LiveWire `File` object provides the capability to access files in the server's file system. You can use `File` to store critical data so that it can be used by LiveWire-external applications and to back up `project` and `server` properties.

`File` objects are created using the `new` operator as follows:

```
var=new File(path)
```

`var` is the variable to which the file object is assigned and `path` is the path to the file, written in the local operating system format. For example, the statement

```
f1=new File("db.txt")
```

creates a new `File` object that can be used to access the `db.txt` file.

TIP   If `f` is a variable that is assigned a `File` object, then `write(f)` produces the name of the file to which `f` refers.

Opening Files

Once a `File` object is created, it must be opened before it can be read or written. The `open()` method of the `File` object opens the `File` object and returns a boolean value indicating whether or not the open was successful. The `open()`

method takes a string parameter that specifies the mode in which the file is to be opened. These mode strings are defined in Table 27.7.

TABLE 27.7   Mode strings for the `open()` method of the File object

String	Description
a	The file is opened in write-only text mode. All data that is written to the file is appended at the end of the file. If the file does not exist, then it is created.
a+	The file is opened in text mode for both reading and writing. All read and write operations occur at the end of the file. If the file does not exist, then it is created.
r	If the file exists, then it is opened in read-only text mode. Reading starts at the beginning of the file. If the file does not exist, then `false` is returned.
r+	If the file exists, then it is opened in read-and-write text mode. Reading and writing starts at the beginning of the file. If the file does not exist, then `false` is returned.
w	The file is opened as an empty file in write-only text mode. Writing starts at the beginning of the file. If the file does not exist, then it is created.
w+	The file is opened as an empty file in read and write text mode. Reading and writing start at the beginning of the file. If the file does not exist, then it is created.

On Windows platforms, the argument b may be appended to any of these mode strings to open the file in binary mode instead of text mode.

Suppose the f variable is assigned the `File` object created from `db.txt`. If `db.txt` exists, the following statement opens the file for reading and writing. The `open()` method returns `true` if `db.txt` exists and `false` otherwise.

```
status=f.open("r+")
```

Closing Files

The `close()` method is used to close a file after access to the file is no longer needed. It returns a boolean value indicating the success or failure of the close operation.

Accessing Files

The `File` object provides several methods for reading and writing files. These methods are summarized in Table 27.8. The `byteToString()` and `stringToByte()`

methods are static. This means that they apply to the `File` object type and not to specific `File` objects. Thus, you must precede static methods by the name of the object type instead of the name of an object instance. For example, the following statement converts the number 49 to its corresponding ASCII string and assigns it to the `str` variable.

```
str=File.byteToString(49)
```

TABLE 27.8   Methods of the `File` object

Method	Description
`byteToString(n)`	A static method that returns the ASCII string corresponding to the byte value *n*.
`clearError()`	Resets any errors or end of file conditions associated with a file.
`close()`	Closes a file that was previously opened.
`eof()`	Returns `true` if the file pointer is passed the end of the file and `false` otherwise.
error()	Returns operating system-specific error status codes.
`exists()`	Returns `true` if a file exists and `false` otherwise.
`flush()`	Writes any buffered output to a file.
`getLength()`	Returns the length of a file.
`getPosition()`	Returns the current position of the file pointer.
`open(`*modeString*`)`	Opens a file for reading or writing (see Table 27.7).
`read(n)`	Reads *n* number of bytes from the file starting at the pointer position. The data is returned as a string. The pointer is moved by the number of characters read.
`readByte()`	Reads the next byte in a file that is opened in binary mode. The byte is returned as an integer and the file pointer is incremented by one byte.
`readln()`	Reads a line of characters from a file and returns it as a string. Moves the file pointer to the beginning of the next line.
`setPosition` (*position[,reference]*)	Sets the file pointer to *position*. The optional *reference* parameter specifies the relative location of *position*. If *reference* is 0 then *position* is relative to the beginning of the file. If *reference* is 1 then *position* is relative to the current position. If *reference* is 2 then *position* is relative to the end of the file.

TABLE 27.8 Methods of the `File` object (continued)

Method	Description
`stringToByte`(*string*)	A static method that converts the first character of a string to its ASCII byte value.
`write`(*expression*)	Writes the string value of *expression* to a file and advances the file pointer by the number of bytes written.
`writeByte`(*n*)	Writes the byte specified by integer *n* to a file that is opened in binary mode. The file pointer is advanced by one byte.
`writeln`(*expression*)	Writes expression as a line of text. The file pointer is advanced by the number of bytes written.

Many of the `File` methods make use of a mechanism known as the file *pointer*. The file pointer is the position within a file at which the next read or operation is to take place. When the file pointer is positioned past the last character of a file, it is said to be at the end of the file.

Locking File Access

Since application files may be shared by several concurrently executing script instances, it is important to implement precautions designed to prevent file access conflicts. The project- and server-locking mechanisms can be used to prevent these conflicts.

- When you invoke `project.lock()`, all other application script instances are prevented from accessing files. These scripts must wait until `project.unlock()` is invoked before resuming execution.

- If a file is shared by two or more applications, use `server.lock()` and `server.unlock()` to prevent scripts from one application from conflicting with the file accesses being made by scripts of another application.

A Fuller Example: *"diskette"*

In this section, you'll develop an application that uses all of the objects of the LiveWire object framework, uses the `File` object to store application data, and integrates client- and server-side JavaScript. This application, which I call *The Diskette Center*, is an online storefront that specializes in the sale of high-density, double-sided, 3.5 inch diskettes. This application takes user orders and stores them in a disk file. Although the application is quite simple—it was designed that way—it illustrates many important aspects of LiveWire application development. A real online ordering application would dress up the site with fancy graphics and provide a mechanism for online payment.

The application name is *diskette*. The next section introduces the files that make up this application. The section after that shows how to build, install, and run the application.

Up until now, I've asked you to run an application before I explained how it works. In the *diskette* application, I'm going to reverse this process. When you study the diskette application files, see if you can visualize how they work in advance of compiling and running the application. This will give you a more thorough understanding of how each of the individual application files work together.

The Files of the *diskette* Application

The diskette application is made up of the following four files:

- `start.htm` — This file is the default page for the diskette application. It presents a price list and order form to the user. When the order form is submitted, the form data is sent to `process.htm`.

- `process.htm` — This file processes the data entered by the user in the order form of `start.htm`. It combines client- and server-side JavaScript to display the user's order. It then prompts the user to enter name and address information. This information is combined with the locally calculated price of the user's order and submitted to `display.htm`.

- `display.htm` — This file takes the form data submitted by `process.htm` and stores it in `client` properties. It then displays the data collected by `start.htm` and `process.htm` so that the user may check their order.

- `finish.htm` — This file writes the user's order to the `orders.txt` file and thanks the user for their order.

These files are analyzed in the following subsections.

start.htm

The start.htm file is shown in Listing 27.8. It is a simple HTML file that displays a tabular price list and an order form. The only distinguishing feature of this file is that the ACTION attribute of the form points to an HTML file (process.htm) instead of to a CGI program. This is possible because process.htm is part of the diskette application and it uses server-side JavaScript to access the data submitted in the order form.

Listing 27.8. The opening page of the diskette application (start.htm)

```
<HTML>
<HEAD>
<TITLE>Diskette Center</TITLE>
</HEAD>
<BODY BGCOLOR="white">
<H1 ALIGN="CENTER">Welcome to Diskette Center</H1>
<P ALIGN="CENTER"><I>The cheapest diskettes on the Web.</I>
</P>
<P>All orders are sent COD.</P>
<H2>Price List (High Density Double-Sided Dikettes)</H2>
<TABLE>
<TR><TH>Quantity</TH><TH>Price per diskette</TH></TR>
<TR><TD>1-20</TD><TD>25 cents</TD></TR>
<TR><TD>21-100</TD><TD>20 cents</TD></TR>
<TR><TD>101-500</TD><TD>15 cents</TD></TR>
<TR><TD>500-1000</TD><TD>10 cents</TD></TR>
<TR><TD>over 1000</TD><TD>7.5 cents</TD></TR>
</TABLE>
<H2>Place your order and click Continue.</H2>
<FORM ACTION="process.htm">
Number of diskettes:
<INPUT TYPE="TEXT" SIZE="10" NAME="number">
<INPUT TYPE="Submit" VALUE="Continue">
</FORM>
</BODY>
</HTML>
```

process.htm

The process.htm file is shown in Listing 27.9. It is an example of how application processing can be divided between client and server scripts.

In the head of `process.htm` is a client-side script that contains the `display-Order()` function. This function displays a breakout of the cost of the user's order. It calculates the total cost of the order and assigns it to the `total` variable. The function has a single argument that identifies how many diskettes the user ordered.

The body of `process.htm` begins with server-side JavaScript that uses the `write()` function to generate client-side JavaScript. The generated JavaScript is a call to the `displayOrder()` function with the number of diskettes ordered by the user passed as a parameter. This number is passed to `process.htm` as `request.number` where number is the name of the field in the order menu of `start.htm`. The `request.number` property is assigned to `client.number`. This enables the value to survive the life span of the request object and be available in subsequent application Web pages.

The body of `process.htm` displays a form which requests name and address information from the user. The form is submitted to the `display.htm` file. Note that the form contains a hidden field named `total`. The value of this field is set in the client script that immediately follows the form, using the total value calculated by the `displayOrder()` function as the result of earlier processing. This is a good example of how a client-side script is able to send a locally calculated result to a server-side script.

Listing 27.9. Combining Client- and Server-Side JavaScript (process.htm)

```
<HTML>
<HEAD>
<TITLE>Diskette Center</TITLE>
<SCRIPT language="JavaScript">
function displayOrder(n) {
 with(document) {
  if(n<21) rate=.25
  else if(n<101) rate=.2
  else if(n<501) rate=.15
  else if(n<1001) rate=.10
  else rate=.075
  subtotal=n*rate
  subtotal=Math.round(subtotal*100)/100
  total=subtotal+10
  write("<H2>You ordered:</H2>")
  write(n+" disks at $"+rate+" per disk: "+subtotal+"<BR>")
  write("Tax: included"+"<BR>")
  write("Shipping: $10"+"<BR>")
```

```
    write("Total: "+total+"<BR>")
  }
}
</SCRIPT>
</HEAD>
<BODY>
<SERVER>
client.number=request.number
write("<SCRIPT language='JavaScript'>")
write("displayOrder("+client.number+")")
write("</SCRIPT>")
</SERVER>
<H2>Please fill out the following information.</H2>
<FORM ACTION="display.htm">
First Name: <INPUT TYPE="TEXT" NAME="firstName"><BR>
Last Name: <INPUT TYPE="TEXT" NAME="lastName"><P>
Address:<BR>
<INPUT TYPE="TEXT" NAME="addr1" SIZE="40"><BR>
<INPUT TYPE="TEXT" NAME="addr2" SIZE="40"><BR>
City: <INPUT TYPE="TEXT" NAME="city">
State: <INPUT TYPE="TEXT" NAME="state" SIZE="5">
Postal Code: <INPUT TYPE="TEXT" NAME="zip" SIZE="10"><BR>
Country: <INPUT TYPE="TEXT" NAME="country"><P>
Phone: <INPUT TYPE="TEXT" NAME="phone"><P>
E-mail address:   <INPUT TYPE="TEXT" NAME="email" SIZE="40">
<INPUT TYPE="HIDDEN" NAME="total"><P>
<INPUT TYPE="SUBMIT" VALUE="Continue">
</FORM>
<SCRIPT language="JavaScript">
document.forms[0].total.value=total
</SCRIPT>
</BODY>
</HTML>
```

display.htm

The display.htm file contains a server-side script that assigns the form data of process.htm to client object properties. Note that the hidden total field of process.htm is also stored as a client property. This value was calculated locally by the displayOrder() function of process.htm.

The second half of the server script displays the client properties to the user so that they can review their order. The server script is followed by a form that contains a Continue button. This form is submitted to finish.htm.

Listing 27.10. Using the client object to store data between Web pages (display.htm)

```
<HTML>
<HEAD>
<TITLE>Diskette Center</TITLE>
</HEAD>
<BODY>
<H1>Please check your order:</H1>
<SERVER>
client.firstName=request.firstName
client.lastName=request.lastName
client.addr1=request.addr1
client.addr2=request.addr2
client.city=request.city
client.state=request.state
client.country=request.country
client.zip=request.zip
client.phone=request.phone
client.email=request.email
client.total=request.total
write(client.firstName+" "+client.lastName+"<BR>")
write(client.addr1+"<BR>")
write(client.addr2+"<BR>")
write(client.city+", "+client.state+" "+client.zip+"<BR>")
write(client.country+"<BR>")
write(client.phone+"<BR>")
write(client.email+"<P>")
write(client.number+" diskettes<BR>")
write("$"+client.total+" US dollars<BR>")
</SERVER>
<FORM action="finish.htm">
<INPUT TYPE="SUBMIT" VALUE="Continue">
</FORM>
</BODY>
</HTML>
```

finish.htm

This file saves the user's order in the `orders.txt` file on the server. It begins by locking the `project` object to prevent any conflicts with other concurrently executing scripts. The `project.nextOrder` property is used to assign a number to each customer order. It is a `project` property because it is shared among all clients.

The if statement checks `project.nextOrder` to see if it is null. This is the case when the application is started or restarted. In this case, it is initialized to 1000. The `client.order` property is set after incrementing `project.nextOrder`.

NOTE The properties of the `request`, `client`, `project`, and `server` objects are stored as strings. Use the `parseInt()` and `parseFloat()` functions to convert from string to integer and floating point values.

A `File` object is created for the file `orders.txt` and assigned to the f variable. The file is opened in append mode. The `writeln()` method is used to write the user's order to the file. The file is closed and the `project` object is unlocked.

The file ends with the user being thanked and informed of the order number.

Listing 27.11. Saving customer orders in a file (finish.htm)

```
<HTML>
<HEAD>
<TITLE>Diskette Center</TITLE>
</HEAD>
<BODY>
<SERVER>
project.lock()
if(project.nextOrder==null) project.nextOrder=1000
project.nextOrder=parseInt(project.nextOrder)+1
client.order=project.nextOrder
f=new File("orders.txt")
f.open("a")
f.writeln(client.order+" "+client.number+" "+client.total)
f.writeln(client.firstName+" "+client.lastName)
f.writeln(client.addr1)
f.writeln(client.addr2)
f.writeln(client.city+" "+client.state+" "+client.zip)
f.writeln(client.country)
f.writeln(client.phone)
f.writeln(client.email)
f.close()
project.unlock()
</SERVER>
<H1>Thank you for your order!</H1>
<H2>Your order number is <SERVER>
```

```
write(client.order)
</SERVER>.</H2>
</BODY>
</HTML>
```

Building and Running the *diskette* Application

Use the following command to compile the *diskette* application.

```
lwcomp -v -o diskette.web start.htm process.htm display.htm
finish.htm
```

Next move `diskette.web` to your server. Use Application Manager to install it, and set the default page to `start.htm`.

Run the *diskette* application by clicking on the Application Manager Run link. It displays the Web page shown in Figure 27.19. Enter the number of diskettes you want to order and click on the Continue button.

FIGURE 27.19

The order form prompts you to enter the number of disks you are ordering. (Listing 27.8)

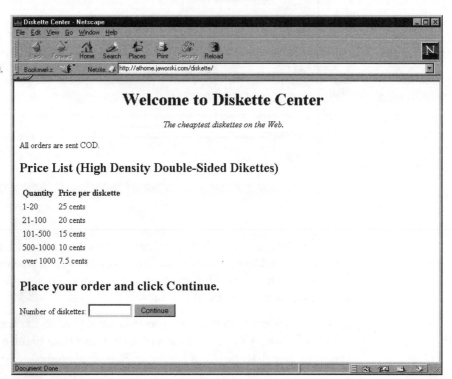

Welcome to Diskette Center

The cheapest diskettes on the Web.

All orders are sent COD.

Price List (High Density Double-Sided Dikettes)

Quantity	Price per diskette
1-20	25 cents
21-100	20 cents
101-500	15 cents
500-1000	10 cents
over 1000	7.5 cents

Place your order and click Continue.

Number of diskettes: [   ] [Continue]

The number of diskettes ordered is passed to `process.htm` and the Web page shown in Figure 27.20 is displayed. Note how the server-side JavaScript displays the user's order information. This is an example of how client-side JavaScript can be used to take some of the processing load off the server. Fill out the name and address information and click on the Continue button.

FIGURE 27.20

This form collects name and address information from the user. (Listing 27.9)

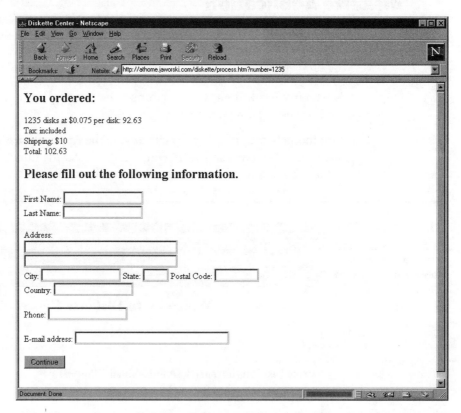

The information provided in the name and address form is forwarded to `display.htm` along with the calculated total price and the number of diskettes from the first form. This information is displayed, as shown in Figure 27.21. Go ahead and click on the Continue button.

The data collected in previous forms is forwarded to `finish.htm`. The JavaScript code in `finish.htm` writes the order data to the `orders.txt` file. A Web page like that shown in Figure 27.22 is displayed.

FIGURE 27.21

The order information
is displayed to the
user for confirmation.
(Listing 27.10)

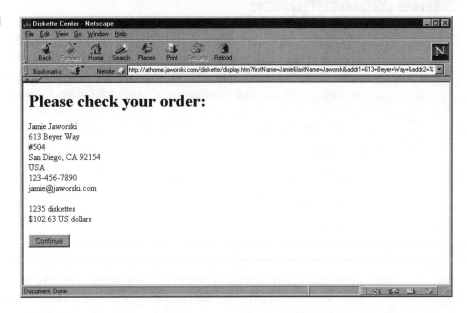

FIGURE 27.22

The user is thanked and
informed of the order
number. (Listing 27.11)

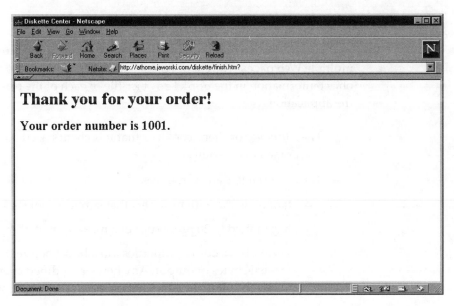

State Maintenance

A popular application that serves many browser clients simultaneously may need a great deal of memory to store client information. The Client Object Maintenance field of Application Manager's Add Application form allows LiveWire applications to choose between five different approaches to storing client information:

- Client-Cookie
- Client-URL
- Server-IP
- Server-Cookie
- Server-URL

LiveWire provides these five alternatives so that you can choose the particular approach that is best suited for your application. The following subsections describe these approaches and summarize the advantages and disadvantages of each approach.

The Client-Cookie Approach

In Chapter 8, you learned how to use cookies to maintain state information across multiple Web pages. The client-cookie approach uses cookies to store `client` object information in the `cookies.txt` file of each of the browsers accessing the application.

+ The *advantage* of client-cookie is that it is client-based and does not require server memory resources.

— The *disadvantages* are as follows:

— It only works with browsers that support cookies.

— It is limited to 20 properties of a maximum of 4K bytes each.

— The `client` object properties must be set before the application generates 64K bytes of output. Any new or modified client properties after the application has generated 64K bytes of output will be lost.

— It increases network traffic.

The Client-URL Approach

In the client-url approach, LiveWire encodes the `client` object properties as *name=value* pairs that are appended to the URLs used to link to other application pages. When these URLs are requested by a browser, the encoded information is sent back to the browser.

+ The *advantages* of this approach are as follows:

  + It is client-based and does not require server storage.

  + It works with all browsers.

  + The `client` object information does not expire.

− The *disadvantages* of this approach are:

  − The `client` object properties are transmitted multiple times if the generated Web page contains multiple URLs. This may significantly increase network traffic for some applications.

  − The size of a URL is limited to 4K bytes. The actual number of bytes available for client object storage is slightly less than 4K bytes.

  − It does not work correctly with forms.

  − The `client` object properties must be set before the application generates 64K bytes of output. Any new or modified client properties after the application has generated 64K bytes of output will be lost.

  − Dynamically generated links must add the client properties to the URL via the `addClient()` function.

The Server-IP Approach

In this approach, the client's IP address is used to index `client` object information on the server.

+ The *advantage* of this approach is that it does not place any limit on the number or size of cookie properties.

− It has the following *disadvantages*:

  − The `client` object information is lost when the server is restarted.

  − It consumes server memory resources.

— It may malfunction with applications that use frames.

— It does not work correctly with browsers that are proxied by a firewall.

— It may malfunction for browsers on hosts that do not have fixed IP addresses.

— It may malfunction on hosts that support multiple concurrent browser sessions.

WARNING In most cases, server-ip is the least reliable way to maintain `client` object information.

The Server-Cookie Approach

In the server-cookie approach, a single cookie value is generated and sent to the browser. This value is used as an index to `client` object information that is stored on the server.

+ The *advantage* of this approach is that it does not place any limit on the number or size of cookie properties.

— The *disadvantages* of this approach are:

— The `client` object information is lost when the server is restarted.

— It consumes server memory resources.

— It may malfunction with applications that use frames.

— It only works with browsers that support cookies.

The Server-URL Approach

The server-url approach stores an index on the browser. This index is used to access `client` object information that is stored on the server. The index is stored by encoding application URLs in the same way as the client-url approach.

+ The *advantages* of this approach are:

+ It does not place any limits on the number or size of client properties.

+ It works with all browsers.

— The *disadvantages* of this approach are:

— The `client` object information is lost when the server is restarted.

— It consumes server memory resources.

— It may malfunction with applications that use frames.

— It does not work correctly with forms.

— Dynamically generated links must add the index to the URL via the `addClient()` function.

Which Approach Should I Use?

With five different approaches to maintaining `client` object properties, each with their own advantages and disadvantages, you may wonder what approach to use for your application. Your decision process is driven by the following questions.

- Do I need to take advantage of client storage capabilities?

- Can I limit my application to browsers that support cookies?

If you need to take advantage of client storage, then your options are client-cookie and client-url. If the application can be limited to cookie-capable browsers, then choose client-cookie, since it eliminates all of the overhead associated with URL encoding.

If you don't need to take advantage of client storage, then your choices are server-ip, server-cookie, and server-url. The required assumptions for using server-ip are so limiting that it should never be considered as a viable option unless you have complete control over all clients that could access an application. This leaves server-cookie and server-url. If the application can be limited to cookie-capable browsers, then choose server-cookie, since it eliminates problems associated with URL encoding.

Server Functions

LiveWire provides several functions that can be used in server-side scripts. These functions are in addition to the functions provided by client-side JavaScript.

addClient(*URL*) When the client-url or server-url approach is used to maintain client object properties, these properties must be encoded as *name=value* pairs in application URLs. If you dynamically generate a URL and are using client-url or server-url, then you must use `addClient()` to add the client properties to the URL. The `addClient()` function returns a string that contains the URL with the client properties appended as a query string.

debug(*expression*) This function is used in conjunction with the Application Manager's Debug command. It writes the value of the expression to the Application Manager's Debug window.

flush() When the `write()` function is used to generate HTML, its output is buffered in 64K chunks before being sent to the browser. The `flush()` function causes buffered output to be immediately sent to the browser. All `client` object properties should be set before invoking `flush()`.

getOptionValue(*name,n*) The `getOptionValue()` function returns the text of the *n*th option of the HTML selection list of the specified name.

getOptionValueCount(*name*) The `getOptionValueCount()` function returns the number of options selected in the select list of the specified name.

redirect(*URL*) The `redirect()` function redirects the browser to immediately load the specified URL. All subsequent JavaScript statements are ignored.

write(*expression*) The `write()` function generates the HTML specified by the expression.

NOTE LiveWire provides additional functions for accessing external functions written in other languages, such as C and C++. Consult the *LiveWire Developer's Guide* for more information on accessing external functions.

Summary

In this chapter, you learned how to use LiveWire to create Web applications that eliminate the need for CGI programs. You learned how to use JavaScript's server programming capabilities to process data received from browsers, and to dynamically return new Web pages to browsers. You also learned how to combine client- and server-side JavaScript to develop server-based Web applications that maximize the use of browser programming capabilities. In the next chapter, you'll learn how to use LiveWire Pro to develop Web applications that connect to online databases.

CHAPTER

TWENTY-EIGHT

28

Accessing Databases with LiveWire Pro

- ■ Databases vs. Files

- ■ LiveWire Pro to the Rescue

- ■ Setting Up the Informix Online Workgroup Server

- ■ Using LiveWire Pro

- ■ The `database` Object

- ■ Structured Query Language (SQL)

In the previous chapter, you learned how to develop server-side JavaScript scripts and integrate them into LiveWire applications. For example, you developed the *diskette* application, which took customer orders and wrote them to a server file. Such file-based applications are expedient for small projects, but they are limited in capability, and are often unsuitable for larger applications. You can go beyond these limitations of file-based storage by developing Web applications that make use of advanced database capabilities—by using Netscape's *LiveWire Pro*.

In this chapter, you'll learn how to use LiveWire Pro to access online databases. You'll learn how to use the `database` object to open database connections, add data to databases, and perform database queries. You'll be introduced to the Structured Query Language (SQL) and learn how to execute SQL statements using the methods of the `database` object. You'll then update the previous chapter's *diskette* application to use an online database, and you'll develop two new applications to query and update the database. When you finish this chapter, you'll be able to use the database capabilities of LiveWire Pro in your own Web applications.

Databases vs. Files

Many small computer applications are centered around the creation, development, management, and display of documents that are organized into files. Your word processor is used to create and manage word processing documents. Your HTML editor is used to develop Web pages. Your spreadsheet program is used to work with spreadsheets. And so on.

Most personal computer programs are perfectly suited to file-oriented applications, since the focus of the application is the application *document*. However, for medium to large-scale applications that focus on the collection, analysis, and reporting of information, a simple file-based approach is quite limiting.

As an example, consider the *diskette* application of the previous chapter. It merely took customer orders and appended them to the end of the file `orders.txt`. This simple application works well for recording orders, but it wouldn't fit all of the needs of the "Diskette Center" business as described in Chapter 27. For example, those employees who are responsible for filling orders would need a capability to view the `orders.txt` file. (Of course, they could always write an application to display the contents of `orders.txt` in some formatted fashion.)

Other employees would be required to maintain the status of the individual orders. (These employees could write an application to update `orders.txt` with status information.) And of course, management would need to get involved in determining how well (or not well) the whole process works. A script that could provide the capability to analyze `orders.txt` would also be helpful.

Are you starting to get the picture? Most file-oriented systems break down when a few different groups need to maintain the file information for different purposes. The main deficiencies of file-oriented systems are that they are structurally rigid, difficult to maintain, less reliable and secure, and do not support custom information sharing.

- File-oriented systems are *structurally rigid and difficult to maintain,* because once a file format has been developed, its very difficult to change the format without having to change everybody's file access scripts.

- They are *less reliable and secure,* because anyone with access to the file has access to the entire contents of the file. All it takes is one individual with an update script that malfunctions to ruin the data used by everyone else.

- File-oriented systems *do not support custom information sharing,* because with file-oriented systems you have two query options: use an existing query script or write your own. For those who do not have the resources to write their own scripts, the available options become rather limited.

Database management systems remove many of the limitations of file-oriented systems. A database management system, abbreviated as *DBMS,* is a system of software tools for storing, updating, retrieving, analyzing, reporting, and managing information. A good DBMS would provide all of the employees at the imaginary "Diskette Center" with the capabilities they need to efficiently carry out their work. For example, compare these characteristics of a DBMS with the drawbacks mentioned above for file-oriented systems:

- A typical DBMS is much more flexible when it comes to structural changes. You can change the structure and organization of your database without losing any of your data. For this reason, a database is usually much easier to maintain.

- A good DBMS promotes reliability by validating data before adding it to the database. Many DBMSes usually have security features for limiting user access to certain types of database information.

- Probably the most compelling reasons for using a DBMS are the capabilities that it provides for querying and reporting information. Many database management systems provide a query language, such as the Structured Query Language or SQL, for asking a database about the information it contains. The query language is often integrated with a set of report-generation tools, which take the results of database queries and format them into custom reports.

Figure 28.1 contrasts DBMS-oriented systems with that of file-oriented systems.

Among the various types of database management systems, the *relational* database management system, or RDBMS, has become the most successful and popular. The

FIGURE 28.1

DBMS-oriented systems have many advantages over file-oriented systems.

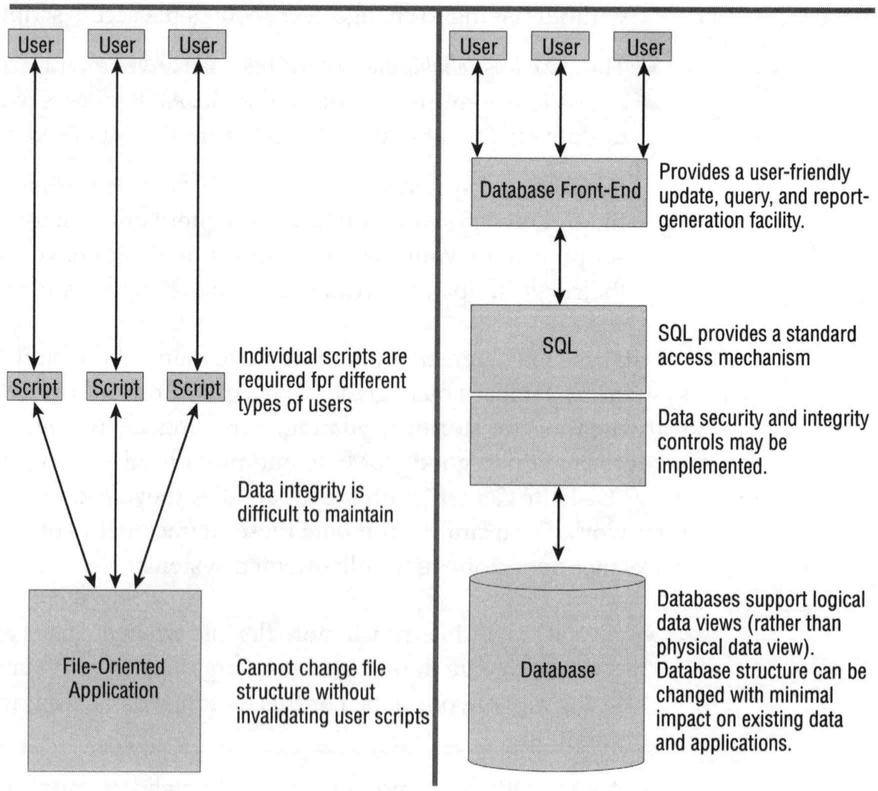
User
User
User
Script
Script
Script
Individual scripts are required fpr different types of users
Data integrity is difficult to maintain
File-Oriented Application
Cannot change file structure without invalidating user scripts
User
User
User
Database Front-End
Provides a user-friendly update, query, and report-generation facility.
SQL
SQL provides a standard access mechanism
Data security and integrity controls may be implemented.
Database
Databases support logical data views (rather than physical data view). Database structure can be changed with minimal impact on existing data and applications.

success of such systems lies in the use of a relational model for organizing the information contained in the database. In the relational model, a database is organized into one or more *tables*, which contain data that is arranged according to the table's *columns*. Each *row* of the table represents an individual table *record*. For example, a database of taxpayers' names and addresses may have the following table columns: taxID, address, city, state, zipCode, and country. A record about me in that table would consist of the following *row*:

taxID	address	city	state	zipCode	country
123-45-6789	613 Beyer Way #504	San Diego	CA	92154	USA

One or more of the columns of a table are used as *keys* for the table. A key is a column group of columns that uniquely identify each row of the table. Take note of that qualifying word "uniquely": in the above taxpayer table, the `taxID` column could be a key, but the `city` column cannot, since a `city` value of San Diego could easily identify hundreds, if not thousands, of table entries. Figure 28.2 summarizes the organization of a relational database.

FIGURE 28.2

Relational database systems are organized into a series of tables.

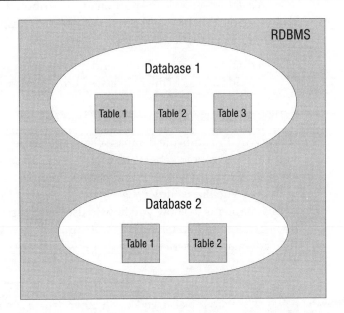

> **NOTE** A DBMS can manage more than one database at a time.

The reason for the popularity and success of relational database management systems is that their tabular approach allows databases to be defined in ways which promote consistency by eliminating redundant information. RDBMs are also storage-efficient and are easily updated and queried.

LiveWire Pro to the Rescue

With all the benefits of using an RDBMS, you're probably wondering why the capability to work with databases was left out of LiveWire. The answer is that it wasn't; in fact, LiveWire provides a `database` object that can be used to access online databases. What LiveWire *is* lacking is the database client and server.

- *A database server* is the portion of a distributed database system which manages the database and provides service by responding to database update and query requests.

- *A database client* is used to send queries and updates to the database and to provide access to the responses of the queries and updates.

These concepts are illustrated in Figure 28.3.

LiveWire Pro adds the database client and server software to LiveWire and provides a useful report-generation tool. The database server that is included with LiveWire Pro is the *Informix Online Workgroup Server*. Other software included with LiveWire Pro is the *Crystal Reports Professional Version 4.5*. Since the purpose of this chapter is to show you how to use JavaScript to access online databases, I do not cover the Crystal Reports software. The LiveWire Pro documentation more than adequately describes the use of this software.

> **NOTE** LiveWire Pro also works with other database servers, such as those provided by Oracle, Sybase, and Microsoft.

FIGURE 28.3

Distributed database
systems use a client/
server approach.

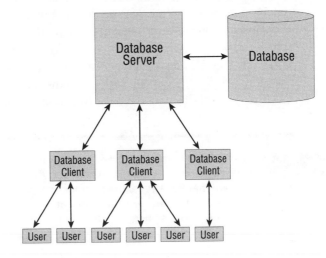

FIGURE 28.3

Distributed database
systems use a client/
server approach.

Before continuing with this chapter, you should download a copy of LiveWire Pro from Netscape's Web site. Follow the links from *http://home.netscape.com* to get to their software download area. The following section shows you how to install the Informix Online Workgroup Server.

> **WARNING** You'll need Windows NT 3.51 (with all service packs installed), Windows NT 4.0, or a compatible Unix platform to install LiveWire Pro. It does *not* work with Windows 95. I use Windows NT 4.0 for the examples in this chapter.

Setting Up the Informix Online Workgroup Server

While Netscape makes it easy to download a trial version of their LiveWire Pro software, Netscape's software installation documentation is less than adequate. After taking two days to get it working right, I've settled on these installation procedures.

First, you'll need to write down the serial number and key for the Informix database included with LiveWire Pro, because you'll be asked for it (in step 4 of these instructions). These items are disclosed in the LiveWire `readme.txt` file, which can be found in your `\Netscape\Server\LiveWire\` folder after you've installed the LiveWire package. If you've installed LiveWire from a CD, the same readme file will also appear in the top-level folder of the first LiveWire CD (the one that does not have the Informix database software).

> **NOTE**
>
> Note that these installation instructions assume that you'll be installing LiveWire Pro on the same host as your Netscape server. This is fine for development systems. In a production system, however, you'll probably want to run your Netscape server and database server on separate hosts for performance reasons.

1. Set up your Netscape Web server (FastTrack or Enterprise) to run as a user service under Windows NT. It runs as a local system service, by default. Use the Services applet of Control Panel to locate your server in the server list and click the Startup button. Set the server to log on as your account. When you are finished, restart your system.

2. Run the self-extracting LiveWire Pro file (`livewirepront.exe`) to create the self-extracting installation files for the Informix server and the Crystal Reports software. Read the `README.TXT` file.

3. Run the self-extracting `ows712nt4.exe` Informix installation software and follow the installation instructions. You should install the database server as `ol_host` where you replace *host* with the name of your Windows NT host. Make sure you write down any passwords that you enter. (I use *"informix"* as the password for the Informix account in the examples of this chapter. If you use a different password, you'll have to substitute your own password for *"informix"*.) You can change this password any time after the database server is set up.

4. Enter the serial number and key mentioned at the beginning of this discussion when requested by the Informix software.

5. Restart your system once the Informix software has been installed.

Now even though you've set up your database server, you still won't be able to use it in any applications. You'll need to use the *Informix Command Center* program to turn the server on (it's in the Informix program group, and is accessible from the Start menu). You'll also need to create a database and a database table. I'll show you how to do that in the sections "Creating a New Database" and "Creating a New Database Table" later in this chapter.

Using LiveWire Pro

Now that you've installed the Informix Online Workgroup Server, you're probably wondering how you go about using LiveWire Pro. The possible uses of LiveWire Pro are limitless. The Informix database server is a high-performance, top-of-the-line server and the Crystal Reports software is one of the best HTML report generation tools for Web applications. Both can be used in numerous ways without writing a single line of JavaScript. However, for the purposes of this chapter, I'm limiting the discussion to how to use JavaScript to access the Informix database server. This involves the following steps:

1. Create a database on the database server.

2. Create one or more database tables to store information.

3. Use the `database` object within a JavaScript script to connect to the database.

4. Use the methods of the `database` object to add data to the database, view data stored in the database, or modify or delete database information.

   The first two steps involve the use of the Informix *Database Explorer* and are covered later in this chapter. Don't worry, the Database Explorer is easy to use—I'm only putting it off so that I can show how to use it in the context of an example.

   The third and fourth steps involve the use of the `database` object, which is covered in the next section. The fourth step also involves the use of SQL statements. A quick and dirty introduction to SQL is provided in the section "Structured Query Language" later in this chapter.

The *database* Object

The database object is a server-side JavaScript object. There is only one database object; it is named database. To use it, you must invoke its connect() method to connect it to a database. This is accomplished as follows:

```
database.connect("INFORMIX","ol_host","user","password","database")
```

In the above statement, ol_*host* is the name you gave the Informix server during installation, *user* is the name of the Informix user account ("informix" by default), and *password* is the password for this account ("informix" by default). The database parameter is the name of a database on the server—it's a database you still have to create.

NOTE   If you use a database other than Informix, such as Oracle, you'll need to substitute the database name for INFORMIX as the first parameter of the connect method.

The invocation of the connect() method marks the beginning of all database activity. After connecting, you'll use the methods of the database object to interact with the database and then disconnect from the database when finished. Table 28.1 summarizes the methods of the database object. The following subsections show how to use these methods.

TABLE 28.1   The methods of the database object

Method	Description
beginTransaction()	Start a new database transaction.
commitTransaction()	Commit all actions since the last beginTransaction() method was invoked.
connect(*dbType, databaseServer, user, password, database*)	Connect to a database.
connected()	Determine whether you are currently connected to a database.

TABLE 28.1   The methods of the `database` object (continued)

Method	Description
`cursor`(*sqlSelect* [,*updateable*])	Create a `cursor` object that contains the result of the *sqlSelect* statement. The *updateable* parameter specifies whether the cursor is updateable.
`disconnect()`	Disconnect from the database.
`execute`(*sql*)	Execute the *sql* statement and return an error status code.
`majorErrorCode()`	Return the major error code that is provided by the database server in response to a failed method invocation.
`majorErrorMessage()`	Return the major error message that is provided by the database server in response to a failed method invocation.
`minorErrorCode()`	Return the minor error code that is provided by the database server in response to a failed method invocation.
`minorErrorMessage()`	Return the minor error message that is provided by the database server that in response to a failed method invocation.
`rollbackTransaction()`	Undo all database modifications since the last `beginTransaction()` method was invoked.
`SQLTable`(*sqlSelect*)	Display the results of the *sqlSelect* statement as an HTML table.

NOTE   You can only access one database at a time in JavaScript. For most applications, however, a single database is sufficient. If you need to access multiple databases, you can do so sequentially, by disconnecting from one and then connecting to another.

Locks and Connections

Two types of database connections may be used to access a database from JavaScript—*standard* or *serial*.

- A standard connection occurs when the `project` object is not locked.

- A serial connection occurs when the `project` object is locked.

Under the standard approach, only one connection is required per application—all script instances of the same application share the single connection. This approach lets LiveWire and the database server handle any issues that may be related to concurrent access to the database; it also greatly simplifies database access. However, it has the disadvantage that you may too easily reach the maximum number of database connections allowed by your database license. In addition, all database connections share the same user name and password and therefore all have equivalent database access.

Under the serial approach, only one script instance is allowed to access the database at a time. The script instance acquires the project lock and retains access to the database until the project is unlocked. Each script instance connects individually and therefore can be assigned different user names and passwords. The drawback to this approach is the overhead required for the project locking and for establishing the database connections.

NOTE   The examples in this chapter use the standard approach, but add additional checks to ensure that a database connection is established before performing any database operations.

Executing SQL

Once a connection to a database has been established, the `execute()`, `SQLTable()`, and `cursor()` methods can be used to execute SQL statements which update or query the database.

The `execute()` method takes a string containing a SQL statement as an argument, executes the statement, and returns an error status code. The SQL statement may be any SQL statement that does not return an answer set. These statements are database updates rather than queries. The "Error Handling" section later in this chapter shows how to handle the error status codes returned by methods that execute SQL statements. An example of the `execute()` method follows:

```
database.execute("DELETE FROM custorder WHERE orderno < 2000")
```

The above statement tells the database server to delete all rows in the custorder table where the value of the orderno column is less than 200.

The `SQLTable()` method is an invaluable tool for querying a database. It takes a SQL `SELECT` statement as a parameter, executes the statement, and displays the result of the query as an HTML table. For example, the following statement queries the database for all rows of the custorder table sorted by the orderno column.

```
database.SQLTable("SELECT * FROM custorder ORDER BY orderno)
```

The `cursor()` method can be used to query or update a database. It takes a SQL `SELECT` statement as a parameter and an optional `boolean` value, indicating whether or not the cursor is updateable. It executes the SQL statement and stores the resulting answer set as a `cursor` object. The `cursor` object can be used to perform subsequent database operations, as described in the next section. An updateable `cursor` object is one that can be used to update the database. A `cursor` object that is not updateable (the default case) can only be used to query the database. The following statement creates a `cursor` object that contains all rows of the custorder table for which the status column is `open`. This cursor is updateable.

```
database.cursor("SELECT * FROM custorder WHERE status = 'open'",true)
```

Using the Cursor

A `cursor` object is created as the result of invoking the `cursor()` method of the `database` object. The `cursor` object contains the answer set which results from a SQL SELECT statement. The properties and methods of the `cursor` object can then be used to perform operations on the answer set. The methods of the `cursor` object are summarized in Table 28.2.

T A B L E 2 8 . 2   Methods of the `cursor` object

Method	Description
`close()`	Closes the cursor object and releases memory resources that it used.
`columnName(n)`	Returns the name of the *n*th column of the cursor object (starts at 0).
`columns()`	Returns the number of columns in a cursor object.
`deleteRow(table)`	Deletes the row in *table* corresponding to the current row of the cursor. Returns an error status code. The cursor must be updateable.
`insertRow(table)`	Inserts the row in *table* corresponding to the current row of the cursor. Returns an error status code. The cursor must be updateable.

TABLE 28.2 Methods of the `cursor` object (continued)

Method	Description
`next()`	Moves to the next row of the answer set associated with the cursor. Returns `false` if the current row is the last row of the cursor (before movement) and `true` otherwise.
`updateRow()`	Updates the row in *table* corresponding to the current row of the cursor. Returns an error status code. The cursor must be updateable.

The `cursor` object is associated with a pointer, which indicates the rows in the `cursor` object's answer set. This pointer is initially placed before the first row. The `next()` method is used to move the pointer to the first row and then to subsequent rows. The current row is the row at which the pointer is currently located.

NOTE LiveWire Pro automatically closes all cursor objects at the end of a client request.

The columns of a `cursor` object are properties of the `cursor` object. They can be referred to by name or by indexing the `cursor` object. For example, suppose the rows variable is assigned a `cursor` object as the result of the following statement:

```
rows=database.cursor("SELECT orderno, status, lastname FROM
➡ custorder")
```

The answer set has the three columns orderno, status, and lastname. You can refer to the column values of the current row using `rows.orderno`, `rows.status`, and `rows.lastname`. You can also refer to these values using `rows[0]`, `rows[1]`, and `rows[2]`.

Each of the columns of the current row is itself a `cursorColumn` object with two methods—`blobImage()` and `blobLink()`, as described below. (The acronym *BLOb* stands for *Binary Large Object*; it refers to large objects, such as images and multimedia objects, that are stored in the database.)

blobImage() The `blobImage()` method causes the value of the `cursorColumn` object to be displayed using an `<img>` tag. Its syntax is as follows:

```
cursor.column.blobImage(format [, alt] [, align] [,width]
➡ [,height] [,border] [,ismap])
```

The *format* parameter may be GIF, JPEG, or any other MIME image format. The *alt*, *align*, *width*, *height*, and *border* attributes specify the corresponding attributes of the image tag. The *ismap* parameter is boolean; if it's true, then an ISMAP attribute is added to the image tag.

To see how blobImage() works, consider the following code:

```
rows=database.cursor("SELECT imageID, title, image FROM imageTable")
rows.next()
write(rows.image.blobImage("GIF"))
```

The above code generates an image tag containing the name of a temporary .gif image generated by the database from the BLOb contained in the image column of the first row of the cursor object assigned to the rows variable.

blobLink() The blobLink() method is used to create a hyperlink to a BLOb. Its syntax is as follows:

```
cursor.column.blobLink(mimeType, text)
```

where *mimeType* is the MIME type of the BLOb, and *text* is the text to be used in the link. For example, the following code:

```
rows=database.cursor("SELECT imageID, title, image FROM imageTable")
rows.next()
write(rows.image.blobLink("image/gif","Click here to see an image."))
```

creates a hyperlink to the .gif image contained in the BLOb with the text *"Click here to see an image."*

Transaction Processing

Most databases allow database updates to be performed as *transactions*. A transaction consists of one or more database operations that are grouped together. Transaction processing causes the transaction to be performed as a single unit. A lock is acquired during the processing of the transaction and prevents other script instances from creating conflicts with the transaction that is in progress. Transactions are also used to perform database operations that can be undone if an error occurs before all steps of the transaction are completed. The database object supports transaction processing.

Invoke the beginTransaction() method to start a transaction and the commitTransaction() method to end the transaction. If you want to undo a transaction before it is committed, invoke the rollbackTransaction() method.

If transaction processing is not specified, it is implicitly performed on a statement-by-statement basis, as each SQL statement is executed.

> **NOTE** A transaction is automatically committed when the HTML page containing the script of the transaction processing is no longer being processed.

Error Handling

Error status codes are returned for the following methods of the `database` object:

- `beginTransaction()`
- `commitTransaction()`
- `execute()`
- `rollbackTransaction()`

Error status codes are also returned for the following methods of the `cursor` object:

- `deleteRow()`
- `insertRow()`
- `updateRow()`

An error status code of 0 indicates a successful database operation. When the error status code is 5 (server error) or 7 (vendor library error), you can use the following methods of the `database` object to find out more information about the error:

- `majorErrorCode()`
- `majorErrorMessage()`
- `minorErrorCode()`
- `minorErrorMessage()`

The major and minor error codes are the primary and secondary codes returned by the server. The major and minor messages are the messages associated with these error codes.

Structured Query Language

So far you've learned how the methods of the database and cursor objects can be used to update and query an online database by executing SQL statements. You've seen some examples of SQL statements in the descriptions of these methods. But what exactly is SQL?

SQL is a language for accessing RDBMSes that was developed by IBM during the early days of RDBMS research. It was standardized during the later 1980s and has become the de facto standard query language for RDBMSes. The following URL is the SQL Standards Home Page and contains links to all types of information about SQL:

http://www.jcc.com/sql_stnd.html

The next URL contains a great tutorial on learning SQL. If you are new to SQL, I highly recommend taking this tutorial:

http://w3.one.net/~jhoffman/sqltut.htm

> **NOTE** The SQL acronym is pronounced *"sequel."*

While an introduction to SQL is a book in itself, in this section I'll try to give you enough of a background to get you going. For a more thorough introduction, I recommend taking the aforementioned tutorial and browsing the SQL Standards Home Page.

In any database application there are a number of core operations that you'll want to perform:

- Create and modify a database
- Create and modify a database table

- Add rows to the table

- Delete rows from the table

- Update rows in the table

- Query tables

There are SQL statements that allow you to do each of the above. Once you learn how to use these statements, you will have a basic knowledge of database programming.

NOTE In the following paragraphs I'll present the basic information you'll need for performing these core operations. For the first two operations, however—creating or modifying a database or a database table—refer to the special expanded discussions in the sections "Creating a New Database" and "Creating a New Database Table" later in this chapter.

Adding, Deleting and Updating Rows

You add rows to a table using the INSERT statement, delete rows from a table using the DELETE statement, and update a table row using the UPDATE statement. Pretty simple.

For the purposes of this section and the next, let's suppose our database consists of a single custorder table with the following columns: orderno, status, firstName, lastName, addr1, addr2, city, state, zip, phone, and email. Let these columns correspond to the client properties of the *diskette* application of Chapter 27.

The *INSERT* Statement

There are two forms for the INSERT statement. The syntax of the first form is

```
INSERT INTO table VALUES (value1, value2, …, valuen)
```

where *table* is the name of the table into which the row is to be inserted and *value1* through *valuen* are the values of the row. For example, the following statement inserts a row into the custorder table.

```
INSERT INTO custorder VALUES ('1001','open','Don','Woodbridge',
➡ '714 Elm Street', 'Apartment B', 'Scranton', 'PA', '18504',
➡ 'USA', '717-555-5555', 'woody@work.com')
```

Note that a value for each column is specified. To enter a row without specifying all of the columns, use the second form of the INSERT statement, the syntax of which follows:

```
INSERT INTO table (columnA, columnB, …, columnJ) VALUES (valueA,
➡ valueB, …, valueJ)
```

The values for *columnA* through *columnJ* are the names of the columns into which data is inserted, and *valueA* through *valueJ* are the values to be placed in these columns. All other columns in the row are assigned a null value. For example, the following statement inserts a row into custorder with the orderno column set to 1111, the firstName column set to Fred, and the lastName column set to Masters.

```
INSERT INTO custorder (orderno, firstName, lastName) VALUES
➡ ('1111', 'Fred', 'Masters')
```

The *DELETE* Statement

The syntax of the DELETE statement is as follows:

```
DELETE FROM table [WHERE condition]
```

The *condition* specifies a condition that must be met for a row to be deleted. The following are examples of using the DELETE statement.

```
DELETE FROM custorder WHERE orderno < 1001
DELETE FROM custorder WHERE lastName = 'Jones'
DELETE FROM custorder WHERE orderno > 5000 AND status = 'open'
```

WARNING If the WHERE clause of the DELETE statement is omitted then all rows of the table are deleted.

The *UPDATE* Statement

The syntax of the UPDATE statement is as follows:

```
UPDATE table SET [columnA = valueA, …, columnJ = valueJ] [WHERE
➡ condition]
```

The *columnl* = *valuel* expressions specify how selected columns of a row are to be updated. The *condition* selects the rows that are to be updated. If the WHERE clause is omitted, all rows of the table are updated. An example of the UPDATE statement is as follows. It sets the status column of all rows where the zip code is 9000 or higher to West Coast.

```
UPDATE custorder SET status = 'West Coast' WHERE zip >= 9000
```

Querying Tables

SQL provides in the SELECT statement all of the capabilities that you'll likely need for querying data from a database. The SELECT statement returns rows consisting of selected columns from one or more tables that meet certain conditions. The rows returned from a SELECT statement are referred to as an *answer set*. In JavaScript, the answer set is either displayed by the SQLTable() method or returned as a cursor object.

While a complete treatment of the SELECT statement is beyond the scope of this section, I'll present a limited description of the SELECT syntax that will get you started. For a more detailed treatment of the SELECT statement, check out the Web tutorial identified in the "Structured Query Language" section earlier in this chapter.

The following is a limited description of the SELECT statement syntax that is used in typical database queries:

```
SELECT columnList FROM tableList [WHERE condition] [ORDER BY column]
```

In the above description, *columnList* is a comma-separated list of columns and *tableList* is a comma-separated list of tables. The answer set generated by the SELECT statement contains exactly those columns specified. These columns may come from one or more tables. The rows in the answer set must meet the *condition* of the WHERE clause and are sorted by the *column* specified in the ORDER BY clause.

The following is an example of the SELECT statement that returns an answer set consisting of the order, status, lastName and phone columns from the custorder table. These rows must have open as the value of the status column and are sorted by the orderno field.

```
SELECT orderno, status, lastName, phone FROM custorder WHERE
➥ status = 'open' ORDER BY orderno
```

Updating the *diskette* Application

Now that we've covered all of the required background information, let's update the `diskette` application of Chapter 27 to take advantage of LiveWire Pro. We'll create an `orders` database and a custorder table within the database. We'll then update `diskette` to add customer orders to the database.

After porting `diskette` over to LiveWire Pro, we'll create two new applications—`orders` and `updateDB`—which will let employees of the imaginary "Diskette Center" view the contents of their database and update the database using SQL. You can use these two new applications to experiment with and learn SQL on your own.

Creating a New Database

The first thing that you need to do is to make sure that your database server is online. Start the *Informix Command Center* program (it is accessible from the Windows NT 4.0 Start menu) and put the database server online. Then close Command Center and start the Informix *Database Explorer*. Select your database server (ol_*host*) in the left frame of the Database Explorer window, and click on the little green and yellow database icon. This will create the New Online Database dialog box shown in Figure 28.4. Enter `orders` for the name of the database, and click OK.

After creating the database, your Database Explorer window should contain the orders database in the right frame, as shown in Figure 28.5. Congratulations, you've just created your first Informix database. Don't close Database Explorer yet. You'll need it in the next section.

FIGURE 28.4

The New Online Database dialog box is where you enter the name of a new database.

FIGURE 28.5

The Database Explorer displays the databases for each database server.

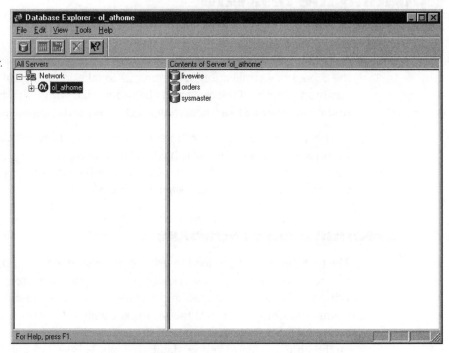

Creating a New Database Table

The Table Editor is the easiest way to create and update database tables. Follow these steps:

1. With Database Explorer opened as shown in Figure 28.5, select Table Editor from the Tools pull-down menu. This launches the Table Editor application.

2. In the Table Editor application, select New from the Table pull-down menu. This launches the Select Database dialog box.

3. Click on the ol_*host* database server to see a list of databases.

4. Select the orders database and click on the Select button. The table editor spreadsheet is launched.

5. Use the table editing spreadsheet to specify the table columns as shown in Figure 28.6.

6. Save the table as `custorder` and then exit the Table Editor and Database Explorer.

FIGURE 28.6

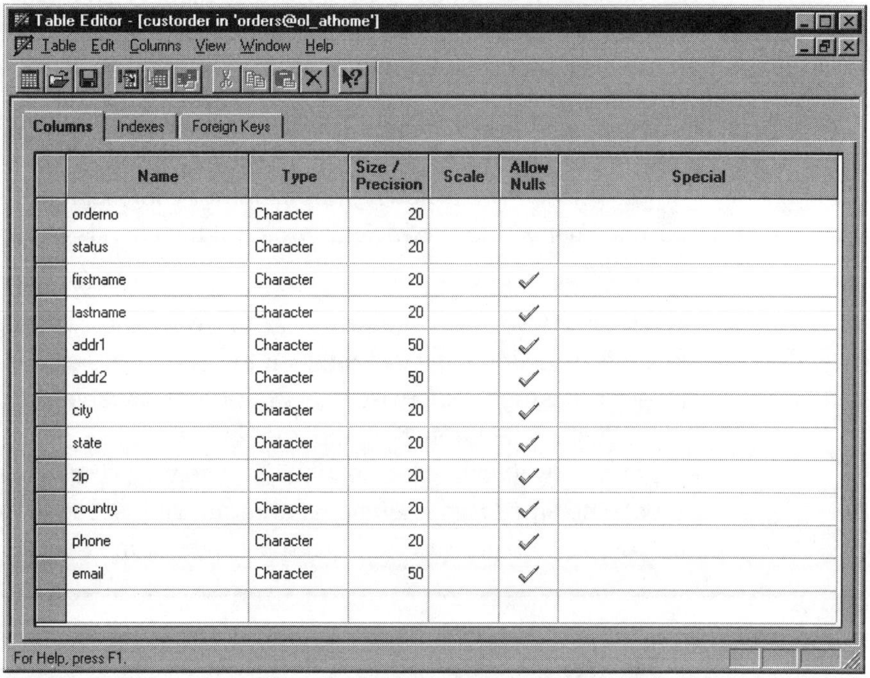

Creating and updating tables is easy with the Table Editor.

Name	Type	Size / Precision	Scale	Allow Nulls	Special
orderno	Character	20			
status	Character	20			
firstname	Character	20		✓	
lastname	Character	20		✓	
addr1	Character	50		✓	
addr2	Character	50		✓	
city	Character	20		✓	
state	Character	20		✓	
zip	Character	20		✓	
country	Character	20		✓	
phone	Character	20		✓	
email	Character	50		✓	

Adding Database Support to *diskette*

Now that you have an `orders` database and `custorder` table to work with, let's update *diskette* to work with the database instead of with a text file. The `start.htm`, `process.htm`, and `display.htm` files of Chapter 27 will not need to be modified. Only `finish.htm` will need to be changed. Go ahead and update it as shown in Listing 28.1. Also create the `thanks.htm` and `error.htm` files shown in Listings 28.2 and 28.3.

What Are the Changes to *finish.htm?*

The first thing that you'll notice is that the `project` object is locked just long enough to update and read the `project.nextOrder` property. This is because we don't need to use project locking for the database. LiveWire Pro and Informix work together to support transaction logging.

The `connected()` method is used to determine whether the database is currently connected. If it is not, then the `connect()` method is used to connect to the `orders` database. Note that you'll have to change `ol_athome` to `ol_host`, where `ol_host` is the name of your database server. You'll also have to change the *informix* password for the user to whatever password you are using.

The second invocation of `connected()` determines whether the `connect()` method succeeded. If it did not, then the `error.htm` file is loaded to display an error message. Otherwise, the `insertSQL` variable is used to build a SQL `INSERT` statement from the properties of the `client` object. The `execute()` method is invoked to execute the SQL statement. The resulting error status is used to determine whether the `thanks.htm` file is loaded to thank the user or the `error.htm` file is loaded to display an error message.

Listing 28.1. Updating finish.htm to use the orders database (finish.htm)

```
<HTML>
<HEAD>
<TITLE>Diskette Center</TITLE>
</HEAD>
<BODY>
<SERVER>
project.lock()
if(project.nextOrder==null) project.nextOrder=1000
project.nextOrder=parseInt(project.nextOrder)+1
client.orderno=project.nextOrder
project.unlock()
```

```
client.status="open"
if(!database.connected())
 database.connect("INFORMIX","ol_athome","informix","informix","orders")
if(database.connected()){
 insertSQL="INSERT INTO custorder VALUES ("
 insertSQL+="'"+client.orderno+"',"
 insertSQL+="'"+client.status+"',"
 insertSQL+="'"+client.firstName+"',"
 insertSQL+="'"+client.lastName+"',"
 insertSQL+="'"+client.addr1+"',"
 insertSQL+="'"+client.addr2+"',"
 insertSQL+="'"+client.city+"',"
 insertSQL+="'"+client.state+"',"
 insertSQL+="'"+client.zip+"',"
 insertSQL+="'"+client.country+"',"
 insertSQL+="'"+client.phone+"',"
 insertSQL+="'"+client.email+"')"
 errorStatus=database.execute(insertSQL)
 client.errorStatus="Execute error: "+errorStatus
 if(errorStatus!=0) redirect("error.htm")
 redirect("thanks.htm")
}else{
 client.errorStatus="Can not open database."
 redirect("error.htm")
}
</SERVER>
</BODY>
</HTML>
```

Listing 28.2. Thanking the user for the order (thanks.htm)

```
<HTML>
<HEAD>
<TITLE>Diskette Center</TITLE>
</HEAD>
<BODY>
<H1>Thank you for your order!</H1>
<H2>Your order number is <SERVER>
write(client.orderno)</SERVER>.</H2>
</BODY>
</HTML>
```

Listing 28.3. Displaying an error message to the user (error.htm)

```
<HTML>
<HEAD>
<TITLE>Diskette Center</TITLE>
</HEAD>
<BODY>
<H1>Sorry! Your order could not be processed.</H1>
<H2><SERVER>write(client.errorStatus)</SERVER></H2>
</BODY>
</HTML>
```

Compiling and Running *diskette*

If you are using Site Manager, be sure to add thanks.htm and error.htm to the site being managed. Compile the site and then deploy it to your Web server in the same location used in Chapter 27. If you don't use Site Manager, you can use the following command to compile the application:

```
Lwcomp -v -o diskette.web start.htm process.htm display.htm finish.htm
    thanks.htm error.htm
```

Launch Application Manager, and then modify the *diskette* application to give it at least one database connection. When you're finished, restart *diskette* and then run it by clicking on the Run link of Application Manager. Use *diskette* to add a few orders to the database. (I know this is boring, but do it anyway—you'll need some data to work with in the next section.) When you add each order, you should receive a customer order number, as shown in Figure 28.7.

Viewing the Database

So far all we've done is update *diskette* to use the orders database instead of the orders.txt file. We need to provide a way for the employees of the Diskette Center to view the contents of the database so that they can see what orders need to be filled. That's what we'll do in this section. We'll do it by creating a new project, called *orders*, that will let users view all or part of the custorder table of the orders database.

FIGURE 28.7

Each order added to the database results in a new order number being generated. (Listing 28.2)

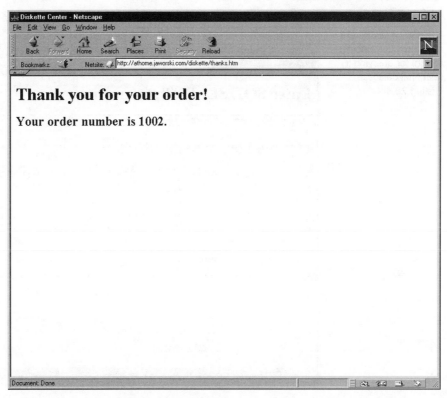

This project illustrates the power and simplicity of using a SQL-capable database with server-side JavaScript. It consists of the single file, `viewdb.htm`, shown in Listing 28.4. Compile the file using either Site Manager or the following command:

```
lwcomp -v -o orders.web viewdb.htm
```

and move the `orders.web` file to your Web server. Start Application Manager, and add the *orders* application. Be sure to give it at least one database connection. When you run *orders*, it displays the contents of your database, as shown in Figure 28.8. Experiment with the SQL SELECT statement to view different subsets of the database.

FIGURE 28.8

The SQL SELECT state-
ment provides a power-
ful tool for querying a
relational database.
(Listing 28.4)

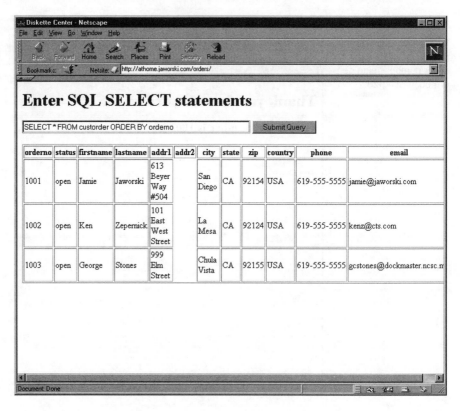

Listing 28.4. Using the SQL SELECT statement in your database applications (viewdb.htm)

```
<HTML>
<HEAD>
<TITLE>Diskette Center</TITLE>
</HEAD>
<BODY>
<H1>Enter SQL SELECT statements</H1>
<FORM ACTION="viewdb.htm">
<INPUT TYPE="TEXT" SIZE="60" NAME="sql"
 VALUE="SELECT * FROM custorder ORDER BY orderno">
<INPUT TYPE="SUBMIT">
</FORM>
<SERVER>
```

```
if(!database.connected())
 database.connect("INFORMIX","ol_athome","informix","informix","orders")
if(database.connected())
 if(request.sql==null)
  database.SQLTable("SELECT * FROM custorder ORDER BY orderno")
 else
  database.SQLTable(request.sql)
else write("<H1>Could not connect to database.</H1>")
</SERVER>
</BODY>
</HTML>
```

How *viewdb.htm* Works

The body of `viewdb.htm` consists of a simple HTML form that contains a text field for entering SQL SELECT statements. The default value of the field is a SQL statement that selects all rows and columns of the `custorder` table. The form is submitted to itself for processing.

The server script within `viewdb.htm` begins by connecting to the `orders` database. It checks to see if the value of the `sql` text field submitted is `null`, which is the case the first time `viewdb.htm` is loaded. In this case, it selects all columns and rows of custorder.

If the value of the `sql` field is not `null`, then the submitted SQL statement is executed.

Providing SQL Access to *orders*

We now can add data to `orders`, using the *diskette* application, and view its contents, using the *orders* application, but there's still something missing. We need to add the capability to update specific rows of the database and to directly insert and delete table rows. To do this, we'll build an *updateDB* application that will consist of three files—getsql.htm, dosql.htm, and error.htm. The getsql.htm file is shown in Listing 28.5, dosql.htm is Listing 28.6, and the error.htm file is the same as that shown earlier, in Listing 28.3. The getsql.htm file is the default page for the *updateDB* application.

Compile the three files to create updateDB.web using the following compiler command:

```
lwcomp -v -o updateDB.web getsql.htm dosql.htm error.htm
```

Move `updateDB.web` to your Web server and create the *updateDB* application, using Application Manager. When you run *updateDB*, it displays the Web page shown in Figure 28.9. Enter a couple of SQL UPDATE and DELETE statements to update your database. You can use this application to practice your SQL.

FIGURE 28.9

SQL statements can also be used to update a relational database. (Listing 28.5)

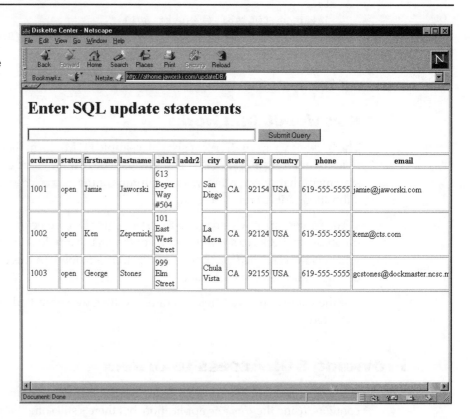

Listing 28.5. Getting a database update command from the user (getsql.htm)

```
<HTML>
<HEAD>
<TITLE>Diskette Center</TITLE>
</HEAD>
<BODY>
<H1>Enter SQL update statements</H1>
<FORM ACTION="dosql.htm">
```

```
<INPUT TYPE="TEXT" SIZE="60" NAME="sql">
<INPUT TYPE="SUBMIT">
</FORM>
<SERVER>
if(!database.connected())
 database.connect("INFORMIX","ol_athome","informix","informix","orders")
if(database.connected())
 database.SQLTable("SELECT * FROM custorder ORDER BY orderno")
else write("<H1>Could not connect to database.</H1>")
</SERVER>
</BODY>
</HTML>
```

Listing 28.6. Processing the database update command (dosql.htm)

```
<HTML>
<HEAD>
<TITLE>Diskette Center</TITLE>
</HEAD>
<BODY>
<SERVER>
if(!database.connected())
 database.connect("INFORMIX","ol_athome","informix","informix","orders")
if(database.connected()){
 errorStatus=database.execute(request.sql)
 if(errorStatus!=0){
  client.errorStatus="Error: "+errorStatus
  redirect("error.htm")
 }else redirect("getsql.htm")
}else{
 client.errorStatus="<H1>Could not connect to database.</H1>"
 redirect("error.htm")
}
</SERVER>
</BODY>
</HTML>
```

How *updateDB* Works

The getsql.htm file is similar to viewdb.htm in that it consists of a SQL entry form, followed by a server script. In the case of getsql.htm, the SQL entry form is used to enter SQL UPDATE, DELETE, and INSERT statements. The form is submitted to `dosql.htm` for processing. The server script that follows the form uses the `SQLTable()` method to display the entire contents of the `custorder` table. This allows you to view the effects of any database updates.

The `dossql.htm` file processes the `getsql.htm` form data by executing the SQL statement entered into the `sql` field using the `execute()` method. Errors are processed by loading `error.htm`. If no errors occur, the `getsql.htm` file is reloaded.

Summary

In this chapter, you learned how to use LiveWire Pro to access online databases. You learned how to use the `database` object to open database connections, add data to databases, and perform database queries. You were introduced to the Structured Query Language (SQL) and learned how to execute SQL statements using the methods of the `database` object. You updated the *diskette* application to use an online database, and developed two new applications to query and update the database. You have now learned how to use most of the features of LiveWire and LiveWire Pro. In the next chapter, you'll learn how to apply this knowledge to design and develop fully distributed Web applications.

CHAPTER TWENTY-NINE

Creating Distributed Applications

- **Characteristics of Distributed Systems**

- **Advantages of Distributed Applications**

- **Distributed Applications and the Web**

- **Building and Running a Distributed Scheduling System**

Now that you know how to use JavaScript to develop client- and server-side scripts and interface with database systems, we're going to use this knowledge to develop a distributed Web application. In this chapter, you'll learn about the three-tiered architecture of distributed systems and how to use JavaScript to implement the client, functional, and database layers. You'll then put this knowledge together to develop a distributed scheduling system. When you finish this chapter, you'll be able to structure your Web applications so that they take advantage of distributed processing capabilities.

The Three-Tiered Architecture of Distributed Systems

Most user applications can be organized into three fundamental parts:

- User interface

- Functions performed by the application

- Information storage and retrieval capability

Take a word processing program, for example. The user-interface layer consists of a WYSIWYG display of the document that you're working on combined with pull-down menus and dialog boxes. The functional layer includes functions for document editing, reformatting, and printing. The information storage and retrieval layer reads and writes document files using the local file system.

A word processing program is an example of a *nondistributed* application—the user, functional, and storage layers usually all run on the same computer. *Distributed* applications, on the other hand, separate these three layers and execute elements of each layer on different computers. For example, consider a hypothetical medical information system:

- The user-interface layer displays patient records and allows doctors to prescribe tests and treatments for patients. This layer is implemented on personal computers that are located in doctor's offices and nurse's stations.

- The functional layer consists of software that schedules patients for tests and treatments. Part of this software is located on the same PCs as the user-interface layer. However, most of the software resides on mid-level to high-end servers, located in various hospital departments, such as the blood lab, X-ray facility, and physical therapy.

- The storage layer is implemented using database servers that are located at various levels within the hospital system. Some departments, such as the blood bank, may maintain a local database that tracks all of the blood work that is performed within the department. The results of the blood work may be stored with patient records in a hospital-level database. Cost information about patient tests and treatments may be maintained on a database at a central billing facility that performs billing for multiple hospitals within a hospital network.

The medical information system is an example of a distributed system because it executes elements of each layer—user-interface, functional, and storage—on different computers.

Characteristics of Distributed Systems

There are a number of characteristics that distinguish the medical information system from the word processing application, the most obvious of which is **size**. A word processing program is typically under 50 megabytes in total size. Medical information systems are in the gigabyte range for very small systems, and extend into the terabyte range for larger systems. In general, distributed applications are usually much larger than nondistributed applications. It is possible to develop a small distributed application (as you'll see in this chapter's example); however, in order to do so, you need to build the application on top of existing client and server software.

Distributed applications tend to be **enterprise-wide**, while nondistributed applications, because of their very nature, are limited to individual use. The hypothetical medical information system extends throughout the various hospital departments. While a word processing program may be used on all of an organization's PCs, each instance of the program is a nondistributed application.

Since distributed applications tend to be enterprise-wide, they are almost always **multiuser** applications. Adding another user to the application is often as simple as adding another user interface client. In the example medical information system, multiple users are supported through individual PCs, each running separate copies of the user interface software. While multiuser word processing systems do exist, most word processing applications operate in single-user mode.

Distributed applications are characterized by their capability to **share information**. Most go beyond simple data sharing and provide the capability to **distribute information**. Information distribution is the process of assembling the information that users need and providing them with the information when they need it. In medical systems, the distribution of information in a timely manner is a must—any delays could result in adverse impacts on patient care. In word processing applications, documents are often distributed as shared files and e-mail attachments. Some people still swap disks and print out hard copies of documents.

Distributed applications are also characterized by the fact that they are in **continuous operation** 24 hours a day and 365 days a year. Medical information systems are noted for their continuity of service—even during power outages and natural disasters. Nondistributed applications, such as word processing programs, are only in operation during the performance of a task.

Security is often a major concern for distributed applications. This is a consequence of the fact that they are multiuser and share information. Security mechanisms are used to limit access to information to authorized individuals and to ensure that information is available when it is needed. Most medical information systems include access controls that safeguard patient privacy and ensure that patient records are protected from unauthorized modification. Word processing programs generally support security by providing the capability to encrypt documents.

As a final consideration, many distributed applications tend to be **mission-critical**—a failure on the part of the application has a significant impact on the organization's capability to conduct business. This is especially true in medical information systems where even a partial system failure can have an adverse effect on patient care. Nondistributed applications *can* be mission-critical, but most are not. There are few companies that have gone out of business because of the failure of a word processing program.

Advantages of Distributed Applications

Distributed applications have numerous advantages—some of those you've probably gleaned from the characteristics described in the previous section. These advantages are mostly of the "-ability" variety—e.g., availability, scaleability, upgradeability, etc. These -abilities describe capabilities of distributed applications that set them apart from nondistributed applications.

Survivability

One of the most obvious benefits of distributed applications, for organizations that count on them, is their survivability. This survivability does not mean that they'll continue to operate through a nuclear war, but it does mean that they will continue to operate when one or more application hosts fail. The most common failure, and the easiest to handle, is the failure of a user-interface component. The solution generally involves using another client workstation until the failed one is repaired or replaced. Failure of application and database servers is usually handled through the use of duplicate, redundant, and backup servers.

Duplicate servers are operational servers that take over the processing of other servers when the primary servers become overstressed or fail. They are like the players of a hockey team—when one or more players get sent to the penalty box, the other players regroup until the missing players can be brought back into the game.

Redundant servers run in the background, waiting for a failure to occur before they are called to action. They are similar to baseball pitchers in the bullpen—they're warmed up and ready to go.

Backup servers are similar to a third string quarterback—they sit on the bench collecting dust until the first and second string quarterbacks are out of commission. Only then are they brought into the game.

Availability

The survivability of distributed applications helps to ensure that they are continuously available. Availability goes beyond the fact that there is adequate backup for system components. It includes a management *commitment to support* continuous operation. This commitment is reflected in the use of sufficient network bandwidth, the availability of backup communication capabilities, and the availability of system support 24 hours a day and 7 days a week.

Scaleability

Many distributed systems are infinitely scaleable. To add another user, just add another user workstation. To increase system storage capacity, upgrade the system file and database servers. To increase system performance, upgrade or increase the number of your application servers.

Upgradeability

Distributed applications are easily upgraded. In many cases, the user interface may be upgraded by switching to a newer version of the client software or by replacing user interface scripts. Functional and storage layers can be upgraded by switching to a new version of the application or database server, or by replacing server or SQL scripts with new and improved ones.

Maintainability

Since distributed systems are organized into user interface, functional, and storage components, they are more modular and easier to maintain. Maintenance changes often take the form of new or improved scripts, or the installation of new client or server software.

Use of Heterogeneous Components

Most distributed applications benefit from their ability to use products that are vendor-independent. This benefit is realized when distributed systems are developed using open standards. For example, the developer of a Web-based distributed application may use a Netscape, Microsoft, or public-domain browser to implement the user-interface layer. He or she may run the browser on a Windows, Macintosh, or Linux platform. They have even more hardware and software choices for Web and database servers. As long as the application developer can stick with open standards and avoid proprietary solutions, she or he will be able to enjoy the luxury of being platform-independent in regard to both hardware and software.

Distributed Applications and the Web

The Web is a distributed application. In fact, it is one of the world's largest distributed applications. It provides the capability to globally publish information on Web servers which can be universally accessed via Web browsers. The browser implements the user-interface layer and the Web server implements the storage layer. The functional layer is split between the browser and the server—browsers execute JavaScript scripts, Java applets, plug-ins, and other executable content in support of the functional layer; Web servers execute CGI programs, server-side JavaScript and Java, and server-side plug-ins in carrying out their share of the functional layer.

Newer and more advanced Web applications have extended the capabilities of Web servers via database systems. This extension is primarily in terms of the information storage layer, but also applies to the functional layer. Figure 29.1 illustrates the relative extents of the three tiers of the distributed application architecture in comparison to the architecture of a database-enhanced Web application.

As shown in Figure 29.1, the user layer is not affected by the use of a database server and remains with the browser. The storage layer extends from the Web

FIGURE 29.1

The extents of the distributed application layers in relation to the Web client-server architecture

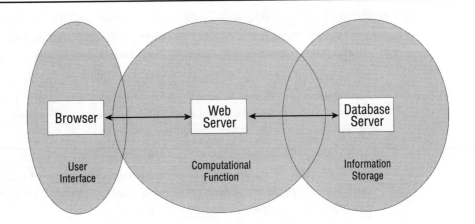

server to include the database server. The Web server retains responsibility for file storage and retrieval, while the database server adds a new dimension to the information that is available to Web applications. The functional layer is extended to the database server to include application functionality that is implemented in SQL.

Implementing the User-Interface Layer on Web Browsers

For many distributed applications, Web browsers are the ideal platform for implementing the user-interface layer:

- They're available for almost all hardware and software platforms.

- They support a full range of networking and multimedia capabilities.

- They're easy to program in support of distributed applications.

- For the most part, they conform to open standards.

Although Netscape Navigator tends to establish standards rather than conform to them, it is the browser of choice for implementing distributed applications. Its principal advantages are that it is supported on almost all major operating system platforms, it is the world's most popular browser, and it is available at a reasonable price.

The bulk of any browser-based user interface should be written in HTML. HTML provides the capability to quickly and easily lay out the user interface and implement user-interface controls, such as form elements.

JavaScript takes over where HTML leaves off. It should be used to handle user-interface events and to integrate and control Java applets and plug-ins. Java applets may be used to implement custom interface elements that are not available in HTML and cannot be synthesized using JavaScript.

Finally, other client-side programming languages and plug-ins may be used to implement some interface controls. The disadvantage of using plug-ins and platform-dependent programming languages is that you lock yourself into a vendor-specific operating system platform.

Implementing the Functional Layer Using Web Clients and Servers

As shown in Figure 29.1, the functional layer of a distributed application can be implemented across Web browsers and servers and also database servers.

The browser can implement client-side functions, such as data validation, dynamic display generation, and the processing of special MIME types. These functions can be implemented in JavaScript, Java, plug-ins, or other client-side programming languages. JavaScript's strengths are in event handling, local form processing, and in dynamic HTML generation.

The Web server implements functions which process and act upon data received from browsers. These functions may be implemented using traditional CGI programs, LiveWire, or other server-side programs. The advantage of using LiveWire is that it integrates client- and server-side functions into a single consolidated Web application.

If the Web application makes use of a database server, then the functional layer extends to the database server. SQL scripts are a standard mechanism for database programming. LiveWire Pro allows SQL statements to be generated by server-side JavaScript and greatly simplifies the process of integrating database capabilities with Web applications.

LiveWire Pro combines browser, Web server, and database server functions into a single Web application. It also eliminates the messy interface programming associated with the use of cookies, URL decoding, the CGI, and accessing databases. This allows you to develop distributed applications without having to worry about the interfaces between browser, Web server, and database server components of the functional layer.

Implementing the Database Layer

The information storage layer is implemented on Web and database servers. Web servers retrieve files that are requested by browsers. These files are identified by URLs. Web servers may also upload and store files that are submitted with the POST method. Database servers store information in and retrieve information from database tables. The database queries and updates are specified using SQL statements.

The information storage layer does not require much programming. Both Web and database servers are designed to simplify information storage and retrieval. Database servers are accessed using SQL statements that are generated by Web server programs. LiveWire Pro applications generate SQL using the `database` object. The `cursor` object is used to access data that is retrieved from a database.

A Distributed Scheduling System

In the previous sections of this chapter, we've discussed the advantages of distributed applications and described how to implement each of the three application layers using browsers, Web servers, and database servers. In this section, we'll develop a distributed application, with LiveWire Pro, that provides the capability for the employees of a company to share their daily schedules. The application makes use of JavaScript's browser, Web server, and database server programming capabilities. The scheduling application is supported by a second administrative application that adds employees to and deletes them from the company's employee database.

The following section walks you through the administrative and scheduling applications and shows you how they are used. The section after that provides a summary description of the files that are compiled to produce the applications. Later sections provide a detailed description of the application code.

How the Scheduling Application Works

This section shows you how the scheduling application works so you'll know what to expect when you start to build it. As mentioned in the previous section, the scheduling application consists of administrative and user components. These components are actually implemented as separate LiveWire applications, `admsched` and `schedule`. This separation allows server access controls to be applied to the administrative application without placing unnecessary restrictions on the user application.

The Schedule Administration Application

The schedule administration application, `admsched`, provides the capability to manage the employees that are allowed access to the scheduling application (*schedule*). The *admsched* application allows you to add, delete and list the employees in the `schedule` database's `employee` table. It also allows you to remove old scheduling information (referred to as activities) from the `activity` table of the `schedule` database. Don't worry about learning about all this now—we'll cover these details later in the chapter.

To start the *admsched* application, you'll open the URL *http://your.server.com /admsched/*, substituting the host name of your Web server for *your.server.com*. Figure 29.2 shows the schedule administration opening display. The left frame provides the administrative commands and the right frame provides forms for entering the commands.

FIGURE 29.2

The schedule administration opening display

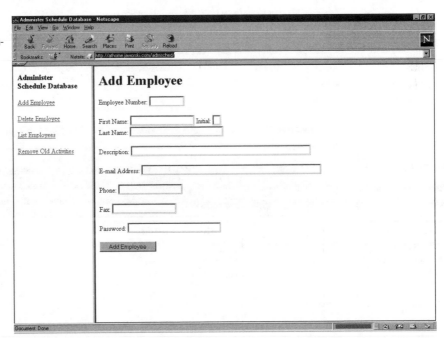

In order to use the scheduling applications, you'll need to add employees to the database. Figure 29.3 provides an example of how this form is filled in. When you click the Add Employee button, the employee is added to the database and a confirmation like that shown in Figure 29.4 is displayed.

FIGURE 29.3

Use the Add Employee form to add an employee to the database.

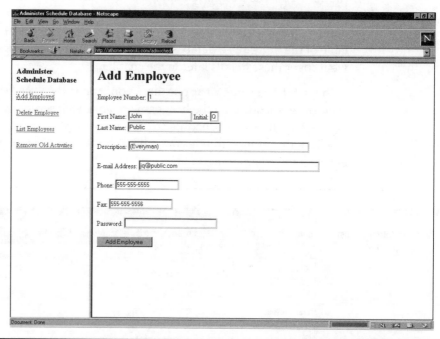

FIGURE 29.4

When you submit the Add Employee form, the schedule administration application informs you of the success or failure of the add operation.

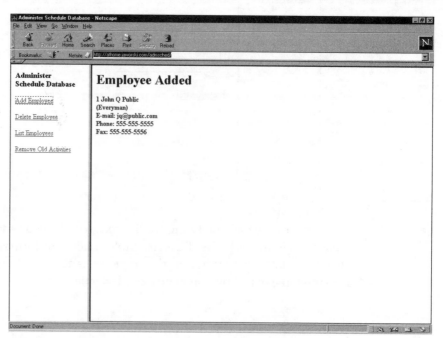

The List Employees command is used to obtain a tabular listing of the employees that are in the database. Refer to Figure 29.5. When you run the `admsched` application and add your own employees, you'll be able to verify the information you've entered using the List Employees command.

FIGURE 29.5

The List Employees command results in a tabular listing of the employees that have been added to the database.

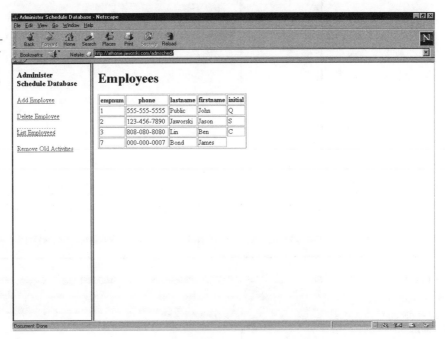

Use the Delete Employee command to delete employees from the database. Refer to Figure 29.6. Enter the employee number of the employee to be deleted, and click on the Delete Employee button. A deletion confirmation is displayed, as shown in Figure 29.7.

The Remove Old Activities command allows you to delete all employee schedule information that is prior to a specified date. To use this command, enter a date in the *mm/dd/yy* format and click on the Remove button. Refer to Figure 29.8.

FIGURE 29.6

The Delete Employee form is used to delete employees from the database.

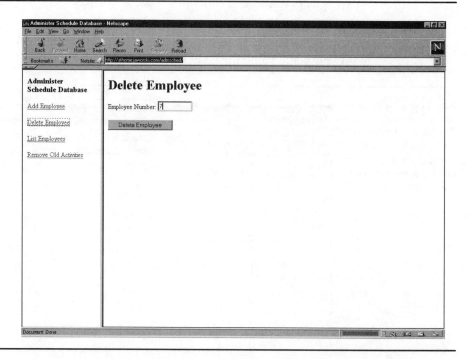

FIGURE 29.7

The schedule administration application provides confirmation of an employee deletion.

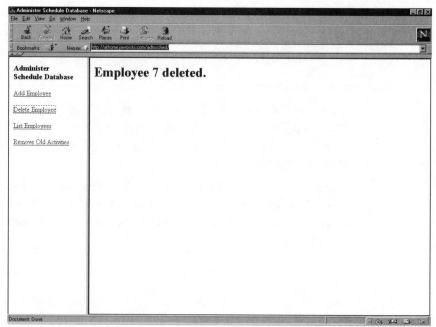

FIGURE 29.8

The Remove Old Activities form is used to delete old schedule information from the database.

The Online Scheduling Application

The online scheduling application enables you to enter personal schedule information in your calendar and also to view the schedules of other employees. The schedule information is stored in the activity table of the `schedule` database. To start the scheduling application, you'll open the URL *http://your.server.com/schedule/*. Figure 29.9 shows the scheduling application opening display.

In order to use the scheduling application, employees are required to enter their employee number and password. This prevents one employee from modifying the schedule of another. Once you've successfully logged in, you'll see the Web frames shown in Figure 29.10.

The top frame displays your employee information and allows you to change it and view the schedules of other employees.

The lower left frame provides a clickable calendar that you can use to view or update schedule information. The date displayed in red identifies the day for which calendar information is displayed in the right frame. The buttons above the calendar allow you to switch from one month to another.

FIGURE 29.9

The scheduling application opening display

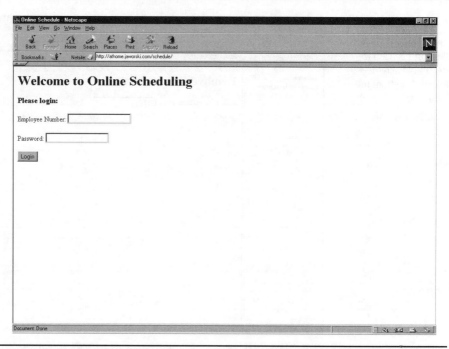

FIGURE 29.10

Logging in to the scheduling application as John Q Public

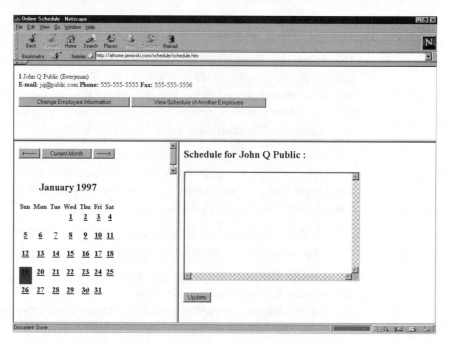

The lower right frame displays schedule information for the date selected in the lower left frame. The update button is used to save schedule information in the database.

When you click the Change Employee Information button, a form is loaded into the top frame, as shown in Figure 29.11. You can use this form to change your employee information. Figure 29.12 shows the results of changing the employee's schedule message. This message can be used to provide general information for those who view your schedule.

To update your schedule information, enter it in the lower right frame and click the Update button, as shown in Figure 29.13. You can click on the calendar dates to enter schedule information for future dates, as shown in Figure 29.14. You can also use the calendar buttons to change the month for which schedule information is being entered. Refer to Figure 29.15.

The View Schedule of Another Employee button, located in the top frame, allows you to look at the schedules of other employees. When you click on the button, the form shown in Figure 29.16 is displayed. If you click on the List Employees button a tabular list of employees is displayed, as shown in Figure 29.17.

FIGURE 29.11

The application allows you to change employee information.

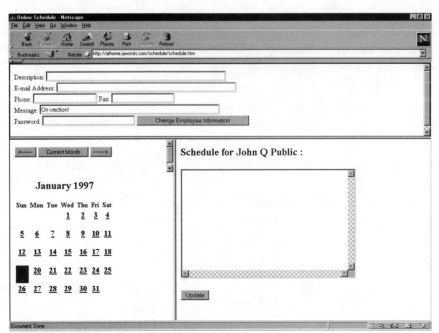

FIGURE 29.12

The updated employee information is displayed.

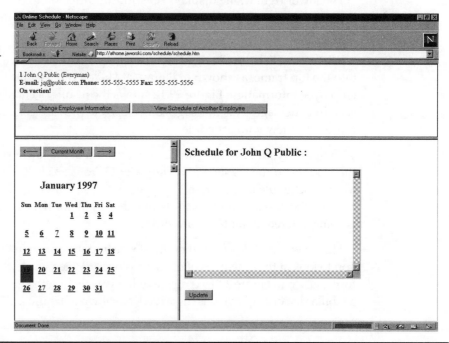

FIGURE 29.13

Enter schedule information in the text area and click the Update button.

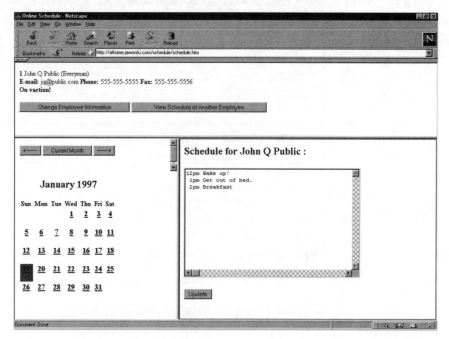

FIGURE 29.14

Click the calendar dates to enter future notes and schedule information.

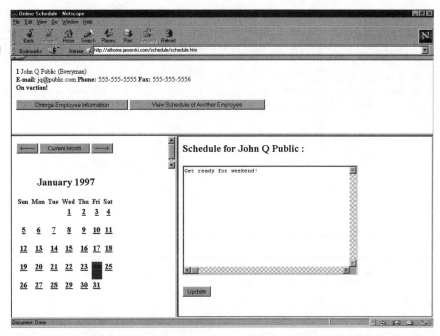

FIGURE 29.15

Click the calendar buttons to switch between months.

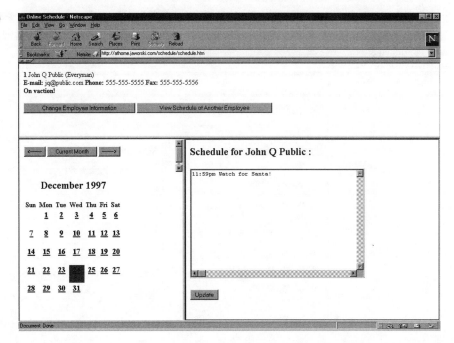

FIGURE 29.16

Use the View Schedule of Another Employee button to access the schedules of other employees.

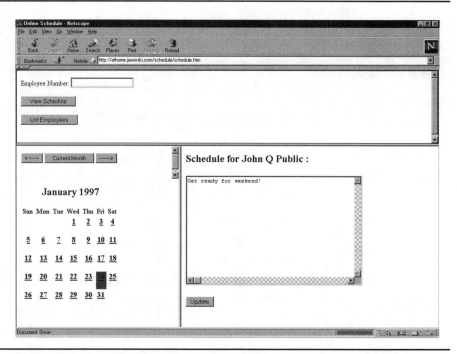

FIGURE 29.17

Use the List Employees button to obtain an employee listing.

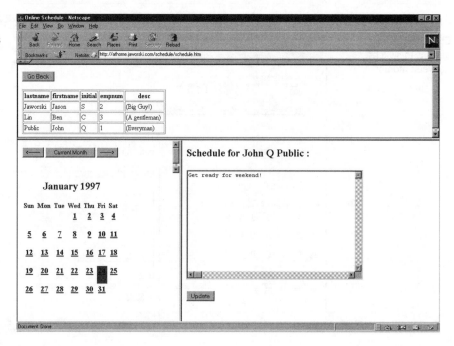

When you enter an employee number and click on the View Schedule button, the schedule of another employee is displayed, as shown in Figure 29.18. Note that no controls are displayed to allow you to change the employee information or schedule of the employee being viewed.

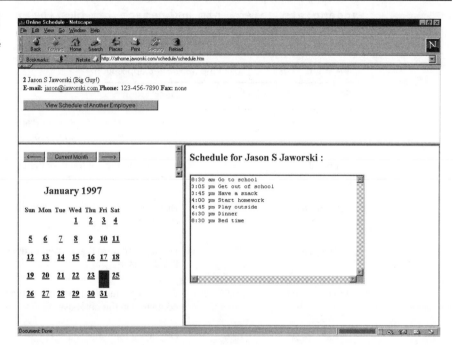

Overview of the Files Used to Implement the Scheduling Application

The *admsched* and *schedule* applications are larger than previous applications that you've developed. The *admsched* application consists of 10 files and the *schedule* application consists of 18 files. These files are described in Tables 29.1 and 29.2.

The *admsched* Application

The admsched.htm file is the default page of the admschsd application. It sets up a two-frame set with commands.htm loaded in the left frame and addemp.htm loaded in the right frame.

The `commands.htm` file provides links to the files that display forms and query results in the right frame. These files are `addemp.htm`, `delemp.htm`, `listemp.htm`, and `remact.htm`.

The files `saddemp.htm`, `sdelemp.htm`, and `sremact.htm`, contain server-side scripts that process the form data submitted by the forms displayed by the `addemp.htm`, `delemp.htm`, and `remact.htm` files. The `error.htm` file is used to notify the user of any errors that occur.

TABLE 29.1   Files of the *admsched* application

File	Listing	Description
`admsched.htm`	29.1	Default page for the *admsched* application. Sets up the two-frame set for the application user interface.
`commands.htm`	29.2	Loaded into the left frame of the user interface. Provides links to the schedule administration commands.
`addemp.htm`	29.3	Displays the form that is used to add an employee to the database.
`delemp.htm`	29.4	Displays the form that is used to delete an employee from the database.
`listemp.htm`	29.5	Generates a tabular listing of the employees that are contained in the database.
`remact.htm`	29.6	Displays a form that is used to get the date before which all schedule information is to be removed.
`saddemp.htm`	29.7	Processes the information entered into the Add Employee form and adds an employee to the database.
`sdelemp.htm`	29.8	Processes the information entered into the Delete Employee form and deletes an employee from the database.
`sremact.htm`	29.9	Processes the information entered into the Remove Old Activities form and deletes all schedule information prior to a specified date.
`error.htm`	29.10	Used to display error messages to the user.

The *schedule* Application

The login.htm file is the default page of the *schedule* application. It displays the login form shown in Figure 29.9.

The slogin.htm file processes the login information collected by login.htm and determines whether a valid employee number and password was entered by the user. If the login information is valid, then the schedule.htm file is loaded. Otherwise, an error is reported, using error.htm.

The schedule.htm file creates a two-row frame set with ownsched.htm loaded in the upper row and updcal.htm loaded in the lower row. The ownsched.htm file provides buttons that allow you to change your employee information or view another employee's schedule. The updcal.htm file sets up the two-column frame set displayed in the lower left and right of the Web page shown in Figure 29.10.

The ownsched.htm file loads chginfo.htm when the Change Employee Information button is clicked. The chginfo.htm displays the form shown in Figure 29.11. The schginfo.htm file processes the data entered into the form and updates the employee table of the schedule database.

The ownsched.htm file loads selemp.htm when the View Schedule of Another Employee button is clicked. The selemp.htm file displays a form that allows you to enter an employee number to view that employee's schedule or to obtain a tabular listing of all employees in the database (as the result of loading listemp.htm). The sselemp.htm file checks the employee number to make sure that it is in the database and loads othsched.htm to display the schedule of the selected employee.

The updcal.htm file loads cal.htm in the lower left frame and blank.htm (a blank file) in the lower right frame. The cal.htm file splits the lower left frame into two rows. The top frame displays the calendar buttons and the bottom frame displays the calendar. The control.htm file is loaded in the top frame and a blank file is initially loaded in the bottom frame.

The control.htm file displays the calendar buttons and, after initializing a hidden form with the current date, loads calendar.htm in the bottom frame and act.htm in the lower right frame.

The calendar.htm file displays the clickable calendar, and the act.htm file displays schedule activities in a text area box. The sact.htm file processes schedule updates and stores them in the activity table of the schedule database.

TABLE 29.2 Files of the *schedule* application

File	Listing	Description
login.htm	29.11	The default page of the *schedule* application. Provides a form for employee login.
slogin.htm	29.12	Checks login information and loads schedule.htm to load the rest of the *schedule* application.
schedule.htm	29.13	Divides the display into a two-row frame set. Loads ownsched.htm into the upper frame and updcal.htm into the lower frame.
ownsched.htm	29.14	Displays employee information, the Change Employee Information button, and the View Schedule of Another Employee button in the top frame.
chginfo.htm	29.15	Loaded when the Change Employee Information button is clicked. Displays a form that allows the employee to change his or her own employee information.
schginfo.htm	29.16	Processes the data entered into the form of chginfo.htm and updates the employee table of the schedule database.
selemp.htm	29.17	Loaded when the View Schedule of Another Employee button is clicked. Displays a form that prompts for an employee number to be entered. Provides the View Schedule and List Employees buttons.
sselemp.htm	29.18	Validates the employee number entered into the form of selemp.htm and loads othsched.htm to display the schedule of another employee.
listemp.htm	29.19	Loaded as the result of the clicking of the List Employees button. Provides a tabular listing of all employees in the database.
othsched.htm	29.20	Displays information about a selected employee and loads the employee's schedule in the lower right frame.
updcal.htm	29.21	Sets up the lower left and right frames. Loads cal.htm in the left frame and blank.htm in the right frame.
cal.htm	29.22	Organizes the lower left frame into two rows. Loads control.htm in the top frame and blank.htm in the bottom frame.

TABLE 29.2 Files of the *schedule* application (continued)

File	Listing	Description
`blank.htm`	29.23	A blank document.
`control.htm`	29.24	Displays the calendar buttons and loads `calendar.htm` in the lower left frame and `act.htm` in the lower right frame.
`calendar.htm`	29.25	Displays the clickable calendar.
`act.htm`	29.26	Displays employee schedule activities in a text area box.
`sact.htm`	29.27	Processes updates to employee schedule information.
`error.htm`	29.10	Displays error messages.

The *schedule* Database Structure

Now that you have a good idea of how the *admsched* and *schedule* applications work (i.e., understand the user interface and functional layers), we'll cover the application's database structure (i.e., delve into the information storage layer).

The name of the database used in the application is simply named `schedule`. The `schedule` database has two tables—`employee` and `activity`—that are described in Tables 29.3 and 29.4. The `employee` table maintains general employee information and is keyed on the `empnum` (employee number) column. The `activity` table stores employee schedule activities and is keyed on the `empnum` and `date` columns.

The *admsched* and *schedule* applications use both tables. The *admsched* application is primarily concerned with maintaining the `employee` table, but it is also used to purge the `activity` table (in response to the Remove Old Activities command). The *schedule* application maintains both tables.

In order to use these tables in your application, you'll need to define them using the Informix Table Editor. Figures 29.19 and 29.20 show how the Table Editor window looks when each table has been defined.

TABLE 29.3 The employee table structure

Column Name	Type	Size	Description
empnum	Integer	-	Employee number
firstname	Character	20	Employee's first name
lastname	Character	30	Employee's last name
initial	Character	1	Employee's middle initial
desc	Character	60	Description of employee
email	Character	60	Employee's e-mail address
phone	Character	20	Employee's phone number
fax	Character	20	Employee's fax number
password	Character	30	Employee's password
message	Character	60	Message that is displayed with employee information

FIGURE 29.19

The employee table definition

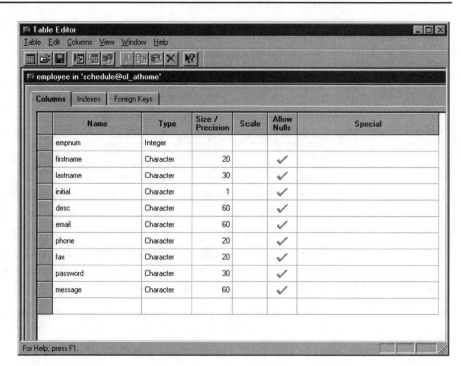

TABLE 29.4 The `activity` table structure

Column Name	Type	Size	Description
empnum	Integer	-	Employee number
date	Date	-	Date to which schedule information applies
activity	Character	1024	Text which identifies the activities scheduled for the specified date

FIGURE 29.20

The `activity` table definition

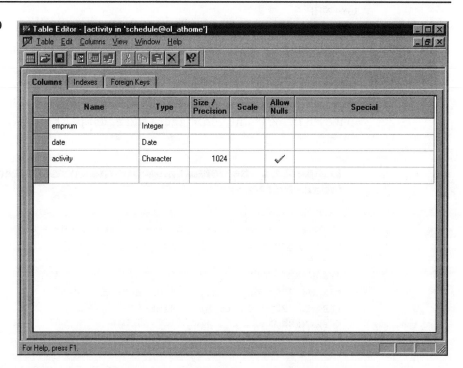

Description of the Scheduling Application Code

The scheduling application code is organized into the files shown in Tables 29.1 and 29.2. Although there are a total of 28 files in both the `admsched` and `schedule` applications, most of these files are quite short and are easy to understand.

However, some files contain both server- and client-side JavaScript and require some explanation. Others use JavaScript to generate SQL statements that are used to access the database server. These also require closer examination. The following sections list and describe each of the files contained in the *admsched* and *schedule* applications. When you examine the listings for these files, see if you can identify the code used to create the user interface, implement application functions, and program the database server. By doing so, you'll be able to appreciate the high degree of browser, Web server, and database server integration provided by LiveWire Pro. To get an even better appreciation of LiveWire Pro's benefits, imagine what it would take to build a similar application using CGI programs, instead of server-side JavaScript.

The *admsched* Application

admsched.htm The admsched.htm file is the default page for the *admsched* application. It simply sets up the two-column frame set, loading commands.htm in the left frame (named commands) and addemp.htm in the right frame (named forms).

Listing 29.1. The default page for the admsched application (admsched.htm)

```
<HTML>
<HEAD>
<TITLE>Administer Schedule Database</TITLE>
</HEAD>
<FRAMESET COLS="200,*">
<FRAME SRC="commands.htm" NAME="commands">
<FRAME SRC="addemp.htm" NAME="forms">
</FRAMESET>
</HTML>
```

commands.htm The commands.htm file provides four links for the four *admsched* commands. Note that the target of these links is the forms frame.

Listing 29.2. The left frame links to the schedule administration commands (commands.htm)

```
<HTML>
<HEAD>
<TITLE>Administer Schedule Database</TITLE>
```

```
</HEAD>
<BODY>
<H3>Administer Schedule Database</H3>
<A HREF="addemp.htm" TARGET="forms">Add Employee</A><P>
<A HREF="delemp.htm" TARGET="forms">Delete Employee</A><P>
<A HREF="listemp.htm" TARGET="forms">List Employees</A><P>
<A HREF="remact.htm" TARGET="forms">Remove Old Activities</A>
</BODY>
</HTML>
```

addemp.htm The `addemp.htm` file provides a form for entering information for a new employee. Note that a short client-side script is used to validate the employee number field.

Listing 29.3. A form to add employees to the database (addemp.htm)

```
<HTML>
<HEAD>
<TITLE>Add Employee</TITLE>
<SCRIPT LANGUAGE="JavaScript">
function addEmployee() {
 n=parseInt(window.document.addEmp.empnum.value)
 if(n>0) window.document.addEmp.submit()
 else alert("Employee Number must be a positive integer.")
}
</SCRIPT>
</HEAD>
<BODY>
<H1>Add Employee</H1>
<FORM NAME="addEmp" ACTION="saddemp.htm">
Employee Number: <INPUT TYPE="TEXT" NAME="empnum" SIZE="10"><P>
First Name: <INPUT TYPE="TEXT" NAME="firstname" SIZE="20">
 Initial: <INPUT TYPE="TEXT" NAME="initial" SIZE="1"><BR>
Last Name: <INPUT TYPE="TEXT" NAME="lastname" SIZE="30"><P>
Description: <INPUT TYPE="TEXT" NAME="desc" SIZE="60"><P>
E-mail Address: <INPUT TYPE="TEXT" NAME="email" SIZE="60"><P>
Phone: <INPUT TYPE="TEXT" NAME="phone" SIZE="20"><P>
Fax: <INPUT TYPE="TEXT" NAME="fax" SIZE="20"><P>
Password: <INPUT TYPE="PASSWORD" NAME="password" SIZE="30"><P>
<INPUT TYPE="BUTTON" VALUE="Add Employee"
 onClick="addEmployee()">
```

```
</FORM>
</BODY>
</HTML>
```

delemp.htm   The `delemp.htm` file displays a simple form for deleting an employee from the database. It uses that person's employee number as an index into the `employee` and `activity` tables. Note that the simple client-side script validates the employee number entered by the administrator.

Listing 29.4. A form to delete employees from the database (delemp.htm)

```
<HTML>
<HEAD>
<TITLE>Delete Employee</TITLE>
<SCRIPT LANGUAGE="JavaScript">
function delEmployee() {
 n=parseInt(window.document.delEmp.empnum.value)
 if(n>0) window.document.delEmp.submit()
 else alert("Employee Number must be a positive integer.")
}
</SCRIPT>
</HEAD>
<BODY>
<H1>Delete Employee</H1>
<FORM NAME="delEmp" ACTION="sdelemp.htm">
Employee Number: <INPUT TYPE="TEXT" NAME="empnum" SIZE="10"><P>
<INPUT TYPE="BUTTON" VALUE="Delete Employee"
 onClick="delEmployee()">
</FORM>
</BODY>
</HTML>
```

listemp.htm   The `listemp.htm` file provides a short server-side script to generate a table of all employees contained in the employee table. Note that only a subset of the available employee information is displayed. This is the result of the SQL `SELECT` statement used to query the database.

Listing 29.5. A file which uses SQL to generate a table of employees (listemp.htm)

```
<HTML>
<HEAD>
```

```
<TITLE>Employees</TITLE>
</HEAD>
<BODY>
<H1>Employees</H1>
<SERVER>
if(!database.connected())
 database.connect("INFORMIX","ol_athome","informix","informix",
 ➡ "schedule")
if(database.connected()){
 selstmt="SELECT empnum, phone, lastname, firstname, initial"
 selstmt+=" FROM employee ORDER BY empnum"
 database.SQLTable(selstmt)
}else write("<H1>Could not connect to database.</H1>")
</SERVER>
</BODY>
</HTML>
```

remact.htm The remact.htm file displays a simple form for obtaining a date value from the application administrator.

Listing 29.6. A form to remove old schedule activities (remact.htm)

```
<HTML>
<HEAD>
<TITLE>Remove Old Activities</TITLE>
</HEAD>
<BODY>
<H1>Remove Old Activities</H1>
<FORM NAME="remOldAct" ACTION="sremact.htm">
Remove activities before (date):
<INPUT TYPE="TEXT" NAME="fromDate"><P>
<INPUT TYPE="SUBMIT" VALUE="Remove">
</FORM>
</BODY>
</HTML>
```

saddemp.htm The saddemp.htm file is an example of a server-side script which updates the employee database. After connecting with the database, the script deletes any previous employee information that is associated with the employee number received (request.empnum) from the form generated by addemp.htm. It then constructs a long SQL statement using the data submitted with the form. A series of `write()` statements are used to generate a Web page whose purpose is to confirm the success of the add employee command.

Listing 29.7. A server-side script for adding employees to the database (saddemp.htm)

```
<HTML>
<HEAD>
<TITLE>Add Employee</TITLE>
</HEAD>
<BODY>
<SERVER>
if(!database.connected())
 database.connect("INFORMIX","ol_athome","informix","informix",
 ➥ "schedule")
if(database.connected()){
 del="DELETE FROM employee WHERE empnum = "
 del+=request.empnum
 database.execute(del)
 insertSQL="INSERT INTO employee VALUES ("
 insertSQL+="'"+request.empnum+"',"
 insertSQL+="'"+request.firstname+"',"
 insertSQL+="'"+request.lastname+"',"
 insertSQL+="'"+request.initial+"',"
 insertSQL+="'"+request.desc+"',"
 insertSQL+="'"+request.email+"',"
 insertSQL+="'"+request.phone+"',"
 insertSQL+="'"+request.fax+"',"
 insertSQL+="'"+request.password+"','')"
 errorStatus=database.execute(insertSQL)
 client.errorStatus="Execute error: "+errorStatus
 if(errorStatus!=0) redirect("error.htm")
 write("<H1>Employee Added</H1>")
 write("<B>"+request.empnum+" "+request.firstname+" ")
 write(request.initial+" "+request.lastname+"<BR>")
 write(request.desc+"<BR>")
 write("E-mail: "+request.email+"<BR>")
 write("Phone: "+request.phone+"<BR>")
 write("Fax: "+request.fax)
}else{
 client.errorStatus="Can not open database."
 redirect("error.htm")
}
```

```
</SERVER>
</BODY>
</HTML>
```

sdelemp.htm   The `sdelemp.htm` file uses the employee number (`request .empnum`) received from the form generated by `delemp.htm` to delete all information maintained about the employee in the employee and activity tables. A `write()` statement is used to relay the success of the deletion command to the application administrator.

Listing 29.8. A server-side script for deleting employees from the database (sdelemp.htm)

```
<HTML>
<HEAD>
<TITLE>Delete Employee</TITLE>
</HEAD>
<BODY>
<SERVER>
if(!database.connected())
 database.connect("INFORMIX","ol_athome","informix","informix",
 ➥ "schedule")
if(database.connected()){
 table="employee"
 del="DELETE FROM "+table+" WHERE empnum = "
 del+=request.empnum
 errorStatus=database.execute(del)
 client.errorStatus="Execute error: "+errorStatus
 if(errorStatus!=0) redirect("error.htm")
 table="activity"
 del="DELETE FROM "+table+" WHERE empnum = "
 del+=request.empnum
 errorStatus=database.execute(del)
 client.errorStatus="Execute error: "+errorStatus
 if(errorStatus!=0) redirect("error.htm")
 write("<H1>Employee "+request.empnum+" deleted.</H1>")
}else{
 client.errorStatus="Can not open database."
 redirect("error.htm")
}
</SERVER>
</BODY>
</HTML>
```

sremact.htm   The `sremact.htm` file deletes all entries in the activity table that have a date-column entry prior to the date submitted in the form of `remact.htm`.

Listing 29.9. A server-side script for removing old schedule information (sremact.htm)

```
<HTML>
<HEAD>
<TITLE>Remove Old Activities</TITLE>
</HEAD>
<BODY>
<SERVER>
if(!database.connected())
 database.connect("INFORMIX","ol_athome","informix","informix",
 ➥ "schedule")
if(!database.connected()){
 client.errorStatus="Can not open database."
 redirect("error.htm")
}
remdate="'"+request.fromDate+"'"
delSQL="DELETE FROM activity WHERE date < "+remdate
errorStatus=database.execute(delSQL)
if(errorStatus!=0){
 client.errorStatus=errorStatus
 redirect("error.htm")
}
redirect("remact.htm")
</SERVER>
</BODY>
</HTML>
```

error.htm   The `error.htm` displays an error message to the user via a server-side `write()` statement.

Listing 29.10. A script for displaying error messages (error.htm)

```
<HTML>
<HEAD>
<TITLE>Error Message</TITLE>
</HEAD>
<BODY>
<H1>Error!</H1>
```

```
<H2><SERVER>write(client.errorStatus)</SERVER></H2>
</BODY>
</HTML>
```

The *schedule* Application

login.htm The login.htm file is the default page of the *schedule* application. It displays a simple form that requires an employee to enter their employee number and password in order to log in to the schedule application.

Listing 29.11. The default page of the schedule application (login.htm)

```
<HTML>
<HEAD>
<TITLE>Online Schedule</TITLE>
</HEAD>
<BODY>
<H1>Welcome to Online Scheduling</H1>
<H3>Please login:</H3>
<FORM NAME="login" ACTION="slogin.htm">
Employee Number: <INPUT TYPE="TEXT" NAME="empnum" SIZE="20"><P>
Password: <INPUT TYPE="PASSWORD" NAME="password" SIZE="20"><P>
<INPUT TYPE="SUBMIT" VALUE="Login">
</FORM>
</BODY>
</HTML>
```

slogin.htm The slogin.htm file contains a server-side script that checks to see if there is a row in the employee table that has the employee number and password that was entered in the login.htm form. It uses the SELECT COUNT(*) SQL statement to count the number of rows that meet the search criteria specified in the WHERE clause. If there is at least one row with the specified employee number and password then some client properties are initialized and the schedule.htm file is loaded. The client.empnum property identifies the employee that is logged in to the online scheduling session. The client.target property identifies the employee whose schedule is to be displayed. The client.selmonth, client.selyear, and client.selday properties identify the current month, year, and day at the time of the login. The client.seldate property is assigned a single-quoted text string that contains the date in the *mm/dd//yy* format.

Listing 29.12. A script to verify a employee's ID and password (slogin.htm)

```
<HTML>
<HEAD>
<TITLE>Online Schedule</TITLE>
</HEAD>
<BODY>
<SERVER>
if(!database.connected())
 database.connect("INFORMIX","ol_athome","informix","informix",
➡ "schedule")
if(!database.connected()){
 client.errorStatus="Can not open database."
 redirect("error.htm")
}
empnum=parseInt(request.empNum)
if(empnum<=0){
 client.errorStatus="Invalid employee number."
 redirect("error.htm")
}
pwcheck="SELECT COUNT(*) FROM employee WHERE empnum = '"
pwcheck+=request.empnum+"' AND password = '"+request.password
pwcheck+="'"
cursor=database.cursor(pwcheck)
cursor.next()
numRows=parseInt(cursor[0])
cursor.close()
if(numRows>0){
 client.empnum=request.empnum
 client.target=client.empnum
 client.view="own"
 today = new Date()
 client.selyear=today.getYear()
 client.selmonth=today.getMonth()
 client.selday=today.getDate()
 seldate="'"+(parseInt(client.selmonth)+1)+"/"
 seldate+=parseInt(client.selday)+"/"
 seldate+=parseInt(client.selyear)+"'"
 client.seldate=seldate
 redirect("schedule.htm")
}else{
 client.errorStatus="Failed login."
```

```
    redirect("error.htm")
    }
    </SERVER>
    </FORM>
    </BODY>
    </HTML>
```

schedule.htm   The `schedule.htm` file sets up the top and bottom rows of the schedule application's user interface. The `ownsched.htm` file is loaded into the top frame, and the `updcal.htm` file is loaded into the bottom frame.

Listing 29.13. Setting up the top and bottom frames of the schedule application (schedule.htm)

```
<HTML>
<HEAD>
<TITLE>Online Schedule</TITLE>
</HEAD>
<FRAMESET ROWS="175,*">
<FRAME SRC="ownsched.htm">
<FRAME SRC="updcal.htm">
</FRAMESET>
</HTML>
```

ownsched.htm   The `ownsched.htm` file combines client- and server-side JavaScript and SQL. It is short, but it's also somewhat complex. The server-side script in the document's body retrieves information about the logged in employee (`client.empnum`) into a `cursor` object. It then uses this information to display information about that employee in the top form of the schedule application window. An HTML form is then displayed which provides the user with two buttons—Change Employee Information and View Schedule of Another Employee. The clicking of these buttons is handled by the client-side JavaScript functions specified in the script contained in the document's head. The form is followed by a single-line client-side script that causes the entire lower frame set to be reloaded.

Why is the lower frame set reloaded? The reason for this is to allow an employee to switch between viewing his or her own schedule and that of another employee. When an employee switches back to viewing his or her own schedule, the lower frame set is reloaded.

The script in the document head loads `chginfo.htm` when the user clicks on the Change Employee button and loads `selemp.htm` when the user clicks the View Schedule of Another Employee button.

Listing 29.14. Displaying employee information (ownsched.htm)

```
<HTML>
<HEAD>
<TITLE>Online Schedule</TITLE>
<SCRIPT LANGUAGE="JavaScript">
function changeEmpInfo(){
  window.location.href="chginfo.htm"
}
function viewEmployee(){
  window.location.href="selemp.htm"
}
</SCRIPT>
</HEAD>
<BODY>
<SERVER>
info="SELECT * FROM employee WHERE empnum = '"
info+=client.empnum+"'"
cursor=database.cursor(info)
cursor.next()
name=cursor.firstname+" "
name+=cursor.initial+" "
name+=cursor.lastname
client.name=name
write("<B>"+cursor.empnum+"</B>"+" "+client.name+" ")
write(cursor.desc+"<BR>")
write("<B>E-mail:</B> "+cursor.email)
write(" <B>Phone:</B> "+cursor.phone)
write(" <B>Fax:</B> "+cursor.fax+"<BR>")
write("<B>"+cursor.message+"</B><P>")
cursor.close()
</SERVER>
<FORM NAME="controls">
<INPUT TYPE="BUTTON" VALUE="Change Employee Information"
  onClick="changeEmpInfo()">
<INPUT TYPE="BUTTON" VALUE="View Schedule of Another Employee"
  onClick="viewEmployee()">
</FORM>
<SCRIPT LANGUAGE="JavaScript">
```

```
    parent.frames[1].location.reload(true)
    </SCRIPT>
    </BODY>
    </HTML>
```

chginfo.htm The chginfo.htm file provides a form that allows an employee to change some of the information about himself or herself that is maintained in the employee table of the schedule database. Note that an employee is not allowed to change their employee number or name. The form is submitted to the schginfo.htm file for server-side processing.

Listing 29.15. A form to change employee information (chginfo.htm)

```
    <HTML>
    <HEAD>
    <TITLE>Online Schedule</TITLE>
    </HEAD>
    <BODY>
    <FORM NAME="chgEmp" ACTION="schginfo.htm">
    Description: <INPUT TYPE="TEXT" NAME="desc" SIZE="60"><BR>
    E-mail Address: <INPUT TYPE="TEXT" NAME="email" SIZE="60"><BR>
    Phone: <INPUT TYPE="TEXT" NAME="phone" SIZE="20">
    Fax: <INPUT TYPE="TEXT" NAME="fax" SIZE="20"><BR>
    Message: <INPUT TYPE="TEXT" NAME="message" SIZE="60"><BR>
    Password: <INPUT TYPE="PASSWORD" NAME="password" SIZE="30">
    <INPUT TYPE="SUBMIT" VALUE="Change Employee Information">
    </FORM>
    </BODY>
    </HTML>
```

schginfo.htm The schginfo.htm file contains a server-side script that updates the information contained in the employee table for a particular employee. The client.empnum property is used to select whatever information is available about the employee. The selected information is stored using a cursor object. The information in the cursor object and the data submitted in the form generated by chginfo.htm is then combined to build a SQL statement that will be used to update the employee's information. If the form data is not blank, then it is added to the SQL statement. Otherwise, the cursor data is used. All existing employee information is deleted before the new employee information is added to the employee table. When the update is completed, the ownsched.htm file is loaded.

Listing 29.16. A server-side script to change employee information (schginfo.htm)

```
<HTML>
<HEAD>
<TITLE>Online Schedule</TITLE>
</HEAD>
<BODY>
<SERVER>
info="SELECT * FROM employee WHERE empnum = '"
info+=client.empnum+"'"
cursor=database.cursor(info)
cursor.next()
insertSQL="INSERT INTO employee VALUES ("
insertSQL+="'"+cursor.empnum+"',"
insertSQL+="'"+cursor.firstname+"',"
insertSQL+="'"+cursor.lastname+"',"
insertSQL+="'"+cursor.initial+"',"
if(request.desc=="") insertSQL+="'"+cursor.desc+"',"
else insertSQL+="'"+request.desc+"',"
if(request.email=="") insertSQL+="'"+cursor.email+"',"
else insertSQL+="'"+request.email+"',"
if(request.phone=="") insertSQL+="'"+cursor.phone+"',"
else insertSQL+="'"+request.phone+"',"
if(request.fax=="") insertSQL+="'"+cursor.fax+"',"
else insertSQL+="'"+request.fax+"',"
if(request.password=="") insertSQL+="'"+cursor.password+"',"
else insertSQL+="'"+request.password+"',"
if(request.message=="") insertSQL+="'"+cursor.message+"')"
else insertSQL+="'"+request.message+"')"
del="DELETE FROM employee WHERE empnum = "
del+=client.empnum
database.execute(del)
errorStatus=database.execute(insertSQL)
client.errorStatus="Execute error: "+errorStatus
if(errorStatus!=0) redirect("error.htm")
cursor.close()
redirect("ownsched.htm")
</SERVER>
</BODY>
</HTML>
```

selemp.htm The `selemp.htm` file displays a form that gives the user the option of entering the employee number of the employee whose schedule is to be viewed or obtaining a listing of the employees in the `employee` table. If an employee number is entered, the form is submitted to the `sselemp.htm` file and the View Schedule button is clicked. If the List Employees button is clicked, the `listemp.htm` file is loaded.

Listing 29.17. A form to select an employee number (selemp.htm)

```
<HTML>
<HEAD>
<TITLE>Select Employee</TITLE>
<SCRIPT LANGUAGE="JavaScript">
function listEmployees(){
  window.location.href="listemp.htm"
}
</SCRIPT>
</HEAD>
<BODY>
<FORM ACTION="sselemp.htm">
Employee Number: <INPUT TYPE="TEXT" NAME="empnum"
  SIZE="20"><P>
<INPUT TYPE="SUBMIT" VALUE="View Schedule"><P>
<INPUT TYPE="BUTTON" VALUE="List Employees"
  onClick="listEmployees()">
</FORM>
</BODY>
</HTML>
```

sselemp.htm The `sselemp.htm` file contains a server-side script that validates the employee number entered in the form displayed by `selemp.htm`. It does this by executing the `SELECT COUNT(*)` SQL statement to count the number of employees that have the specified employee number. It then checks to see whether an employee is trying to view their own schedule or that of another. In the case that the employee is trying to view their own schedule, the `client.view` property is set to own and the `ownsched.htm` file is loaded. In the case that the employee is trying to view the schedule of another, the `client.view` property is set to `other` and the `othsched.htm` file is loaded.

Listing 29.18. A server-side script to validate a selected employee number (sselemp.htm)

```
<HTML>
<HEAD>
<TITLE>Select Employee</TITLE>
</HEAD>
<BODY>
<SERVER>
empnum=parseInt(request.empnum)
if(empnum<=0){
 client.errorStatus="Invalid employee number."
 redirect("error.htm")
}
sql="SELECT COUNT(*) FROM employee WHERE empnum = '"
sql+=request.empnum+"'"
cursor=database.cursor(sql)
cursor.next()
numRows=parseInt(cursor[0])
cursor.close()
if(numRows>0){
 client.target=empnum
 if(client.target==client.empnum){
  client.view="own"
  redirect("ownsched.htm")
 }else{
  client.view="other"
  redirect("othsched.htm")
 }
}else{
 client.errorStatus="Invalid employee number."
 redirect("error.htm")
}
</SERVER>
</BODY>
</HTML>
```

listemp.htm The listemp.htm file invokes the SQLTable() method of the database object, passing it a SQL statement that selects each employee's name, employee number, and description from the employee table. The SQLTable() method generates an HTML table that displays this information arranged in employee-name order.

Listing 29.19. A server-side script to generate an employee listing (listemp.htm)

```
<HTML>
<HEAD>
<TITLE>List Employees</TITLE>
</HEAD>
<BODY>
<FORM>
<INPUT TYPE="BUTTON" VALUE="Go Back"
 onClick="window.location.href='selemp.htm'">
</FORM>
<SERVER>
sql="SELECT lastname, firstname, initial, empnum, "
sql+="desc FROM employee "
sql+="ORDER BY lastname, firstname, initial"
database.SQLTable(sql)
</SERVER>
</BODY>
</HTML>
```

othsched.htm The othsched.htm file is similar to the ownsched.htm file, except that the othsched.htm file displays the employee and schedule information of other employees. In doing so, it eliminates the capability for one employee to modify the employee or schedule information of another. Like ownsched.htm, it contains client- and server-side JavaScript and generates SQL statements for searching the database.

Listing 29.20. A server-side script to display information about other employees (othsched.htm)

```
<HTML>
<HEAD>
<TITLE>Online Schedule</TITLE>
<SCRIPT LANGUAGE="JavaScript">
function viewEmployee(){
 window.location.href="selemp.htm"
}
</SCRIPT>
</HEAD>
<BODY>
<SERVER>
info="SELECT * FROM employee WHERE empnum = '"
```

```
info+=client.target+"'"
cursor=database.cursor(info)
cursor.next()
name=cursor.firstname+" "
name+=cursor.initial+" "
name+=cursor.lastname
client.name=name
write("<B>"+cursor.empnum+"</B>"+" "+client.name+" ")
write(cursor.desc+"<BR>")
write("<B>E-mail:</B> <A HREF='mailto:"+cursor.email+"'>")
write(cursor.email+"</A> <B>Phone:</B> "+cursor.phone)
write(" <B>Fax:</B> "+cursor.fax+"<BR>")
write("<B>"+cursor.message+"</B><P>")
cursor.close()
</SERVER>
<FORM NAME="controls">
<INPUT TYPE="BUTTON" VALUE="View Schedule of Another Employee"
 onClick="viewEmployee()">
</FORM>
<SCRIPT LANGUAGE="JavaScript">
parent.frames[1].location.reload(true)
</SCRIPT>
</BODY>
</HTML>
```

updcal.htm   The updcal.htm file splits the lower frame of the *schedule* application window into two columns. The cal.htm file is loaded into the left column and a blank file is loaded into the right column.

Listing 29.21. Setting up the lower left and right frame sets (updcal.htm)

```
<HTML>
<HEAD>
<TITLE>Monthly Calendar</TITLE>
</HEAD>
<FRAMESET COLS="400,*">
<FRAME SRC="cal.htm">
<FRAME SRC="blank.htm" NAME="activities">
</FRAMESET>
</HTML>
```

cal.htm The `cal.htm` file splits the lower left frame of the *schedule* application window into two rows. The `control.htm` file is loaded into the top row and a blank file is loaded into the bottom row.

Listing 29.22. Organizing the lower left frame set (cal.htm)

```
<HTML>
<HEAD>
<TITLE>Monthly Calendar</TITLE>
<FRAMESET ROWS="77,*" BORDER="0">
<FRAME SRC="control.htm" NAME="control">
<FRAME SRC="blank.htm" NAME="calendar">
</FRAMESET>
</HTML>
```

blank.htm The `blank.htm` file is used to initialize a frame to a blank document.

Listing 29.23. A blank document (blank.htm)

```
<HTML>
<HEAD>
<TITLE></TITLE>
</HEAD>
<BODY>
</BODY>
</HTML>
```

control.htm The `control.htm` file is adapted from the calendar example presented in Chapter 13. It displays buttons for controlling a calendar that is loaded into the lower left frame. The `onLoad` event identified in the body tag causes the `calendar.htm` file to be loaded in the bottom frame and the `act.htm` file to be loaded in the lower right frame.

The `control.htm` file combines both client- and server-side JavaScript. The document body uses server-side JavaScript to initialize the values of hidden form fields to contain the current date selected by the user. Buttons are implemented that allow the user to switch to past or future months or to easily return to the current month. The client-side JavaScript contained in the document head handles the clicking of these buttons. When the form is submitted, it is submitted to the `act.htm` file. The results of the form submission are displayed in the lower right frame named `activities`. The values of the hidden form fields are used to notify `act.htm` which date is to be used to display schedule information.

Listing 29.24. Implementing the calendar buttons (control.htm)

```
<HTML>
<HEAD>
<TITLE>Monthly Calendar</TITLE>
<SCRIPT LANGUAGE="JavaScript"><!--
function loadCal(){
 parent.frames[1].location.href="calendar.htm"
 parent.parent.frames[1].location.href="act.htm"
}
function updateCalendar(month,year) {
 document.forms[0].monthValue.value=month
 document.forms[0].yearValue.value=year
 parent.frames[1].location.reload(true)
 window.document.changeDate.submit()
}
function previousMonth() {
 month=document.forms[0].monthValue.value
 year=document.forms[0].yearValue.value
 --month
 if(month<0) {
  if(year==0) month=0
  else{
   --year
   month=11
  }
 }
 updateCalendar(month,year)
}
function currentMonth() {
 var today=new Date()
 updateCalendar(today.getMonth(),today.getYear())
}
function nextMonth() {
 month=document.forms[0].monthValue.value
 year=document.forms[0].yearValue.value
 ++month
 if(month>11) {
  if(year==99) month=11
  else{
   ++year
   month=0
  }
 }
```

```
    updateCalendar(month,year)
}
// --></SCRIPT>
</HEAD>
<BODY onLoad="loadCal()">
<FORM NAME="changeDate" ACTION="act.htm" TARGET="activities">
<SERVER>
write('<INPUT TYPE="HIDDEN" NAME="monthValue" VALUE="')
write(client.selmonth+'">')
write('<INPUT TYPE="HIDDEN" NAME="yearValue" VALUE="')
write(client.selyear+'">')
write('<INPUT TYPE="HIDDEN" NAME="dayValue" VALUE="')
write(client.selday+'">')
</SERVER>
<INPUT TYPE="BUTTON" NAME="previous" VALUE="<-------"
 onClick="previousMonth()">
<INPUT TYPE="BUTTON" NAME="current" VALUE="Current Month"
 onClick="currentMonth()">
<INPUT TYPE="BUTTON" NAME="next" VALUE="------->"
 onClick="nextMonth()">
</FORM>
</BODY>
</HTML>
```

calendar.htm The calendar.htm file is also adapted from Chapter 13. The most significant change is the fact that the writeDate() function produces a link for each of the calendar dates displayed. The clicking of these links is handled by the setDay() function, which is specified in the script of the document head. The setDay() function updates the hidden fields in the form of control.htm with the date selected by the user. The form of control.htm is then submitted. The submission of control.htm causes the lower right frame to be reloaded using the HTML generated by act.htm.

Note that the hidden form fields of control.htm are read in the client-side script contained in the document's body. This date information is used to determine what month and date are to be displayed by the calendar functions in the document head.

Listing 29.25. Displaying the clickable calendar (calendar.htm)

```
<HTML>
<HEAD>
<TITLE>Monthly Calendar</TITLE>
<SCRIPT LANGUAGE="JavaScript">
```

```
function setDay(n) {
 formRef.dayValue.value=""+n
 parent.control.document.changeDate.submit()
}

function Calendar() {
 var len = Calendar.arguments.length
 if(len == 2){
  this.month = Calendar.arguments[0]
  this.year = Calendar.arguments[1]
 }else{
  today = new Date()
  this.month = today.getMonth()
  this.year = today.getYear()
 }
 this.display = displayCalendar
}

function displayCalendar() {
 document.writeln("<TABLE BORDER='0' BGCOLOR='white'>")
 displayCalendarHeader(this.month,this.year)
 if(displayCalendar.arguments.length>0){
  var day = displayCalendar.arguments[0]-1
  displayDates(day,this.month,this.year,true)
 }else displayDates(0,this.month,this.year,false)
 document.writeln("</TABLE>")
}

function displayCalendarHeader(month,year) {
 var days = new Array("Sun","Mon","Tue","Wed","Thu",
  "Fri","Sat")
 var months = new Array("January","February","March","April",
  "May","June","July","August","September","October",
  "November","December")
 document.writeln("<TR><TH COLSPAN='7'><H2 ALIGN='CENTER'>")
 document.writeln(months[month])
 document.writeln(" 19"+year+"</H2></TH></TR>")
 document.writeln("<TR>")
 for(var i=0;i<days.length;++i)
  document.writeln("<TH> "+days[i]+" </TH>")
 document.writeln("</TR>")
}
```

```
function displayDates(day,month,year,shade) {
 d = new Date(year,month,1)
 var startDay = d.getDay()
 var numDays = numberOfDays(month,year)
 var numRows = Math.floor((numDays+startDay)/7)
 if((numDays+startDay)%7 > 1) ++numRows
 var currentDate=0
 for(var i=0;i<numRows;++i) {
  document.writeln("<TR>")
  for(var j=0;j<7;++j) {
   if(shade && day==currentDate)
    document.write("<TD BGCOLOR='red'>")
   else document.write("<TD>")
   if(currentDate>=numDays) document.write(" ")
   else if(currentDate>0){
    ++currentDate
    writeDate(currentDate)
   }else if(i*7+j>=startDay){
    ++currentDate
     writeDate(currentDate)
   }else document.write(" ")
   document.writeln("</TD>")
  }
  document.writeln("</TR>")
 }
}

function numberOfDays(month,year) {
 var numDays=new Array(31,28,31,30,31,30,31,31,30,31,30,31)
 n = numDays[month]
 if(month == 1 && year % 4 == 0) ++n
 return n
}

function writeDate(n) {
 document.write("<H3 ALIGN='CENTER'>")
 document.write("<A HREF='calendar.htm' onClick='setDay(")
 document.write(n+")'>")
 document.write(n)
 document.write("</A>")
 document.write("</H3>")
}
</SCRIPT>
```

```
</HEAD>
<BODY LINK="black" VLINK="black" ALINK="black">
<SCRIPT LANGUAGE="JavaScript">
formRef = parent.frames[0].document.forms[0]
month = parseInt(formRef.monthValue.value)
year = parseInt(formRef.yearValue.value)
day = parseInt(formRef.dayValue.value)
cal=new Calendar(month,year)
cal.display(day)
</SCRIPT>
</BODY>
</HTML>
```

act.htm The `act.htm` file produces the form shown in the lower right of the scheduling application. This form displays the employee's schedule for the date selected in the calendar that appears in the lower left frame.

The `act.htm` file first checks to see if it is being loaded in response to the submission of the form of `control.htm`. It does this by checking to see if the `dayValue` request property is not `null`. In this case, it updates the `selmonth`, `selyear`, `selday`, and `seldate` properties of the `client` object, using the data that was submitted with the form.

The `act.htm` file uses the date selected by the user to search the `activity` table to see if any schedule information is available for that date. If information is available, then it is displayed as the default text of a text area tag. This tag, and the form containing it, is generated by server-side JavaScript `write()` statements.

The schedule information is encoded when it is stored in the database. New-line characters are encoded using the "\" character followed by an "n". The "\n" character strings are converted into new-line characters before being set as the default text of the text area form element.

If the employee is viewing his or her own schedule (as indicated by the `client.view` property being set to own) then a button is provided which allows that employee to update their schedule information. Clicking the Update button results in the schedule information being submitted to the `sact.htm` file.

Listing 29.26. A form to display and update schedule activities (act.htm)

```
<HTML>
<HEAD>
```

```
<TITLE>Daily Activities</TITLE>
</HEAD>
<BODY>
<SERVER>
if(request.dayValue!=null){
 client.selmonth=request.monthValue
 client.selyear=request.yearValue
 client.selday=request.dayValue
 seldate="'"+(parseInt(client.selmonth)+1)+"/"
 seldate+=parseInt(client.selday)+"/"
 seldate+=parseInt(client.selyear)+"'"
 client.seldate=seldate
}
info="SELECT * FROM activity WHERE empnum = '"
info+=client.target+"' AND date = "
info+=client.seldate
cursor=database.cursor(info)
activity=""
if(cursor.next()){
 s=cursor.activity
 t=""
 for(i=0;i<s.length;++i){
  ch=s.charAt(i)
  if(ch=="\\"){
   if(i<s.length-1) {
     if(s.charAt(i+1)=="n"){
      ++i
      t+="\n"
     }else t+="\\"
   }else t+="\\"
  }else t+=ch
 }
 activity=t
}
cursor.close()
write("<H2>Schedule for "+client.name+": <H2>")
write('<FORM NAME="act" ACTION="sact.htm">')
write('<TEXTAREA ROWS="14" COLS="50" NAME="actext">')
write(activity)
write('</TEXTAREA><P>')
if(client.view=="own") write('<INPUT TYPE="SUBMIT" VALUE="Update">')
write('</FORM>')
```

```
</SERVER>
</BODY>
</HTML>
```

sact.htm   The `sact.htm` file updates the `activity` table of the `schedule` database using the data submitted in the form generated by `act.htm`. Due to the way that this information is submitted by Navigator, some format processing and encoding is required.

Navigator has a tendency to pad the data submitted in the text area field with blank characters. Sometimes up to 1000 blank characters are appended to the field contents. A `for` statement is used to remove these trailing blanks and to convert carriage returns (ASCII 13) into "\n" character strings. The static `stringToByte()` method of the `File` object type is used to convert string characters to their ASCII numeric values.

The database is updated by first deleting the previous schedule information for the specified date and then inserting a row containing the updated schedule information into the `activity` table. The `act.htm` file is then reloaded to redisplay the updated information.

Listing 29.27. A server-side script to update schedule information (sact.htm)

```
<HTML>
<HEAD>
<TITLE>Daily Activities</TITLE>
</HEAD>
<BODY>
<SERVER>
s=request.actext
t=""
u=""
for(var i=0;i<s.length;++i){
 n=File.stringToByte(s.charAt(i))
 if(n==32) u+=" "
 else if(n==13){
   t+=u
   u=""
   t+="\\n"
 }else if(n>32){
   t+=u
   u=""
```

```
     t+=s.charAt(i)
    }
   }
   client.activity=t
   delSQL="DELETE FROM activity "
   delSQL+="WHERE empnum = '"+client.empnum+"' AND date = "
   delSQL+=client.seldate
   database.execute(delSQL)
   insertSQL="INSERT INTO activity     VALUES ("
   insertSQL+=client.empnum+","+client.seldate+",'"
   insertSQL+=client.activity+"')"
   database.execute(insertSQL)
   redirect("act.htm")
   </SERVER>
   </BODY>
   </HTML>
```

error.htm   The error.htm file used in the schedule application is the same as the one used in the *admsched* application (discussed earlier in the chapter).

Building and Running the Scheduling Application

In order to build and run the *admsched* and *schedule* applications, you'll need to do the following:

1. Create the schedule database, employee table, and activity table as described in "The schedule Database Structure" section earlier in this chapter.

2. Compile the files listed in Table 29.1 earlier in the chapter to create the admsched.web file.

3. Use LiveWire's Application Manager to install *admsched*. (Make sure that you give yourself at least one database connection and that you use the Informix Command Center to turn on the database server.)

4. Run *admsched* by opening the URL *http://your.server.com/admsched/* (replacing *your.server.com* with the name of your server).

5. Use the Add Employee command to add a few employees to the employee database.

6. Compile the files listed in Table 29.2 earlier in the chapter to create the `schedule.web` file.

7. Use LiveWire's Application Manager to install *schedule*.

8. Run *schedule* by opening the URL *http://your.server.com/schedule/*.

9. Play with the application by adding schedule information for your employees. Also, check an employee's schedule while being logged in as another employee.

Note that these applications are truly distributed. You may run the Informix database server on one host, the Netscape Web server on another host, and Netscape browsers on multiple hosts. When I ran the database server, Web server, and Navigator 4 on a single host (Pentium 133 with 64 MB RAM running Windows NT Server 4.0), the *schedule* application crawled to a snail's pace. However, when I ran the browser on a separate host, the response time was normal.

Summary

In this chapter, you learned about the three-tiered architecture of distributed systems and how to use JavaScript to implement the client, functional, and database layers. You then used this knowledge to develop a distributed scheduling system. In the next chapter, you'll learn about some of the application components that are available via the Web and how to use those components as building blocks for your Web applications.

CHAPTER

THIRTY

30

Integrating Existing Application Components

- Netscape ONE

- Internet Foundation Classes (IFC)

- Using AppFoundry

- JavaBeans and Portable Applications

- A Word about Plug-Ins

It's very rewarding to start from scratch and develop an advanced Web application. The feeling of accomplishment that you get from laying out your Web pages, writing the HTML and JavaScript, and assembling the pages into a final application is inspiring. It motivates you to go on to try more advanced JavaScript features in your next Web applications. You may soon find yourself becoming a JavaScript hacker (in the good sense of the word). But as rewarding as it may be to write your own JavaScript, the easiest way to put together a sophisticated Web application is to use components that have been developed by others. By using these components, you can free yourself to spend more time focusing on what you want to build rather than on how to build it. This is one of the goals of the *Netscape Open Network Environment*, or *Netscape ONE*.

In this chapter, we'll investigate Netscape ONE and discuss its support for building advanced Web applications using prebuilt components. We'll then introduce Netscape's *AppFoundry* and discuss how to use AppFoundry components in your Web applications. We'll finish up the chapter by looking at a new Web technology called *JavaBeans* which will make it even easier to work with reusable Web components. When you finish this chapter, you should be ready to make use of components built by others in the Web applications that you develop.

Netscape ONE

Netscape has carefully documented its strategy for building applications for an organization's intranet. This strategy is aimed at the rapid development and deployment of platform-independent applications that use open standards. Netscape refers to these applications as *network-centric* since they are applications that are associated with the network as a whole, rather than any particular host on the network.

Netscape ONE is the development environment for these network-centric applications. It makes use of the technologies that you've been studying in this book—HTML, JavaScript, and Java—as well as supporting technologies that make it possible to extend and tailor HTML, JavaScript, and Java in order to develop secure network-centric applications. These supporting technologies are described briefly below:

- *Open communication protocols* technologies, such as the Simple Mail Transfer Protocol and other protocols, allow e-mail and Usenet news to be integrated into Web applications.

- *Security services,* such as the Secure Sockets Layers and digital certificates, provide the secure communication and access controls needed to implement business critical functions.

- The *Netscape Internet Foundations Classes* (IFC) provides the basis for component building. This topic will be covered in detail in the next section.

NOTE Check out the URL *http://home.netscape.com/comprod/one/ white_paper .html* for a white paper that documents Netscape Corporation's vision of its open networking environment.

Internet Foundation Classes

The set of Internet Foundation Classes, or IFC, is a key component of Netscape ONE insofar as it provides the basis for developing reusable Web components. The IFC is a set of Java classes that support the development of platform-independent objects and services that can be accessed from Java and JavaScript. These classes provide the following platform-independent capabilities:

- Prebuilt GUI controls, such as sliders

- GUI control event handling and redrawing support

- Dialog boxes for the selection of fonts and colors

- A multifont text object that is capable of displaying embedded images

- Support of native windows within Java

- Animation support

- Drag-and-Drop support

- Concurrency support

- Support for saving and restoring object states

- Support for using local resources

You may use the IFC to develop stand-alone Java applications or applets. In order to use the IFC in your Web application, you must use the IFC classes as part of a Java applet. In order to access IFC components from JavaScript, load an applet containing the components and use LiveConnect to access the Java objects which comprise these components.

NOTE The Netscape IFC is available for download at the URL *http://developer .netscape.com/library/ifc/index.html.*

Installing the IFC

To install the IFC, download it from the Web at the following URL:

http://developer.netscape.com/library/ifc/downloads/downloads.html

If you are installing on Windows 95 or NT, then you should download the file ifc10.zip. Unzip the file to a directory that you've created especially for the IFC on your computer (for example, c:\ifc10\). You then need to set the CLASSPATH variable:

- On Windows 95 systems, add the following line to the end of your AUTOEXEC.BAT file:

  ```
  SET CLASSPATH=c:\ifc10\classes.zip; %CLASSPATH%
  ```

- On Windows NT systems, use the System applet in the Control Panel to set the CLASSPATH environment variable.

After setting up your CLASSPATH variable, reboot your system to make sure the changes take place.

The IFC Developer's Guide is included with the IFC classes. It provides excellent documentation on how to use IFC classes in Java applets and applications. It is available in HTML format and is located in the \ifc10 \documentation\developerguide\ directory.

Using AppFoundry

Netscape created AppFoundry as a repository for Web components (and for information and tools for using those components). The AppFoundry is available at the following URL:

http://home.netscape.com/one_stop/intranet_apps/

The Web components contained in AppFoundry provide platform-independent network-centric solutions to common business needs, and are provided as reusable applications that may be freely downloaded and tailored to your particular requirements. These components are written in HTML, JavaScript, and Java.

Sample AppFoundry Applications

In order to show you what's available through AppFoundry, we'll take a tour of some of its sample applications. To start the tour, open your browser to the AppFoundry home page (listed above). Figure 30.1 displays this page. In the lower left frame you will notice a number of links to AppFoundry applications. Click on the Application Overviews link to read an overview description of the available applications. Figure 30.2 shows the summary information that is provided on this page.

FIGURE 30.1

The AppFoundry home page is the starting point for learning about AppFoundry.

Let's look at some information on the sample applications. Click on the Travel and Expense Reporting link in the lower left frame. This causes the Web page shown in the right frame Figure 30.3 to be loaded. The *Travel and Expense Reporting Form* (*TERF*) application is one of my favorites. I do a lot of traveling with my day job, and filling out paper expense forms is no fun. I wish my company would show some initiative and adopt an application similar to the one contained in the AppFoundry.

NOTE   While you have the Travel and Expense Reporting page open, click on the download link to download the expense report application file. You'll need it for the example of the next section.

FIGURE 30.2

The AppFoundry Application Overviews page summarizes the applications that are available through AppFoundry.

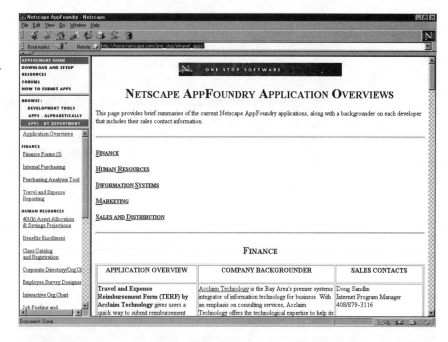

FIGURE 30.3

The Travel and Expense Reporting application can make filling out expense reports more convenient.

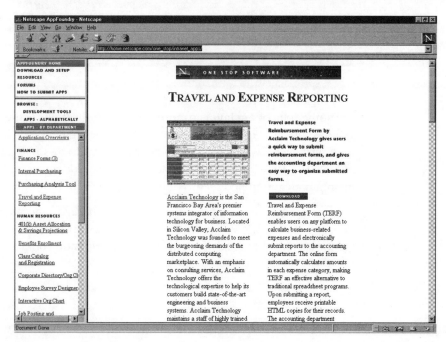

When you have finished downloading the expense report application file, click on some of the other applications. Figure 30.4 shows the description of the *Interactive Organization Chart*. This is a very useful application for companies that frequently reorganize.

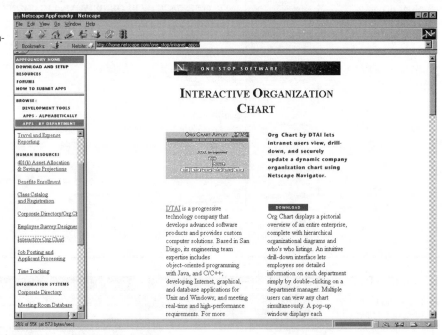

Another one of my favorite AppFoundry applications is the *Time Tracking* application shown in Figure 30.5. One of my biggest challenges is to turn in my paper time card every two weeks. There always seems to be some reason why I have to redo it. The Time Tracking application is a must for any company that needs to maintain an automated record of its employee's time charges.

As a final example, consider the *Personal Start Page Builder* shown in Figure 30.6. This application lets you build a personalized start page for the Internet. It is a great example of the use of client-side JavaScript and cookies.

FIGURE 30.5

The Time Tracking application sure beats filling out paper time cards.

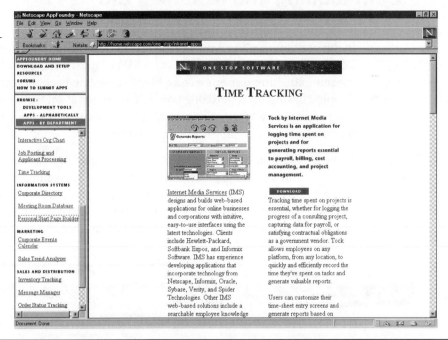

FIGURE 30.6

Use the Personal Start Page Builder to give employees the capability to easily create their own start pages.

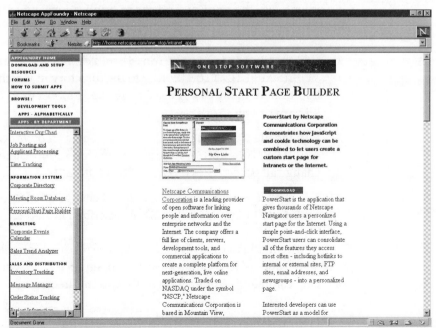

Downloading and Installing the TERF Application

In the previous section, you were asked to download the Travel and Expense Reporting application from Netscape's Web site. This application is contained in the self-extracting `expense.exe` file. To install it, execute `expense.exe` by double-clicking on it. A dialog box will appear that prompts you for the name of the directory to which the application files are to be installed. Pick a subdirectory under your LiveWire applications directory.

The installation creates three directories: `admin`, `images`, and `user`. The `user` directory contains the files used to create the `terf` application. The `admin` directory contains the files used to create the application (`admterf`) used to administer the `terf` application. It is similar, in function, to `admsched` of the previous chapter. The `images` directory contains images that are used in the applications.

> **NOTE**   TERF was developed by Acclaim Technology. Their home page is located at *http://www.acclaim.com*.

In order to use the `terf` and `admterf` applications, you need to make a few small changes.

1. Edit the file `admin\function.js` and change all occurrences of the string `<FULL APPLICATION HOME>` to the directory in which you installed the application. In my case, I use `e:/netscape/server/LiveWire/jscript/ch30/terf`.

2. Edit the file `use\function.js` and change all of *its* occurrences of `<FULL APPLICATION HOME>` as described in step 1 immediately above. Also change all occurrences of `<APPLICATION HOME>` to `/admterf`.

3. Edit the file `use\formput.html` and change all of *its* occurrences of `<FULL APPLICATION HOME>` as described in step 1.

Once you've made the above changes, you're ready to compile the `admterf` and `terf` applications. To compile `admterf`, open up a DOS window and enter the following commands from within terf's `admin` directory:

```
lwcomp -v -o ..\admin.web admin.html function.js
```

To compile `terf`, enter the following command from within terf's `user` directory:

```
lwcomp -v -o ..\user.web final.html formput.html function.js
```

Now open the LiveWire Application Manager and add the `admterf` and `terf` applications, as shown in Figures 30.7 and 30.8. (Make sure that you substitute your own path for the Web File Path field shown in Figures 30.7 and 30.8.) The default page for the `admterf` application is `admin.html`. The default page for the `terf` application is `final.html`.

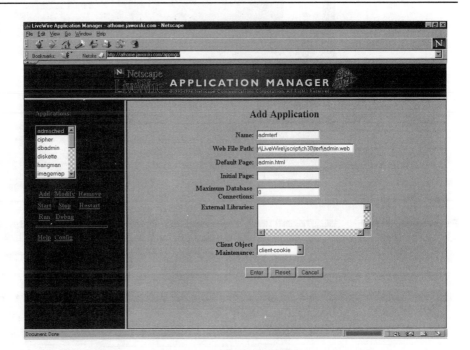

Running the TERF Application

To see how TERF works, first open the `terf` application using the URL *http://your.server.com/terf/*, replacing *your.server.com* with the name and domain of your own server. The expense report form is displayed. Fill out the form by entering values in the form fields. My expense report form is shown in Figure 30.9. Note that the totals are automatically updated each time you update a form field. Scroll down to the bottom of the form and click on the Send to Accounting button. The expense report summary shown in Figure 30.10 is displayed. (Bet you can't wait to get your expense check!)

FIGURE 30.8

Adding the `terf`
application

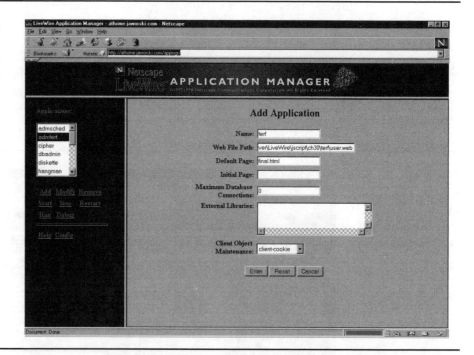

FIGURE 30.9

My expense report

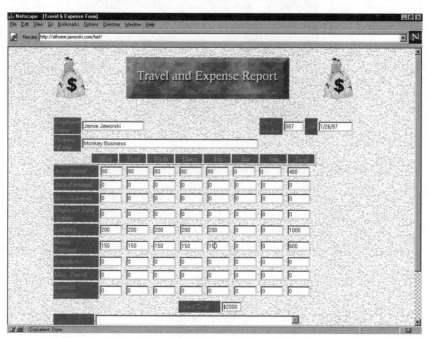

FIGURE 30.10

My expense report
summary

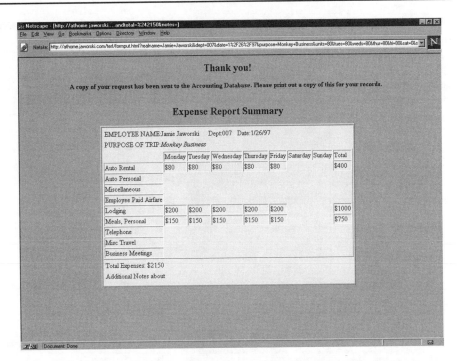

Let's see what forms the accounting department is working on. Open the URL
http://your.server.com/admterf/. The expense reports that are currently being
processed by accounting are displayed as shown in Figure 30.11.

WARNING

Note that the links to individual expense reports in TERF might not work.
This is a bug in the `admterf` application. It assumes that the expense
report summary files it creates are accessible to your Web server.

Tailoring the Application

The TERF application is a good example of a useful application component that
you may want to tailor to the needs of your particular organization. In what ways
should the application be tailored? First of all, *security* is important. You may want
to protect it with a user ID and password so that you'll have some assurance that
expense reports are submitted only by the person whose name is on the form.

FIGURE 30.11

The expense reports that have been submitted to accounting are listed in tabular form.

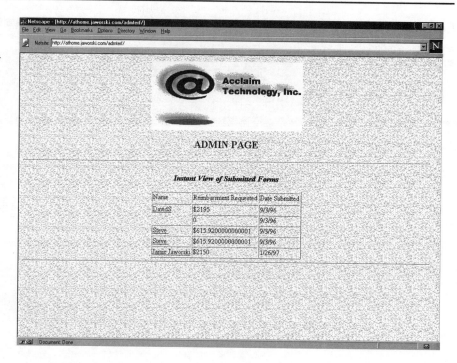

After securing TERF, the next thing that I would do is to interface it with a *database*. This would allow it to be integrated with other financial applications and provide a more reliable approach to tracking expense reports.

The final thing that *I* would do would be to tailor it to my company's needs. Since I work for a defense contractor that ties expense allowances to the city being visited, I would add a link to a table of allowed per diem rates by city.

The specific ways that you decide to modify TERF will depend on your organization's needs. You can choose to modify some of it, all of it, or none of it. No matter what modifications you make, the important point is that you aren't working from scratch—you're using components built by others to create your Web applications.

If you are seriously interested in tailoring TERF to your needs, print the application HTML and JavaScript files that are contained in the `admin` and `user` directories. You can then study these files to see how they work and how they can be improved to fit your needs.

JavaBeans and Portable Applications

One of the most impressive approaches to creating Web applications with reusable components has recently been introduced by Sun. Their approach, referred to as *JavaBeans*, extends the benefits associated with Microsoft's VBX and OCX to the Web and beyond.

Java Beans are components, written in Java, that are specially designed for maximum reuse. They can be custom visual controls, specialized algorithms, or complete subsystems. They can be embedded in an applet or used as part of a stand-alone application. They can be run anywhere that Java can be run, which is just about everywhere.

JavaBeans uses a component/container software assembly model similar to those of Microsoft's Visual Basic and Borland's Delphi. In this model, software components are designed in such a way that they can easily be combined into larger components and applications. Components are organized into containers. Containers provide the basis for component display and interaction. Containers can also be used as components and placed in larger containers.

Java has supported a component/container framework since its inception. JavaBeans extends this framework with the following features:

- *Component interface exposure and discovery.* Java Beans can dynamically inform other objects of their interface (exposure) and find out about the interfaces of other objects (discovery).

- *Component persistence.* Java Beans can have properties, such as foreground and background colors, that can be read or set by other objects.

- *Component event handling.* Java Beans can handle events that occur local to the bean and generate events that are handled outside the bean.

- *Persistence.* Java Beans can be stored in such a way that their state remains intact during storage.

- *Application builder support.* Java Beans expose their interfaces and properties to application builder tools so that they can be easily combined into larger application containers.

- *Component packaging.* The Java Archive file format (. JAR) is used to package all of the classes of a Java Bean into a single distributable file.

Java Beans provide a powerful capability for building Web applications. They enable applets to be easily composed as component containers. Since applets are accessible to JavaScript via LiveConnect, they can be combined with client-side scripts to develop advanced Web applications more quickly and easily.

As an example, consider the online scheduling application of Chapter 29. The bulk of the JavaScript code of this application is in the calendar widget. This widget is a perfect candidate for a Java Bean. It could be implemented once as a bean and then reused in many Web and stand-alone applications.

NOTE   For a good introduction to JavaBeans, check out the white paper at *http://splash.javasoft.com/beans/WhitePaper.htm.*

A Word about Plug-Ins

Plug-ins are another important component for developing Web applications. As you learned in Part 5, plug-ins are used to display files of special MIME types, such as multimedia files, and to implement custom Web components.

Plug-ins are a great addition to any Web application. The number and variety of plug-ins grows larger every day. The only drawback to using plug-ins is that they are platform-specific. This can be a serious problem if you intend for your application to run on multiple platforms.

On the other hand, if you are developing an intranet application and your company uses only Windows 95-based PCs, then you are in luck—most plug-ins are written to run on Windows 95. The bad news is, most organizations do *not* limit themselves to a single operating system platform. The bottom line on using plug-in components is that they can provide exceptional capabilities, but only if you are able to limit your application to a single OS.

Summary

In this chapter, we covered Netscape ONE and discussed its support for building advanced Web applications using prebuilt components. We explored Netscape's AppFoundry and described how to tailor AppFoundry applications to your needs. We finished the chapter by looking at JavaBeans and the benefits that it provides for developing Web applications using prefabricated components. In the next chapter, we focus on the intranet, and discuss how JavaScript can be used to satisfy an organization's requirements for sharing information.

Building an Intranet

- Intranet Sites vs. Internet Sites

- Exploring the Airius Virtual Intranet

- The Internal Web vs. the External Web

When the Web first became popular, there was no "intranet." The focus of every company was to get its home page on the World Wide Web for *everybody* to see. It didn't take long, however, for companies to realize the value of Web technologies for publishing information for more specialized audiences. The intranet was born out of the tremendous benefits gained from using the Web for *company-internal* communication.

In this chapter, we explore the intranet and look at the differences between intranet and Internet publishing. We describe the typical services provided on an intranet and identify the type of information that is published there. We then take a tour of Netscape's showcase—the *Airius Virtual Intranet*—which is an example intranet of a hypothetical company. We discuss JavaScript's role in the intranet, and look at the additional possibilities that an intranet provides for developing JavaScript-based applications. When you finish this chapter, you'll have a better understanding of the differences between intranet and Internet applications and how to use JavaScript to build your organization's intranet.

Intranet Sites vs. Internet Sites

We hear a lot about the differences between an intranet and the Internet and about new Web technologies that are targeted to the intranet. But what exactly *is* an intranet? Here's a good working definition:

> An intranet is that part of an organization's internal network that supports Internet services and is intended for organization-internal use. In other words, it's an organization's "internal Internet."

Although intranets are usually associated with companies, they are used in all kinds of organizations. There are university intranets, government intranets, and military intranets. There are even elementary school intranets. Because an intranet is intended for organization-internal use, it is commonly protected by a *firewall*. The firewall separates an intranet from the Internet at large, limiting access to intranet services to authorized users.

While an intranet uses the same services as the Internet at large, some of these services are used in significantly different ways, as discussed in the following paragraphs.

E-Mail   The most popular service on the Internet is e-mail. The appeal of Internet e-mail when compared with the telephone is that in most cases it is less expensive than the telephone, especially for communication beyond your area code. The drawback to e-mail is its asynchronous nature: you can't usually expect an immediate response to your e-mail messages.

Other than its lack of immediacy, however, e-mail has certain distinct advantages, and these are especially well used by the e-mail programs being put to use over intranets. In fact, within some companies intranet e-mail has surpassed the telephone for company-internal communication; it is not uncommon for people to send e-mail to the person in the cubicle next to them! This can be explained by the fact that e-mail is simply better than the telephone for some communications. For instance, *because* it asynchronous, e-mail actually obviates certain problems that are associated with synchronous communication mediums like the telephone. For example, with e-mail, you can avoid the game of "phone tag" you end up playing when you're trying to make a voice call but the other person is not available. Further, most business e-mail programs offer a digital record of all your communications. It is also quite easy to direct your e-mail communications to specific groups of people, something that usually takes extra effort and cost when you attempt the same with a telephone.

Newsgroups   Company-internal newsgroups have been around for a number of years. Groupware was popular before the Internet revolution but was mostly based on proprietary standards. Netscape helped to pioneer the use of open standard newsgroups with its Collabra server, bringing Usenet-style newsgroups to the company intranet. The major advantage of Collabra over actual Usenet newsgroups is its security services.

Usenet-style newsgroups on an intranet differ from Internet-wide newsgroups in that they tend to be more focused, and much more attention is given to the identity of the person submitting a message.

File Transfer/File Sharing   File transfer is a popular Internet service, and the File Transfer Protocol (FTP) is the most popular protocol for Internet file transfer. However, on an intranet, FTP's popularity has waned. Since most intranets use MS Windows of some sort (Windows for Workgroups, Windows 95, or Windows NT), Microsoft's file and printer sharing protocol (SMB—Symmetric Message Block) is the predominant means of intranet file sharing and file transfer. While SMB may also be used over the Internet, its use has not become popular, because it is slower than FTP and raises additional security concerns.

E-mail file attachments have also become a popular means of intranet and Internet file transfer.

Remote System Use Remote system use has always been a popular Internet service. The telnet and rlogin protocols have traditionally been the most common way of logging in and using a remote system using a command-line interface. The X Windows System added new possibilities for accessing remote systems that use windowed applications.

The Microsoft Windows family of operating systems provides no native remote-control services similar to telnet or X Windows. However, some products, such as Laplink 95, provide the capability to remotely control Windows platforms over the Internet and intranet. While these products certainly work over the Internet, their performance is affected by the slow speeds that characterize much Internet communication. Over an intranet, on the other hand, speed is exponentially better, due to better connections; thus remote-control products work great over an intranet. They can be an invaluable aid in providing internal user support.

Intranet Websites

In the daytime, I work for a fairly large company—I'm employee number 48,062. We have an internal web, which is similar to other company-internal webs, in that its websites focus on facilitating communication between the company and its employees. Company-related information is provided in a central location for all to see. By using Web technologies, it can be quickly updated as needed. My company makes tremendous use of its internal web, publishing all sorts of valuable information:

- Information about what's new in the company.

- Information about company projects, products, and services.

- Company policies and procedures.

- General help information.

- Links to different departments within the company.

- An online company directory.

The online company directory is of immeasurable help. If I need to find an employee's phone or fax number or e-mail address, I can quickly do a search on the employee's name. The department links are also a great help. Suppose that I want to find out who is involved in network security. I can do a departmental search on security, find the network security department, and find out who works in the department.

My company's internal website is typical of first-generation internal websites. It focuses on publishing information and supports simple web applications, such as search engines.

Second-generation internal websites go beyond simple publishing and searching to provide true network-centric web applications. These applications are typified by those showcased in the AppFoundry—travel and expense reporting, electronic time cards, and dynamic organization chart development. Fully functional web applications such as these are being fielded now and are changing the way companies use their internal websites. The following section provides a glimpse at a second-generation company intranet and illustrates the latest use of company-internal web applications.

Exploring the Airius Virtual Intranet

In order to spur the development of second-generation internal websites which use their products, Netscape has put together an example of a hypothetical company's intranet. This example shows how technologies such as client- and server-side JavaScript and Java, and server-accessible databases, can be combined to produce the network-centric applications of Netscape ONE. Some of the sample AppFoundry applications are also included in the example intranet.

The example explores an intranet of the fictitious Airius Aircraft company. The starting point for our virtual intranet tour is the following URL:

http://home.netscape.com/comprod/at_work/vip/index.html

Open it with your browser and you'll see the web page shown in Figure 31.1.

This page provides an overview of the example and discusses how to make the most of your visit. The Click to Begin button leads to the registration page shown in Figure 31.2. It's somewhat of an inconvenience, but go ahead and register. (You need to register to get access to the rest of the demo.)

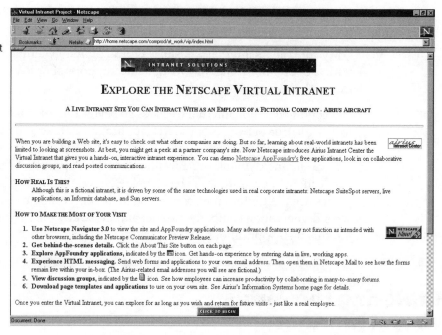

FIGURE 31.1

The opening screen of Netscape's demo intranet

Once you register, you'll see the web page shown in Figure 31.3. This is the home page of the Airius Aircraft company. The home page uses frames to provide access to intranet applications. The left frame is an index to these applications and is organized according to company functions. Use your browser's View Document Source command to take a look at how the top-level frame set is organized. You may also want to explore some of the documents loaded in the individual frames.

Run your mouse over the individual topics in the left frame. Notice the little boxes that appear, briefly explaining the content of each link. Figure 31.4 provides an example. This feature is implemented by displaying a new image in response to the `onMouseOver` event.

Click the Daily Essentials link in the left frame and a new web page is loaded in the right frame, as shown in Figure 31.5. There is a wealth of useful applications on this page. I recommend that you try them all. In the next section I'll show you the first pages from a few of these links.

FIGURE 31.2

The registration page

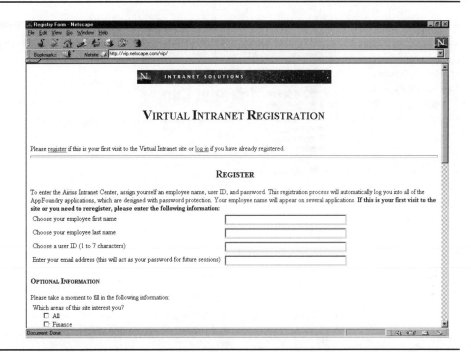

FIGURE 31.3

The fictitious company's home page

FIGURE 31.4

An onMouseOver event
controls the display
of brief explanatory
material for the links.

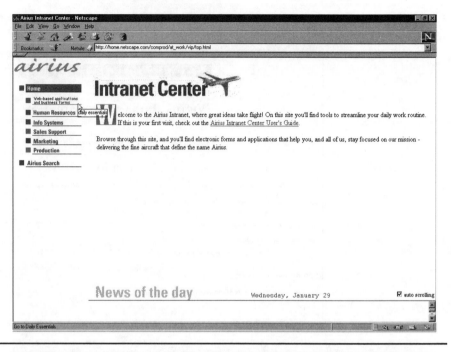

FIGURE 31.5

We'll be checking out the
links under this page's
Frequently Used Forms
and Applications topic.

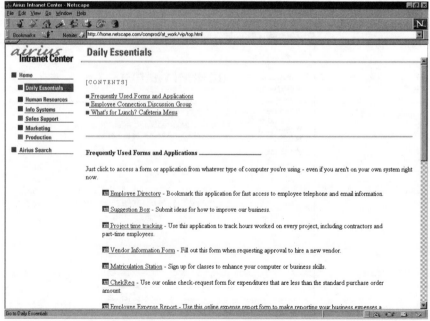

The Airius "Daily Essentials" Page

On the Airius Daily Essentials page, click the Employee Directory link. A new window is created, as shown in Figure 31.6. All intranet webs should have an application of this kind. Try an employee search to see how it works. When you're finished, close the window and return to the Daily Essentials frame.

FIGURE 31.6

The Employee Directory link from the Daily Essentials page takes you to this interactive search page.

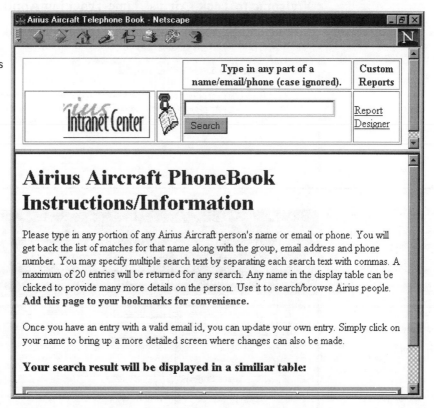

Click on the Project Time Tracking link. The window shown in Figure 31.7 is created. You can use this application as an online time card. Click the Preferences link to get started. The web page shown in Figure 31.8 is displayed. Fill out the form's fields to identify the projects you are working on. When you're finished with this application, close the window and return to the Daily Essentials frame.

FIGURE 31.7

The Project Time Tracking
link from the Daily Essentials page takes you to
this application screen.

FIGURE 31.8

The Preferences form
for the Time Tracking
application

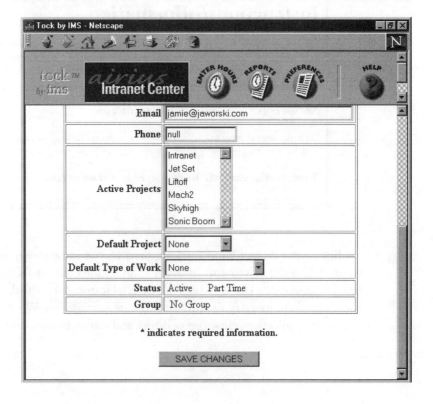

Click on the Employee Expense Report link. The window shown in Figure 31.9 is created and displayed. Try submitting an expense report of your own.

FIGURE 31.9

The Employee Expense Report link from the Daily Essentials page takes you to this application.

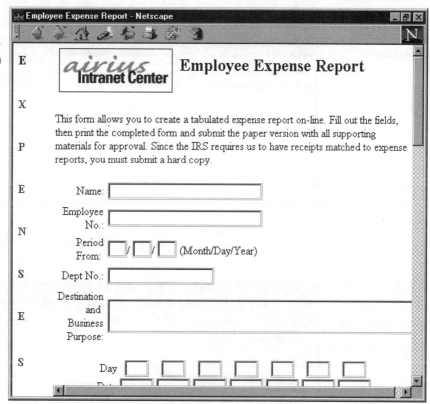

FIGURE 31.9

The Employee Expense Report link from the Daily Essentials page takes you to this application.

One last application, before we go on to other company functions. Click on the Employee Connection Discussion Group link. The Netscape Newsgroup application is launched, as shown in Figure 31.10. Wouldn't it be great to have a newsgroup capability like this for your organization? Try sending a message to the newsgroup. When you've finished, close the newsgroup window.

The Airius "Human Resources" Page

Back at the Daily Essentials page, click on the Human Resources link in the left frame. The page shown in Figure 31.11 is loaded. This page provides a number of interesting human resources applications.

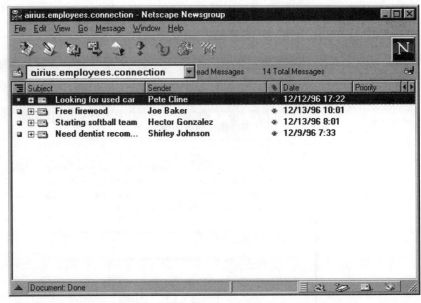

FIGURE 31.10

The Employee Connection Discussion Group link from the Daily Essentials page connects you to the Netscape Newsgroup application.

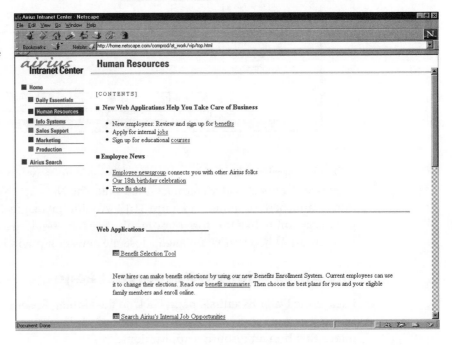

FIGURE 31.11

The Airius intranet's Human Resources page

Click on the Benefits Selection Tool link. A new window like that shown in Figure 31.12 is displayed. Click on the Employee Benefits link. The multiframe document shown in Figure 31.13 is loaded. Try some of the links to get some ideas for your intranet. When you're finished, close the window.

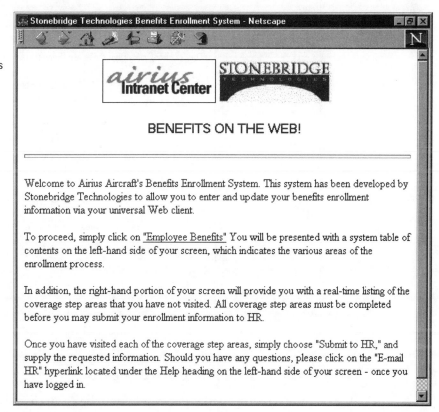

Back at the Human Resources page, click on the Jobs link to load the Job Listing Center web page shown in Figure 31.14. This page provides three different views of the hiring process. Click on the Job Seeker button to access a very useful summary of the current job openings at Airius. Close the window before continuing.

FIGURE 31.13

Clicking on the previous page's Employee Benefits link takes you to this multi-featured page.

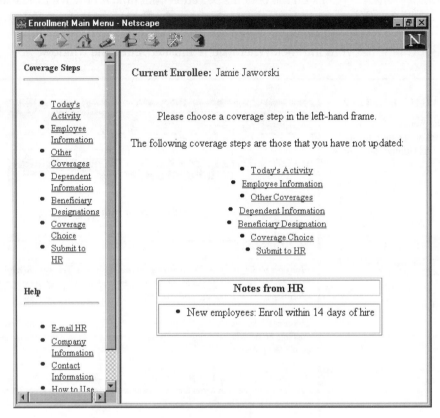

The Airius "Sales Support" Page

Let's move on to the Sales Support link from the Airius home page. Back at the home page, click on the Sales Support link in the left frame to load the page shown in Figure 31.15. Several sales support applications are provided via this page. Click on the *Marketing and sales tools management system* link. The colorful "Sales KnowledgeSite" web page shown in Figure 31.16 is loaded. This application provides valuable information for the company's sales force.

FIGURE 31.14

The Jobs link from the Airius Human Resources page leads you to this screen.

FIGURE 31.15

The Airius Sales Support page

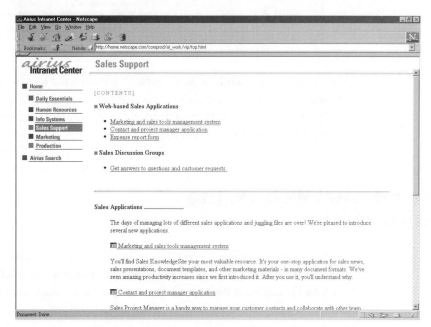

FIGURE 31.16

The appealing "Sales
KnowledgeSite" web page

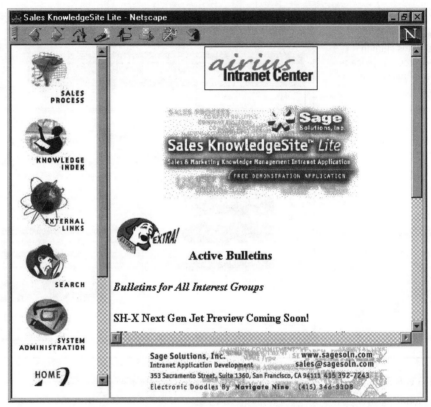

FIGURE 31.16

The appealing "Sales
KnowledgeSite" web page

This completes a random walk through some of the top-level pages of the
Airius intranet. It should give you some good ideas on how you might want to
build your own organization's intranet. For more ideas and information, go back
and explore some of the other Airius links.

The Internal Web vs. the External Web

The Airius virtual intranet provides a great example of a second-generation internal web. It combines document publishing and search capabilities with JavaScript-
based and Java-based Web applications to provide comprehensive support of

business-related functions. My mouth watered when I first looked at the online time tracking and expense-reporting capabilities. While keeping the Airius virtual intranet example in mind, let's look at some of the differences between internal websites and the Web at large.

Focus

The most obvious and most significant way in which internal and external websites differ is in their focus. The Web at large defies convention—anything goes. You can find Web pages on almost any subject, ranging from the serious to the silly. On an intranet, there is much less variety and levity. The focus is on the organization, with emphasis on communication, information distribution, and business applications.

To this end, internal websites share the same structure and many common features. For example, consider the Airius virtual intranet and imagine how you could apply it to your organization. If your organization is a company, then you can probably use the Airius web pages as a template and just replace Airius information with that of your company. If you work for a different type of organization, then you will have to replace the business functions (production, marketing, sales, etc.) with those of your organization. However, you will still be able to borrow quite a bit from the Airius example.

Standardization

One of the advantages of developing content and applications for an intranet is standardization. You can select a standard Web browser, Web server, mail system, directory server, and so on, for use throughout your organization.

Standardization is important. With standardization, you can be sure that all users will be able to use an intranet web in the same way, that your web applications are portable between servers and can be developed in the same manner, and that organizationally-dispersed intranet segments are interoperable.

While there are open standards on the Internet and Web at large, there are many gradations of capabilities within these standards. Take browsers, for example. There are text-mode browsers and graphical browsers. There are browsers that are JavaScript- and Java-capable and browsers that are not. Even within the same product line, there are browsers of different versions with different capabilities.

The variety of browsing capabilities found on the Web usually results in a least-common-denominator approach to determining which capabilities are used. In other words, most Web content designers try to limit the features used in their applications to those that are supported by the largest possible set of browsers.

The alternative to the least-common-denominator approach is to develop Web pages with different feature levels. You've probably seen pages with links such as "Click here for a text-only version" and "Click here for a Java-enhanced version." While this approach supports multiple levels of browser capabilities, it also requires you to develop multiple versions of the same Web page.

Standardization enables intranet applications to take advantage of the latest in browser and JavaScript capabilities. This allows you to develop your applications with the assurance that all users will be capable of using them. By using a standard intranet web browser, then you can develop web applications that take advantage of the latest browser features without having to pander to low-capability browsers.

Bandwidth

Communication bandwidth is another major difference between an intranet and the Internet. This difference means that you can use multimedia files on an intranet that would be highly impractical on the Internet. For example, you can include a video of the company receiving a prestigious award or an audio file of the president's last speech in your company's What's New page.

With advances in networking technology, differences between the intranet and Internet will remain, but will change in scale. While typical Internet access rates will soon be in the 0.1 to 100 megabit per second range, gigabit per second speeds will be used on an intranet.

Since bandwidth limitations are a primary reason for browser-side programming, you may wonder whether the need for browser-side JavaScript will diminish as bandwidth limitations are eased—especially on an intranet. The answer is emphatically no. Browser-side programming is still needed to support custom event handling and to access browser objects. In addition, any processing that can be performed on the browser reduces the load on the server. This is especially important in an intranet environment where many users may be using the same application concurrently.

Mission-Critical Nature

While external websites are critical to some companies, this is only true for a small fraction of those that are on the Web—the ones that actually use the Web to conduct their main business. For example, if the Super Web Shopper site goes down, then the site owner's will lose business. On the other hand, if Coca Cola's site is unavailable, there probably won't be much difference in the company's bottom line.

Internal websites (what I call "intrawebs") are currently not very critical to business success. First-generation intranet websites that focus on information distribution can go down without much impact on the business operation. As companies transition to second-generation internal webs, the importance of the intraweb to business operation will increase. Web-based applications, such as those shown in the Airius intranet, will begin to take over common business functions. Eventually, as more critical functions are implemented in terms of web applications, the intraweb will become indispensible to business operation.

Need for Security

Security is an important consideration for any networked application, and the Web is no exception. Security on the Web at large is concerned with protecting business transactions, protecting websites from hacker penetration, and protecting users from damage by malicious code.

On an intranet, security is focused on user identification, authentication, and privilege controls:

- *User identification* and *authentication* is needed to verify that users are who they say they are. These are very important for such applications as online timecards and expense reports where you wouldn't want one user posing as another. The traditional user ID and password are still the most popular type of user identification and authentication. In the near future, "digital certificates" will be the predominant mechanism for identification and authentication.

- *Privilege controls* are needed to allow different users to have different capabilities in certain applications. For example, consider a more advanced expense report application in which additional functions are provided for reviewing, approving, and processing expense reports. Ordinary users may only be allowed to prepare expense reports that are in their own name. Supervisors may be given the capability to review and approve the expense reports for the people they supervise. A select few employees may be given the capability to process expense reports and cut expense checks.

Summary

In this chapter, you examined the differences between intranet and Internet publishing. You learned about the typical services used on an intranet and the type of information that is published there. You took a tour of the Airius virtual intranet and sampled some second-generation intranet applications. You then covered JavaScript's role on the intranet and looked at the additional possibilities that an intranet provides for developing JavaScript-based applications. In the next and final chapter, you'll learn a little about Web security and some of the steps that you can take to secure your Web applications.

CHAPTER

THIRTY-TWO

Security Considerations

- Internet Security Threats

- Web Security Issues

Congratulations, you've made it to the last chapter of this book! If you've worked your way through the previous chapters, then by now you are adept at client- and server-side JavaScript and have been exposed to CGI and database programming. With these new skills, you are probably eager to go out and develop your own Web applications. The purpose of this chapter is to temper your enthusiasm with some practical cautions related to Web security vulnerabilities.

This chapter covers Web security from two perspectives—the Webmaster's and the user's:

- The Webmaster-oriented discussion describes issues related to Web site security and emphasizes server-side application development.

- The user-oriented discussion describes the security risks associated with using the Web and identifies ways to protect your personal computer from Web-based attacks.

When you finish this chapter, you'll be able to develop your Web applications with a better understanding of the security issues involved.

Internet Security Threats

Threats to the Website Manager

As a Web content developer *and* as a user, the Internet security threats that you face depend on who you are and what you have to protect. For example, if you are the Webmaster for a high-profile organization, such as the CIA or the U.S. Department of Justice, then you'll be the target of hackers merely for the challenge you present; many hackers want the fame associated with penetrating one of the big guys. Even if your Web site is not in the hacker "Top 40," if it is not well protected, it may be penetrated just because it is an easy target.

If your Web site is involved with any type of financial transactions or controls any valuable assets, directly or even indirectly, then your Web site could be the target of a more professional type of criminal than the recreational hacker. These cyber thiefs may try to penetrate your Web site in order to get access to such things as credit card numbers, software, sensitive information, or physical assets, such as products which may be purchased through your Web site.

An attack on your Web site may be the first stage of a concerted attack on your organization as a whole. If your Web server is inside your organization's firewall, then a penetration of your Web server could lead to a serious security breach of site-internal networks. If your Web server is outside your organization's firewall, then an attacker may attempt to install clandestine software to monitor network traffic at the firewall's external interface.

With the growing importance of the Web to commerce, a company's ability to conduct business can be affected by attacks on its Web site. While most businesses don't prey on each other through the Internet, a third party *could* manipulate a company's Web presence to reap financial gain.

Threats to the Web User

The security threats faced by the individual user are somewhat different than those of the Webmaster. First of all, there isn't much prestige in breaking into someone's PC. This rules out some, but not all, recreational hackers. If someone wants to get access to your PC, then it is probably someone who is intent on collecting information about you or sabotaging the data on your PC. This special someone could be an acquaintance, a competitor, or anyone else who has an interest in knowing or stopping what you're doing. With the rise of electronic commerce on the Web, it's likely that some electronic pickpockets will surface. These small time cyber thiefs will snoop on user's PCs in order to collect credit card numbers, passwords, and information that can be used to forge digital certificates.

Most indiscriminate attacks on individuals come in the form of malicious software, such as viruses—yes, they are still out there. Future attacks will probably include executable Web content (JavaScript, Java, ActiveX) and executable e-mail, such as that supported by Netscape Messenger.

Web Security Issues

To some, the Internet itself is just one big security vulnerability. However, for most of us, it is a vulnerability that we have to live with. While a complete treatment of Internet security vulnerabilities is beyond the scope of this book, the following subsections describe Web-specific security issues from the point of view of the Webmaster and the user.

The Webmaster's Perspective

Running a secure Web server is not an easy task. Security vulnerabilities can, potentially, exist anywhere—in CGI programs, in the server setup, or in the Web server itself. These vulnerabilities could lead to embarrassing modifications to Web content, the theft of sensitive information, or the complete shutdown of your Web site.

To run a secure Web site, the Webmaster must keep abreast of the latest Web vulnerabilities and implement security countermeasures as needed. The World Wide Web Security FAQ, located at *http://www.genome.wi.mit.edu/WWW/faqs/www-security-faq.html* can help you get started. It discusses many of the known Web vulnerabilities and offers good advice on how you can protect your Web site.

Server Software

Website security begins with the Web server. Unfortunately, not all Web servers are secure. Security holes have been identified in both commercial and public domain servers. Although these holes have been patched in later versions of the server software, the potential for the introduction of new vulnerabilities cannot be dismissed.

Publicly available Web servers, such as the CERN, Apache, and NCSA servers, offer a high level of security and reliability. However, if security is of paramount concern, then you may want to consider a commercial server, by a major vendor, such as Netscape. While commercial servers are not immune to security flaws, reputable vendors tend to respond quickly to security holes once they are identified, in order to stay in business.

Server Capabilities

New server products continue to add features, such as server-side JavaScript, server plug-ins, and database connectivity, which increase the overall complexity of the server software. While the Webmaster looks at the capabilities of a Web server and visualizes all of the ways in which these capabilities could be used to build a better Web site, the penetrator examines each capability in terms of how it could be used to circumvent, defeat, and disable the security of the server as a whole.

Server-side *includes* are an example of a server feature which is also a bonus to the penetrator. A server-side include is a sequence of commands that are embedded in an HTML document. When the document is requested by a Web server, the server scans the document for the embedded commands and executes them.

The results of the command execution are used to update the HTML document before it is sent to the browser. One of the commands, `exec`, allows arbitrary operating system commands to be executed. This capability is very powerful—to both you and the penetrator. With server-side includes enabled, a person with minimal Web publishing capabilities gains the extra privilege of being able to execute operating system commands.

The best way to avoid security vulnerabilities with new server features is to assess the capabilities provided by each feature and determine which ones pose unacceptable security risks. As a minimum, you must consider the following to be risks:

- If the feature can be used to execute external programs or operating system commands.

- If the feature can be used to read or write arbitrary files located on the server.

- If the feature maintains client information on the browser using cookies or URL encoding.

The above risks only determine whether the feature has the *capability* to cause security problems—it doesn't mean that the feature is necessarily insecure. For example, both CGI programs and LiveWire applications are risky according to all three risk indicators. Once you identify a feature as risky, you have to determine whether secure applications can be built using the feature despite its inherent risks, and whether the benefits provided by the feature are worth taking a chance. In the case of CGI programs and LiveWire applications, the answer is usually yes.

CGI Programs

There is nothing inherently insecure about the CGI itself. However, CGI programs are a prime source of server-side vulnerabilities. By deploying a CGI program, you are allowing others to execute programs on your Web server. From the penetrator's perspective, every CGI program is a potential tool with which to attack your system. Any security flaws in your CGI programs are directly and continually accessible, and penetrators are free to repeatedly probe and cajole these flaws until they succeed in accomplishing their clandestine objectives.

Do flaws exist in CGI programs? You bet. Some flaws let attackers read data that should otherwise be concealed. Other flaws let hackers trash data that is collected from Web users. The most devastating flaws let penetrators remotely execute operating system commands and programs of their choosing.

How do flaws in CGI programs occur? How are they exploited? In many cases, these flaws occur because of poor parameter checking and faulty assumptions on the part of the programmer. For example, consider the case where a CGI program invokes a search program and passes it the value of a decoded query string. The programmer assumes that the search program will simply search for whatever value is passed. But when the query string is passed, the following is executed:

```
search string; cat /etc/passwd
```

In this case, the CGI program returns much more than the search results—it appends the contents of your password file to the search results. The penetrator can then use a password cracking program to find a password that will let him log into your system.

You may wonder why anyone would develop CGI programs that would allow such serious breaches of security. Some programmers don't know any better—they are oblivious to the fact that their programs may be misused. Some are so focused on developing their Web applications that security is put on the back burner—permanently. However, the biggest problem, by far, is that in most CGI programs, security flaws are difficult to spot. In the cases where they are found, they are often dismissed. "But no one would ever do that" is a common justification for failing to remove an exploitable flaw.

Another problem facing CGI programmers is the fact that the odds are heavily stacked against them. The programmers must eliminate *all* possible security flaws in order to make their CGI programs secure. The penetrator need only find a single exploitable flaw in order to break into the Web server.

LiveWire Applications

Although LiveWire applications provide the same capabilities as CGI programs, they are far less prone to security vulnerabilities. There are a number of reasons why LiveWire applications are inherently more secure.

1. LiveWire automatically parses data that is passed to applications and makes it available in an easy-to-use manner. This reduces the likelihood of a flaw occurring in the input parsing functions.

2. LiveWire does not provide any native capabilities to execute other programs or operating system commands. (It does, however, let you add these capabilities using external functions.) This reduces the possibility of a LiveWire

application being used to execute commands and programs for which it was not intended.

3. LiveWire applications have predefined objects at their disposal, which reduce the complexities of maintaining client information, sharing data between clients, and sharing data between applications. By making it easier to perform common server-side functions, LiveWire helps you to develop more reliable and error-free code, thereby lowering the likelihood of an exploitable security flaw.

4. LiveWire applications are written in JavaScript. This eliminates the potential problems associated with using a second, less familiar, language for writing CGI programs. The less experience a programmer has with a language, the more likely s/he is to make mistakes—potentially exploitable ones.

The above features significantly reduce the likelihood of security vulnerabilities in LiveWire applications. However, the potential for some vulnerabilities still exists. For example, suppose a LiveWire application is designed in such a way that a LiveWire `redirect()` method takes a client property as a parameter. A penetrator could modify client properties (client cookies or URLs) to cause the `redirect()` function to return a file of the penetrator's choosing.

Server-Side Plug-Ins

Netscape and Microsoft Web servers provide other server-side programming features, such as Java and server-side plug-ins. In general, *any* server-side programming mechanism has the potential to be exploited.

Server-side plug-ins are compiled and integrated with the Web server software. They allow server-side applications to be developed that perform better than LiveWire applications and CGI programs. This is because they are called directly by the server instead of being run as a separate process.

The performance gain of server-side plug-ins is offset by the difficulty of developing them. Because server-side plug-ins are closely integrated with the server, any errors in the plug-in could easily result in the complete failure of the server.

Web Application Access Controls

Most Web servers provide the capability to control access to certain Web pages and, in the case of LiveWire, to Web applications. These controls may be based on host name, IP address, user name and password, or other identification and authentication mechanisms. Failure to implement restrictions on some applications, such as your server's management software or Application Manager, could lead to serious security holes.

File Permissions

Operating-system file permissions are closely related to Web-application access controls. These permissions determine which files users and applications are able to read, write, and execute. These controls are important to protecting your Web site. In particular, write permission to the directories containing CGI programs and server-configuration files should be limited to the most trusted users. Failure to do so weakens the security of your Web server, opening it up to a a broader spectrum of attacks.

If your server stores financial information, such as credit card data, the permissions of these files should be set to prevent them from being read by other applications. If at all possible, these files should be made write-only.

In the event that your server is penetrated, the privileges of your server become those of the penetrator. Therefore, the login privileges of the Web server itself should be limited to the minimum needed to perform its function.

Other Server-Side Security Considerations

In addition to the vulnerabilities mentioned in the previous sections, Web servers are vulnerable to a wide range of attacks aimed at their application services and communication protocols. If a Web server supports other Internet services, such as telnet or FTP, then the server inherits all of the vulnerabilities of these services. The good news is that you can eliminate these vulnerabilities by turning off the additional services.

If a Web server is on the Internet, then it, by definition, must support the Transmission Control Protocol/Internet Protocol (TCP/IP). TCP/IP is notorious for its security vulnerabilities. These vulnerabilities include susceptibility to spoofing, session hijacking, and session monitoring. While these vulnerabilities are common to all systems that are on the Internet, they need to be considered when assessing the risk of setting up a Web server. If the perceived risk is too high, then you may want to implement a firewall or other network security countermeasures.

As a final consideration, the operating system platform on which the Web server runs is also a potential source of security vulnerabilities. In general, multi-user operating systems, such as Unix, pose a higher risk than single-user sytems, such as the Macintosh and Windows 95. The security of most multiuser systems depends on the reliability and trustworthiness of all system users. If a single user is careless or untrustworthy, then the security of the entire system could be jeopardized. Most multiuser operating systems provide security controls, such as file permissions, that prevent a user from viewing or modifying the files of others. However, to be effective, these controls must be correctly applied.

Although Web servers exist for the Macintosh, Windows 95, and Windows 3.1 platforms, most mid-level to high-end servers run on Windows NT and Unix platforms. This is because Windows NT and Unix provide a fuller set of operating system services for implementing more complex and capable server software.

Both Windows NT and Unix have advantages and disadvantages as far as security goes. The main advantage of Windows NT is that it does not support (without additional software purchases) many of the services, such as telnet, Internet mail, and the X Windows System, that are provided out of the box with Unix systems. These services may be used by a penetrator to gain remote access to a Unix system.

The primary advantage of Unix is its maturity. It has been subjected to hacking for many years, including years before Windows NT was conceived. As a result, most of the Unix security bugs have been identified and countermeasures have been implemented. Under a security-conscious system administrator, a Unix Web site can be made as secure as it would be using other operating-system platforms.

The Web User's Perspective

Although the risk of using the Web is small, it still merits some consideration. The basic question that you need to ask is, "What do I have to lose?" If you use your PC purely for recreation and don't perform any financial transactions over the Web then the answer is, "Not much." However, if you use your PC to store your diary and sensitive company documents and use the Web to make online purchases, then you may want to examine your risk more closely.

For users, Web security begins with the browser and, for most of us, that means a Netscape or Microsoft browser. Netscape Navigator and Microsoft Internet Explorer provide a number of features that go beyond simple Web page display. Both browsers support executable content—Java and of course JavaScript. Microsoft supports a limited version of JavaScript that they call *JScript*. Microsoft also supports VBScript as part of its ActiveX strategy. In addition to executable content, both browsers support plug-ins (Internet Explorer supports Navigator plug-ins in addition to its own), cookies, Secure Sockets Layer (SSL) communication, and digital certificates. Each of these features has implications for user security, as described in the following subsections.

Dealing with Executable Content

When most people think of browser vulnerabilities they think of Java, JavaScript, and ActiveX. For most of us, the thought of opening a Web page and automatically having a program load and execute on their computer is a bit frightening. There is a good reason for this fear—it is very difficult to allow executable content without leaving yourself wide open to a Trojan horse attack.

A Trojan horse is a program that appears to provide a useful function while, in reality, it is attacking your system. The name comes from the legend of the huge wooden horse that was left as a gift at the gates of Troy: when the Trojans opened the gates of their city to bring in the horse, Greek soldiers who were hiding inside the horse poured out and attacked the Trojans.

Each of the major three browser programming technologies use a different approach to protecting against Trojan horses:

- Java code executes in the Java Virtual Machine (JVM) which is part of the Java runtime system. The runtime system is designed to prevent operations that would violate the browser's security policy.

- JavaScript eliminates Trojan horse code by not providing objects or methods that could be used to cause damage or violate the user's privacy.

- ActiveX components do not provide any inherent protection against damage. Instead, these components are digitally signed. The signature provides a degree of assurance that the component originated from the organization that it claims.

Navigator 4 also supports signed Java applets. The signature can be used to determine whether the applet should be given extra privileges beyond those allowed by the default Navigator security policy.

Of the three approaches, JavaScript's is the most secure. By not providing a mechanism for creating damage, it is able to prevent the damage from occurring. But how do we know that no object or method can be used to cause damage? The answer is extensive analysis and testing. Could something have been overlooked? Try writing a JavaScript script that could damage your system.

Java's approach is next best when it comes to security. The Java runtime system is capable of supporting multiple security policies. For example, Java programs that are loaded from your hard disk are allowed more privileges than applets that are loaded over the network. Signed applets are given more privileges than unsigned applets. Java's approach, in allowing multiple security policies to be enforced, is daring. Except for a few early flaws, the Java runtime system has held up to its claims of security.

ActiveX uses the least secure of the three approaches. The signature attached to an ActiveX component does not provide any assurance that the component won't destroy your system, it just tells you who to go after in the case that it does.

Both Navigator and Internet Explorer provide the capability to selectively turn off these browser programming capabilities. If you simply can't take the chance of Trojan horse software being loaded into your computer, then you should take advantage of this option.

Plug-In Vulnerabilities

There are nearly two hundred plug-ins that are available for Navigator and Internet Explorer. These plug-ins execute as native code extensions to the browser. As such, plug-ins can do anything that your browser can. From a penetrator's perspective, this means that a plug-in can cause any sort of damage. With nearly two hundred available plug-ins to choose from, what do you think the chances are that one of them contains an exploitable security vulnerability? With the capability to invoke plug-in functions from Java and JavaScript, what do you think the likelihood is of a plug-in vulnerability being exploited?

As an example of the risk associated with plug-ins, consider the programs that are available for viewing Microsoft Word documents. With the capability to embed macros in a Word document, what do you think the likelihood is that a macro virus could be injected into your system via a Word document?

Plug-ins pose a potential risk to browser security. The more plug-ins you use, the greater the risk. Fortunately, there is an easy way to lower this risk—only install the plug-ins that you absolutely need.

Protecting Financial Information

If you plan on purchasing any merchandise or performing other types of financial transactions over the Web, you should be aware of the security mechanisms being used by your browser. The lower left corner of the Navigator window displays an indicator that shows the level of security that is currently in force. A broken key indicates that no encryption is being used. A solid key with a single tooth indicates that international security (40-bit) encryption is in use. A solid key with two teeth indicates that domestic security (128-bit) encryption is in use.

Both international and domestic security use the Secure Sockets Layer (SSL) for encryption. SSL uses public key cryptography to exchange keys that are used for private key encryption. Digital certificates are used to verify the identity of the organization with which you are communicating.

How strong is the security provided? If no encryption is used, then you should assume that whatever information you send can be intercepted.

If international (40-bit) encryption is used, then your encrypted communication is probably secure from a hacker without much computational resources, but not from anyone else. This encryption scheme has already been broken several times.

If domestic (128-bit) encryption is used, then you are probably secure from most eavesdroppers. However, absolute security cannot be guaranteed. SSL only protects information while it is in transit. Whatever information you send is unprotected before it is transmitted by your browser and after it is received by the server.

Maintaining Privacy

How private is your interaction with the Web? Not very private. Whenever you request a document from a Web server, your request is usually logged by that server. The log record doesn't identify you by name, but it does include your IP address. If you use a static IP address then, you are positively identified. If you use a dynamic IP address, then the log information could apply to other users of your Internet service provider.

Both Navigator and Internet Explorer support cookies. When cookies were first introduced, they were the subject of some concern. Since they can be used to maintain information about a user on the user's browser, cookies were looked at as the instrument of Big Brother. As it turns out, cookies *can* be used to maintain information about users—that was their original intent. Is this a problem? It depends. If you look at cookies as a way to improve Web services, then you'll want to keep them. If you look at cookies as a means to spy on you then your best bet is to periodically delete the `cookies.txt` file. This will let you use cookies when you need to and will make it difficult for anyone to maintain consistent information about you.

Summary

In this chapter, you learned about Web security from the perspective of the Webmaster and the user. You learned about the security issues related to Web site development and how to protect your personal computer from Web-based attacks. You should now be able to develop your Web applications with a better understanding of the security issues involved.

This is the final chapter of the book. Thanks for staying the course. I hope that it helped you to learn JavaScript well enough that you'll be able to use it effectively and creatively in your Web applications. Be sure to check out the book's Web page at *http://www.jaworski.com/javascript/*. If you have any questions, you can e-mail me at *jamie@jaworski.com*.

PART VIII

Appendixes

HTML Reference

- Document Structure and Text Markup

- Anchors and Links

- Images and Image Maps

- Forms, Tables, and Embedded Objects

- Scripting

- Applets

- Style Sheets, Layers, and Character Entities

- Colors

This appendix is a quick reference manual for the Hypertext Markup Language. It shows you the basics of creating HTML documents and discusses popular tags in summary form. Note that JavaScript-specific event-handling attributes are not covered. These attributes are identified and discussed in Chapter 4.

Document Structure

HTML documents begin with the `<HTML>` tag and end with the `</HTML>` tag. Between these tags you may define a document head by using the `<HEAD>` and `</HEAD>` tags, a document body by using the `<BODY>` and `</BODY>` tags, or a frame set by using the `<FRAMESET>` and `</FRAMESET>` tags. If a head is supplied then it must precede the body or frame set. A document may not contain both a body and a frame set. Only one head, body, or frame set may be included in a single document.

Document Head

The document head contains tags that apply to the document as a whole (rather than tags for specific markup). Tags that may be placed in the head are as follows:

- The `<TITLE>` and `</TITLE>` tags identify the document's title.
- The `<STYLE>` and `</STYLE>` tags identify a style sheet.
- The `<LINK>` tag references an external document, such as an external style sheet.
- The `<SCRIPT>` and `</SCRIPT>` tags reference embedded scripts, such as JavaScript.
- The `<ISINDEX>` tag creates a one-field search form.
- The `<BASE>` tag identifies the document's base URL.
- The `<META>` tag identifies document properties.

NOTE   The `<STYLE>` and `<LINK>` tags are covered in the "Style Sheets" section later in this chapter and the `<SCRIPT>` tag is covered in the "Scripting" section.

Document Body

The <BODY> tag defines the following attributes:

- BACKGROUND—The document's background image.
- BGCOLOR—The document's background color.
- TEXT—The default text color.
- LINK—The color of unfollowed links.
- ALINK—The color of activated links.
- VLINK—The color of visited links.

The body of an HTML document also contains HTML tags that are used to *mark up* the document layout and display. These tags are organized into the following categories:

- **Text Markup**
- **Links**
- **Images and Image Maps**
- **Forms**
- **Tables**
- **Embedded Objects**
- **Scripts**
- **Applets**
- **Layers**
- **Styles**

The tags corresponding to each of the above categories are discussed in subsequent sections of this appendix.

Frame Sets

The <FRAMESET> and </FRAMESET> tags are used to identify multiframe documents and replace the <BODY> tags. The <FRAMESET> tags surround zero or more `<FRAME>` tags, which specify the documents to be loaded within the frames of a frame set.

The attributes of the `<FRAMESET>` tag include the ROWS and COLS attributes. These attributes describe the size of the rows or columns that comprise the frame set. Their values are written in the form "`p1,p2,...pn`", where `p1` through `pn` identify the size of the frame as a row or column. The `*` value may be used for `p1` through `pn` to indicate "whatever space remains."

The attributes of the `<FRAME>` tag are NAME and SRC. The NAME attribute names the frame so that it can be referenced within HTML and JavaScript. The SRC attribute identifies the document to be loaded into the frame.

NOTE Multiple nested frames can be created by identifying documents that contain next-level frame sets, via the SRC attribute of the `<FRAME>` tag.

The `<NOFRAMES>` and `</NOFRAMES>` tags display alternative text for frames.

Comments

HTML comments begin with `<!--` and end with `-->`.

Text Markup

The body of an HTML document may contain the following text markup tags:

- **Headings**—Six levels of headings are supported, identified as H1 through H6. The tags `<Hn>` and `</Hn>` are used to identify level *n* headings where *n* is 1 through 6. The heading tags define the ALIGN attribute, which is used to align the heading as LEFT, CENTER, or RIGHT.

- **Paragraphs**—Marked using the `<P>` and `</P>` tags. Paragraphs use the ALIGN attribute in the same way as headings.

- **Line Breaks**—Marked by `<BR>`. The CLEAR attribute (LEFT, RIGHT, ALL) specifies that the line break should move down past floating images in the left, right, and both margins. The `<WBR>` tag is used to identify a possible breaking position. The `<NOBRK>` and `</NOBRK>` tags are used to identify where line breaks should not occur.

- **Division**—The `<DIV>` and `</DIV>` tags identify a block of text. The `ALIGN` attribute may be used in the same way as headings.

- **Centered Text**—The `<CENTER>` and `</CENTER>` tags identify a division of centered text.

- **Spacing**—The `<SPACER>` tag is used to insert blank space into a document. Its `TYPE` attribute specifies the direction of the space (`HORIZONTAL`, `VERTICAL`, or `BLOCK`). The `HEIGHT`, `WIDTH`, and `SIZE` attributes specify its dimensions. The `ALIGN` attribute identifies how spaces of type `BLOCK` are to be aligned with respect to surrounding text.

- **Multicolumn Text**—Marked by `<MULTICOL>` and `</MULTICOL>`. The `COLS` attribute identifies the number of columns. The `WIDTH` attribute identifies the column width. The `GUTTER` attribute specifies the number of pixels between columns.

- **Addresses**—E-mail or postal addresses are identified using the `<ADDRESS>` and `</ADDRESS>` tags.

- **Block Quotations**—Marked using the `<BLOCKQUOTE>` and `</BLOCKQUOTE>` tags.

- **Preformatted Text**—Marked using `<PRE>` and `</PRE>`.

- **Example Listings**—Marked by `<XMP>` and `</XMP>`, `<LISTING>` and `</LISTING>`, or `<PLAINTEXT>` and `</PLAINTEXT>`.

- **Lists**:

  - Unordered lists—The `<UL>` and `</UL>` tags surround individual list items which are identified using the `<LI>` tags. List items are marked with bullets as specified by the `TYPE` attribute. The `COMPACT` attribute specifies that a list's display should be compacted when possible. It may be used with any type of list.

  - Ordered lists—The `<OL>` and `</OL>` tags surround individual list items which are identified using the `<LI>` tags. List items are numbered using the numbering style specified by the `TYPE` and `START` attributes.

- Directory lists—The `<DIR>` and `</DIR>` tags surround list items that are to be formatted as a multicolumn directory listing.

- Menu lists—The `<MENU>` and `</MENU>` tags surround list items that are to be formatted as a text menu.

- Definition lists—The `<DL>` and `</DL>` tags surround individual list items which are identified using the `<DT>` and `</DT>` and `<DD>` and `</DD>` tags. The `<DT>` and `</DT>` tags identify the term being defined. The `<DD>` and `</DD>` tags provide the term's definition.

- **Logical Formatting Tags**:

  - Emphasis—`<EM>` and `</EM>`.

  - Strong emphasis—`<STRONG>` and `</STRONG>`.

  - Definition—`<DFN>` and `</DFN>`.

  - Program code—`<CODE>` and `</CODE>`.

  - Sample output—`<SAMP>` and `</SAMP>`.

  - Text entered by a user —`<KBD>` and `</KBD>`.

  - Variables—`<VAR>` and `</VAR>`.

  - Citations—`<CITE>` and `</CITE>`.

- **Physical Formatting Tags**:

  - Boldface—`<B>` and `</B>`.

  - Italic—`<I>` and `</I>`.

  - Underline—`<U>` and `</U>`.

  - Strikeout—`<STRIKE>` and `</STRIKE>`.

  - Teletype—`<TT>` and `</TT>`.

  - Blinking—`<BLINK>` and `</BLINK>`.

- **Font Properties**:

  - Base font—`<BASEFONT>`. The `SIZE` attribute may be 1 through 7 to set the base font size.

  - Font—`<FONT>` and `</FONT>`. Sets the font for selected text based on the `SIZE` and `COLOR` attributes.

- Bigger font—`<BIG>` and `</BIG>`.
- Smaller font—`<SMALL>` and `</SMALL>`.
- Superscript—`<SUP>` and `</SUP>`.
- Subscript—`<SUB>` and `</SUB>`.

Anchors and Links

The destination anchor of a link is inserted into a document using the `<A>` and `</A>` anchor tags. These tags surround the text or image that is to serve as the anchor. The `NAME` attribute is used to name the anchor.

The `<A>` and `</A>` tags are also used to identify the source anchor of a link. When used in this manner, the `HREF` attribute is set to the URL of the link's destination. The `TARGET` attribute is used to identify the window or frame in which the destination document is to be displayed.

NOTE An anchor can be used as both a source and destination of a link.

Images and Image Maps

Images are inserted into documents using the `<IMG>` tag. This tag has the following attributes:

- `SRC`—Identifies the URL of the image.
- `NAME`—Identifies the image's name.
- `ALT`—Identifies alternative text to be displayed in place of the image.
- `BORDER`—Identifies the width of the image's border in pixels.
- `HEIGHT` and `WIDTH`—Identifies the dimensions of the image display area.

- HSPACE and VSPACE—Identifies the horizontal and vertical spacing of the margins around the image.

- LOWSRC—Identifies the URL of a low resolution image to be loaded while the higher resolution image specified by the SRC tag is being loaded.

- ISMAP—Identifies an image as a server-side image map.

- USEMAP—Identifies the URL and name of a client-side image map. The attribute value is written as *URL#name* where *name* is the name of the map.

- ALIGN—Used to specify the alignment of the image. Values are LEFT, RIGHT, TOP, ABSMIDDLE, ABSBOTTOM, TEXTTOP, MIDDLE, BASELINE, or BOTTOM.

Horizontal Rules

The <HR> tag is used to insert a horizontal line in a document. It takes the following attributes:

- ALIGN—Specifies the alignment of the line as CENTER, LEFT, or RIGHT.

- NOSHADE —Specifies that the line is not to be shaded.

- SIZE—Specifies the thickness of the line in pixels.

- WIDTH—Specifies the width of the line in pixels.

Client-Side Image Maps

The <MAP> and </MAP> tags are used to identify a client-side image map. The NAME attribute identifies the image map's name so that it can be referred to in a URL. <AREA> tags are placed between the <MAP> and </MAP> tags to associate URLs with specific areas of a client-side image map. <AREA> tags have the following attributes:

- NAME—Names the area.

- SHAPE—Identifies the geometrical shape of the area (RECT, POLY, CIRCLE, or DEFAULT).

- COORDS—Specifies the shape's geometrical coordinates.

- HREF—Identifies the URL associated with the area.

- NOHREF—Specifies that the area is not to be associated with a URL.

- TARGET—Identifies the window or frame where the results of an image map link are to be displayed.

When the SHAPE attribute is set to RECT, the COORDS attribute takes a value of the form "x1,y1,x2,y2" where (x1,y1) is the upper left corner of a rectangle and (x2,y2) is its lower right corner.

When SHAPE="POLY" then COORDS may be used to specify the vertices of a polygon of up to 100 sides. The attribute value is of the form "x1,y1, ..., xn,yn" where (x1,y1) through (xn,yn) represent adjacent vertices of the polygon. The last vertex (xn,yn) is connected to the first vertex (x1,y1) to close the polygon.

When SHAPE="CIRCLE" then COORDS is set to a string of the form "x1,y1,x2, y2" where (x1,y1) is the center of the circle and (x2,y2) is a point on the circle's perimeter.

When SHAPE="DEFAULT" then COORDS is not used.

Server-Side Image Maps

Server-side image maps are identified by including the ISMAP attribute in an <IMG> tag and surrounding the <IMG> tag by <A> and </A> tags. The HREF attribute of the <A> tag is set to the URL of the server's image map program. A file is specified on the server to map geometrical areas to URLs. The name of this file and syntax of the image map file varies according to the server vendor.

Forms

Forms are identified using the <FORM> and </FORM> tags. The <FORM> tag has the following attributes:

- NAME—The form's name.

- ACTION—The URL to which the form's data is to be submitted.

- METHOD—The HTTP method associated with form submission.

- ENCTYPE—The encoding to be used with the form's data.

- `TARGET`—The name of the window or frame to which the form's output is displayed.

Individual form elements are specified using the `<INPUT>`, `<SELECT>`, and `<TEXTAREA>` tags.

The `<INPUT>` Tag

The `<INPUT>` tag is used to specify a range of form elements depending on the value of the `TYPE` attribute:

- `BUTTON`—The `VALUE` attribute is used to label the button.

- `CHECKBOX`—The `CHECKED` attribute is used to set the default state of the checkbox to checked. The `VALUE` attribute specifies the value associated with the checkbox.

- `FILE`—The `VALUE` attribute specifies the default name of the file to be uploaded.

- `HIDDEN`—The `VALUE` attribute specifies the initial value of the field.

- `IMAGE`—The `SRC` attribute identifies the URL of the image. The `ALIGN` attribute may be set to `LEFT`, `RIGHT`, `TOP`, `BOTTOM`, `BASELINE`, `MIDDLE`, `TEXTTOP`, `ABSMIDDLE`, or `ABSBOTTOM`.

- `PASSWORD`—The `VALUE` attribute specifies the default value. The `MAXLENGTH` attribute specifies the maximum field length. The `SIZE` attribute specifies the size of the displayed field.

- `RADIO`—The `CHECKED` attribute identifies whether the button is checked by default. The `VALUE` attribute identifies the value associated with the radio button.

- `RESET`—The `VALUE` attribute identifies the button's label.

- `SUBMIT`—The `VALUE` attribute identifies the button's label.

- `TEXT`—The `VALUE` attribute specifies the default value. The `MAXLENGTH` attribute specifies the maximum field length. The `SIZE` attribute specifies the size of the displayed field.

The `NAME` attribute is used to name all input elements. When used with radio buttons, it names the radio button group.

The <SELECT> Tag

The <SELECT> and </SELECT> tags are used to identify selection lists. The <SELECT> tag has the following attributes:

- NAME—Names the selection list.
- SIZE—Identifies the displayed size of the selection list.
- MULTIPLE—Allows multiple selections from a list.

The <SELECT> tags surround list elements that are specified using the <OPTION> and </OPTION> tags. The VALUE attribute of the <OPTION> tag identifies the value that is returned when the option is selected. The SELECTED attribute identifies an option as selected by default.

The <TEXTAREA> Tag

The <TEXTAREA> and </TEXTAREA> tags define a multiple-line text area. The text surrounded by these tags is displayed as default text in the form element. The NAME attribute names the text area. The ROWS and COLS attributes display the dimensions of the text area. The WRAP attribute may be set to OFF, HARD, or SOFT to identify how text is to be wrapped in the text area.

The <KEYGEN> Tag

The <KEYGEN> tag is used with forms to submit a public key and challenge string with a form. The NAME attribute names the key/challenge as a form element and the CHALLENGE attribute identifies the challenge string.

Tables

The <TABLE> and </TABLE> tags mark the beginning and end of a table. The <TR> and </TR> tags mark individual rows of a table. The <TD> and </TD> tags mark the beginning and end of a table cell. The <TH> and </TH> tags mark heading cells. The <CAPTION> and </CAPTION> tags appear between the <TABLE> and </TABLE> tags and identify the table's caption.

The `<TABLE>` tag has the following attributes:

- `ALIGN`—Align table on `LEFT` or `RIGHT` margins.
- `BGCOLOR`—Table background color.
- `BORDER`—Size of table border.
- `CELLPADDING`—Space between cell border and content.
- `CELLSPACING`—Space between individual cells.
- `HEIGHT`—Height of table.
- `WIDTH`—Width of table.
- `HSPACE`—Left and right margins.
- `VSPACE`—Top and bottom margins.

The `<TR>` tag has the following attributes:

- `ALIGN`—Align `LEFT`, `CENTER`, or `RIGHT`.
- `BGCOLOR`—Row background color.
- `VALIGN`—Specifies how text is to be vertically aligned within table cells: `BASELINE`, `BOTTOM`, `MIDDLE`, or `TOP`.

The `<TH>` and `<TD>` tags have the following attributes:

- `ALIGN`—Align `LEFT`, `CENTER`, or `RIGHT`.
- `BGCOLOR`—The background color of the table cell.
- `ROWSPAN`—The number of rows spanned by a table cell.
- `COLSPAN`—The number of columns spanned by a table cell.
- `NOWRAP`—Specifies that lines within a cell not be wrapped.
- `VALIGN`—Specifies how text is to be vertically aligned within table cells: `BASELINE`, `BOTTOM`, `MIDDLE`, or `TOP`.

The `ALIGN` attribute of the `<CAPTION>` tag may be set to `BOTTOM` or `TOP`.

Embedded Objects

Embedded objects are identified using the <EMBED> tag. Its attributes are as follows:

- ALIGN—Alignment of text around the object. (LEFT, RIGHT, TOP, or BOTTOM).

- BORDER—Size of border in pixels.

- FRAMEBORDER—Does the embedded object have a frame border? ("YES" or "NO").

- HEIGHT—Height of the display area in pixels.

- HIDDEN—Is it hidden? (TRUE or FALSE).

- HSPACE— Size of the left and right margins in pixels.

- NAME—The name of the embedded object.

- PALETTE—Color palette to use. (FOREGROUND or BACKGROUND).

- PLUGINSPAGE—URL of plug-in installation instructions.

- SRC—URL of the embedded object.

- TYPE—The MIME type of the embedded object.

- VSPACE—Top and bottom margins in pixels.

- WIDTH—Width of the display area in pixels.

The <NOEMBED> and </NOEMBED> tags surround text that is to be displayed by browsers that are incapable of using a plug-in.

Scripting

Client-side scripts are included in an HTML document using the <SCRIPT> and </SCRIPT> tags. The LANGUAGE attribute is set to the type of scripting language being used. The SRC attribute identifies the URL of a file containing script code.

The <NOSCRIPT> and </NOSCRIPT> tags specify alternative text for browsers that do not support the scripting language.

The `<SERVER>` and `</SERVER>` tags are used to insert server-side JavaScript into a LiveWire document.

Applets

Java applets are included in HTML documents using the `<APPLET>` and `</APPLET>` tags. The `<APPLET>` tag has the following attributes:

- `ALIGN`—Alignment of the applet with respect to the document margins and surrounding text. Values are `LEFT`, `RIGHT`, `TOP`, `ABSMIDDLE`, `ABSBOTTOM`, `TEXTTOP`, `MIDDLE`, `BASELINE`, or `BOTTOM`.
- `ALT`—Alternative text to be displayed by browsers in lieu of the applet.
- `ARCHIVE`—The URL of a Java archive file.
- `CODE`—The URL of the applet code.
- `CODEBASE`—The default location where applet resources can be found.
- `HEIGHT` and `WIDTH`—The dimensions of the applet display area.
- `HSPACE` and `VSPACE`—The horizontal and vertical spacing around the applet.
- `MAYSCRIPT` —Allows an applet to access JavaScript via LiveConnect.
- `NAME`—The name of the applet.

The `<PARAM>` tag is used to pass values to an applet. This tag is inserted between the `<APPLET>` and `</APPLET>` tags. The `NAME` attribute names a variable being passed to the applet and the `VALUE` attribute identifies its value.

Style Sheets

Both JavaScript and cascading style sheets are identified in a document's head using either the `<STYLE>` and `</STYLE>` tags or the `<LINK>` tag. The `<STYLE>` tag specifies document-internal style sheets and the `<LINK>` tag specifies document-external style sheets.

The `TYPE` attribute of the `<STYLE>` tag identifies the type of style sheet being defined. JavaScript style sheets have the value `text/javascript`. Chapter 23 covers JavaScript style sheets. Cascading style sheets set the value of `TYPE` to `CSS`. Cascading style sheets are covered in "The W3C Recommendation, Cascading Style Sheets, level 1," which is available at the following URL:

http://www.w3.org/pub/WWW/TR/REC-CSS1

The attributes of the `<LINK>` tag when used with style sheets are:

- TYPE—Set to text/javascript or CSS.
- REL—Set to STYLESHEET.
- HREF—Set to the URL of the style definitions.
- TITLE—Assigns a title to the external file.

The `<SPAN>` and `</SPAN>` tags are used to apply a style to selected text. The attributes of the `<SPAN>` tag are:

- STYLE—Defines a style to be used with the `<SPAN>` tag.
- CLASS—Applies a class of styles to the spanned text.
- IDS—Applies a uniquely identified style to the spanned text.

Layers

Document layers are identified using the `<LAYER>` and `</LAYER>` tags or the `<ILAYER>` and `</ILAYER>` tags. The contents of the layer is inserted between the tags. The `<LAYER>` and `</LAYER>` tags identify fixed position layers. The `<ILAYER>` and `</ILAYER>` tags identify a layer that is formatted in the natural document flow. Both sets of tags have the same attributes:

- BGCOLOR—The layer's background color.
- BACKGROUND—The layer's background image.
- NAME—The name of the layer.

- LEFT and TOP—The horizontal and vertical position of the layer (absolute or relative).

- SRC—The URL of a layer's contents.

- Z-INDEX, ABOVE and BELOW—The ordering of the layer with respect to other layers.

- WIDTH—The width of the layer's display area.

- CLIP—The viewable clipping rectangle of the layer.

- VISIBILITY—Whether the layer is visible or hidden.

Chapter 24 covers the use of layers.

Character Entities

Special characters are inserted into HTML documents using character entities. Two types of entities are supported—named character entities and numbered character entities. A complete list of these character entities may be found at the following URL:

http://developer.netscape.com/library/documentation/htmlguid/entities.htm

Colors

The named color values supported by Netscape Communicator are specified by JavaScript, and are listed at the end of the JavaScript appendix (Appendix B). Examples and descriptions of these colors may be found at the following URL:

http://developer.netscape.com/library/documentation/htmlguid/colortab.htm

APPENDIX

B

JavaScript Reference

- Objects

- Functions

- Color Constants

This appendix provides a quick reference manual for the objects, properties, methods, events, and functions of the JavaScript 1.2 language. Properties, methods, and event handlers are described with the objects to which they apply. The functions and predefined JavaScript colors are listed at the end of this appendix.

Objects

The following sections describe the predefined JavaScript objects.

In this appendix, you'll notice that some object names are capitalized (e.g., `Form` and `Frame`) while others are not (e.g., `document` and `location`). This is consistent with Netscape's convention of capitalizing object names. Object names appear in lowercase if they are used as a property of a higher-level object. Object names are capitalized if they are not a property of a higher-level object. For example, there is a `window.document` property but there is no `window.Frame` property.

All objects have the `eval(string)`, `toString([radix])`, and `valueOf()` methods:

- If the string value passed to the `eval()` method is an expression, then `eval()` returns the value of the expression. If the string value is a statement then the statement is executed.

- The `toString([radix])` method returns a string representation of the object. The optional radix parameter converts numeric values to the specified radix notation.

- The `valueOf()` method returns a primitive value associated with the object, or the object itself if no primitive value is associated with the object.

Since the `eval()`, `toString()`, and `valueOf()` methods are common to all objects, they are not identified in the following sections.

> **NOTE**
>
> Throughout this appendix, the properties that are described in the form of a question are properties whose attributes take a boolean value. For example, the description of the `complete` property of the `Image` object is, "Is the loading of the image complete?". The value of the `complete` attribute is set to `true` when the loading of the image is complete and `false` when the loading of the image is incomplete.

Anchor

Description: The destination (target) of a link.

Property of: `document`

Properties: None.

Additional Methods: None.

Event Handlers: None.

Applet

Description: A Java applet.

Property of: `document`

Properties: None.

Additional Methods: None.

Event Handlers: None.

Area

Description: An area of a client-side image map.

Property of: `document`

Properties:

- `hash`—The name of an anchor included in the associated URL.
- `host`—The full name or IP address of the host part of the URL.
- `hostname`—The *host:port* part of the URL.
- `href`—The entire URL.
- `pathname`—The path part of the URL.
- `port`—The port of the URL.
- `protocol`—The protocol part of the URL.
- `search`—The query string part of the URL.
- `target`—The target attribute of the link.

Additional Methods: None.

Event Handlers:

- `onMouseOut`
- `onMouseOver`

Array

Description: A JavaScript array.

Property of: This is not a property of any object.

Properties:

- `length`—The number of elements in the array.
- `prototype`—Used to create additional properties.

Additional Methods:

- `join([separator])`—Joins the elements of the array into a string. The optional separator is inserted between the array elements.
- `reverse()`—Reverses the elements of an array.
- `sort()`—Sorts the elements of an array.

Event Handlers: None.

Boolean

Description: Object representation of a boolean value.

Property of: This is not a property of any object.

Properties:

- `prototype`—Used to create additional properties.

Additional Methods: None.

Event Handlers: None.

Button

Description: A button of a form.

Property of: Form

Properties:

- form—The form containing the button.
- name—The button's NAME attribute.
- type—The button's TYPE attribute.
- value—The button's VALUE attribute.

Additional Methods:

- blur()—Removes focus from the button.
- click()—Simulates the clicking of the button.
- focus()—Adds focus to the button.

Event Handlers:

- onBlur
- onClick
- onFocus

Checkbox

Description: A checkbox of a form.

Property of: Form

Properties:

- checked—Is the checkbox checked?
- defaultChecked—The default status of the checkbox.
- form—The form containing the checkbox.
- name—The checkbox's NAME attribute.

- `type`—The checkbox's TYPE attribute.
- `value`—The checkbox's VALUE attribute.

Additional Methods:

- `blur()`—Removes focus from the checkbox.
- `click()`—Simulates the clicking of the checkbox.
- `focus()`—Adds focus to the checkbox.

Event Handlers:

- `onBlur`
- `onClick`
- `onFocus`

Date

Description: An object representing a date and time.

Property of: This is not a property of any object.

Properties:

- `prototype`—Used to create additional properties.

Additional Methods:

- `getDate()`—Returns the day of the month of the `Date` object.
- `getDay()`—Returns the day of the week of the `Date` object.
- `getHours()`—Returns the hours value of the `Date` object.
- `getMinutes()`—Returns the minutes value of the `Date` object.
- `getMonth()`—Returns the month value of the `Date` object.
- `getSeconds()`—Returns the seconds value of the `Date` object.
- `getTime()`—Returns the number of milliseconds of the `Date` object since New Year's 1970.

- `getTimezoneOffset()`—Returns the local time zone offset.

- `getYear()`—Returns the year of the `Date` object.

- `parse(dateString)`—Converts *dateString* to the number of milliseconds since New Year's 1970.

- `setDate(dayOfMonth)`—Sets the day of the month of the `Date` object.

- `setHours(hours)`—Sets the hours value of the `Date` object.

- `setMinutes(minutes)`—Sets the minutes value of the `Date` object.

- `setMonth(month)`—Sets the month value of the `Date` object.

- `setSeconds(seconds)`—Sets the seconds value of the `Date` object.

- `setTime(time)`—Sets the time value of the `Date` object as the number of milliseconds since New Year's 1970.

- `setYear(year)`—Sets the year value of the `Date` object.

- `toGMTString()`—Returns the Universal Coordinated Time (UTC) value of the `Date` object as a string.

- `toLocaleString()`—Returns the string value of a `Date` object using local conventions.

- `UTC(year, month, day, [, hours] [, minutes] [, seconds])`—Returns the number of milliseconds since New Year's 1970 for the specified parameters.

Event Handlers: None.

document

Description: A document displayed in a window or frame.

Property of: `window`

Properties:

- `alinkColor`—The `ALINK` attribute of the document body.

- `anchors`—An array of all anchors in the document.

- `applets`—An array of all applets in the document.

- bgColor—The BGCOLOR attribute of the document body.
- cookie—The cookie values associated with the document.
- domain—The domain name of the host from which the document was retrieved.
- embeds—An array of all plug-ins of the document.
- fgColor—The TEXT attribute of the document body.
- forms—An array of all forms in the document.
- images—An array of all images in the document.
- layers—An array of all layers in a document.
- lastModified—The date when the document was last modified.
- linkColor—The LINK attribute of the document body.
- links—An array of all links in the document.
- referrer—The URL of the document from which the referenced document was linked.
- title—The document's title as specified by the <TITLE> tag.
- URL—The URL of the document.
- vlinkColor—The VLINK attribute of the document body.
- Named anchors, applets, image map areas, forms, images, and links are also properties of the document object.

Additional Methods:

- open([*mimeType*])—Opens the document for writing and associates it with the specified MIME type. The default MIME type is text/html.
- close()—Closes the document, causing the document to be updated with any previously written output.
- write(*expression1*, [... *expressionN*])—Writes the expression(s) to the document object.
- writeln(*expression1*, [... *expressionN*])—Same as write(), except that a new line character is appended to the output.

Event Handlers: None.

event

Description: An object representing an event.

Property of: This is not a property of any object.

Properties:

- x—The x-coordinate of the mouse when the event occurred.
- y—The y-coordinate of the mouse when the event occurred.

Additional Methods: None.

Event Handlers: None.

FileUpload

Description: A form's file upload element.

Property of: Form

Properties:

- form—The form containing the FileUpload object.
- name—The element's NAME attribute.
- type—The element's TYPE attribute.
- value—The element's VALUE attribute.

Additional Methods:

- blur()—Removes focus from the form element.
- focus()—Adds focus to the form element.

Event Handlers:

- onBlur
- onChange
- onFocus

Form

Description: An HTML form.

Property of: document

Properties:

- action—The form's ACTION attribute.
- elements—An array of form elements.
- encoding—The form's ENCTYPE attribute.
- length—The number of elements on a form.
- name—The form's NAME attribute.
- method—The form's METHOD attribute.
- target—The form's TARGET attribute.
- Form objects also have properties associated with named form elements.

Additional Methods:

- reset()—Simulates the clicking of the form's reset button.
- submit()—Submits the form.

Event Handlers:

- onReset
- onSubmit

Frame

Description: An HTML frame.

Property of: window

Properties:

- frames—An array of all sub-frames of a frame.
- name—The frame's NAME attribute.

- length—The number of sub-frames of a frame.
- parent—The frame of window containing the current frame.
- self—The current frame.
- window—The current frame.

Additional Methods:

- blur()—Removes focus from the frame.
- focus()—Adds focus to the frame.
- setTimeout(*expression, milliseconds*)—Creates a timeout and returns a timeout ID. The identified expression is evaluated after the specified number of milliseconds.
- clearTimeout(*timeoutID*)—Clears the identified timeout.

Event Handlers:

- onBlur
- onFocus

Function

Description: An object that is used to create functions.

Property of: This is not a property of any object.

Properties:

- arguments—An array of arguments to the function.
- caller—The function that invokes the referenced function.
- prototype—Used to create additional properties.

Additional Methods: None.

Event Handlers: None.

Hidden

Description: A hidden form field.

Property of: Form

Properties:

- form—The form containing the hidden field.
- name—The field's NAME attribute.
- type—The field's TYPE attribute.
- value—The field's VALUE attribute.

Additional Methods: None.

Event Handlers: None.

history

Description: A list of recent documents loaded into a window.

Property of: window

Properties:

- current—The URL of the current entry in the history object.
- length—The number of entries in the history object.
- next—The URL of the next entry in the history object.
- previous—The URL of the previous entry in the history object.

Additional Methods:

- back()—Go back one entry in the history list.
- forward()—Go forward one entry in the history list.
- go(relPos | string)—Go to a relative position within the history list (e.g., -2 or +3) or go to the closest URL matching string.

Event Handlers: None.

Image

Description: An image that is inserted in an HTML document.

Property of: `document`

Properties:

- `border`—The image's BORDER attribute.
- `complete`—Is the loading of the image complete?
- `height`—The image's HEIGHT attribute.
- `hspace`—The image's HSPACE attribute.
- `lowsrc`—The image's LOWSRC attribute.
- `name`—The image's NAME attribute.
- `prototype`—Used to create additional properties.
- `src`—The image's SRC attribute.
- `vspace`—The image's VSPACE attribute.
- `width`—The image's WIDTH attribute.

Additional Methods: None.

Event Handlers:

- `onAbort`
- `onError`
- `onLoad`

layer

Description: A document layer.

Property of: `document`

Properties:

- `above`—The layer above the referenced layer.
- `background`—The background image of the layer.

- `below`—The layer below the referenced layer.
- `bgcolor`—The background color of the layer.
- `clip`—The clipping region of the layer.
- `height`—The height of the layer's display area.
- `layers`—An array of sublayers of the referenced layer.
- `left`—The horizontal position of the layer.
- `name`—The layer's name.
- `parentLayer`—The layer that contains the referenced layer.
- `siblingAbove`—The layer above the referenced layer that has the same parent as the referenced layer.
- `siblingBelow`—The layer below the referenced layer that has the same parent as the referenced layer.
- `src`—The URL of the layer's contents.
- `top`—The vertical position of the layer.
- `visibility`—Is the layer visible?
- `width`—The width of the layer's display area.
- `zIndex`—The z-order of the layer.

Additional Methods:

- `offset(deltaX, deltaY)`—Moves the layer by the specified offset.
- `moveTo(x, y)`—Moves the layer to the specified position.
- `resize(width, height)`—Resizes the layer to the specified dimensions.
- `moveAbove(layer)`—Moves the referenced layer above the specified layer.
- `moveBelow(layer)`—Moves the referenced layer above the specified layer.

Event Handlers: None.

Link

Description: A hypertext (or image-based) link.

Property of: document

Properties:

- hash—The name of an anchor included in the associated URL.
- host—The full name or IP address of the host part of the URL.
- hostname—The host:port part of the URL.
- href—The entire URL.
- pathname—The path part of the URL.
- port—The port of the URL.
- protocol—The protocol part of the URL.
- search—The query string part of the URL.
- target—The target attribute of the link.

Additional Methods: None.

Event Handlers:

- onClick
- onMouseOut
- onMouseOver

location

Description: The URL of the document that is loaded in a window.

Property of: window

Properties:

- hash—The name of an anchor included in the URL.
- host—The full name or IP address of the host part of the URL.

- `hostname`—The host:port part of the URL.
- `href`—The entire URL.
- `pathname`—The path part of the URL.
- `port`—The port of the URL.
- `protocol`—The protocol part of the URL.
- `search`—The query string part of the URL.

Additional Methods:

- `reload([true])`—Causes the document that is currently loaded in a window to be reloaded.
- `replace(url)`—Loads the document specified by *url* over the current document in the history list.

Event Handlers: None.

Math

Description: A library of mathematical constants and functions.

Property of: This is not a property of any object.

Properties:

- `E`—Euler's constant.
- `LN2`—Natural log of 2.
- `LN10`—Natural log of 10.
- `LOG2E`—Base 2 log of E.
- `LOG10E`—Base 10 log of E.
- `PI`—Ratio of the circumference of a circle to its diameter.
- `SQRT1_2`—Square root of ½.
- `SQRT2`—Square root of 2.

Additional Methods: (Note: all trigonometric functions return radian values)

- `abs(x)`—The absolute value of x.

- `acos(x)`—The arc cosine of x.

- `asin(x)`—The arc sine of x.

- `atan(x)`—The arc tangent of x.

- `atan2(x,y)`—The angle from the x-axis to (x,y).

- `ceil(x)`—The least integer greater than or equal to x.

- `cos(x)`—The cosine of x.

- `exp(x)`—The exponential function of x.

- `floor(x)`—The greatest integer less than or equal to x.

- `log(x)`—The natural logarithm of x.

- `max(x,y)`—The greater of x and y.

- `min(x,y)`—The lesser of x and y.

- `pow(x,y)`—Returns x raised to the y power.

- `random()`—Returns a random number between 0 and 1.

- `round(x)`—The value of x returned to the nearest integer.

- `sin(x)`—The sine of x.

- `sqrt(x)`—The square root of x.

- `tan(x)`—The tangent of x.

Event Handlers: None.

MimeType

Description: An object representing a browser-supported MIME type.

Property of: `navigator`

Properties:

- `description`—The MIME type's description.

- enabledPlugin—The Plugin object corresponding to the MIME type.
- type—The name of the MIME type.
- suffixes—A string of possible file name extensions associated with the MIME type.

Additional Methods: None.

Event Handlers: None.

navigator

Description: A top-level object corresponding to the browser and its configuration and capabilities.

Property of: This is not a property of any object.

Properties:

- appCodeName—The browser's code name.
- appName—The browser's name.
- appVersion—The browser's version number.
- mimeTypes—An array of MIME types supported by the browser.
- plugins—An array of plug-ins installed on the browser.
- userAgent—The user-agent header associated with the browser.

Additional Methods:

- javaEnabled()—Is Java enabled for the browser?
- taintEnabled()—Is data tainting enabled for the browser?

Event Handlers: None.

Number

Description: An object representation of a number.

Property of: This is not a property of any object.

Properties:

- MAX_VALUE—The largest number.
- MIN_VALUE—The smallest number.
- NaN—Not a number value.
- NEGATIVE_INFINITY—Negative infinity.
- POSITIVE_INFINITY—Positive infinity.
- prototype—Used to create additional properties.

Additional Methods: None.

Event Handlers: None.

Option

Description: A form's select list option.

Property of: Form

Properties:

- defaultSelected—Is the option selected by default?
- index—The index of the option in the selection list.
- selected—Is it currently selected?
- text—The option's text label.
- value—The value returned by the option when selected.
- prototype—Used to create additional properties.

Additional Methods:

- blur()—Remove focus from option.
- focus()—Add focus to option.

Event Handlers:

- onBlur

- `onChange`
- `onFocus`

Password

Description: A password field of a form.

Property of: `Form`

Properties:

- `defaultValue`—The default value of the field.
- `form`—The form containing the field.
- `name`—The field's `NAME` attribute.
- `type`—The field's `TYPE` attribute.
- `value`—The field's `VALUE` attribute.

Additional Methods:

- `blur()`—Remove input focus from the field.
- `focus()`—Add input focus to the field.
- `select()`—Selects the field's contents.

Event Handlers:

- `onBlur`
- `onFocus`

Plugin

Description: A browser plug-in.

Property of: `navigator`

Properties:

- `description`—A description of the plug-in.

- `filename`—The file name of the plug-in.
- `length`—The number of MimeType objects associated with the plug-in.
- `name`—The plug-in's name.

Additional Methods: None.

Event Handlers: None.

Radio

Description: A radio button of a form.

Property of: `Form`

Properties:

- `checked`—Is the button checked?
- `defaultChecked`—Is the button checked by default?
- `form`—The form containing the button.
- `name`—The button's NAME attribute.
- `type`—The button's TYPE attribute.
- `value`—The button's VALUE attribute.

Additional Methods:

- `blur()`—Remove input focus from the button.
- `click()`—Simulates clicking of the button.
- `focus()`—Add input focus to the button.

Event Handlers:

- `onBlur`
- `onClick`
- `onFocus`

Reset

Description: A form's reset button.

Property of: `Form`

Properties:

- `form`—The form containing the button.
- `name`—The button's `NAME` attribute.
- `type`—The button's `TYPE` attribute.
- `value`—The button's `VALUE` attribute.

Additional Methods:

- `blur()`—Remove input focus from the button.
- `click()`—Simulates clicking of the button.
- `focus()`—Add input focus to the button.

Event Handlers:

- `onBlur`
- `onClick`
- `onFocus`

Select

Description: A selection list of a form.

Property of: `Form`

Properties:

- `form`—The form containing the selection list.
- `length`—The number of option values of the list.
- `name`—The selection list's `NAME` attribute.
- `options`—An array of the list's option value objects.

- selectedIndex—Index of the first selected option.
- type—The selection list's TYPE attribute.

Additional Methods:

- blur()—Adds input focus to the selection list.
- focus()—Removes input focus from the selection list.

Event Handlers:

- onBlur
- onChange
- onFocus

String

Description: A string object.

Property of: This is not a property of any object.

Properties:

- length—The length of the string.
- prototype—Used to create additional properties.

Additional Methods:

- anchor(*anchorName*)—Creates a named anchor.
- big()—Returns a string that is displayed using the <BIG> tag.
- blink()—Returns a string that is displayed using the <BLINK> tag.
- bold()—Returns a string that is displayed using the <B> tag.
- charAt(*index*)—Returns the character at the specified index within the string.
- fixed()—Returns a string that is displayed using the <TT> tag.

- `fontcolor(color)`—Returns a string that is displayed using the `<FONT COLOR="color">` tag.

- `fontsize(size)`—Returns a string that is displayed using the `<FONTSIZE="size">` tag.

- `indexOf(matchValue [,start])`—Returns the first index of the position where the string specified by `matchValue` is found within a string. The optional `start` parameter specifies where in the string searching should begin.

- `italics()`—Returns a string that is displayed using the `<I>` tag.

- `lastIndexOflink(matchValue [,start])`—Returns the last index of the position where the string specified by `matchValue` is found within a string. The optional `start` parameter specifies where in the string searching should begin.

- `small()`—Returns a string that is displayed using the `<SMALL>` tag.

- `split([separator])`—Returns an array of substrings separated by the separator character. If the separator is omitted then a one-element array is returned.

- `strike()`—Returns a string that is displayed using the `<STRIKE>` tag.

- `sub()`—Returns a string that is displayed using the `<SUB>` tag.

- `substring(i,j)`—Returns the substring from index *i* to index *j*.

- `sup()`—Returns a string that is displayed using the `<SUP>` tag.

- `toLowerCase()`—Returns a lowercase copy of the string.

- `toUpperCase()`—Returns an uppercase copy of the string.

Event Handlers: None.

Submit

Description: A form's submit button.

Property of: Form

Properties:

- `form`—The form containing the button.

- `name`—The button's NAME attribute.
- `type`—The button's TYPE attribute.
- `value`—The button's VALUE attribute.

Additional Methods:

- `blur()`—Remove input focus from the button.
- `click()`—Simulates clicking of the button.
- `focus()`—Add input focus to the button.

Event Handlers:

- `onBlur`
- `onClick`
- `onFocus`

Text

Description: A text field of a form.

Property of: `Form`

Properties:

- `defaultValue`—The default value of the field.
- `form`—The form containing the field.
- `name`—The field's NAME attribute.
- `type`—The field's TYPE attribute.
- `value`—The field's VALUE attribute.

Additional Methods:

- `blur()`—Remove input focus from the field.
- `focus()`—Add input focus to the field.
- `select()`—Selects the field's contents.

Event Handlers:

- onBlur
- onChange
- onFocus
- onSelect

Textarea

Description: A text area field of a form.

Property of: Form

Properties:

- defaultValue—The default value of the field.
- form—The form containing the field.
- name—The field's NAME attribute.
- type—The field's TYPE attribute.
- value—The field's VALUE attribute.

Additional Methods:

- blur()—Remove input focus from the field.
- focus()—Add input focus to the field.
- select()—Selects the field's contents.

Event Handlers:

- onBlur
- onChange
- onFocus
- onSelect

window

Description: A browser window.

Property of: This is not a property of any object.

Properties:

- `closed`—Is the window closed?
- `defaultStatus`—The window's default status message.
- `document`—The document that is loaded into the window.
- `frames`—An array of all frames contained in the window.
- `history`—The `history` object associated with the window.
- `length`—The number of frames in a window.
- `location`—The window's `location` object.
- `name`—The name of the window.
- `opener`—The name of the window which caused the referenced window to be opened.
- `parent`—The window containing the referenced window.
- `self`—This window.
- `status`—A window status message.
- `top`—The top-level window containing the referenced window.
- `window`—This window.
- Named `Frame` objects are also properties of a window.

Additional Methods:

- `alert("message")`—Displays an alert dialog box with the specified message.
- `blur()`—Removes input focus from the window.
- `clearInterval(intervalID)`—Clears the specified timeout interval.
- `clearTimeout(timeoutID)`—Clears the specified timeout.
- `close()`—Closes the window.

- `confirm("`*`message`*`")`—Displays a confirm dialog box with the specified message.

- `focus()`—Adds input focus to the window.

- `moveBy(`*`deltaX,deltaY`*`)`—Move the window by the specified offset.

- `moveTo(`*`x,y`*`)`—Move the window to the specified position.

- `open(`*`url, name`* `[,` *`options`*`])`—Opens a new window loading the document at the specified URL, assigning the window the identified name, and using the specified options. Returns a `window` object reference to the newly opened window.

- `prompt("`*`message`*`",` `[`*`defaultValue`*`])`—Displays a prompt dialog box with the specified message and default value.

- `resizeBy(`*`deltaX,deltaY`*`)`—Resize the window by the specified amount.

- `resizeTo(`*`width,height`*`)`—Resize the window to the specified dimensions.

- `scroll(`*`x,y`*`)`—Scroll the window to the specified position.

- `scrollBy(`*`deltaX,deltaY`*`)`—Scroll the window by the specified amount.

- `scrollTo(`*`x,y`*`)`—Scroll the window to the specified position.

- `setInterval(`*`exprOrFunc,milliseconds,` `[arguments]`*`)`—Repeatedly evaluates the expression or function after the specified number of milliseconds. If a function is specified then a comma-separated list of arguments to the function may also be supplied.

- `setTimeout(`*`exprOrFunc,milliseconds,` `[arguments]`*`)`—Evaluates the expression or function after the specified number of milliseconds. If a function is specified then a comma-separated list of arguments to the function may also be supplied.

Event Handlers:

- `onBlur`

- `onError`

- `onFocus`

- `onLoad`

- `onUnload`

Functions

The seven predefined JavaScript functions are described in the following sections.

escape(*string*)

Encodes a string in a suitable form to be passed as a query string of a URL.

Parameters:

- String to be encoded.

Return value: Encoded string value.

isNaN(*value*)

Returns `true` if the value passed to the function is not a number. Returns `false` otherwise.

Parameters:

- Value to be examined.

Return value: Boolean identifying whether the examined value is not a number.

parseFloat(*string*)

Parses a string and returns a floating-point number.

Parameters:

- String to be parsed.

Return value: Floating-point number parsed from the string.

parseInt(*string* [,*radix*])

Parses a string and returns an integer.

Parameters:

- String to be parsed.
- Radix of return value.

Return value: Integer parsed from the string.

taint(*element*)

Taints a JavaScript language element. Tainting prevents the element from being disclosed to a host other than the server from which the script originated.

Parameters:

- Element to be tainted (object, property, method, variable, or function).

Return value: A copy of the referenced element.

unescape(*string*)

Reverses the encoding performed by the `encode()` function.

Parameters:

- String to be decoded.

Return value: Decoded string.

untaint(*element*)

Removes tainting from a JavaScript language element.

Parameters:

- The element from which tainting is to be removed.

Return value: A copy of the referenced element.

Color Constants

The following JavaScript color constants are defined. A visual description of these colors can be found at the following URL:

http://developer.netscape.com/library/documentation/htmlguid/colortab.htm

aliceblue	darkgreen	gray
antiquewhite	darkkhaki	green
aqua	darkmagenta	greenyellow
aquamarine	darkolivegreen	honeydew
azure	darkorange	hotpink
beige	darkorchid	indianred
bisque	darkred	indigo
black	darksalmon	ivory
blanchedalmond	darkseagreen	khaki
blue	darkslateblue	lavender
blueviolet	darkslategray	lavenderblush
brown	darkturquoise	lawngreen
burlywood	darkviolet	lemonchiffon
cadetblue	deeppink	lightblue
chartreuse	deepskyblue	lightcoral
chocolate	dimgray	lightcyan
coral	dodgerblue	lightgoldenrodyellow
cornflowerblue	firebrick	lightgreen
cornsilk	floralwhite	lightgrey
crimson	forestgreen	lightpink
cyan	fuchsia	lightsalmon
darkblue	gainsboro	lightseagreen
darkcyan	ghostwhite	lightskyblue
darkgoldenrod	gold	lightslategray
darkgray	goldenrod	lightsteelblue

lightyellow	olive	seagreen
lime	olivedrab	seashell
limegreen	orange	sienna
linen	orangered	silver
magenta	orchid	skyblue
maroon	palegoldenrod	slateblue
mediumaquamarine	palegreen	slategray
mediumblue	paleturquoise	snow
mediumorchid	palevioletred	springgreen
mediumpurple	papayawhip	steelblue
mediumseagreen	peachpuff	tan
mediumslateblue	peru	teal
mediumspringgreen	pink	thistle
mediumturquoise	plum	tomato
mediumvioletred	powderblue	turquoise
midnightblue	purple	violet
mintcream	red	wheat
mistyrose	rosybrown	white
moccasin	royalblue	whitesmoke
navajowhite	saddlebrown	yellow
navy	salmon	yellowgreen
oldlace	sandybrown	

Java 1.1 Reference

- ■ Program Structure and Terminology

- ■ Program Elements

- ■ Statements and Local Variable Declarations

- ■ Operators

- ■ Java 1.1 API

This appendix provides a quick reference to the Java language and API (Application Programming Interface). It covers the Java Development Kit, version 1.1. For a formal (and complete) definition of the Java language, consult the Java Language Specification, available at JavaSoft's Web site: *http://www.javasoft.com*.

Program Structure and Terminology

Java programs consist of one or more compilation units, which are organized into packages. A *compilation unit* is a source-code Java file that declares classes and interfaces. A *class* is a collection of variable and method declarations. A *variable* is used to store data, and a *method* is used to perform operations on data. An *interface* specifies a set of methods that are to be implemented by a class. A *package* is a group of compilation units that have a common name space.

The *package* Statement

The `package` statement is used to identify the package to which a compilation unit belongs. It is the first statement in a compilation unit. Its syntax is as follows:

```
package PackageName ;
```

If a `package` statement is not identified in a compilation unit, then the compilation unit is put into a package with no name.

The *import* Statement

The `import` statement allows classes and interfaces that are declared in other packages to be used in the current compilation unit. Its syntax has three forms:

```
import PackageName.*;
```

or

```
import PackageName.ClassName;
```

or

```
import PackageName.InterfaceName;
```

The first form enables all classes and interfaces declared in *PackageName* to be used in the current compilation unit. The second and third forms are used to reference a specific class or interface within *PackageName*. A class or interface must be declared as `public` in order for it to be referenced outside of its package. Only one `public` class or interface is allowed in a compilation unit.

The *CLASSPATH*

The `CLASSPATH` environment variable is used to locate compiled Java classes that are declared in other packages. It consists of a list of directories and files that are separated by semicolons (Windows platforms) or colons (Unix platforms). When Java tools (compiler, interpreter, etc.) look for a particular class, they look in the directories identified in the `CLASSPATH`. For example, I put the following statement in my Windows 95 `AUTOEXEC.BAT` file to set the `CLASSPATH`:

```
SET CLASSPATH=.;C:\jdk1.1.1\lib\classes.zip
```

The above statement tells the Java tools to look first in the current directory (represented by the period) and then in the file `C:\jdk1.1.1\lib\classes.zip` to find referenced classes.

When Java is searching for the class, the package name is appended to the directories of the `CLASSPATH`, and each period in the package name is replaced by either a back slash (for Windows platforms) or a forward slash (on Unix platforms). For example, suppose my `CLASSPATH` is as specified above and that I reference the class `x.y.z`. In this case, the class `z` is identified as being in the `x.y` package. Based on the `CLASSPATH` and the `x.y` package name, Java tools will look for the `x\y\z.class` file in the current directory or in the files contained in the zipped file `C:\jdk1.1.1\lib\classes.zip`.

The *main()* Method

The entry point for a Java program is the `main()` method of the class that takes the name of the Java program. The `main()` method is declared as follows:

```
public static void main(String args[]) {
  . . .
}
```

The `args[]` array is an array of `String` objects that are used to pass values to the program. The first value is passed via `args[0]`.

Program Elements

Java programs are written in the Unicode character set (Version 2.0), which is upward-compatible with ASCII. The following subsections describe the elements of a Java compilation unit.

Comments

Java provides three kinds of comments. The first two forms are used in the same manner as JavaScript:

```
// This comment continues till the end of the current line.

/* This comment
   spans multiple
   lines. */
```

The third comment form is used to identify information to be used by the Java documentation tool (javadoc):

```
/** This is
a multi-line comment
that is used by the javadoc tool. */
```

It begins with /** and ends with */.

Java comments cannot be nested.

Identifiers

An identifier is a Java name. Identifiers are used to name Java language elements such as classes, variables, methods, etc. An identifier is a sequence of one or more characters that can include letters (including Unicode letters), digits, the underscore character (_), or the dollar sign character ($)—but see the following note for why you should actually avoid using the dollar sign. An identifier can be of any length, but it *must* begin with a letter or the underscore character.

An identifier cannot have the same spelling as a keyword (listed in the following section), or the literal values true, false, or null.

> **NOTE**
>
> **$** The reason you should not use a dollar sign with Java identifiers is that dollar signs are meaningful in a different way to a Java compiler, and the compiler may act in a way you didn't intend when it comes to dealing with them.

Keywords

The following keywords are reserved by Java and cannot be used as identifiers:

abstract	default	if	private	throw
boolean	do	implements	protected	throws
break	double	import	public	transient
byte	else	instanceof	return	try
case	extends	int	short	void
catch	final	interface	static	volatile
char	finally	long	super	while
class	float	native	switch	
const	for	new	synchronized	
continue	goto	package	this	

Data Types

Java supports two basic types of data: *primitive* types and *reference* types, as described in the following sections.

Primitive Types and Literals

Java supports eight primitive types. They are described in Table C.1.

Integer constants may be written in octal or hexadecimal using the same conventions as JavaScript.

Character literals are represented by putting the character within single quotes. The single quote, double quote, and back slash character are escaped. The back slash character is the escape code. Table C.2 lists the Java escape codes.

TABLE C.1   Primitive Java Types

Type	Bits	Literal Values	Description
byte	8	Integer constants.	1-byte signed integer.
char	16	Character constants.	2-byte Unicode character.
short	16	Integer constants.	2-byte signed integer.
int	32	Integer constants.	4-byte signed integer.
long	64	Integer constants. Use '1' or 'L' suffix to indicate long.	8-byte signed integer.
float	32	Floating point constants.	4-byte floating point value.
double	64	Floating point constants.	8-byte floating point value.
boolean	—	true false	Boolean data type used for logical expressions.

NOTE: The constant NaN is a numeric value that stands for "not a number." It is used to indicate numerical errors or overflows.

TABLE C.2   Character Escape Codes

Escape Code	Character
\b	backspace
\f	form feed
\n	line feed
\r	carriage return
\t	tab
\'	single quote
\"	double quote
\\	back slash

Unicode characters can be escaped by following a back slash with a 16-bit octal value or by '\u' or '\U' followed by a 4-digit hexadecimal code.

String Literals String types are not primitive types in Java. Strings are objects of the String class. String literals are enclosed in double quotes.

The *null* Literal The null value is used to indicate that a variable does not reference a primitive value or an object.

Reference Types

Reference types consist of references to Java objects: arrays, class instances, and interface instances. All three support the methods of the Object class, which is the top-most class in the Java class hierarchy.

Arrays The elements of arrays are accessed using references of the form *arrayName*[*indexValue*], where *arrayName* is the name of the array and *indexValue* is an expression that evaluates to a positive integer.

Class Instances Instances of classes are created using the new operator. The variables and methods of classes are referenced using the object.variable and object.method() notation used in JavaScript.

Interface Instances An interface is a set of methods and constant declarations. Interface references are to instances of classes that implement a particular Java interface.

Variables

Variables are identifiers that refer to typed storage locations. They can hold primitive values; they can refer to arrays, class instances, or interface instances; or they can refer to the null reference type.

Declarations

Declarations are used to introduce language elements into a compilation unit. Typical declarations include class declarations, variable declarations, constructor declarations, method declarations, and interface declarations.

Class Declarations

Classes are declared using the following syntax:

```
[modifiers] class name [extends superclass] [implements
interfaceList] {
    class body
}
```

Modifiers are optional keywords (`abstract`, `public`, and `final`) that specify the class's behavior. The `abstract` keyword is used to indicate a class that cannot be instantiated because it is incomplete. Abstract classes are used to develop partial classes whose implementations are completed by subclasses. The `public` keyword is used to identify a class that can be accessed outside of its package. The `final` keyword is used to identify a class that cannot be subclassed.

The *name* identifies the class name. The optional `extends` clause is used to identify the direct superclass of a class. The optional `implements` clause is used to identify one or more interfaces implemented by a class. The *class body* may contain variable, constructor, and method declarations.

Variable Declarations

Variables are declared using the following syntax:

```
[modifiers] type name [initialization] ;
```

Allowed variable *modifiers* are `public`, `private`, `protected`, `final`, `static`, `volatile`, and `transient`. The `public` modifier allows a variable to be referenced anywhere that the class can be referenced. The `private` modifier limits access to a variable to the class in which it is defined. The `protected` modifier limits access to a variable to the class in which it is defined and its subclasses. The `final` modifier is used to identify a variable as a constant. The `static` modifier is used to identify a variable that applies to the class as a whole and not to any specific class instances. The `volatile` modifier is used to identify variables that may be updated asynchronously. The `transient` modifier identifies variables that should not be saved when an object is written to permanent storage.

The *type* may refer to a primitive data type, a class name, or an interface name. The variable *name* may be followed by one or more bracket pairs [ ] to indicate that the variable refers to an array. The optional *initialization* is used to assign a value to the variable. An array is initialized by assigning it to a comma-separated list of values enclosed by curly braces { }.

Constructor Declarations

A constructor is declared using the following syntax:

```
[modifiers] className([parameters]) [throws exceptions] {
  constructor body
}
```

Constructor *modifiers* are `public`, `private`, and `protected`. They are used the same way they are with variables. The *className* is the name of the class to which the constructor applies. The *parameters* are a comma-separated list of parameter declarations of the form `type parameterName`. The optional `throws` clause is used to identify the exceptions that may be thrown by the constructor. Exceptions are used to indicate errors or other anomalous conditions.

The constructor body consists of local variable declarations and statements. The first statement in the constructor body may be of the form `this(parameters)` or `super(parameters)`. A statement of the form `this(parameters)` causes a constructor of the current class that matches the parameter list to be invoked. A statement of the form `super(parameters)` causes a constructor of the superclass of the current class that matches the parameter list to be invoked. If neither of these statements appear as the first statement of a constructor, then the `super()` constructor is invoked by default.

Method Declarations

Non-constructor methods are declared using the following syntax:

```
[modifiers] type name(parameters) [throws exceptions] {
  method body
}
```

The allowed *modifiers* are `public`, `private`, `protected`, `abstract`, `final`, `static`, `native`, and `synchronized`, as described below:

- The `public`, `private`, and `protected` modifiers are used in the same way as variables.

- The `abstract` keyword is used to identify a method that has no body. You must use a semicolon (`;`) in place of the missing body and its surrounding brackets. Abstract methods are only declared in abstract classes and interfaces.

- The `final` modifier identifies a method that cannot be overridden in a subclass.

- The `static` modifier is used to identify a method that applies to the class as a whole and not an instance of the class. Static methods can only access static variables.

- The `native` modifier identifies a method that is implemented outside of Java.

- The `synchronized` keyword is used to support concurrent access to objects.

The *type* identifies the type of the value returned by the method invocation. The `void` type may be used to identify that a value is not returned.

The *name* identifies the method name.

The *parameters* and *throws* clause are used the way they would be used with constructors.

The *method body* consists of the local variable declarations and statements used to implement the body.

Interface Declarations

Interfaces are declared using the following syntax:

```
[modifiers] interface name [extends extendedInterface] {
    interface body
}
```

The allowed interface *modifiers* are `public` and `abstract`. However, since all interfaces are `abstract`, the `abstract` modifier does not need to be specified. A `public` interface may be accessed outside of its package. The *name* is used to identify the interface. The `extends` clause identifies any interface that the current interface extends. If one interface extends another interface then the declarations of the extended interface apply to the extending interface. The *interface body* consists of method and `static` variable declarations.

Statements and Local Variable Declarations

Java statements are identified in the bodies of constructors and methods. Java provides a number of statements that are very similar to those of JavaScript. A Java statement is terminated by a semicolon.

Statement Block

A statement block consists of zero or more statements or local variable declarations enclosed within curly braces { }. A statement block may appear anywhere that a single statement may appear. Because the closing brace serves to indicate the end of the block, a statement block does not need to be followed by a semicolon of its own.

Local Variable Declarations

Local variables are declared in the same manner as class variables except that local variable declarations do not include modifiers. The `this` variable is a predefined variable that refers to the current object. The `super` variable is a predefined variable that refers to the superclass of the current object.

Statement Labels

A statement may be labeled by preceding it by an integer or an identifier and a colon. The syntax of a labeled statement is as follows:

```
identifier: statement
```

or

```
integer: statement
```

Empty Statement

The empty statement performs no action. It consists of a single semicolon (;).

Assignment Statement

An assignment statement assigns a value or object reference to a variable. Its syntax is as follows:

```
variable = expression ;
```

The value or object reference resulting from the expression must be consistent with the variable's type.

Method Invocation

A method invocation statement invokes a method and optionally returns a value. The method may be invoked for a class (static method) or an instance of a class. The syntax of a method invocation is the same as in JavaScript.

If Statement

JavaScript supports if statements using the same syntax as JavaScript:

```
if (booleanExpression) statement1 else statement2
```

Either of the alternative statements, *statement1* or *statement2*, may be a statement block. If an alternative statement is not a statement block (i.e., if it is a single statement), then it must be terminated by a semicolon.

Switch Statement

JavaScript supports switch statements using the same syntax as JavaScript:

```
switch(expression) {
case value1: statements
   .
   .
   .
case valuen: statements
default: defaultStatements
}
```

The last statement in each group of statements is usually a break statement. The break statement is used in the same way as in JavaScript—to cause the remaining statement groups of the switch statement to be skipped so that program execution jumps to the statement following the switch statement.

For Statement

The syntax of the for statement is the same as it is in JavaScript:

```
for(indexAssignment ; loopTest ; iterationAssignment)
➡ iteratedStatement
```

Since Java requires all variables to be declared, the *index assignment* usually includes a declaration of the index variable.

While Statement

The syntax of the `while` statement is the same as it is in JavaScript:

```
while(booleanExpression) iteratedStatement
```

The *iterated statement* may be replaced by a statement block. In this case, the `while` statement does not require a terminating semicolon.

Do Statement

The syntax of the `do` statement is the same as it is in JavaScript:

```
do iteratedStatement while(booleanExpression) ;
```

Break Statement

The syntax of the `break` statement is the same as it is in JavaScript:

```
break [label] ;
```

Continue Statement

The syntax of the `continue` statement is the same as it is in JavaScript:

```
continue [label] ;
```

Try Statement

The Java `try` statement is used to try to execute a group of statements and catch any exceptions that may occur. Its syntax is as follows:

```
try {
  statements
}
[catchClauses]
[finallyClause]
```

At least one `catch` clause or a `finally` clause must be provided.

A `catch` clause is used to catch exceptions and provide exception handling code. The syntax of a `catch` clause is:

```
catch(Exception variable){
    statements
}
```

A `catch` clause declares a variable of an exception class to indicate which exceptions are handled by the statements specified in the `catch` clause.

The `finally` clause provides code that is always executed whether or not an exception occurs. Its syntax is:

```
finally {
    statements
}
```

Return Statement

The syntax of the `return` statement is the same as it is in JavaScript:

```
return [expression] ;
```

The optional *expression* must yield a value that is consistent with the method's return type.

Operators

The operators used by Java are virtually identical to those used in JavaScript. These operators are as summarized in Table C.3.

TABLE C.3   Java Operators

Category	Operators	Description
Arithmetic	+	Addition
	-	Subtraction
	*	Multiplication
	/	Division

TABLE C.3 Java Operators (continued)

Category	Operators	Description
	%	Modulus
Relational	>	Greater than
	<	Less than
	==	Equals
	<=	Less than or equals
	>=	Greater than or equals
	!=	Not equals
Logical	!	Not
	&&	And
	||	Or
Bit	~	Complement
	&	And
	|	Or
	^	Exclusive or
	<<	Left shift
	>>	Right shift
	>>>	Zero-filled right shift
Assignment	=	Assignment
	++	Increment & assign
	−	Decrement & assign
	+=	Add & assign
	-=	Subtract & assign
	*=	Multiply & assign

TABLE C.3   Java Operators (continued)

Category	Operators	Description
	/=	Divide & assign
	%=	Take modulus & assign
	|=	OR & assign
	&=	AND & assign
	^=	XOR & assign
	<<=	Left shift & assign
	>>=	Right shift & assign
	>>>=	Zero-filled left shift & assign
Selection	? :	If/then selection
Creation	new	Object creation

In addition to the operators in Table C.3, the caste operator, (`type`), may be used to change the type of a value or object to a compatible *type*. For example, suppose variable x is of type `short` and y is of type `long`; in this case the value stored in x can be converted to `long` in an assignment statement by using the (`long`) type caste as follows:

```
y = (long) x ;
```

The `instanceof` operator returns a boolean value indicating whether or not an object or value is a member of a particular type. For example, x `instanceof` `String` returns `true` if x refers to an object of type `String`.

Java 1.1 API

The Java 1.1 application programming interface consists of 23 predefined packages. These packages declare classes, interfaces, and exceptions that you can use to develop your own Java applets or programs. A significant part of learning Java consists of learning to use these packages. These packages are summarized in Table C.4.

TABLE C.4   The Java 1.1 API Packages

Package	Purpose
java.applet	Applet development
java.awt	Creation and display of GUI components
java.awt.datatransfer	Clipboard operations
java.awt.event	GUI event handling
java.awt.image	Image processing
java.awt.peer	Access to native windows implementation
java.beans	Development of reusable components
java.io	Input and output
java.lang	System access
java.lang.reflect	Access to class and interface definition
java.math	Math package for big numbers
java.net	TCP/IP client-server programming
java.rmi	Remote method invocation
java.rmi.dgc	Distributed garbage collection
java.rmi.registry	Remote Registry access
java.rmi.server	RMI server development
java.security	Encryption/digital signature calculation
java.security.acl	Access controls
java.security.interfaces	Digital Signature Algorithm interfaces
java.sql	Database access
java.text	Internationalization support
java.util	General utilities
java.util.zip	Compression utilities (for zipping/unzipping files)

APPENDIX

D

ECMA Standardization
of JavaScript

- The Development of JavaScript

- JavaScript Standardization and ECMA

- Limits of Standardization

- Online Updates

D

While both Netscape *Navigator* and Microsoft *Internet Explorer* are both JavaScript-enabled, the level of JavaScript support provided by these two browsers, and by different versions of these browsers, differs significantly. To help standardize the development of this type of scripting language, a leading international standards organization, The European Computer Manufacturers' Association, or ECMA, has been called on to provide assistance and advice.

The Development of JavaScript

Internet Explorer 3.0 provides the same level of JavaScript support as Navigator 2.0. This version of the language is referred to as **JavaScript 1.0**.

With the development of Navigator 3.0, Netscape added more objects, methods, properties, and functions to JavaScript. The JavaScript language corresponding to Navigator 3.0 is referred to as **JavaScript 1.1**. Microsoft fell behind Netscape in their support of JavaScript when Netscape released Navigator 3.0. Rather than catching up with Netscape, Microsoft renamed their version of JavaScript as *JScript*.

JavaScript 1.2 was introduced with Netscape *Communicator*. The Navigator 4.0 component of Communicator added support for layers, JavaScript style sheets, and other features.

JavaScript Standardization and ECMA

In order to standardize the rapidly evolving JavaScript language, Netscape, Microsoft, and other companies approached the European Computer Manufacturers' Association, or ECMA. The ECMA, founded in 1961, has supported the standardizing of information and communication systems for over 35 years—a long history in a young field. The home page of ECMA is *http://www.ecma.ch*.

Technical Committee 39 (TC39) of the ECMA was formed to "standardize the syntax and semantics of a general purpose, cross-platform, vendor-neutral scripting language." The standardized language is currently referred to as *ECMAScript*. A new name may be selected in the future. It is intended that the standardized language be submitted to the International Standards Organization/International

Electrotechnical Commission Joint Technical Committee 1, or ISO/IEC JTC 1. This will result in full international standardization of ECMAScript.

As of this writing, both Netscape and Microsoft have submitted language standardization proposals to the ECMA. Netscape's JavaScript language specification is available at the following URL:

http://home.netscape.com/eng/javascript/index.html

Microsoft's JScript specification can be found at the following URL:

http://www.microsoft.com/jscript/frn/techinfo/standards.htm

Netscape's Specification

Netscape's JavaScript specification is based on JavaScript 1.1. It formalizes the syntax and semantics of the language as well as standard objects and functions. The specification does not cover *implementation-specific* objects. Unfortunately, it is the implementation-specific objects that form the heart of the Navigator object hierarchy, and they are key to providing platform-independence of JavaScript-based Web applications. Server-side JavaScript (i.e., LiveWire) is not included in the specification. Table D.1 provides an overview of the chapters of the Netscape JavaScript Specification.

TABLE D.1   The Netscape JavaScript Specification

Chapter	Summary
1 Introduction	Introduces the specification, presents the notation used for the JavaScript grammar, and lists applicable references.
2 Lexical Structure	Specifies fundamentals such as the character set, literal values, keywords, identifiers, and operators.
3 Types, Values, and Variables	Covers primitive and reference types, variables, and name scope.
4 Expressions	Discusses the evaluation of expressions.
5 Object Model	Describes functions, object prototypes, constructors, and object creation in terms of the JavaScript object model.

TABLE D.1 The Netscape JavaScript Specification (continued)

Chapter	Summary
6 Statements	Describes the statements of JavaScript 1.1.
7 Built-in Functions and Objects	Covers built-in functions, arrays, the `Date` object, and the `Math` object. Discusses boolean, numeric, and string types as objects.
Appendix A - JavaScript Grammar	Specifies a formal grammar for the JavaScript language.

Microsoft's Specification

Microsoft's JScript specification is noticeably shorter than Netscape's specification. Netscape's is 114 pages while Microsoft's is 47 pages. The Microsoft specification does not even contain the word "JavaScript." Instead, the term "JScript" is used throughout the document.

Microsoft's specification contains 14 sections that cover JScript syntax and semantics and provide examples and informal discussion of the language. These sections are summarized in Table D.2.

TABLE D.2 The Microsoft JScript Specification

Section	Summary
1 Notational Conventions	Describes the notation used throughout the document.
2 Source Text	Discusses the character set used by JScript.
3 Types	Covers primitive and reference types.
4 Conversion Operators	Identifies how one type is converted to another.
5 Lexical Conventions	Describes the use of comments, keywords, identifiers, and literals.
6 Variable Scoping	Discusses the scoping rules of JScript.
7 Primary Expressions	Describes how expressions are created and evaluated.
8 Statements	Covers the syntax and semantics of JScript statements.
9 Function Definition	Identifies how functions are defined.

TABLE D.2   The Microsoft JScript Specification (continued)

Section	Summary
10 Program	Lists the syntax for JScript programs.
11 Native JScript Objects	Provides a placeholder for adding information on native objects. This section is currently empty.
12 Language Syntax Summary	Currently empty.
13 References	Brief list of references.
14 Index	Index to document.

Comparing the Two Specifications

The Netscape and Microsoft specifications differ significantly. Netscape obviously put more time and effort into their specification. As a result, it is significantly more complete. The Microsoft specification has two completely empty sections. Other differences are summarized as follows:

- Microsoft's specification is based on the Unicode character set while Netscape's uses ASCII.

- Netscape's specification covers predefined objects and functions. Microsoft's does not.

- Microsoft introduces statements, such as the switch statement, that are not part of JavaScript 1.1.

- Netscape provides a formal language grammar. Microsoft does not.

- In some cases, the syntax and semantics of JavaScript and JScript differ.

The above differences, while significant, are not insurmountable. Use of the Unicode character set would make ECMAScript more suitable to international Web application development. Other differences can be resolved by taking the least upper bound of the two specifications—the two specifications can be combined with conflicts being resolved in favor of the more general and consistent approach.

Limits of Standardization

While ECMA standardization of JavaScript is likely, it is uncertain what its impacts will be. Netscape has already introduced JavaScript 1.2 with Communicator, and JavaScript 1.2 contains additional statements and other language changes that are not covered in its ECMA proposal.

Microsoft, on the other hand, has fallen further behind Netscape in its JScript language support. VBScript and ActiveX are the focus of attention of the Microsoft browser.

Even with ECMA standardization, Web applications will continue to be incompatible between different browsers. This is because browser-specific objects are not part of the ECMA standardization. For example, Navigator 4.0 supports layers, JavaScript style sheets, and other objects that are unavailable in other browsers.

In the absence of common vendor-independent browser objects, the question arises as to which object set Web applications should be written for. This question is further complicated by the fact that different versions of the same company's browsers have differing capabilities with respect to JavaScript.

If you want your Web applications to have the widest possible audience—i.e., general Web applications—then you should use JavaScript 1.0 or JavaScript 1.1. Unfortunately, the capabilities provided by JavaScript 1.0 are very limited, and those provided by 1.1 do not take advantage of appealing newer features, such as layers and style sheets.

If your Web applications are targeted for an intranet where all users have Netscape Communicator, then you have the best possible environment for developing JavaScript-based applications. In this environment, you can use all of the latest JavaScript 1.2 features without having to make trade-offs to deal with compatibility concerns.

In practice, most Web applications will fall between these two extremes. In these cases, you should attempt to use the minimum set of objects and language features needed to build the application, trading off the use of newer objects for more widely supported alternatives.

Online Updates

The publisher of this book, Sybex Inc., is closely following the standardization of ECMAScript. Online updates about the progress of this effort may be found at their Web site for this book, via the following URL:

http://www.sybex.com

Click on the Catalog on the Sybex home page to follow the links to this book's own Web pages.

INDEX

Note to the Reader: Throughout this index **boldfaced** page numbers indicate primary discussions of a topic. *Italicized* page numbers indicate illustrations.

SYMBOLS

& (ampersands)
 in assignment operators, 80
 in bit operators, 79
 for entities, 40
 in form data coding, 741
 in logical operators, 78
 precedence of, 87
< > (angle brackets) in HTML, 10
* (asterisks)
 in assignment operators, 80
 for comments, 41, 671
 for multiplication, 78
 precedence of, 87
` (backquotes) for LiveWire, 776–777
\ (backslashes)
 in Java, 1011–1012
 in string values, 54
{ } (braces)
 for entities, 40
 for functions, 101
 for if statements, 92
 in Java, 1017
 for with statements, 108
[ ] (square brackets) for arrays, 68
^ (carets)
 in assignment operators, 80
 as bit operator, 79
 precedence of, 87

: (colons)
 in conditional expressions, 81
 precedence of, 87
 in URLs, 301
, (commas) for parameters, 168
" (double quotes)
 for attributes, 121
 in Java, 1011–1012
 for string values, 54
= (equal signs)
 in assignment operators, 80
 in comparison operators, 78–79
 in form data coding, 741
 precedence of, 87
! (exclamation points)
 for comments, 35
 for comparison operators, 78
 for logical operators, 78
 precedence of, 87
/ (forward slashes)
 in assignment operators, 80
 for comments, 35, 41, 671
 for division, 78
 in HTML, 10
 precedence of, 87
 in URLs, 15–16, 301
> (greater than signs)
 in assignment operators, 80
 as bit operator, 79
 in comparison operators, 79
 precedence of, 87

A

B

(

E

G

H

I

K

L

M

N

O

P

Q

R

T

table0 constructor—textyle.htm file

X

Y

Z

Java™ Development Kit
Version 1.1.1
Binary Code License

This binary code license ("License") contains rights and restrictions associated with use of the accompanying software and documentation ("Software"). Read the License carefully before installing the Software. By installing the Software you agree to the terms and conditions of this License.

1. **Limited License Grant.** Sun grants to you ("Licensee") a non-exclusive, non-transferable limited license to use the Software without fee for evaluation of the Software and for development of Java™ compatible applets and applications. Licensee may make one archival copy of the Software. Licensee may not redistribute the Software in whole or in part, either separately or included with a product. Refer to the Java Runtime Environment Version 1.1.1 binary code license (http://www.javasoft.com/products/JDK/1.1/index.html) for the availability of runtime code which may be distributed with Java compatible applets and applications.

2. **Java Platform Interface.** Licensee may not modify the Java Platform Interface ("JPI", identified as classes contained within the "java" package or any subpackages of the "java" package), by creating additional classes within the JPI or otherwise causing the addition to or modification of the classes in the JPI. In the event that Licensee creates any Java-related API and distributes such API to others for applet or application development, Licensee must promptly publish an accurate specification for such API for free use by all developers of Java-based software.

3. **Restrictions.** Software is confidential copyrighted information of Sun and title to all copies is retained by Sun and/or its licensors. Licensee shall not modify, decompile, disassemble, decrypt, extract, or otherwise reverse engineer Software. Software may not be leased, assigned, or sublicensed, in whole or in part. **Software is not designed or intended for use in on-line control of aircraft, air traffic, aircraft navigation or aircraft communications; or in the design, construction, operation or maintenance of any nuclear facility. Licensee warrants that it will not use or redistribute the Software for such purposes.**

4. **Trademarks and Logos.** This License does not authorize Licensee to use any Sun name, trademark or logo. Licensee acknowledges that Sun owns the Java trademark and all Java-related trademarks, logos and icons including the Coffee Cup and Duke ("Java Marks") and agrees to: (i) to comply with the Java Trademark Guidelines at http://java.com/trademarks.html; (ii) not do anything harmful to or inconsistent with Sun's rights in the Java Marks; and (iii) assist Sun in protecting those rights, including assigning to Sun any rights acquired by Licensee in any Java Mark.

5. **Disclaimer of Warranty.** Software is provided "AS IS," without a warranty of any kind. ALL EXPRESS OR IMPLIED REPRESENTATIONS AND WARRANTIES, INCLUDING ANY IMPLIED WARRANTY OF MERCHANTABILITY, FITNESS FOR A PARTICULAR PURPOSE OR NON-INFRINGEMENT, ARE HEREBY EXCLUDED.

6. **Limitation of Liability.** SUN AND ITS LICENSORS SHALL NOT BE LIABLE FOR ANY DAMAGES SUFFERED BY LICENSEE OR ANY THIRD PARTY AS A RESULT OF USING OR DISTRIBUTING SOFTWARE. IN NO EVENT WILL SUN OR ITS LICENSORS BE LIABLE FOR ANY LOST REVENUE, PROFIT OR DATA, OR FOR DIRECT, INDIRECT, SPECIAL, CONSEQUENTIAL, INCIDENTAL OR PUNITIVE DAMAGES, HOWEVER CAUSED AND REGARDLESS OF THE THEORY OF LIABILITY, ARISING OUT OF THE USE OF OR INABILITY TO USE SOFTWARE, EVEN IF SUN HAS BEEN ADVISED OF THE POSSIBILITY OF SUCH DAMAGES.

7. **Termination.** Licensee may terminate this License at any time by destroying all copies of Software. This License will terminate immediately without notice from Sun if Licensee fails to comply with any provision of this License. Upon such termination, Licensee must destroy all copies of Software.

8. **Export Regulations.** Software, including technical data, is subject to U.S. export control laws, including the U.S. Export Administration Act and its associated regulations, and may be subject to export or import regulations in other countries. Licensee agrees to comply strictly with all such regulations and acknowledges that it has the responsibility to obtain licenses to export, re-export, or import Software. Software may not be downloaded, or otherwise exported or re-exported (i) into, or to a national or resident of, Cuba, Iraq, Iran, North Korea, Libya, Sudan, Syria or any country to which the U.S. has embargoed goods; or (ii) to anyone on the U.S. Treasury Department's list of Specially Designated Nations or the U.S. Commerce Department's Table of Denial Orders.

9. **Restricted Rights.** Use, duplication or disclosure by the United States government is subject to the restrictions as set forth in the Rights in Technical Data and Computer Software Clauses in DFARS 252.227-7013(c) (1) (ii) and FAR 52.227-19(c) (2) as applicable.

10. **Governing Law.** Any action related to this License will be governed by California law and controlling U.S. federal law. No choice of law rules of any jurisdiction will apply.

11. **Severability.** If any of the above provisions are held to be in violation of applicable law, void, or unenforceable in any jurisdiction, then such provisions are herewith waived to the extent necessary for the License to be otherwise enforceable in such jurisdiction. However, if in Sun's opinion deletion of any provisions of the License by operation of this paragraph unreasonably compromises the rights or increase the liabilities of Sun or its licensors, Sun reserves the right to terminate the License and refund the fee paid by Licensee, if any, as Licensee's sole and exclusive remedy.

About This CD

In addition to all the *listings* (scripts, code, and supporting files and graphics) presented and discussed in this book, the attached CD contains Sun's *Java Developers Kit* (complete, version 1.1.1); an excellent editor—*TextPad* (shareware version)—for creating and editing HTML and JavaScript files; and *reference files* detailing the latest developments in HTML, JavaScript, and related standards.

- **Example scripts and code (The listings):** All the book's example files can be read and used directly from this CD. To speed access to the listings, however, you may want to copy them to your hard drive. To make this easy for you, we have provided a self-extracting compressed file containing all the listings, which you can copy to your hard drive in one easy operation. Simply double-click on `MJScript.exe` to extract all the files at once to the directory of your choice on your hard drive.

- **The Java Developers Kit:** From Sun Microsystems. This is the complete JDK, version 1.1.1. To use this software, run `\java\jdk1_1_1-win32-x86.exe` from this CD to start the JDK 1.1.1 setup program, and follow its instructions to install the JDK software on your Windows 95, Windows NT, Linux, or Unix machine.

- **TextPad editor:** From Helios Software Solutions. This is a shareware version of an excellent editor for creating and editing HTML and JavaScript files. To use the software, run `\textpad\win95\setup.exe` from this CD to start the TextPad setup program, and follow its instructions to install the program on your Windows 95, Windows NT, Linux, or Unix machine. (To run the program on a Windows 3.1 machine, run `\textpad\win31\setup.exe` instead.)

For warranty and support information, refer to the book's software license/warranty page and to the readme and license files in the individual providers' directories on the CD. Where specified in files on the CD, the owners retain copyright of their specific contents. Where not otherwise noted, all contents are copyright 1997 Sybex Inc.

The *Mastering JavaScript* CD is formatted in such a way that it can be read from machines operating under Windows 95, Windows NT 4.0, Linux, and most variations of Unix—which covers most of the platforms we expect a serious JavaScript developer might be using.

Note to Windows NT 3.51 users: If you are using Windows NT 3.51 (or earlier), you will not be able to read this CD format successfully. However, you *can* use the CD's contents if you obtain them via the Web instead of from the CD—just use your browser to access the Sybex home page (at *http://www.sybex.com*), then click on *Downloads* and follow the links to *Mastering JavaScript*. The files available for downloading include the complete and unmodified listings (i.e., all the book's scripts, code, and supporting files and graphics). Links to the other contents of the CD are also displayed.